FAMILY FORTUNES

P 25   451
37
114
131
148
191
260
395

403
415
429

445

Women in Culture and Society

A Series Edited by

Catharine R. Stimpson

FAMILY FORTUNES

Men and women of the English middle class, 1780–1850

Leonore Davidoff and Catherine Hall

The University of Chicago Press

The University of Chicago Press, Chicago 60637
Unwin Hyman Ltd., London W1V 1FP
© 1987 Leonore Davidoff and Catherine Hall
All rights reserved. Published 1987
University of Chicago Press paperback 1991
96 95 94 93   543

Library of Congress Cataloging-in-Publication Data

Davidoff, Leonore.
  Family fortunes.

  Bibliography: p.
  Includes index.
  1. Middle classes—England—History—18th century—
Case studies   2. Middle class women—England—History—
18th century—Case studies.   3. Middle classes—England—
History—19th century—Case studies.   4. Middle class
women—England—History—19th century—Case studies.
I. Hall, Catherine.   II. Title.
HT690.G7D38   1987   305.5'5'0942   86-30874
ISBN 0-226-13732-5 (cloth)
ISBN 0-226-13733-3 (paperback)

♾ The paper used in this publication meets the minimum
requirements of the American National Standard for
Information Sciences—Permanence of Paper for Printed
Library Materials, ANSI Z39.48-1984.

For our families and friends

especially
in memory of my nephew, Jonathan Davidoff 1959–1985
L. D.

and
for my mother, Gladys Barrett
C. H.

Contents

Foreword   9

Acknowledgements   11

Prologue   13
  Introducing James Luckcock of Birmingham – What was the
  English middle class? – Concepts and methods

Setting the scene   36
  Places: The town – Birmingham – The countryside – Essex and
    Suffolk
  People: The family shop – the Cadburys of Birmingham – The
    family pen – the Taylors of Essex

Part One   RELIGION AND IDEOLOGY   71

Introduction   73

1 'The one thing needful': religion and the middle class   76
  Church and chapel activity – The Evangelical revival and serious
  Christianity – Church against Dissent – The religious community

**2 'Ye are all one in Christ Jesus': men, women and
   religion**   107
  Doctrines on manliness – Doctrines on femininity – The ministry
  – The minister's wife – John Angell James: 'bishop' of Birmingham
  – Church organization: women voting and women speaking –
  Laymen and women

**3 'The nursery of virtue': domestic ideology and the
   middle class**   149
  The Queen Caroline affair – Middle-class readers and writers –
  William Cowper and Hannah More – Local writers on separate
  spheres – Domestic ideologies of the 1830s and 1840s

**Part Two   ECONOMIC STRUCTURE AND
                      OPPORTUNITY**   193

Introduction   195

4 'A modest competency': men, women and property   198
Enterprise organization – Land and capital – Enterprise finance –
Providing for dependants – The interdependence of enterprise,
family and friends – The role of marriage in the enterprise – Training
for the enterprise – Retirement from the enterprise

5 'A man must act': men and the enterprise   229
Middle-class men and occupations – The search for a 'sound
commercial education' – Commerce and trade – Banks and
banking – Manufacture – Farming – The professions – The salaried

6 'The hidden investment': women and the enterprise   272
Women and property – Women's contribution to the enterprise –
The education of women and its effects – Women as teachers –
Women as innkeepers – Women in trade – The marginal place of
women in the economy – Women, men and occupational identity
– How did women survive?

Part Three   EVERYDAY LIFE: GENDER IN ACTION   317

Introduction   319

**7 'Our family is a little world': family structure and
        relationships**   321
The role of marriage in family formation – Fatherhood –
Motherhood – Children – Brothers and sisters – The role of wider
kin

8 'My own fireside': the creation of the middle-class home 357
What was a home? – The separation of home from work – The
meaning of the garden – The lay-out of the home – Running the
home – The question of servants

**9 'Lofty pine and clinging vine': living with gender in the
        middle class**   397
Manners and gentility – Changing attitudes to sexuality – Mobility
and gender – Gender and the social occasion – Gender as
appearance

10 'Improving times': men, women and the public sphere 416
James Bisset of Birmingham – Voluntary associations –
Philanthropic societies – Leisure and pleasure – Men, women and
citizenship

Epilogue   450

Appendices
   1   Three poems by local authors – 2   Sources for the local study
   – 3   Tables   455

Notes and references   470

Select bibliography   542

People index   560

Subject index   566

Foreword

In 1849 Charlotte Brontë published *Shirley*, a historical novel set in the England of 1811–12, a convulsive political and economic period. To the immediate east and south, England was fighting in the Napoleonic Wars. Much further to the west, it was about to engage in the War of 1812 with the United States. At home, England was creating industrial capitalism, its middle class, and the families of that class. The very word *capitalist* was only twenty years old. Brontë dramatizes these epochal events through the stories of two young women, their courtships and marriages. One of these women, Caroline, the sweet niece of a clergyman, loves Robert, an ambitious mill owner. After they are engaged, Robert imagines their future: she will run a Sunday-school; he a company town. He glories: 'The copse shall be firewood . . . the beautiful wild ravine . . . a smooth descent . . . there shall be cottages in the dark ravine . . . the rough pebbled track shall be an even . . . road, bedded with the cinders from my mill . . . my mill shall fill its present yard . . . .'[1]

Family Fortunes is a momentous history of the birth of nonfictional Carolines and Roberts, and of the formation of that middle class between 1780 and 1850. The book's centers of gravity are the city of Birmingham and two adjoining provincial counties, Essex and Suffolk. Town and country have a variety of inhabitants, but *Family Fortunes* most closely attends to the Cadburys of Birmingham, who made their money in shopkeeping and food manufacturing, especially of a chocolate drink, and to the Taylors of Essex, who made their money in ministering, writing, and publishing.

Leonore Davidoff and Catherine Hall have deliberately selected families as the lens through which to refract the growth of the middle class, rather than individuals or couples or such public institutions as a school or factory, for the authors' great and legitimate concern is the inseparability of class and gender in modern society. Together, class and gender structure production and consumption, toil and leisure, work space and living space, hierarchy and equality, citizenship, public identity, subjectivity, private identity, and finally culture and 'normal' behavior. The values the middle class preferred were rationality (in men), comfort, stability, and Christian morality. Class and gender come together and sustain themselves within the family. As the middle class prospered and cohered, it increasingly treasured a sexual division of labor. Although men worked for and with their families, women became more detached from the processes of production, a separation that moving the home to the suburbs both symbolized and insured.

Davidoff and Hall have amassed a vast range of facts from archival and literary sources to prove how compelling their theory about history is.

Family Fortunes is as spacious, and yet as humanly detailed, as a massive realistic novel. It first examines the churches and the religious ideology of the middle class, which together offered not only an active sense of belonging to an orderly community, but a justification of sexual difference. The book then takes up the economic forms, such as liquid capital and consumer services, that the middle class used and refined. If these opportunities helped the middle class, they hurt employees and displaced craft workers. Davidoff and Hall also show how these forms molded masculinity one way, femininity another. Inheritance laws, for example, kept women from accumulating wealth. In its last section, *Family Fortunes* analyzes the institutions of gender as they worked themselves out in everyday life: in courtship and marriage; child bearing and child rearing; eating and dressing; giving and taking, including the orders that women gave to servants in those comfortable suburban homes.

In a scene in the middle of *Shirley*, the two heroines refuse to go to church on a warm, still evening. Standing in the churchyard, they revise the figure of Eve that Genesis and *Paradise Lost* have imposed upon them. 'Milton was great,' one says, and then adds, ' . . . but was he good?' They are not feminists, but they speak as if they might be. At the end of *Family Fortunes*, Davidoff and Hall ask, once more, about the belief in sexual difference that the English middle class burnished and practiced. For that belief was not, could not be, stable and monolithic. Its volatile tensions and contradictions were overtly codified in the 'Woman Question.' The period that began with Mary Wollstonecraft's *A Vindication of the Rights of Woman* (1792) was to end with John Stuart Mill's *The Subjection of Women* (1869). The women who helped to build the middle class left their granddaughters a sense of class that buoyed many, but a sense of gender and of a division between public and private spheres that constricted them as well. The consequences of the revolt of some of these granddaughters are still emerging in the late twentieth century. Among them is the resolve to write a full, deep history of both men and women, an indispensable history, like *Family Fortunes* itself.

Catharine R. Stimpson

1. Charlotte Brontë, *Shirley* (Harmondsworth: Penguin Edition, 1974), p. 597. Though complex, Brontë's sympathies are middle class.

Acknowledgements

The origins of this study lie in the Women's Liberation Movement and the questions which feminist history has raised over the past fifteen years. We continue to be deeply indebted to the existence of the feminist movement.

We would like to thank the Economic and Social Research Council and the Nuffield Foundation for supporting the research on which the book is based, in particular, John Malin and Patricia Thomas.

We are grateful to those who have generously given their time to read and comment on parts of the text: Sally Alexander, Veronica Beechey, Rosalind Delmar, Stuart Hall, Cora Kaplan and David Lockwood. Robert Moris's generosity in sharing his broad knowledge of the British middle class has been invaluable. Ellen Ross took on the Herculean task of reading the book in draft; her encouraging but critical editorial eye spurred on the project and our debt to her is immense.

Friends and colleagues have listened and supported us over the years, encouraging us when the task seemed too great: David Albury, Joan Busfield, Ida Davidoff, Anna Davin, Diana Gittins, Elaine Jordan, Ludmilla Jordanova, Jean L'Esperance, Diana Leonard, Jane Lewis, Judy Lown, Susie Meikle, Sonya Rose, Margaret Rustin, Alison Scott, Barbara Taylor, Paul Thompson, Martha Vicinus, Judy Walkowitz and all at North East London Polytechnic Cultural Studies Department.

We would like to thank the following for help with specific items: Gladys Barrett, Clive Behagg, Wendy Bradshaw, William Bramwell, George Bunting, Jane Caplan, Ed Copeland, Brenda Corti, Geoffrey Crossick, Geoff Eley, Esther Goody, Michael Ignatieff, Michael Lane, Jules Lubbock, Hugh McLoed, Michael Mann, Judith Netown, Mary Poovey, John Saville, Leonard Schwarz and Oriel Sullivan.

It would not be possible to carry out such a study without the expert knowledge and good will of local historians and local residents to whom we have a special obligation:

Birmingham: Patrick Baird, John Kenrick, Ian Christie Lee, John L. Moilliet, Barbara Smith.
Essex and Suffolk: John Bensusan-Butt, Nancy Briggs, David Clarke, Shani DeCruze, David Dymond, Jean Harding, Philip Hills, Andrew Phillips, John Penfold, David Ransome, Hilda Sebastian and Elaine Strutt. Arthur Brown's enthusiasm and willingness to share his immense store of information was never failing. Janet Gyford's generous and specialist help with the history of Witham has been much appreciated.

Staff at the Local Studies Department in Birmingham, the Essex, Ipswich and Bury St Edmunds Record Offices, the Colchester Borough Library Local Studies Collection, Essex Archeological Society Library, Friends House Library and Dr William's Library have been consistently helpful as have the Inter-Library Loan Departments at the University of Essex and North East London Polytechnic. Rosemary Procter organized the copying of the 1851 census through the Birmingham Genealogical Society and Manpower Services.

Michael Anderson and his staff at the University of Edinburgh gave us help and encouragement with the census data. Eric Tannenbaum and Phil Holden at the University of Essex have been towers of strength in coping with the quantitative data sets. Peter Dickinson, Martin Greenway and Mel Read patiently provided computing assistance.

We owe special thanks to the University of Essex Sociology Department secretaries: Sandra Dyson, Linda George, Mary Girling and especially Carole Allington for typing and re-typing such a long, complicated manuscript and coping cheerfully with our authorial demands.

Finally, but not least, thanks to the editors, Sarah Conibear and Claire L'Enfant, for making it all happen.

Leonore Davidoff
Catherine Hall
October 1986

Prologue

Family Fortunes is a book about the ideologies, institutions and practices of the English middle class from the end of the eighteenth to the mid nineteenth centuries. It concerns both men and women. It looks at the place of the family and the delineation of gender difference at a time of rapid economic, political and social change. The principal argument rests on the assumption that gender and class always operate together, that consciousness of class always takes a gendered form. Of course the articulation of class and gender is never a perfect fit. Indeed, tension between class aspirations and feminine identity was one of the powerful forces in the development of mid nineteenth-century feminism.

We are particularly sensitive to middle-class people's division of the world into public and private spheres. This is not primarily the political debate about the state versus private interest; it is rather the common-sense distinction between the realm of morality and emotion and that of rational activity, particularly conceived as market forces. We attempt to move beyond this public/private divide to show how middle-class men who sought to be 'someone', to count as individuals because of their wealth, their power to command or their capacity to influence people,[1]* were, in fact, embedded in networks of familial and female support which underpinned their rise to public prominence.

While many facets of middle-class formation are explored, this is not a study of the relation between the middle class and other strata, an important but different story. It has little to say about middle-class men as employers, about relations within the workplace or the organization of the labour process. Rather it argues for the centrality of the sexual division of labour within families for the development of capitalist enterprise. It also traces how new conceptions of sexual difference were built on existing traditions and maps the social and institutional effects of those beliefs.

Introducing James Luckcock of Birmingham

At the centre of our project are the men and women of the middle class whose lives we have tried to uncover and understand. By way of introduction we may take one such man, James Luckcock, a Radical Birmingham jeweller, who died in 1835, aged 74.[2] Well-known for his politics, his Unitarian sympathies and his upright business practice, he had lived his last fifteen years in domestic retirement in the suburb of Edgbaston, just over

* Superior figures refer to the Notes and references beginning on p. 470.

Plate 1   James Luckcock, manufacturer of jewellery, 1761–1835

a mile from the town centre. His life, recounted in his publications, his autobiography, his poems as well as his more didactic lectures, allows us to build up a picture of what he did and how he saw himself and his family. Luckcock's beliefs, his conduct, the philosophy of life which he distilled out of experience, the domestic and social relations within which he lived, offer us crucial insights into some of the unexamined terrains of late eighteenth- and early nineteenth-century middle-class provincial life. His story provides clues to the deep connections between religious belief, political practice, commercial activity and family life. These connections must be followed if we are to unravel the complicated inner dynamics of middle-class culture.

Luckcock's narrative fits neatly into the established picture of radical politics, religious dissent and manufacturing enterprise typical of the existing account of the provincial middle class. He seems an all too recognizable, if minor, figure in the story of Birmingham's rise to civic pride and prosperity. In his 20s, he came under the influence of Joseph Priestley, the celebrated chemist and theologian. Priestley was the minister of Birmingham's Unitarian New Meeting until he was forced to leave in 1791 when prominent Radicals and Dissenters were attacked by the mob in the name of Church-and-King. Inspired by Priestley's commitment to education, Luckcock, together with a group of like-minded friends, established a Sunday Society which offered instruction in writing, arithmetic, book-keeping, geography and drawing as well as moral and religious education to those who had a basic Sunday school training. This project evolved into the Birmingham Brotherly Society whose purpose was to train teachers for Sunday schools, provide managers for the benefit clubs attached to the schools and assist in 'the general promotion of knowledge and virtue'. The society aimed to promote both manufacture and active benevolence in its young men. The members eschewed all 'trifling unmanly behaviour', foppishness in dress, bad company and gambling and promoted commitment to work and obedience to parents and masters.[3]

Luckcock's view of what constituted manliness (masculinity), rested on deeper foundations than dress or behaviour. His connections with Unitarianism and the Birmingham Book Club were expressive of his radicalism. In the 1790s he was associated with the reforming group in the town which managed to survive the reaction following the Priestley Riots. In 1810, he wrote a pamphlet on the folly of war and following the re-emergence of radical organizations after the French wars in 1815, he joined the public call for reform and in 1819, became treasurer of the Birmingham Peterloo fund. He espoused in some ways impeccably radical views: he was attached to Tom Paine and hostile to Malthus, for liberty and against the replacement of labour by machinery, critical of corrupt government, suspicious of taxation, hostile to self-seeking aristocracy. He had a horror of debt and pawning, was committed to anti-slavery and to defence of the weak and of animals, and to representation of the people. Not surprisingly, he won the title of 'the Father of Birmingham Reform' from Thomas Attwood himself (one architect of 1832 Reform). His portrait, appropriately, hangs today in the corridors of Birmingham's Corporation building.

Yet Luckcock combined radicalism with a language of reciprocal duties and obligation more resonant of Burke or the older moral economy than of Paine. His collected poems contain an attack on self-serving politicians who refused to face the issues of unemployment and poverty. But the 'Father of Birmingham Sunday Schools', as he was called, included as a hymn in the same volume:

> Who kindly took us by the hand,
> And taught us truth to understand,
> And ev'ry gen'rous purpose fann'd?
> Our Patrons.

And at the final Mercy seat,
When all mankind as equals meet,
Enraptured may we rise to greet,
                              Our Patrons.[4]

Such jostling together of the concepts of liberty with those of patronage
and deference, echoed by many in the early nineteenth-century middle
class, is a reminder of the contradictory ways in which purer discourses of
philosophers and idealogues are reworked within common sense.

Luckcock was born, as he tells us, in 'humble life'. Apprenticed to a
Birmingham plater, he later joined his brother in buckle making before
moving into the manufacture of jewellery. In time he reached the position
of manager in a substantial firm and by 1809 was earning £400 per annum,
a prelude to being invited into partnership. His first printed work on
practical book-keeping for apprentices and small tradesmen, exemplified his
motto, Pope's 'Order is Heaven's first law'.

In 1811, to his dismay, his employer decided to retire propelling Luckcock to use his savings to set up in business for himself, aided by customers
from the old firm. Relying on his two eldest sons and his wife, he was able
to establish a prosperous business. Though he did his own designing and
being, as he tells us, clever at alloying gold so as to produce the best
appearance at the least expense, he nevertheless found his chief gratification
in keeping accurate accounts, guaging his profits, and being able to plan
for six months ahead. When in need of extra capital, he borrowed from
friends but always repaid promptly.

By 1820 he found his business overcapitalized and resolved to invest in
property, building two houses in Edgbaston, one for himself and his family,
one to let. By now possessed of a 'moderate independence' and enjoying
some leisure, he looked forward to a comfortable old age, intending to
withdraw from the business and leave his son, Felix, and the manager he
had appointed as equal partners. Felix, however, 'took a dislike to the
whole' and despite all his father's efforts left the warehouse. This forced
the 59-year-old Luckcock to sell up on disadvantageous terms leaving him
only a modest income and feelings of bitter mortification. 'I had established
the business with the most ardent anxiety', he wrote,

I had nursed it with all the fondness of a parent to his child – I had brought more
mind into the concern than my natural energies could well allow: and had, I
believe, injured myself by intense application and solicitude. I had all along built
my hopes upon it for the future prosperity of the family. . . .[5]

Conventional economic and political histories would stop at this point.
Much attention has been paid to middle-class men as captains of industry,
protagonists of reform, active members of voluntary associations contributing to the formation of their class through the exercise of social power.
Luckcock's own language, however, points to the central importance of
another, less well documented aspect: the family and the dynamics of sexual
difference. For Luckcock, the purpose of business was not the avid pursuit
of profit, but the provision of a 'modest competency' so that his family
could live in a simple but comfortable way. As Defoe had argued, 'that

tradesman who does not delight in his family, will never long delight in his business'. It was the affections of his wife and children which would make him 'hunt the world for business'.[6] For Luckcock, too, business existed to provide for his family. His politics were devoted to ensuring the representation of heads of households like himself. The point of his philanthropic endeavours was to encourage young men to be like him; responsible bread-winners whose manhood was legitimated through their ability to secure the needs of their dependants.

By 1815, Luckcock believed he had achieved the 'utmost ambition of the desires of my whole life'. This ambition was neither a new rate of profit nor new measure of reform, but rather, a 'small comfortable house, and a good sized garden'.[7] In the early days of his own business, he had lived in a house without a garden near to his workplace which was convenient since his wife helped out to save on extra wages. As soon as profits allowed, she gave up working in the business and he was able to afford another house with its own land which, though not far from the warehouse, was thoroughly insulated from all view of the town and its annoyances.

By 1820 spare cash from the business allowed him to embark on his ultimate dream of creating a home and garden far from the town centre. Situated in Lime Grove, in the residential suburb of Edgbaston, the foundation stone was laid by his daughter Irene, with the same silver trowel with which Luckcock had laid the foundation stone for the new Unitarian Sunday school. His object was to make a 'snug and comfortable' home. 'In my own premises', he wrote,

I have all my heart could wish. The house and garden planned by myself, the situation picturesque, secluded and charming; the aspect, a southern slope; the soil deep and highly productive; and the whole plantation rapidly rising to beauty and perfection. . . .[8]

The 'mansion' was actually a modest white stuccoed house, on one side attached to its neighbour. Here Luckcock lived the life that he had long idealized in his mind's eye: reading, writing, gardening, keeping detailed household accounts, talking to his old friends, making occasional forays into town but for the most part entirely satisfied with domestic pursuits. All associations with commerce were gradually left behind. He sold his canal shares because the canal at the bottom of his garden thrust thoughts of business too intrusively into his poetic retreat. His rustic arbours were embellished with statues of Flora and Ceres. Inscriptions 'To Domestic Harmony', 'To Public Virtue', to his favourite poets and politicians decorated urns, vases and benches. Here Luckcock was surrounded by his household; his wife, his daughter still at school, his third son, Howard, apprenticed to a prominent Unitarian attorney, and his two servants. His brother pursued scientific interests in a small house visible on the other side of the canal.

The Luckcocks were a family organized around the idea of sexual difference, expressed through the proper forms of manliness and femininity. Men and women occupied separate spheres because they were naturally different. Mrs Luckcock, whose name we do not know, worked briefly in the family enterprise, but when circumstances permitted, retired to the home. She had no visible public life, no portrait was painted of her, none of her thoughts, ambitions and dreams have survived in her own words. Not long before her death her husband wrote of her:

We have lived together nearly thirty years – have rejoiced and sorrowed together – economised together – reflected together – sympathised together – and we will speed hand in hand together to our final home. Equal in property – equal in importance – equal in good intentions – equal in fidelity and affection – equal in the estimation and favour of Heaven.[9]

Equal in the eyes of Heaven they may have been. Equal in property and importance they certainly were not. As a married woman, Mrs Luckcock had no rights to property and her life was spent in domestic obscurity. Her daughter was equally invisible to the public eye. Her son, Howard, however, followed in his father's footsteps, becoming a stalwart of Birmingham, a JP, a trustee of the Botanical and Horticultural Society, the chairman of the Fire Insurance Company – a veritable public man, a fit and proper person.

If we are to understand middle-class culture in this period, we cannot rest content with Luckcock the reformer, the Radical, the prominent Unitarian, the entrepreneur. We must go behind the public man to discover the private labours on which new forms of capitalist enterprise were built, new patterns of social life established. We need to watch Luckcock and his wife struggling in the early days to set up a business on a shoestring; he always trusting her to economize at home, to make the clothes and darn the stockings, to provide cheap meals and keep the house clean. We must trace the sources of Luckcock's powerful investment in domestic harmony as the crown of the enterprise as well as the basis of public virtue. We must uncover the beliefs and activities of the silent Mrs Luckcock and the thousands like her, so essential to their men and yet so unable to speak on their own behalf. Families like the Luckcocks were the very pivot of middle-class society. In order to understand the dynamics of their lives, however, it is first necessary to place the English middle class in the general context of the period.

What was the English middle class?

The provincial middle class took shape during the turbulent decades of the late eighteenth and early nineteenth centuries. It was the crises of these decades which brought out common interests and drew its disparate membership together; the vicissitudes of war and trade cycles, the near breakdown of the old Poor Law, the pressure from the growing body of wage labourers. Although the eighteenth-century middling groups had many affinities with aristocracy and gentry, the basis of their property and their value system and, not least the nonconformity of many in their ranks, set them apart.[10] These differences coalesced in the growing desire for independence from the clientage of landed wealth and power.

In the heady early days of the French Revolution, the cry for liberty appealed to many sections of the middling ranks from commercial men to déclassé gentry on small incomes; people as diverse as William Cowper,

Mary Wollstonecraft and William Wordsworth. It stirred an echo among provincial clergymen and doctors, apprenticed attorneys, tradesmen, booksellers and merchants. Many came to feel that the fruits of liberty could not be guaranteed unless a man (*sic*) had a say in the political decisions which affected him and his family. Court circles around the Prince Regent symbolized the corruption of the governing class, made painfully evident by the madness and withdrawal of the king whose domesticated lifestyle had contrasted so sharply with his son's debauchery.

However, in the 1790s, the growth of a native revolutionary movement and the campaign for political reform, together with the excesses in France, produced a backlash which drew all property owners together. The radicalism of those sections of the middling ranks who had found inspiration in France ebbed as fears for their property grew and Paineite doctrines became more firmly embedded in the artisan communities of Sheffield, Norwich or London. The celebrated rationalist and Unitarian theologian, Joseph Priestley, Luckcock's mentor, was driven out of Birmingham by Church-and-King mobs, never to return to England.

The war with France proved to be a 'cultural watershed comparable to that of the Great War'.[11] Vast numbers of men were involved and after 1815 demobbed soldiers flooded the country. Fear of invasion had rocked coastal communities. Some trades had been decimated by blockade while others had flourished; entrepreneurs and merchants found new markets as continental rivals lost out. War profits buoyed up many a business and farming family, fuelling the desire for social recognition. As the price of bread soared, however, the position of labourers worsened and widened the gap between them and the lower ranks of the middling strata. War, and the fervent patriotism which came to be associated with it, sharpened ideas of social place. The idealized position of women was a central theme in nationalistic claims to English superiority advanced by radicals and conservatives alike. The effeminacy of the French was held up to derision, including the accusation that they had used women as soldiers.[12] The enlarged role of the military enhanced masculine virtues; local male worthies were called on to assist in recruitment and organization. Nonconformists were excluded from serving as officers in local militia, further isolating them, heightening the search for alternative masculine forms of activity.

It was only after years of struggle that the heads of middle-class households were incorporated politically by the Reform Act of 1832, significantly the first explicit exclusion of women by its limitation of the franchise to 'male persons'. Middle-class interests were prominent in the new Poor Law (1834) and reform of municipal government (1835). The latter, together with the repeal of the Test and Corporation Acts (1829), removed civil disabilities from nonconformists, locally and nationally, opening the way for wider social participation for a critical sector of the middle class.[13]

Nevertheless, land remained a unique form of property, conferring a special status, a 'dignity and a set of duties . . . which are peculiar to itself'.[14] Although land could be purchased, the association of name and birth with land as in the Great House, provided the model of leadership. King Property had reigned supreme throughout the eighteenth century, consolidating the rights to absolute property with a range of legislation

from enclosures to the Black Acts. Although landed groups extended their
wealth by investing in consols and other liquid forms of property or
developed their assets as ground landlords, their major revenues continued
to be derived from agricultural rents. The middle class depended on different
sources of wealth, but they, too, built on the concept of absolute property
rights. However, when they bought land it was often more of an investment
or asset to produce income for enlarging a business or farming operation,
as collateral on loans or for paternalistic schemes for their workpeople.[15]

There were other important differences in the use of these varied property
forms. Commercial and professional interests were most vulnerable to the
instability of the fledgling market system, buffeted as they were by natural
disasters, fluctuating trade cycles and constant failure of inadequate financial
institutions. Basic concepts such as *credit* and *cost accounting* were still
rudimentary. 'Monied men' and factors, Cobbett's reviled 'stock jobbers',
still aroused fierce suspicion, while commercial families struggled to stay
free of debt and retain independence.[16] Perhaps the single greatest distinction between the aristocracy and the middle class was the imperative for
members of the latter to actively seek an income rather than expect to live
from rents and the emoluments of office while spending their time in
honour-enhancing activities such as politics, hunting or social appearances.
The liquid form of middle-class property which had to be manipulated
to ensure its survival, much less growth, encouraged a different ethos,
emphasizing pride in business prowess.

The belief in the importance of new business practices and the benefits
which they could bring to the whole community, whether through specialization and the division of labour, the use of new marketing techniques or
the introduction of new machinery, found echoes in the language of political
economy. A Birmingham miller's son, scarred by the attack of a hungry
crowd on the family mill, left the business but continued to find solace in
reading Adam Smith. Smith's *Wealth of Nations* must have comforted many
a corn merchant or miller caught between the pincer of popular belief in
the 'just price' and laws of the new market economy since Smith's justification made self-interest the basis for an expansionist economy and society.
The attack on apparently traditional rights and liberties could be couched
in the language of long-term benefits for all. Yet another favourite author
of the miller's son was William Cowper, the Evangelical poet of domesticity,
who abhorred the development of a cash economy and longed for a return
to a paternalistic idyll.[17]

The growing commitment to new commercial forms among sections of
the middling ranks jostled with fears and anxieties of the dangers inherent
within them. Those dangers encompassed the clash between masters and
men as well as the fear of bankruptcy and failure. This unease found its
voice in an attachment to some aspects of traditionalist and paternalist
thinking.

The mental map of James Luckcock included the celebration of the rural
and the belief in the home as haven from the market. Aspects of such
middle-class thinking were premised on the separation between market and
family, but this was highly contradictory since at the same time the market
itself was structured by the organization of sexual difference. The tension

at the heart of much middle-class thinking – between a belief in a free
market economy and a commitment to the importance of maintaining ties
of belonging to a social order – perhaps goes some way to explaining the
persistence of paternalist thinking among many employers. Some refused
an exclusive reliance on the language of class conflict and the struggle
between capital and labour. Many influential middle-class men stressed
the importance of winning the consent of their workers to new forms of
organization, new divisions of labour. Employers could be the 'providers'
not only for their wives, children and servants, but also for their employees.
Wives, children, servants, labourers, all could be described in the language
of paternalism as the dependants and children of their father, their master,
their guardian.[18]

Aristocratic claims for leadership had long been based on lavish display
and consumption while the middle class stressed domestic moderation. In
particular, aristocratic disdain for sordid money matters, their casual attitude to debt and addiction to gambling which had amounted to a mania in
some late eighteenth-century circles, were anathema to the middling ranks
whose very existence depended on the establishment of creditworthiness
and avoidance of financial embarrassment. Court circles around the Prince
Regent, the 'Fashionables' among whom high class prostitutes openly
appeared in public, also outraged provincial decorum. But so too did the
London-based opponents of the Regent's lifestyle, the Dandies. This all-
male social clique had its own aesthetic, disdaining coarse womanizing, but
was opposed to business pursuits or habits, ostentatiously even refusing to
wear a watch, and spurning all domestic burdens. The Dandies set their
mark on London Society with their fashionable elegance and concern with
clothes, the antithesis of domesticated masculinity dedicated to business.[19]
These conflicting ideals of masculine leadership came to a head over the issue
of duelling. The use of the sword in issues of private honour symbolized all
that was repellent to the pacific, religious and commercial sense of the
middle-class provincial.[20]

Opposition to elements in the aristocratic code, however, had also arisen
within the aristocracy itself. As Lawrence Stone has argued, in the early
eighteenth century, some were beginning to elevate a domesticated lifestyle,
influenced by the urban gentry and merchant patriciate.[21] The revival of
Puritan doctrine within the Evangelical movement, many of whose early
adherents came from the margins of the gentry, encouraged forms of domesticity which had much in common with middle-class practice. However,
while for the landed family, this might be a choice, for the middle class it
was mandatory.

The 'oppositional culture' of the provincial middle classes cannot be
understood outside a religious context.[22] Middle-class men and women were
at the heart of the revivals which swept through all denominations. Their
most vocal proponents had their sights fixed not on gentry emulation but
on a Heavenly Home. The goal of all the bustle of the market place was
to provide a proper moral and religious life for the family. The dynastic
ambitions of the aristocratic model fitted neither moveable capital nor
conceptions of immortality. For many middle-class parents, their childrens'
inheritance should be their education and religious principles.[23] The cold-

blooded pursuit of profit was as deeply suspect on moral grounds as was the desire to shed the taint of trade. A wealthy shopkeeper's son started the process of mobility which ended with the marriage of his own son into the Essex gentry by choosing to train for the law. He framed his decision on ethical principles, claiming that a legal profession, being free from 'perpetual attention to profit and loss', had fewer temptations to vice and 'the most intimate connections with morality'.[24]

Examples of aristocratic vice provided potent lessons for the middling ranks. In 1812, an Essex heiress, one of the wealthiest women in England with a putative income of £80,000 a year, married the aristocratic but dissolute nephew of the Duke of Wellington. The wedding outfit costing almost £1000, with entertainments to match, had all the splendour of a fairy tale and the couple drove away scattering coins to the tenantry. But within ten years he had wiped out the fortune and Wanstead House had to be sold to pay for gambling debts and other dissipations. In a blaze of publicity, the wife and young family were deserted, and soon after she died, reputedly of a broken heart.[25] Such a case received maximum local and national publicity and enhanced middle-class determination to build their homes into havens of comfort, stability and morality where wives and children would be protected and controlled.

The concern among people in the middle ranks with control over behaviour was partly a result of uncertainty, arising not only from shifting economic fortunes but also from the depredations of illness and accident. Despite a relatively high standard of living, they suffered from waves of fever and the cholera epidemics, while death from consumption was an ever present threat. The survivors of both financial and mortal disaster might easily find themselves sunk into the ranks of those who had little but their labour to sell.

By this period, control by guilds or the state over the terms of labour and prices had virtually disappeared and the gap was growing between masters and farm servants or journeymen increasingly unable to set up on their own. Those who could muster a modest independence, particularly when motivated by religious enthusiasm, spent their small margin on increasing literacy, widening horizons and extending vision. Involvement in the market drew men – and some women – to travel, made easier by better roads and cheaper forms of conveyance. Labourers were more often tied to their locality through the decline in apprenticeship and farm service as well as the harsh dictates of revised settlement laws.[26] Above all, the more affluent and aspiring were concentrating more of their energies on the management of materials, time and workforce rather than working as craftsmen who depended on their own hand work.

Middle-class attitudes to work and its meaning subtly shifted as the degradation associated with manual tasks increased. Cobbett, the nostalgic radical, fumed at young people 'too clever to *work*', who despised that highest agricultural skill, ploughing. 'What, young gentlemen go to plough! They become *clerks*, or some skimmy-dish thing or other. They flee from the dirty *work* as cunning horses do from the bridle.'[27] While some artisans followed Cobbett's line, especially when their own trades were declining, others, like Luckcock, made the transition into the lower ranks of the middle class.

Marriage and courtship patterns, too, were changing. 'The distance between the mores of ordinary people, and those of the educated elite had never been greater.'[28] Working-class men and women were often now bereft of community support and more reliant on charity or the Poor Law. Meanwhile, the middle class, bolstered by networks of family, kin and the religious community, aspired for inclusion in the governing stata if only in the parish vestry. Like Luckcock, they inserted themselves into the public gaze through a myriad of societies devoted to religion, philanthropy, education, science and cultural activities. The second and third decades after peace saw further distress with falling grain prices and rural wages. Class distance took solid form as the more prosperous watched the night skies flare with burning ricks or saw Chartist crowds sweep past their comfortable parlour windows.

Despite these differences from both gentry and nascent working class, at the beginning of the period, the middle strata canno. be seen as a block. It was criss-crossed by differences of interest and riven with internal dissension. The large sector of professionals and merchants in London differed from manufacturing families in the north and Midlands whose experience differed again from the market town tradesmen and solicitors or the farmers whom they serviced. Divisions between Anglicans (themselves split between Evangelicals and traditionalists) and nonconformists were compounded by a multitude of nonconformist sects. While ostensibly based on doctrinal issues, these denominational divisions often covered latent social distinctions. Political alignments ranged from Radical through Tory, often partly reflecting a division between those whose livelihood rested on the production and handling of material goods – manufacturers and farmers – and tradesmen and professionals who dealt in services and did not directly confront a waged labour force. Yet by the middle of the nineteenth century, these disparate elements had been welded together into a powerful unified culture.

The early nineteenth-century middle groups were stratified in a gradation of status with sharper divides at certain levels of income. It is, however, notoriously difficult to pinpoint income bands which will clearly identify a specific group. In this period, estimates of the incomes appropriate to middle-class membership put forward by historians have ranged from £100 a year to 'as low as a few £1,000 a year'[29] depending on the context of the discussion. James Luckcock was convinced that it was impossible to maintain any semblance of gentility under £50 a year, a sum which matched the lower limit for taxable income when income tax was introduced in 1802.[30] Family income was made up of a variety of sources which increases the difficulties of estimation. Top rates of tax started above £200 and most historians agree that from £200 to £300 per annum secured a place within the middle class for an average family.

The proportion of the population who could be included as middle class varied from place to place, but generally appears to have been expanding in the eighteenth century. Brewer estimates that by the start of the period, the population with family incomes of from £50 to £400 a year increased from 15 to 25 per cent. Morris claims that the 13 per cent of £10 a year household heads registered as voters increased to 25 per cent by 1847. This fits with Corfield's mid century figure of 18 per cent for Norwich and Foster's estimate of 20 to 30 per cent for northern industrial towns, and Burnett's claim of 23 per cent for the whole country. These proportions tally with our local study, one-sixth of the population of Birmingham according to Eversley and our own findings of 17 to 20 per cent for Colchester and an Essex village.[31]

Our research confirms the divisions observed by others into a higher and lower strata within the class, although the breaks are not always easy to establish empirically. For example, one important distinction was between those who could supply loans and those at the bitter end of credit chains.[32] Our analysis of wills and the 1851 census gives a breakdown similar to Burnett's of two-thirds in the lower and one-third in the higher strata with the latter broken down again to 3 to 5 per cent in the wealthiest, most powerful positions.[33]

The centrifugal forces in such a wide range of circumstances could be,

Table 1 *Internal divisions within the middle class*

Lower ranks	Higher ranks
Single person enterprise	Partnership or trust
Use mainly family labour	Employer of workforce
Farm 50–300 acres	Farm over 300 acres
Leave real property at death	Leave property in trust for dependants at death
Invest in houses and buildings	Invest in government securities, land or other
Limited credit, short-term back up from suppliers/friends	Credit from banks, long-term, regional or London
Men educated small private day school or free grammar school	Men educated private academy, fee paid grammar school
Methodist, Baptist, Independent Anglican	Quaker, Unitarian, Congregational or Anglican
Tory or radical or non-political	Tory or Whig, depending on interest
Live in city centre	Middle-class enclave in city centre or suburb
Social circle local	Social circle also in other towns, sometimes London
Rank-and-file in voluntary societies	Leadership in voluntary societies
Wives help in enterprise or have own business/skill	Wives full time at home

however, counteracted by both common material interests and fundamental values. The more affluent provided models for the lower ranks who modified these codes to suit more modest circumstances. Family and kinship ties could further bridge the gap, as did similar education, reading matter, and exposure to sermons. The practice of sending daughters of small farmers and tradesmen into domestic service in the houses of the higher ranks meant that notions of gentility were carried back into their own homes.

❧ One of the strongest strands binding together urban and rural, nonconformist and Anglican, Whig, Tory and Radical, manufacturer, farmer and professional, wealthy and modest, was the commitment to an imperative moral code and the reworking of their domestic world into a proper setting for its practice. In the early part of the period this did not necessarily mean that women had to be confined within this domestic sphere or that men had no part in it. But the home was strongly associated with a form of femininity which was becoming the hallmark of the middle class, although much of it drived from a traditional inheritance.

Ideas of a woman's place were underpinned by legal, political and social practices which subordinated women. This was combined, however, with a recognition of their economic worth in the family enterprise. The Puritan metaphor of man as sun and woman as moon captures the relative positions of male and female. The draper's daughter helping in the shop, the farmer's wife running the dairy, the printer's widow carrying on his business, all were well established routes for women. As recent research has emphasized, almost no guilds excluded women completely, but custom decreed that their access to trades was through their husbands and fathers and their guild membership never carried the same status or privileges as it did for men. Whether in fifteenth-century London, sixteenth-century Oxford, seventeenth-century Yarmouth or eighteenth-century Birmingham, women's work opportunities were closely constrained in relation to their position within the family and the path was never easy for would-be independent spinsters.[34]

The evangelical revival of the eighteenth century had made a religious idiom the cultural norm for the middle class by the mid nineteenth century. At its heart was concern with individual salvation, only to be won by active struggle. This thrusting religion cut through both the fatalism of the labouring poor and the indifference of the rich. As Obelkevich has noted, unlike high Anglicanism or traditional nonconformity, it offered a passionate belief in a future life to counter discarded pagan prophecy.[35] Since all were worthy to be saved, the plight of slaves – souls at a convenient distance – became a major crusade. This outlook fostered humanist compassion for the helpless and weak: women, children, animals, the insane, the prisoner. However, this benevolent concern was tempered with the drive to control these same groups who were regarded as closer to nature and peripheral to, if not outside the social order.[36]

The moral order became a central battle ground for the provincial middle classes. They set God's design and the power of prayer against fortune telling, conjuring, ghosts, witches, wizards and other manifestations of that 'prior culture' which was so deeply embedded in the English countryside and followed the working class into the cities.[37] Clergymen joined doctors and scientists in the attack against these seemingly reactionary forces. As this alliance indicates, a religious mentality was not yet regarded as opposed to scientific thought. On the contrary, committed Protestants were concerned with novel forms of creating an ordered existence. They recast notions of diurnal, weekly and annual time in harness to their greater purpose. Holy Days, still 'plaited with pagan good cheer',[38] were transmuted to the anniversary celebrations of family, church or voluntary society. 'Accounts' were continually cast up with God: had the year been 'time spent in the pleasures of sin for a season or endeavouring to obtain the favour of the Shepherd of Israel?'[39]

Religious belief thus supported a rational outlook and the active pursuit of commerce. Those Christians most attracted to the rational discourse of the Enlightenment moved to Unitarianism, rejecting the God in Christ but remaining within a broadly Christian framework. In local records, the young men travelling as representatives of the family machinery or biscuit firm on weekdays, held impromptu prayer meetings on evenings and Sundays.[40] Nor were religious beliefs incompatible with the study of Nature. In Cowper's words, quoted by a local author, the science of botany demonstrated that 'not a flower, but shows some touch . . . of His unrivall'd pencil'.[41] Religion, that 'great engine of belief', could dictate from the pulpit the course of action that was likely to be 'profitable to the soul'.[42]

Given their involvement in production, design and building, it is not surprising that the middling ranks were the chief exponents of a rational and scientific world view. Nature was to be understood and controlled although not desacralized. In combination, these values sharpened their perceived distance from the easy going, haphazard gentry or the feckless, superstitious working class. Although provincial, the middle-class 'country of the mind' was far removed from the linguistic localism of labourers.[43]

Commercial activity provided much of the impetus to formalize and codify the middle-class world. City merchants, with a background of accounting for profit and loss, carried their experience into 'retirement' to estates, agreeing with Adam Smith who equated local prejudice against larger farming units with 'popular terrors and suspicions of witchcraft'.[44] The war, necessitating mobilization on a grand scale, further rationalized methods of estimating needs for men and materials. By the early nineteenth century, foreign visitors were struck by this spirit: the prevalence of measuring instruments, the clocks on every church steeple, the 'watch in everyone's pocket', the fetish of using scales for weighing everything including one's own body and of ascertaining a person's exact chronological age.[45] A less likely derivation of quantitative thought was the probability theory developed by gamblers but transmuted by the serious to estimating survival for the new mortality tables and life assurance.[46]

This categorizing mentality became associated with all that was progressive. Rural culture, often represented to the middle class by their domestic servants, became the repository of 'folklore, fairy tale, the supernatural and dark local family histories'.[47] Similarly, elements of boisterous play and carnival were separated and circumscribed, appropriated only for children and the inferior who were childlike. Sexuality, regarded as one of the most irrational forces, was relegated to the inner core of marriage and sexual play became the ultimate antithesis of rational work.[48] Women, particularly when pregnant and thus incontrovertibly sexual beings, were associated with animalistic nature, incompatible with the serious work of the world.[49] Categories of purity and pollution, the separating of the useful from waste, weeds and rubbish were invoked by scientific and sanitary movements to control noxious materials, sights, sounds, smells – and people.[50]

This powerful combination of religious, commercial and scientific ideologies can be traced in the reforming figures of the period: the serious Christians, Arthur Young at the new Board of Agriculture, John Rickman at the new Registrar General's office, William Morgan, actuary of the first insurance office, Equitable Assurance, or the later Utilitarians, the sanitary reformer Edwin Chadwick and Rowland Hill, Postmaster General. Their ordered, active and committed lives and the hundreds of their provincial counterparts, were extended by an array of publications which combined moral themes with scientific reasoning and commercial appeal. These were replacing, for example, the old style almanacs with their proverbial wisdom. In all these endeavours, a male intelligence analysed a feminized 'Nature'. Men framed rational scientific practice just as they pushed forward quantitative thought; it was their birthright, seen as an inborn, natural quality of masculinity.[51]

Women partook equally of the religious framework of order and duty. They were expected to act rationally in housekeeping and money matters, especially those related to consumption. Yet they were also seen as the embodiment of both the positive and negative qualities associated with irrationality. By the early nineteenth century, women in rural areas were regarded as the last bearers of traditional culture in their 'Old Wives Tales'. Young men might ridicule feminine adherence to old style cures and nostrums, yet feminine love and 'knowledge of the heart' was women's greatest asset.

By the early nineteenth century, this peculiar blend of evangelical religion and rationalism was joined by ideas and images now often labelled romantic, but which appealed far wider than the usual association of that term with artists and writers. The core of romanticism was also individual identity. It appeared in a variety of forms, but it was the colourful nationalism of Scott which especially appealed to the provincial middle class. The distancing from local culture to prove gentility, the rejection of proverbs as a speech form and guide to behaviour was being softened by a rediscovery of folk culture as an objective study (just as much a distancing mechanism). The search for individual autonomy and liberty in Byron's heroes had a strong appeal to people carving out a destiny, even if it was as a provincial shopkeeper. The glory of war enhanced these images, although the seriously religious, committed to Christ's army, were uneasy in its unqualified celebration.

The contradiction between, on the one hand, the disruption and squalor caused by manufacture and urban development which were the bread and butter of the middle class and, on the other, the intense desire for order and moral superiority, was bridged by the romantic vision. Young chemists and attorneys could leave their mundane occupations for walking tours in the mountains and, more sedately, with their sisters or sweethearts, passionately experience sunsets or seaside vistas. This romantic anti-urbanism built on existing traditions of revulsion against the sophistication of urban life for a 'dream of the pastoral' stretching back through the poetry of William Cowper to James Thomson's *The Seasons*, still favourite authors of the provinces.[52] This longing for rural tranquility versus urban restlessness and corruption closely followed the dichotomy between Home and World, both associated with the overarching categories of masculine and feminine.

Women, like children, represented the innocence of the natural world which active masculinity must support, protect – and oversee. Scott's romanticism touched off a wave of pseudo-chivalry which promoted a masculine identity which could mask, if not deny, the commercial origins of its most devoted adherents.[53] A similar impetus coloured the often self-serving paternalism of many a manufacturer, farmer or local merchant. The romantic imagination indelibly fixed the image of a rose-covered cottage in a garden where Womanhood waited and from which Manhood ventured abroad: to work, to war and to the Empire.[54] So powerful was this dual conception that even the radical fringe subscribed.

A similar vision moulded ideas of taste and beauty. In the mid eighteenth century, Edmund Burke, building on earlier models, had conceived beauty as small in size, smoothness, sweetness, bright colours, delicacy and the general lineaments of the 'infantine'. He posed this conceit against the grander virtues of the sublime: judgement, wisdom and strength which had an angular, even terrifying aspect.[55] These obviously gendered connotations were later attached to moral qualities, so although femininity remained the model of beauty, immorality in women as expressed by independent action was, by definition, ugly. Classical learning added a further dimension through the exposure of some men to Latin and Greek in their youth. The celebration of masculine virtues and the ignoring or trivializing of women's concerns in classical texts compounded the already complex views of masculinity and femininity.

This rich and potent mixture became the epitome of refinement in middle-class life. In the mid eighteenth century, people of rank had not yet needed to be so particular. Even early Evangelicals had been of an earthier hue, not so far removed from the coarseness of hunting field or coffee house. As Thomas Hood ruefully remarked in the 1830s after he and Charles Lamb had been publicly censured for their satirical handling of domestic topics, 'I am born out of time. I have no conjecture about what the world calls delicacy.'[56] For by his time, the middle-class view was becoming the triumphant common sense of the Victorian age.

Concepts and methods

In this study we have attempted to reconstitute the world as provincial middle-class people saw it, experienced it and made sense of it; to accurately reconstruct an emerging culture. Our purpose has been to develop analytic and explanatory frameworks which allow us to understand why that world was as it was, how it was structured, what were the processes and conditions on which middle-class experience rested and why these were the prevailing moral and cultural forms. Inevitably this attempt has been guided, as all historical work is, by present concerns. In particular our concern has been to give the neglected dimension of gender its full weight and complexity in the shaping and structuring of middle-class social life in this period.

A variety of working concepts has framed our study, some at a more general level of abstraction and others specific to the historical time and place. We start from the premise that identity is gendered and that the organization of sexual difference is central to the social world. Distinctions between men and women are ever present, shaping experience, influencing behaviour, structuring expectations. As a generation of feminists has argued, every individual's relation to the world is filtered through gendered subjectivity. That sexual identity is organized through a complex system of social relations, structured by the institutions not only of family and kinship but at every level of the legal, political, economic and social formation. Neither these identities nor institutional practices are fixed and immutable. 'Masculinity' and 'femininity' are constructs specific to historical time and place. They are categories continually being forged, contested, reworked and reaffirmed in social institutions and practices as well as a range of ideologies. Among these conflicting definitions, there is always space for negotiation and change although often differing interpretations are covered by a seemingly unified 'common sense'.[57] Violations of accepted gender boundaries by either men or women were, and are, subject to sanctions ranging from ridicule to violence.

It has been exceptionally difficult to insert these concerns into the main agenda of social and historical analysis. Our work confronts both the commonly accepted division of the world between *public* and *private* and the related theoretical categories of *production* and *reproduction*, the latter mainly elaborated in socialist feminist theory in an attempt to correct exclusive concentration on the former. Traditional Marxist scholars have paid scant attention to the family, the private, the home, the place to which women have been conceptually relegated. The world of production and the state has been systematically privileged as central to historical understanding. Many social scientists as well as historians have inherited this 'double view' of the social order and consign women to the home and family, sites which are accorded no conceptual or analytic importance in social theories. Women are defined by their sexuality while men remain gender neutral and are defined by class.[58]

An approach informed by Marx's concepts but shorn of reductionist and economistic formulations, offers one way out of this unhelpful dichotomy. His emphasis on the circuit of production with its necessary reproduction of labour power, of distribution and exchange, reminds us of the full cycle of capital and thus the central importance of consumption. That process of social reproduction depends on the family and women's labour, a form of labour which, however, is hidden by its categorization as private. And yet, the creation of the private sphere has been central to the elaboration of consumer demand, so essential to the expansion and accumulation process which characterizes modern societies. The recent work which has analysed consumption as a process of 'cultural production', looks not only at its role in reproduction but also at the creation of need and the ways in which particular desires and pleasures come to define social identities and to be represented as cultural products.[59] This approach has necessarily emphasized the gender dimension. Furthermore, consumption is instrumental in forming and maintaining status, the 'relational' element of class, the continual claim and counter claim to recognition and legitimation.[60] Gender classification is always an important element in the positioning of groups and individuals and the competition for resources which takes place at every level of society. Women, in their association with consumption, are often seen as creators as well as the bearers of status.

In an historical study of a society increasingly encompassed within industrial capitalism, inevitably *class*, the relation to the means of production, distribution and exchange and related cultural forms, became our second major conceptual axis. The theoretical debates of the last two decades have highlighted the importance of a non-reductionist analysis of class and have focused on questions of moral and cultural authority. Yet class has continued to be analysed without sexual specificity. Even E. P. Thompson's classic study of England in this period, with its important stress on cultural aspects of class, pays scant attention to the different positioning of men and women within the working class.[61] Our focus is on the gendered nature of class formation and the way sexual difference always influences class belonging. In this we follow Mary Ryan, whose study of the middle class in early nineteenth-century New York State argues that the domesticated family provided the 'cradle' for a new class culture.[62] Other studies of the development of domesticity have stressed political, ideological and bureaucratic factors; important but not sufficient to explain major change.[63]

The English middle class was being forged at a time of exceptional turmoil and threatening economic and political disorder. It is at such times that the endemic separation of social categories which exaggerate differences between groups, including men and women, produces intensified efforts to create a 'semblance of order'.[64] Claims for middle-class recognition were refracted through a gendered lens.[65] Middle-class farmers, manufacturers, merchants and professionals in this period, critical of many aspects of aristocratic privilege and power, sought to translate their increasing economic weight into a moral and cultural authority. Their claim to moral superiority was at the heart of their challenge to an earlier aristocratic hegemony. They sought to exercise this moral authority not only within their own communities and boundaries, but in relation to other classes. Their 'proud pretensions', their critique of the established dominance of the landed class and their belief in their capacity to control and improve the working class, which was at the centre of their claims, was articulated within a gendered concept of class. Middle-class gentlemen and middle-class ladies each had their appointed place in this newly mapped social world. The privileges and duties for a *lady* differed in crucial ways from those of a *gentleman*. A heavily gendered view of the world was utilized to soften, if not disavow, the disruption of a growing class system as the master and household head was transmuted into employer on the one hand and husband/father on the other.[66] Masculine identity was equated with an emerging concept of 'occupation', while women remained within a familial frame.[66]

It follows from this that *family* as an historical and analytic category becomes a crucial concept in this book. The variability of family forms cannot be overstressed; there is no essential 'family', but always 'families'. The work of the Cambridge Group has taught us to differentiate clearly between family and household. Miranda Chaytor's work on early modern households, in particular, has drawn attention to the 'fragility and imperma-nency of most domestic arrangements'.[67] Her work is critically extended by feminist insights and chronicles the differing experience of men and women, children and elders, both within the family and in relation to other institutions. In the early eighteenth century, as Kussmaul notes, no word existed which meant 'only kin' within a household; servants, lodgers, visi-tors, pupils, shopmen or unrelated children might well be included.[68]

This unit was under the authority of the paterfamilias: husband, father and master who represented his dependants to the wider body politic. Only gradually was he himself considered part of, rather than outside, that unit. Nor were either family or houshold necessarily coterminus with the group which ate or even slept under the same roof.[69] A multitude of inns and 'public houses' provided accommodation while informal visitors and casual dining at the tables of relatives and friends was constant. The boarding or part-boarding of all types of supernumeraries makes any such rigid distinc-tions historically untenable. Such a flexible concept of family was important when demographic failure, incompetence or disinclination of their own offspring to join the productive enterprise could be made good by giving opportunity to others from networks of kin and friends. Later in the nineteenth century, the middle class may have operated a tighter definition of family and loyalty to a business house, but this must be empirically established.

While we take the family as a central institution for the middle ranks at this time, we are aware of its flexible make-up and permeable boundaries. Familial inclusion and exclusion was a social principle around which female sexuality and reproduction, property and political status were organized.[70] Within the family, the dominance of the male is clear through inheritance (patrimonialism) and naming practice (patrilineality). Nevertheless, women were clearly central to the family's survival. Only by such unpicking of the concept of family, can we see women as well as men in the reality of their everyday lives and relationships, outside as well as inside the familial setting.[71]

Historical studies of family and economy which have focused on the working class, have been based on a conceptual separation between family and economy using an 'essentialist' view of the family, often seen as a pre-industrial enclave or survival.[72] A similar conception frames the sparser studies of entrepreneurs and professionals. Traditional economic historians have recognized the role of the family in providing capital and personnel for the firm. Their focus on economic growth or stagnation, however, usually deflects following this up and the object of study has remained the individual entrepreneur or industrial group. More recently, some studies of the wider middle class in various local settings have begun to include the family as part of a distinctive middle-class culture.[73] Few, however, have matched Dorothy Crozier's early and meticulous investigation of mid nineteenth-century Highgate indicating the interrelationship of family and firm.[74] Recently, R. J. Morris has stressed how not only consumption decisions but savings and allocation to different forms of investment were shaped by family events as well as production needs.[75]

It was the family which mediated between public and private and connected the market with the domestic. Well into the nineteenth century the family remained the basis for most economic activity. The guild, livery and joint stock company were all-male institutions which carried out only specific and limited functions. Most production for profit was through the *family enterprise*, a social entity which has been the special focus of our research. The forms of property organization and authority within the enterprise framed gender relations through marriage, the division of labour and inheritance practices. This necessarily included the 'production' of children. In the widest sense, the structure of property can be regarded as a powerful 'relational idiom' in the creation of both gender and class, placing men as those with power and agency, women as passive dependants.[76]

Increasingly, the enterprise was caught up in *market relations* – for labour, materials, capital, credit and sales. The elaboration of that market had grown in previous centuries but from its inception it was basically masculine in form and personnel. Far from the market being separate from the family, the two were locked into a set of elaborate connections. Contrary to the usual conception, the market never was 'sex blind'.[77]

In all societies, family organization has been embedded in systems of *kinship*. Kinship bonds, however, can also be flexible and extended by marriage particularly where there is an element of choice in marriage partner. Kinship recognition widens available resources and exchanges of services, especially welcome in lightening the burdens – or reaping the rewards – of parenthood. Such 'pro-parents', that is kin or fictive kin who take on some parental function, may draw closer to biological parents, thus increasing the density of the social web.[78] Intermarriage and a wide kinship network implies that some may be chosen and others quietly forgotten or even actively defied, an equally effective mechanism whether in far flung Quaker communities or a tightly knit village.[79] Strong kinship commitments tend to cut across class divisions since inevitably some will rise and some fall within the social structure. In a class-based society, flexibility in recognition of kin is a necessity but even residual ties serve to temper class antagonisms.

Kinship and family relationships, by definition, usually contain both men and women. Indeed, they are an important way of delineating gender. On the whole, women have been more often contained within these relationships; men move beyond them into all-male locations and organizations. American feminist historical research has highlighted the vitality of women's relationships to each other both within and across the boundaries of the family and the importance of such bonds in establishing a feminine identity and female-oriented culture.[80] Our study, too, recognizes the importance of women's ties to one another, among family members, kin and friends. While we have uncovered little evidence of an exclusively female culture in practice, nevertheless, in a society dominated by institutions framed to give men power, authority and rewards, women continued to find ways of expressing their needs and desires, often in terms of their claim for a separate sphere. Such claims, however, have tended to avoid any direct expression of sexual antagonism.

Recognizing the flexibilities of family and kin also draws attention to other historically specific relationships. Together with the emphasis on gender this has required us to be alert to mediating concepts appropriate to the period. *Sponsorship* and *patronage* were still important social bonds, particularly used in placing the young. These relationships were slowly taking on new meanings within the middle class, for example, in the notion of *stewardship* or *trusteeship*. One of the latent consequences of such practices was to tie together the patrons, or adults, in common concern and control of dependants or petitioners. Under aristocratic dominance, these vertical ties had been defined as *friendship*.[81] We have, however, noted a shift in meaning of that term towards more horizontal ties, used between more equal individuals as an extension or reaffirmation of kinship but including non-kin, often within a religious community. Such usage is an indication of the adaptable social forms adopted by a middle class whose status was not fixed at birth.

In conceiving and carrying out this study, we have attempted to move beyond the nineteenth-century inheritance of 'separate spheres'. But a particular problem stems from the tendency for gender terms to be used as stand-ins for socially valued or derogated attributes as when strength or independence are conceived of as 'manly' and weakness as effeminacy. Conversely, institutions and organizations which are in reality gendered are put forward as neutral or gender free as we have seen in the case of the market. Picking a way through this forest of 'mutual metaphorization' necessitates keen perception and a sense of proportion.[82]

Special sensitivity is also needed to grasp the interconnections which are masked by language expressive of the ideological divide. For example, women's domestic tasks which took place in the private sphere of the home have been unacknowledged as *work*. The contribution which married women made, and still make, to the family enterprise through their labour, their contacts and their capital was equally obscured.[83] As long as 'production' is narrowly defined, such connections literally cannot be seen. The world of production fed on consumer demands inspired by the bourgeois family for brass, for garden tools, curtains and wallpaper. Public men were constantly cared for and serviced by wives, daughters, sisters and female servants. The apparently autonomous individual man, celebrated in both political economy and evangelical religion, was almost always surrounded by family and kin who made possible his individual actions.

Similarly, men had to come to terms with the private world. Many men valued and enjoyed domesticity; others defined themselves in opposition to it. Middle-class homes were built on the expropriation of working men and women's labour, whether in the public world of the workplace or the private workplace of the home which employed the majority of the female workforce as servants well into the twentieth century. Public was not really public and private not really private despite the potent imagery of 'separate spheres'. Both were ideological constructs with specific meaning which must be understood as products of a particular historical time.[84]

Historical research which seeks to explore and deconstruct the divide between public and private has been hampered by the way records are categorized according to one or the other. Sources for family history have tended to be separated from those of economic, business or political history. Archives and subject indexes follow the division. In order to form a picture of people living the complexities of gender and class, it seemed necessary to turn to the local community where everyday behaviour as well as specific institutions could be observed. Since the underlying assumption was that capitalist enterprise was a dynamic factor in the constellation of class and gender in this period, we chose to study an urban and rural area where the latter was firmly embedded in market relations. Thus we could apply our analysis to a wider spectrum than the usual urban focus of middle-class historiography. The differences as well as similarities between the two areas have illuminated the general argument.

Our study concentrates on the industrial town of Birmingham and the agricultural counties of Essex and Suffolk whose economy was based on arable agriculture (see Maps 1–4). By the end of the period, Birmingham had a population of about 250,000; the eastern counties roughly double that number. These communities covered a range of occupational and religious groups but were compact enough to supply detailed knowledge of individuals, families and organizations. In addition to general coverage of the two areas, we made a detailed study of Birmingham's premier suburb, Edgbaston. The scattered evidence for the rural area at county level was counteracted by special attention to a market town, Colchester, and a representative village, Witham in Essex.

Within each area, we used a three tier approach.[85] The first covered named individuals and families and the relations between them. It was based mainly on qualitative material supplemented by a sample of wills. The second focused on the local communities: their physical lay-out, economic, political, religious and social profile and their local organizations. The third gave a quantitative framework within which to place more qualitative interpretation. It was based mainly on a sample of middle-class households from the 1851 census, the first census to give reliable household and occupational data.[86] This provided a sobering corrective to reliance on family papers. Separate files on individuals, family enterprises and organizations were constructed from these varied sources for each area. These were then consolidated into four area files: Birmingham, Essex, Suffolk and Witham. (For more detailed description of sources, see Appendix 2.)

Despite the attempt to draw a complete picture, gaps and distortions remain. In particular, the fact that we were not able to use solicitors holdings or court records has possibly resulted in a more harmonious picture than would otherwise have emerged. We are aware that less is said about the lower ranks of the middle class than the wealthier or better educated since their lives were less well recorded. By definition, the findings focus on those families who were successful rather than the many who failed and were swept out of the historical record.

Although we have concentrated on the two local areas, this is not meant to be a purely local study. Where evidence was thin, as it necessarily often was for women's experience, we have not hesitated to use sources from other places, although these are almost entirely confined to the Midlands and south-east, areas with a similar economic and social structure. The study addresses questions to the whole of English society even though the answers mainly concern a specific section of the provincial middle class. While there were undoubtedly local variations and, in particular, London with its concentrated commercial and professional enclaves may be somewhat different, nevertheless, we feel that the basic argument is generally applicable. By these various means we have attempted to draw a rounded picture of middle-class men and women as they followed their daily pursuits and carried on their individual lives at a time when they were both agent and object of major historical change.

'Birmingham Town Hall', Samuel Lines, 1821

Setting the scene

Places

The town – Birmingham

Towards the end of his journeys Mr Pickwick's negotiation of a certain delicate matter necessitated a visit to Birmingham. As he and his friends approached the 'heart of the turmoil' of 'this great working town' their senses were forcibly struck by 'the sights and sounds of earnest occupation'.

The streets were thronged with working people. The hum of labour resounded from every house, lights gleamed from the long casement windows in the attic stories, and the whirl of wheels and noise of machinery shook the trembling walls. The fires, whose lurid sullen light had been visible for miles, blazed fiercely up, in the great works and factories of the town. The din of hammers, the rushing of steam, and the dead heavy clanging of engines, was the harsh music which arose from every quarter.[1]

Birmingham was well known for the 'harsh music' of anvil and stamp, of press and lathe, of hammer and file. Its name had become synonymous with brass, just as Manchester was known for cotton. Visitors to the town regularly remarked on its 'uninviting and monotonous' appearance, its 'sooty artisans', its absent beaumonde, and contrasted these with the dazzling displays of steelware and plated goods in the shops, its wondrous character as far as nails, pins, screws and jewels were concerned.[2] Birmingham, commented its first historian, was 'well able to *fabricate* gentlemen, but not to *keep* them'. One had only to breathe the air of Birmingham to turn from an idle character to a diligent and productive one. Any hint of a profit and a Birmingham man would sniff it out.[3] Birmingham's interest, as described in 1836, was not in its churches, its streets, its institutions and its public buildings, for every town had these. Rather it lay in its products, whose technological innovation, scientific ingenuity, tasteful and skilful design, 'impress the mind with the conviction of the mighty and almost measureless powers of the human intellect'.[4] Birmingham might be a cultural desert but it was a paradise for the useful arts.[5]

Many of Birmingham's useful arts were designed to grace the houses of the middle class. From the cast iron coffee mills patented by Kenrick's West Bromwich family business to the plated ware suitable for breakfast, dinner and dessert services made in the workshops of the Ryland family, from the brass candlesticks, lamps and casters supplied by brass founders such as Robert Martineau, the brother of the famous writer Harriet, to the jewellery of James Luckcock, from the hinges of the wrought iron gate to the

Map 1 England, showing the main places mentioned in the text

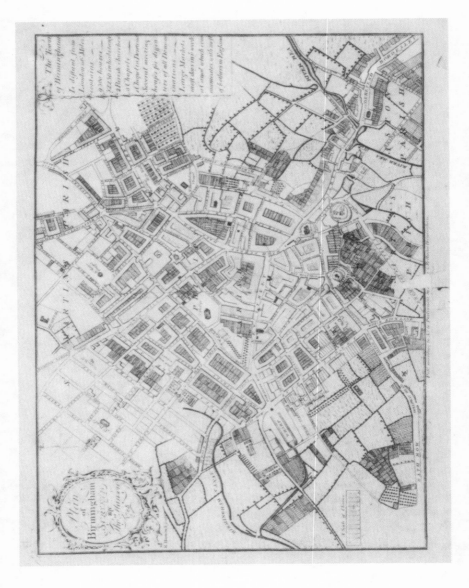

Map 2 Birmingham, 1787. Houses and workshops jostle together in the town centre with the canal and river acting as main arteries of communication

chemicals for the bleach and soap so essential to new standards of cleanliness, from the kettles and pots to the needles and screws, from umbrella stands to plate glass, all these were made in Birmingham.

Birmingham's place in the metal industries was well established by the seventeenth century, known particularly for its guns and swords. The expansion of the town in the eighteenth century rested on the development of the Staffordshire coal and iron industries and the improvements in transport which opened up the markets of the south and west as well as the colonies. Birmingham's jewellery and plate, pistols and daggers, buttons and buckles, seals, chains and charms of all kinds, known collectively as the toy trade, employed approximately 20,000 by 1759 and relied particularly on the new colonial markets.[6] The absence of gild and corporation restrictions facilitated development and particularly encouraged skilled Dissenters to settle in the town.[7] Between 1740–80 the town had already doubled in size and the population of around 35,000 in 1780 had grown to nearly 70,000 by 1800. Like several other industrial towns its peak period of growth was between 1821–31 when the population expanded by over 41 per cent (see Appendix 3).

It was the varied industries associated with metals that provided some of the work for this expanding population and filled the streets of the town with noise and smoke. Birmingham specialized in finishing work, for the primary stages in iron manufacture were usually done in the towns of the coal and iron fields. Finishing processes ensured the continued importance of skill combined with an extensive subdivision of work, so that small masters were able to survive for some time. Contemporaries noted that well into the nineteenth century there were few large but many smaller capitalists.[8] By 1810, however, concentration was beginning, connected to the price of new machinery, as in the glass industry. Between 1800–50 larger establishments were introduced into most of the town's staple trades and in boom years there was more investment in new plant. Between 1815 and 1838 there was a considerable increase in steam power and by the 1840s a number of large, efficient firms had emerged which aimed at low cost per unit of output. Increasingly, small masters could not compete and were driven into a dependent relationship on larger businesses for orders and credit, leading to the decline of an independent artisanate and a sharpening demarcation between wage earners and the petit bourgeoisie.[9]

Birmingham's early historian was struck by the absence of a local aristocracy and the speed with which gentlemen who made their fortune left the town.[10] The period from 1780–1850, however, saw the emergence of an increasingly articulate and indigenous middle class, determined to make Birmingham a place worth living in. In the late eighteenth century visitors to the Birmingham vicinity headed for Boulton's factory at Soho, a wonder of the new mechanical world with its water power used not only to drive the machinery but also to fill an ornamental lake.[11] There was little to feast the eyes on in the town. But merchants, professionals and manufacturers were united in their concern to improve the amenities of their Midland toyshop. Successive Improvement Acts gave the oligarchic elite, the Street Commissioners, the powers to deal with nuisances, to light and to clean, and to reorganize the markets.[12] Private housing developments, first in

Map 3 Birmingham, 1848. The town has now spilled over into the surrounding countryside with development along the main roads. To the east (right) the railway links Birmingham with the rest of the country. In the south west (lower left) Edgbaston's orderly growth is visible

select areas of the town centre, then further from the 'heart of the turmoil' in areas such as Handsworth, Harborne and Edgbaston sought to both stimulate and satisfy the increasing middle-class demand for homes separated from the workplace, from noise, smoke, and the presence of working-class neighbours.[13] Private associations raised funds for an imposing Grecian Town Hall, a purpose built Corn Exchange, new reading rooms and subscription libraries. The transformation of New Street, one of the town's principal streets, showed what could be done. It was a busy commercial thoroughfare by the late eighteenth century but offered little architecturally that would 'polish or enlighten' as well as being the regular market place for pigs, sheep and horses. From 1800 the first paving stones were laid, the Theatre Royal was much improved after a fire, the old established Hen and Chickens became a handsome new hotel with a stone front and was later further improved with a frontage and a portico. The animals were sent off to a newly built Doric Market Hall. At the top of the street where New Street met Paradise Street rose the new Anglican Christ Church. The grammar school was rebuilt in Gothic style, pavements were raised with railings, gas lighting was introduced, shops were remodelled with impressive showrooms and corinthian columns. By 1851 a Birmingham poet could wax lyrical on New Street, a fitting main thoroughfare for a prosperous, liberal and civilized town:

> In every building of this gorgeous street, Grace,
> beauty, fashion all combine to meet. . . .[14]

This poem, 'Birmingham', was dedicated to William Schofield, one of the town's first MPs after the Reform Act of 1832, and was an expression of radical, liberal pride in the achievements of the Birmingham men of reform. Its narrative of improvement, inspired by radicals and Dissenters, would have met with much resistance, for the period from 1780–1850 was marked by times of bitter political and religious division in the town. The Priestley Riots of 1791, when a mob proclaiming itself in favour of Church-and-King had attacked the homes and businesses of leading Dissenters on the grounds of their sympathy for the French Revolution, left a deep scar. As one of the victims wrote,

These unhappy riots . . . have astonished all Europe, as a shameful attack upon private property, which, in all civilised nations, is held sacred.[15]

Working-class Jacobinism survived in the town, though Birmingham never achieved the level of militancy of Sheffield or London, but middle-class reformers were severely shaken by the attack on the sacred shibboleth of private property and the failure of the authorities to protect them.

   The riots had marked the high point of the smouldering hostility between the Church and Dissent. It was not to re-emerge with the same force until the 1830s with the eventual success of Dissenting attempts to stop the payment of church rates. Meanwhile, there were many efforts by enthusiastic Anglicans and nonconformists to work together on commonly defined matters of Christian interest. Dissenters could always command considerable power and influence in the town, although the 1851 religious census revealed that nearly half the church-goers were Anglican, a high proportion for an industrial town and undoubtedly connected with the efforts of Anglican Evangelical reformers.[16] In improving and philanthropic activities, however, Dissenters were always to the fore and there were a number of influential Quaker and Unitarian families who were central to the town's economic, social and political life. There are few Anglican equivalents to the names of Cadbury, Lloyd, Kenrick, Ryland and Phipson, all assured a place in Birmingham history and able to make their mark in successive generations.

Religious divisions by no means mirrored political divisions. Churchmen were often Tories but Dissenters were divided between Whigs and Radicals. The series of Improvement Acts from 1769 had named wealthy and prominent citizens as Street Commissioners, responsible for some town services. These were men united by their ownership of property worth £1000 but divided in their religious and political affiliations. Few were involved with the rise to prominence of the Birmingham Political Union which depended on an alliance of Tories with Radicals, industrialists with bankers, masters with men, and engaged few of the established Birmingham elite in its struggle for the vote. This campaign for political representation led directly to the claim for incorporation and a demand for representative town government. The granting of borough status was a triumph for the Radicals who dominated the council until 1851, led by small manufacturers and traders. Meanwhile, the Commissioners continued to operate, with control over the major areas of town government, and it was not until 1851 that this oligarchic body was abolished and the council given real power.[17] By then the threat from the Chartist movement was over and the attempts to build alliances between sections of the middle class and sections of the working class had, for the moment, broken down. Erstwhile middle-class Radicals who had led a class alliance against the 'lordlings and scions of nobility' had become the protagonists of law and order, the established rulers of their great Midland town.[18]

The religious and political divisions which had fractured the Birmingham middle class did not prevent the emergence of a common culture. In 1780 when Joseph Priestley came to Birmingham, the Unitarian chapel of which he was the minister was in the centre of the town; his large and comfortable house was in the style of a modest country gentleman, close to open land. For men of his generation there were only two choices, to live in the town centre, as did many of the merchants and manufacturers with their warehouses and workshops attached or next to their dwelling, or to move to the outskirts. For the generation of young men influenced by Priestley, men like James Luckcock, a new alternative had arisen; to live in a middle-class suburb, haven of domestic tranquility. In Edgbaston and suburbs like it, Luckcock was joined by professionals, by those active in commerce and manufacture, and by ladies and gentlemen of independent means. Their families comprised the missing middle class of an earlier time, families who stayed and worked to build a town renowned not only for its brass, but also for the culture which brass could buy.

The countryside – Essex and Suffolk

At first sight, nothing could be further from Birmingham's dynamism than the flat, coastal lands or 'picturesquely undulating' western regions of Essex and Suffolk with their 'pleasing succession of fine rural landscapes' dotted with country seats of minor gentry and city gentlemen.[19] Compared to Birmingham, larger towns like Colchester were open and clean, situated on or near rivers winding through meadows fringed with woodland. The remains of walls, priories and churches partly built from Roman ruins were constant reminders of their antiquity. In these counties, woollen textiles had been the staple industry of the seventeenth and early eighteenth centuries. Their economies were already tied to London and overseas trade routes.[20] By the end of the eighteenth century, however, competition from abroad and the drift of textile production to the north-west had reduced the trade which was finally extinguished by the blockade imposed by France during the war. But the blow to the wool trade simultaneously cut off grain imports, opening opportunities to local agriculturalists. In the space of a few decades, arable farming became the mainstay of the area's economy.[21] Market activity which was already well served by canal, river and coastal traffic was improved by road transport based on turnpikes: coaches, goods waggons, vans and carts of every description.[22] Woollen merchants, many of whom had farmed on the side, turned their energies and capital to farming, while agriculture in the eastern region also attracted City investment.[23] Fulling mills for cloth were rapidly converted to grinding corn.[24]

Essex, in particular, lent itself to farming for profit. Many common lands had long been enclosed yet most parishes were not dominated by a single landowner.[25] Very large acreages and tiny plots alike were losing out to medium sized but substantial farms, averaging 150 to 300 acres.[26] When rented by an enterprising farmer, these were large enough to take advantage of new developments in agriculture, concentrating on corn and barley with a sharp fall in butter and cheese.[27] The scale of production and pull of the London market, made Essex and Suffolk the first areas to adopt drainage, crop rotation and root vegetables, the elements of improved farming.[28] Arable farming on this scale demanded more labour, not of the continuous kind needed for animal care but less skilled hands at planting, hoeing and harvest. As a result, Essex had one of the highest rates of employment of wage labour on the land.[29] For those farmers and their landlords able and willing to make the change, profits were golden until the 1820s when cessation of war, combined with poor harvests, reversed the high price of corn and the less well capitalized went to the wall. Nevertheless, the more secure recovered and continued to flourish. This wage-employing 'agricultural bourgeoisie'[30] stimulated the related manufacturing operations of milling, malting, brewing, ironfounding and transport and encouraged professional services: land surveying, land management, conveyancing, auctioneering, banking and engineering.

In the eastern region of breckland or marshes, new lands were drained for grain production and farmsteads located in the open country. But for the most part, farmers continued to live and work from villages, even town centres. In Thaxted, Essex, in the 1790s, a third of all 'traders' listed in the directory were farmers. Even in Colchester there were seventy-two farmers

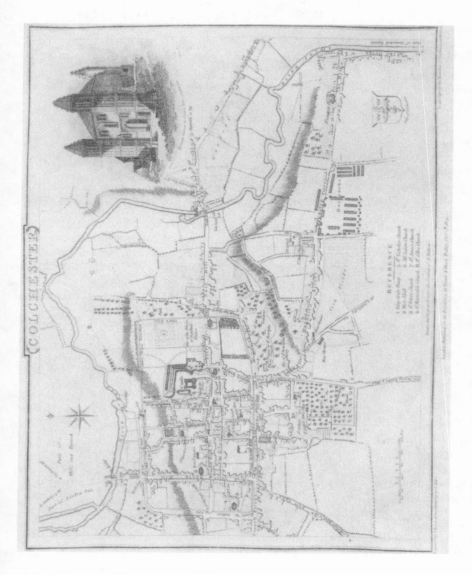

Map 4 Colchester, 1805. Most building was still within the town walls with large open spaces between streets

Plate 2 Colchester from the north in the 1820s

Plate 3 Colchester High Street in the 1820s

living within the town boundaries in 1851.[31] Rural industrial development
was steady but undramatic, often located in isolated canal sidings or river
basins.[32] Mills, powered by wind, river or tides, provided much of the
motor force for processing agricultural products.[33]

These developments were reflected in the distribution of the growing
population which rose from 436,868 in 1801 to 706,533 in 1851.[34] The larger
market towns of between 20,000 and 30,000 were headed by Colchester in
Essex and Ipswich in Suffolk, followed by Chelmsford, administrative and
judicial focus of Essex, and Bury St Edmunds, Suffolk's social and ecclesiastical centre. The remainder of the population was spread over smaller
towns, villages and hamlets whose fortunes waxed and waned with the local
economy. Some had been depopulated with the decline of the wool trade.
Others like Witham in Essex, were revitalized in the late eighteenth century
as stopping places en route from London, many to be upstaged again by
the railway within forty years.

A market town like Colchester, which served the rural hinterland, was
peopled with artisans and small retail shops. Farmers, professionals,
merchants and prosperous shopkeepers dominated the economic and social
scene. A silk mill and distillery were the only large industrial works in the
town.[35] The upsurge in the fortunes of towns like Colchester from the late
eighteenth century could be sensed in its bustling streets now extending
beyond the crumbling town walls. Brick fronted houses and bow-windowed
shops, the buying and selling in the High Street central market, the people
pouring in to attend the numerous fairs, all were witnesses to the prosperity
brought by rising grain prices and army contracts.

Early nineteenth-century activity brought a new breed of grand public
buildings: the workhouse beyond the northern town gate, the porticoed
hospital to the west, the theatre and new church to the south. Dominating
the top end of the High Street was the pillared front of the combined Corn
Exchange and Essex and Suffolk Insurance Society building, crowned with
a clock commissioned by Colchester's Evangelical Tory MP, Robert
Thornton, and made by one of the town's best-known clock manufacturers.[36] Despite in-filling in the main town streets, early nineteenth-century
Colchester still had a green and leafy atmosphere. The substantial houses
of the middling ranks were surrounded by gardens and orchards. The
open ground where wool merchants had dried their cloth was now market
gardens.

While towns like Colchester and Ipswich may have been bypassed by
industrial production, they were by no means rural backwaters. The army
presence during the war, the influx of retired City families, the relative
proximity of the metropolis encouraged a wider outlook. In eastern districts
of London nonconformist communities, some with Hugenot influence and
encouraged by the commercial atmosphere, had grown up in areas like
Islington, Hackney and Stoke Newington, extending into Essex through
Wanstead and Walthamstow. Their large, wealthy congregations and ministerial training centres were important sources of contacts and support for
Essex and Suffolk Dissenting families.

By the 1820s, almost forty coaches a day were on their way to or from
east London through south-east Essex,[37] routes later taken by railway

development. Even with stage coaches, it was possible for people living in the vicinity of Colchester to be at The Bull, Aldgate by mid-morning and return the same evening after a day shopping, attending meetings or visiting friends.[38] Personal and business correspondence was delivered twice a day by mail coach while London newspapers supplemented the *Ipswich Journal* and *Chelmsford Chronicle*, the established local papers, soon extended by a range of other local publications of every persuasion.[39] For the worldly minded there were balls at the Assembly Rooms, visits to the theatre or races. For the more serious there were lecture series, reading rooms, museum displays, the botanical gardens. Weekday and Sunday sermons crossed a wide spectrum of religious allegiance. For men, there were social and political clubs meeting in numerous public houses.

Large villages like Witham in Essex with a population of between 2000 and 4000 also throve on agricultural prosperity with markets, mills, maltings, cyder plants, tanneries and brickworks. Rents of agricultural land in Witham had risen by 40 per cent between 1770 and 1805.[40] Witham had the added advantage of lying about 40 miles on the main route out of London. Large coaching inns and a variety of hostelries dotted Newland Street, the main road which extended for about two-thirds of a mile, where the majority of the town's population lived. Here open fields ran to the backs of the brick-fronted town houses and shops and farms lined either side of this wide, grass-verged thoroughfare. A large coach builder, a modest spa and a mental asylum were the only 'industries' aside from a small brush manufactory whose owner did not mix with the town elite and most of whose employees were immigrants to the area.[41]

Towns like Witham also had their complement of bookshops, literary clubs and visiting shows and people could easily go to nearby Chelmsford for more sophisticated facilities. Gentry families, particularly widows and unmarried daughters, inhabited the top end of Newland Street in large houses which had been renovated with new staircases, plaster work and other elegant details.[42] In the 1840s, Jacob Pattisson, an attorney from a local family who had made its wealth in shopkeeping, developed an area branching off Newland Street with a church, school, police station and many new houses, suitable for the new breed of white-collar lower middle-class family.[43] Social circles in Witham clustered around membership of church and chapel as much as income. The dominance of agriculture and the gentry in their midst made it, in the words of Henry Dixon, an aspiring doctor and newcomer, 'a smart little town with rather high aristocratic pretentions'.[44] Like Dixon, the majority of professionals, many tradespeople and some resident gentry had been born outside the town, many outside the region.[45]

Much of the rural population lived further from main routes. For example, Saffron Walden, with a population little larger than Witham, nestled in the north-west corner of Essex, its fortunes based largely on barley for Quaker breweries in London. The town was approached through a ring of clay pits, small brickfields, lime kilns and a gypsy encampment. Common lands where sheep grazed and cricket was played lay on the margins of the town centre, a square where the inhabitants gathered to gossip on summer evenings. On the other side, numbers of allotments were tended by labourers in a field let out by a prosperous Quaker brewer. The Allotment Society was patronized by the aristocratic and major landowner Lord Braybrooke, also president of the local Agricultural Society who had built the museum and Agricultural Hall which was run by a Quaker trustee.[46]

Many smaller villages were still more remote. The literate culture of the middle class may have been slower to reach outlying hamlets and farmsteads on the marshy coastline of Essex or wooded uplands of north-west Suffolk, but a thin network of like-minded families travelled to Sunday services, visited and made themselves well informed far beyond the daily working round. As farmers and tradesmen broadened their outlook and raised their standard of living, inevitably social barriers rose between them and agricultural wage labourers. But minor gentry and the clergy who had assumed social leadership also had to re-evaluate their position in the social order in relation to the novel self-confidence of the middling ranks. Not surprisingly this economic and social jostling took on a political cast although it was often reflected through complicated religious alliances.

Late eighteenth-century market towns were run mainly by self-selected corporations dominated by party interest, ripe with patronage which verged on outright corruption. Colchester's Anglican Tories held the town so tightly that many early nineteenth-century improvements such as paving, lighting and water supplies were instigated by mainly nonconformist tradesmen as private companies or taken on by Improvement Commissioners.[47] In the 1830s, following national legislation allowing Dissenters to hold office and reforming municipal government, the more liberal element succeeded in capturing the corporation. However, after a few years of the liberals' notoriously inefficient rule, Colchester's Tory oligarchy were triumphantly returned and maintained control beyond mid century.[48] Ipswich's liberal nonconformists fared better for, building on a minority Whig presence, they gained and held power for over a decade.[49]

In the countryside, larger farmers dominated through control of the vestry and as overseers of the poor. At national level, the agricultural interest overrode party divisions as Whig landowners joined with Tories in support of protection for grain prices. In the 1830s and 1840s, local opposition mainly took the form of anti-Corn Law agitation championed by a handful of independently minded nonconformists, many already bitter over religious issues. Some Whig farmers, while supporting the Corn Laws, vigorously promoted a free market in trade and labour. The wealthy Witham farmer, William Hutley, would have stopped all out-relief through the winter months even in the cruel conditions of the 1820s depression. But he was opposed by the more paternalistic Tory clergy.[50] Municipal Reform in 1835 released the energies of many nonconformist men. By 1836, nine out of the sixteen-member council of Saffron Walden were Quakers or Independents, five from one chapel, one of whom became the town's first Dissenting mayor.[51]

Nevertheless, radical support was best able to emerge at parliamentary level, backed by commercial and professional men, free from direct agricultural pressure. Together with a few nonconformist farmers, they rallied behind D. W. Harvey, a reforming attorney who repeatedly stood as MP for Colchester and was finally returned in the 1830s. Like other middle-class Whigs, however, once in office he gave tacit support to the new Poor Law.[52] The Reform Act had actually reduced the number of artisan voters in Colchester and resentment which had simmered through the lean years of the 1820s flared at the imposition of rigorous Poor Law enforcement, feeding support for Colchester's moderate Chartism of the 1830s. Chartism in Essex and Suffolk was mainly an artisan movement, but had the backing of a handful of middle-class men such as a dynamic minister of Colchester's largest Independent chapel as well as the self-styled Owenite and professed historical materialist, J. Barmby.[53]

Through the 1830s a frail Chartist–Liberal alliance survived, managing to support crowds of up to 3000 at a meeting on universal suffrage which packed Colchester town centre in 1838. But the activities of more militant Chartists elsewhere in the country frightened middle-class sympathizers. In the countryside, the Chartist cause found a small following in selected villages urged on by Barmby. It was the only political movement in the region which made any effort to actively involve women. But the movement began to dwindle as artisans' energies turned to nascent trade unionism. In any case, by the 1840s, fortunes made in farming, trade and the professions, even by nonconformists, had become respectable. Party politics may have continued at the hustings, but in the great work of enlightening and controlling the labouring classes Colchester Tories like the Rounds joined with nonconformist Liberals such as the Tabors and Savills in Sunday school and philanthropic efforts, as joint members of a solid mid Victorian provincial middle class.[54]

Although the economy of the two areas was based on products as diverse as grain and metals, their involvement in regional and national markets had laid the groundwork for a similar social structure where medium-sized manufactories were matched by medium-sized farms. Obviously, the several hundred thousand inhabitants of Birmingham were more closely concentrated physically than their matching numbers scattered over the countryside and market towns of the two counties. Moreover, the manufacturing town had expanded two and a half times more during the period of national maximum growth in the 1820s and 1830s (see Appendix 3).[55] In both areas, however, a good deal of expansion had come from migrants seeking new opportunities and these dynamic newcomers seem particularly numerous among the middle class.[56]

Both Birmingham and the county towns of Essex and Suffolk were well placed for easy contact with the Metropolis (see Maps 1–4). They had trade and transport links with other regions; Birmingham's canals being matched by Essex and Suffolk coastal routes. The latter, however, were more exposed to threat of invasion which inevitably gave greater immediacy to the French wars, although both areas benefited from a war economy.

Despite these basic similarities there were significant differences in relations between classes. The sheer concentration of labourers and artisans in the manufacturing town made the groups above them acutely aware of their condition which was a constant source of concern. The diffused, quiescent agricultural labourers could more easily be ignored until the crisis conditions of the post-war years brought open attacks on property in the brief reign of 'Captain Swing'.[57]

At the other end of the spectrum, the gentry as landlords formed a greater presence in the countryside and a strong influence in market towns where many tradesmen and professionals owed their livelihood to aristocratic patronage. Birmingham, by contrast, was a more self-contained community. With its aggressively philistine reputation, it was not a town favoured by resident gentry. Into the early years of the new century, it lacked the elegant facilities of a social centre like Bury St Edmunds, only a tenth its size. There was no ancient university casting influence as did Cambridge in the eastern region where the sons of quite modest families might make their way to be educated.[58]

Aristocratic leadership and the presence of Cambridge University were connected to the higher profile of the established church in the countryside, both its traditional and Evangelical wings. These factors, plus the thinly scattered presence of middle-class families, may partly account for the greater number of local writers on domestic subjects we have found in Essex and Suffolk. The compact Birmingham middle class was actively building a domestic culture in manufacture and trade, in suburbs and voluntary societies. The curate, doctor, farmer or country tradesman and his female relatives in village or county town were more likely to propagate these ideas in writing.

People

The generations born into the middling ranks in the 1780s and 1790s experienced the full impact of the evangelical movement. Their childhood and youth were permeated by the early excitement and later revulsions surrounding the French Revolution and the uncertainties of a society constantly at war. Their families were often newcomers to the communities where they grew up. Their prosperity was closely tied to middle-class consumption since in many cases they lived by producing goods and services which formed the lineaments of the middle-class culture of which they were a part.

The two families here described in detail both followed this pattern, although one lived from shopkeeping and food manufacture and the other from ministering, writing and publishing. In both cases, these activities became family traditions which extended over three or four generations. One branch of the Cadburys of Birmingham dealt in drapery to be made into the respectable clothing of middle-class display. Another sold tea and coffee, soon specializing in the manufacture of chocolate which in this period was consumed solely as a hot beverage and deliberately promoted as a wholesome family drink, an alternative to the stimulant of alcohol. The Taylors of Essex lived by producing cultural items: lectures, sermons, engraving, writing and publishing ideas about correct middle-class morality and behaviour.

The following detailed description of these two families draws together the lived experience of the various themes later explicated in the text.

The family shop: the Cadburys of Birmingham[59]

'God has placed men in families'   George Cadbury 1839–1922

In 1794 Richard Tapper Cadbury, the son of a Devon Quaker serge-maker, arrived in Birmingham and set up in business as a draper. This marked the beginning of the long connection between the Cadbury family and Birmingham, a connection that still exists today. Richard Tapper Cadbury, born in 1768, had left home at 14 to be apprenticed to a draper in Gloucester and then moved to London where he worked in linen drapers in the City. At the age of 34 he managed to set up independently and settled with a partner in Birmingham, no doubt hoping that the rapidly expanding town would provide a good business base. In 1796 he married Elizabeth Head of Ipswich and in 1800 they moved, together with their first child Sarah, to the good sized house with some garden above their shop in Bull Street, a major shopping street in the town centre (see Plate 4). Over the years they managed to build up a flourishing business and at the age of 60, Richard Tapper Cadbury was able to retire with a 'modest competency', as his son John described it, and leave the shop in the hands of his eldest son Benjamin.[60]

From the beginning the Bull Street shop was a family business. The premises, combining workplace and home, were run as a joint enterprise by Richard and Elizabeth, though Elizabeth, as a married woman, could not be a full partner. She was always ready to be called on in emergencies, however, and to help in the shop when needed. In her husband's absence she oversaw the business, checking on orders, receiving news from him as to wholesale purchases and dealing with callers. Meanwhile, she carried responsibility for the running of the house with its growing number of children, its apprentices and the various relatives and Friends who lived there from time to time. In the fourteen years between 1797 and 1811 Elizabeth had ten children, eight of whom survived to adulthood so that she must have been more or less continually pregnant or nursing. She had to cope with the death of two children, one at 3 and one at 13 as well as that of her own mother who was living with them. In a letter to one of his daughters, away at school, Richard described her as recovered from an illness and able to 'bustle about all day'. With water to carry, a house to keep clean, meals to prepare, servants to supervise, clothes to make and mend, apprentices to keep in line, little children to nurse and teach and a watchful eye required for the business, she must have needed to be constantly on the move.[61] Her care of the physical needs of family and household enabled Richard to focus on the business which supported them all. Whether greeting his customers in the shop, going to London to choose new fabrics, training his apprentices in cutting, placing his adverts in the local press or, as the business expanded, investing the profits in property and shares, he knew that he could rely on the support of the family.

The immediate family could be called on to help in the shop. Daughters Maria and Ann lent a hand when needed. Little boys could be used to run errands and take messages. As the sons grew they were sent as apprentices to learn different aspects of retailing. The eldest, Benjamin, returned to take over the business, the second son, John, set up as a tea and coffee

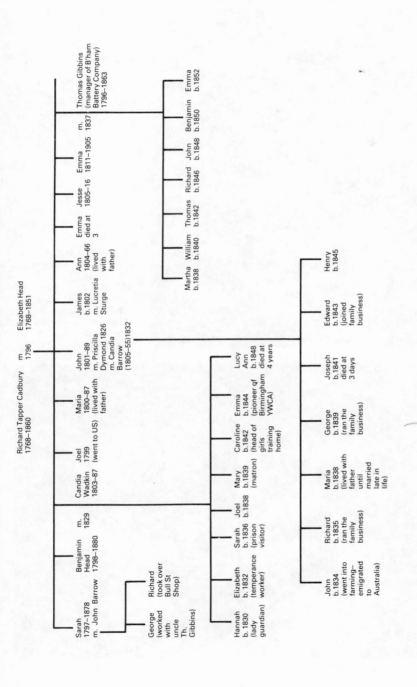

Figure 1 *Cadbury family tree*

Plate 4 The Cadbury shop and house, Bull Street, central Birmingham, 1824

Plate 5 A family portrait of Benjamin Head and Candia Wadkin Cadbury (m. 1829) and their children, whose fortunes were based on the drapery business. Photographed c. *1850*

Plate 6 A Cadbury family home in Calthorpe Road, Edgbaston, photographed about 1860. Several Cadbury households were set up in this part of Edgbaston

The Contented Pair

A cottage, with a steeple nigh,
A little brook that bubbles by,
A garden full of fruits and flowers,
Of mossy beds and shady bowers;
An orchard richly stored with fruit,
That any lady's taste may suit;
Daises o'erspread th' enamel'd ground,
Diffusing fragrance all around.

attributed to *John Cadbury*

Plate 7 'A Contented Pair', attributed to John Cadbury, 1801–89

merchant next door. The extended family also provided aid of various kinds which the Cadburys reciprocated. Sister Sarah, married and living in London with her silkmercer husband, provided a metropolitan base. Her son Samuel was apprenticed to Richard. Family acted as trustees and executors, advisers and consultants. After the marriage of Benjamin to Candia Wadkin of Lancaster, advice on business affairs flowed between Richard and her father, the two fathers-in-law. Recommendations as to the arrangement of fire insurance or the right time to buy railroad shares were as important a part of family letters as the news of relatives and friends. Daughter Sarah's two sons were both taken into aspects of the growing family business.

Friends also could be relied on for support in business matters. The Cadburys had been Quakers since the early eighteenth century. The Quaker network provided not only a religious community but also a social world across the country. All the Cadbury children who married, entered well established Quaker families, from the Sturges and Gibbins of Birmingham, corn merchants and bankers respectively, to the Wadkins and Barrows of Lancashire. Indeed, when appropriate partners were not chosen, marriages did not take place. Emma Cadbury recorded that her two sisters Maria and Ann both had lovers who were not acceptable; they remained single, looking after their father in his widowhood. The Quakers in Birmingham were a coherent and self-conscious community, sharing their particular habits in worship at their regular social events and in their daily lives. They talked together, ate together, shared their high days and holidays. For Thomas Southall, Quaker chemist and founder of the Southalls family business, it was natural to lodge with the Cadburys when he first arrived in Birmingham and set up his shop opposite them in Bull Street.

The Quaker community gave strength and assistance to its members, but it by no means cut them off from the rest of society. Like James Luckcock, Richard Tapper Cadbury played a significant part in the public institutions and voluntary associations that were so central to the middle class in this period. He was named as a Street Commissioner, one of the elect of the town. He was never a party man in any simple sense, though he stood unsuccessfully as a Tory candidate for Edgbaston in the municipal elections of 1838. His main commitment was to philanthropic issues and he was active in the anti-slavery and temperance movements as well as working for institutions such as the General Hospital, the Deaf and Dumb Asylum, the Eye Infirmary and the Infant School. He was ready and willing to work in an interdenominational context and campaigned with Anglican Evangelicals such as the Rev. William Marsh to improve and moralize the town. He was widely recognized as one of the 'fit and proper' men of Birmingham, present at town meetings on important matters, a well-known figure for whose funeral all the shops in Bull Street were closed as a mark of respect.

For his son John, however, his beloved father's 'most interesting and important feature . . . was to be found in his consistent private walk in the bosom of his family'.[62] But the nature of that 'private walk' was changing. The relative success of the drapery business allowed Richard to rent a second house from 1812, in Islington Row on the edge of Edgbaston, at that time effectively the country. Here the younger children spent a good deal of their time keeping pigeons, rabbits, a dog and a cat. The parents joined them whenever possible. Elizabeth was running two households, constantly moving between the two of them, enjoying gardening and fruit preserving as well as childcare and home improvements, completely occupied in the world of family and Friends. Richard was increasingly engaged in the public and civic scene, a domain that was rapidly expanding. In 1829, on the marriage of their eldest son Benjamin, Richard effectively retired from the business and he and Elizabeth settled, with their daughters Maria, Ann and Emma, in a new house in Edgbaston. Benjamin and Candia moved in over the shop and brought up their six daughters and one son in the refurbished family house, sometimes renting a country cottage for the summer months somewhere nearby. In the 1840s they too moved into Edgbaston.

Meanwhile, John, the second son, had returned from his training in Leeds and London. In 1824, with the help of a modest capital from his father, he set up in trade as a tea and coffee merchant next door to the old family shop. Initially he lived above the shop with his first wife whose premature death left him alone. In 1832 he married Candia Barrow and for the first two years of their marriage they stayed in Bull Street. At the time Candia regarded this as entirely natural, but later a daughter explained this life over the shop in terms of her mother's desire not to be separated from her husband. After the birth of their first child they moved into a small house in Edgbaston. They subsequently found a house, rather cottage-like in appearance, on Calthorpe Road only a few doors away from Richard and Elizabeth and with many alterations and additions it remained the family home for over forty years (see Plate 6). Here Candia and John brought up their five sons and one daughter Maria. 'Our home was one of sunshine' wrote Maria, in her evocation of her childhood, written for her own nieces and nephews, 'Home was the centre of attraction to us all, and simple home pleasures our greatest joy.' Her parents loved their home and garden and Candia busied herself with domestic life, children and gardening but

our Father was greatly occupied with business and town affairs and other interests and he had very little time during the week, for enjoying his garden.[63]

The married life of John and Candia was significantly different in one respect from that of their parents' generation. Living as they did in Edgbaston, Candia had no direct relation to the business and John left home each day to go to work, coming home in the evening. Suburban living meant an evening meal rather than a midday dinner. Their business was still a family business in the sense that it supported the family, that its managerial personnel was mainly drawn from the family and that its ownership remained within the family. But Candia did not help in the shop or look after apprentices, she was not concerned with the running of the factory which John set up in 1831, where the beans were roasted and ground for the famous cocoa drink. Her children did not run errands and help in the shop. Candia's presence, however, was still essential for the success of the business. Her practical and emotional support enabled John to work well until her death in 1855 when the family fortunes plummeted. This business decline was explained in terms of the widower's unhappiness and it was only halted when sons Richard and George took over the firm completely, utilizing an inheritance from their mother as an additional capital. In the terms of Richard's biographer this was a test of their manliness. They 'pushed like men', he wrote, and 'put their shoulders to the wheel'.

Their wholesome training in self-discipline, thoroughness, and attention to detail, as also the habit of abstinence from alcohol and tobacco, and from any pursuits which might weaken their physical and moral fibre, stood them now in good stead.[64]

Their self-discipline was rewarded with the new factory at Bournville, an achievement that depended on hard work and austere living. As George later wrote,

If I had been married there would have been no Bournville today – it was just the money that I saved by living so sparely that carried us over the crisis.[65]

In 1872, once the business was on a firm footing he married and established his own comfortable home. His wife, like her mother-in-law, had no direct relation to the business. Indeed George Cadbury was strongly opposed to the employment of married women and refused to have them working at Bournville.

Elizabeth Head Cadbury had seen the business as part of her life. As she wrote in 1828 when the Bull Street premises were being altered and they were worried as to the effects this would have on the light in the parlour, 'I suppose we must not complain as it is for the business.'[66] Her daughters-in-law and granddaughters had somewhat different attitudes to the work that women should do. For Candia and her sisters-in-law married life started over the shop, but the physical separation between workplace and home which affected all of them at some point in their lives symbolized the more rigid demarcation of male and female spheres which was taking place. As long as Emma Cadbury Gibbins lived next door to her husband's battery works in Digbeth her home was the site of partners' dinners, impromptu meetings, and could contain an idle cousin who was supposed to have responsibilities in the factory. But such a home meant an uncomfortable proximity not only to a fire at the works but also to strikes and Chartist demonstrations. Life in Edgbaston removed the felt dangers of town centre life, but left Emma's relation to the family enterprise considerably attenuated. The increasing contemporary stress on the professional nature of motherhood found its echoes in the comfortable Cadbury homes and leafy gardens of Edgbaston, an early example of middle-class suburbia, where women were free to focus their time and attention more exclusively on hearth, husband and children.

When 'woman's mission' was defined as within the family what choices were there for those women who did not marry? Elizabeth's daughter Maria remained single and lived with her parents until they died, caring for her father in his last years. Her will provides a testimony of the social and emotional world of a single woman of modest independent means in an extended and close family. Her favourite family memorabilia were left to her beloved sister Emma (her other sister Ann with whom she lived for many years had died before her), and precious teaspoons, sauce ladles and sugar tongs were left to her many nieces and nephews. Her nieces were her especial financial responsibility, together with an old servant and the philanthropic societies with which she had been associated – the Ladies' Negroes' Friends Society and the Society for the Relief of Aged and Infirm Women each had a legacy of £10. Her life was one of service to family and friends, her financial support came from that family enterprise she indirectly succoured.

For her nieces, however, growing up in the 1830s and 1840s, there were new possibilities. Her brother Benjamin had seven daughters, to each of whom she left £300. The six who survived took up philanthropic work as a profession, an option that did not exist for their aunts who had to pioneer the right of women to engage with issues such as anti-slavery. Their aunt Candia had so disliked public activities that she had pursued her philanthropic works silently and unostentatiously, though in her own family 'she shone bright as the wife and mother'. For the next generation of Hannah the lady Guardian, Elizabeth the temperance worker, Sarah the prison visitor, Mary the matron, Caroline the head of a Friends mission in Syria and Emma the pioneer of the Birmingham YWCA, such modesty in the public world of service could be eschewed since philanthropy had become the quintessential sphere of the single woman.

Hannah's mother, also Candia, wrote to her when she was away at the Quaker girls' school in Lewes in the 1840s. She stressed to her the continuities between the generations in their family. 'Affectionate feeling', she wrote, 'sweetens many a trial thro' life . . . may we all continue to be as our dear Parents and their children are and have been a family of love. . . .'[67] To the Cadburys that love may have seemed a natural and timeless phenomenon, born of their Christian faith, their commitment to family life and their honest business practice. But it was a love framed by particular legal and economic institutions, by particular ideas about families, the proper relations between the sexes, and the nature of men's and women's work. It was a love which legitimated certain courses of action and not others, which shaped the possibilities for both men and women, which had its costs as well as its benefits. And it was a love intended to enhance the 'family' of employees which would not admit conflict of interests. It was a vision of family warmth powerfully symbolized by the steaming cup of hot cocoa, prepared by a caring mother for her husband and children on a cold winter's night.

The family pen – the Taylors of Essex[68]

> Lord, what is Life? – if spent with thee
> In duty, praise and prayer,
> However short or long it be
> We need but little care,
> Because Eternity will last
> When Life and death itself are past.
>
>   Jane and Ann Taylor, 1806

Isaac and Ann Martin Taylor, born in the mid eighteenth century, were

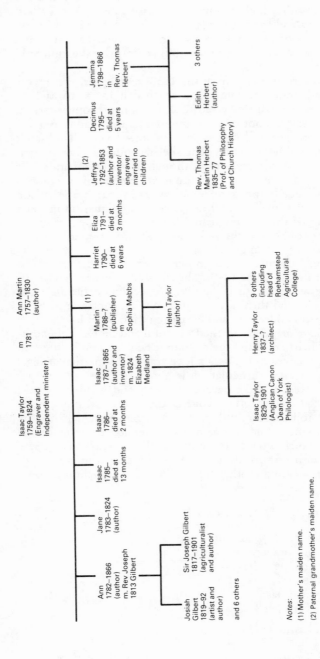

Figure 2 *Taylor family tree*

Notes:
(1) Mother's maiden name.
(2) Paternal grandmother's maiden name.

representative of the new culture which enlivened the Essex and Suffolk countryside. Isaac's family were highly placed goldsmiths; his father, who moved from Worcester to London, earned his living in the new craft of copperplate engraving. His eldest brother, Charles, edited a popular dictionary of the Bible and became the first secretary of the London Library, and a younger brother, Josiah, made a fortune in publishing. It was a family steeped in a literate, religious milieu. Through his mother's people from south-east Essex, Isaac was related to Milton and Raikes, the founder of the Sunday school movement. The copy of Dr Watt's *Divine Songs for Children*, given to Isaac's grandmother by the Puritan divine when she sat on his knee as a young child, was a family heirloom.

Isaac himself went through a conversion experience in his early teens. He had wished to become a minister, but being prevented by illness carried on the engraving taught by his father. Ann Martin came from a family of minor gentry and clergy. Her father had lost his patrimony in building speculation and set up as an estate agent in London. He had been converted by Whitfield in boyhood and his religious faith was the major inheritance left at his early death. Ann's mother's remarriage and subsequent children left the young girl isolated and the chapel became the focus of her life. Through chapel activities the couple had exchanged verses. By 1781 they were married although Isaac's only support was regular engraving commissions from his brother Charles, some freelance work plus a nest egg of £30. Ann brought £100 and some furniture with which they settled in Islington.

Within five years of marriage, two of the four children born had died. Determined to move to less expensive, healthier country surroundings, Isaac inquired through the Congregational connection and chose the village of Lavenham in Suffolk, about 60 miles from the capital. Thanks to mail and transport improvements, Isaac could continue his engraving with only the occasional personal visit to London. In Lavenham, the Taylors were leading members of the chapel where Ann opened a Sunday school and Isaac arranged week day services and lectures. The couple was more literate and cosmopolitan than most of the sleepy villagers, although they found friends among some substantial tradespeople and farmers. Among these, their two eldest bright and uninhibited little girls were much admired. The family had little capital but education, skill and a formidable energy fuelled by active religion which centred on raising their children and enlightening their community. Their London contacts remained an invaluable life-line and Ann Martin still sorely missed her friends.

Much of Isaac's engraving was exported to France so that upheavals of revolution and war badly affected their income. Then in 1792 he was struck down by a near fatal fever. The young couple had sunk their savings in renovating a house; doctors' expenses mounted to £30. Ann Martin was left to face ruin with children of 10, 9, 5 and a 6 month old baby. She nearly broke down and lost her faith at this time. She had no choice, however, but to reluctantly leave the children with what servants they could afford and nurse Isaac to recovery.

Three years later, Isaac was persuaded to become minister to a small Colchester congregation. For the rest of his life he served as an Independent

Plate 8   Jane and Ann Taylor, painted by their father, Isaac, 1792

minister, but he always set up a workroom and continued engraving to support the growing family. Decimus, the tenth child, was born the month they arrived in the busy market town and Jemima, the last, three years later. In all, only six of the eleven children born survived. In Lavenham, Isaac had trained apprentices, but they lived at home leaving the Taylors their valued family privacy. In Colchester there were always apprentices and usually a few pupils in the tall rambling old weaver's house just off the High Street. Individual attic rooms were fitted up for both boys and girls as a retreat for private study and prayer.

Isaac himself always spent from 6 to 7 a.m. and 8 to 9 p.m. in prayer and contemplation. His life was highly organized to fit his multifarious activities and to accord with his religious convictions. He always kept a lexicon, gazetteer and encyclopaedia handy to answer queries. In addition to his preaching and pastoral work, he taught and lectured regularly as well as maintaining the engraving business. He wrote books of advice to young men, on travel and natural history with titles such as *Where Does It Come From?* and *The History of the Brown Loaf*. He devised teaching aids such as flash cards of plants and animals and engraved outline drawings for the

Plate 9 Isaac Taylor, 1787–1865, son of Isaac and Ann Martin Taylor, minister, author and inventor

pupil to colour and fill in with names of parts: anatomical, botanical, even military. His son, in recalling Isaac's prodigious accomplishments, maintained that 'method, arrangement, regularity in everything were the characteristics of his mind'.[69] Despite this schedule, Isaac saw a great deal of his children; at meal times, for lessons, in the workroom, on daily walks or special excursions, family evenings and amateur theatricals.

Ann Martin shared many of his activities but necessarily was preoccupied in running the household with minimum help from a single servant and occasional parishioner, always with a precarious income. She, like Isaac, had vowed to bring up their children in a new way, giving them attention, kindness and joyous religious faith. Both consciously broke with the cold, strict but neglectful atmosphere of their own childhoods. Early in the marriage, she had felt the duties of wife and mother, 'these important relations', absorb all her energies and thoughts.[70] Although from her mid 20s to 30s she was continually pregnant, bearing children and coping with toddlers, she had early heeded the warning of an older woman friend about becoming a drudge and losing the companionship of her husband. To counteract the physical and emotional strain, she took to reading aloud at

meals, a practice followed by the family from then on, even the baby
learning to sit quietly in its high chair. But the strain on health and spirits
was unmistakeable and she nearly broke down completely with her last
pregnancy at the age of 41. Despite the Taylor's celebration of family
life, there are hints that these large families raised under tight financial
circumstances extracted a high price. Ann Martin had to rely on help from
a younger step-sister and her older children. The eldest daughter, Ann, at
16 became the adoring surrogate mother to the last baby, Jemima. Ann
Martin rallied, sustained by her belief in the importance of family life and
eventually expressed these ideas in print. Urged by her husband and children, in late middle age she wrote a series of highly successful books on
domestic life (see Chapter 3).

When the Taylors arrived in Colchester they found a lively market town
of about 10,000, served by a dozen parish churches as well as several
nonconformist chapels. Despite this, the Taylors thought the atmosphere
torpid in both secular and religious affairs. They turned to the handful of
more enlightened inhabitants such as the antiquarian, vegetarian, amateur
artist, musician and agnostic, Benjamin Strutt, who lived on the High Street
in a house fitted with medieval features. The Taylors continued, too, to
visit like-minded friends and family in London and other parts of Essex and
Suffolk: publishers, writers, medical families and ministers. Their intense
nonconformity precluded political activity and they had left the town by
the time more organized scientific or literary groups such as the Colchester
Philosophical Society, were founded, many of them building on groundwork laid by Isaac's lectures and teaching.

In 1807, Isaac's father died leaving a small legacy, although most of the
property went to the already prosperous London brothers and Chancery
proceedings seem to have tied up Isaac's share for years. In 1810, one of
the periodic schisms rent the Colchester congregation, pitting friend against
friend and cousin against cousin. Isaac was forced to leave and the following
year was called to an even smaller, more rural congregation at Ongar, about
20 miles from London. Here the family adapted a farmhouse to their
workroom/study pattern and Isaac devoted more time to Sunday schools,
a book club, week night prayer meetings and lectures. He ministered in
Ongar until his death in 1829 when one of his successors extended into
missionary work and in the 1830s, David Livingstone emerged as Ongar
chapel's most illustrious product.[71]

When the family had moved to Colchester in 1796, the elder Taylor
children had just been entering their teens. Their childhood had been
moulded by religious duties and study but their regime also included much
physical and imaginative play. Ann and Jane, the two eldest and only
eighteen months apart, were exceptionally close playmates, divided from
Isaac junior by a four year gap caused by the death of two infants. From
their earliest years they played made up games, the persona ranging from
'Moll and Bett', two poor but respectable washerwomen, to the 'Miss
Parkes', ladies who did good to their poor neighbours and just occasionally,
royal princesses. From about the age of 7, they began scribbling verse and
prose. But they were also expected to follow their mother in carrying out

domestic duties, 'learning at once the reason and practice of all that was done'.[72]

All the children were educated at home but the boys were also sent to day school. As each child reached middle teens, she or he was taken on in the workroom to train in engraving and help with Isaac's work. For this they received board, lodging and a small wage. At the time, this seemed normal, but in middle age Ann wrote defensively that her father thought he was thus fitting the girls for self-support 'not otherwise than feminine; and in keeping us around him at home he retained a domestic feeling strong in everyone of us'.[73] The boys used spare time to cultivate an allotment, wander the countryside and experiment with rudimentary mechanical invention in their attic chambers. The girls were expected to help in the house. Ann and Jane took turns to be engraver one week – 'Supra' – and to do housework the next – 'Infra' (preferable to being dubbed 'Betty' as when the scheme began). Their own writing was done in snatches between tasks, walks, family gatherings and by finally persuading Isaac to put back the rigid supper time by half an hour. Far from resenting this close supervision, the girls were proud of their housekeeping abilities and scorned fine literary ladies.

As they grew to young adulthood, the children made their own friends. Ann and Jane's close circle in Colchester included daughters of a Unitarian Doctor Stapleton, of a woolstapler and of an Anglican shopkeeper as well as the non-religious Strutt children. Spurred on by Isaac senior, they formed the Umbelliferous Society (technically many blossoms on one stem). Here papers were read and issues of the day debated by both boys and girls. In fine weather the group got up picnics and 'gypsy rambles'. When Dr Stapleton's family moved the 9 miles to Dedham, the friends would walk over to visit and were introduced to the family of the wealthy cornfactor, Golding Constable. They greatly admired son John, several years their senior, handsome and fascinating as a practising artist.

But around 1807, the circle was riven by that scourge of young people, tuberculosis. The four Stapleton girls, two of the Strutt daughters and another pair of sisters died within a year as well as the youngest Taylor brother from typhoid fever. The young Taylors turned inward and their religion became a more vivid reality. As Jane wrote of this time, they seemed more like 'the possessors of some lone castle in the bosom of the mountain than the inhabitants of a populous town'.[74] In 1809, Martin came of age and was apprenticed to a London publisher while young Isaac was sent to learn miniature painting. Left behind, Jane wrote to her brother, 'You, engaged in business and surrounded by friends cannot feel as we do on this subject.'[75] A few years earlier, Ann had won a writing competition in a young people's almanac, *Minor's Pocket Books*. The publishers, Darnton and Harvey who specialized in children's books, asked for more and Ann, Jane, even Isaac at 14, became regular contributors. Ann and Jane then collaborated on their first book, *Original Poems for Infant Minds* in 1804. By the time they left Colchester seven years later they had published nine children's books, mainly the work of the two sisters but with contributions from Isaac junior, Jeffrys and even Jemima. Through London contacts these were widely distributed, becoming extremely popular. (They included the two poems for which the Taylors are still remembered, 'Twinkle twinkle little star' and 'My Mother' – see Appendix 1.)

Ann and Jane had met Josiah Conder, son of a London bookseller, through the Strutts. In 1810 together they collaborated in a book of poetry for adults, *The Associate Minstrels*.[76] (See 'Remonstrance', Ann's poem on relations of the sexes in Appendix 1.) Both Josiah's father who published the book and Isaac senior as well as Josiah's future wife contributed. London publishing contacts through the Conders, Darnton and Harvey, and Uncle Charles Taylor were crucial in promoting the literary enterprise of all the Taylors but particularly for Ann and Jane – young, female and isolated in the provinces. The sisters had received small lump sums, £5 to £10, for their early work although sometimes they were also paid in gifts of fish or fruit. Their ambivalence about professional authorship is seen in the proud claim that they never stipulated a price for their work, leaving it to their publishing 'friends'. Even when all their savings invested with a publisher were lost, Jane wrote: 'Ah well, it is God who determines what I am to have.'[77]

About the time of the move to Ongar, Ann and Jane spent some time in London studying for their project of opening a school. However, like the Brontë sisters a generation later, they had insufficient capital and few prospective pupils. With relief, they returned to Ongar where Jane retired behind her 'paper screen'. Within a year, young Isaac showed signs of consumption and was sent off to Devon accompanied by his elder sisters. In Ann's absence, the senior Taylors were approached for her hand by Joseph Gilbert, Independent minister and middle-aged widower, who had been attracted by Ann's religious expression in her writing. Sight unseen and relying on her parents' judgement, Ann accepted him believing that love would follow spiritual union. In 1813 at the age of 31, she married and followed him to various northern ministries. She ran the household of eight children (born within eleven years), her husband's first wife's teenage niece and the ubiquitous pupil-boarders. For long she wrote little, unable to seclude herself or 'nurse up' (*sic*) her mind for writing, always attentive to a baby's voice. From early in her marriage she had hoped to combine writing with domestic duties but 'if one must suffer, it should certainly be the literary'. Her son reports her taking comfort: 'Never mind, the dear little child is worth volumes of fame.'[78] Nevertheless, from letters to her more famous sister, there are hints of unease over this subject.

Except for a petition to the queen on Free Trade from the women of Nottingham – woman to woman – she published only a few reviews, a school story and reissues of her poetry. In addition to household duties, however, she undertook her husband's correspondence and helped with his popular life of a Puritan divine. As her children grew older, she took an active part in religious and philanthropic affairs, visiting the sick and teaching in Sunday schools, running meetings for mothers. She was a member of the Local Provident Society, Free Trade Library, Blind Asylum and Anti-Slavery Society as well as managing the property of a friend who had left the area. Ann stayed in close touch with the Ongar family, paying visits, having Jemima to stay for months and sending her eldest son, Josiah, to live with his grandparents from the age of 5 to 15 (a contact which confirmed his inheritance from Isaac senior's brother, Josiah, for whom the boy presumably had been named).

Jane never married, her central 'business in life' being to restore Isaac junior to health, with 'self-denying, indefatigable and tender assiduity'.[79] During this time she continued to write including her only novel, *Display* (1815), and a book length collection of moral essays in rhyme. But she always found it hard to regard herself as professional, being too timid even to enjoy teaching at the Ongar Sunday school. Her first known poem at age 8, seems to recognize a prohibition against female authorship:

> To be a poetess I don't aspire
> From such a title I humbly retire
> But now and then a line I try to write. . . .[80]

As a girl, like Charlotte Brontë, she had castigated herself for 'castle building'. Only religious conviction overcame her diffidence. In the tradition of Dr Watt and Mrs Barbauld (the eighteenth-century nonconformist writer of children's poems living in Suffolk whom Jane had met), she pursued her 'ministry of the press', for she believed that single women had a special mission to 'care for things of the Lord'.

Her writing had also begun to contribute to the family exchequer. *Hymns for Infant Minds* brought in £150 in 1810, more than most curates and country schoolmasters could command in a year. From 1816 to 1822, she was editor of an Evangelical magazine for young people which included Mrs Sherwood and the Suffolk Quaker poet of domesticity, Bernard Barton, among its contributors. She also helped her mother's writing ventures, all activities which could be carried on in the bosom of the family. In her early 30s, she became involved in 'an attachment' which for some reason could not proceed to marriage. Shortly afterwards, she developed cancer of the breast and was instructed by her medical adviser, father of a friend, to give up all literary work, but she did write occasional poems until her death at age 41 in 1824.

Isaac and Ann Martin had not wished their daughters to become authors, despite the family tradition. They thought professional literary work both precarious and inappropriate. In deference to their wishes, all Ann and Jane's early publications were anonymous. Their brother Isaac was more supportive, once chiding Ann that the stockings she was mending were too costly in terms of lost literature. Yet he made it clear that he, like Ann's husband who also urged her to keep up her writing, disdained ladies who indulged in literary airs.

Isaac junior, even when ill in his early 20s, had been offered posts as a draughtsman on an expedition abroad as well as a ministry. He became a well known miniaturist as well as author of scientific, philosophical and theological works; his *Natural History of Enthusiasm* became a classic of the genre. He married at age 37, almost immediately after Jane's death, Jemima claiming that he would never have done so if his sister had lived. He moved to the next village to Ongar and joined with his nephew Josiah Gilbert in various inventions including a beer spigot and printing press eventually used for Manchester cottons. The eldest of his eleven children, another Isaac, became an Anglican canon and philologist, two other sons an architect and scientist. Martin was the only Taylor who did not write but remained in publishing. Jeffrys wrote and illustrated many popular books for children on natural history and continued to invent machinery. Jemima took care of her parents in Ongar until their death when she was 31 when she went to Ann's and there married a nonconformist minister and had five children, including a clerical son and author daughter.

The Taylor's work was mainly illustrated by their own drawing and engraving. Their products were highly successful, many going into thirty or more editions before being revised and reissued well into the late nineteenth century. There were over 100 editions of *Original Poems* and *Original Hymns* in England and America alone as well as numerous translations and the poems remained in print until the 1930s. Walter Scott and Southey used the little books with their own children, Keats recommended Jane Taylor to his young sister, Browning wrote a poem based on one of her stories and considered her poems for children as the most perfect of their kind. Numerous references are made to their works by people in our local study.

Between them, the Taylor parents and children produced seventy-three books. While all wrote for young people, the two Isaacs and Jeffrys also took on scientific, philosophical and theological subjects. Unlike their predecessor, Mrs Barbauld, who wrote both children's books and radical pamphlets, however, Ann Martin and her daughters wrote exclusively for women and girls or nursery aged children. Ann's first published piece in her late teens was an election manifesto for the Evangelical Tory candidate for Colchester, but she never tackled such subjects again in print. A swelling canon of genteel femininity had begun to impose limitations on women of this generation. As Isaac wrote of his sister Jane:

she continued to address herself to childhood and youth, not merely because she thought that to be the work for which she was fitted; but in great measure because within this humble sphere she felt safe; and that, while she moved not out of it, the dreaded charge of presumption could not well be brought against her.[81]

The Taylors are a particularly dramatic example of middle-class experience. They were socially isolated and somewhat cut off from their families of origin by their fervent religious commitment and from their neighbours by their superior education and metropolitan background. They had known much personal insecurity. In the 1790s, pro-Church-and-King feeling turned the Lavenham villagers against them so that they fled their home. In Colchester, fear of Bonaparte's invasion reached a pitch so that in 1802 the older children were sent to the country for safety. Isaac senior's serious illness had underscored their financial vulnerability. There was the loss of five of their eleven children and the illness and death endemic among their contemporaries. In Ann Taylor Gilbert's words, 'all comforts [were] exposed on the brink of a precipice with a loose and crumbling soil. Disease and accidents have keys for every door'.[82]

Their defence and sense of place came through their religion and their family. In expounding and defending these institutions through pulpit, lectures, books and engravings, they also enlarged their fortunes by the 'family pen'. The message they created, packaged and sold played its part in the creation of the early nineteenth-century provincial middle class.

Part One

Religion and Ideology

Introduction to Part One

English middle-class men in the late eighteenth century lived in a world which denied them substantive public power. Influential as they might be in their own business or profession, that influence could not necessarily be cashed in the political or social arena. But professionals, merchants, manufacturers and farmers, marginal to the world of rank and land, increasingly established their own associations and networks which gave meaning to their lives and in the process challenged the existing apparatus of power. For many of them it was religious faith which was the ultimate judge of stature, neither pedigree or particular material possessions. It has been argued that in the eighteenth century, 'the nation', those 'people' who had consented to the settlement of 1688 and constituted the responsible governors who defended the traditional rights of freeborn Englishmen, had been extended to include all those who could aspire to join 'polite society'. But being a member of 'polite society' required an independent income whether from land or the City of London.[1] By the end of the eighteenth century this association of gentility with an income and style of life requiring neither mental nor manual labour was no longer acceptable to many of the middling ranks. A new claim was asserted, that *salvation* was the mark of gentility, that an artisan's son from a rural backwater who managed to educate himself and become a minister, had as much right to that epithet as an aristocrat.

Methodism had been the first portent of religious revival in the eighteenth century but Methodism was associated with the lower orders and the poor. Anglican Evangelicalism, the revival which both began and remained within the established church, had very different social origins. Declassé gentry, from families of declining status and wealth, were significant among its protagonists and this ensured that Evangelicalism never suffered as Methodism had in gaining a firm holding among the middling ranks. Evangelicalism's success among merchants and manufacturers, professionals and farmers, was matched by that of the New Dissenters, the Independents particularly, and Old Dissenters, especially Unitarians and Quakers, in winning or holding middle-class support. Religious belonging grew to be a central plinth of middle-class culture.

Men's claim to act as stewards and trustees for God, to demonstrate their faith through their church and chapel duties, their public works and their business practices, provided a basis for later claims for other kinds of influence and power. A man who could be a trustee for God and caretaker of the financial affairs of the chapel could certainly fill other positions of public responsibility. By the early nineteenth century the traditional concept of *stewardship* associated with aristocratic patronage and the devolution of obligations from the lord to his agent was transposed into religious discourse. The trustee and the steward in this definition were only responsible directly to God. There was no secular authority that stood between such a man and his Lord. Nonconformist rejection of the intervention of the state in their affairs sprang from the conviction that no secular power had that right; religious liberty must mean not only the right to worship in peace but also the right to run their own business, to marry in their own chapels and to stand for public office if they so chose.

Despite the traditional hostilities between Church and Dissent, there were new aspirations in this period which allowed people to feel a sense of religious community. Enthusiastic Christians of different denominations found they could work together, could identify with moral causes which they saw as cutting across old chasms. Networks of serious Christians were created which linked rural and urban communities, Anglican with Dissenter. Even Unitarians, far distant from any association with religious revival, could share the belief that it was religious force and moral probity which allowed men to make the claim that 'Christian men emerging from the bosom of their families carry Godliness with them.'[2]

The linkage of Christianity, godliness and the family was crucial. In the new alliances and alignments of the early nineteenth century, when it was possible for Anglicans to be fighting over church rates with Dissenters one day and co-operating with them on philanthropic initiatives on another, when Quakers could continue to insist on their special forms of address but work together with other denominations to remake the educational map of town and country, Christians shared a core of beliefs in the central importance of the family. The precise doctrines on manliness, femininity and the family within different religious groupings varied as will be seen, but there was enough common ground to allow for the emergence of a series of beliefs and practices as to the distinct and separate spheres of male and female which provided the basis for a shared culture among the middle class by mid century.

Divisions within the middle class were cut across by assumptions as to the 'natural' consequences of sexual difference. Anglicans, Congregationalists, Quakers and Unitarians could all agree that the home must be the basis for a proper moral order in the amoral world of the market, that the new world of political economy necessitated a new sphere of domestic economy, that men could operate in that amoral world only if they could be rescued by women's moral vigilance at home. Such beliefs informed the creation of a network of institutions and associations which formed the basis for a distinctive middle-class culture. Claims for the power of salvation and the force of moral influence were premised on ideas which did not necessarily belong to any one class. Banker or pauper, 'lady' or 'female', slave or free, all could claim salvation.

But the meaning of salvation, the effects of salvation in practice, depended on the class positions to which it was linked. 'The rich man in his castle, the poor man at his gate' must know their place in the heavenly hierarchy of the saved. The stability of the eighteenth-century world was broken apart by the combined effects of the American and French Revolutions with their intellectual overtones of the Enlightenment and the impact of economic change. In particular, the 1780s and 1790s were decades of acute social, political and economic disturbance and disruption associated with significant shifts in class relations and political power. They were also decades when questions of sexual difference and sexual antagonism came to the fore, when assumptions about marriage and the family were questioned, when novel kinds of relations, involving different forms of social organization, seemed not only possible but desirable. What constituted the proper relations between the sexes was a central question whether for the conservative Hannah More or the radical Mary Wollstonecraft.

The debate between conservative and radical elements was to surface once more in the stormy decades of the 1830s and 1840s when Evangelicals engaged in public dispute with socialists, when John Angell James the prominent Independent minister of Carrs Lane, Birmingham, battled with Utopian feminists. Frequently the political lines which were drawn cut across other established political and religious allegiances for few Radicals were feminists and many Tories were not Evangelicals. But the debate over sexual difference, the 'woman question' as it came to be called, occupied a central place in the hearts and minds as well as spiritual life of the English middle class.

During this period there had been significant change. The active men and women of the 1780s and 1790s, people profoundly moved by the experience of the French Revolution and often experiencing religious conversion in adulthood, were a different breed from the activists of the 1830s and 1840s, many of them 'cradle Christians', born into a society already affected by the evangelizing activities associated with the revival. By this period new kinds of secularism as well as reactions within the church were at work. Although many would have echoed the Evangelical Essex curate who insisted that socialism was the same old enemy, however dressed up, the political and social map of England looked very different from that of the 1790s.[3] Middle-class men had gained representation in parliament, nonconformists had won the right to office, middle-class people had established a whole cultural world, class relations had decisively shifted.

In this part, Chapter 1 deals with the place of religion within middle-class culture. It argues that religious belonging carried with it many benefits both spiritual and material and examines the denominations which were central to the middle-class men and women of Birmingham and the eastern counties and the shifting alliances and fractures between these groups. Chapter 2 deals with the doctrines and practices of the religious in relation to sexual difference, arguing that the demarcation of separate spheres was a central concern for all groups whether spelt out in doctrine or maintained in practice. Chapter 3 steps away from religious doctrine as articulated by the clergy and looks at the closely related field of domestic ideology. Using the example of the affair of Queen Caroline to demonstrate changes in public attitudes to marriage and sexuality, it establishes the routes of ideological transmission within the middle classes and then examines domestic ideology as doctrine and as it was translated into 'common sense' for ordinary middle-class men and women.

1 'The one thing needful': religion and the middle class

My boast is not that I deduce my birth
From loins enthroned or rulers of the earth
But higher far my proud pretensions rise
The Son of Parents passed into the skies

William Cowper

The religious census of 1851 made it abundantly clear that attendance at church or chapel was a practice much more associated with the middle than the working classes.[1] As many historians of religion have pointed out, religious belief had become 'a character and function of class' rather than a basis for a wider social unity. Religious belonging gave distinctive identity to particular communities and classes in a society which was increasingly aware of its divisions and in which the established church was gradually losing its claim for national rather than sectarian status.[2] Foremost among those distinctive identities was the association between the middle class and a Christian way of life so that by mid century adherence to evangelical protestant forms had become an accepted part of respectability if not gentility. Attendance at church or chapel was a social necessity even when it was not a religious imperative. Respectability was coming to include church going, family worship, the observance of the Sabbath, an interest in religious literature. As the Tory journalist T. W. Croker commented in 1843, there was a kind of 'Christian tint over the general aspect of society'.[3]

This 'tint' had its effects on many who were not themselves subject to the waves of religious enthusiasm which swept England in the late eighteenth and early nineteenth centuries, for the zeal of the serious Christians played a vital part in establishing the cultural practices and institutions which were to become characteristic hallmarks of the middle classes. In the 1840s an Essex farmer in his 70s was constrained to note guiltily in his diary that he had shot a partridge on a Sunday, an activity he had learnt to feel uncomfortable with.[4]

Why was religious belief and practice so appealing to the men and women of the middle class? How did it become defined as 'the one thing needful'? First of all it offered individuals an identity and a community to which they could attach themselves in a society which was changing rapidly. Gilbert's argument in relation to nonconformity, that it was able to satisfy 'the profound associational and communal needs of people experiencing anomie and social insecurity in a period of rapid social change and dislocation', can be applied more generally to 'serious Christianity', the revival which affected both Anglicans and Dissenters in our period.[5] Religious belief gave confidence as to how to behave, how to know what was right and what was wrong. The strength of religious belief of an Essex shop-keeper's wife enabled her to face ridicule in a public coach when she demanded that a man should stop swearing.[6] It gave Dissenters the courage to deal with the hostility and contempt they confronted until they were able to insist on their rights. As Binfield argues, serious religion 'provided a manner of living and a reason for it which owed little to established modes and made sense in a senseless society'.[7]

Both religious beliefs and practice gave tenant farmers, small manufac-turers and professionals who were struggling to establish themselves, a certainty about their claims and a reason for rejecting some of the values of the aristocracy and gentry. It gave middle-class women a particular identity distinctive from the aristocratic ideal of the lady. For serious Chris-tianity, despite the political conservatism of many of its adherents, was profoundly meritocratic. Any individual, male or female, could be redeemed through Christ. Whatever the hierarchy established within the church or chapel, the heart of that religious community was spiritual equality, for all had access to the Lord. Finally, it was religious and moral practice which provided the basis for distinctive middle-class demands for status and power. The sanction of their worth came from Heaven. It was an Essex tanner's daughter who noted a verse from that most favoured poet William Cowper:

> My boast is not that I deduce my birth
> From loins enthroned or rulers of the earth
> But higher far my proud pretensions rise
> The Son of Parents passed into the skies.[8]

If religious belief offered individuals a sense of identity and a community, it also offered personal comfort and security in an unstable and unsafe world. When facing death or bankruptcy, two of the most common disasters for middle-class families, religious belief provided meaning and explanation, religious institutions provided care and support. The satisfactions which religion offered were timeless, not subject to the vicissitudes of health and wealth. Martha Gibbins, the widow of a Birmingham banker, one of whose sons had continued in his father's line of business, wrote to one of her daughters in the wake of the terrible financial crisis of 1825–6 at a time when the bank was on the brink of collapse. Reflecting on the difficulties faced by her son, she commented,

I much desire his late very severe trials, when fully ended, may prove a lesson of deep and lasting instruction, so to limit his earthly views that he may set his affections more on eternal durable riches, and the joys of Heaven rather than on the fading uncertain accumulation of wealth.[9]

Such a view was commonplace among the religious for belief in things eternal gave succour.

Plate 10 Carrs Lane Congregational chapel, Birmingham, presided over by John Angell James

Church and chapel activity

It was the evangelical revival starting in the late eighteenth century which made religion so central to middle-class culture.[10] That revival featured in both town and country life. It can be marked in the growth of charities, the increase in religious literature, the development of Sunday schools, the increase in church and chapel buildings and the numbers in their congregations. Between 1790 and 1820 over 100 new religious periodicals were established.[11] Often these were the main vehicles of literacy and culture available to people. The only reading matter in the home of a poor farmer in a remote Essex village in the 1790s was the nonconformist publication, *The Evangelical Magazine.*[12]

By 1800, it is estimated, there were between 300 and 500 clergymen encouraging parochial activities from the setting up of Sunday schools to the establishment of societies and meetings.[13] From the 1780s in both Birmingham and the eastern counties there was a steady development in the building of new churches and chapels and the enlarging of both Anglican and Dissenting facilities. In 1782 William Hutton tells us that there were fourteen places of worship in Birmingham catering for a population of about 35,000: six Anglican churches, some of them endowed quite recently to serve the rapidly growing town, three Old Dissenting chapels, a Quaker meeting house, a Baptist and a Methodist chapel, a Roman Catholic church and a Jewish synagogue.[14] Between 1782 and 1819 ten more Dissenting places of worship were set up in the town, so that Birmingham could boast of four Baptist, four Methodist and four Independent congregations as well as a number of smaller groupings.[15] Two young women visiting from Cornwall in 1819 were astonished by the level of Dissenting activity in the town. 'There seems to reign in this place', one of them recorded,

Plate 11   Edgbaston parish church, one of the Birmingham churches to come under Evangelical influence

a latitudinarianism in religion and politics, which quite startles our more aristocratic and less liberal views; not English law and liberty, but liberty and no law seems the ruling principle here. It is a perfectly dissenting republican place, – Presbyterians, Quakers, Independents, Unitarians, all seem placed here on the same level; the last we fancy have rather the preference. The poor Church alone seems the object of prejudice and animosity. . . .[16]

Catherine Fox was right not to underestimate the power of the Unitarians in Birmingham, but, as a nonconformist, she did not have a clear view of the Anglican position. As one of the new industrial towns with clearly inadequate church provision, Birmingham benefited both from local patrons and government grants. Christ Church, for example, with a town centre site donated by a local landowner and funding from public subsidy was consecrated in 1813 and was specifically designed to accommodate the working classes with free seating in the whole of the downstairs area. The Parliamentary Church Building Committees were responsible for four churches in the 1820s, one in the centre and three on the outskirts. By the 1830s the Church Commissioners were encouraging local initiatives such as the diocesan building societies. In 1838, with provision established for only one-seventh of the inhabitants, the rural dean of Birmingham initiated the building of five further churches in the next ten years.[17] Despite these efforts, however, the working classes continued to stay away from church. As McLeod points out, 'in both towns and countryside the non-Church goers came mainly from the working class population, and middle class church attendance remained high until the end of the century'.[18]

The revival in the Anglican church cannot, of course, be measured only in terms of attendance but also by the growth of charitable societies, by church building and extension and the recorded activities of the energetic clergy. William Marsh, a personal friend of Wilberforce and Simeon and a prominent activist among the first generation of Evangelical clergy, was the enthusiastic rector of St Peter's, Colchester, in the 1820s and was responsible for the renovation of the church, the addition of a gallery and provision for 300 extra seats. In 1829 he went to Birmingham where he was the first incumbent of the new church of St Thomas, built specifically to provide for the working class, where the celebrated 'Millenarian Marsh' was able in time to build up a devoted following as he had in Colchester.[19] Like other Evangelical clergy, he placed great store on extra services; up to three on Sundays with weekday evenings for prayer meetings, Bible readings and other forms of devotional exercises which shaded into philanthropic activities.

Much of this Anglican effort, both locally and nationally, was in response to activity within the Dissenting churches. The membership of the New Dissenting groups, that is the Congregationalists or Independents and some Baptists, increased rapidly from the 1780s and peaked between 1850–75. Nationally by 1800 there were about 300,000 nonconformists, including Methodists, in a population of about 10 million. The increase in Dissenting congregations was particularly marked in the provinces. 90 per cent of the strength of the Independents, according to a survey of 1778, was concentrated in the south, the south Midlands and East Anglia. Essex had the highest concentration in the country; the county at that time had forty-seven Independent congregations and Suffolk, twenty-six. Whereas in the north the established church was very weak and the Methodists managed to gain at the expense of all other groups, in the belt from Dorset and Wiltshire through the south Midlands and East Anglia the church's presence was felt but uneven, leaving gaps which allowed the evangelizing Independents to move in. Thus Birmingham, Essex and Suffolk lay within this band with the highest rate of religious practice in 1851; it was, as Gilbert notes 'the religious cockpit of England'.[20]

The effects of this level of religious activity were striking. By 1850 in Suffolk, for example, 40 per cent of the Anglican clergy were living in parsonages within the parish and there were only fifteen cases of non-residence, a marked change from the earlier period. Similarly, whereas in 1830 only eighty-six of the Suffolk parishes celebrated Sunday services both morning and evening, by 1850, 235 parishes had reached this level of parochial zeal. Indeed, Colchester boasted the highest level of religious attendance of any town in 1851.[21] Birmingham lay on the edge of this belt of evangelizing activity. According to the 1851 census, fewer than one in ten people were worshippers and almost half of these church-goers were Anglican.[22] But what the city lacked in numbers it made up for in visibility, for among the publicly known members of the middle class, few were prepared to admit that they were not believers. Just as the Dissenters in Colchester were seen to be the majority in the town despite evidence that in 1829 they in fact constituted 27 per cent of the population, so in Birmingham serious Christianity appears as a dominant influence in the local press and local societies.[23] There was, of course, opposition to evangelical influence, particularly marked in the turbulent years of the 1790s and the 1830s and 1840s, but nevertheless serious Christians had managed to put their insignia on many aspects of middle-class cultural affairs, to cast their 'Christian tint' over society.

The social basis of the evangelical Christians varied. The Evangelicals, that is to say the reformers within the Anglican church who espoused a conversionist and intensely active faith, were initially drawn from the margins of the lesser gentry and from merchants. Indeed, it has been argued that among the first generation there was a marked sense of social inferiority; those who were attracted to the movement were concerned about a decline in their status.[24] By the late eighteenth century, civil servants, officers in the armed services, bankers, merchants and professionals were drawn to Evangelicalism as were some manufacturers and farmers, the main support tending to come from the upper ranks of the middle class.[25]

Evangelical nonconformity had a somewhat less elevated constituency. The majority of their support came from within the middle and lower middle class; the aristocracy and the unskilled labouring poor were scarcely represented in their ranks. The Independents had a larger minority of the upper strata than did the Methodists. Artisans may have been the backbone of nonconformity in terms of rank-and-file membership but theirs were not the influential voices in the large chapels and developing national societies. The Unitarians and Quakers were a special case. In terms of numbers both groups were in decline in early nineteenth-century Birmingham as elsewhere, especially in comparison with the growth of New Dissent. But their members 'became more and more disproportionately represented in the upper middle classes, among the wealthier merchants and manufacturers of industrial England and within the radical municipal oligarchies which emerged after the Municipal Corporation Act of 1835 to challenge the traditional Tory–Anglican elites'.[26]

Among the identifiable middle class of Birmingham and East Anglia in this period, religious allegiance was divided between the Anglicans, the Independents, the Unitarians and the Quakers, with only a small percentage attached to the Baptists and Methodists. Of those within our study with a recognized religious affiliation, 40 per cent were Anglican while 54 per cent were outside the established church. The occupational breakdown illustrates that professionals, as would be expected, tended to align themselves to the established church or the Unitarians (a traditionally high status group) as did the upper echelons of the middle class such as merchants and bankers, while tradesmen, manufacturers and the less well-to-do professionals such as solicitors found themselves more at home among the Independents and Quakers. Among the Quakers in Birmingham, however, were also a good sprinkling of wealthier merchants and bankers (see Tables 2 and 3, p. 82).

The Evangelical revival and serious Christianity

The Anglican Evangelicals made an impact on the religious state of the nation as early as the 1780s. Responding in part to Methodism with its conversionist appeal and emphasis on revealed religion, the Clapham sect, the first recognizable grouping, was spearheaded by William Wilberforce and Hannah More who, with their mercantile and gentry backgrounds, were able to break the association of enthusiastic Methodism with the

Table 2 *Religious affiliation in the local areas (percentages)*

	Essex and Suffolk	Birmingham	Total in areas
Anglican	47	34	40
Unitarian	2	34	17
Independent	30	8	17
Quaker	20	10	18
Baptist/Methodist	0	4	2
Don't know	1	10	6
Total	100	100	100

Note: N = 192
Source: Essex and Suffolk File; Witham File; Birmingham File.

Table 3 *Religious affiliation by occupation in the local areas (percentages)*

	Clergy	Lawyers (estate agents)	Medical	Merchant/ banker	Manu- facturer	Trade	Farm
Anglican	53	46	62	39	29	12	53
Unitarian	16	35	11	13	31	8	0
Independent	31	15	4	9	13	38	21
Quaker	–	0	4	26	14	38	26
Baptist/Methodist	0	4	4	0	2	4	0
Don't know	0	0	15	13	11	0	0
Total	100	100	100	100	100	100	100

Note: N = 186
Source: Essex and Suffolk File; Witham File; Birmingham File.

lower social orders. Initially a small group, their influence was nevertheless extensive, partly because of their access to power and partly because of their level of activity. 'It is better to wear out than to rust out' was the maxim of one of their later prominent figures and might have stood as a motto for the group.[27] A Unitarian journal commented somewhat sourly in 1808,

They have invaded the Navy, they thrive at the Bank, they bear sway at the India House, they count several votes in Parliament, and they have got a footing in the Royal Palace. Their activity is incredible.[28]

The extent of the Evangelical drive was associated with the crisis they felt confronted English society, particularly after the French Revolution. The nation, they believed, was suffering from moral degeneracy. Events in France were a warning of what was to come if individuals did not inspire a revolution in the 'manners and morals' of the nation, a transformation which must begin with individual salvation.

Starting from a conviction of man's sinfulness, Evangelicals stressed the importance of the conversion experience and individual spiritual life which could be transformed by an infusion of grace. They believed that the spirit could work through other means than the trappings of the church. Individual faith was the key to moral regeneration, and the primary setting for maintaining faith was a religious family and household. By implication the Evangelicals criticized many aspects of church policy and practice, so that, despite their social and political conservatism, they were unpopular with High Churchmen in particular. Wilberforce's critique of 'nominal Christianity' and appeal for 'real religion' can hardly have made comfortable reading for many of the church establishment.[29]

Initially the Evangelicals aimed to make their influence felt by admonition of the great and the powerful but increasingly, particularly in the context of the political crises of the 1790s, they sought to extend their message. Through their establishment of the Cheap Repository Tract Society and the British and Foreign Bible Society they tried to make their literature widely available, and through the appointment of clergy sympathetic to their cause they hoped to transform parish life.

Evangelicals' view of the parish was significantly different from that of their contemporaries. They believed that the parish should be an active arena within which the clergyman should regularly celebrate divine worship and instruct and care for his parishioners. The parish should be a scene of ceaseless effort to win the souls of all, not only through church services and private visiting, but also by the development of Sunday schools, clubs and meetings which would make real religion available to everyone.[30] In this task all help and support should be encouraged, whether clerical or lay, whether male or female. This view of the parish and the clergy's role was in clear opposition to the easy going hunting and shooting 'squarson' or the scholarly cleric immersed in esoteric theological debates. It castigated the non-resident clergy by example. The new emphasis on the parish and clerical activity was associated with the fears aroused by the divisiveness of a growing cash nexus, directly experienced in the countryside as well as the town with the shift to waged day labour, the commutation of tithes in kind and the growth of middlemen such as corn factors and agents. The parish could de-emphasize class distinction, for all souls within its boundaries were bound together for the same Heavenly Home.

One of the earliest concerns of the Evangelicals was to place their adherents in crucial clerical positions, a project demanding money and influence. The powerful Cambridge Evangelical preacher and teacher, Charles Simeon, established a trust in 1817 through which advowsons could be bought and supporters well placed. Prior to this they had had to rely on personal influence, as, for example, in the case of St Peter's Colchester where the living was owned by the Thornton family (close friends of Wilberforce and prominent Tory Evangelicals). St Peter's had been presented to an Evangelical as early as 1783, and in 1814 Rev. William Marsh, a member of the Simeon Trust, became its highly influential rector until his departure for Birmingham in 1829. In time, an Evangelical network spread over southern East Anglia, influenced by Simeon who sent his students and disciples through the Cambridge, Essex and Suffolk hinterland; a project made easier

by the 'flood of livings' released from the patronage of the Corporations
by the Municipal Reform Act of 1835.[31] Organizations such as the Bible
Society acted as meeting points for these enthusiasts, while letter writing
as well as informal meetings kept them in touch. Lay supporters were able
to make contributions by gifts of land and money to buy yet more livings.
For example, relative newcomers to the area such as the Rounds of Colchester who had been publishers and merchants in London and who had
become a prominent banking family in the locality established one of their
sons in an Evangelically co-opted Colchester church.[32]

A similar network took much longer to establish in Birmingham where
there was initially less fertile ground. The appointment of Henry Ryder,
an Evangelical, to the bishopric of Coventry and Lichfield in 1824 made a
crucial difference. Nationally Evangelical support was at a low ebb then,
although it is estimated that approximately one-eighth of the clergy were
sympathizers.[33] Their support increased in the crisis decade of the 1840s
and they reached the summit of their influence in the mid 1850s when
Sumner, who was friendly to Evangelicalism, was the Archbishop of
Canterbury and Shaftesbury, one of their best known second generation
public figures, was stepson-in-law to the prime minister.[34] Ryder's Midlands
appointment marked the first bishopric for an Evangelical; its late date an
indication of their weakness in the church hierarchy as opposed to among
the laity. His position made possible some strategic patronage which strengthened the position of 'The Saints', as they were popularly known, in
Birmingham. Ryder chose George Hodson, the Evangelical incumbent of
Christ Church, a new church built expressly to provide more accommodation for the working classes in the centre of Birmingham, as one of his
archdeacons.[35] In 1827 he named his friend, William Spooner, Archdeacon
of Coventry, within whose jurisdiction Birmingham lay. Spooner came
from the well-known Evangelical family whose original money was made
in Birmingham banking. Barbara Spooner had married William Wilberforce
and they were closely related to the Calthorpes, one of the most significant
landowning families in the town and keen supporters of the Evangelicals.
The combination of Spooners and Calthorpes meant that Birmingham had
a powerful lay Evangelical base. The Calthorpe patronage in the developing
suburb of Edgbaston secured not only new churches but also for the most
part Evangelical incumbents.[36]

In 1829 the death of the aged and inactive rector of Birmingham's old
parish church, St Martins, created an opening. Ryder appointed a conscientious Evangelical who occupied the living until 1846 and was able to witness
the establishment of a clear Evangelical ascendancy in the town. From his
arrival this rector provided Sunday evening services, a greater emphasis on
preaching, the provision of more seats for the poor and support for the
Evangelical societies such as the Church Missionary and Bible Societies.
More important, however, was the power of patronage associated with his
church. St Martins was a rich living, long established and in the centre of
the town. Its value had risen substantially. In 1829 the advowson was given
to Evangelical trustees and the parish was then divided in order to endow
three new districts. These became the churches of St Thomas, given to the

Evangelical 'Millenarian Marsh', St Georges and All Saints, both of which also had Evangelical appointments.

This successful extension of Evangelical patronage did not go unnoticed. The Evangelicals' most articulate opponent in the town was Walter Hook, at this point in the early stages of his clerical career but later to become a well-known figure in the church. Hook was much influenced by the Tractarians, that reforming group within the Anglican church in the 1820s and 1830s who explicitly rejected much Evangelical doctrine, sought a return to ritual and the sacraments, and emphasized the special duties of the clergy and their separation from the laity. Hook was opposed, for example, to the attempt by The Saints to establish a ladies' committee for the Birmingham penitentiary in 1827 and he was concerned about Evangelical success in gaining control of advowsons.[37] By 1851, Evangelicalism claimed significant numbers of Birmingham clergy, compared to the three in 1829. The Saints, with their confidence and certainty in their own moral probity, were indeed in command.[38]

Evangelical militancy was in part inspired by the growing power and support which Dissent could command, for if serious Christianity was making headway among Anglicans it was also winning recruits to the new Dissenting congregations. John Angell James, the best known of Birmingham's Independent clergymen and minister of the town centre's Carrs Lane chapel, was able to firmly pronounce that 'the cause of dissent is progressive and triumphant in the middling classes of society'.[39] The membership of Tacket Street Congregational church in Ipswich was typical of the kind of people the Independents were most successful in attracting, and comprised 'multiple drapers, maltsters and millers, large farmers, solicitors, engineers and shipowners, printers', hardworking men and their families, some of whom also held office in the municipality and were local leaders, living in new villas on the new avenues of Ipswich.[40]

The Dissenters of the eighteenth century had tended to be on the fringes of national and regional politics, increasing their commercial and manufacturing interests but not as yet occupying positions of civic or national power. By the mid nineteenth century this had decisively changed and nonconformity was organized as a powerful auxiliary pressure group in support of successful reform movements. The shift from 'Dissent' to 'nonconformity' implied a change from the oppositional and radical connections of the late eighteenth century to a politics dominated by religious issues more narrowly defined, and the slow move to incorporation.[41] Bunyan's Pilgrim, with his critique of a whole society, became the single issue campaigner seeking redress on church rates. Independent support was growing from the 1780s and Carrs Lane, for example, which in 1791 had nineteen members could boast a membership of 815 in 1851 and their buildings had been through successive enlargements and extensions.[42] This was in part due to the inspired evangelicalizing of John Angell James, but it also reflected a national phenomenon.

Becoming a member of a nonconformist congregation required individual choice. All members of the parish were potential communicants of the local Anglican church, but attending a nonconformist chapel meant going against the establishment and subscribing to a chosen body of doctrine. The congregation provided a community within which this voluntary choice could be made and would provide subsequent support in maintaining those beliefs. The Independent revival of the early nineteenth century stressed, as did the Evangelicals, the personal relationship with Christ at the centre of the conversion experience. The union of the individual 'saint' with Christ, the experience of rebirth was at the heart of the revival. The strict Calvinism of the earlier period with its emphasis on the elect had somewhat softened. Edward Williams's, a pastor of Carrs Lane before James, wrote an influential treatise, *Divine Equity and Sovereignty*, which showed 'the difference between Christ as mediator providing salvation for all and Christ as a surety, securing salvation of the elect'.[43] In the period after 1800, new recruits to Independent churches tended to be less disciplined and severe than their predecessors, less intellectual, more emotional and enthusiastic. The manner of preaching changed from read sermons to oral presentations and new evening classes, services and prayer meetings were introduced with the use of more music. Independents were hostile to all forms of ritual and to stated forms of worship, they laid great emphasis on the Bible, on the sanctification of Sundays, on family worship and on personal introspection with individual prayer morning and evening. Their doctrine emphasized personal responsibility as in the right use of 'talents', of time and money, which was a moral imperative. Failure in business was seen as faulty stewardship, for goods were in trust for God and 'nothing but probity will support credit'. This sense of responsibility extended to belief in the support of dependants; wives, children and servants.[44]

Each Independent chapel was seen as a community of believers; membership was only on the basis of being received into the fellowship and the church was 'an organised Society of persons professing personal faith in the Lord Jesus Christ'.[45] The 'visible church' was 'a Congregation of faithful men' argued Bennet, the historian of the Independents, unconsciously pinpointing in his formulation some of the ambiguities as to male and female forms of belonging to that fellowship.[46] The membership exercised discipline over themselves and elected their minister, whom they also paid, and deacons. Over the period, however, this fundamentally democratic form of organization became more hierarchical. As local congregations joined into regional federations, the power of the minister and the elders considerably increased.

In comparison with the Anglicans and Independents, the Quakers were a tiny grouping, but their small numbers were offset by their wealth and influence. There were about 20,000 Quakers in England and Wales in 1800, only half as many as at the end of the seventeenth century but this membership was predominantly middle class.[47] The decline in numbers had carried with it no loss of internal cohesiveness and by tradition the Quakers were separated from the rest of the community, by dress and speech. For the most part they lived within their own communities, relying on their large families and extended networks of Friends for support of every kind. Quakers became members by birth or conversion and could lose their membership by voluntary resignation or expulsion. Marrying out of the Friends meant leaving, thus the practice of extensive intermarriage within the group. Voluntary severance was hard, as Mary Wright Sewell of Suffolk commented having left the Quakers, 'Oh I was lonely – almost all my friends and acquaintances were Friends.'[48] Power was exercised through the local monthly meetings and a yearly meeting took place in London open to all Quakers. Quaker ministers were a non-professional group and were never paid; ministry depended on inspiration and was open to both men and women. Despite the quietist and mystical traditions of the Quakers, an influential tendency among them, headed by the Norfolk banker John Joseph Gurney, was affected by the evangelical revival. This grouping, most active in the period from 1830–85, shared the evangelicals' emphases on the importance of good works, the concept of original sin and the importance of the Bible and also laid stress on the conversion experience. This moved the Quakers closer to the rest of the religious world; they became more a part of the serious Christian brotherhood.[49] Hannah Ransome, for example, daughter of an Ipswich iron foundry owner, as a young woman was part of the evangelical Quaker community. She engaged in a dispute with the local vicar on the question of baptism, but also worked with him, visiting the poor, helping with the British School and the Penny Club. The vicar, impressed by her ardour, tried to woo her to the Church of England.[50]

Serious Christians, whether Anglican or nonconformist, found much to agree on and large arenas within which, despite other disagreements, they were fully able to co-operate. The shared core of their belief systems focused on their conviction of original sin and the possibility of redemption through the divine mission of Christ. At the heart of the serious Christian experience was conversion, which was felt as the flooding of the soul with God's grace, the melting of self or individual identity and individual will, being guided by and leaning completely on God's will and his mercy, through Jesus Christ. 'The Holy Spirit', wrote an Essex Quaker, and wife of a shopkeeper,

must work a change in the natural man before he can stand approved in the sight of a Being of infinite purity and self must be renounced and laid in the dust that Christ may be all in all.[51]

This renunciation of self and fusion with Christ was constantly stressed, particularly by women writers, as an essential part of the rebirth that could be experienced through conversion. The practice of self-denial and the putting aside of self was less problematic for women than men since it went along with their dependent position and the importance attached to the influence which their weakness and need for protection would have on men. The ultimate stage of such immolation of self was illness and death, for only thus could both the self be completely dissolved and purity from the taint of the world be assured, a process of bringing the soul back to Christ. It was in this spirit that death was welcomed as a moment of birth.[52]

The 'undivided surrender' of the heart to 'holy obedience' was the aim of the serious Christian matched by a constant fear of backsliding. From this concern with the pervasiveness of sin, the sense of oneself as depraved, weak and inadequate came the obsession with self-examination. 'I ought to think it a rich mercy', wrote the Rev. John Breay, an Evangelical clergyman in Birmingham, 'that one spark of enjoyment, throughout my life, is afforded to such a worm as I am.' 'Real religion', he taught his children, 'teaches and inclines us to put *self last*.'[53] But this self-abnegation was contradictory since in order to check on the state of one's soul it was necessary to be perpetually vigilant for signs of falling away from grace. Evangelicalism thus encouraged a powerful sense of self, but a self which was transformed and made anew. It was this which made possible the creation of significantly changed patterns of behaviour, based on a new code of morality. Serious Christians waged a constant struggle with their unreconstructed selves, valiantly confronting their weaknesses and denying their baser impulses. 'When will my *will* be slain', wrote one young Essex Quaker woman and another Anglican from Colchester reflected in her diary in 1827, 'I want to have no will of my own in anything but to find the Lord's will precious to me even when it crosses me.'[54]

In this struggle for the better self, serious Christians attributed pride of place to the power of prayer. Relying on prayer oneself and teaching others, whether one's children or the poor, how to pray, was a central part of the evangelizing effort.[55] Amy Camps, an ardent Evangelical and one time member of William Marsh's Colchester congregation, married late in life and went to live in the remove fastness of the Isle of Ely. She had an implicit belief in the power of prayer. 'The weather in harvest time becoming unusually wet', she recorded in her diary, 'prayer was set before me as the means of staying the calamity.' She rose at 5 a.m., prayed and waited on the Lord, 'til he raised up the north wind and gave us a clear sky'.[56] The scrupulous emphasis on diary keeping, on New Year's resolutions, on birthday books and the annual casting up of accounts before God were all part of the effort to watch over one's own soul, and for mothers to watch over the souls of their children. On 1 January 1834, Jane Ransome Biddell, an Ipswich farmers' wife, gave her 15-year-old daughter such a printed blank memorandum book in which to keep her spiritual 'accounts'. At the beginning of the little book Jane Biddell wrote a poem for her daughter the first and last stanzas of which read:

> The Memorandum, brief yet clear
> The record of each hour so dear
> Spent as the conscience best can tell
> On which remembrance loves to dwell
>
> That the ensuring year may tell
> That thou has spent the period well
> Little will thou avail the time
> Alloted in this nether clime
> If true improvement marks each year
> And fits us for a nobler sphere.[57]

Such meticulous overlooking of self and children was extended in the context of the congregation to the overlooking of members' personal and business concerns. The clergyman and senior male members of the church or chapel watched over the rest, judging when necessary. This close connection between personal morality and secular concerns (for Independents and Quakers could be expelled for irregularities in money matters) established a coherence in the careful regulation of life which could bring both psychic and material rewards. As Jane Ransome Biddell wrote in her commonplace book in 1809 under 'Lines written in a Ladies Pocket Book at the close of the year', in facing the troubles and storms of the past and future, only true religion could 'bid the turmoil cease' and she prayed that each hour would bring her closer to her God.[58]

Clergymen and religious fathers were more than ever the symbol and representative of the divine Father. The writer Mary Wright Sewell, in recalling her childhood on her father's farm, claimed that 'he has helped me to understand the Fatherhood of God. *He* is very pitiful and of tender mercy and so was my dear father'.[59] This potent overlapping was intensified still more for the children of clergymen. Catherine Marsh and her sisters undertook to write their father William's biography as a 'sacred duty'. For her, 'the holy Father and earthly Father are one'.[60] This imagery spread beyond the household and was deliberately used to frame the idea of the congregation of believers as a family. The smaller the congregation, the more personal power potentially wielded by the minster. Isaac Taylor at Ongar in Essex, with its tiny membership, was both loved and feared for the exercise of his 'patriarchal' authority, in the words of one of his parishioners. He had no hesitation 'in recommending the removal from Church membership of those lacking in loyalty to public worship and the observance of the sacraments and also those falling short of the Christian standard in home and business dealings'.[61]

The overlooking of 'home dealings' was particularly important since every serious Christian knew that the one place where moral order could be maintained and recalcitrant time and nature be brought more securely under control was in the home. Mid eighteenth-century resistance to allowing a form of church service outside church buildings had been overcome and various forms of family worship were being suggested through the latter part of the century. Family prayers within the four walls of home were more decorous than Wesley's open air preaching, but no less revolutionary in their results. The shift to family worship across all denominations, even in preference to individual prayer, the spread of 'parlour' as well as cottage worship, marked the growing prominence given to the family. The family would collectively pray over each member's successes and failures, each individual would be collectively called to account.[62] Family prayer stood between public worship and private devotion. The father and head of household marshalled his dependants, wife, children, servants and perhaps apprentices, thus contributing to the

good order of families, to the discharge of relative duty, to the improvement of the young, to the morals of servants' and to the welfare of the community at large.[63]

Doctrinal differences were overlooked as the great nonconformist moralists appeared in the hymn collections used in the home by Anglicans and Dissenters alike. The Anglican Evangelical, Edward Bickersteth, included in his *Christian Psalmody* of 1832 hymns based on verse by Watts and Dodderidge, Puritan divines, as well as William Cowper and John Newton, Anglican Evangelicals; a powerful mixture of various denominations.[64]

Cowper, Watts and Dodderidge were standard fare in the commonplace books of both Anglicans and Dissenters from the local area. Little Catherine Marsh, aged 5, William's daughter, in the ultra-Evangelical Colchester nursery, learned to read using Isaac Watt's verse, 'How doth the little busy bee improve each shining hour'. Her parents found it perfectly appropriate to their needs and expressive of their views.[65]

Serious Christians also shared a preoccupation with the precariousness of life in this world and the overwhelming importance of life everlasting often conceived as the Heavenly Home. Ministers made use of such fears as a way of keeping the faithful active and attached to the church. In March 1823 a farmer's wife recorded in her diary that the vicar 'gave us a short account of the sudden death of Mrs Cook to let us know how careful we ought to live'.[66] More emphasis was put on the joys of heaven and heavenly reunions with loved ones, however, than on the fears of hell. For a man like the Quaker shopkeeper from Ipswich, John Perry, the chief comfort after the death of his wife when they were in their 50s was that she was now in Heaven. This was particularly important in his case since his business failure had probably hastened her death with constant removals and financial worries. Even the scientific and rational Witham doctor, Henry Dixon, was awed by the strength of belief shown by his young wife dying agonizingly of TB. 'She enjoys the sweetest comfort with Christian resignation as to her eternal state', he commented in his diary.[67]

All serious Christians were exhorted to turn their backs on 'the world', but opinion varied as to where 'the world' began. The strictest eschewed sport, the theatre and card playing, some refused all novels, and some forbad even music in the home and pictures on the walls. All were agreed that domestic seclusion gave a proper basis for a truly religious life and since women were seen as naturally occupying the domestic sphere this was one of the reasons why women were seen as more 'naturally' religious than men. The experience of conversion was often described as a process of cleansing and purification from the pollutions of the world. 'Wash me, Oh Saviour', wrote Maria Marsh, the pious wife of William Marsh, 'cleanse me and I shall be whiter than snow'.[68] 'What a comfort that a fountain is open to wash in when sin has defiled our garments', wrote an Essex woman, warning that 'the enemy, if there is not a watch, will prevent if possible the operation of the means appointed to purify and cleanse'.[69] The concept of purity had taken on a special resonance for women partly because of fears associated with the polluting powers of sexuality. One of the distinguishing characteristics of the middle class was their concern with decorum in bodily functions and cleanliness of person. Thus, maintaining purity and cleanliness was both a religious goal and a practical task for women.

Serious Christianity, however, demanded private space for individual introspection and this could present problems for women concerned with the everyday tasks of running a household and bringing up children. The pleasures and privileges of daily 'entering into her chamber, and shutting the door' were always in danger of becoming a luxury.[70] While the home could be to some extent a scene of retreat and seclusion for men, for middle-class women it was the site of their responsibilities. Women who had encountered real religion were often worried about the effects which marriage would have on their spiritual lives, whether they would become too concerned with worldly matters, with the management of their households, with entertainment and dress, to allow enough space for spiritual life.[71] There is no doubt that the maelstrom of family life, with the large numbers of children born at frequent intervals and the wife's continued involvement in the productive enterprise could hardly have been conducive to a quietly contemplative religious experience. 'A dear young family with a number of daily interruptions, seems to allow very few opportunities for making memorandums of religious progress and the state of the individual soul' wrote one Essex shopkeeper's wife and she was echoed by many.[72]

For men the problems associated with the call to retreat were different since their daily lives necessarily involved frequent forays into the threatening worldly sphere and purity was not part of men's 'natural' inheritance. One strategy, as adopted by William Wilberforce, was to organize daily routines so carefully that time was always kept for self-examination and prayer.[73] A second possibility was for men to rely on their womenfolk to do some of the spiritual work for them. A Baptist farmer and miller constantly worried about the state of his soul, carrying his Bible, hymn book and copy of *Pilgrim's Progress* with him as he travelled on business with his horse and trap. He wrote his fiancée in the 1820s of his gratitude that she would be able to keep him from worldliness. 'I am engaged extensively with business of the world', he wrote, 'and too apt to have my affections fixed upon the vanities of it, therefore I need a double watch.'[74] Men also relied on their wives to take on much of the spiritual responsibility of parenthood. The father of the famous preacher Charles Spurgeon, clerk to a coal merchant in Colchester, was preoccupied with his public duties as a lay preacher and deacon. He returned home one evening anxious about the neglect of the religious education of his seventeen children but going quietly upstairs he heard his wife's voice:

She was engaged in prayer with the children. I heard her pray for them one by one by name. . . . I listened till she had ended her prayer and I felt 'Lord, I will go on with thy work. The children will be cared for.'[75]

Faced with the contradictory demands of public work and private spiritual life a third strategy for men was to retire from business as soon as a 'modest competency' had been achieved and enjoy the fruits of the years of work, leaving a son or nephew in charge of the business. John Talwin Shewell was a prosperous Ipswich draper, active as a Quaker minister, but in his 50s he retired to build his own home at Rushmere, just outside the town. There he resolved to be 'a good steward of my time and means'. On the one hand he wanted to be at liberty to enjoy the 'sweets of repose' to which he felt his 'earnest work' of earlier days had entitled him, while he continued with his preaching and other religious activities. He saw the turning *towards* domestic life as a turning away from the world. This had been the dream of his youth and like many others he quoted from Cowper's *The Task*, which best expressed the aspiration that domestic and rural life would bring men nearer to God.

Oh blest seclusion from a jarring world
What could I wish that I possess not here
. . . Not slothful, happy to deceive the time
Nor waste it, and aware that human life
Is but a loan to be repaid with use [note: meaning
interest]
When He shall call His debtors to account.

He regarded his retirement as a 'sort of vestibule in which to put off the
things of time and put on the things of eternity'.[76]
The stress on an individual relation to Jesus and concern with the individual soul tended to take attention away from more secular matters and
committed religionists tended to be apolitical, for politics could be another
worldly trap. The political energies of the serious Christians were focused
on moral issues (or church politics) and those with explicit party commitments were the minority. The tremendous energies which were poured into
such campaigns as anti-slavery, while radicals ridiculed the 'white slavery'
that flourished in England, was based on the belief that slaves, too, had
souls. But the belief in the primacy of the soul and the inevitability of social
hierarchies could lead to a profound conservatism. Ann and Jane Taylor,
ended their children's poem 'The Child of Poverty' with these lines:

Give me an humble pious mind
A meek and lowly heart. . . .[77]

This view of the world was shared by the Anglican Marsh and the Independent James, the latter maintaining 'that to a certain extent the distinctions
of society must be maintained'.[78]
Linked to the evangelical emphasis on salvation, was a millenarian strain.
A preoccupation with miracles and prophecy was a thread running through
the thought of Cowper, that most popular of middle-class poets. Signs
and portents must be properly attended to and understood. The Lisbon
earthquake was interpreted in *The Task* as a direct admonition from God
and a warning of chaos to come, and sectarians like Joanna Southcott kept
alive such traditions.[79] Not surprisingly the events of the 1790s were given
a similar reading. Henry Kett's book on prophecy in 1799, which linked
the beast of Revelation with infidelity and Jacobinism, marked a common
serious Christian response to the French Revolution.
Dissenters, however, tended to be more ambiguous and many went
through a phase of sympathy with the revolution. From the best-known
national figures such as Priestley to little-known locals, the effects of the
revolution were profound. Samuel Newton, the Independent minister of
Witham, had suffered serious doubts after reading Priestley in the 1780s.
Influenced by Godwin, who had been a pupil of his father when young
Newton was still at home, he resigned his chapel in the wake of 1789 but
managed to re-order his faith.[80]
The political conservatism of religionists and their insistence on a different
kind of agenda for change from that of the reformers is well illustrated by
co-operation between Anglicans and nonconformists in Birmingham in the
troubled decades of the 1830s and 1840s. It was indeed the firm conviction

of Catherine Marsh, William Marsh's Evangelical daughter, that her father, together with his band of serious Christian friends, were responsible for saving Birmingham from the horrors of Chartism and disorder. The town, 'from being the scene of Chartist riots', had become 'peaceable and well-ordered' and it was evangelicalism which had effected this cure.[81] The great demonstrations of the Birmingham Political Union and the famed Bull Ring Riot of 1839, together with the consistent threat posed by socialists and Owenites, had meant that the struggle was a hard one, but the Army of Christ had won through. The impressive work of serious Christians, faced with a world of unbelievers, allowed even such a radical as Joseph Sturge to think that it would be a terrible loss for Birmingham if Marsh were to leave.[82] Similarly, the Essex Quaker brewer James Hurnard, an admirer of Marsh when he was in Colchester, wrote a poem to him as a symbol of respect, despite the fact that Hurnard was a radical and secretary of the local Anti-Corn Law League.[83]

As early as 1819, John Angell James, observing the demonstrations and the agitation for reform which was galvanizing Birmingham, argued from the pulpit for the established nonconformist tradition of non-participation in politics. 'The Crisis', he insisted, was associated with neglect of piety, with immorality, with drunkenness and swearing rather than the problems of wages and labour which the reformers discussed. He saw around him insubordination to the laws and authorities of the realm and asserted the wisdom of the few in the face of the passions of the multitude. 'We must turn to God', he argued, in this crisis, for 'piety is patriotism and wickedness is treason'.[84] Faced with the political upheavals of the 1830s, James became willing to co-operate with the Anglican Evangelicals in the town, whose position and influence were steadily increasing, despite his fundamental disagreements with them and his distrust of the established church. As he wrote to one of his friends:

One of the most extraordinary circumstances associated with the Church of England, is the vast increase of evangelical clergymen, in connexion with a system so manifestly and notoriously corrupt as is the Church of England. I cannot interpret the circumstance; a vast nucleus of piety has been forming in the midst of surrounding evils of an enormous character.[85]

In the 1820s Evangelicals and Dissenters co-operated in a sustained attempt to win people to a Christian way of life. They worked together in the Bible Society and the Birmingham Infant School Society. James would appear on the platform of the Church Missionary Society. They made anti-slavery and temperance their common cause. From 1838 they co-operated over the Town Mission, and between 1846–59 James and the new Evangelical rector of St Martins, John Cale Martin, were very close.[86] Similarly, the Rev. John Charlesworth, an enthusiastic Anglican Evangelical, travelled all over east Suffolk, often with a nonconformist 'brother minister', both standing up 'amidst village listeners in a barn or large room of an inn', preaching the word wherever there was an audience to listen.[87] Such men formed the Army of Christ, sharing their belief in the centrality of the conversion experience and of personal religion. They also shared a revulsion for socialist politics. Their mission was to challenge the Owenite and

Chartist influence and to re-interpret the political crisis of the 1830s and 1840s in moral and religious terms, just as their forefathers had done in the 1790s. The problem, as James said so eloquently, was sin, not political representation.[88]

Birmingham had a strong Owenite presence. By the 1840s the central concerns of the Owenite movement had shifted from action through trade unions to communal experimentation and the dissemination of propaganda. Religious free thought, women's rights, marriage reform and working-class education had moved to centre stage. The Owenites were purveyors of a new way of life, their membership had to be born again in a similar way to evangelicals. They used an evangelical propaganda mode to put across a message which was directly subversive of orthodox Christian attitudes. Many of the socialists and feminists associated with Owenism had themselves been through a religious experience but were re-interpreting that encounter in more radical ways, insisting that the new commonwealth must abolish competition and that woman's mission must become woman's power. In the late 1830s and 1840s there were constant public confrontations between Owenites and evangelicals, and one of the aims of the religiously inspired town missions set up in this period was to counter the spread of socialist and infidel ideas among the working classes.

Birmingham was not immune from these developments. The town had housed an Equitable Labour Exchange, had been the headquarters of the socialist builder's union and provided the editorial office for *The Pioneer*. In 1840 a group of women petitioned the Birmingham Mechanics Institute for classes but this petition was refused. The women turned to the Owenites who provided them with classrooms and instructors at their Hall of Science.[89] Furthermore, Birmingham was to become a 'Chartist Metropolis'.[90] The alliance between sections of the middle class and sections of the working classes on the issue of reform, which had been held together by the organization and activities around the Birmingham Political Union, was breaking down by the late 1830s. The support for Chartism among the membership of the BPU collapsed by the time of the Chartist National Convention, which was moved from London to Birmingham in 1839, and the Bull Ring Riots completed the process of alienating 'respectable opinion'.[91]

Serious Christians responded to the twin challenge of Owenism and Chartism with vigour. James, who chose to focus on the godless character of the French Revolution and of Owen, was only one among many who believed that the only way to counter socialism was through 'real religion'.[92] The Rev. Charles Craven, preaching at St Peter's Birmingham in 1843 on the subject of the vital importance of new church building, noted that the rioters in the manufacturing districts were all non-church attenders. The manufacturing towns had become 'hotbeds of vice' and the money which should have been spent earlier on churches and schools was now being spent on the police force and prisons. 'The present crisis demands', he proclaimed, 'that all Clergy and Laity, Rulers and Subjects, should with one heart and one mind, join in a simultaneous effort to stem the tide of impiety and ungodliness that is threatening to deluge the land – for these are emphatically days of trouble, rebuke and blasphemy.'[93] As Millenarian Marsh thundered, in a sermon delivered at St Thomas's in 1841, the French Revolution was Anti-Christ. He appealed to his beloved brethren to recognize that

perilous times *are* come. What is Chartism but opposition to all human government? What is Socialism, but opposition to all moral and religious control, or infidelity under its most dangerous form, because whilst it approaches its victims in the garb of philanthropy, it leaves unrestrained all the sinful passions of man, and then charges on religion the evils which religion alone could mitigate or remove.[94]

Such sentiment was echoed by the Evangelical Rev. Charles Tayler in his Suffolk parish, who maintained in his tract *Edward or almost an Owenite* that the socialism of the 1840s was 'the same old poison in fresh bottles . . . *community of goods, community of wives and − no religion*'.[95]

The struggle of the serious Christians to save England from impiety and ungodliness was couched in religious terms. Catherine Marsh observed the 'thrilling' events of 1848, commented on the 'infidel and satanic origin' of the revolutionary movement and its tendency above all in her view to degrade women to slavery, but she never thought of herself as political in the conventional sense. 'I never talk *party* politics', she wrote in later years, having spent a lifetime trying to convert the working classes,

for this conclusive reason that I *have* none! I have only anti-Bradlaugh-ics and Gordon-ics, and so on − things that seem to me to be bound up with morals and religion and honour, and all the rest of the things that go to make up English and Christian character.[96]

The evangelical struggle for English hearts and minds was conducted not through the political meeting, the ballot box or the hustings, but through the sermon, the tract, the Sunday school, the auxiliary society and the philanthropic visit. It was a struggle which engaged significant sectors of the middle class, both male and female, in constant labour as the ungodly were exhorted, admonished and reproved. 'If the flame of Faith is not fanned by the works of love, it will soon be extinguished' wrote one pious young man in the commonplace book of his young sister-in-law on her Essex farm.[97] The conviction that 'works', inspired by Christian love, could regenerate English society was shared by evangelicals of all denominations and made possible the alliance of middle-class Anglicans and nonconformists in the bid to rescue those otherwise condemned to eternal damnation.

Church against Dissent

Such an alliance would have been hard to predict given the historic tensions between the established church and Dissent. Indeed some Dissenters kept their distance, particularly the Unitarians. Unitarians were never willing to join in the chorus of approval for the efforts of serious Christians. While admiring the exemplary way in which many evangelical clergy carried out their duties they regarded them as 'bigoted and intolerant'.[98] They heartily disliked the zeal and enthusiasm of the evangelicals, particularly the ways in which they relied on an appeal to emotion rather than reason, and Unitarians were often feared and reviled in return.

For Unitarians the discovery of truth could only be made through reason.

Freedom of thought was, therefore, a necessary prerequisite and the education of the mind and the faculty of reason a primary consideration. Unlike the evangelicals, Unitarians were intellectual in their orientation, influenced by science and philosophy, and admiring analytic skills in their ministers. Their chief doctrinal emphasis was on the human nature of Jesus Christ, the belief that made them so different from all other denominations and subject to unending persecution. For them the Bible was the sole source of authority in religion. They were not against 'the world' nor were they anti-pleasure in the mode of many evangelicals, for they enjoyed music and dancing, the theatre and other public entertainments. It has long been recognized that the rationalist tradition to which they belonged brought Unitarians close to the Utilitarians. They shared with the latter a belief in the perfectability of man and society. Not surprisingly, Unitarians were predominantly middle class, and indeed tended to attract the patriciate of that group in Birmingham. However, their emphasis on self-education and self-improvement also attracted a considerable following among respectable artisans and small masters.[99]

Essex had a small but well established Unitarian connection in the late eighteenth century, facilitated by Unitarian settlement in Stoke Newington, a development on the Essex side of London. This was an area which had always attracted Dissenters who could afford it, sited as it was near the City but with the advantages of fresh air and rural surroundings. The scattered and small-scale nature of Essex and Suffolk Unitarianism can be explained partly by the low level of support in rural areas. It contrasts with the powerful concentration of Unitarians in Birmingham, centred around two influential town centre congregations, the Old and New Meetings. Joseph Priestley's ministry at the New Meeting in the late eighteenth century marked one of the most active periods of hostility between church and Dissent in the town, with the Dissenting interest being led by the famed chemist and theologian. A series of conflicts between the two groups, about control of Sunday schools, about the buying of controversial theological texts for the Birmingham Library and about the possibility of successfully agitating for the repeal of the Test and Corporation Acts, all evidence the deep divisions between church and Dissent at this time.[100] Furthermore, there were divisions between Unitarians and other Dissenters, particularly on the issue of the divinity of Christ, but a fragile alliance was built with the aim of campaigning for the repeal of the Test and Corporation Acts, legislation which adversly affected the civil rights of all Dissenters. In 1790, inspired by the news from France, many were convinced that their liberation from the restrictive hand of church and state must be imminent.

But the news from France had roused the Anglicans in another direction. Their fears as to potential disturbances in England, following in the wake of the French, inspired them to view the efforts of Dissenters to abolish civil disabilities as tantamount to revolution. 'Presbyterian principles are unquestionably republican' argued one cleric, while another foretold the imminent demolition of the whole fabric of Christianity.[101] Tempers were high and Evangelicals across the country warned of the dangers of the French example. Political and social disorder were threatened; the rector of Stanway, preaching at St Peter's Colchester, warned,

Marriage was of course desecrated and degraded; and by necessary consequence all the charities of father, son and brother which emanate from it.[102]

The effects of this in Birmingham were to silence middle-class supporters of reform even before the development of artisan radicalism, as government repression silenced them elsewhere.[103]

The fright which the radical Birmingham Unitarians had received in 1791 gave them significant reasons to treat politics with more care and to retreat into social and even for some political conservatism. This was a pattern repeated across the country. Their unorthodox religious beliefs were enough to deal with and they sought moral respectability through family and domestic life. A minority group such as the Unitarians had strong reason for devotion to the family since their religion excluded them from many aspects of public life. The contemporary accounts of the riots from those who suffered, pay marked attention to the destruction of their homes, the 'calm retreat' of their private lives which inevitably preoccupied them more in the dangerous days of the 1790s when middle-class reformers went in constant fear.[104] As E. P. Thompson argues, 'after 1792 there were no Girondins to open the doors through which the Jacobins might come'.[105] Middle-class radicalism had retreated and this splitting of the traditional lines of connection between radicalism and Dissent was to have extensive consequences. In the stormy days of the 1790s, simply to be a Dissenter was to indicate support for some of the dangerous ideas associated with France, as Isaac Taylor and his family discovered in the remote Suffolk village of Lavenham. The Independent Taylors, newcomers to the village, were driven to seek refuge with the local vicar when attacked as outsiders, the bearers of dangerous ideas.[106]

With the increased separation of politics and religion buttressed by the Evangelical drive, relations between the church and Dissent were on the whole amicable until the 1820s.[107] The energies and efforts of the Anglican Evangelicals were not matched within the church establishment. Despite the fears aroused by the French Revolution, the governing classes were slow to act on the need for reform, not because the abuses were unrecognized but because they assumed that the church did not have to be popular and certainly did not have to accept public opinion.[108] The 1820s, however, marked a turning point and it was clear to all that the church was in crisis. Middle-class public opinion had become more evident and influential, whatever the views of the aristocracy and gentry. Furthermore, liberalism and radicalism had become more widespread. The Evangelicals within the church were sounding a less cautious and conservative note in their publications and, frustrated by their continued marginalization, were turning to questions of reform. The repeal of the Test and Corporation Acts and the granting of Catholic Emancipation significantly altered the religious balance of power. The clergy were shocked, they felt let down by their political leaders and saw the old relation between church and state being ruptured. Dissenters and Catholics could now sit in Parliament, implying that they could legislate in relation to the Church of England. The passing of the Reform Act in 1832 after the bishops had been highly identified with its opposition (since the new towns tended to be identified as centres of nonconformist criticism of the church), marked a low point for the church establishment.

It was the 1830s which saw a widespread demand for the disestablishment of the church. Dissenters still had many grievances; only Jews and Quakers could be married outside the parish church, the state registration of births was only on parish church records, it was difficult to be buried outside a Church of England burial ground, the universities were tied to the church and every citizen was liable to a rate to repair the parish church. It was this last issue which galvanized most opposition in the 1830s. The rate had to be voted by a parish meeting and every occupier of property had a right to vote, church or chapel, male or female. Many meetings refused to levy the rate and in the face of this the ecclesiastical authorities were powerless. There had been expectations that the church rate would have been abolished after the Reform Act. When this was disappointed there was strong local reaction, led by the nonconformists. Many of these had quickly gained ascendancy after Municipal Reform and nonconformists had also begun to take their turn as overseers of the poor and in other public offices.[109]

Having achieved this degree of integration, the issue of the payment of church rates, and, for nonconformist farmers the continued irritation of the tithe, came to a head in the turbulent atmosphere of the late 1830s. From 1834 to the early 1840s Samuel Courtauld, the Unitarian silk manufacturer in Essex, led the church rate issue centred on the village of Braintree, an action for which he paid by social ostracism. He brought the test case for non-payment which finally reached the House of Lords in 1853, virtually putting an end to the rate where nonconformists were in the majority.[110]

Church rates were not actually abolished until 1868, but in many places, including Birmingham, no attempt was made to collect them after the early 1840s. The church rates issue was a popular one in Birmingham and in 1836, for example, 6000 people attended an anti-rate meeting at the Town Hall. Some of the supporters of abolition linked their attack on the established power of the church with the struggle for popular rights and representation. A liberal poet characterized the struggle in his poem, 'Birmingham', dedicated to the Birmingham Political Union MP William Scholefield, as one in which the poor were saved from their oppression by the establishment:

> For let us not, upon the Church, intent,
> Forget to pay our tribute to Dissent;
> For 'tis to this we owe our high renown –
> This lends a noble spirit to the town;
> To this is due the honour we achieved,
> When from the church-rates we the poor relieved
> Its influence lends a healthful moral tone
> For which we stand unequalled and alone.[111]

But support for the church rates issue ranged across the Whig/Radical spectrum among the Dissenters. Evangelical nonconformists united with Unitarians on this issue and crucial to their alliance was a moderate version of reform which insisted on the civil rights of Dissenters and the legitimate interests of the Dissenting commercial classes. On this basis John Angell James could agree with the patrician minister of the New Meeting, who heartily disliked James's enthusiasm in religious terms, as well as with the minister of the Old Meeting, who was a well-known radical and took an active part in Birmingham political life.[112] Such an alliance was also effective in preventing the exclusion of Dissenters from the government of King Edward's School in the 1830s and provoking a serious debate as to the kind of education the school should provide.[113] Clearly, the Dissenting middle class still had important interests in common which allowed them to co-operate extensively on certain issues.

Faced with the strength of the Dissenting opposition, the church establishment responded in varied ways. The development of the Oxford Movement was part of this response. Their principal beliefs were in the doctrine of apostolic succession and consequently in the sinfulness of allowing non-clergy to interfere in spiritual matters, and in the importance of the sacraments. All these were in direct opposition to Evangelical doctrines, despite the centrality of men from second generation Evangelical families in the heartlands of Tractarianism. They were deeply hostile to the Evangelical mobilization of lay women, though willing to countenance the establishment of protected 'sisterhoods'.[114] A second establishment response was the growth of a moderate reforming group within the church who hoped that by a combination of some legislative reform and the adoption of the Evangelical view of the importance of the parish as a worshipping community, the church would be able to roll back the tides of nonconformity and preserve social stability.[115]

It was not until the 1860s that it became clear that the Anglican church could never hope to reinstate itself as the national church, inevitably it was becoming denominational.[116] Many middle-class men and women had religious affiliations but belonged to varied denominations of which Anglicanism was but one. Religious discourses, however, remained central to the belief systems of the articulate middle class and avowed atheists were few in the period up to 1850. Furthermore, as will be seen, the religious practices associated with these varied groups permeated respectable middle-class culture.

The religious community

Membership of church or chapel, it has been argued, provided men and women with a community of like minded people, albeit a community based on moral superiority. For all denominations, religious activity was rewarded by links with a wider network, which in the case of the Quakers was highly organized across the country, while Evangelicals, Independents and Anglicans were all concerned to build up closer ties in the early nineteenth century.

'Serious Christians' separated themselves from existing society and their critique of 'the world' meant that they had a considerable ideological investment in trying to construct an alternative culture. Such a project necessarily focused initially on the home and the church or chapel with its ancilliary

institutions. Similarly, Unitarians shared beliefs which were unacceptable
to many and they too relied on the creation of networks of their own, where
their intellectual interests and social concerns were welcomed. Religious
networks in all cases meshed with both kinship and business ties, almost
completely in the case of Quakers, but in significant ways for other Christian groups.

Religious networks could provide an entire world for the individuals
involved in them. It was a world which stretched not only across England
and involved yearly gatherings of the faithful at the great May meetings such
as those at Exeter Hall, but to the missions which were being established
overseas.[117] Above all, the community of believers reached beyond the
world and to Heaven, promising reunion in the life everlasting. The constant
Christian meetings, gatherings and events provided alternative structures to
the social calendar of the aristocracy and gentry with their hunts and race
meetings linked to the agricultural seasons, and to the clubs and coffee
houses frequented by middle-class men in the eighteenth century. 'Serious
Christians' needed to construct a social order in which the scenes of
domestic or church life would always be preferred to 'the gaieties and follies
of an ensnaring world' and this meant building a framework within which
individuals could find help, care and support.[118] A young trainee minister,
visiting Carrs Lane Independent chapel in Birmingham in the early nineteenth century, was impressed by the range of invitations he received and
the numbers of social events he attended. He dined out and took tea
regularly and liked 'the manners of the social circles at Birmingham very
much'. He met many attractive young ladies whom he was delighted to be
able to advise, and was charmed to receive 'a very acceptable offer from a
Gentleman, a Bookseller to visit at any time his reading room. It is not a
public library and only a select number of the *literate* of the town are
admitted'.[119] Young women attached to the congregation could not expect
to enjoy the same kind of social round, but even for them church societies
provided many opportunities for meetings and activities.

The religious community could be particularly important for adolescents
and young people, most frequently men, living away from home in another
town or village. The church or chapel could act as a kind of religious
'family', often providing accommodation, friendship and emotional support
as well as initial business contacts. Single women could also find membership of a religious 'family' especially rewarding, for example a woman like
Amy Camps, the Colchester Evangelical, who for many years built her
social and emotional life completely around the church.[120] Religious
networks were also, not surprisingly, important sources for potential
marriage partners since for many young women they represented their main
social contact outside of kin. Receiving communion or becoming a member
of a chapel provided an important stage in the lifecycle of men and women.
A young man finishing his apprenticeship and starting up in business might,
in addition, mark his entry to full adulthood by becoming a member of a
chapel. A young woman with less opportunity for public recognition associated with the taking on of new household responsibilities might find chapel
membership and the adoption of Sunday school teaching or other chapel
related duties part of the process of growing up. Young people growing

away from their parents might register rebellion by moving to another church or chapel.

Kinship groups were often well established within a church or chapel and poor relations were often kept afloat by eliciting a religiously inspired sense of duty from more prosperous kin, whether or not members of the same congregation. Poorer individuals might make up for their lack of material success by giving time and energy to the church. In case where different material fortunes could have been a divisive factor within families, membership of the same religious community could help to bind them together. This amalgam of kinship and religious community was strongest among the Quakers who could travel anywhere in the British Isles or even abroad and find a welcome in the Quaker congregation. Take the Suffolk Quaker woman Ann Watkins who started married life with her shopkeeper husband in Belgium. On their return to England he became the manager of a Birmingham business but this employer turned out to be a fraud and they were left with nothing. Ann was faced with an ill husband, several small children and no help. The Birmingham Friends rallied and supplied food, clothes and cash amounting to £40 in small sums which allowed time for her husband to recover and take up new work as a commercial traveller.[121] When such a sense of community was strengthened by family ties it provided formidable advantages which go a long way to explain Quaker commercial prominence.

When members of a family did badly and relatives, despite institutional and moral injunctions did not step in to help, however, disappointed expectations were proportionately greater. The very closeness of family and religious ties meant that on occasion family and religious loyalties could come into conflict. This occurred when the Congregational church in a small Essex village was caught in a bitter dispute between the minister and the deacons over some aspects of the minister's conduct. This struggle between the Rev. Fielding and his most senior male church members brings out some of the difficulties inherent in a religious grouping which drew many of its features from the family form and yet was voluntaristic. Fielding feared losing both his material support and his social identity if he were forced to leave his ministry. Long residence and his connection with the chapel had provided a 'kind of home and a domestic circle for him' as for so many others. Fielding's wife's cousin had been persuaded to join the opposition to the minister and this shook Fielding to the core. 'We see here a violation of the ties of flesh and blood', he protested,

Due regard of *relationship* is among the first lessons of morality. Love of *kindred* are generally esteemed the basis and foundation of social affections. *Family alliances* are commonly reckoned *sacred* and not to be wantonly torn asunder.

Meanwhile, the deacons' party berated Fielding's wife's nephew for putting his family allegiances above his religious conscience and continuing to support the minister.[122]

Wealthy members of a congregation were also expected to help out the poorer and less successful. Sometimes this would be organized on an individual basis, sometimes collectively as with the financial aid which the New Meeting in Birmingham offered to its aged and needy members.[123] The

Anglican clergy had always had a good deal of patronage at their disposal and the handing out of contracts associated with local charities was one such gift. Small tradesmen and farmers could benefit from their association with a church in this way, as did the Ipswich baker Jeremiah Howgego. He was genuinely interested in religious matters if not a devout church-goer and supported Sunday school treats and special services of various kinds associated with different denominations, trying out attractions such as hearing 'a black man' preach and sampling a 'Unitering' service when in London. He was, however, a conscientious member of Ipswich's Evangelical St Margaret's church and as a baker had large orders through his association with church charities.[124] This kind of patronage gradually became less important as demands for regulation of such contracts increased but religious connections could directly facilitate business prosperity. The Bentall's drapery concern at Maldon on the Essex coast 'added quite a new class of trade to business' from timber merchants and farmers when the family joined the local Independent chapel.[125]

Nonconformist men, acting as chapel trustees and paying the bills, could acquire a healthy reputation for worth and probity. Professionals, struggling to establish themselves with fee paying clients could find a church or chapel connection rewarding. The Birmingham Quaker community had their own dentist as early as the 1780s and Witham's Dr Henry Dixon, who like his fictional counterpart in *Middlemarch* disliked selling drugs to supplement his income and wanted to depend on his professional skills alone, found the patronage of his chapel minister, Samuel Newton, and that of the wealthy Congregational lawyer's family of Pattisson, an invaluable introduction.[126] Similar advantages came to the Anglican doctor, Richard Mackintosh, in Colchester, whose wife was a friend of Mrs Marsh. He was himself part of the local Evangelical network and Mrs Marsh senior's personal physician. Mackintosh was treasurer of the Castle Library, vice-president of the Colchester Philosophical Society, a manager of the savings bank, active member of the Botanical and Horticultural Society and of the Colchester and East Essex Bible Society. He was also a founder member and voluntary physician of the Essex and Colchester Hospital. At the hospital, medical staff worked in close connection with the board of directors, primarily staffed by clergymen. Although free church ministers were allowed their turn in conducting hospital services, the connections were mainly with high ranking Anglicans and this considerably widened the potential professional network of doctors.[127]

The overlap between religious and entrepreneurial networks was not automatically an advantage, however. The strict overlooking of honesty, industry and competence meant that bankrupts could find themselves shunned by their fellow members as well as outcasts in the business world. Furthermore, religious communities would sometimes overlook in a way that directly challenged the profit motive. The Galtons, a well established Quaker family in Birmingham with a gun manufactory, were unwilling to have their business affairs interfered with by the religious scruples of their Friends. Their factory was directly dependent on the slave trade, the abolition of which was a subject dear to the hearts of many Quakers. Varied attempts were made to appeal to the Galton conscience and in 1795 Samuel

Galton was visited by Sampson Lloyd and Joseph Gibbins, two of the most senior members of the Birmingham Meeting. They invited him to discuss their scruples but Galton was unmoved. He argued that his major concern must be with making a living and that the trade in slaves nor the sale of arms did not imply approval of their use. 'The trade *devolved* upon me', he insisted,

as if it were *an inheritance*, . . . not easily assignable, or convertable to other purposes. . . . Will any Person, for a moment suppose, that as a Manufacturer, it is my object to encourage the *Practice*, or the *Principle* of War, or that I propose to myself any other end, than that which all commercial persons propose, viz. the acquisition of property?

Galton capital stayed tied up for some time in gun production but the family was also careful to diversify.[128]

Membership of a religious community could also confer position and status in English society at a time when the middle class was challenging traditional aristocratic and gentry routes to social honour. Religion, in theory at least, was 'the one thing needful'. It gave both men and women a sense of identity and a community which provided social and economic benefits and gave individuals the strength to assert demands, offering new identities in public and private worlds. The increased sense of power and purpose in private was associated with the existence of religious convictions which allowed for Cowper's plea that claims to honour were derived not from earthly but from heavenly inheritance. The public activity was associated for serious Christians, particularly men, with religious demands on their time. In the early nineteenth century Dissenters in the Essex countryside could still popularly be referred to as 'pork dumplings'.[129] But by mid century the deaths of prominent nonconformist men in Essex and Birmingham heralded public funerals when business in the town more or less came to a standstill while tribute was paid. On 17 March 1852, John Angell James's brother, James James, a well-known manufacturer and philanthropist, was buried. A local clerk noted in his diary that this 'man of great influence and respectability' was followed to his grave by a procession of 2000 or 3000 tradesmen and gentlemen. The event was orchestrated by his brother the minister, whose public appearance on such an occasion confirmed his power and standing in the town. In 1859 John Angell James himself died. Tens of thousands were said to have lined the streets for his funeral. It was a major public spectacle, attended not only by his family, friends and congregation but also by large sections of the town's population. Such events were public confirmations of nonconformist values.[130]

Anglican clergy already had a well established public presence and were prominently represented at civic occasions, such as at the end of the war or a coronation, spectacles which provided ways of demonstrating and consolidating power. The selection of the groups who would walk in the procession expressed public recognition and the clergy were prominent in the forefront. Increasingly, Dissenting clergy were invited to join these processions as in the opening of the Essex and Colchester Hospital in 1820.[131] Together with the civic dignitaries in a town, the street commissioners and public officials, town councillors, aldermen and mayors in incorporated boroughs, the clergy were the recognized elite. The fairly extensive building of new Anglican churches in the early nineteenth century gave their clergy ample opportunities for public visibility, and for showing off their links with the county gentry, who would usually turn out for ceremonial occasions. The stone laying of Birmingham's Christ Church in 1805 was followed by a dinner at the Royal Hotel when 'the nobility, gentry and clergy' were 'joined by a large party of gentlemen of the town and neighbourhood'. The consecration of the church in 1813 provided another occasion for public celebration and the service was followed by a 'public' dinner in the afternoon.[132] Such 'public' dinners were not of course public in the sense of open. They were public occasions which the rest of the town, meaning those tradesmen and artisans who were not 'gentlemen', the working classes, Dissenters and women could watch. Ladies were an important part of the audience at the services, but they were not usually invited to attend the dinners. The 'public' was propertied men. Women contributed by swelling the ranks and providing an admiring and respectable crowd.

Despite the increasing respectability of nonconformists, there was still more prestige attached to the Anglican church. The socially mobile might well acquire pew rights with their rental of a house and appearance in one's own pew was a way of augmenting social visibility. It was a not uncommon pattern for nonconformists who became very wealthy and wanted to mix with the upper middle classes for social or political reasons, to abandon their chapel and join the church. The Rylands were a well-known Birmingham Unitarian family with long associations with the New Meeting. Louisa Ryland, the only child and daughter of the wealthy Samuel Ryland, was educated into the church, while Samuel continued to attend the New Meeting. Her cousin commented wryly in his memoirs:

Being a young lady likely sometime to be very rich, and may be form some high connection, they, I suppose, thought it best to make her a member of the Established Church. This, we will hope, has been satisfactory to her, as it certainly has been to the Church.[133]

It must have been particularly satisfactory to the church as Miss Ryland never married and was well known for her philanthropic activities. Similarly, William Henry Pattisson, the wealthy Witham lawyer, perhaps finding the nonconformist circle and the Congregational chapel in Witham somewhat restricting, resigned over a disagreement in 1825 and quickly joined the Anglican church. He gave land for the new church of All Saints and was a founder of its building fund. He established a recognized position for himself within the Anglican elite and his son was able to marry into the local gentry.[134]

The kinds of status which religious belonging could confer did not always, however, have such a worldly definition. Serious Christians were genuinely concerned with demonstrating their piety and denial of self. Their status as 'truly religious' came not from their rank but from their subjection of self to God's will. Such beliefs could pose problems since despite this respect for true religion, few went so far as to deny that rank was important or that morality must be expressed in appropriate levels of dress and behaviour. The recognition of equality in Christ had to be combined with a healthy respect for social hierarchy, a contradiction often explored in novels of the period.[135] The desire for social status and the way in which it conflicted with the humbling of self demanded in conversionist theology presented potent problems to serious Christians. Were they sufficiently willing to refuse considerations of social position and lose themselves in Christ? A Witham couple decided to relinquish their membership of the Congregational chapel in 1848 and join the Primitive Methodists, admiring the capacity of that sect to deny themselves. 'No other denomination', they argued,

was so plain and quite so willing to stoop so low, as to go out into the highways and hedges and compel the Poor and needy and outcasts of Society to come into the field of Christ.[136]

Jane Taylor, the Colchester author, in her novel *Display* was preoccupied with the social and status connotations associated with 'embracing Christianity'. What kinds of relationships were appropriate between people of high and low degree who were members of the same chapel? Taylor was critical of 'unbecoming familiarity' and applauded her fictional alehouse keeper's daughter who knew her place and had 'no inclination' to step outside it. But she also disliked the patronizing ways of the upper classes. Taylor was articulating in this novel, published in 1815, the values of the respectable middle class, their fear of vulgarity, insincerity and worst of all, display. Such behaviour could not be part of a proper Christian practice. Elizabeth, one of the central characters in the novel, was forced to undergo a drop in social status and was even expected by her husband, officer turned tradesman, to help serve in his shop. Jane Taylor based part of *Display* on the Hill sisters of Colchester. 'Elizabeth' in her novel was one of the Hills, who had ostentatiously left Isaac Taylor's (Jane's father) chapel to join the Baptists. The Baptists, felt Taylor, expressed their signs of grace 'coarsely', lacking as they did education and delicacy. 'Some religionists' she wrote,

certainly [were] not attractive in themselves – plain good people but low in manners.

They suffered from narrow views with a tendency to what was the 'bane of Colchester', namely, 'high antinomian doctrine'. Miss Hill would walk arm in arm with some of their leaders who occupied a low grade in life. But her spiritual pride came before a fall. Both in the novel and real life the young woman was attracted by the golden epaulets of an officer, married hastily and returned to Colchester a broken woman. In real life, the husband installed his mistress in the house. In *Display* this too shocking immorality is transmuted into the husband's bad debts which lead to the abandonment of the army and entry into trade. In the novel 'Elizabeth' had to learn that even the humiliation of standing behind a counter could be dealt with through true religion. Taste and understanding, she came to learn, were not dependent on money or position but rather on qualities of mind, of reason and culture. They could even be found behind a counter, so demeaning in social terms for a genteel woman. Furthermore, she learnt that it is only religion which can guarantee a true understanding, freed from the trammels of rank, prejudice and party.[137] Real religion required an independence of mind, an ability to go forth on one's own, unaffected by other social interests, with the claims of reason, truth and the spirit to the fore. Religion was indeed the 'one thing needful', able to free individuals from the patronizing and dependent practices of the old society, able to assert their claim that their 'proud pretensions' stemmed from their faith. Serious Christians or committed believers of whatever denominational persuasion agreed that whether their beliefs stemmed from faith or reason they were right to have the courage of their convictions.

2 'Ye are all one in Christ Jesus': men, women and religion

There is neither Jew nor Greek, there is neither male nor female for ye are all one in Christ Jesus.

Gal. 3, 28

Religion may have been the 'one thing needful' for men and women of the middle class but it was not experienced by them in the same way. Indeed, discussions on the proper place of men and women in the public and private sphere were a central part of religious practice at this time. Seventeenth-century Puritanism, with its emphasis on the individual believer and the importance of the religious family and household, had inaugurated a debate on the relative places of men and women in the church. The more radical – Familists, Ranters and Diggers – were soon silenced, but there remained a belief in individual freedom of conscience and a commitment to spiritual equality, that men and women were 'all one in Christ Jesus'. This formed a base line for discussions on the religious natures of men and women, their relative rights in church or chapel and their appropriate practice in the world. Many voices were heard, ranging from those of the Evangelical Anglicans to the Primitive Methodists and even Owenite feminists, but it is noticeable that the more radical tended to become muted as nineteenth-century orthodoxies about woman's place became established. Among the millenarian movements of nineteenth-century England, for example, the importance of women as preachers and teachers had been recognized but, where such movements outgrew their enthusiastic origins and became more bureaucratic, the women were usually pushed to the margins.[1]

Nevertheless, the numbers of women attending churches and chapels in comparison with the numbers of men was noted and it was widely believed that women were more susceptible to religion. Obelkevich has explained this as the decline of community and the rise of class society. When church attendance had been a public duty, it was usually undertaken by the husband, representative of his family and household. When communal obligations had been overtaken by class and religious practice became a matter of individual decision, the way was open for women to play a more active role. This was particularly the case among the Primitive Methodists where women were able to play a greater part than in the Anglican church, even if within a recognizably 'woman's sphere'. Within the established church as well, the balance of the sexes within public worship had shifted, in part through the actions of the clergy, so that women's activities increased as those of men were reduced. Women's enlarged role was, therefore, a by-product of the clergy's attempt to increase their power over their congregations. For Obelkevich, the key factor in this change was the increasing importance of individual decision in religious practice. Faced with the decline of their productive activities and the strong desire to be genteel, the ambitious farmer's wives of south Lincolnshire turned, not just to the parlour, but also to the church.[2]

In his analysis of the differential attendance of men and women, McLeod, in contrast, emphasizes the positive reasons which women had for choosing to be religious; within the church or chapel they could find one public arena from which they were not excluded. The personal morality which was at the heart of Christian concerns in the nineteenth century accorded well with the situation of most middle-class women, locked as they were into a world of family and friends, while groups such as prayer societies offered a woman's subculture of validation and support. Men, meanwhile, had many places other than church or chapel in which to meet and be active, their business interests were often in contradiction to religious precepts and their male subcultures were structured around forms of masculinity which might well present problems in religious terms.[3] Despite these possible checks on the involvement of middle-class men, large numbers were religious, and church and chapel leadership remained masculine with women in the rank-and-file. Given the belief in spiritual equality, how was this differentiation between male and female spheres constructed, on what religious doctrines was it based and within what practices was it enshrined? The separate spheres of men and women were not already given, they were created through belief and practice.

Doctrines on manliness

Wives submit yourselves unto your own husbands, as it is fit in the Lord. Husbands, love your wives and be not bitter against them. Children obey your parents in all things: for this is well pleasing unto the Lord. Fathers, provoke not your children to anger, lest they be discouraged. Servants, obey in all things your masters according to the flesh, not with eyeservice, as men pleasers; but in singleness of heart fearing God. . . .

Col. 3 18–22

These verses, from St Paul's Epistle to the Colossians, were a favourite passage in collections for family prayers.[4] All Christians should discharge their duties according to their rank. Within the household it was natural that the husband should command and the wife, children and servants should obey. These were the laws of God and of man. Such a view was built on the assumption that the household was the basic unit of society and that within most households there was a family, including servants. To be lasting, religious knowledge needed to be based within that household, and as Henry Thornton, a member of the Evangelical Clapham Sect, argued it was through families that the knowledge of God and of his laws was handed down from generation to generation.[5]

The Puritan belief in the spiritualization of the household as a necessary prerequisite in a society dominated by a church establishment with little enthusiasm for Puritan doctrine survived as a central aspect of serious religion in the late eighteenth and early nineteenth centuries.[6] This assumption as to the *naturalness* of the family as the primary form of social organization underpinned Christian thinking. The earthly family, moreover, was an extension of the heavenly family. Good Christians could enjoy, 'an unshaken belief in a future life where the members of the household would meet again and would recognise each other and be eternally happy'.[7] As an Essex Quaker noted, 'Family celebrations could contribute to the building of the little kingdom of heaven on earth, the looking forward to the heaven above.'[8] It was within the power of the household head to create a happy family home, and as Birmingham's Rev. George Bull argued, he had never met an atheist with a contented home and family.[9] The domestic circle was the 'school of character' and who could hope for responsible and well-adjusted adults if religious knowledge and piety had not been imbibed almost with the mother's milk.

The stress on the importance of religious practice being firmly embedded within the family became more urgent as work became separated from the home. 'How often', bemoaned the editor of *Leisure Hour* in 1852, 'it seems to be taken for granted that when the business of the day is begun, in a large concern, all family scenes and all religious thoughts must wait until the day is over'.[10] Family prayers were a way of signifying the place of religion at home. The celebration of family prayers became increasingly popular as the nineteenth century progressed and Henry Thornton's *Family Prayers* was only one of a genre that went through successive editions.[11] The occasion itself marked the recognition, which St Paul had urged, of the power and authority of the father and household head, as his dependants knelt before him. 'Every family', argued the Birmingham Independent minister, John Angell James,

when directed as it should be, has a sacred character, inasmuch as the head of it acts the part of both the prophet and the priest of his household, by instructing them in the knowledge, and leading them in the worship, of God; and, at the same time, he discharges the duty of a king, by supporting a system of order, subordination and discipline.[12]

James strongly advised his church members to engage in family prayers, early enough in the morning so as not to interrupt business and not too late in the evening so that participants would not be fatigued. He was concerned that excessive eagerness in 'commercial pursuits' was interfering with morning prayers and fashionable habits of late visiting were disturbing evening worship. Some members of his congregation clearly took his exhortations seriously: family prayers in the household of the Phipsons, for example, a modest metal manufacturing family who were enthusiastic members of James's congregation, were seen as crowning the domestic arrangements of their household and serving as an expression of all that was most delightful in family life.[13]

Serious Christians assumed that the male head of household had certain responsibilities and duties. Evangelical clergy, of every denomination, were concerned to elaborate Christian doctrine as they saw it in relation to masculinity. In this task they were assisted by the mainly female lay-writers

who produced a myriad of tracts and pamphlets. Preoccupation with forms
of manliness was never as central and overt an issue as forms of femininity
for Christian preachers and writers, since man's nature was seen as in God's
image while woman was defined as 'other'. There were several reiterated
elements, however, in serious Christian discourses on the subject, which
show a coherent, if contradictory, set of ideas about male character which
made possible the construction of a new subject – the Christian middle-
class man. Christian manhood had to be created anew from the tissue of
ideas associated with masculinity in the eighteenth century. Many of the
values associated with evangelical Christianity – the stress on moral earnest-
ness, the belief in the power of love and a sensitivity to the weak and the
helpless – ran counter to the worldly assumptions and pursuits of the
gentry. Masculine nature, in gentry terms, was based on sport and codes
of honour derived from military prowess, finding expression in hunting,
riding, drinking and 'wenching'. Since many of the early Evangelicals came
from gentry backgrounds they had to consciously establish novel patterns
of manhood.

Many more were in middle-class occupations, often of a sedentary type.
Evangelical men could hope to exercise considerable power and influence
but of a new kind. Their rewards were not political or material, but moral
and religious. One soul converted was worth more than an income. The
Rev. John Breay in his town centre church in Birmingham with its relatively
low stipend was offered a more valuable, less precarious living in 1839, but,
despite his financial worries with his growing family, he felt bound to
refuse. He had not received a 'call' and his spiritual duties in the insalubrious
town courts remained more important than material considerations.[14] Such
a view depended on a strong belief that a man's work was God's work.
Even those Evangelicals who lived off property still had work to do in the
world, the work of winning others to salvation. Such was the responsibility
of all serious Christians, not only the professionally engaged clergy.

The religious influence associated with serious Christianity opened novel
opportunities for men. William Marsh, the friend of Simeon and Wilberforce and minister in both Colchester and Birmingham, provided an
example of the new kind of male identity. According to his daughter
Catherine (probably writing with more explanatory hindsight than
veracity), even in his early childhood he was noted for his 'tender sensitive-
ness' which gave him an 'almost feminine grace' in his later years. He was
known to his schoolmates as 'Bible Billy' and on one occasion, taunted by
a man servant that 'Master Billy' was not man enough to swear, the boy
was stung into complicity to prove his manhood and then wept with
contrition for having given in. Destined, like his elder brothers for the
army, he responded to his conversion and his religious call in masculine
terms and undertook 'another and higher commission in the service of the
Great Captain of his salvation, and fought under His banner against sin'.
Such a call gave him steadfastness and the power of self-sacrifice which
helped to balance the 'infantile measure of his feminine sensitivity', and 'by
the Grace of God' he was 'moulded into an example of real manliness as
consisting of all that is pure and true and strong and tender and lasting'.[15]

This Christian manliness represented a sharp break with the traditional association of the parson with the jollities of country life. In one Suffolk village, for example, the parson, who was also a landowner, had always joined the Horkey or harvest festival. He contributed £5 to the 'frolic' held at the local inn and engaged heartily with the other 'jolly good fellows', performing a song about the man who 'takes his glass at night', who 'lives as he ought to live and dies a hearty fellow' as opposed to the sober spoil sport.[16]

The Evangelical clergyman had to turn his back on this pattern and in so doing, he risked his masculine identity. His new persona might be interpreted as weakness and could alienate his natural upper-class fellows. Yet as an active minister he had to regularly mix with his inferiors, made one with them in Christ's fellowship. Only the passionate commitment of Evangelical belief could carry him over these barriers. Men like Marsh could, however, demonstrate their masculinity in other ways. His active ministry fostered wide travel and he preached to large numbers both at home and away. His new church of St Thomas in Birmingham, initially almost empty, was soon packed with enthusiastic supporters, and on a return visit to Colchester after a twenty-three year absence the road from the station to the town centre was lined with ex-parishioners and friends who gave him a hero's welcome. His widely publicized saving of the bank in Colchester in 1825 was the kind of public action which confirmed a manly presence based on moral authority rather than physical prowess or the power of wealth and office.[17]

Nevertheless, Evangelical manhood, with its stress on self-sacrifice and influence, came dangerously close to embracing 'feminine' qualities. In the heady days of conversionist excitement, the fervent singing, praying and weeping as public displays of religious emotion outraged upper- and middle-class secularists and traditionally religious alike. Gradually concern with order and control in every aspect of life made such outbursts, particularly in men, appear excessive and vulgar. In late eighteenth-century local records we find Evangelical 'tender hearted' men moved to tears by the Waverley novels or by the first sight of Norwich cathedral.[18] By the 1820s, men's weeping in public was more problematic. In a Suffolk curate's moral tale, a studious farmer's son throws himself on the ground and sobs on hearing that the patrimony is wasted by his profligate brother, but he soon regrets his 'unmanly' action. The minister/narrator, on the contrary, admires the youth's manliness in abandoning his own ambitions to take on the debt for his father.[19] By mid century, when Romanticism and emotionalism were losing favour, such behaviour was shifting to a more controlled version of the Christian gentleman. In a letter, Matthew Arnold's sister wrote rather maliciously about him at this time:

Matt is stretched at full length on one sofa, reading a Christian tale of Mrs. Gaskell's which moves him to tears, and the tears to complacent admiration of his own sensibility.[20]

If the manliness of emotion was elevated by Evangelicalism so too was the concept of work. The *religious calling*, drawing on established Protestant tradition, was an important part of Evangelical belief. Work was not to be despised, rather it was to be seen as doing God's duty in the world. Work was dignified, serious and a properly masculine pursuit. Such a concept was necessary to the growing middle class, whose livelihood so often derived from the despised activities of commerce. Honour and competence in business and professional dealings became more closely associated with both manhood and respectability, a combination exemplified by the Quakers. The upper-class Evangelical and friend of the Clapham Sect, Thomas Gisborne, in his *Enquiry into the duties of men in the higher and middle classes of society* (1794) was at pains to deal with the Christian duties of not only the old and established professions but also with 'persons engaged in trade and business', bankers, merchants agents and manufacturers. Probity in business was their most important virtue, he argued, and it was vital that all employers take moral and religious responsibility for their workforce, attending to their cleanliness and domestic lives. Middle-class Christian men, whether professionals or in commerce, were engaged in vital work. Like Adam Smith, a man whom he much admired, Gisborne was convinced that moral purpose overrode issues of pecuniary gain.[21] The commercial world might not have the glory associated with the battlefield in the past, or the political arena in the present, but it was a world that mattered.

There were, however, contradictory elements in this elevation of honest toil and its rescue from disdain by the rich. A key aspect of Evangelical thinking was its refusal of the 'world' and consequent turn to domesticity. While celebrating the rural and the domestic, William Cowper clearly felt the need to justify this emphasis on retreat away from the heat of battle, whether it was military, political or commercial. Hazlitt indeed complained that Cowper's poetry was not heroic or 'even masculine'.[22] Cowper defends the domesticated man as not an idler or of little worth and excuses his lack of ambition and thrusting action in the world:

> The man whose virtues are more felt than seen,
> Must drop indeed the hope of public praise,
> But he may boast what few who win it can,
> That if his country stand not by his skill
> At least his follies have not wrought her fall.[23]

The real reward for the private man would, of course, be in the world to come and this belief must have helped many converted men to hold to their religion despite attacks on their manliness or even virility. Similarly, the champions of the underdog, whether slaves or hunted foxes, were taunted with softness or weakness. Thomas Clarkson, the Suffolk based anti-slavery campaigner, in defending the Quakers' opposition to blood sports, again quoted Cowper:

> . . . Detested Sport!
> That owes its pleasure to another's pain.[24]

The refusal of blood sports was the kind of 'healthy moral feeling' welcomed by evangelicals, which they associated with 'manly sensibility', to be sharply contrasted with 'effeminate sentimentalism'. Manliness and sweetness could

go together, tenderness was a truly Christian *and* male attribute. As the
Rev. Samuel Newton, Congregational minister of Witham, was described
in his own home,

When he conducted the evening family worship we were all edified by the manly,
scriptual and glowing devotion with which he led us to the throne of grace.[25]

This enactment of Christian manliness was least problematic for the
clergy since there was no disjunction between their spiritual work and their
livelihood. Their church or chapel could be seen as a professional extension
of their own home and family. Unlike women, however, men had to be
careful that they did not become too attached to the home, for although
'the preservation of a tender love for home and its occupants, has proved
in some cases the last tie to virtue, and a last preservation from ruin', yet
too much affection for home would promote feebleness of character and
dependence, characteristics that could never be associated with manliness.[26]
For whatever the respect for tenderness, love and care, his authority derived
from God, the master in Heaven, and the rights of household heads associated with it were enshrined in law and custom.

In part this was the old language of paternalism, but articulated to a
different code. The rights which had been attached to property, and to land
in particular, now belonged elsewhere. There was nothing wrong with
property, providing the propertied fulfilled their duties, but it was not
necessary to be a member of the landed gentry to qualify for gentility. Real
gentility, like real manliness was a matter of the inner state, not the outer
casing. Without salvation men could not aspire to be truly 'fit and proper
persons' for in their inner lives they were lost. With salvation they could
combine in themselves the authority of God and man. As the Rev. John
Angell James said, it was 'bliss' for a family to have a godly father and
master. 'Religion', he told the young men in his congregation in a series of
sermons prepared especially for them,

will fit you to preside with dignity over your household: it will add the sanctity
of the Christian to the authority of the parent and the master, and render obedience,
on the part of your children and servants, more pleasant and easy, as given to one
who has such high claims to it. How will your family prayers tend to keep up,
in all other respects, family order! Piety will strengthen and soften every domestic
tie, as well as consecrate every domestic occupation. It will lighten the cares of
business, brighten the scenes of prosperity, and yield consolation in the dark
season of family sorrow. If called to leave your wife and family, it will mitigate
the pang of separation by the prospect of eternal union in a world where death
has no power; or if required to surrender a pious wife or children, it will prevent
the sting of that sorrow which has no hope. What a bliss then to a family, what
a benign and heavenly inmate, is sincere, consistent, eminent religion, as it shines
forth in the form and character of a godly father and master.[27]

James was in one sense only explicating the words of St Paul to the Colossians, masters in their households must rule in God's name; but at the same
time he was enunciating the principles which should characterize Christian
manhood in the early nineteenth century – piety, domesticity, a proper
sense of responsibility about business – these were the attributes of the new
man.

Doctrines on femininity

If a man's ability to support and order his family and household lay at the heart of masculinity, then a woman's femininity was best expressed in her dependence. Dependence was at the core of the evangelical Christian view of womanhood, and the new female subject, constructed in real religious terms, was the godly wife and mother. As with men, elements within these new concepts had a long history. Puritan divines had preached and written about the importance of a loving marriage and a concerned mother who would supervise the religious education of her children, in contrast to the more secular notions of domesticity among the eighteenth-century mercantile and upper classes.[28] In reiterating the words of St Paul on women's subordinate position evangelicals were drawing on traditional ideas. What was new was the context in which the evangelicals explicated 'women's sphere' and the particular combination of elements they saw as 'naturally' feminine.

The primary religious explanation for woman's subordination to man lay in the Fall. Eve had introduced transgression to the world and must suffer for it. Indeed, childbirth was seen by some religious thinkers as 'woman's hour of sorrow' when, in conditions of 'peculiar agony', each mother would reflect upon that fall and experience her pain as 'a lasting memorial' of Eve's fate and 'an impressive comment on the evil nature of sin'.[29] But childbirth could also represent a woman's access to salvation since Mary, the mother of Jesus, had through her maternity raised women from despair. Christian notions of womanhood thus assumed a link between the godly woman and her family duties. A woman's salvation lay in her responsibilities as mother, wife, daughter or sister; through her services to the family she could suppress the dangerous parts of herself, associated with her sexuality, which linked her back to Eve. As John Angell James put it, 'To be a good wife is a high attainment in female excellence: *it is woman's brightest glory since the fall.*'[30] Women, therefore, needed to be contained within families, whether their family of origin, their family of marriage, or the family of the church. Lack of attachment to a family would mean that women were exposed to being 'surplus', with no meaning to their lives, and with the additional dangers of uncontained sexuality.

Serious Christians did not doubt that women were and should be subordinate to men socially. This was established biblical teaching. At the same time, however, they firmly believed in the right of all women to salvation and the spiritual equality of men and women. The crucial distinction was between spiritual equality and social subordination. These beliefs were firmly stated in a series of essays on women in *The Christian Lady's Friend* in 1832:

In her spiritual character, as created anew in Christ Jesus, and made complete in Him, she is the undoubted equal to man, though subordinate to him, as relatively viewed in the important stations of wife or daughter. The Holy Scriptures have not left us to our own conjectures on these momentous subjects. They have plainly asserted the natural equality of woman with man, and, as viewed in connexion with her salvation by grace, a fellow heir with him of the grace of life, while her relative and social duties are most exactly defined. . . .[31]

The Christian Lady's Friend was perhaps being a little disingenuous in suggesting that everything was straightforwardly stated in the Bible for, as will be seen, biblical texts and their interpretation were open to different readings. The magazine was insistent, as were many serious Christians, that subordinate did not mean inferior. Subordination in marriage did not imply that women were less important than men, but only that they were operating 'in a different department and sphere of action'.[32] Men and women were in separate spheres and those spheres were not hierarchical; the contribution of women in the home and family was quite as vital as that of men in the world outside.

Male preachers and teachers tended to less positive interpretations of biblical meanings in relation to women than did female; the tension between the fall and the possibilities for salvation were given prominence. As James wrote in a memoir of a pious Christian woman,

The same blessed page which proclaims your dishonour in the sin of your first mother, displays the glorious part you are to bear in the instrumentality of saving a lost world. . . .[33]

It was widely believed that Christian societies had played a vital part in raising the status of women and that Protestantism, in particular, manifested a high level of civilization in terms of its attitudes about them. Woman had been created for man, indeed for one man, and there was a necessary inference from this that *home* was 'the proper scene of woman's action and influence'.[34] The advances in English society which made possible this retreat of women, away from the dangers of the 'world' into the home which they could construct as a moral haven, was thus a mark of progress. The idea of a privatized home, separated from the world, had a powerful moral force and if women, with their special aptitude for faith, could be contained within that home, then a space would be created for true family religion. Women were more open to religious influence than men because of their greater separation from the temptations of the world and their 'natural' characteristics of gentleness and passivity. Home must therefore be the first and chief scene of their mission. 'There are few terms in the language', argued James,

around which cluster so many blissful associations as that delight of every English heart, the word HOME. The elysium of love – the nursery of virtue – the garden of enjoyment – the temple of concord – the circle of all tender relationships – the playground of childhood – the dwelling of manhood – the retreat of age; where health loves to enjoy its pleasures; wealth to revel in its luxuries; poverty to bear its rigours; sickness to endure its pains; and dissolving nature to expire; which throws its spell over those who are within its charmed circle; and even sends its attractions across oceans and continents, drawing to itself the thoughts and wishes of the man that wanders from it at the antipodes: – this, – home – sweet home – is the sphere of wedded woman's mission.[35]

In this peculiarly English setting of the home, women could wield their moral influence and thus save not only themselves, but men as well, from the fall which they had brought about. In the domestic retreat and the seclusion of a pious family, women, like violets on a sheltered bank, could reveal their true nature. Women's 'natural' characteristics would contribute to the effectivity of their influence, which would work through the 'passive power of gentleness'.[36]

Women's profession was, as Hannah More the celebrated Evangelical put it, to be wives and mothers, but once this work was properly done they could consider doing some religious and philanthropic work outside.[37] Family, however, must always come first, while within that family the demands of individual spiritual life had somehow to be balanced with the responsibilities of motherhood. A further issue was the vexed question of women's employment. In the Bible, as the Rev. Binney, a self-educated bookseller's son and popular Congregational minister of Weigh House chapel in the City (attended by several Essex people), observed, the good wife is shown in 'profitable employments, securing advantages in barter and merchandise and investing the proceeds in real property'. How was this to be reconciled with the evangelical view that a woman's place was in the home as a safeguard to the morality of all? Binney was constrained to argue that the biblical model in this case was not to be taken literally. In the days when the Bible was recorded it might have been part of the character of a 'virtuous woman' to be engaged in buying and selling but this was no longer the case. He argued that,

All matters of business in merchandise belong, for the most part, exclusively to the husbands of English wives: nor are they expected to be able, in any way, to make, independently, a fortune for themselves. . . .

Women did not need the accomplishments of men, they did not need to be involved with parts of his work or take his responsibilities in either the public world or the world of the church, but they could expect to influence him and thus assist in fulfilling the duties given him by God. 'Women are not to be men', Binney wrote elsewhere, 'in character, ambition, pursuit or achievement: but they are to be *more*; they are to be the *makers* of men.' Binney then ended with the extraordinary statement: 'The Mother is the father of the child', thus claiming women's influence as equal to the power of men.[38] John Angell James never made such a grandiose claim for his female members, but preaching to his predominantly lower middle-class congregation, he felt bound to argue that there was nothing inherently wrong in women assisting their husbands in the business when this help was needed, but the inference was that it was better to avoid doing so.[39]

Evangelical clergy did not want to overemphasize this point, however, since they were aware that a woman's labour was often essential in a family business. In a moral tale by a Suffolk curate, 'The Merchant's Wife', a young wife, in addition to offering religious consolation to her husband during his financial troubles, insisted on staying with him, refusing to let him carry the burden alone, 'as a man – and as a Christian'. In the early morning, to avoid mixing with the clerks, she went down to the counting house from the rooms where they lived above, saying, 'I do not understand business but will do whatever you will employ me about' and soon 'her husband found she could assist him very essentially'. Together they tried to save something from the bankruptcy. The author strongly justified not only her passive influence in urging religious morality on her husband, but also her active intervention:

A young and delicate female, bearing up against the storms of misfortune is a beautiful sight; she is not out of her element. Where could the peaceful Halcyon appear so lovely as on the raging water?

By the end of the story the wife is supporting the whole family with her millinery shop; a 'little humiliating but Lucy possessed a mind which dignified every employment'.[40]

There was then, some ambiguity among evangelicals as to the strict definitions of male and female responsibilities. It was clear that women were subordinate, yet they had influence; it was evident that the home and children were their sphere, yet sometimes they had to engage in male pursuits and help to support, or indeed entirely support, a family. It was this ambiguity on the finer points of detail that made the precise delineation of woman's role a matter of negotiation, rather than a fixed code. Between the recognition of influence and the marking out of the female sphere there was contested ground. For the Protestant ethic endowed women with a strong sense of self, a belief in their individual responsibility for their own souls which could inspire action among the weakest. Indeed the possibility that serious Christianity might give women too much power through moral influence was a continuing point of tension. It is brought out in the viciously satirical view of the Newcome establishment at Clapham in Thackeray's novel of that name. Thomas Newcome, having married a banker's daughter and become a partner, is, in fact, a cipher, 'the gardeners touched their hats, the clerks at the bank brought him the books, but they took their orders from her not him'. His managing wife not only runs the elaborate household and takes part in all the causes of 'enslaved Negro, Jews, Infidels and Papists and indifferent washerwomen', but takes over as virtual manager at Threadneedle Street, and in a passage of pure fantasy is described as sweeping into the bank in a scene of complete female domination, her henchman being a soft spoken, unctuous clergyman, in strong contrast to the manly bluff army officer who is the hero.[41]

These powerful, if open-ended beliefs about the nature of true religious femininity were expounded throughout England from the 1780s. The urgency of this mission was partly in opposition to other formulations of the period, such as those of Mary Wollstonecraft. Across the country, sermons were preached on texts from the price of a virtuous woman being above rubies to the Lord God ruling that man should have a helpmeet, while panegyrics to pious women at their death rolled from the same pulpits. Numerous memoirs and biographies also immortalized the gentle influence of particular wives, mothers and daughters. Such memoirs served as a female counterpart (even though many were written by men) to the outpourings of the clergy on the subject of the proper division of labour between the sexes, determined as it was, 'by reason and by revelation'. They represented, together with the published journals and letters of religious women, a kind of extended 'makeshift pulpit' as Mary Ryan has called the deathbed scene, when the family gathered around a dying woman and listened attentively to her words. They gave religious women a voice as much as their novels, poetry and tracts.[42]

But that voice was primarily defined as being within the family, the audience of a married woman was her own husband, children and servants; that of unmarried women their brothers, nephews and fathers together with the family of the church. As the Rev. Binney argued, in a little book which he presented to all the young women in his church, woman's mission was by influence, tasteful economy, intelligent piety and faith to inspire and animate, sooth and resuscitate their men, so that 'the mighty engine of masculine life may be aided in its action and its results'.[43] Man's sphere, on the other hand, was to guide that mighty engine, to emerge from the bosom of their families carrying their Godliness with them and exercise their trust in the world with 'manly determination and resolution'.[44] Such were the spheres of serious Christian men and women in doctrine; what then in practice?

The ministry

As the professional exponent of Christian doctrine, the clergyman or minister was situated at the heart of Christian practice. His conduct and his household stood open to inspection; he was the exemplar of Christian manliness, the man of 'consecrated character'. However, the definition as to what constituted righteous behaviour varied according to the denomination. Unitarians were less interested in the doctrinal discussion of the place of the family and the relative spheres of men and women, but in practice they made clear distinctions and assumed many of the same 'natural' divisions as other groups. Reacting against the laxness associated with much of the clerical establishment in the eighteenth century, Anglican Evangelicals argued for a more vital parish life and an active, committed clergy who would regard their work as a vocation. The duties of the minister should be pastoral as well as spiritual and the Evangelicals were the first to emphasize the importance of visiting in the parish and extending church activities from basic Sunday services to a range of associated clubs and societies which dealt with the educational and temporal needs of parishioners.[45] The ministry, they insisted, was a specific vocation. The clergy were to lead parish worship, celebrate the sacraments, preach and teach, care for their parishioners and take part in local public life. The clergy were indeed becoming far more professional, with their increasingly specialized functions and established patterns of training including a classical and preferably Oxbridge education, out of reach for many young men who might otherwise have been attracted to a career which combined spiritual and professional life. The difficulties posed by the need for such an education pushed some converts towards nonconformity, where the Dissenting academics and later the training colleges such as Hackney offered a more flexible and less expensive route into the ministry.

Entering the ministry also offered young men possibilities of social advancement, opportunities not lost on ambitious youth. The favourite game of a Wolverhampton boy was to stand on a stool and pretend to preach, for even the young had a shrewd idea of where power lay.[46] William Burgess, a grocer in Colchester, married a woman with some capital which he used to expand his business to several shops. He was a strong Evangelical, encouraged and sponsored by William Marsh. Burgess went to Cambridge when he was 38, making use of Marsh's connections with the university, and took orders. He became the vicar of a village near Colchester where he preached Evangelically-inspired sermons on the duties of the minister and his people. *His* duties, Burgess argued, were to lead his congregation to the Holy Spirit, his principle object was to preach the Gospel, their temporal and spiritual welfare was in his care. *Their* duties were obedience to his ministerial authority, submission to his instruction and a proper view of the ministerial character. Burgess was claiming considerable power and authority in his parish, power which he used in such projects as renovating the vicarage and establishing Sunday schools, gaining a status which he could not have possessed as a grocer.[47]

The patronage of an established figure such as Marsh was one of the recognized routes to the ministry. In his fifteen years at Colchester, Marsh claimed to have sent out twenty-two missionaries and clergymen, inspired by his preaching and aided by his contacts.[48] Family connections were also useful. For example, the Essex farming family of Blomfield had a long nonconformist connection. Around 1800, Bezaliel Blomfield became a well-known Essex Independent minister and later a missionary. Inter-cousin marriages as well as the marriage of a Blomfield woman to another minister, increased their clerical connections and the family met regularly, often at religious functions.[49] Women were instrumental in such alliances, keeping alive both family and religiously inspired friendship contacts. The daughters of clergymen seem to have had a strong propensity to marry into the clergy, while sons followed fathers, uncles or grandfathers into the ministry. There was not a family business in the normal sense to inherit, and partnership was illegal for the clergy, but the cultural capital of the clergyman's son, his education, knowledge and contacts, were often worth a great deal. Family and friendship connections were frequently the route into a curacy for a young Anglican clergyman[50] and the revitalized church with its new ministries and accompanying positions offered wide opportunities for enthusiastic young men. Such opportunities were, of course, closed to women except among the Quakers with their non-professional ministry. Indeed, the point of the rigorous training that was gradually evolving for Dissenting ministers was to ensure an appropriate preparation for their work, and this route served to exclude others, whether they were unsuitable men or just women. As so often, increased formality led to the increasing marginalization of women. Yet the clerical enterprise remained a family affair, i . ways that reproduce, but with a particular ideological emphasis, the patterns of organization in other professions.

Wealthier parents were not always keen, however, for their sons to enter the ministry since a comfortable livelihood could not be assumed. John Savill, from a family in the Essex woollen industry, met opposition from his parents when he wanted to go into the church. He had been destined for the family business and his father, 'being desirous of all things that his sons might attain wealth by business', apprenticed him to a wholesale linen draper. In 1799, however, he had a conversion experience, left trade and entered the Independent ministry, despite lack of family enthusiasm.[51] Only the successful could hope to occupy a living or be the minister in a chapel which would fully support a family and there were considerable divisions between those in well funded livings, or wealthy urban chapels and the poor curates with their large families immortalized by Trollope, or the poverty stricken Dissenting ministers supported by tiny congregations.

The relationship of Anglican and Dissenting clergy to their flock differed. The Anglican cleric relied on the church establishment for his support; his livelihood came from endowments and trusts and was administered by the church. The Dissenter, on the other hand, was directly supported by his congregation; he was chosen, paid, and had to satisfy them while the Anglican clergy were dependent on patronage. Nevertheless, within both the Anglican and Dissenting ministry there were clear demarcations associated with money and status. At the top end of Birmingham's Anglicans, for example, was the Rev. Isaac Spooner. Born in 1808, he was the son of the Midlands MP Richard Spooner, one of the scions of the Spooner banking family, a daughter of whom married William Wilberforce. His mother had been the daughter of the Dean of Hereford. He was educated at prestigious schools as well as having private tutors, and then went to Cambridge. He married the daughter of one of Birmingham's wealthiest solicitors. In 1837 he became vicar of St George's, Edgbaston, one of the new suburban churches funded by Evangelical money, and in 1848 vicar of Edgbaston parish church. In 1849 a new vicarage was built for him, a handsome house with good land attached and at his death in 1884 he left over £28,000 to his wife. Spooner belonged to the cream of Anglican society and had links with the gentry. Few clergymen could aspire to such heights. Further down the Birmingham hierarchy can be contrasted the positions of the rector of St Thomas's and his curate in 1851. The rector was a well-known Tory Radical who accepted the position at St Thomas's in 1847. In 1851 he was living on the Hagley Road, in the select new area of Edgbaston. He had a large house, its rateable value was £55 (Spooner's was rated at £119 plus £60 for the land), with a cook and a housemaid. His curate was living in a much smaller house, with a rateable value of £23, on the edge of Edgbaston and had taken in four boarders to help eke out his stipend, a common pattern among the less well paid sections of the clergy.[52]

Similar contrasts can be found among Dissenters. Joseph Priestley when he came to the New Meeting in 1780 was offered a stipend of £100. This could not conceivably have covered the expenses of his comfortable middle-class establishment with costs augmented by his scientific work. Priestley was able to rely on his richer friends and relatives to support him. He and his family lived in a large house on the edge of the town and after the destruction associated with the riots of 1791 his claim for damages to property amounted to well over £1000. In contrast, other Unitarian ministers in the town had to supplement their income in the usual pedestrian ways, running schools and taking in pupils.[53]

Supplementing a clerical income by teaching or by giving public lectures was a favoured way of making ends meet. Ministers had both the education and a ready source of pupils in their churches. In the late eighteenth and early nineteenth centuries this practice was as common among Anglicans as Dissenters. As claims for the importance of the minister's work among his congregation increased, however, this became less acceptable, and was seen as a distraction from proper duties. For Anglicans the gradual improvement in the value of livings associated with agricultural productivity and tithe commutation, together with the increase in the stipends of curates, made paid work outside less essential by mid century,[54] but it remained difficult for many nonconformist ministers to survive financially without additional means of support.

Unitarians were less concerned than serious Christians about their ministers seeking supplementary support elsewhere for their view of the functions of their preachers differed. Their focus was on the minister as teacher and preacher, rather than spiritual guide and mentor. A proper education through the Dissenting academies and colleges and perhaps graduation from a Scottish university had always been seen as central to their training, for they looked for intellectual skills in preference to religious enthusiasm. By the end of the eighteenth century the established authority of the old Presbyterian ministry, some of whom moved into Unitarianism, had declined. In the circumstances of the late eighteenth century, Unitarianism came to cover many doctrinal differences and congregations offered shelter to rationalists of many persuasions. Religious toleration was essential within the group and the minister could not, therefore, have the role of purveyor of the single truth. Furthermore, Unitarian congregations did not believe in supervisory moral functions and the minister was not expected to rule on his hearer's conduct. He was not seen as a man apart, but his authority derived from his intellect and power as a preacher.[55]

A clergyman, whatever his position within the hierarchy, could hope for considerable status deriving from his post. For those with upper-class backgrounds and connections, with wealthy livings or private incomes, it was obviously easier to establish themselves in a local community. The census from the local areas makes it clear that a high proportion of clergy and their wives came from outside the areas in which they were living which meant that while more work had to be done in making a position for themselves, the upwardly mobile could start with a fresh slate. The moral and political stature of such men could be considerable, as the repeated story of William Marsh's intervention in the 1825 bank crisis illustrates. As with so many country banks in that year, the farmers and other depositors gathered in Colchester on market day, and on hearing the news of other bank failures rushed to draw out their money. One of the bank clerks ran across the street to the vicarage to ask aid from the 'friend of Colchester'. Marsh had a large sum of money in the house collected for a charity. He drew a cheque for the amount on his London banker and sent it to one of the church wardens thus marking it as his own. Then taking the bags of gold and silver out into the street held high for the crowd to see, he told them he was not afraid to deposit it with the bank. Confidence was restored and the Colchester bank survived the crisis.[56]

Marsh's influence in the local community, first in Colchester and then in Birmingham, was underpinned by devotion from individual parishioners. The minister was a significant figure in the lives of his flock. The Marsh family doctor, Charles Boutflower, named his second son William Marsh Boutflower, just as the son of a farmer was named after his father's revered minister at a Colchester Independent chapel.[57] A pastor's visits were treasured, his words carefully heeded. For a woman like Colchester's Amy

Camps, a spinster until her middle age when she married and was soon widowed, the church was a substitute family. After her husband had died, with no male relatives to call upon, her minister took over her business affairs. In her early 20s when she had found herself orphaned and alone, William Marsh was like 'balm' to her. 'If ministers knew how their conversation was marked', she wrote, 'they would look to their words.'[58] Even a farmer's wife whose life was full with friends and family, treasured the words of her clergyman.[59] For such women, the combination of superior education, social status, fatherly authority and spiritual sanction was potent. Members of church and chapel would vie to offer service from cleaning the building to sewing or providing food for the pastor's family. Isaac Taylor, with his modest Colchester congregation, had help with the starching of finer linens by a devoted chapel member.[60]

However, clergy could not always ensure the respect they claimed. They wished to be regarded as providers of a better way of life, as 'culture carriers' bringing enlightenment to rural backwaters and urban ghettos. As a Suffolk vicar claimed, they were the cultivators who 'found the place a wilderness and left it a promising garden', who renewed the parched ground with the 'Water of Life'.[61] The Rev. Fielding, however, was locked into a bitter dispute with much of his congregation in Coggeshall in Essex in 1815. The deacons accused Fielding of not visiting chapel members enough, of having particular friendships within the chapel, of not being enthusiastic about the Bible Society, of ill-prepared sermons and neglect of charity schools, and of having money troubles from which the congregation had to rescue him. This last is hardly surprising with an income of £40–50 per annum with a wife and seven children to support. As a result, the deacons tried to make Fielding leave after eighteen years in office. Outraged, Fielding defended himself in print, arguing that his particular enemy, a substantial farmer, had organized a faction against him, shouted at him and slandered him in a village shop and in the Sunday school room on the Sabbath as well as trying to malign him to his own family and relatives.[62]

The hawk like eye which Dissenting tradesmen and farmers kept on the minister's income and expenditure helped demystify the relation between congregation and clergy, including the spending habits of ministerial families.[63] Such disputes are far removed from the idealized portrait of the clergy which dominates the literature. Mary Ann Hedge, the Evangelical daughter of a Colchester clockmaker, described the ideal village vicar as one who,

puts aside his studies and hides his abilities to enter the lives and problems of his poor parishioners. . . . In consequence of this self-sacrifice his influence over the affections of his flock is unbounded.[64]

Fielding's influence over the affections of his Coggeshall flock was severely limited and records of disputes and splits within many Dissenting congregations echo this.

Within the Anglican church, by mid century, it was hoped that every parish would have a resident clergyman, preferably married with a family, to set an example and the cleric would devote his whole time and energy to the ministry. Marriage for clergy was vital for it ensured 'the common endearments of domestic life', the absence of which was a major source of attack on the celibate Catholic clergy.[65]

Marriage and a resident clergy meant it was necessary to provide a house for those parishes which did not possess a parsonage and improvements started to be made from the end of the eighteenth century. Across the country existing facilities were done up, new houses were purchased, new rectories built, a movement traced in local records from building plans to census listings.[66] In 1847, Bishop Wilberforce insisted that a church without a parsonage was incomplete. He felt that the people should be able to reach the clergy as well as the clergyman having contact with his parishioners. The clergyman's life should illustrate his doctrines and give 'the example of the amenities of family life' especially where there were few resident gentry.[67] (Unfortunately, keeping the parsonage so close to the church often meant that the health of clerical families living in the vicinity of the churchyard was at risk.) In his statement, Wilberforce draws attention to the many features illustrated in practice. The increasing emphasis on the parochial duties of the clergy and need for accessibility meant that clerical homes became a kind of busy, public place. The clergyman's household had to be carefully organized to accommodate both secular and spiritual concerns. His private sphere, his haven, necessarily could not be fully private. His family, too, had to act as example. In commenting on her childhood, the daughter of an Evangelical Suffolk vicar noted: 'in how many cases is the influence of a godly Pastor weakened, when the villagers observe the flippant modern manners and showy *dress* of his daughters?'.[68] The clergy were to demonstrate proper gender-specific behaviour in every aspect of their lives.

The minister's wife

The professionalization of the ministry and the increased emphasis on the specific duties of the clergyman brought with it a new attentiveness to the position of the clergyman's wife. In her popular novel of 1809, *Coelebs in search of a wife*, Hannah More, that most celebrated of Evangelical women, painted a picture of the perfect clergyman's wife. Dr Barlow was the Evangelical rector of the country parish where much of the novel was set; an active minister all the week, he was zealous in fighting ignorance, a genuine Bible Christian, preaching clearly and knowing his parishioners. Dr Barlow was happy in an excellent wife whose first contribution had been the capital she brought, enabling her husband to enlarge his sphere of activity.[69] Maria Marsh was able to do the same for her husband, as did the wife of the Independent minister at Witham and the first and second wives of John Angell James.[70] As in all family enterprises among the middle class in this period, a good marriage could make a substantial material difference. But far more important that this material contribution, claimed More, was Mrs Barlow's character of piety and prudence. This enabled her to identify wholly with her husband's work and to support him in every way. Her management of household affairs meant that he was able to devote himself more fully to his public duties.

It was a common regret for the wives of serious Christian ministers that their husbands' constant occupation kept them so frequently from home. Maria Marsh regretted William's absence, but she willingly took on extra domestic responsibilities knowing that, 'although his Master's service gives me less of his society now, I shall enjoy it more when we reach our home'.[71] Furthermore, Mrs Marsh organized the household for maximum hospitality. Her daughter Catherine remembered that her father liked to be hospitable without grudging,

on a scale which his income could hardly have met, but for the careful, though generous, economy and simplicity with which my mother ordered her household, for the sake of never narrowing of her husband's numberless gifts to the needy, in various classes, and in his Master's service. Scarcely one third of their income was consumed by their household expenses.[72]

Maria Marsh was, indeed, the exemplary clerical wife, organizing the household of five children, three or four servants, a mother-in-law next door and innumerable visitors, often young men who were her husband's disciples and stayed for long periods. Maria saved her husband from having 'any thought or trouble in making the necessary arrangements and took her own part in the duties and privileges of each day'.[73] Before she had children she was able to devote much time to directly helping her husband with the myriad organizations and meetings. He was always ready to instruct her, sympathize with her and pray for her.

One of Mrs Marsh's most important activities was the religious instruction of her servants and children, which included praying individually with each one for wrong doing. The younger children were her special responsibility, while Marsh took more responsibility as they reached adolescence. Since the moral influence of mothers was the linchpin of religious regeneration, it was a particularly sacred trust for clerical wives. In addition to daily religious lessons, Mrs Marsh taught her own younger children on Sunday afternoons, giving Bible lessons round the fireside in winter, in the garden in summer, when they were joined by a few children of the more genteel Colchester families. On Saturday afternoons she gave religious instruction to tradesmen's children.

Maria Marsh, and after her death her daughter Catherine, taught Sunday schools in the converted carriage house next to the rectory (for the family had deliberately given up keeping a carriage to save money for charity). The Marsh women, with the combined force of their gentry paternalistic background and evangelical faith (typical of the first generation of the Saints), also counselled the poor, distributed soup from the kitchen, provided refreshment between services on Sunday for parishioners who came from afar in the laundry place behind the house, and 'heartily aided' husband and father in the Bible, Missionary, Conversion of the Jews, Prayer Book, Homily, Religious Trust, Anti-Slavery Societies and other endeavours, often leading separate ladies committees. They presided over large gatherings held at the vicarage to mark, in good Puritan tradition, the anniversaries of each society, when accounts were cast up (both temporal and spiritual) and enthusiasm renewed, while friends and fellow workers exchanged information and strengthened commitment to their common cause. Mrs Marsh, in her capacity as fellow worker, on several occasions met and subsequently corresponded with Hannah More, for whom she had the greatest admiration.

The three Marsh daughters were as wedded to the Evangelical family enterprise as their mother. After Maria's early death, Catherine, particularly following the marriage of her two sisters to clergymen, tried to take her mother's place. From their earliest days the Marsh girls had been trained as auxiliaries of the clergy: 'My dear girls are going on delightfully', wrote Mrs Marsh in 1827, 'they spend all their pocket money on the poor'.[74] In a different era, Catherine Marsh, who never married, would have made a powerful woman minister, but such aspirations were impossible for her. Indeed, several daughters of ministers, like other religious girls, recall the shocked realization that unlike their brothers, their 'preaching' games would come to nothing. They would never be allowed to interpret the word directly.[75] Catherine Marsh, like many others, dealt with contradictory feelings about the limits of her sphere by an exaggerated admiration for her father. Her 'working parties' for young ladies ended with Rev. Marsh coming in to address them, and she would never willingly speak when a clergyman was present. Catherine was carrying on in the tradition of her mother. At a sewing party in Ipswich attended by Maria in 1824, the subject of 'hindrances to the lively exercise of prayer' was set as the topic of discussion: 'the ladies work the gentlemen talk' until the ladies were specifically requested to say something.[76] Maria and Catherine Marsh held clear views on 'the duty of women to the ordained ministry', and, like Elizabeth Fry, their female duties could only be overridden if there was certainty that they had been 'called'.[77] The human sanction of the clerical father, husband or brother was usually necessary before the 'call' could be verified.

Many clergymen's daughters found their vocation in making a home for their clerical brothers, fulfilling much the same parish function as a wife. Since the age at marriage for clergy was so late, opportunities for this service were common. Sometimes, however, there was no suitable brother available and both widows and daughters were vulnerable to being left at the minister's death with no means of support. (For the dependence of a high proportion of clergymen on their stipends, and their early support of life assurance see Chapter 4.)[78] The female relatives of the clergy are well represented in writing in a religious genre since, being usually well educated, they often attempted to make a living or add to the exchequer by writing, although such literary efforts were often presented as part of their religious mission. Towards mid century, female relatives of clergy also played a part in the spread of more organized district visiting and in the sisterhoods attached to the Tractarian movement.[79] But, like Catherine Marsh, they accepted the authority of the male hierarchy, regarding their role as secondary and supportive.

The public positioning of the female supporters of the clergy is well illustrated in the headstone of the Birmingham Evangelical minister J. G. Breay and his wife Phyllis. The Rev. Breay came to Christ Church, close to the town centre, in 1832. He was an archetypical Evangelical enthusiast, working seven days a week to expand the activities of his church and in this he was ably supported by his wife who took special responsibility for school work and clothing clubs, did much private visiting and was involved

with the Magdalen. Breay died suddenly in 1839 leaving his widow with
five children. She remained in Birmingham and was actively involved in
Evangelical causes until her death in 1870, yet she was remembered as *his*
widow and helpmeet, the mother of his children, as recorded on their
gravestone at Christ Church.[80]

John Angell James: 'bishop' of Birmingham

Over the period, the position of both clergy and their female supporters
was shifting. Ann Douglas has recorded a related change in America where
the disestablishment of the church and the expansion of the commercial
economy weakened the dominance of the clergy. This coincided with the
consignment of middle-class women to the margins of the economy and
the sphere of personal experience. Ministers and literary women allied to
reassert influence through the 'feminization of American culture'.[81]

In England, the gradual disappearance of the national church drew forth
new claims for legitimacy by the Anglican clergy, while the rise of New
Dissent demanded a similar response from Old Dissent. Like their American
counterparts, English women were being marginalized from production.
Many of them found a place in alliance with the clergy in the sphere
of moral influence. But with the religious revival, English clergy of all
denominations had increased their authority, political potential and
professional status. Despite wide differences of income, status, political
and doctrinal commitment, the clergy had become public 'somebodies',
recognized as spokesmen for respectable middle-class culture in the provincial world and displaying a novel masculinity based on moral seriousness.
Through their involvement with educational and philanthropic activities,
they won a powerful place for themselves in middle-class institutions. A
central part of their message was their concept of the proper spheres for
men and women. The support the clergy drew from women and the division
of labour in clerical households, reflected their beliefs about women's role.
Its power can be seen in its adoption by the Unitarians as much as other
serious Christian households since Unitarians emphasized the minister as
intellectual and preacher, as impossible a place for women to occupy as
that of spiritual leader.

The public and private life of Birmingham's best-known nonconformist
minister, John Angell James (dubbed the unofficial 'bishop' of Birmingham), is a story of the new possibilities which were opening for men in
the ministry and the extent to which these were built on the hidden contribution of women. Born in 1775, James was the son of a Dorset draper, his
mother a pious Baptist. After a sketchy education, he was apprenticed to
a draper and he became a practising Christian. He started Sunday school
teaching and decided to enter the ministry. His father opposed the scheme
having invested in the apprenticeship but eventually agreed. After studying
for two years, in 1804 he was invited to Carrs Lane, a small Independent
congregation in the centre of Birmingham, recently split over an internal
dispute. Thus at the age of 20, poorly educated and with little experience,
John Angell James became leader of his chapel. By 1812, however, when
he made a well received speech at the annual meeting of the Birmingham

Auxiliary of the British and Foreign Bible Society, his reputation as a powerful preacher grew as did the fortunes of the Carrs Lane congregation.[82]

James's initial stipend was £120 a year, adequate for a young bachelor in lodgings. In 1806, he married the daughter of a respectable Birmingham physician who had inherited a comfortable income from her father and this much improved his financial situation. Carrs Lane did not provide a manse and after James's marriage he went to live in his wife's home which she had inherited. In 1819 his wife died leaving a surviving son and daughter, and in 1822 James was remarried to a well-to-do London widow with a fortune of £20,000. Probably at this time the family moved into the house in Hagley Row, on the edge of the new suburb of Edgbaston where they were to stay for the rest of James's life. Moving out to Edgbaston represented a significant shift. In the early days of the chapel, the members had tended to live in the area immediately around it. But the growth of the town and the movement of the better off sections of the middle class to the outskirts meant that some sections of the membership began to live slightly further away. Carrs Lane was not a particularly wealthy church and the preponderance of its membership came from the lower end of the middling ranks so James was making a choice which signalled his special status.

In 1818, when church membership was rising and the political crisis over proper religious provision was at its height, the decision was made to build a new and larger church. The original chapel built in 1746 had been substantially rebuilt in 1802 and galleries had been added in 1812 to accommodate the increasing congregation. This last expansion coincided with a period of great activity. James had become extensively known in the town. He was active on many fronts – from missionary movements at home and abroad to benevolent societies, anti-slavery, prison reform, temperance, the Infant School Society and even more secular activities such as the Society of Arts and agitation against the opium trade.

James's powerful, if ornate and rhetorical style of preaching and speaking was clearly one of the sources of his influence. He also seems to have inspired strong reactions from people – whether of loyalty and respect, or hostility. A local poet, who had listened to James as a child, captures the combination of the minister's powerful yet blinkered vision:

> Twas from his lips I first was taught to know
> That life was vanity, the world a show:
> That there's a brighter region in the skies,
> To which he trained my youthful hopes to rise:
> And when by trouble and misfortune pressed,
> I've proved him true to what he has professed,
> What though he only knows one narrow way,
> And his poor flock may go at times astray:
> Still let us venerate the earnest man,
> Who ends his honoured life as he began.[83]

Others were less kindly in their evaluations, recalling, for example, that James always enunciated his own thoughts 'as if they were absolutely

true and incontrovertible', which indeed he believed they were.[84] George
Holyoake remembered that all he was taught in five years of James's Sunday
school was the hymns of Dr Watts, the Bible and to be content with his
own station, a lesson the Radical clearly failed to learn.[85]

James had ambitious views on the position of the minister and used his
influence within his own church, in the region and even nationally, to
propagandize these. He regarded himself as the leader of his flock and
adopted a strongly admonitory tone in church meetings. In 1841, for
example, addressing the church meeting he proclaimed that it was his 'wish
and intention to form a "Maternal Society" in which Mothers may meet
together and pray for their children, and to receive instructions from me
as to their education. . .'. On Wednesday afternoons he proposed 'to visit
households of young families to commune with and instruct them'. At
another meeting in 1842 he complained about the low attendance on Sunday
evenings at the service: 'I expect all who can do so, to hear me in the
evening, as well as the morning', he informed them.[86] The pastor, he argued,
should be treated with great respect – he was not simply another brother.
His belief in ministerial authority was firmly based on the necessity of a
'call' to the ministry, reserved for the select few. James's insistence on the
importance of the pastor's role was not confined to his own congregation.
He worked for a more general appreciation of the proper status of the
ministry bolstered by improved ministerial education. Despite (or perhaps
because of) his own inadequate schooling, and deep anti-intellectualism, he
was influential in establishing Spring Hill College in Birmingham in 1858,
expressly designed for the training of ministers.

James's work as a pastor was always more important to him than his
public duties and he likened the church to his family. The ministry, in his
view, was the greatest of all human employments. In the pastoral charge
which he delivered for his brother, the Rev. Thomas James, at his ordination
in London in 1816, he preached on ministerial duties and recommended
that clergy must be careful to visit their congregations impartially, to avoid
staying too long, to lounge or gossip. Private friendships must not interfere
with their obligations. They should never visit late in the evenings and they
should always sup at home. 'Our character', he proclaimed, 'like that of a
female, must, to be reputable, be without suspicions. . . . We occupy a
very public station; like the angel standing in the sun, we must be seen.'[87]
One suspects that James would have much appreciated the description of
him offered by his Evangelical friend J. C. Miller, the rector of St Martin's,
at the sermon a week after James's death when he characterized him as a
'beautiful specimen of sanctified humanity, such as is seldom seen in this
fallen world'.[88]

James saw it as his task to give detailed advice on all subjects to his
congregation. He was their monitor in their daily lives, whether in domestic
matters, commercial or public affairs. Their behaviour on Sundays was one
of his gravest concerns. 'Some of our members', he admonished, 'give
unspeakable pain to their pastors by the irregularity of their visits to the
house of God'.[89] He acted as their conscience, a conscience which did not
cease to scold. James firmly believed that congregations should offer their
pastors liberal support, that this was an explicit scriptual injunction, and

that it was wrong for ministers to be put in a situation where they had to run a school or find other means of income when the chapel could afford to give them a decent livelihood. This was the payment of a just debt rather than charity. James himself, because of his marriages, was comfortably off and even kept a carriage at the end of his life, but in his earlier days, according to his son, he had maintained a plain style of living.

Not surprisingly James had very strong views on the role of the minister's wife. 'She is the wife of a man', he argued, 'whose master is God, whose business the salvation of souls, whose scene of labour the church of Christ, and the consequences of whose exertions, whether they succeed or fail, are infinite and eternal; LET HER ACT ACCORDINGLY.'[90] His own description of his first wife combined patronage with Christian benevolence:

This dear and eminent woman had few personal charms, but her countenance was intelligent and thoughtful, with a cast of mild and reserved benevolence. Her character, spirit, and temper were a combination of matured female excellence. She had little sprightliness or vivacity; was not obtrusive in conversation, yet was not taciturn, but ever ready with invariable good sense to bear her part in the ordinary subjects of discourse. Her demeanour was grave, but by no means gloomy. Profoundly humble, and beautifully meek, she could never offend, and was rarely offended; . . . her prudence, sound good sense, sobriety of mind, and correctness of judgement were exemplary. All this was veiled by a delicate and invariable modesty, and sanctified by eminent piety.[91]

The pastor's wife, he believed, was next in influence to her husband by virtue of her relationship to him, an honourable station. Excepting him,

she has the greatest opportunity of any member of the church to do good or harm. As a wife she should be a bright pattern of all that tender affection, that unsuspicious confidence, that cheerful obedience, that undivided devotedness to her husband's comfort, which such a relationship implies; a lovely, spotless exhibition of connubial virtue.[92]

She must also have no favourites within the congregation and be prudent about talking, especially given the information she gained by being the minister's wife. While the minister had ever increasing opportunities for public speech, his wife must even be careful as to her private words. James saw this prohibition on talking as particularly difficult for women, since he regarded gossip as a purely female activity. If she were a mother she must 'strive to excel in every maternal excellence' (his emphasis), and as a female head of her household she must direct it with judgement and order. This was particularly important since a minister derived part of the respect of his congregation from the state of his family life. 'Lovely . . . home scenes' would 'form a beauteous halo round . . . the orb of his public character'.[93]

The special task of the pastor's wife in relation to the church was to deal with auxiliary activities designed for females. In this way she mirrored the division of labour between laymen and women in relation to the church. Furthermore, 'her influence should be discreetly exerted in forming the general and pious habits of the younger females', and she should often be seen 'in the chambers of those of her own sex, when they are visited with sickness'. Mrs Sherman, the wife of a colleague of James's, represented his ideal of an active minister's wife. She had formed four classes, one for the poor mothers fortnightly, one for the mothers 'occupying superior stations in life' which took place monthly at her house, one for young ladies from the congregation, and one for servants and other young persons who had left Sunday school, stratified activities which helped to construct class and status distinctions. She was also busy with the clothing clubs and Dorcas societies attached to the church.[94]

James's second wife, according to varied accounts including his, was the perfect helpmeet for her husband's ministerial work. 'His dignity and the influence of his character and position was increased by his having such a wife.' James's co-pastor and biographer writes that she was influential in not allowing her husband to become overblown by his success.

Having no young children requiring constant attention at home she was able to devote the greater part of her time to the visitation of the sick and the poor.[95]

Her formal positions included being an officer of the Ladies Association of the British and Foreign Bible Society and a member of the ladies committee of the Infant School Society and Carrs Lane Sunday school.

Such was the life of John Angell James. Coming from a modest West Country family he was able to raise himself, with a little education, two advantageous marriages and a great deal of religious enthusiasm, to a position of local and even national influence. His most famous book, *The Anxious Enquirer after Salvation*, was said to be the most popular religious book in England after *The Pilgrim's Progress*. His congregation came to number over 1000 and his funeral was a major public event in Birmingham. He was a man the revitalized ministry could be proud of. He was also a man of the middle class who firmly believed, both in theory and in practice, in the separate spheres of men and women.

Church organization: women voting and women speaking

Perhaps the most distinctive feature of Dissenting chapels, in contrast with the established church, was their self-governing constitution. 'Membership' of the Anglican church did not require any formal joining; only 'confirmation' was necessary to become an active communicant since all parishioners were potentially part of that congregation. But to become a member of a Dissenting chapel meant a decision to reject the established church and commit oneself to an alternative community, the gathered church of the believers. Those believers were responsible for the running of their chapel or meeting house. Their pastor was chosen by themselves or their representatives, his stipend raised by them, the building maintained by their efforts, their officers chosen from among them. Church membership was vital to proper religious practice and fellowship, 'the instituted way of making a public profession of the faith and hope of the Gospel'.[96]

Members had both privileges and duties. Their privileges included participation in the Lord's supper, the right of assisting in the choice of pastor, some part in the election of officers and the admission and exclusion of members as well as rights to pastoral oversight and the sympathy and prayers of the church. Their duties included leading a visibly Christian life both in their public and private activities and playing their part in the church. These elements, in one form or another, informed the practice of Dissenting congregations. Since congregations were self-governing, the precise pattern varied and different sects had different emphases but all congregations, of whatever kind, tended to privilege some male members over others and all male members over female. As Mark Rutherford wrote of his fictional congregation:

for although women were members as well as men, it was always an understood thing at Tanner's Lane that they were to take no part in the business of the community.[97]

Precisely what part women were or were not to play in 'the business of the community' was, however, by no means a clear issue and the debates over the proper place of women were a regular feature of the late eighteenth and early nineteenth centuries. Spiritual equality, as women were constantly reminded, did not mean social equality, but what were the implications for the organization of the chapel of the recognition of the centrality of individual salvation, or, as in the case of the Unitarians, of individual conviction? Given the numerical preponderance of women over men in the active life of the religious in this period, this was a pressing item on the agenda.

In any case, it was not always agreed what part different men should play in the government of the chapel. It was hardly surprising that this should be an issue since the question as to what form representation should take was one of the key political questions of the period. Should the rich carry more weight when it came to making decisions? Should their greater financial contribution entitle them to more formal recognition in addition to their informal influence? What rights should subscribers, who made a regular donation, have, and how should those rights compare with those of the members who were the active participants in the chapel community? How much control belonged to the minister and what part should he play in church meetings? There were no simple rules to follow as these questions were argued and antagonistic interpretations offered of biblical authority, different conclusions drawn as to correct practice. The concept of the individual saint, united with Christ, opened the way for *all* believers, whether rich or poor, male or female, to claim a part in the organization of the religious community. But as John Knox had realized, if women were given voting rights on this basis they would then have power over men. For Knox, such a proposition had been unthinkable, but for later generations it could be a thorny issue.[98]

At the Carrs Lane Independent church in Birmingham, established after a strict Calvinist secession from the Old Meeting in 1747 and having a fairly rocky existence before the arrival of John Angell James in 1805, the voting rights of male members were firmly established. This did not mean, however, that the church was run in an open and democratic way. In 1822 James outlined his own principles of church organization in the *Christian Fellowship or the Church Member's Guide*. His motto at the beginning came from St Paul: 'Ye are all one in Christ Jesus. Walk in Love.' James was quick to point out that this did not mean absolute equality. Attacking 'the absolute impropriety of a few rich men attempting to lord it over God's heritage', he argued that it was equally inappropriate for those who were young or immature to assert 'their claim to equal rights, upon every occasion in a vehement, contentious manner'. In all societies, he insisted, there must be some individuals who had more influence than others, but this should be the result of 'character and usefulness' rather than 'station'.[99] James was engaged in an argument against the claims of rank and wealth, in favour of wisdom and merit. To that extent his rhetoric had a radical edge. But he was also concerned to advance the claims of the elder, as against the young, and those with knowledge, experience, and 'character'. James was in part justifying the emergence of a male elite in the church, directly under his leadership, who, in effect, ruled the church from above. That elite, consisting of the male deacons who were elected by the male members, were drawn from the better-off sections of the congregation. Most of them served for long periods and were noted for their loyalty to James. One was his brother, James James, a prosperous screw manufacturer, another his relative by marriage, Joseph Phipson.[100]

James encouraged his flock to value and esteem their pastor. His efforts were aided by his public prominence and his long tenure of office, for frequent changes of minister gave more weight to those who made the choice. The church minute book suggests that he tended to get his way. He usually had tea with the deacons on the evening of every church meeting and sorted out the business. On Sundays he met with them in the vestry before the service. The major items of business were usually the admittance of new members and the disciplining of existing ones, or those who had lapsed.[101]

James was asserting the power of the pastor against the independent claims of congregations vis-à-vis their 'leaders'. The damaging secession suffered by Carrs Lane in 1802 was over the position of the then pastor, the Rev. Brewer. Brewer, charged with improper behaviour by members of the chapel, called only the brethren of the church to a meeting. Such issues were not for the ears of women members. There he was charged with taking 'indecent liberties with a female' and was forced to resign, although not on a unanimous vote. Shortly afterwards another meeting was called by the supporters of Brewer and all church members were requested to attend. As frequently happened when the men could not agree among themselves the women were brought in to make up the numbers. This, however, raised difficulties. 'Several of the sisters' attended this meeting, 'some of whom claimed a right to vote at the Church Meetings'. This claim was resisted but 'much altercation ensued' and no vote was decided. Mr and Mrs Brewer left the meeting which then broke up in a disorderly fashion. Subsequently, Brewer seceded with some of the members and established a new chapel.[102]

Such schisms were a commonplace of chapel life in this period, though the particular grounds were unusual. What is interesting is the insight this dispute gives into the contested arena of women's rights. This was hotly debated among Independents as in the *Congregational Magazine* in a series of articles and letters in 1837. The contributors focused on the interpretation of St Paul's injunction to the Corinthians,

Let your women keep silent in the churches: for it is not permitted unto them to speak; but *they are commanded* to be under obedience, as also saith the law. And if they will learn any thing, let them ask their husbands at home: for it is a shame for women to speak in the church.[103]

The readings of this passage were many and varied. Some thought that female preaching was expressly forbidden, quite as much as were 'drunkeness and idolatry' and that it represented a 'gross violation of nature', deeply injurious to female modesty. Opinions were mixed as to the Quaker acceptance of such practices; some defended it, others wryly pointed to the curious situation whereby 'this doubling of the number of preachers, by admitting both sexes, has ended in silent meetings'. But there were voices ready to defend a more liberal reading of St Paul as did one who thought the rule implied women were not to *chat* in church, but it would be quite acceptable for them to preach and it was the translation of the original Greek which had been at fault.[104]

J. A. James was ready to join the liberal phalanx; his understanding of the passage was that it had been 'wrongly interpreted' and there was an apostolic prohibition on teaching but this should not be extended, as it had been, to the right to vote in church assemblies. 'In the nature of things', he asserted,

it seems but reasonable that as women are equally competent, equally interested to give their vote, they should be allowed to exercise a privilege, which does not oppose the dictates of reason, the authority of revelation, the analogies of civil society, or the general principles of church government. 'Whether male or female', says St. Paul, 'we are all one in Christ Jesus'.[105]

These were generous words, but in practice the congregation at Carrs Lane did not follow these 'dictates of reason' and the 'analogies with civil society' would, indeed, not have encouraged them so to do. James's distinguished co-pastor in his later years is categorical in his biography of James that only men could vote at church meetings. When he himself was invited as minister in 1844 the letter was signed by 222 male members of the congregation. Furthermore, the trust deed of the chapel stipulated that the financial matters of the church should be submitted yearly to a special meeting of the male members, a reflection of the commonplace assumption that women were not able to manage the dealings associated with property and money.[106]

James's good management ensured that despite the contradictions of theory and practice in the government of Carrs Lane his reign was calm. The Congregational church at Witham in Essex, however, had some stormy moments over similar issues. This chapel was able to boast 100 members in 1714 and had expanded to 340 by 1790. Between 1825 and 1847, 215 new members were admitted and in 1840 £1700 was spent on rebuilding the premises. The congregation comprised the families of shopkeepers, maltsters, millers, schoolmasters, farmers, some doctors, an exciseman and even the master of the workhouse.[107] In 1822 the sudden death of the well-established pastor the Rev. Samuel Newton sparked a controversy over how his successor was to be chosen. The deacons judged that they, as the appointed representatives of the male members of the church, elected in a church meeting, should have the right to issue an invitation to a young man to come on trial. Some of the subscribers, however, were not happy with this arrangement and wrote to the deacons challenging the right of the male members of the church to have the exclusive right of choosing the pastor. They demanded that the subscribers should carry an equal vote. The deacons retorted that only members could be allowed the final decision but that they were willing to canvass the views of subscribers. To bolster their case they sought the advice of two neighbouring ministers, both of whom were of the definite opinion that 'mere subscribers have no scriptural right to vote equally and conjointly with the members of the Church'. A church meeting then decided that the members should make the choice, discuss it with the subscribers and if the latter objected the members should reconsider but would have the right to their original candidate. Meanwhile, the issue was raised: which church members were to vote? Was it 'scriptural that females should vote in the choice of a minister'? A decision was made in the negative but only by a majority of three. A compromise was agreed and a visit was made to all 'those sisters who were widows, single women or whose husbands were not members' to ask them to express their opinions. It was assumed that those who had husbands who were members were already represented. Eventually an agreement was reached by the majority of both members and subscribers and a new pastor was invited.[108]

Evidence from the Independent congregations suggests an absence of scriptural certainty as to male and female rights in church government but a practice which excluded women from voting and decision-making and from the holding of any office. Similar ambiguities reigned in Unitarian meetings. The New Meeting in Birmingham was probably established in 1692 and was situated close to the town centre. Unitarians allowed their ministers less power in the government of the meeting than did other Dissenters. Executive action lay with two bodies, the trustees who were responsible for the property and the financial interests of the chapel, and the vestry who took responsibility for the day-to-day running of the meeting. Both bodies were all male. The trustees, originally thirty-two in number, and the vestry, a smaller group of twelve, were elected by the subscribers. Frequently the same men served in both capacities and such famous Birmingham Unitarian names as Ryland, Phipson, Smith, Clark and Kenrick appeared regularly. These men were the elite of the congregation, commanding between them considerable wealth and prestige. The vestry, together with two chapel wardens, regulated such matters as the letting of seats, the conduct of relations with the Sunday schools, the disposition of gifts to the church, the practicalities of selecting new ministers. The vestrymen were seen as representatives of the congregation and periodic general meetings of subscribers were held to decide, for example, on a new pastor. The ministers attended neither the vestry committee nor the general meetings, but in 1836 it was decided to invite them to the latter though a layman still occupied the chair. Any official tasks were done by men; any official positions were held by men. Subcommittees established to inquire into particular issues were male, gentlemen were occasionally appointed from the meeting to visit subscribers and sound out opinions on policy questions, even the singers in the choir were men.[109]

Yet it would be wrong to see the New Meeting as a straightforward male oligarchy. As early as 1782 Joseph Priestley, one of the ministers of the New Meeting and a powerful protagonist of representative government, argued in a sermon that all those who *subscribed* to the upkeep of the chapel should be involved in its management. 'The people who create must likewise have the power to change their own officers', he suggested, and it was as a result of the discussions following this sermon that the vestry was established. It was decided that anyone who contributed one guinea or more per annum should be registered as a voter to elect this committee. Women who subscribed in their own right were permitted to vote but only by proxy and were not eligible to hold any office.[110] This was indeed a move towards a male property owning democracy and a step away from the older oligarchic pattern. John Seed's research indicates that a similar shift in the organization of other Unitarian chapels was taking place after 1800.[111]

The distinction between the influence of subscribers in Unitarian meetings and members in Independent chapels is instructive for while the Unitarians gave power to those who contributed financially, to the Independents it was the salvation expressed through active membership which counted. On both scores there were problems as to women. Women gave money but they never acted as trustees. Whereas men's contributions were linked to the assumption that as money-makers and managers they would fulfil these same roles in the chapel, women simply gave.[112] Subscriptions only represented one part of the financial resources of chapels such as the New Meeting. Their major source of income was pew rents. The majority of seat holders were men usually in their capacity as household heads and providing seats for their families. There was no bar, however, to women holding seats and indeed we find evidence from wills of these being passed on as treasured parts of an inheritance.

Not surprisingly there is far more evidence of male donations to the chapel than female. After the destruction of the Meeting House in the riots of 1791, for example, the list of donors included thirty-seven names, only three of which were female. But on occasion quite considerable legacies were given to the chapel by women. Mary Bayley left £300 in 1789 to buy property below the Old Meeting House and expand the yard; the sisters, Ann and Jane Giles gave £100 each in 1846 to make possible the widening of Old Meeting Street. In times of emergency the wealthier subscribers would be approached for help. Undoubtedly these 'wealthier' would sometimes be women, since independent widows and spinsters had less drain on their resources than men whose capital was tied up in productive enterprises. It seems possible that the pattern which Prochaska has established in philanthropy, of the significant scale of female financial contributions despite their underrepresentation at every formal level, may well have been at work in Dissenting congregations.[113]

Yet as with taxation, there was no automatic right of representation. For that it was necessary to be male *and* a financial contributor. The record on women's right to vote at the New Meeting is confusing. In the recording of names at early general meetings no women appear, but this may have been because their names were not noted even if they were present. Women were undoubtedly subscribers and thus held formal rights to attend. Initially they were not allowed to vote, but following a debate in 1802 over whether the meeting should have one minister or two, some female signatures appear on a letter discussing the issue. In 1803, Sarah Bache, a New Meeting subscriber, wrote to her sister that she had signed a petition against inviting a new minister. Women could, however, play a part in chapel affairs without voting or speaking in the 'assembly'. Their silent witness expressed by non-attendance, their gossip, their choice of who to call on, who to exclude, could be potent weapons in chapel politics.[114] The appointment of new ministers was a moment of potential conflict since this was one of the times subscribers exercised their power. In 1816 there was again a disagreement over a proposed invitation. A general meeting was called and the ladies' votes were used to carry the motion in favour of the Rev. Yates. The record of this leaves us in no doubt that an unusual practice had been followed. The votes were registered as:

For the motion	53	Against	62
Ladies present	11	Against	0
	64		62

The supporters of the Rev. Yates were presumably driven to establish the dangerous precedent of letting the ladies' vote count. A prominent member of the New Meeting recalled in his reminiscences that the ladies' votes had indeed been used to get Yates in the face of considerable opposition.[115]

Both men and women might potentially wield power and influence in the religious community in ways that would have been difficult in the wider society. Men, who as Dissenters were barred from public office for much of the period, learnt to be active in the chapel, to conduct public meetings, to take minutes and count votes, to debate, discuss and reach compromises, to make factions and build alliances, in short to operate in the complex world of chapel life, that potential training ground for other forms of representative government. For women it was different. Religion offered a vital individual space, a place for self-fulfilment at a time when that was not generally highly valued for the female sex, but without, for the most part, aligning that place with positions of public responsibility. The very confusion, however, as to whether women should speak, should vote, should teach, meant that no closure was formally effected.

The relative autonomy of Dissenting congregations made the whole issue of power and leadership one for constant negotiation and the determination of what part women would play was integral to this process. Despite the doctrinal emphasis on separate spheres, it was possible for women in the context of extremely small congregations to play a leading role. The force of personality, or wealth, in a woman might give her the backing to overcome the unease of herself and others in taking public office. In a fervently evangelical Congregational chapel in Essex, with its active Home Missionary Society already creating scope for women's contribution, a School of Missionaries' Daughters was founded in 1838 by a married couple. The wife was also a deacon of the chapel and secretary to the school from its founding.[116] In another instance, the paralysis of her husband, a vicar in rural Essex, led his wife to take on (in the absence of a curate) as many of his duties as she could. 'She considered', declared her obituary in the

Evangelical *Christian Observer* in 1820, that 'there was a path for her to tread, which, without encroaching upon the functions of the ministry, would promote the great objects of that high calling'. Her funeral was conducted by the Rev. William Marsh who admired the delicate way she had trodden that path between the needs of the parish and strictures of femininity.[117]

But there is some evidence that as ideologies of femininity became more sharply defined it grew more difficult to hold those spaces open. In rural areas, women had occasionally acted as overseers, parish clerks and church wardens, their office dependent on their position as landowners and farmers. Saffron Walden, for example, boasted the notable widow who dealt with 165 applicants for relief in a single meeting.[118] Such women were almost always widows, yet even they came to be unacceptable and those nominally eligible increasingly appointed a proxy. Such parish offices, their status downgraded *vis-à-vis* the new brand of clergy, were increasingly held by male small farmers and shopkeepers. For enthusiastic Christians seeking to reform the church and ensure respect for church government, it was disturbing to have women in parish offices. It was seen as unnatural, a sign of the backward uncivilized condition of a parish organization. It evoked comparison with the more extreme forms of Methodism where female office holding and public preaching were permitted and taken by others as signs of vulgarity.[119] When the zealously Evangelical Rev. John Charlesworth took over an isolated parish in Suffolk in 1814, he saw its population as barbaric, prey to poaching and drunkenness and without a dame school to instil basic education. His biographer, another Evangelical Suffolk clergyman, emphasized the degree of 'degradation' of the village by noting that

no labouring man being able to read tolerably, when Mr. Charlesworth first entered his reading desk *a woman* [his italics] acted as the clerk, giving out the responses.

Along with both Rev. and Mrs Charlesworth's charge that 'the people had to be taught cleanliness, neatness and common manners', they also had to learn appropriate sexual divisions. Rev. Charlesworth removed the woman clerk and replaced her with an almost illiterate farmer.[120]

There is similar evidence from other denominations. The few women deacons traced among Baptist chapels in the 1780s disappeared.[121] It became more difficult for women preachers among the Methodists. The main body of Methodism stopped women preaching in 1803 and it was only localized breakaway groups such as the Bible Christians in the south-west who regularly allowed such practices.[122] Even in the special case of the Quakers the predominance of women ministers over men, which had been marked in the early nineteenth century, dropped away.[123] The justification for Quaker women preaching rested on the belief that the Holy Spirit could empower either man or woman and impart the inspiration to preach. Preaching was thus marked off from every other kind of public speaking. As Joseph John Gurney commented to his family after hearing women speaking on the anti-slavery issue in the US,

I do not approve of ladies speaking in public, even in the anti-slavery cause, except under the immediate influences of the Holy Spirit. *Then*, and then only, all is safe.[124]

His sister, Elizabeth Fry, wrote that she could only speak comfortably when 'much covered with love and power'; a 'cover' which protected her from the attacks of her own family, members of the Quaker community and the world outside when she stepped out of a woman's sphere.[125]

The ministry of Quaker women was widespread and powerful in the late eighteenth and early nineteenth centuries. It was often a family tradition handed down from mother to daughter, much as son followed father in a religious calling in other denominations. The large Quaker community in Saffron Walden produced three sisters who were ministers within the grocer's family of Green. One of them, Susanna, married a Suffolk minister and together they preached extensively all over East Anglia.[126] Sara Grubb was also married to a fellow minister, living first in Bury and then in Chelmsford. She was an exceptionally gifted preacher, described as the 'powerful Grubb that sounds her master's praise in streets, in markets, prisons and highways'. In 1802 Elizabeth Fry, herself not one to shirk from incessant religious activity, noted that when Sara Grubb brought in her account of her late visit to the monthly meeting she requested to go out yet again and 'it appears as if she could never rest'.[127] In December 1818, an Ipswich diarist noted that John and Sara Grubb 'shone in the ministry' and on another occasion that she was 'eminently favoured', while in 1837 a meeting of over 1000 gathered to hear her preach.[128]

Thomas Clarkson, the anti-slavery campaigner who had retired near Ipswich, although an Evangelical Anglican, had worked closely with Quakers and wrote a three volume *Portrait of Quakerism* in 1807. In it he defended Quaker women as more spiritual than men and especially praised their modesty in conversation, looks, behaviour and dress which set them apart from females of the world. Nevertheless, he admitted that Quaker women 'have that which no other body of women have, a public character'.[129] Herein lay the problem. Could a public engagement with a Christian ministry be combined with the proper performance of feminine duties? Would a lady's delicacy and refinement of mind be tainted by contact with the outside world? This was not an issue which could be easily resolved. Much of the voluminous public discussion of Elizabeth Fry focused on whether she had forfeited her femininity by her ministry. For the Rev. Charles Tayler, the Evangelical curate in Suffolk who was proud of his acquaintance with Fry, the answer was unequivocal. For him, religious considerations could override even genteel femininity. If he had seen her only at home with her children, so tender, 'so feminine in all her ways', he might have supposed that 'her sphere was in the retirement of home with its quiet occupations. . . . But there was another sphere *divinely* appointed and a very different one to which she was evidently called and for which she was eminently qualified'.[130]

The letters, diaries and memoirs of women ministers abound with evidence of tensions between the public path of their call and private duties. Anna Braithwaite, a child of the prominent Lloyds, born in Birmingham in 1788, married in 1808 into the Braithwaites, another well established Quaker family in Kendal. She had seven surviving children of her own and after 1822 felt responsible for the seven young children of her dead sister, yet felt compelled to place her religious duties uppermost. Only her 'constraining sense of the love of Christ' allowed her the strength to overcome her sense of female propriety and speak in public. In 1823, despite the death of her sister and the fact that her own children were still 'at that susceptible age in which the character is being formed', and in which 'the mother's influence is of the greatest importance' she travelled to the US to preach.[131]

Such commitment to an independent life inevitably had effects. Another daughter of the Lloyds who became a minister in 1840 was both physically and emotionally separated from her children as a result. One of her daughters recalled that she and her sisters were much attached to their governesses

and made them our confidantes almost more than our parents. Mamma's engagements as a minister separated her a good deal from her children. We could not enter into the conflict of mind that preceded them, we only knew she was absorbed and grave, and easily distressed if things went wrong.[132]

This daughter registers none of the bitterness which surfaces in the complaints of parts of the Fry family about Elizabeth's neglect of home and children. But the social climate of the nineteenth century was increasingly unfavourable to women preaching, their capacity to interpret the word was severely curtailed. Bernard Barton, the Quaker Suffolk poet and bank clerk, discussing in a letter in 1843 the famous Pauline injunction as to women's silence, argued that St Paul himself was inconsistent on the subject and that, 'in our Society, I can only say that I believe that it has worked well; that some of the most powerful, effective and persuasive ministers in the Society have been women – and still are'. He even went so far as to argue that women's general habits, training and experience made them especially qualified for the ministry. But by then Barton was almost 60, and in the atmosphere of the mid nineteenth century public ministry did not appeal to many women.[133] By this time the evangelical enthusiasm which had renewed the Quaker movement had waned, while the canons of gentility made it difficult for women to continue such public displays even within their own community. The Quaker belief in the seed of God residing in all spirits, regardless of their sex, did not lead them to believe in social equality. Quakers had a strong sense of sexual difference, reflected in their forms of organization, down to the separate seating for men and women. Separate men's and women's meetings were held, the Monthly Meeting providing the focus for local executive power and dealing with issues such as birth, marriage, death and finances, the Yearly Meeting for central legislative power. From 1754 Quaker women argued that their Yearly Meeting should be properly constituted; the men refused until 1784. But the winning of a formal constitution did not prevent the men's meetings from continuing to enjoy the monopoly of power.

Quaker women were no more the decision-makers in their denomination than their Anglican, Congregational or Unitarian sisters. Their power to preach and pray was a special dispensation, which could, with increasing difficulty, be allowed to coexist with notions of feminine propriety. John Bright, one of the most prominent Victorian Quakers, was described by a contemporary as conventional in his views on relations between the sexes. 'He could worship what he called charming women', it was said,

but he could *never* bear women to assert themselves. He did not think his sisters had a right to think for themselves with regard to any offer of marriage. . . .
He once told me that daughters had no right to have the money their fathers had left them if it would be of use to their brothers in business.[134]

Undoubtedly there would have been many male voices, like that of Barton, ready to challenge such an account. But the fissure between the inner light of spiritual equality and the outer structures of the social world ran deep.

Laymen and women

For most serious Christian men, as indeed for rational religionists, the choice was not to enter the ministry but to live a life active in the service of the congregation, a life which could combine faith with works in the world. There were many opportunities to be active on behalf of church or chapel. A miller from Witham, who had left the Church of England in 1787 to join a Congregational chapel and was so pious that his father almost disinherited him in disgust, created a religious atmosphere in his home by instigating family prayer. Having considerable material resources, he was able to support his chapel community by opening his home to the surrounding local ministers, making available to them his hospitality, giving personal advice and financial help, and offering his excellent library. He also took on the secretaryship of the Benevolent Society for the relief of the necessitous widows and children of Protestant Dissenting Ministers in the Counties of Essex and Hertford. Together with his cousin, he gave freely of his time and money to the founding of the Essex Congregational Union, an organization vital to the linking of the disparate cells of the gathered church.[135]

Beyond the formal offices associated with parish or chapel there were numerous openings for men with the time and inclination to take their improving zeal into the community. Whether as evangelists, as carriers of culture to the labouring poor or as improvers within their own class, the activities associated with churches and chapels give substance to the claim that this was indeed the age of societies.[136] This range of enterprises, mobilizing not only material wealth but the skills and experiences of thousands, was one of the most powerful weapons in the evangelical armoury. In the early days of Evangelicalism, Simeon, one of its founding fathers, had recommended to John Venn, one of his friends in the Clapham Sect, that he should galvanize the seventy or so elders in his congregation. 'Make use of *them*', he suggested,

both male and female. Dear Amelia [Venn's aunt] will conduct the female department where 20 or 30 are ready to work under her. The males will work under you.[137]

For Anglicans, this was a revolutionary suggestion. To make use of laymen, never mind laywomen, broke with the traditions of the established church and veered dangerously close to the vulgar enthusiasms of Methodism. Evangelicals, however, were ready to welcome female activity, provided always that it remained within its proper sphere.

Take a woman like Amy Camps, born in Colchester in 1800 and brought up first 'under' an early Evangelical, Rev. Robert Storry, and then William Marsh, both at St Peter's. Unmarried until her 50s and devoting her whole life to religion, she could carve out a niche for herself under the enlarged Evangelical view of the parish. Starting with visiting 'dear Mrs. Marsh's' school for poor children, she gave life long support to the Bible Society and hospital visiting. Her specially chosen avocation of visiting the sick and dying gave her an ear to parish affairs which could be relayed to the minister and other church dignitaries. 'My sick people keep dying off', she wrote in her diary in 1838, 'Fresh ones occupy my time which is a mercy as no time is left for useless conversation.' In the 1840s she went into an unnamed Colchester church where, presumably under the influence of a Tractarian minister, she saw workmen setting up images of the Apostles which she called 'idols'. She interviewed the vicar and, with the force of her belief in God directing her every action, persuaded him to remove them. Amy Camps was a personal friend of several local ministers and their wives and in old age, after her marriage took her to live in the Isle of Ely, she gave hospitality to Charles Spurgeon, the enthusiastic young evangelist from Colchester who took London by storm in the late nineteenth century. Thus Amy Camp's Evangelical involvement spanned almost the whole century.

Fervent female adherents moved to the heart of the Evangelical experience and although they could not preach in public, they could convert in private. From her own household staff, to her close friends, neighbours, the local poor, the people she met travelling by coach, boat, or in inns, women like Amy Camps never ceased to put forward the gospel in person and in their often widespread correspondence. If, like Camps, she was successful (and she was not a little proud of that success) she would then have to hand on her charges to the male minister. Any attempt of such women to shift from this informal persuasion to a more formal setting was made under the control and direction of professional men and dependent on their good will or hostility. At 21, Amy Camps, modelling herself on an older spinster friend who saw herself as a 'sick visitor', started going to the Colchester workhouse and speaking to the inmates. Typically, this 'career' was broken when she was confined to home to care for her dying widowed mother. After her mother's death, she did become a visitor and Sunday school teacher, positions created by men like William Marsh who followed Venn's advice and made full use of lay support.

Her greatest opportunity came in 1834 when she started visiting at the recently opened Essex and Colchester Hospital. Three years later she notes that an 'unexpected door has been opened by my friend, the Reverend Dr. Seaman', when she was allowed to visit the poor formally at the new Union House. However, in November 1842, her access to hospital visiting was cut off by the arrival on the committee of a clergyman with stricter ideas of woman's place, who denounced her as the 'preaching and praying woman'. The hospital was moved to make a rule that only ministers of religion were allowed to pray with patients. But Camps appealed to divine guidance for her self-appointed mission and turned to her Bible which opened at Ecclesiastics x. 4:

If the Spirit of the ruler rise up against thee, leave not thy place.

Her clerical supporters rallied, the vicar of St Peter's, who had replaced Marsh, promised to make her a life member of the hospital rather than see her prohibited from her work. With an increasing eye to the public, Amy Camps tried publishing her experiences but was rejected by a tract society. Discouraged, she turned to a clerical friend who suggested she print a tract herself which soon sold out.[138]

A woman like Amy Camps constructed life around religious causes, but there were lesser ways in which women, in spite of their formal invisibility, could be active in a congregation. A minister who was unpopular could be ostentatiously snubbed. Those who were approved derived support from hospitality and spreading of the good word on social networks. At times women could act as an informal 'court of appeal', soothing tensions and settling disputes behind the scenes. In the conflict at the Coggeshall Congregational chapel in 1818, when an influential deacon led a sustained attack on the minister, the chapel community was deeply divided and the attendance and non-attendance of the deacon's female relatives became a sore issue. In the highly public drama of hurled epithets, whether in the local shop or the chapel itself, women made up an important part of the unrecorded but influential audience.[139] A woman's respect and appreciation of her pastor might be expressed in gifts, the presentation of a hand worked gown to be worn in the pulpit, or the leaving of a small bequest to a favourite preacher.[140] Scattered evidence from membership and subscription lists suggests that the women of a family might often be the first converts. They carried the message back to their menfolk and inculcated serious religious behaviour into their children.[141] The limitations on public activities of women directed many of them towards a more informal role, acting as information networks, keeping the formal officers up to date. The middle-aged farmer's wife, who was an indefatigable walker and dropper-in for tea, was able to tell her vicar when certain parishioners were ill or in trouble so that he could then visit. She was diffident, however, when requested to 'take the Book' for the collecting committee of the local charity. The vicar's wife had to tell her, woman-to-woman, that the vicar very much wanted her to take up this office. This farmer's wife keenly felt the departure of a previous minister when he went to India as a missionary. She viewed the new pastor with some suspicion until she had heard him preach several times. The final accolade came when she entertained him to supper complete with 'ham, fowles and tarts' of her own baking.[142] To accept or reject in this way, and to use hospitality as the measure, was one weapon in the passive armoury of women.

When men and women were both involved in activities associated with a church or chapel there were clear lines of demarcation. A day and Sunday school treat organized by the Witham Congregational chapel relied on the men for some arrangements, the women for others. A gentleman was to approach the local dignitary, Mr Pattisson, and ask him for the use of his park. Another was to sort out the tables, others were to purchase the meat and to carve, others were to receive the children on the day and keep them in order. The ladies, on the other hand, were to solicit their friends to make plum puddings, lend urns and make tea. They were to ask the local doctor for a gift of free potatoes for the 250 little mouths, they were to beg pots and pans, supply the salt, make cakes and allow the bread and butter to be cut in their homes.[143] The men were dealing with the formal arrangements, the premises and the meat, the keeping of order; the women were dealing with the rest of the food. Such a division mirrors the assumptions which pervaded the workings of voluntary organizations from Provident Associations to Sunday schools, from clothing societies to tract distribution and the visiting of the poor. Men would deal with the formal, women with the informal. Men would be decisive, women would be supportive. Men would take their proper place in the world, women would remain associated with the home.

Such expectations permeated the many activities initiated and encouraged by John Angell James at Carrs Lane. Here theory and practice were united, men and women contributed in their different but appropriate ways. Carrs Lane established its own 'Sabbath schools' in 1813 but James believed that for the schools to have their proper effects, the sexes must be strictly segregated, for the sake of both teachers and pupils. He stressed the importance of,

the most punctilious regard to all the rules of modesty and reserve, between male and female teachers. A schoolroom is not the place, nor is the Sabbath the time, for gossip between young men and women. Nothing can be more improper than to see young men intruding into an apartment appropriated to the instruction of girls, and there nodding, laughing, or talking to a female acquaintance. Before an assembly of poor children, one of whose greatest dangers arises from a want of proper and delicate reserve between the sexes, and who are ready to copy with avidity any want of decorum in their teachers, the very smallest deviation from the strict rules of propriety is a crime, not only against their manners, but against their morals.

Female teachers, he warned in his best-selling *Sunday School Teachers' Guide,* should be especially careful as to their clothes and always be modest and neat. There was a danger that the mixed society of the Sunday school community might 'expose young females' to unsuitable acquaintances and connections, but with care this could be avoided. Mixed meetings of teachers were quite unnecessary and all branches of activity should take place in their separate spheres.[144] Similar principles underpinned the common practice of providing separate accommodation for boys and girls when new buildings were put up, and even of having different times and places when the minister would be available to see the different sexes.

The boys' school at Carrs Lane was run by a gentlemen's committee, the girls' by a ladies', but both were formally subject to the men. A committee consisting of James, the church treasurer and ten gentlemen was established as the 'general committee' with responsibility for the day-to-day running of the boys' school, and with overseeing the girls'. The ladies' equivalent, staffed by Mrs James, the wives of several deacons and some unmarried enthusiasts, regularly reported to the gentlemen's secretary. He passed on anything that he thought was necessary and kept the only minutes up to date. There was similar organization in the plethora of pursuits followed at Carrs Lane. There were societies supporting missionaries, distributing tracts, visiting the poor, supplying child bed linen, providing Bibles, Provident Societies, Benefit Societies, all masterminded by James and his 'judicious and experienced' deacons, many of them relying on the support of faithful females.

James saw district visiting societies, benevolent institutions for temporal and spiritual instruction and relief, and Bible and Missionary Societies as all appropriate activities for women. Tract distribution was acceptable if care was taken as to the sites visited, calling on the poor and the sick was women's especial task. 'Here', he argued,

there *can be* nothing in opposition to female modesty, nothing that can minister to female vanity. The seclusion of the scene prevents all this: no rude or inquisitive gaze follows her there: no language of fulsome compliment or sickly adulation is addressed to her there: she is alone with sorrow, or witnessed only by her conscience or her God.[145]

This conviction that the more private the near public activities of Christian women were, the easier they were to defend as not breaking with feminine propriety, underpinned the practices of multiple zealous enterprises. As long as James, or an equivalent figure, were there to front, to organize, to present, the day-to-day work could be done by women. Women were never the trustees or the financial genius's, those who designed, raised the money for and built the new institutional complexes, but they were sent round as collectors to help pay debts on new chapels. In fifty years the ecumenical Ipswich Auxiliary Bible Society managed to raise £55,000 and distribute over 188,000 Bibles. Its Ladies Auxiliary raised £2574 and distributed 6818 Bibles. It was pointed out that these latter figures were particularly impressive since the ladies' labours were 'noiseless and untiring', and furthermore performed 'free of expense' to the society.[146]

Upper middle-class women often organized and paid 'Biblewomen' to distribute tracts or Bibles for them, but a woman like Amy Camps carried her own supply wherever she went and for years paid out of her own modest resources for tracts to supply to her 'friend', a peddlar who carried them with his wares around the villages of Essex.[147] As the expectation that ladies did not work for pay increased, so the importance of the voluntary principle of women's contribution was emphasized. When the magistrates eventually offered Sarah Martin, a self-educated dressmaker who had started voluntary prison visiting in Great Yarmouth, a £12 per annum stipend she refused. Until then she had been accepted by the prisoners as a disinterested and religiously inspired missionary and felt she could not risk being branded as a 'jail functionary', the only possible term for a woman paid to do such a job; she would lose the power of feminine grace.[148]

Unitarians shared none of the evangelical zeal of the real religionists, but they had a strong commitment to improving the working classes. The New Meeting Sunday school was set up in 1778, following the collapse of the attempt to run Birmingham Sunday schools on non-denominational lines. Its stated aim was to

> prepare the poorer classes for enduring with a Christian spirit the hardships and privations attendant on a life of poverty . . . [and producing] that temperate and peaceful demeanour for which the operatives of this town and neighbourhood are pre-eminently distinguished in the land.[149]

Such a determinedly Utilitarian approach was somewhat mitigated by the way in which the schools were actually run, since the more open syllabus and the focus on non-religious teaching ensured that the New Meeting schools were more successful in keeping their numbers than most of their rivals. The original committee established to run the separate schools for boys and girls was composed of Priestley and his co-pastor, together with twenty-seven other gentlemen. Initially one male and one female teacher were appointed; they were supervised by visitors, who provided the connection between congregation and school. They were the representatives of the masculine elite of the meeting, organizing their subalterns, the lower middle-class and artisan male and female teachers. The women teachers are represented in the minutes as 'females', the visitors as 'ladies'; similarly the men are 'males' and 'gentlemen'. The visitors gave regular reports to the committee on how the schools were progressing, what new items were needed, what the children had been doing. It was the committee which made policy and organized the finances. The girls' school was, therefore, only indirectly represented and it was assumed that the gentlemen would necessarily know best.

The assumption that women would support the initiatives of men rather than independently pursuing separate aims and ventures was reflected not only in the formal organization of the New Meeting Sunday schools but also in the provision of facilities for Sunday school teachers. Despite the relatively progressive view of female education which was a characteristic of Unitarian thinking, few attempts were made to encourage women to educate themselves as did men. Priestley was so advanced as to set up an evening discussion group, open to young men and women. The male friendships maintained in this group spilt out into a range of other enterprises such as the Brotherly Society promoted by James Luckcock. Such bodies were vital for self-education, but the female teachers had no equivalent. The extent to which independent thinking was encouraged among the men is reflected in the conflicts between the teachers and the Sunday school committee in the early 1830s which culminated in the secession of the boys' school from the umbrella of the New Meeting. The teachers objected to the committee's interference, to its assumptions that it had the right to hire and fire teachers, to its monthly meetings where *their* work was discussed. The committee believed that the troubles were the result of too much lassitude on their part, too much autonomy being granted to the male teachers. They were relieved that no such developments threatened at the girls' school where there were no extra-curricula activities for the teachers, no apparent sense of independence.[150]

As with female clerical relatives, religious women could extend their activities beyond teaching and sick visiting by writing. The keeping of a

private spiritual record was a tradition of serious Christianity, often starting
in childhood with the keeping of birthday books and diaries, and it could
continue through life. The daughter of a Colchester tradesman and wife of
a modest Ipswich draper, left several volumes of 'pious effusions' at her
death. Amy Camps kept a considerable part of her small inheritance for
the posthumous publication of her diary. Mothers published memoirs of
their daughters who died young, daughters published volumes celebrating
the spiritual lives of their mothers.[151]

The purpose of such writing was in part self-exploratory, but publication
also implied that the example should be diffused through the Word. The
death of the pious young of both sexes was a powerful reminder of the
necessity to keep the world at bay and constantly prepare one's soul for
Heaven. However, the death of young women had a particularly strong
message, combining resignation, purity and the paradoxical strength of
weakness and humility illustrated in Bernard Barton's poem written in 1828
for his dying cousin, daughter of a Suffolk banker.

> If gentle cheerfulness in pain
> And weakness, silently can teach;
> Believe not thou hast liv'd in vain
> Nor mourn that thus thy life should preach.
>
> For this to do, and this to bear
> Requires far more strength of nerve;
> And those a rich reward shall share,
> Who *thus by weak endurance* 'SERVE'
>
> That life might eloquently preach
> To thoughts attentive ear;
> But death, e'en death like thine should teach
> And Bid the thoughtless hear.[152]

Sometimes it fell to a male relative or friend, as in this case, to point to the
example of the pious young woman. Pastors frequently published funeral
sermons to stand as exempla, complete with a record of the faith and works
of the dead. Such portrayals of female excellence, in the most modest
domestic circles, could act as hope and inspiration.

There were other less private channels of women's religious expression,
ranging from poems, hymns and tales privately or locally printed to those
reaching a wide circulation. Writing provided a form of intervention for
women at a time when other kinds of public speech were increasingly
difficult. Some, like Amy Camps, paid to have their own writings published. Others raised subscriptions on the basis of their little volumes. A
few women were able to reach a wider audience still or a more professional
status. Mary Wright Sewell, born in 1800, the daughter of a Quaker farmer
on the Suffolk/Norfolk border, sister-in-law of the famous Mrs Ellis and
mother of Anna Sewell of *Black Beauty* fame, moved on from the organization of mother's meetings, Biblewomen and temperance work to publish,
after persuasion, her *Thoughts on Education* in the 1850s. In the 1860s she
started writing her set of tracts, of which *Mother's Last Words* sold over a

million copies and *Our Father's Care* 750,000.[153] The best known of the
local women who wrote in this genre were the sisters Ann and Jane Taylor,
specializing in works for children, a peculiarly feminine sphere. It was even
possible for a few women to branch out into magazine editing and
publishing either for a local audience or a national readership, a course
much eased by contacts with a sympathetic religious publisher as when Jane
Taylor edited *The Youth Magazine or Evangelical Miscellany* in the 1820s.
But the question of women's appearance in print, even with a religious
impetus, was fraught with problems about the exposure of self and the
admission of worldly ambition, to be eschewed by men but doubly
dangerous for women. One way of containing this risk was to limit the
audience and the genre, a self-limitation not practised by eighteenth-century
writers.

The possibilities for such writing, together with the clubs, societies and
auxiliaries of the church and chapel worlds provided women with a space.
Such activities might become an avenue of real, if narrowly defined power
and recognition within the local community. Maria Charlesworth, daughter
of the Rev. John Charlesworth of Flowton, Suffolk, was particularly
involved with the religious 'family enterprise'. In later life she wrote a
fantasy based on aspirations for women such as herself in her popular
volume of stories, *The Female Visitor to the Poor*. This was designed to
be a practical guide for those in neglected country parishes, but tells us
much about her frustrations and wishes. In these tales, the genteel middle-
class woman can give Bible classes for the wives of labourers or the
pastor's daughter can give extra classes on Sunday evenings, staying on to
take tea alone in the vestry waited on by pious cottagers' wives. For
Charlesworth, the Sunday school fête, of which the pastor's daughter
(herself) is the chief organizer, becomes the acme of the year, replacing the
boisterous pagan harvest feast. Her subordinates are the farmer's wives who
make and donate the food, the schoolmistress who solicits funds. The
minister's daughter is left to bestow rewards for good work and pronounce
banishment from the fête since it is she who gives out the individual
invitations to attend. The whole village turns out to decorate the barn where
the proceedings are to be held. A special throne for her, decorated with
green boughs, is placed on a raised dais from which she 'bestows praise,
reproof or counsel'. Even the girls who had left to go into service were
invited with their mistress's permission, after 'enquiry had been made as to
their conduct' and the proceedings finished with tea provided for 'superior
visitors' in the farmhouse while the Sunday school teachers had theirs in
the barn.[154]

In this fantasy, the moral and religious force emanating from the truly
religious woman is used to re-establish a village 'community' with each
group in their appropriate place and where she, as the rector's daughter,
takes the place of the lady of the manor. Reading between the lines,
however, this is an almost totally female community. Strikingly absent is
the male power upon which the support (or obstruction) of real women so
much depended. Not all women would have shared Maria Charlesworth's
feminized version of paternalism, but all could share her dream of a world
in which women could matter, could be somebody, could act on others as

men did. Religion offered the key to such a world, where women could be valued for their spiritual worth if not their material power, where a 'religious career' could give meaning to women's experience and express some of their aspirations.

3 'The nursery of virtue': domestic ideology and the middle class

Domestic happiness, thou only bliss
Of Paradise that has survived the Fall
... thou art the nurse of virtue

William Cowper, *The Task*, Book 3

'Home ... the nursery of virtue'

John Angell James

Church and chapel were central to the articulation and diffusion of new beliefs and practices related to manliness and femininity. But late eighteenth- and early nineteenth-century society was peopled by many other ideo- logues, who sought to map out new forms of social and familial order. Public attitudes to private morality shifted markedly, as is demonstrated by the case of Queen Caroline and the resolute attack on the double standard for men and women associated with it. Such changes in the terms of public debate on the family and sexuality were connected with new ideas about the place of men and women in the pamphlets, manuals, novels and maga- zines so avidly read by the middle class. Two eighteenth-century Evangelical writers, William Cowper and Hannah More, were influential in setting the terms for the characterization of domesticity and sexual difference. They were followed by a host of minor writers, pre-eminently women, who explored the ways in which such values could be translated into the daily practice of the home, whether in nursery or kitchen. Their writing, in their different ways, was concerned with and explored the contradictions between the claims for women's superiority and their social subordination, a tension which could not be resolved within early Victorian society. Writing on sexual difference was by no means confined to the protagonists of separate spheres but increasingly the language of *woman's place* and *woman's mission* dominated debates over womanhood itself. Womanhood was a contested site, not only intellectually but in practice. By the 1830s and 1840s the language used was increasingly secular and the belief in the natural differ- ences and complementary roles of men and women which had originally been particularly linked to Evangelicalism, had become the common sense of the English middle class.

The Queen Caroline affair

In 1820 'the most perplexing domestic question' galvanized English society. 'It was the only question I have ever known', wrote Hazlitt, 'that excited a thorough popular feeling. It struck its roots into the heart of the nation; it took possession of every house or cottage in the kingdom. . .'. As the Evangelical *Christian Observer* bewailed, 'this contaminating topic has polluted every newspaper, and found its way to every hamlet in the kingdom'.[1] This 'perplexing domestic question', this 'contaminating topic', concerned the sexual adventures and infidelities of kings and queens. It was about scandal in high places, marriages without love, the exotic pleasures of the rich. More specifically, it concerned the attempt by the unpopular George IV to divorce the wife he had never liked, Caroline of Brunswick, by bringing an action against her in the House of Lords, consequently exposing her supposed misdeeds to the inquisitive eyes and ears of the expanding literate public.

George and Caroline had married in 1795 and their only child Charlotte was born nine months later. It was a marriage of convenience. As one of the political pamphleteers who were to pour out pamphlets, broadsheets and songs on the subject later put it in the language of popular romantic melodrama, 'The great G- weds the charming and amiable C- because he was in debt: he pockets the cash and leaves her to the stings of neglect and disappointment.'[2] The couple separated almost immediately, but whereas George's public lovelife could be pursued almost indiscriminately, his wife's careless friendships and indiscreet talk had more profound consequences. In 1806 a 'Delicate Investigation' was set in motion which failed to prove that Caroline had borne an illegitimate son, but despite this clearing of her name she left England. At the death of George III, however, Caroline decided to return. Angered by her husband's insistence that her name should be excluded from the liturgy, she sailed for England and landed in a storm of public controversy, determined to claim her rightful place as queen. Unable to secure a negotiated compromise, George insisted on attempting to divorce her, despite the anxieties of his ministers. His own well-known infidelities meant that it was impossible to appeal to the ecclesiastical courts and so recourse was made to a special procedure in the House of Lords, a Bill of Pains and Penalties, which provided a way of punishing a person without legal trial.

On 17 August 1820 the trial began. All peers were required to be present. The queen herself attended the trial and was the only woman in a chamber packed with men. There was huge public excitement, large demonstrations attended Caroline as she went to and from the court each day, the newspapers across the country, from *Aris's Birmingham Gazette* to the *Ipswich Journal* provided blow by blow accounts of each day's revelations. There was widescale popular feeling for the queen. 'The agitation', wrote Macaulay, 'spread to the farthest corner of the island'. The country waited: had Caroline committed adultery with her servant Bergami? Could the foreign witnesses be trusted to tell the truth? Did the couple make love on the boat? Did he help her to dress and undress for a masque? Would the king succeed in his plan to be rid of her? In the end the queen was virtually acquitted for the bill was passed by such a small majority that his Majesty's government felt compelled to withdraw it. From urban centres like Birmingham to small rural villages there were bonfires, illuminations and celebrations. 'All here is ecstasy', enthused the young Macaulay from Cambridge to his well-known Evangelical father, ' "Thank God the country is saved" is written on every face and echoed by every voice.'[3]

This episode has traditionally been seen as an important moment in radical politics with the royal divorce proceedings symbolizing the corruption of the political system. But, as Laqueur has argued, the affair was something more than 'the farce that would expose Old Corruption'. Much of the rhetoric employed relied on the notion that the people's claim to political participation arose from their virtue. Conversely, the government's moral degradation provided evidence of the decadence of the whole system. The famous Green Bag, the bag that contained the fabricated evidence of hired informers, became a symbol of all that was rotten in the state of England. But the 'radical parable' went wrong. It was 'deluged by royal melodrama and romance' and the agitation ended with a conservative triumph. Only seven months after the end of the trial the queen was unable to mobilize support when she tried to attend George's coronation and she died, 'broken-hearted', not long after.[4] The political narrative which the radicals had tried to construct, resting on a denunciation of corrupt governments and ill famed kings, 'was overwhelmed by a more compelling, a more culturally complex, and politically safe version of the story as domestic melodrama and royalist fantasy'.[5] The queen was saved from the king's evil ministers, her honour was restored, her virtue reasserted. The story had a happy ending which restabilized the monarchy and allowed George a triumphant coronation.

The case for Caroline rested on her innocence of the charges levelled against her, combined with a denunciation of the double standard which called her to account while her husband remained unscathed. Proving her innocence necessitated her presentation as a hapless victim, 'a poor forlorn woman' as she described herself.[6] Her mistreatment by some men made it imperative that other men should rescue her from an ill deserved fate. Caroline was the virtuous heroine, the symbol of dependent womanhood. The 'manly' and the 'courageous' must rise up and protect her. It was an insult to the nation's manhood to see the queen so insulted by men:

The beauty – the goodness – the very helplessness of the sex are so many claims on our support, are so many sacred calls on the assistance of every manly and courageous arm . . . whilst an example is held up to every ruffian in the land to absue and insult the wife, that he promised to cherish and protect, is it unreasonable to apprehend the degeneracy and decay of our national morals?[7]

The tenderness and respect with which women were treated in England, it was argued, were the mark of England's advanced state of civilization, and the brightest ornament of that civilization was its 'domestic virtue'.[8] The people of England must support this 'poor wronged female', the men to prove their manhood, for, as the Radical, Burdett argued at a packed Middlesex County meeting, as fathers – as husbands – as brothers – as men they were called upon by the voice of nature to stand firm in a woman's cause (loud cheers).[9]

Meanwhile, the women must rally too, for if virtuous British wives were to defend their rights they must see that Caroline was not wronged. As one of the many popular songs put it,

> Attend ye virtuous British wives,
>   Support your injured queen;
> Assert her rights; they are your own,
>   As plainly may be seen.[10]

The majority of addresses presented to Caroline from her loyal female subjects, however, tended to rely on an appeal to chivalry, and an assumption that men would act for them. The most prevalent image was of the 'unprotected female' assailed by the might of the crown.[11]

Such an image was somewhat incongruous given what is known of Caroline. One of George's objections to her from the start was her lack of control, her verbal indiscretions, her openness as to her feelings. These were characteristics far removed from the fragile, dependent, passive virtues increasingly associated with femininity. In the public spectacle of the trial, Caroline came to stand for an ideal of womanhood which had little relation to her ('Nobody cares for *me*' as she said of the proceedings in the House of Lords),[12] but which expressed a view of marriage and domesticity which was becoming increasingly powerful. The reaction to the whole episode marks one of the first *public* moments at which one view of marriage and of sexuality was decisively rejected in favour of another. Public opinion sided with 'John Bull' in 1820 in his 'Ode to George the Fourth and Caroline his wife':

> A *Father* to the *nation* prove,
>   A *Husband* to thy *Queen*,
> And safely in thy people's Love,
>   Reign tranquil and serene.[13]

The 'people' wanted George to fulfil his domestic obligations, only then could he be a proper father to his country as well. The domestic had been imprinted on the monarchical.

George's father, George III, had become a popular monarch by the time of his death in 1820. In his later life he had embraced all those virtues increasingly adopted by the middling sorts: piety, dignity, honesty and the love of a proper domestic life.[14] His attachment to domestic duties was particularly commented upon in obituaries. In contrast one of the most unpopular personae of his unpopular son was 'despiser of domestic ties'.[15] Indeed Regency London represented everything that was the opposite of serious middle-class life, particularly in its provincial guise. The high-class prostitutes, the boxes at the opera, the carriage drives in the park designed to advertise sexual wares, the life of ease and wit, the rude vigorous open enjoyment of sexuality, all of this was anathema to serious Christians.[16]

The public examination of the queen's life was bound to deeply offend such people and it is one of the ironies of the event that Liverpool, a committed Evangelical, was obliged to head the king's action. Wilberforce worked hard in an attempt to persuade the queen, through her attorney general Brougham, to make a settlement, but was unsuccessful. One of the most painful aspects of the case for Evangelical Tories was the exposure of moral malpractices connected with the monarchy, for it was deeply disturbing to their view of the king as head of the church.[17]

Faced with a Regent who despised domesticity, popular hopes for a better time ahead had rested on Princess Charlotte, the only daughter of George and Caroline and heir to the throne. In 1817 Charlotte died in childbirth after a brief but seemingly happy marriage. Her death was a signal for poets and sermonizers to laud her for her untainted femininity. Implicit comparisons with her father were made as her 'abhorrence of the depraved maxims and dissolute habits of fashionable life' were dwelt upon. 'She enjoyed', it was believed, '(what is not always the privilege of that rank) the highest connubial felicity'. Her pleasure in simple domestic duties, charitable activities, and the creation of a beautiful home and garden for herself, her husband and her prospective child were chronicled. She would have been a monarch such as the middling classes sought, sharing their values, enjoying their pastimes. As an Anglican clergyman and teacher at King Edward's School Birmingham wrote at her death,

> Our Western Isle hath long been famed for scenes
> Where bliss domestic finds a dwelling place;
> Domestic bliss, that like a harmless dove,
> Honour and sweet Endearment keeping guard,
> Can centre in a little quiet nest
> All that desire would fly for thro' the earth;
> That can, the world eluding, be itself
> A world enjoyed. . . .[18]

That notion of the world as a quiet domestic nest represented the polar opposite to the Regent's world of public entertainment and lax morality. It was those two worlds which were in conflict in 1820 with the unlikely figure of Queen Caroline representing the rejection of aristocratic moral standards and the defence of a more rigorous sexual practice.

The support for the queen cut across some of the usual political lines and prefigured later alliances built on moral rather than purely political consensus. It was difficult for Tories to support her since her main defenders were the Radicals who threatened public order. Nevertheless, even the *Christian Observer* had its correspondents who were prepared to do so and the whole episode was in part interpreted as evidence of the decadence in high places and the urgent need for moral reform.[19] But it was difficult to dismiss all her supporters as wild radicals seeking the downfall of the whole social system. 'The people all favour the Queen', wrote Lady Palmerston, 'including the respectable middle ranks.'[20]

In Birmingham, sections of the local middle class organized celebrations when the case was dropped against the queen. In rural Essex, Samuel

Courtauld, the Unitarian silk manufacturer, helped to arrange illuminations and a procession; a symbolic burning of the Green Bag took place on the village green and toasts were drunk to the local nonconformist worthies who had given their assistance.[21] It was the middle-class Radicals and nonconformists who were most prominent, but by no means exclusively so. The Utilitarian James Mill rushed to the queen's defence on the grounds of unacceptable legal procedures being used. The Evangelical Charles Tayler, a curate from Essex, attended the trial and found himself at a pro-Caroline gathering in London attended by Mme de Stael, symbol of female achievement. Some of the bishops refused to vote with the government on the grounds that they could not defend divorce. The moral issues raised, the defence of the virtuous female victim, the defence of marriage, the refusal of divorce meant that, for a precarious and short-lived moment, a moral majority was produced, too powerful for the king and his government. John Bull had triumphed in his insistence that the king must be a husband too.[22]

Nine months after the end of the trial, Caroline was dead. Her death provoked a last flurry in her defence. On 16 August, Colchester paid the queen its last respects as her remains were taken on the journey to Harwich, ready for embarkation to Germany where she had wished to be buried. People flocked from the neighbouring areas, the bells of the different churches tolled, business generally was suspended and at five o'clock a procession reached the town preceded by about 200 people on foot and twenty on horseback. Dinner had been ordered at the Three Cups for more than a hundred and the High Street was lined with spectators. On arrival in the town the corpse was taken to the parish church of St Martins, the scene of the last public altercation over the unfortunate queen. After the coffin had been deposited, the queen's household, her great supporter Alderman Wood and the public looked on while a plate was screwed on the coffin with an inscription: 'Caroline of Brunswick, the injured Queen of England, departed this life 7th August, in the year of our Lord, 1821, aged 53 years'. This wording, not surprisingly, disturbed the government representatives and it was requested that it should be removed and replaced with the official plate. The queen's supporters, however, refused and eventually the plate was removed at dead of night after the pressing crowd of spectators had subsided.[23]

The 'injured queen' had made her mark. After the death of George, the English crown provided a 'bright model' for the middle classes. William and Adelaide, who subscribed to domestic ideals, were celebrated in local records, and the death of Adelaide in 1849 evoked paeans of praise to her wifely qualities.[24] Her behaviour, commented an Anglican clergyman in Birmingham, provided a perfect pattern which the 'wives of England' would do well to follow. She had been a fond and loving wife, not distracted from her duties by the high position she held. When her husband was dying she nursed him, gave him medicine, smoothed his pillow, read the Bible to him, said prayers with and for him.[25] This notion of the queen as a model was much played on in the years following the accession of Victoria, the 'Rosebud of England', when the wives and mothers of England could all claim to be queens in their own homes, however modest, and to follow the young queen in her celebration of marriage.[26] Public opinion had decreed that the royal family must indeed be a family; kings and queens must be fathers and mothers in their own home if they were to be fathers and mothers to the people.

Middle-class readers and writers

The Queen Caroline affair marked a significant moment in terms of public attitudes to marriage and sexuality, an assertion of belief in the unblemished nature of English womanhood, an insistence that femininity meant virtue and honour. But how did these particular meanings come to be attached to marriage, manliness and femininity? And why did they triumph over others; for example, the eighteenth-century preoccupation with rampant and voracious female sexuality?[27] A stress on domestic virtues, on marriage, home and children was by no means new. The Puritan divines had led the way in formulating doctrines on the proper place of home and family from the early seventeenth century, their ideas finding echoes among domestic ideologues of the eighteenth and nineteenth centuries. Some of those ideas had been taken up by the upper echelons of the bourgeoisie, the hierarchy and even sections of the aristocracy from the late seventeenth and early eighteenth centuries onwards.[28] But from the late eighteenth century there was a significant reworking of established ideas.

Clergy were in the vanguard in formulating rules of male and female behaviour. But in addition to clerical writing and preaching, there were lay writers on domesticity, often religiously inspired, who played a vital part in establishing the social codes which informed middle-class propriety for many generations. Some of these writers came to be household names, as in the case of William Cowper or Hannah More. Others were less well known, sometimes with local rather than national reputations, often enthused by the better known prophets of domesticity. In their works, in the view of the world they propounded, these domestic ideologues contributed to a set of beliefs as to the proper and different place of men and women. These beliefs played a part in the shaping of social institutions and practices, and had effects on material reality. Their ideas were, however, contested. Discourses on manliness and femininity were not closed; reading and writing could become dangerous ground, for women particularly.

Writers were themselves trying to make sense of their own changing world and came from a wide spectrum. Mary Wollstonecraft's problems about employment underpinned her fears in *A Vindication* as to the marginalization of women from economic production. Her eloquent plea on behalf of her sex was to have ripples for generations.[29] James Luckcock was attracted by new ideals of domesticity and became a minor writer in this field himself. He made choices about his life, the organization of his business, the relation between his home and his work, which were informed by his beliefs. His domestic ideology had real effects on his behaviour and the lives of his family, while in his writings he encouraged others to interpret changes according to his lights.[30]

Reading had an important place in middle-class life by the end of the eighteenth century. 'General literature now pervades the nation through all its ranks', Dr Johnson had remarked, every house was 'supplied with a closet of knowledge'.[31] A declining interest in literature after the Restoration was reversed and the now predominantly middle-class reading public expanded in the early eighteenth century. In towns particularly, the growing ranks of modest shopkeepers, traders, and clerical employees were brought into the orbit of middle-class culture previously the preserve of the wealthy minority.

These were the people who were sensitive to the injunction of divines such as Isaac Watts that 'lost and wasted time' would have 'painful and dismal consequences' and that it was more fruitful to pass their leisure hours in reading and discussion. Protestantism had always been a 'book religion', laying emphasis on the importance of private reading and thought. The greatest single category of books published in the eighteenth century were religious works, but many readers began with religious reading and passed on to wider interests. The success of the *Gentleman's Magazine* and *The Spectator*, catering for the middle class and providing 'practical information about domestic life and a combination of improvement with entertainment', bore witness to the increased interest in a secular literature, as did the expansion in the newspaper and the novel.[32] Improvements in education also played a part, and the Dissenting academics encouraged the reading habit, producing a significant element of the audience 'soberly concerned for private morality and an improved society'.[33] The need for information and guidance in the increasingly complex everyday world encouraged advice manuals covering all aspects of business and private life. In short, any claim to participate in the 'polite world' depended in part on a capacity to read, think and speak correctly.[34]

As early as the 1730s, Birmingham had seven booksellers and by the 1740s the first of its local newspapers, *Aris's Birmingham Gazette*. The period between 1760–74 saw a rapid growth in local newspapers and magazines, and the nine printers in the town enjoyed a booming business. The town was well served with libraries, both the more specialist private subscription variety such as the Birmingham Library established in 1779 and reorganized by Joseph Priestley, which contained an impressive number of serious theological and scientific works, and the commercial libraries which numbered nine in 1800.[35] Lucas's Circulating Library, advertising in the *Gazette* in 1790, claimed a stock of 2353 books, ranging from romance and novels through history and travel to art and science. All this was available in the town's prime shopping street for only 12 shillings per quarter.[36] Several of the libraries were well supplied with political literature and John Lowe's catalogue of 1796 lists Wollstonecraft's response to Burke as well as the *Vindication of the Rights of Woman*.[37]

The eastern counties shared in this widening culture of the book. Colchester Castle Library was established by the mid eighteenth century with thirty or so members paying 2 guineas membership fee, enjoying free admission and the right to order books. In 1794, ten of the thirty members were clergy, underlining their importance in the transmission of knowledge, four were bankers and membership included at least one grocer, one apothecary, one clockmaker and one captain. Ipswich had a bookshop that served as meeting place for the group of friends around the local poet Bernard

Barton. Even a village such as Thaxted had its book society, established in 1805, its members a handful of farmers and the free church minister who met six times a year 'on or before full moon' to exchange books bought from London. Their topics had begun as religious but by the 1830s their diet was less restricted.[38]

The evidence of the availability and importance of books is matched by the weight given to reading and to favourite authors in local memoirs, diaries and letters. The provincial audience was increasingly literate, more politically aware and more open to works dealing with 'oppositional themes' of all kinds. The heady political engagement of some sections of the middle class, well represented in a place such as Birmingham, was offset by another grouping, oriented around the country interest, uneasy about both London's court circles and the presence of manufacturing towns.[39] The celebration of nature by poets such as James Thomson with his immensely popular *The Seasons* (1730) (the favourite reading of Birmingham's Dr Withering on walks during his courtship) was reinfused with Evangelical ardour, particularly in the works of William Cowper.[40]

Cowper is easily the most quoted writer in the local records from both areas, mentioned specifically by twenty-three people and usually occupying a place of honour. Exemplifying the concern with individual salvation combined with the celebration of the domestic setting, Cowper's best-known poetry reflected on the calm minutiae of everyday life in the home, the garden, the fields and woods. Like the little anonymous verse copied in a 17-year-old Essex farmer's daughter's commonplace book, Cowper's central themes were the humility, comfort and peace to be found in the whitewashed cottage.[41] For generations of serious Christians born in the 1780s and 1790s, Cowper became the emblem of all their hopes and fears. Arthur Young, his near contemporary from Suffolk and fellow adult convert, commented that 'Cowper is invaluable to a country gentleman that would enjoy his residence without the world's assistance'.[42] But the families of bankers, shopkeepers, manufacturers, farmers, tanners, brewers, millers and clergymen also found succour and inspiration in Cowper, whether their politics were radical or conservative. With him, Quakers, Independents, Unitarians, Baptists and Anglicans all found food for thought. He was reputed to be Jane Austen's favourite author and Marianne Dashwood was 'animated by Cowper'.[43]

'God made the country, man the town', perhaps Cowper's best-known maxim inspired such different people as the Evangelical conservative Maria Marsh with a gentry background and the radical minded Birmingham greenhouse manufacturer Thomas Clark Junior. Maria Marsh, having moved from the bustling centre of Colchester to a home in leafy Edgbaston a little distant from her husband's town church, was moved to quote Cowper:

> the calm retreat, the silent shade
> With prayer and praise agree
> And seem by Thy sweet bounty made
> For those who follow Thee.[44]

Thomas Clark, whose Birmingham business had benefited much from

Cowper's recommendation of the greenhouse ('Who loves a garden loves a greenhouse too'), retired to the country having made a comfortable income, leaving 'Rose Villa, Edgbaston' for the calm of Surrey. There he wrote his poem 'Town and Country':

'*God* made the country, *man* the town'
So has the poet Cowper sung,
And none the sentiment disown
Who can distinguish right from wrong.[45]

Jane Taylor, mortally ill, made a pilgrimage from Ongar, Essex to Cowper's garden in Olney in 1822, a visit which inspired one of her last poems.[46] The Quaker bank clerk in Suffolk, Bernard Barton, dubbed 'the poet of domesticity', wrote several imitations including 'On some Illustrations of Cowper's "Rural Walks" '.[47] Cowper's *Olney Hymns*, co-authored with the Evangelical cleric John Newton, and his poems, letters and essays were given as gifts, bought with precious savings and appeared in many local library collections. His couplets dot the pages of commonplace books and diaries. His most famous poem *The Task* was a favourite for reading aloud, as in the Birmingham banking family of Galton, in 1788.[48] In celebrating domesticity, Cowper crossed political, religious and economic divisions and established himself as the most beloved writer of the period.[49]

Cowper seems to have inspired more devotion than his female counterpart Hannah More, but her books of instruction were seen as excellent gifts for young women, as to the daughter of a Birmingham manufacturer, and her only novel *Coelebs* was very widely read and was, indeed, 'the book of the day' in Colchester two years after it appeared in 1809.[50] She remained the favoured author of such influential figures as Birmingham's John Angell James.[51] More specifically religious works continued to be popular. *Pilgrim's Progress* remained a stand-by, and the early eighteenth-century meditations on mortality, Edward Young's *Night Thoughts* appealed to more serious Christians. Ann and Jane Taylor's poetry for adults and children was enjoyed by many including the Quaker Sturges in Birmingham whose radical politics were seriously at odds with the sisters' social conservatism.[52] Another poet frequently quoted or referred to was Felicia Hemans, known as 'the poetess of domesticity' and a personal acquaintance of her male analogue, Suffolk's Bernard Barton.[53]

The desire for liberty from the patronage of the powerful and the aristocratic, fuelled by religious belief, was a strong impulse for large sections of the middle class. This made Mrs Barbauld popular particularly in the 1790s and 1800s and turned Scott into a great favourite for the later generations, except for the ultra religious who would not read novels. James Watt was a great devotee of Scott's and the Galton family passed *Rob Roy* from one to another as soon as it came out, while the *Waverley* novels were consumed by those friends of Bentham, the Hill brothers, keeping their progressive school in Edgbaston.[54] 'How great an obligation do we owe to Sir Walter Scott', wrote a Galton daughter, for raising the tone of light literature, and infusing into it, not only much instruction and information, but noble and elevated sentiments, and a tone of feeling honourable, manly, highly moral, and to a certain degree Christian.[55]

Doubts as to the 'certain degree' of Christianity did not, however, prevent the unlikely figure of Byron from being the second most popular author among the local readers; a powerful reminder of the ways in which fiction might open up dangers which could not easily be resolved, for reading could signify resistance as well as marking acceptance. The Castle Book Club in Colchester carried his works, and even the Thaxted Book Society read his *Life* in the 1830s.[56] His publications were received with emotional enthusiasm not only by those with radical sentiments, such as the daughter of a Birmingham manufacturer who married into the Hill family, but by others for whom his appeal is somewhat more unexpected.[57] Samuel Newton, the powerful Independent minister of Witham Congregational chapel confessed to having picked up Byron's *Hebrew Melodies*, 'I can never again speak of *all* Byron's poetry as bad in its tone.'[58] Jane Ransome Biddell, reader of Hannah More and writer of poetry full of flower images and pious aspirations, with themes centring around home, friendship and other domestic subjects, was such an admirer of Byron that she and her farmer husband named one of their sons 'Manfred' to honour the Byronic hero. Nor did she and others like her seem to be unduly worried by the disclosures of Byron's outrageous social and sexual behaviour. Jane Biddell's poem, 'After Reading Childe Harold', appeared the year after its publication and the first verse of her 'To the death of Lord Byron' expresses something of his appeal:

> Well might she (England) mourn, for he had led
> Her youth the tyrant's yoke to spurn
> And bade on Freedom's altars spread
> The fire that hailed her glad return.[59]

An Essex Quaker tanner's wife compared her adored husband to Byron in looks and temperament, despite their sober domesticated lifestyle with nine children, while Mary Wright Sewell, daughter of a strict Quaker farmer, read Scott, Southey and Byron with delight.[60]

The son of a Quaker shopkeeper who was later apprenticed to a chemist exemplifies the reading patterns of these sections of the middle class. Each chapter of his memoir was headed by a quotation, many of them from Cowper. He saved his first wages to buy the seventeenth-century Puritan Dodderidge's *Family Expositor*. His aunt gave him Cowper's letters and poems on a birthday and when his apprenticeship was finished his mother celebrated by giving him Thomas Clarkson's *Life of Penn*. He regularly read Scott and Burns in addition to religious works. He joined with other apprentices for walking tours in the Welsh hills and celebrated the sunsets. He gave his young fiancée James Thomson's *The Seasons* and Hannah More's *Practical Piety*. But his favourite was Byron and he subscribed to a reading room so that he might 'obtain an early sight of Byron's poems on issue from the press'.[61] By 1833, a Colchester headmaster's collection of 'poetic gems' for young persons of both sexes included the roll call of middle-class taste: Cowper, Hemans, Barbauld, Nathaniel Cotton, Scott, Barton, the Taylor sisters and Byron.[62]

Progressive middle-class circles turned to the less romantic and more practical world of Miss Edgeworth with her sound common sense and clear grasp of the practicalities of the everyday world. But this was often combined with an attraction to the fanciful as in the case of the Galtons and the Hills, both families addicted to Edgeworth and Scott. A daughter of the banking Galtons, writing to her young brother who was away at school and frequently in trouble with his parents about money, recommended Miss Edgeworth's *Out of Debt out of Danger*.[63] Frederick Hill was delighted when his fiancée's small book for parents received the accolade of the great Miss Edgeworth's approval.[64] For the later generations, Harriet Martineau came to represent similar values. Like the other major writers she too had her local devotees, influenced by her ideas and copying her style.[65]

It is the unorthodox combination of authors favoured by these middle-class men and women that gives access to the contradictory elements in their system of values. The Quaker, Bernard Barton's library included much Wordsworth, Dodderidge, Scott, Coleridge, Hannah More, Keeble and three volumes of Byron in addition to various political and literary journals.[66] His circle of friends embraced the anti-slavery advocate Thomas Clarkson living nearby, the Essex artist John Constable and local Anglican clergymen. He was a close friend of Edward Fitzgerald and corresponded with Charles Lamb, Byron, Southey and Felicia Hemans.[67] His friend and neighbour, Clarkson's agent, the wealthy farmer Arthur Biddell and his wife Jane Ransome Biddell, listed Shakespeare, books of travel and history and, interestingly, Mary Wollstonecraft, in their library in addition to the inevitable Cowper, More and Byron.[68] Another in Barton's Suffolk circle, Charles Tayler, the Evangelical curate of Hadleigh, started his impeccably moral collection of tales for reading aloud in the family circle, with a quotation from 'Childe Harold' while in one story the good older sister reads aloud *The Task* to the naughty younger sister. Tayler suggested a list of reading for girls, which was first to be vetted by papa. This included Thomson's *The Seasons*, Cowper, Young's *Night Thoughts*, George Crabbe and *The Spectator*.[69]

Part of Byron's great appeal was the passionate nature of his poetry. The emotion which poured into conversionist faith was not so far removed from the intensity of romantic sensibility; both focused on the individual and the theme of liberty. Yet there was a vital tension between the two modes. Bernard Barton, who was a clerk in Alexander's Woodbridge bank all his life, in his 'From a Poem addressed to Shelley' regretted the lack of that most important ingredient, religious belief, without which the poet's 'pure bright spirit' lost its 'ethereal ray' and he pleads: 'Ere it shall prove too late, thy steps retrace.' The poet's Muse, even in the heights to which she rises, can never be safe as in Christianity which finds 'the immortal river of life in the deep valley of humility'.[70]

Beauties of language and romantic associations could be dangerous without the countervailing strength of religion with its domestic connotations. Such tensions could be particularly poignant for women. Madame de Stael's passionate tale *Corinne* had an enormous impact on successive generations of women. Celebrating as it did the woman of genius who enjoyed public triumph in the intellectual and artistic freedom of Italy, it stood as a symbol of woman's creative potential. Corinne falls in love with an Englishman, Oswald, who represented all the virtues of home but she renounced her love, let him eventually marry a quiet and modest wife and herself progressed through Italy in public splendour, dancing, speaking, acting, improvising, making music, painting, singing. Corinne was 'the fantasy of the performing heroine', the female Childe Harold.[71] The theme of recognition through art was seductively powerful for successive generations of literary women in England, since for them public success was always a problematic issue. The celebration of the free culture of Corinne's southern Europe had an irresistible pull even for the earnest inhabitants of English provincial homes. In her poem 'Corinne at the Capital', the Anglican, Felicia Hemans (who wrote of Corinne's indescribable power over her), spends five verses extolling the rapturous reception of Corinne in Rome and the beauty of her voice, her appearance, her musical ability. But for Hemans, this extraordinary woman is flawed because she scorns the attractions of home:

> Radiant daughter of the sun! Now thy living wreath is won
> Crown'd of Rome: – O art thou not
> Happy in that glorious lot?
> Happier, happier far than thou,
> With the laurel of thy brow,
> She that makes the humblest hearth
> Lovely but to one on earth![72]

Amelia Moilliet, wife of a prosperous Anglican Birmingham banker and daughter of the well-known chemist James Keir, had a life constructed around her domestic responsibilities, her husband, her children and her home. Brought up to distrust her feelings and always follow the path of duty, she was inspired by her reading of de Stael and particularly admired the stimulus she gave to imagination, a faculty little encouraged in her rationalist world.[73] For her, too, de Stael offered something different, something forbidden. The Independent, Jane Taylor was also subject to the 'magic' of *Corinne*'s pages and wrote that she felt Mme de Stael as 'a friend'. Yet for Taylor, too, the absence of religious feeling separated her world from that of de Stael and her poem on Corinne ends:

> Yes, too much I've felt her talent's magic touch.
> Return my soul, to that retreat
> From sin and woe – Thy Saviour's feet!
> There learn an art she never knew
> All to resign that He denies:–
> To Him in meek submission bend;
> Own Him an all sufficient friend;
> Here, and in holy worlds above,
> My portion – and my only love![74]

For these three women reading was an important experience to which they responded in writing, albeit in different ways. Hemans and Taylor both wrote poems which were published, Amelia Moilliet expressed her feelings in her private journal. They symbolize the importance of reading and writing within provincial middle-class life. Reading was not only a form of instruction, self-discovery and self-definition, it was also a source of profound pleasure, both individually and collectively, but sometimes a source of real confusion. Discussion groups, based on reading, were a common feature of middle-class life; both discussion and reading frequently took place within the family circle. Writing, whether in journals, diaries, letters, memoirs, poetry or prose, was a favoured occupation for large numbers of women and men, a few of whom were to make a living from it, but the vast majority of whom wrote for their own pleasure and edification and that of their relatives and friends.

Writing and publishing were an important and expanding sector of the economy and a division of labour frequently operated within a family business, utilizing the appropriate skills of both male and female members. The young William Hutton, disliking his work as a stockinger, began to bind books, then started to sell them, then to manufacture paper. He himself wrote a famous *History of Birmingham*, his male heirs took over the commercial aspects of the business while his daughter Catherine wrote several novels and was a prolific letter writer.[75] The well-known Birmingham preacher George Dawson, two generations later, relied on his wife to edit and prepare for publication his prayers and sermons while her sister wrote many successful works for children.[76] Such writers and such publications were at the heart of middle-class culture for there was both a national and a local 'cultural marketplace'.[77] Popular writers formed the subject of conversation and letters between people, the imaginative food for thought of individuals. Their works and ideas were discussed, their lives a source of fascination, their homes and gardens places to visit and revere.[78] Such authors answered existing needs from an expanding literate public seeking not only diversion but instruction. They were instrumental in constructing an audience, and in their responses to the changing world they themselves inhabited were defining what came to be understood as specifically middle-class beliefs and practices.

William Cowper and Hannah More

William Cowper (1731–1800) was the most popular named author for our middle-class sample in Birmingham and East Anglia. The eldest son of a gentleman cleric, Cowper received a small inheritance and entered the law, but suffered from mental breakdown and never completed the training. For the rest of his life he lived mainly on the kindness of friends and relatives. For many years Cowper lodged with Mrs Unwin, an enthusiastic Evangelical and follower of John Newton, a leading Evangelical preacher. The household followed Newton to Olney, a Buckinghamshire village. Cowper was always dependent on others – emotionally, intellectually, physically and financially. Socially conservative, his preoccupations intersected with those of the middling ranks and his championship of a quiet and serious

Plate 12 W. Williams, 'Conversation Piece before a house in Monument Lane, Edgbaston', c. 1780. Note the visual representation of the domestic ideal: the rural aspect despite proximity to the town and other buildings, the circular drive, gate and fence, the presence of servants going about their tasks and the informal intimacy of the family group

way of life with religious experience attracted many adherents. *The Task*, his most popular work, was published in 1785 when he was in late middle life. He took no part in London literary life and he has been described as an 'extramundane', living on the sidelines, watching the world, recommending a different kind of lifestyle from that enjoyed by most of his readers,[79] maintaining the tradition of the independent 'disinterested gentleman'.[80]

Cowper offered a serious critique of many aspects of aristocratic and gentry life and, like many Evangelicals, sought a regeneration of the social and political world. Converted in adulthood, his religious faith gave meaning to his life and he saw spiritual salvation as man's 'noblest claim':

> to feed upon immortal truth,
> To walk with God, to be divinely free,
> To soar, and to anticipate the skies. . . .[81]

At the Day of Judgement, when the trumpet sounded, 'arrogant distinctions' would fall and only conscience and conduct would be the arbitrators of man's fate.[82] Cowper's religious message was one which stressed the importance of inner commitment rather than public 'enthusiasm'. Private prayer and a quiet home-centred life were seen as the essential elements. The most important task in life was the task of learning to walk with God; the most important freedom, the freedom to recognize God's works.

This stress on individual liberty as residing in religious belief was vital for it provided an alternative source of recognition and legitimation to the traditional association of honour with rank. Real honour, Cowper argued, rested with religious faith, not with land or wealth. Blended with this notion of liberty and independence was his attachment to Whig values and belief in limited kingship, even reform of the franchise. But kings could not grant 'liberty of heart' for that was derived from Heaven, 'bought with His blood, who gave it to mankind'. Cowper's sympathy with nonconformists seems to have been limited but he did believe in liberty of conscience and his famous poem 'The Negro's Complaint' insisted that even slaves were free in thought; minds were never to be sold.[83]

Cowper strongly believed that the country provided a better location for the religious life than the town ever could. Critical of the court and its manners, particularly of the circles associated with the Prince Regent, he helped to define a form of gentility which had religion in a rural setting at its heart. Moving away from the association of manliness with military prowess and public triumph, Cowper argued for a more modest male demeanour, valuing reflection, peace, the protection of the weak and of animals (he particularly hated hunting, that symbolic enactment of man's power over the animal world), for even the meanest creature was made by God and had a right to live. His notion of patriotism was to live in such a way that his 'virtues are more felt than seen', virtues which aided the helpless and used influence to 'soothe the sorrow'.[84] Critics of Cowper rejected these views as dangerously effeminate and noted with distaste that Cowper took up unmanly pastimes. He walked everywhere rather than rode, liked to garden, to write letters and poems, to drink tea and sit chatting to women. Cowper, Hazlitt thought, 'shrinks from and repels common and hearty sympathy'.[85]

If manliness did not depend on rank or prowess, nor did it depend on making money. The real man for Cowper was the one who could enjoy 'leisure and silence', 'and a mind released from anxious thoughts how wealth may be increased'. In Cowper's world there was certainly no carte blanche for middle-class men to pursue their untrammelled self-interest. It was not business which for him was the serious pursuit in life, rather it was the religious quest. 'The statesman, lawyer, merchant, man of trade', he believed,

> Pants for the refuge of some rural shade,
> Where all his long anxieties forgot,
> Amid the charms of a sequester'd spot.

Cowper recommended rural retirement, not to be idle, for

> Absence of occupation is not rest,
> A mind quite vacant is a mind distressed.[86]

But the mind should be employed with real duties, not those appertaining to making money. Life, he believed, was not for one's own pleasure but should be treated as an 'entrusted talent' and men would be answerable to

God. This did not mean that religion denied pleasure, far from it. Studying, gardening, reading, taking walks, watching Nature, enjoying friendship, all these were 'unnumber'd pleasures harmlessly pursued'. But man was

> form'd for God alone,
> For Heaven's high purposes and not his own.

Only if man recognized and acted upon this could he

> Improve the remnant of his wasted span,
> And, having lived a trifler, die a man.[87]

Cowper's critique of the free play of the market, factories built with blood, trade conducted with the sword, men combined in associations for self-interest, is connected to his strong paternalist inclinations. For him individual liberty of conscience was unproblematically associated with a belief in social hierarchy. For many of those who loved his poetry, however, this chain was broken and the claim for independence in religion indissolubly connected to the claim for political rights. For Cowper, however, born as he was in 1731, defects in the social order were not due to inequality but a failure of the governing classes to act responsibly. The decline of paternalism combined with the growth of a cash economy was at the root of most evils for Cowper. Landed estates were turning into landscapes to be sold, and 'improved' to the detriment of landlord and tenant.[88] The greed of the opulent, displayed in London and fashionable watering places, was contaminating all classes. Cowper had little sympathy for the poor; they should do their work and know their place, but it was up to their betters to properly maintain the social bonds. The country still provided a more hopeful environment for 'the task', the work of living a truly religious life. An Ipswich draper on his retirement from business, quoted Cowper's lines on the country which provided 'blest seclusion from a jarring world. . . . Domestic life in rural pleasures pass'd'.[89]

In one of the most evocative passages of *The Task*, Cowper summoned up the pleasures of the winter evening in the countryside. The post arrived, the newspaper was read and the family settled down for their pastimes:

> Now stir the fire, and close the shutters fast,
> Let fall the curtains, wheel the sofa round,
> And while the bubbling and loud hissing urn
> Throws up a steamy column, and the cups
> That cheer but not inebriate, wait on each,
> So let us welcome peaceful evening in.

The cosy fire, the close fitting shutters keeping out not only wind and rain but the social disorder of the 1780s and 1790s (of which there was a good deal around Olney), the convivial cups of tea, the comfy sofa (which was the original subject of the entire poem), the 'social converse' and the family group were all celebrated. 'I crown thee king of intimate delights/Fireside enjoyments, homeborn happiness.' 'The needle plies its busy task' while someone read aloud, then there was supper and more talk, 'cards were superfluous here'. These were the pleasures of domestic life.[90] But Cowper's love of the domestic was not confined to the interior. It stretched to the garden, where 'Nature in her cultivated trim' could be 'dress'd to his taste'.[91]

Cowper was by no means the first to sing in praise of the fireside. After his first breakdown he had been taken to an asylum in St Albans run by the Evangelical Dr Nathaniel Cotton, author of *Visions in Verse for Entertainment of Young Minds* (1751). One of Cotton's most popular poems, quoted in an early nineteenth-century Suffolk commonplace book, was his evocation of 'The Fireside'. Cotton wrote of the real happiness that could be found in the home as compared with the 'gay world' and its gaudy and superficial pleasures. Life's journey could best be met through marriage, which,

> rightly understood
> Gives to the tender and the good
> A paradise below.

Drawing on established Puritan ideas he stressed the joys and responsibilities of child-rearing, the insignificance of material goods as compared with real friendship and knowledge of God. The family circle was seen as the source of comfort, the home and the fireside were the location and symbol of that warmth. Cotton's book was republished in 1791, the decade when Cowper and More were both publishing; praise of domesticity was in vogue and *Visions* found a ready audience.[92]

Cowper came from the gentry and yet became immensely popular with the middle classes; he did not earn his own living yet spoke for those who did; he never married and had no children yet was the pre-eminent poet of home and domesticity. His marginality, living in the depths of the country, always subject to mental instability, not engaged with active business pursuits or with the sporting life of those around him, made possible the representation of a different, calmer, gentler, purer world in his poetry. His religious commitment was deep but in his writing he softened and made more accessible an Evangelicalism that had frightened some by its enthusiasm, that was too raw and too linked to fears of social disorder, Methodist rabble.

Cowper validated a manliness centred on a quiet domestic rural life rather than the frenetic and anxiety ridden world of town and commerce. For many men, active as entrepreneurs in that market, this would always be a dream, with little possibility of realization but a dream which offered some resolutions to the tensions and contradictions they daily faced. Their suburban garden might be the closest they would ever get to the world of *The Task*. Others, however, did follow Cowper. Having established a 'modest competency' they were only too ready to retire from active business and lead a quieter life of contemplation. The 'entrepreneurial ideal' was after all only one of the available visions of manhood in provincial middle-class society.[93] Cowper had little to say about femininity in itself and indeed his men and women enjoyed many of the same pastimes, but his special appeal to women lay in his form of Evangelicalism which could remain in the private sphere, which indeed defined and elevated the private sphere and asserted that the homely duties and private prayers of domestic life provided the best way to be close to God. Since the 'noblest claim' was 'to walk with God', women could indeed aspire to achieve that dignity.

Hannah More (1745–1833), the second key writer for the provincial public on domesticity, came from a similar background to Cowper. Born into the gentry, her father lost his inheritance and she and her four sisters set up a successful school in Bristol in 1757. For a time More became a successful playwright, friend of Garrick and closely involved with London intellectual life. During the 1780s, however, she was increasingly influenced by Evangelicalism and, like Wilberforce, became a convert. She began to write religious and moral works starting with a successful essay in 1788, *Thoughts on the Importance of the Manners of the Great to General Society*. In the 1790s her conservatism led her to become heavily involved in the struggle to combat Paine and Radicalism. Her Cheap Repository Tracts, written in simple language for the poor, together with her pioneering work in establishing Sunday schools (to the great disapproval of many more staid Anglicans) were widely heralded as having made a vital contribution to the stabilizing of English society in the difficult years after the French Revolution. In her later years she went out of fashion, her religion was seen as too inflexible, her literature too didactic, but from the late 1780s to the early 1830s she was an extremely popular author, widely known and quoted.[94]

In 1807 More anonymously published her only novel, *Coelebs in search of a wife, comprehending observations of domestic habits and manners, religion and morals*. It was an immediate success. Eleven editions were run off in nine months, thirty in the lifetime of More, and 21,000 copies sold.[95] Even abroad a young Englishwoman, married to an officer and resident for several years in India, was enchanted when she read it. Writing to her mother, the wife of an Anglican clergyman with Evangelical sympathies, she enthused,

I have this morning finished reading a book entitled Coelebs in search of a wife, I am more pleased with it than I can possibly describe. . . .

'There is scarcely a page in that book but is an echo of your sentiments', she continued, 'and in saying that I think I pay both yourself (my dearest Mother) and the author the highest compliment.'[96] This young woman's stress on the extent to which *Coelebs* echoed already existing sentiments focuses attention on the way in which the novel brought together existing ideas in a widely available form. More had already written a series of texts on female education, the duties of the upper classes and the proper place of religion in everyday life. She deliberately wrote *Coelebs* to appeal to 'the middle regions of the social landscape . . . the subscribers of the circulating libraries'.[97] *Coelebs* was written as a novel, that pre-eminently middle-class form, with all the characteristics of formal realism. It was located in specific places and at specific times. It concerned real people with characters of their own, even if many of them were close to idealized representations of virtues and vices. More, despite her worries about the dangerous tendencies of the novel form, had been able to take on board the lessons she had learnt from her popular pamphlet writing in the 1790s to reach an audience her earlier didactic writing could never have done.[98]

Coelebs represents the pulling together of More's ideas about the proper relations of men and women in the middle and upper classes, written as a fictional narrative. By the time it was published the fierce struggles of the 1790s were over. Mary Wollstonecraft was dead, the Napoleonic empire was established, middle-class radicals were silent and Jacobin influence was at a low ebb. The combination of Pitt's repression, the French wars and the campaigns to reform manners and morals had achieved some successes. Hannah More could look back on more than twenty years of polemical propagandizing with some equanimity.

Coelebs is the story of a young man with a comfortable landed income whose beloved parents both die. Their belief in domestic happiness leads him to set out in search of a wife. The quest for love has always been a favourite literary topic and *Coelebs* was only one of the versions produced in the early 1800s. Its hero, a serious Christian, was markedly different from the heroes of two of the other most popular writers of this period, Walter Scott and Lord Byron. However, its heroine, beautiful, modest and domestic, was of a type not dissimilar to the heroines of Scott, and later Byron.[99] *Coelebs* was a novel that was intended to instruct, not simply entertain, and its preface, written supposedly by Coelebs himself, refuting love as great passion and trial, argued for love as commanded by reason and religion. More was inspired in her view of sexual difference as well as the place of religion in daily life by *Paradise Lost*. Her reading of Milton, however, was a particular one. Her Garden of Eden had no politics and no sexuality. Her Eve, Lucilla, was obedient and passive, satisfied with influence and with the capacity to inspire male virtues.

> To study household good,
> And good works in her husband to promote. . . .[100]

In the 1780s and 1790s, Evangelicals had argued that the reform of manners and morals must start with the upper classes. The setting for More's novel is provided by comfortable landed society, a world apparently timeless, stable and decidedly pre-industrial – there are no chimneys, no factories, no towns outside London, no middle class and no urban artisans. It is peopled by the gentry and the labouring poor and like so much literature of this kind it idealized those relations as providing an organic community. This organic community was linked to a belief in the *natural* hierarchical social order. Hierarchy, paternalism and dependence were the necessary elements for the stability of the social system; 'mutual affection, mutual benefit and mutual obligation' were the cement which secured the union of the family as well as the state.[101]

The linking of dependence in the family to dependence in the state draws on long traditions of conservative thinking.[102] More herself was a friend of Burke and has been described as effecting with her *Village Politics* for the lower orders what Burke's *Reflections* did for the higher.[103] The landed gentleman was the head of his family, whose wife and children should obediently follow his judgement, whose faithful servants and labourers would value the kindness and consideration of their master. Indeed it was the dereliction of duty in the higher echelons of society which represented for the Evangelicals one of the central problems facing England at the end of the eighteenth century. But More's belief in the potential, wisdom and power of the upper classes was tempered with criticism. Indeed, the favoured characters in *Coelebs* are not the titled, they are the simple gentlemen who are able to act as exempla to their superiors in rank. This implicit critique of the aristocracy must have played some part in making More, like Cowper, so popular among sections of the middle classes.

After the death of his beloved parents, Coelebs visits London. The Metropolis shocks him with its lack of 'real' Christianity, which for the Evangelical was the most vital aspect of religion. For More, as for Milton, the 'prime wisdom' was to be in touch with and in control of everyday behaviour. The spiritual emptiness of London life is reflected for Coelebs in the flighty and ill-educated characters of the young ladies he meets, none of whom he sees as suitable partners. He decides to leave London and go to his father's friends in the country. At 'The Grove' Coelebs finds an establishment which he can admire with all his heart. Mr Stanley, the simple country gentleman ably supported by his wife, conducts a truly religious household.

More believed that men and women occupied separate spheres by nature as well as custom and propriety. Men were naturally formed for 'the more public exhibitions on the great theatre of human life'.[104] Women, by contrast, were best suited to the smaller scale of the domestic, seeing the world 'from a little elevation from her own garden' where she had an exact survey of home scenes.[105] *Coelebs* offered a guide to behaviour for both men and women from a woman of recognized social and religious position. In following the precepts of the novel, no member of the middle class need fear that they would offend gentility. In the portraits of Mr Stanley and Coelebs himself More offered exempla of true manliness. Mr Stanley's most marked feature, noted by all but never in a sneering way, is his real religion, his true piety. 'The Grove' is presented as a happy, cheerful environment, the domestic circle is charming and entertaining, even Sundays are full of a quiet Christian cheer. Seriousness can exist without severity, cheerfulness without levity. Mr Stanley is not of the old school of eighteenth-century gentry living for hunting, shooting, fishing and drunken convivial dinners. He is a landlord with a powerful moral purpose, concerned to improve his property, with the interests of his tenants at heart. In More's characterization there is none of the dissociation between men and emotional sensibilities which later takes place. Coelebs, too, is a feeling man, but subject to reason. The more he discovers how appropriate Mr Stanley's daughter, Lucilla, would be as a wife, the more he feels, for he is also emotional, quite capable of crying when moved, as when memories of his beloved father are aroused. But those characteristics are seen as manly, just as it is manly to be careful and considerate, to be authoritative without aggression, to be thoughtful and to reason with others. Above all it is manly to enjoy domestic life and to willingly take responsibility for the education of both sons and daughters. The neglect of wife and children is to be regretted, the kind of manliness associated with sexual indulgence, with drink and with dissipation is to be abhorred. The model for this virtue is Christ who convinced doubters through faith.

Women also need a rule of life that will facilitate salvation, but their sphere in *Coelebs* is severely circumscribed. Gisborne, another influential Evangelical author, had argued according to Pauline doctrine, that the duties of women were to care for their relatives, to improve their menfolk and to bring up their children on a Christian path.[106] Mrs Stanley's daughters were all educated with the intention of making them good wives and mothers. More, however, was in favour of girls' education provided it had a moral purpose. Coelebs was delighted to discover that Lucilla had learnt Latin with her father, for a man of taste would otherwise have to lower himself in his wife's company.[107] For Coelebs, the point of a woman's education was that she should be a better companion for a man, enhancing the domestic environment and making it more appealing than 'Society' outside. Lucilla is quite able to listen intelligently to serious discussions. Whereas in London young ladies resorted to whispers and giggles, she always listens respectfully to what the men have to say, for in the many pages of discussion on moral and religious issues in the novel the women never speak.

Despite her emphasis on the natural qualities of femininity, More was also insistent that women must learn to be feminine. There is an underlying tension in her writing between what she senses women are and what they ought to be. This is little emphasized in *Coelebs* where More makes her female characters into stereotypical ideals, but in her prescriptive writing she is more aware of the tensions within femininity. Seventeenth- and early eighteenth-century writing on women had stressed rampant and voracious female sexuality, the insatiable desires of womanhood. This view was suppressed, particularly by Evangelicalism; the late eighteenth-century view was that women were not sexually active in themselves, their sexual feelings would only be evoked through love in marriage. Women should express their sexuality only as promise; consequently the emphatic stress on modesty as *the* most valued female characteristic.[108] Men, argued More, preferred their wives to be quiet, virtuous and meek rather than showy and brilliant.[109] Wives who would adopt the modest self, who could accept that their fulfilment must be won through service to others, would find their compensation in the exercise of moral influence. Power was for men, influence for women. Through their example in life women could hope to make those around them, in their family circles, better people. It was *moral influence* which was to allow a reassertion of self for women.

A major influence for More, as for most Evangelicals, was the preaching and teaching of St Paul. St Paul, argued More, bore witness from actual events; his injunctions derived from truth absolute.[110] More derived great strength from this view. She needed this conviction in refuting two alternative views of femininity present in the 1790s. The first was part of society life and the gay world, which she castigated as empty, tawdry and selfish. The second was radical critiques of established forms of femininity, particularly from Mary Wollstonecraft. More argued that neither properly expressed the natural elements of true womanhood. The Society women, met by Coelebs in the Metropolis, are presented as figures of display, self-seeking and hypocritical, concerned only with appearances, finding no ultimate happiness.

The Wollstonecraftian figure in *Coelebs* is Miss Sparkes, a neighbour of the Stanleys, a single lady of 45, who has pretensions to be a scholar, a huntress, a politician, and a farrier, essentially unfeminine characteristics. She is witty, bold, fond of the marvellous and the incredible; she is sure of herself and the only woman in the book to 'speak'. She arrives at The Grove on her horse carrying a whip and wearing a cap, claiming to know all about horses, an essentially male terrain. She likes men better than women, but of course they do not like her. Above all she is contemptuous of domestic economy and her estimation of these 'plodding employments' which 'cramp the genius, degrade the intellect, depress the spirits, debase the taste, and clip the wings of imagination' provokes all the gentlemen at The Grove to a powerful defence of the central importance of domestic skills. But Miss Sparkes is not silenced. She rises to the bait and expresses her envy of the advantages which men have in the world, their access to power and glory.

The portrait of Miss Sparkes is More's refutation of the radical and feminist demands for a voice for women, for their right to be equal citizens with men, for her an absurd demand. For More the emphasis is on sexual *difference*. Women should enjoy their separate sphere rather than struggling against it, make use of their moral influence rather than trying to convert it into power. After Miss Sparkes's departure, the party discussed her refusal of gentleness and passivity, attributes, they were all agreed, which were 'peculiarly Christian, and peculiarly feminine'. Miss Sparkes, like Mary Wollstonecraft, is deviant, marginal, unfeminine.[111]

In some respects, then, More's writing is profoundly anti-feminist. In *Coelebs* not only does she firmly state that the Pauline injunction on women to be obedient is correct, but the structure of the novel itself places women in a clearly subordinate position. The irony, of course, is that the novel was written by a woman, a woman who never married, who carried considerable respect in the public world of religion and letters, ran a successful school and always maintained an independent life. Was she really so committed to the subordination of her sex? The answer to this lies in the contradictory messages which More develops. On the one hand she confined women to the sphere of the private and the domestic, on the other she argued for the central importance of women's influence in nurturing morality in an amoral world. She argued that politics was not for women but asserted that politics began at home, the only way to save the nation was to reform from the bottom up and a truly religious home provided the only sure foundation. She insisted that women were capable of reasoning provided that they were properly educated. Femininity might be natural but it required social and cultural forms of training and expression. Such ideas are by no means inherently conservative and indeed many of them were later detached from this set of theories with its conservative inflection and rearticulated to a more radical view of the potential power of a women's influence. More's argument that philanthropy was the proper calling of a lady, that the care of the poor was her profession had echoes for many years. As Ray Strachey pointed out in 1928:

Without in the least intending to do so, she [More] was marking out a new sphere for the young women of the middle classes, and their revolt against their own narrow and futile lives followed as a matter of course.[112]

We might pause at the judgement that it was all a 'matter of course', but it is as well to be sensitive to the contradictory nature of More's philosophy for it was in part this, and the space it allowed for alternative interpretations of the nature of 'influence', which gave her such powerful appeal.

Local writers on separate spheres

Writers such as Cowper and More clearly played a vital part in codifying ideologies of sexual difference. But they also inspired other writers and thinkers who never became known as widely but were nevertheless active in defining the meanings of manliness and femininity in the home and family. Provincial writers were particularly important in their attempts to interpret domesticity into patterns for daily life for ordinary middle-class people, without the resources of Cowper's and More's gentry folk. It was provincial intellectuals who turned those values stated in more abstract and utopian level in the fantasized world of *Coelebs* or *The Task*, into practicable arrangements for life. They were usually drawing directly on their experience as mothers, as fathers, as ministers of religion, as doctors or designers. They were not intellectuals in the sense of great scholars or writers with national reputations; rather the group that Gramsci would describe as 'organic intellectuals' of the middle class, those people who, by virtue of their literacy and capacity to articulate were able to make sense of experience so as to appeal to large sections of their own class.[113] In this period there were scores of provincial writers publishing pamphlets, manuals, tracts, sermons and poetry, writing in local newspapers and church magazines, in locally published books produced by subscription, in annuals and gift-books. Some became widely known, others remained relatively insignificant, but as a group they operated as intermediaries, translating the aspirations of Cowper and More into autobiographical and biographical accounts and practical advice about daily life. In their writings, domesticity shifted from an abstract utopia to practical wisdom.

One such writer was Mrs Ann Martin Taylor (see Setting the scene, p. 59). She was born 1757, and also came from a downwardly mobile sub-gentry family. Most of her married life was spent in Essex. For her, a central theme was true gentility, the view that people with limited means and many responsibilities could maintain their position in society through religion; in Cowper's phrase, their 'noblest claim' was to walk with God. Writing and publishing were the stock-in-trade of the Taylor family and in middle age she was persuaded to publish her modest thoughts about family life, parents and children. Her husband Isaac's advice book for young men which stressed regularity and steadiness in business could as well have applied to the young woman's domestic occupations as seen in the publications of his wife. Between 1814 and 1818, Mrs Ann Taylor published *Correspondence Between a Mother and her Daughter at School* (co-authored with her daughter Jane), *Maternal Solicitude For a Daughter's Best Interests*, *Practical Hints to Young Females on the Duties of a Wife, a Mother and the Mistress of a Family* and *Reciprocal Duties of Parents and Children* in addition to several didactic novels.[114] Her writing was the fruit of her own experience as a mother. Her chief mentors were Maria Edgeworth and Hannah More.

Mrs Taylor's first book was not originally intended for publication. It was probably written for her daughter, Ann, when in her teens about 1800; she wrote because she found it hard to communicate verbally. Her thoughts came, she said, out of 'that affectionate concern for youth and inexperience, which is *natural* to one, who has been long a Mother' (our emphasis).[115] The substance of all her books was, indeed, concerned with the demonstration of what should be 'natural' to a mother. Like her husband, Ann Taylor had been converted to evangelical Congregationalism, and felt concerned to present the publication of her writings in a religious light. 'As in Christ there is neither male nor female' she argued,

I shall not be charged with impropriety and indecorum should I for your encouragement in the *spiritual* warfare . . . declare that I also have obtained victories over my enemies with my sword and my bow. . . .[116]

With this unexpectedly fighting metaphor from a profoundly socially conservative elderly lady, she went on to insist that struggles in the domestic world were no less important than spiritual struggles elsewhere. Her 'natural' womanly modesty had to be conquered in Christ's name. 'Every true Christian', she argued, 'should make their home into a seminary'.[117] Like Hannah More before her, she maintained that 'to promote domestic virtue, and preserve the domestic happiness of the fireside is an effectual, as well as simple means of increasing national prosperity'. She addressed her books to a vital if less elevated grouping than More, those who were of 'sufficient eminence to render their conduct highly important to society'. Like More she had a simple view of cultural diffusion; the influence of the middle ranks ought to descend like a 'kindly shower' on those beneath them who would then unproblematically aspire to live by such examples.[118]

Taylor saw a proper marital relation as central to religious life. The point of efforts to reorder home life was religious, since the home provided both the best context for salvation and the best hope for reformed manners and morals in the world at large. It was the particular task of the married woman to make the home and fireside an attractive place, for men who had temptations abroad. The married woman, therefore, should clearly *be* at home, an understandable prescription for her since the Taylor home was also the site of the family's engraving business, but one that must have been made in the knowledge that other women were too easily seduced from their duties.

'The man who is not domestic in his habits will rarely be kind', she asserted,

but where are the charms of the fireside; where is that which should give him a taste for its pleasures, if the wife, its chief ornament is absent?[119]

Plate 13 Frontispiece to Jane Taylor's (QQ) Collected writings as editor of an evangelical youth magazine. It is probable that she or her brothers did the etching and that the farmhouse was their home in Ongar, Essex

Taylor even argued that the running of the home might be able to exert a good influence on that of the business:

Perhaps if some portion of that spirit of order, that love of regularity which she displays, were transferred to the shop or the counting-house, it might increase the comfort and secure the permanence of the establishment.[120]

Like More, Mrs Taylor believed firmly in the rule of the father as head of the household. 'There cannot, indeed, be a sight more uncouth', she declared,

than that of a man and his wife struggling for power; for where it ought to be invested, nature, reason and scripture concur to declare.[121]

Plate 14 Frontispiece to one of Ann Martin Taylor's texts on motherhood, *Practical Hints*. The romantic view of mother and child is evident

The stress on the duties of religious parents to their children is given a detailed and practical bent in Mrs Taylor's works. Both parents are seen as having awesome responsibilities, but the duties of the mother are given particular attention. Reflecting on the cultural capital in her own family, she argued that the best inheritance parents can give their children is their industrious habits and independence which can only be learnt through the persevering subjugation of the child's will. Yet at the same time she argued for a willingness to listen to children and to treat them with respect. For her as a mother, it had been the 'business and study' of her life to guide her children in the right direction. This had been her job, just as it had been the job of her husband to be an engraver and Independent minister. Ann Taylor was suggesting in the early nineteenth century the notion of professional motherhood which became more clearly articulated by the 1830s and 1840s. It was 'the grand interest and happiness and amusement of the intelligent mother' she felt, to educate her children. This meant that wives and mothers should themselves be educated. How could they fulfil such important work without proper preparation, without attention to system, without organization and regularity? Hannah More's need for rules and order became more systematized in her thinking, drawing as she also did on the enlightenment tradition of Edgeworth. ' "Let everything be done decently and in order" ', she wrote, 'is a precept that should be extended from our religious concerns to all the affairs of life'.[122]

A properly ordered household had to rely on the direction of the mistress. Taylor was fierce in her denunciation of the practice of entrusting children to servants. Like Edgeworth, she wanted childhood to be peopled not by giants and fairies and fantastical superstitions of the servant class but by reason and godliness. Consequently she believed that home education was best since it allowed parents to maintain control, but boys must be sent to school after an early training at home.

These were the views of people who knew that their values were not shared by the majority. Until such cultural patterns became more widely accepted, the ideologues of domesticity thought of themselves as Christian warriors, using what swords and bows they had at their disposal, in a society which was careless of spiritual life. Mrs Taylor's pen and ink and her connections with evangelical publishing houses were her weapons. She was at one and the same time making sense of her own experience and making it available to others. Her writing, initially for her own purposes, forced her to be self-conscious and explicit about her maternal practices, and she no doubt presented them as more consistent and coherent than they were in practice. In part she was giving the work she had done as a mother a weight and public recognition which had to be fought for. It was women like Ann Martin Taylor who were insisting on the vital tasks associated with motherhood, not men who were imposing it on them.

The contradiction noted in More between the acceptance of a narrow sphere and an assertion of the unbounded potential influence of that sphere, is in full play in Mrs Taylor. 'The foundation stone of public and private felicity should be laid in the nursery', she insisted, adding tartly that this necessitated the 'skilful hand of the intelligent Christian mother', rather than the 'mercenary services of ignorant domestics'.[123] 'In that insignificant chamber', that is the nursery, she continued, 'the future happiness and misery of the fire-side below is (if we may be allowed the expression) manufactured, which may spread from thence far and wide'.[124] Her commercial language in relation to motherhood became a commonplace in later years for being a mother was indeed a business.[125]

Mrs Taylor was also full of practical advice as to the running of a house: 'That house only is well conducted', she declared,

where there is a strict attention paid to order and regularity. To do everything in its proper time, to keep everything in its right place, and to use everything for its proper use, is the *very essence* of good management.[126]

She was firm about the importance of keeping accounts and advised purchasing an account book. Printed ones could now be obtained, with columns for every article and every day of the year and this would ensure an end to the mysteries of business. She recommended the importance of saving, particularly for large sums such as servant's wages, and the desirability of paying tradesmen's bills regularly. Order in the household meant early rising; the mistress should be up and about so that she could check on the servants, meals should always be at stated times and servants must learn to be punctual.

Mrs Taylor's manuals were written out of the experience of running a household with business attached, including apprentices and pupils, and caring for her children. Her writing, cast in the mantle of Hannah More, defined a new path for women, recognizing their capacity and potential while elevating them from drudgery and insignificance.

But the tensions between motherhood as satisfying vocation and as drudgery, between writing as an essential part of the creative self and as secondary to domestic duties, were not easy ones to negotiate. Ann Martin Taylor's daughters, Ann and Jane, both prolific writers as young women, chose significantly different paths in adult life. Ann married and took on the work of household management and the rearing of eight children. She tried to go on writing but found that

every hour I devote in this way now, is almost against my conscience, as I have not the time to spare. My mind is never in that composed careful state which I have always found necessary for writing; my ear is waking perpetually to the voice or cry of the dear child, and continually I am obliged to break off at a moment's notice to attend to him.[127]

Meanwhile, her sister Jane remained at home and with limited domestic responsibilities as daughter and sister, was able to read, write and publish. Ann wrote to Jane in 1817 comparing her own busy family-centred life with the quieter, more contemplative one enjoyed by her sister:

If your fame, and leisure for the improvement of your mind, could be combined with the comfort and pleasures of a larger domestic circle; and if, with a husband and children, I could share a glimmer of your fame, and a portion of your reading, we should both perhaps be happier than it is the usual lot of life to be. . . .[128]

But writers such as the Taylor mother and daughters tended to confine their contradictory feelings, their ambivalent responses to woman's sphere, to their private journals and letters. Only occasionally was there a hint of wider aspirations, an echo of different desires, in their public prose and poetry. Domestic discourses promised women fulfilment within the home and had little space for frustrated ambition or unsatisfied needs.

Mrs Taylor and her daughters became nationally known as writers, but many of the provincial authors remained essentially local figures. In their writings these people were engaged with both defining what was meant by domesticity and confirming selected existing doctrines and practices. A domestic memoir, for example, written for friends and relatives and concerned to mark the private contribution of a loving wife and mother, served both to codify ideas about marriage and motherhood and to act as an example to others. Such texts mythologized particular ways of being husbands, wives, fathers, mothers and children. The reasons for writing and publishing were varied; to make money, to propagandize new ideas, to mark publicly the death of a beloved family member, to express and explore one's own feelings. The body of writing is extensive and appears in private papers and manuscript collections as well as in published form, whether full-scale novel or advice book, or short filler in a local newspaper. Authors often drew on religious inspiration and reflected the repertoire of themes found in Cowper and More.

John Player, for example, one time Congregational mayor of Saffron

Walden, forced to retire due to ill health, published a book length poem in 1838 entitled *Home: or The Months, A Poem for Domestic Life* which drew directly for its inspiration on *The Task*. Its opening line, 'Home is the sacred refuge of our life', made immediate connections to the division between public and private, the home as haven from the turbulent world outside, and the religious nature of the home as a foretaste of the heavenly home above.[129] The vision of home as refuge and haven is found in countless poems and manuals of the period, whether a Birmingham banker's poetic paeans to domesticity or James Luckcock's effusions over 'My House and Garden'.[130] Home was business for women, haven for men. Bankers, manufacturers, clerks all stressed the universality of home, 'Alike in day built shed, or marble hall' according to Jane Ransome Biddell. The 'quiet nest' was dear to all whether rich or poor.[131] The Suffolk bank clerk, Bernard Barton, known nationally as 'the poet of domesticity', evoked in his poem 'To Little Susan' the 'humble home' remembered with love.[132] Homes were contrasted with mere houses for a house could not be home unless it were the site of love and care.[133] Home, indeed, was often defined as where the loved one was, as in this poem by the Taylor's co-author and friend Josiah Conder to his fiancée.

> Tis where thou art, is home to me,
> And home without thee cannot be.[134]

If the home was potentially the one place of peace, then the home in a rural setting was particularly attractive. Cowper's delight in his rural retreat was echoed by many and the semi-rural nature of surburbia was part of its great attraction to the protagonists of domesticity. Mary Ann Hedge, the Colchester author, evoked the standard image in one of her stories of the 'pretty little cottage' standing at the edge of a wood with its thatched roof. 'A rose tree and jasmine were intertwined around a small trellis porch in front of the cottage' and there the widowed grandmother lived with her grandchildren, the boy going out to work and bringing all his earnings home, his sister making the little cottage into a delightful haven, with cheerful logs on the fire and dumplings and potatoes being prepared for supper.[135]

When a country life was impossible, domestic affection could substitute, for in real life many of the middle class were living in city centres. Love, however, could replace nature's charms. In a poem written for her niece, about to marry the partner in her father's iron foundry and leave her Ipswich home set in a large garden for London, Jane Ransome Biddell assured her,

> What though thy future home be not
> Where Nature sheds her glories round,
> Affection tried shall bless the spot,
> And there may brightness still be found.[136]

If home was the physical location of domesticity, marriage was at its emotional heart. A good religious marriage could provide a pathway to Heaven. 'Nurse of domestic bliss', carolled Player,

> best friend to Home,
> Is wedded love! Whether in home or cot,
> In humblest shed or under roof adorned . . .
> A virtuous marriage yields to fallen man
> The richest bliss of earth: and, blessed by God,
> A sweet foretaste of these celestial joys
> Which ever flourish in the realms above.[137]

Marriage provided security and order in personal relationships, the most perfect *friendship*. Furthermore, it created the setting most suited to the bringing up of children, who needed both 'the mother's bosom' and the 'father's knee'.[138] A good marriage rested on the man and woman bringing to it their complementary characteristics. The man would be the 'lofty pine', the woman the 'slender vine', the man would take responsibility for the stormy world of business and politics, the woman would cast her sunbeams over the murky clouds he had to contend with and 'sweetly smile' the cares of the world away.[139]

Parenthood was another major concern of such writers. One of Bernard Barton's poems on motherhood, 'The Mother of Dr Doddridge teaching Him Scripture from the Dutch Tiles', referred his readers to the famous Congregational minister, Doddridge, and the importance of his mother in developing his faith. (This poem was reproduced on handkerchiefs in the 1840s, thus ensuring a wider sale.) The mother is represented as working in tandem with God for the child's salvation:

> Here he beholds the stories he has heard
> From holy lips, embodied to his view;
> Faith surely follows sight, for God's own WORD,
> And a fond mother's, tell him *all is true*!

> Here he beholds his blessed Savour bear
> The cross – there crucified! – his eyes are dim
> With childhood's tears – his silent thought is prayer,
> As her voice whispers, 'It was all for him'.[140]

Such writers were not introducing new themes. Their ideas, and indeed the imagery in their poetry, is predictable, their values familiar. What is important about such writing, however, is the scale on which it existed, the market which it commanded and the evidence it provides as to the centrality of domestic values in middle-class culture. This was the voice of the middle class uniting Anglican and Dissenting audiences. Uniting, furthermore, Radicals, Liberals and Tories from all strata of the occupational spectrum and uniting men and women in a celebration of their different and separate spheres.

Plate 15 'The family of love' as illustrated in an engraving from Mrs Sarah Stickney Ellis's collection of short stories, *Family Secrets*, 1840s.

Domestic ideologies of the 1830s and 1840s

The work of translating the late eighteenth-century domestic utopias to a middle-class public was not confined to lesser known writers of the early part of the period. By the second quarter of the nineteenth century there were also major national figures who had taken the process further towards realization. Mrs Ellis, Harriet Martineau and John Loudon in their very different ways were concerned with transforming the daily lives of middle-class families and finding ways to make domesticity a lived reality. All three were self-conscious idealogues, seeking to form taste and win others to their opinions. Speaking within established genres, they extended their meanings, offered new possibilities and reiterated pieties. Writing in the troubled decades of the 1830s and 1840s, when political and social unrest both at home and abroad was rife, they propagandized for the family as a repository of stability and firm values, just as Cowper and More had done for the 1790s. At a time when some socialists and feminists were seeking new forms of marriage and new kinds of relations between men and women, these thinkers were arguing for a stable family as the way to achieve not only social harmony but also individual fulfilment. Just as in the 1790s, the debates over manliness, femininity, the family and home were constructed around an argument as to the meaning of sexual difference. Were women naturally subordinate to men? If so, what did spiritual equality really mean? Could women be equal to men? Did this mean that they had to behave like men? Was the domestic sphere the only proper place for women? Was it acceptable for women to be 'gainfully employed'?

Cowper and More both envisaged in their writing an organic society, based on the land, in which there would be no substantial separation between production, reproduction and consumption. The household was to unite within it the separate but complementary activities of the two sexes. By the 1830s and 1840s such a vision was no longer appropriate or possible. Middle-class families were increasingly living, or at least desiring to live, not on premises which combined workplace with living space but in homes which were separated from work, away from the pressures of business with the concomitant apprentices and employees.[141] Writers on domesticity by the 1830s and 1840s all assume that this separation has taken place, and that if it has not it is an unfortunate aberration.

Mrs Ellis, therefore, does not like More, write about a whole society peopled by both men and women. Her advice books and novels assume a world in which the domestic sphere is occupied by women, children and servants, with men as the absent presence, there to direct and command but physically occupied elsewhere for most of their time. Similarly, Harriet Martineau assumes a world divided between political economy and domestic economy; John Loudon advises and instructs middle-class families how to build and furnish houses and design gardens which would be suited to a purely domestic life without manufactories or counting houses attached. It was recognized that men would be preoccupied with business, and domesticity had become the 'woman's sphere' rather than, as it is for Cowper, a way of living for both men and women.

A second major shift had occurred by the 1830s and 1840s. The original inspiration for new patterns of behaviour in the home and family lay with the religious revival of the late eighteenth century. First Cowper and More, then Isaac and Ann Taylor and their generation were converted in their adult lives and had all the enthusiasm of the new discoverers of truth. However, for many of the writers of the later period, religion was a given part of their intellectual framework but no longer occupied centre stage. Many of the public protagonists of domesticity still received their inspiration from 'real religion' but for others domestic life no longer had to be framed in predominantly Christian terms, no longer required the revolutionizing force of salvationist religion.

Ellis, Martineau and Loudon, from their very different backgrounds and preoccupations, all exemplify these shifts in the meanings of home and domesticity. Each of them had connections with the middle-class inhabitants of our local areas. Sarah Stickney Ellis was sister-in-law to Mary Wright Sewell, a popular writer herself in the domestic genre, who came from Suffolk and returned there in middle age.[142] Mrs Ellis was a favourite author of John Angell James and provided him with many a rich quotation.[143] Harriet Martineau had strong connections with Birmingham through her brother Robert, a local brass manufacturer. She spent time with his family, took two of his daughters as her companions and had a network of close friends in the town.[144] John Loudon, whose wife came from Birmingham, was so admired by the middle class of Edgbaston that he was invited to design their new botanical gardens in 1831 and so impressed was he by their enterprise that he was willing to do so without payment. Loudon's popular *The Suburban Gardener and Villa Companion* figured prominently in the reading matter of local people; it was found in the holdings of Colchester's Castle Library.[145]

Mrs Sarah Stickney Ellis was probably the best-known idealogue of domesticity, one of a number of women writers in the genre in the second quarter of the nineteenth century. Indeed conservative thinkers were sometimes worried at the extent to which advice books were written by women. 'We doubt much', complained one critic, 'whether women are the best direct preceptors of women'.[146] Yet these women were tremendously popular.[147] Mrs Ellis, born in 1799, was a tenant farmer's daughter. Expected to contribute to the household from an early age, she divided her time between familial responsibilities and writing, from which, by the mid 1830s, she was making a precarious living. At the age of 37, she started to correspond with Mr Ellis, her husband-to-be who was then working for the London Missionary Society. Through her connection with him she became more seriously interested in religion and in 1837 she joined the Congregational church before marrying. She never had children of her own but took major responsibility for her step-brothers and sisters, her nieces and nephews and her three step-children. Her advice to women on childcare was based on long experience, though her insistence on the importance of maternal *instinct* is ironic in the context of her adopted mothering. After her marriage she continued to write prolifically and, furthermore, established a school in their home in the country in 1844 so that throughout her life she contributed economically to the household.[148]

Her best-known books were the series on the wives, mothers, daughters and women of England. Mrs Ellis will soon, commented one unsympathetic reviewer, 'have circumnavigated the female world; every variety of female condition will have had its separate book. . .'.[149] Even in such potentially critical journals as *The Quarterly* she was well received, though her pompous tone and the 'magnificent catalogue of virtues' which she was attempting to inculcate were commented upon with amusement.[150] In more progressive circles there were doubts as to whether her view of women as 'relative creatures' was acceptable, but her general advice on education and household organization was welcomed.[151] What is significant is the extent to which Mrs Ellis's views were seen as a radical departure, an attempt to break with the unhappy state of affairs in the middle-class homes of England, where gentility had been winning too many victories over practicality.

Mrs Ellis was rooted in the middling ranks of the provincial middle class; her father a tenant farmer, her husband a minor professional, herself a struggling writer and teacher. Yet she addressed herself first and foremost to women who did not need to earn. This may have been more to do with her sense of a proper domestic ideal, than with her individual needs. Indeed, she clung with some guilt to her financial independence. 'The middle class' that she addressed represented for her 'the pillar of our nation's strength', renowned for their intelligence and moral power.[152]

She was particularly concerned with those families of traders, manufacturers and professionals where there were one to four servants, where there had been some kind of liberal education, and where there was no family rank. 'False notions of refinement', were rendering their women, 'less influential, less useful, and less happy than they were'. This was a moral crisis for the nation and her concern was to find ways of improving 'the minor morals of domestic life'.[153] Once again the family was to provide a secure basis for national stability. Men did not have the time; they were occupied in the world of business and politics. Women had both the time, the moral capacity and the influence to exercise real power in the domestic world. It was their responsibility to re-create society from below.

A tension between the notion of women as 'relative creatures' and a celebratory view of their potential power lies at the heart of Mrs Ellis's writing and helps to explain her popularity. Like Hannah More her belief in the separate spheres of men and women went together with a conviction that women's influence could be felt far beyond her own limited circle.[154] *Influence* was the secret of women's power and that influence, as wives and mothers, meant that they did not need to seek other kinds of legitimation. Having been criticized for placing women on too low a scale Mrs Ellis responded by arguing that,

I still think that as a wife, woman should place herself, instead of running the risk of *being placed*, in a secondary position; as a mother, I do not see how it is possible for her to be too dignified, or to be treated with too much respect.[155]

The tension between subordination and influence, between moral power and political silence, was one which preoccupied all the protagonists of 'woman's mission'.[156] If the moral world was theirs, who needed the public world of business and politics? Women could find the true meaning of their lives in the family which was a woman's profession, the love that she would find there would answer her needs. For women, wrote Mrs Ellis, love was her very being 'In that *she* lives, or else *she* has no life', unlike a man who had his public character.[157] To love was woman's duty; to be beloved her reward. Women's aim should be to become better wives and mothers. However, much improved education for girls would be necessary for the natural maternal instinct needed training and support. Women should regard good domestic management not as degrading but as a moral task and abandon false notions of refinement, accepting that they had a vital job to do at home, just as their sons and husbands had to do at work. Wives and daughters, 'enclosed, as it were, in the home-garden', should practice the domestic virtues of making others happy.[158]

For herself, Mrs Ellis was never under the illusion that enclosure in the 'home-garden' was enough. She was well aware that in many middle-class households, as indeed in her own, women's financial contribution could make an essential difference. Women in the lower middle class, she argued, should be educated to be useful and active members of society. There was nothing degrading in women's employment if it were essential, and there were fields such as engraving and the drawing of patterns as well as the more common teaching and needlework.[159] But this was a small comment among volumes which argued that woman's place was in the home, and although she prefaced *The Women of England* with the proviso that it was written for those who did not have to work for money, her works, and those of others like her, were taken to apply far more generally. The moral panic engendered in the 1840s by the vision of women working in the mines, mills and factories of England was fuelled by the view that woman's duty was to care for home and children. Mrs Ellis, whether she intended to do so or not, played a part in rigidifying existing views that it was not genteel for women to work. At the same time that she was writing *The Women of England*, she described in a letter the 'blessings of constant employment' her step-daughters, and indeed herself, enjoyed from their teaching as daily governesses.[160] But this also brought guilt and anxiety as to whether her work as a wife and mistress of a household was suffering. Like Mrs Gaskell she felt obliged to make sure that she never allowed those other responsibilities to be neglected.[161]

In some ways Mrs Ellis directly inherited the mantle of Hannah More. She had similar concerns about the nature of marriage, the importance of motherhood, the need for better education for women and the nurturing of their rationality, the advantages of rural life and suspicion of 'society'. But there were also significant differences between them. She did not share Hannah More's conservative politics for, like Ann Taylor in Essex, she was attached publicly to progressive liberal causes and throughout her life remained sympathetic to the Quakers (whose faith she had known as a child) and their preoccupation with issues such as anti-slavery, peace, capital punishment and temperance. Furthermore, she was concerned to address a much wider audience than More had originally envisaged and to make domesticity a more available practice. All women could be mothers, she argued, and

the heart of woman, in all her tenderest and holiest feelings, is the same beneath the shelter of a cottage, as under the canopy of a tree. . . .[162]

This democratization of domesticity was solidly rooted in the homes of the middle class and not in the country estates of the minor gentry. It was no longer tied to a desire for a retreat from the development of towns and industries and a return to a patriarchal rural idyll, but located in the towns and villages of England, among middling manufacturers, traders, professionals and farmers.

A second major difference between More and Ellis also played a vital part in making domesticity the practice of a class rather than of a particular religious group, for she was never evangelical in her religion, remaining within a generally Christian framework but without spiritual inspiration. Rather her primary concern was with morals. Hannah More would never have made this distinction between religion and morality. It was precisely the religious meaning of the minutiae of daily life that had led to More's insistence on rules of habit and behaviour, to the emphasis on every detail of private life and the necessary distinctions between the spheres and duties of men and women. For Mrs Ellis, however, women did not have to be seriously religious to follow her precepts. The loose Christian framework within which she placed her work, her characterization of religious influence or 'atmosphere' including those who 'did not want quite to give up the world, yet not quite to live without God' meant that it was acceptable to many.[163] The tone that Mrs Ellis achieved was precisely that of a respectable moralist with a 'Christian tint', that had come to dominate mid century England, enveloping the language of the proper relations between the sexes.[164]

Sarah Stickney Ellis developed the idea of female satisfaction being achieved through selflessness;[165] Harriet Martineau, from a different tradition, saw other advantages in domesticity. Born in Norwich in 1802, the daughter of a successful Unitarian merchant and manufacturer, Martineau suffered an unhappy and frustrating childhood. Despite her intellectual interests and the relatively progressive position of Unitarians on female education, she was expected to settle into the life of a young lady at home. In an early article 'On Female Education' she refused the belief in the natural mental differentiation of the sexes, as Wollstonecraft had before her, and argued that women had the same mental endowment as men. But at the same time, she believed that the female mind was peculiarly susceptible to religion and virtue and dwelt on the importance of the personal and moral to women.[166] In 1829 the family business collapsed and for Harriet this turned out to be a blessing in disguise. Her surreptitious writing done before breakfast became a serious occupation and source of income.[167] Now, she commented thankfully, she won friends, independence, and an interesting life and was able to feel that she had 'truly lived'. Becoming increasingly interested in political economy, Martineau had the idea of writing tales to popularize the theories of Smith, Ricardo, Malthus and Bentham. Despite her difficulties in finding a publisher for this unlikely female enterprise, the venture was an immediate success with its simple language to explain such issues as the corn laws, the poor law and population. But how did Martineau weld together her newfound commitment to the Benthamites with her Unitarianism and belief in the equality of men and women?

Classical liberalism had been content to combine a belief in the individual rights of propertied men with an acceptance of sexual inequality within the family.[168] Building on this tradition, Bentham had little to say about either women or the family but when he did address himself to such matters he relied on customary morality. 'The sensibility of the female sex appears in general to be greater than that of the male', but women's sympathies went to individuals, not classes or divisions. They were modest, delicate and more superstitious than men, with stronger affections for children. Women, in short, occupied a smaller sphere than men. Finally, and most damning of all, women were less sympathetic to the principle of utility than were men. Bentham was happy to rest with custom when it came to relations between the sexes. Like Hobbes and Locke before him, he thought that marriage must be a contract but that powers would have to rest with the husband who would act as 'master' and 'guardian'.[169] For the most part the political economists were happy with a conventional view of the family as separate from the market and providing a haven from the competitive thrust of the economic world. Martineau recorded that Malthus came to see her after the publication of her tale on taxation:

on purpose to thank me for a passage, or a chapter, (which has left no trace in my memory) on the glory and beauty of love and the blessedness of domestic

life; and that others, called stern Benthamites, sent round messages to me to the
same effect.[170]

It was ironic that this was the moment at which the 'stern Benthamites'
thanked her – for a passage on the 'blessedness of domestic life' of which
she had no recollection.

Martineau's experience of domestic life was mixed; a consistently difficult
relationship with her mother, serious quarrels with most of her siblings,
never interested in marriage and only in later life able to set up a household
on her own terms. Why, then, did she feel the need to celebrate domesticity?
Building as she did on the twin traditions of Utilitarianism and Unitarianism
she took from them a powerful belief in individual rights and a commitment
to rationality. All women should have the right to develop their full potential and she consistently opposed educational and economic discrimination.
But arguments for better opportunities for women must be made from a
spirit of rationality, not from passion and misery. Critical of Wollstonecraft,
who she saw as a poor victim of passion, Martineau's feminism was based
on the need for self-control and self-discipline. The best friends of women's
cause, she insisted, were happy wives and 'busy, cheerful, satisfied single
women'.[171] Every woman who could think and speak wisely and bring up
her children soundly was advancing the time when women's interests in
society would be better represented.

But Martineau firmly believed also in the positive value of domestic life.
'No true woman', she wrote,

married or single, *can* be happy without some sort of domestic life; – without
having somebody's happiness dependent on her. . . .[172]

Her demand for women was for individual fulfilment. For married women
this meant as wives and mothers. While recognizing the need for single
women and working-class women, even those who were married, to work
for pay, she saw home and family as the most satisfying site for married
women of the middle class. Setting the path for John Stuart Mill, she never
seriously queried the division of labour within the family.[173] But if the
family was to be all that it could and should, women must be better
educated to be good wives and mothers. The highest domestic enjoyment,
she asserted, went with the best educated women. In *Household Education*,
published in 1848, she argued that the most ignorant women she had known
had also been the worst housekeepers. A woman of superior mind knew
better than an ignorant one what to require of servants and how to deal
with tradespeople.[174] 'Every woman ought to have that justice done to her
faculties', she wrote, making the classic liberal feminist case,

that she may possess herself in all the strength and clearness of an experienced
and enlightened mind, and may have at command, for her subsistence, as much
intellectual power and as many resources as education can furnish her with.[175]

Martineau saw the artisan household as providing a good model for the
running of a household for there women necessarily had to be heavily
involved themselves and could not leave the upbringing of the children and
the management of the home to servants. The mother would take major
responsibility for the children but the father would be involved when he

came home in the evenings. The children would learn to help from the beginning and girls would learn domestic management the best possible way. Love was the right source of parental authority she thought, and she combined this with advice on breastfeeding, on fresh air and exercise, and the importance of cleanliness. Children should learn regularity and discipline and the importance of making good use of time. In this context Martineau strongly recommended the works of Mrs Ann Martin Taylor.

Martineau's recommendation of Mrs Taylor (despite the latter's evangelicalism to which she was hostile), and her proximity in attitudes to some aspects of the thinking of More and Ellis, gives an indication of the pervasiveness of domesticity. The starting points of these writers were widely different. More and Ellis regarded domesticity as a moral imperative, Martineau argued for a good domestic life in terms of the needs of individuals for fulfilment. None of them wanted for themselves quite what they advised for others. Martineau was wedded to the life of an independent woman writer and determined to succeed in a male literary world. The costs of this included her steadfast refusal of her own sexuality and her labelling as 'eccentric'. More and Ellis also made ambitious claims for women, if on a different plane, and in their own ways advanced women's cause in their separate spheres. For all of them their versions of domesticity were to enhance women's status, not reduce it.

The tensions which were present in the writings of these authors, the contradictions between influence and the narrow sphere, fulfilment and domestic economy, often disappeared, however, in the popularizations of their work. The *Magazine of Domestic Economy*, for example, started in 1835, aimed at a middle-class audience, was priced at 6d and appeared monthly. Its motto read,

We are born at home, we live at home, and we must die at home, so that the comfort and economy of home are of more deep, heartfelt, and personal interest to us, than the public affairs of all the nations in the world.

The aim of the journal, which the proprietors felt had been overlooked by other periodicals, was to explore 'the principle and practice of rendering the enjoyments of home more generally appreciated, and more habitually delightful'. The magazine dealt with domestic economy in its widest sense: the management of the household, the care of children, the fulfilment of social duties, the proper use of time and the management of income all came within its purview. They strongly recommended the 'excellent Miss Martineau' and much of their advice might have come straight from the pages of Mrs Taylor (bar the religion) or Mrs Ellis. But the tone was bland, the tension which informed the more creative writers missing. The magazine demonstrated an acceptance of separate spheres without any moral or political imperatives – it simply was the way to be. The province of men was to find the means to support a home, the province of women was to make the home enjoyable. It was wrong for women to seek to be active in men's sphere and women should not complain about the legal disabilities associated with marriage. 'A woman gives up her worldly possessions', they argued,

in exchange for a determinate station; for protection, for support . . . she gains
station . . . she gains protection. . . .

What else could she need?[176]

In 1852 Martineau wrote a series for *Household Words* based on her
experiences in Birmingham during a long stay with her brother and his
family. One concerned 'A New School for Wives', established through the
efforts of a Unitarian led group of women, friends and admirers of Miss
Martineau. The school aimed to educate married working women, of whom
there were many in the Birmingham metal trades, in the arts of housewifery
as well as the three Rs. It was an initiative which came out of the prevalent
middle-class anxieties as to the nature of working-class family life and the
deleterious effects of married women's employment. This particular school
was a success for Unitarians had a genuine belief in the value of education,
as well as a powerful desire to inculcate their own familial ideals.[177] But
such ventures were frequently inspired by less sympathetic attitudes and it
was no great leap from a dissatisfaction with the state of working-class
homes to a wholesale disapproval of women's employment. The loss of the
political and philosophical imperatives behind the arguments about separate
spheres, whether in the form of a genuine belief in woman's influence or
demand for individual fulfilment for women, and the common-sense
reduction of those beliefs which took place, had very mixed effects for
women by the middle of the nineteenth century.

Mrs Ellis hoped to regenerate society through the benevolent influence of
woman, Harriet Martineau hoped that social progress would be initiated
through the strengthening and improving of individual character, while
John Claudius Loudon hoped that by creating the conditions for a proper
domestic life in the suburbs he would contribute to the promotion of social
virtue. It was material life that Loudon was concerned with, rather than
spiritual. He offered to the English middle classes a way of realizing the
dreams of Cowper and More through the construction of actual homes and
gardens, designed to cultivate the pleasures of domestic life. Loudon, born
in 1783, the son of a Scottish farmer, was apprenticed to a nurseryman and
landscape gardener. Partly self-educated, he founded and ran an agricultural
college as well as creating a family enterprise with the support of his sisters
and later his wife, specializing in gardening, agriculture, horticulture and
design literature. He moved to London when he was 20 but did not marry
until he was 47. His wife was Jane, the daughter of Thomas Webb, a
manufacturer of Birmingham. He designed and built a semi-detached house
in Bayswater (the forerunner of the Victorian semi-detached suburban villa)
for himself and his wife with his three sisters installed next door. From
there he did all his writing and editing, assisted by Jane and the sisters,
whom he had trained to do etching and illustrations for his publications.[178]

Loudon's best-known book was *The Suburban Gardener and Villa
Companion* published in 1838. He wrote consistently between 1804 and his
death in 1846, producing books and pamphlets with subjects ranging from
architecture, gardening, house furnishing, and greenhouses to plant life,
cemeteries and agriculture. In addition he established and edited three

magazines, and engaged in the work of design, particularly botanic gardens and cemeteries, all over the country. Jane Webb Loudon not only helped him to edit and produce his own work but also herself wrote nineteen books including a popular manual, *Gardening for Ladies*. Her *The Lady's Companion to the Flower Garden*, published in 1841, went through nine editions and sold 20,000 copies.[179] She 'did for the outdoor activities of the inexperienced mistress of a Victorian household', it has been claimed, 'what Mrs Beeton's great work did for her indoor economy'.[180] Her husband has been described as 'the virtual arbiter of taste to the new middle classes in the matter of their domestic surroundings'.[181]

Loudon's primary bent was practical. He promised his readers that he would make even technical subjects such as building construction simple and understandable. In *The Suburban Gardener and Villa Companion* he guaranteed 'to treat every subject in such a manner as to be understood by those who have little knowledge of either gardening or country affairs'. 'More especially', he added, 'to adapt it to the instruction and amusement of ladies.'[182] He aimed to 'create and diffuse . . . a taste for architectural comforts and beauties' and thus promote the interests of 'all mankind'.[183] But these grand aims were presented in practical and straightforward terms. How to care for plants, what kinds of furnishings to choose, how to create a consistent whole of home and garden were all dealt with in minute detail. Loudon was fascinated himself by doing things; he and his wife not only designed but dug and planted their garden. His interests ranged from the scientific to the technological to the domestic. He revolutionized the design of hot-houses and conservatories by inventing a flexible wrought-iron sash bar which made curvilinear glazing possible.[184] His books dealt with every aspect of home life, from the planting of garden seeds to the appropriate authors to display on a dining room bookshelf.[185]

His major contribution to middle-class culture was his recognition that domestic life could blossom in the suburb. 'We shall prove in this work', he asserted in *The Suburban Gardener*, 'that a suburban residence, with a very small portion of land attached, will contain all that is essential for happiness'.[186] Initially he had assumed that all would seek the joys of country life and that the working household should operate in a rural setting. City amusements, he believed, had the effect of promoting effeminacy, extravagance and luxury. Indeed, he argued, 'Such is the superiority of rural occupations and pleasures that commerce, large societies or crowded cities may be justly reckoned unnatural.' The main purpose for him of engaging in commerce was to be able to retire to the country where 'man may approach the simplicity of nature and attain the enjoyments and pleasures of pristine innocence'. Following Cowper and More he argued that the man in the country could be more independent, more manly, than in the city, especially in enjoying the 'society of his own amiable family'.[187]

He soon realized that rural life was possible for few; home and work were separating, and the suburb provided a solution. Loudon believed that all members of the household could contribute to the creation of home and garden, consequently it need not involve great expense. Furthermore, there was the satisfaction of doing it oneself: 'It is this which gives the charm of creation and makes a thing essentially one's own', he insisted.[188] Here the idea of private property is closely linked to the idea of the home, but Loudon was well aware that most middle-class property was rented and that turnover tended to be frequent. Therefore his detailed instructions, ranging from the modest to the ambitious, set out to create a flexible template for domestic life.

Suburban living as he envisaged it could have similar aims as the gentry but was on a much more modest scale. 'What can be more rational', he asked his readers,

than the satisfaction which the grown up amateur, or master of the house, enjoys, when he returns home from the city to his garden in the summer evenings, and applies the syringe to his wall trees, with refreshing enjoyment to himself and the plants, and to the delight of his children, who may be watching his operations?

Here he was justifying a certain amount of manual work, just as had Cowper, insisting that it was no detriment to gentility. Suburban living could teach both adults and children about science, through learning to train trees or deal with insects, and it could help with a knowledge of taste and design. Ladies, for example, could discover that the steps from loving flowers to laying out a flower garden were not impassable. The latter, they would find, was no more difficult than cutting out a dress.[189] In concrete terms of walls and hedges he promoted the privacy so important to suburban life; prying eyes and too much interest in other people's business took away from the charms of domesticity.[190] Communal living with its echoes of the easy and promiscuous sociability of the poor was alien. Improving on Cowper, the final purpose of Loudon's design was to subdue wild or barren country in order to control the local labouring population through influence.[191]

Loudon hoped that his books would be read by those in a position to shape the destiny of others and he shared the common view that if they adopted his schemes their practices would unproblematically diffuse downwards in the society. Especially significant for him was his female audience, and the clergy and schoolteachers, whom he saw as having extensive influence.[192] He wanted men and women to work together to create domesticity. Both should enjoy the suburban home, 'the ultimate in point of comfort and enjoyment' for the man of society and his wife, each in their own sphere.

These assumptions were reflected in his encouragement of specialization and segregation within the house. Women were 'naturally' indoor people and men outdoor. Women had a 'natural' love of flowers and colour and indoor gardening was especially associated with them. 'A greenhouse', he wrote,

is in a peculiar degree the care of the female part of a family and forms an interesting scene of care and recreation to a mother and her daughters at a season of the year when there is but little inducement to walk in the kitchen garden and nothing to do in the parterre or shrubbery.

Loudon's domestication of women is linked to his comparison between a plant in the garden bed and the one in a pot. The latter he sees as 'thoroughly domesticated', particularly endearing and capable of 'receiving especial regard'.[193] His imagery of pure home and garden had many resonances and particularly drew on popular biblical evocations of sexual purity in the Garden of Eden.[194]

Loudon was concerned with educating the middle class into the canons of good taste, in which women were to play a special role. 'Nothing contributes more to the moral and political government of the passions', he argued, 'than the rigid disciplines of good taste, which are always in unison with those of good morality.'[195] Without good taste there could be no morality, and women through their influence would be the purveyors of taste. Society could be revolutionized in thirty years, he believed, through family improvement based on the proper private education of women.[196] But women's role did not rest with their capacity to influence others through good taste. They were themselves the ultimate expression of taste, for beauty was best expressed in the female form. 'Supreme beauty', stated Loudon, 'to the mind of man, is only found in a lovely woman; the beauty of all other objects may be termed relative.' In an appendix to a treatise on country residences, he saw beauty as associated with love of possession and considered those qualities as most beautiful,

which approach nearest to that of woman: thus gentle undulations, insensible transitions, smooth and soft surfaces, circular or conical forms, are all termed beautiful, except when they are connected with some moral evil or deformity in relation to man.[197]

For Loudon the most beautiful women were always tender and delicate, as different as possible from men. The translation of this vision of beauty into material form could be achieved by the use of supports, by employing a smaller quantity of materials, as in elegant furniture or columns, by the creation of undulations and smoothness, by the employment of tender ornaments and colours. For Loudon rugged scenery could be sublime but not beautiful, and the opposite of beauty for him was deformity and monstrosity, always linked to a moral judgement. Delicate, shrinking femininity was the only beauty expressing full virtue so that strong, large women depart from both moral and physical standards. Loudon's definition of beauty, which he intended to be literally built into his designs for homes and gardens, thus rested ultimately on morality as exemplified through women.

Like many of the other major protagonists of domesticity, Loudon both elevated the status of women and contained them in a relative sphere. As a male writer that containment was unproblematic. Women's beauty was the arbiter of taste; a chandelier would be judged according to its delicacy, the wrought iron of the conservatories of Birmingham's Botanical Gardens by its feminine curves and undulations. Furthermore, women had the capacity both through their physical presence and their moral influence to inculcate good taste in others, and by the 1840s good taste, the capacity not to be vulgar, was replacing salvation as the mark of special status. But such a doctrine also confined women within a particular notion of femininity, both in their appearance and behaviour. To be large, or loud, or strong, was to be ugly and carried with it notions of moral collapse as well as physical failure to conform.

Woman's virtuosity lay in her containment, like the plant in the pot,

limited and domesticated, sexually controlled, not spilling out into spheres
in which she did not belong nor being overpowered by 'weeds' of social
disorder. That containment carried with it possession; the woman must be
placed within a family, as wife or daughter or sister, protected by her male
guardian. In Loudon, the religious influence of the woman in the evangelical
world, acting as chief purveyor of morality, has been replaced by a secular
counterpart. Woman represents taste without which there is no morality.
But she has also been objectified. In stressing the relation between female
form and moral virtue and providing the material surroundings for such a
belief, writers like Loudon introduced important new elements to concepts
of domesticity. The woman's body was brought back to the centre of
femininity, but it was the body of the contained and domesticated woman.
Loudon's ideal type was not the voracious, sexually active woman of the
eighteenth century. Nor was she Hannah More's spiritually centred
moralist, refusing passion in the interests of influence.[198] Rather, she had a
physical presence, but that presence was only legitimated when it expressed
a proper sense of belonging to a delicate, refined and gentle domestic world.

Part Two

Economic Structure and Opportunity

Introduction to Part Two

Family, hearth and home were both rationale and setting for the business enterprise while domestic ideals increasingly set the terms for economic activity. Economic institutions of this period had evolved from traditional legal, financial and customary forms which privileged men and cast women as subordinates. But it was only when resources were well above subsistence that more than a tiny elite could afford to dispense with women's productive labour. It was the shift to liquid capital and the middle-class reinterpretation of property forms which enabled dependent women to be supported while keeping their capital in circulation. It may be argued that the search for safe income to support dependants – wives, children, younger siblings and adult female relatives – had a marked effect on investment and production decisions of the middle class as a whole, turning them from the sole pursuit of maximum profit. This argument is but a special case of the more general point that a concern with morality and religious values centred on a domesticated lifestyle limited and framed economic activity throughout the early nineteenth century.

Conversely, economic activity profoundly affected the family: the size and location of the enterprise, the workforce and problems of discipline, the type of product and its distribution, the plant and technology, pace of work, mobility of managing personnel, all were intimately linked to family life. The interpenetration of family and production also had strong effects on the emerging class structure. The late eighteenth- and early nineteenth-century middle class flourished partly because the institutions it created produced vast material resources and social confidence at a period when the nation was poised to reap the benefits of an overseas empire. But its methods of production were also highly successful in exploiting the labour of working-class men, women and children, while its ideology proclaimed that such brutal conditions were inevitable. The overriding objective of pursuing a moral and genteel life made it almost impossible for employers to acknowledge the price paid by their employees and displaced craft workers under capitalist industrial expansion. To them, simply living a domesticated and Godly life was justification for existence. The processes, however distasteful, which had made such a life possible were but a means to this divinely sanctioned end.

From the end of the eighteenth century, capital accumulation for the middle class was rising. Income distribution further shifted in favour of recipients of profits and rents during the Napoleonic War.[1] Even after the drop in capital holdings, R. J. Morris estimates that the continued rise in national income indicates that spending on consumer goods and services continued.[2] Middle-class wealth was being created by selling a vast offering of both goods and services both at home and abroad. Many of these goods and services were consumed by the middle class itself, its consumption patterns sometimes leading, at other times following that of the gentry; both strata infused with wealth and tastes brought back from the Indies, east and west.

New methods of production, themselves, created demands for novel products. For example, changes in arable farming in the eastern regions required the use of fertilizers in the form of mash, a by-product of breweries, or extracted as a mineral from local sources. The draining of land meant that tile and clay pipe manufacture could enrich the village brick works out of all recognition, while the redesign and mass production of agricultural tools laid the foundations of several local fortunes.[3] The metal manufacturers of Birmingham produced machines fuelled by steam power and made tools designed for the manufacture of yet other goods. Significantly, however, the same iron foundries also produced kitchen grates and other domestic applicances.

In Birmingham, the articles most commonly made in the eighteenth century were buttons, buckles and toys, swords, guns and papier mâché ware. This range gradually expanded and the town was best known for its finishing work: '. . . almost every metallic article whether used in the shop or in the house . . . is more or less directly connected with some of the Birmingham trades' as one local commentator proudly claimed.[4] The items manufactured ranged from metallic bedsteads to silver plated tableware, from pipes for the plumbing to needles and pins, from steel pens to pots and pans. When brass was introduced the middle class was able to have 'silvered brass and gilt brass above stairs and plain elegant functional brass in the kitchen, stables and outhouses'.[5] Their hooks and hinges, castors and handles, window and door catches, coach fittings and harness fittings, buttons, buckles, coat and hat pins, needle cases and snuff boxes, picture frames and scissors, umbrella handles and walking sticks, tea bells and even dog collars – all of them could be supplied from Birmingham brass, the 'perfect emblem of respectable wealth'.[6]

In both areas the local families studied based their income on the manufacture and sale of such items as clocks, paper, glass for greenhouses, engravings, hollow ware, hymn books, oil paintings, coaches and light vehicles, seeds and plants for the garden. The change in consumption of everyday goods in the period covered was dramatic. In the early eighteenth century, the possession of an item such as a clock or watch would only be within the range of the wealthiest strata. By 1804, an Essex farmer neither particularly well off or literate proudly noted in his diary that he had bought 'a wach of a Jew at the dore cost 3 gns'.[7] Birmingham small masters and respectable artisans were able to buy books, watches and clothes by forming small paying-in clubs.[8]

The fortunes of the middle class rested not only on the manufacture and sale of material goods but also on services. A more active property market and the spate of building in the late eighteenth century created a place for auctioneers and agents, architects and engineers, landscape gardeners and designers, attorneys and bankers. Manufacturers needed industrial designers and scientists to enhance their products, as did the development of better transport, roads, bridges, ships and vehicles. The cultural aspirations of the middle class had an immense effect on the demand for teachers, musicians, painters, and authors. A greater concern with health and a less fatalistic outlook increased opportunities for doctors while the leap in both Anglican and nonconformist membership created many places for clergymen. Some of those who toiled to produce cultural products and services were the forerunners of the experts who strove to explain the middle class to itself in spiritual and material terms, to set out the lineaments of a respectable if not genteel lifestyle. Authors, publishers, booksellers (and ultimately paper manufacturers) made good in this fashion. Many were able to use their connections with religious communities to further their business interests. The son of a Congregational farmer from Essex started a publishing concern which swept the market for nonconformist hymn books promoted through his chapel adherence.[9] Paid positions within philanthropic missions, the writing and publishing of serious Christian material, even the distribution of tracts for a small income were commercial activities promoted by the beliefs and values of the middle class.

Part Two first examines men and women's relation to property, the evolution of the family enterprise and its connection with the demographic structure of households. It goes on to consider the concept of occupation as part of masculine identity which entailed new patterns of education and training. Nineteenth-century occupations emerged from multiple activities, many of them performed as personal services to a patron. Middle-class men's task was to wrest economic independence and public status from these ties. The last chapter focuses on women's relationship to the economy at a time when both social expectations and property forms made it increasingly difficult for women to play a direct part in business and professional activity. It documents the serious consequences of this pattern for those left without support and contrasts this with the ways in which men were able to grasp the expanding opportunities underwritten by women's capital and labour in both home and enterprise.

4 'A modest competency': men, women and property

'Girls', said Mr. Dombey, 'have nothing to do with Dombey and Son'
Charles Dickens, 1848

In this period, the pursuit of profit was in many cases subordinated to the creation and support of an 'establishment', a term used to connote the combined enterprise and family/household. The value placed on domestic life which radiated from religious belief framed early business activity. Economic organization, finance, training and personnel were interwoven with domestic affairs. Men and women were both implicated in the enterprise but their position differed radically, from their relationship to property to the use of their labour. As industrial capitalism developed, forms of wealth and income followed this distribution of power and resources between the sexes.

The England of the late eighteenth century was still dominated by land. Ownership of landed property remained the greatest source of wealth, power and social honour, the real patrimony and the basis of citizenship.[1] Yet by this period, the concept of land itself was undergoing change. Resources on and under land such as minerals and timber were being exploited commercially and land as a basis for urban building meant that ground rents were becoming a form of property. Mortgages, extensively used to circumvent the rigidities of entail, were also coming to be regarded as a liquid asset.[2] The very solidity and stability of land could be a disadvantage compared to these more flexible forms of property; for example, in a crisis when land might have to be sold at a loss.

At the same time, commercial activity had reached the point where older concepts were no longer adequate. Commerce made use of liquid assets, which rested on the notion of credit. But, despite the need for flexibility in borrowing and lending, there was still ambivalence in conceiving credit as an abstraction. The powerful notion of 'personality' as founded on real property – land – as the basis of all virtue and claims to honour remained. Those involved with credit mechanisms were often suspect as creatures of 'passion and fantasy'.[3]

This distrust led to an unease surrounding positions which had grown with commercial and manufacturing society: the agent, baliff and factor. The 'monied men' of the eighteenth century – Cobbett's reviled 'stock jobbers' – were regarded as hirelings of government or aristocratic patronage; their origins in the service of these interests were not to be easily sloughed off. By the early nineteenth century such positions were being transmuted into fee paid quasi-professionals serving more anonymous multiple customers such as canal companies or Municiple Corporations. Public office shifted slowly from sinecure to bureaucratic position.

These novel developments were part of the bid to be free from economic as well as political 'control of the patricians'.[4] They reflected the general early nineteenth-century shift to a more secular, less paternalistic social order hailed by followers of political economy.[5] Manufacturers and market-oriented farmers, dealing with a larger wage paid workforce, too, caught up these ideas, breaking the bonds of traditional expectations for fixed prices and seeking moral justification to follow the dictates of the market if they wished to reject paternalistic ties to the local community.[6]

The brisk dismissal of personal ties within the conceptions of political economy gave force to the middle-class equation of masculine honour with independence. The resulting early nineteenth-century concept of 'manhood' had political as much as sexual connotations. Manhood was to become a central part of claims to legitimate middle-class leadership. This development can be traced in attitudes towards dependency and those positions which continued to imply men's personal services. Male domestic servants were the last category of men to be enfranchised and were banished from organizations such as the Freemasons who were concerned to establish bases for independence as alternatives to paternalistic hierarchies.[7] Manhood also implied the ability and willingness to support and protect women and children. Men would enter the market as free agents but would thus preserve the moral bonds of society in their private and philanthropic capacity.

The stark world of political economy had been conceived within real lives deeply embedded in ties of kinship and traditional, if modified, bonds of patronage.[8] These face to face relationships extracted reciprocal obligations encapsulated in the concept of 'friendship'. But the idea of friendship had been subtly transmuted for the middle class by the equality of the converted soul within evangelical religious circles and the more radical ideas of political equality inspired by the French Revolution.

By the early nineteenth century, middle-class 'family and friends' provided a potent support from which middle-class men could assert their independence from aristocratic patronage. Men were also sustained by new forms of occupational and professional identity in turning to their peers for endorsement. Most of the national and provincial scientific and professional societies were founded in the period between 1750 and 1830 by middle-class men with a sprinkling of dedicated gentry, groups of like minded men who were meeting regularly to 'talk shop and eat dinners'.[9] The use of informal gatherings such as clubs as a transition to more formal institutions is typical of economic life of the period, for eighteenth-century trade and manufacture were 'as uninstitutionalized as politics'.[10] Decisions about the deployment of property and the carrying-on of business remained within the family or household, and only in the nineteenth century were they fully taken into the economic arena and the rule-based sphere of the legal system.[11]

Precedents for business procedure were drawn from the landed estate and much of accounting was based on estate practices. Early merchant

ventures had begun as short lived affairs throwing up temporary partnerships which dissolved when their objective had been fulfilled. Later
merchants and merchant/manufacturers took a more stable form but used
basically similar routines.[12] The more permanent organizations were not
oriented to market operations. The City Livery Companies and Oxbridge
Colleges had been operating under a form of trust for several centuries, but
such corporate trusts were specifically limited to non-profit functions.[13]
Many middle-class institutions, from nonconformist chapels to insurance
companies, were able to make use of the trust, while becoming a trustee
was an excellent entrée into business habits and contacts for middle-class
men. But these trusts, with their limitation to a specific purpose, were
inflexible and expensive to administer. The organization with the greatest
possibility for business expansion had been the joint stock company but
this had been curtailed in the early eighteenth century after the South Sea
Bubble débâcle when stringent laws were passed to make sure that anyone
engaged in market activity would personally take the full brunt of failure.
This both limited possibilities of business expansion and emphasized the
moral qualities desirable in those engaged in such business.[14]

Throughout the late eighteenth and early nineteenth centuries, therefore,
even as business and professional activity rapidly expanded, there was a
dearth of impersonal forms to encompass the enterprise. A business firm
as such did not have a legal existence until well into the nineteenth century,
even though customers, creditors, and employees often acted as if it did.
Thus the personality of the entrepreneur, or partners, *was* the firm. The
rapidity with which firms ceased to exist with the death or withdrawal of
the founder and the expectation of high turnover indicate this amorphous
character.

Enterprise organization

The form which evolved for most business and professional activities was
simple, flexible, and grew directly from the family household. The single
entrepreneur together with his wife, children, other kin and servants
performed commercial, manufacturing or professional tasks. If expansion
was required this unit was reproduced by taking a partner. Partnership
required no formal contract, it was simply a relationship which existed
between people with the aim of making a profit, each partner usually
contributing capital, stock, tools, skill or labour.[15] Much like a family
member, every partner could act as an agent for the other but was also
liable for all debts. 'Partnerships were in some senses *brothers* who
represented each other.'[16]

This familial term is significant. In practice, since most production of
goods and services was carried on as part of a family setting, wives were
de facto 'partners', yet under the common law doctrine of *coverture* a
married woman only existed under her husband's protection, within his
personality. She could not sign Bills of Exchange, make contracts, sue or
be sued, collect debts or stand surety and therefore she could not act as a
partner, since for all practical purposes, on marriage a woman died a kind
of civil death.[17] Because single women would potentially marry, in custom,

they too were very seldom regarded as partners. Even the widow or child of a dead partner (as well as his servant) who received shares or an annuity from the profits of a business was specifically designated as not a partner nor did lending money to a business, even for a share in the profits, make that person a partner.[18] Both Samuel Courtauld's great-aunt and mother had invested in his Essex silk mill at crucial times for the survival of the business but were never considered partners.[19]

The whole thrust of partnership was *active* participation. Its essence was the personal nature of the relationship for no stranger could be substituted.[20] Partners had to be personally responsible as this was the only protection against fraud and business malpractice in a period of widespread financial and social instability. There was a constant fear that lifting this sanction would give unrestrained rein to 'ambitious hopes.and the habit of gambling in shares'.[21] There was also the fear that a form of joint stock would destroy individual enterprise. Thus the household head continued to represent the interests of his family and the partnership remained equivalent to the firm; indeed firms tended to be judged on the quality of their partners, a judgement frequently given moral, even religious overtones.[22]

The fluidity of the institutional framework surrounding English economic organization at this time is noticeable. In the early nineteenth century a variety of alternative forms was being proposed within the middle class and a few even tried in practice, although without much success. Some of these schemes aimed to spread responsibility and soften the impact of market forces on individual entrepreneurs and their families. Some attempted to protect the smaller producer from dominance by the larger, to retain a measure of independence from credit chains. Many still aimed to resist the break between production and consumption at the heart of industrial capitalism; their ideas were not unlike those that fed the early socialist experiments. An early venture calling itself the Birmingham Flour Company put forward 20,000 shares at £1 each. Every member was limited to twenty shares and had to covenant to purchase a certain amount of flour weekly.[23] Samuel Courtauld, the Essex silk manufacturer, planned an American scheme based on Owenite lines but it soon folded and he returned to his traditionally operated mill.[24]

The consequences of continuing to tie the entrepreneur and his dependants so closely to the fortunes of the enterprise were compounded by the particular harshness of English bankruptcy law which demanded personal repayment and often incarceration for debt. A partner in an Essex bank that failed in the panic of 1825, had long since ceased to be active, but had neglected to withdraw his name from the partnership. The bankruptcy commission stripped him of virtually all his fortune, £32,000, returning only £100 and his pocket watch.[25]

The principle of personal responsibility was behind much of the long controversy over the introduction of limited liability and the evolution of the joint stock company. Only with the evolution of public auditing of accounts and the formal registration of companies was it possible to shift the risks from the person and family of the entrepreneur. The final mid century implementation of limited liability was, significantly, made under the aegis of an appeal to laissez-faire doctrine.[26] The separation of individuals and their dependants from personal implication with the main economic form, limiting their rights and responsibilities to that of the formal contract as either managers or shareholders, can be seen as analogous to the shift from personal service to the wage contract in the working class.

In practice, even a modified form of limited liability was difficult to achieve as long as domestic accounting was not distinguished from business. The slow disentangling of finances was associated with the equally uneven physical separation of a home from workplace. Examination of account books shows that even where formal records were kept, items of income and expenditure were often muddled, while household and enterprise purchases were seldom distinguished. The mixed nature of local retail outlets helped to perpetuate such intermingling. From 1818 to 1833, an Essex farmer used an account book in which were entered purchases of food, school fees, rates, wages, horse medicine and nails jumbled with incomings from sales of corn, rents from small property as well as of payment in kind.[27]

The gradual acceptance of more accurate accounting procedures was part of a wider development in the eighteenth- and nineteenth-century mode of looking at the world in a more measurable, even quantitative way. Such a world view was particularly associated with the expansion of business and professional practices. Early merchants had needed to develop simple mechanisms to record imports and exports, to gain some consistent idea about their balance of trade. These needs helped to spread a knowledge of simple arithmetic among this section of the governing classes who had 'hitherto been extraordinarily ignorant of the subject',[28] an ignorance it should be noted, among men as well as women.

Throughout the period there are exhortations for better and more accurate accounting procedures for every aspect of business, including farming. In addition to printed account books, forms were produced for measuring and listing the yields of each field to set against fertilizers and other inputs.[29] The application of such methods to farming is of particular interest since it was advocated by those who saw farming as no longer a 'way of life' but as a capitalist enterprise. For a farmer, the inducement to keep accounts were the same as that for a merchant or tradesman, 'a love of order and the gratification of a thorough knowledge of his own affairs . . . for a farmer is a general dealer in corn and cattle; consequently, regularity and precision in business should be as much expected from the one, as from the other'.[30]

Most accounts kept in this period described assets rather than making calculations of profit, and were modelled on estate management. Nevertheless, even such primitive practice made it possible to formulate future goals for the enterprise and to check its performance.[31] The extension of partnership encouraged long-term planning and quantifiable knowledge since if one partner withdrew or died the total value of the enterprise had to be estimated using rudimentary concepts of depreciation. It encouraged the transfer from day books to ledgers to quarterly accounts, furthering the notion of a balance of profit and loss over time.

Although the enlargement of business practice began to demand such regularized systems of estimating various practices, the drive to keep regular accounts was not only located in economic experience. Production did not necessarily proceed in regular weekly, monthly or yearly spans. Sources of incomes varied widely, drains on resources could leap to cover a business slump, a harvest failure, illness in the family, a child's marriage. Indeed, it may be argued that the force necessary to make men operate within this artificial paper mould primarily came from the dictates of serious Christianity, the fundamental place within Protestantism of 'casting up accounts' with God.[32]

Particularly within Quaker and other nonconformist sects, it was part of religious duty to know one's means and operate within them, in opposition to aristocratic extravagant show and debt. These were the groups at the forefront of campaigns for accurate estimates of values. Quakers, for example, were the first to reject haggling in favour of fixed prices and such attitudes gave them an unrivalled reputation as trustworthy 'men of business'. The devout Congregational shopkeeper, John Kent of Colchester, recorded in his cash book at an end of the year which brought considerable advance in turnover:

Psalm 126, 3. The Lord hath done great things for us, whereof we are glad.

And the following year when there had been a falling off, at the end of his accounts he wrote, 'still be thankful'.[33]

Nonconformist membership gave public sanction to these beliefs in disciplinary procedures which made a member's financial situation a matter of public oversight and financial irregularity or failure a cause for expulsion from the congregation. John Kent's Lion Walk chapel in Colchester took such action in 1823 when the minister recorded:

On account of the bankruptcy of our Brother J.B., he be suspended from holding the office of Deacon for the next 3 months, the suspension is deemed a proper expression of regard to the honour of the Church but short term in recognition of his zeal and unforfeited integrity.[34]

The need for quantitative estimates of income and expenditure to be used as a basis of public accountability was also growing for local authorities faced with new demands for estimating rates and operating larger budgets. Similar developments at the national level were part of the attack on smuggling which had been an important source of income along the Suffolk and Essex coast. The vast quantities of contraband goods coming in threatened to make a mockery of public accounting as well as effecting the exchequer. Both a seriously minded Quaker farmer and a radical agnostic Suffolk doctor appeared to be ambivalent about the question of smuggling in these terms rather than taking a censorious moral stand.[35]

As with smuggling, many of these moves were regarded as an attack by the middle class on those customary practices which had evolved to balance the powers of gentry, farmers and the labouring poor. Nowhere was this as clear as in the marketing of corn, the basis of the people's food. The latter half of the eighteenth century had seen many bitter contests over the fixing of grain prices in the market place where regulation had given traditional rights of purchase to local people.[36] The new system that was evolving by-passed such protection. As a result, the careers of middlemen such as auctioneers and corn factors flourished. A contemporary making a tour of the eastern counties in 1815 was struck by the introduction of more sophisticated marketing: 'The custom of selling corn by sample in lieu of the ancient mode of bringing it in waggons to the market place, is now becoming universal.'[37] The pillared porticos of the new Corn Exchanges, built by conglomerates of middle-class men, dominated the once open street market. Such men, often also operating flour mills, became the focus of attack as the symbol of the new economic order. Pickard's mill in Birmingham was the scene of a riot in 1799, while during the war, Chelmsford corn factors and millers were vilified for keeping prices high and a Quaker corn merchant was physically assaulted in Chelmsford town centre.[38]

If products were given uniform cash values, they had to be made comparable; thus standardization of weights and measures became an aim of many reformers. Arthur Young, native of Suffolk and passionate adherent of the new agriculture, was an indefatigable proponent of both standardization and serious Christianity. In his report on Essex for the newly formed Board of Agriculture at the turn of the century, he noted that until a few years ago, each type of grain was sold with a different measure.[39] Many progressive landowners shifted their method of estimating gross income from the number of rents to the interest charged on capital and labour annually expended. This calculation of profitability, enforced by cost conscious estate agents and baliffs, influenced farmers. An Essex man who farmed over 1000 acres saw himself 'more in the nature of a person employing capital than a farmer'.[40]

The Napoleonic War gave further impetus to these trends. In the eastern counties, under threat of invasion, vicars were called upon to make valuations of local assets,[41] while the wartime creation of income tax necessitated dividing various categories of wealth and income. The Ordnance Survey of the 1790s, although mainly carried out for military purposes, had the added effect of giving far more accurate knowledge of land holdings. This was complemented by the widespread mapping which had started with estimates for enclosure, then extended in the negotiations over tithes, and culminated in the surveying for railway lines in the 1830s and 1840s. The estimates made for the 'commutation of tithes', officially recognized by law in 1836, are a particularly striking example of a shift to quantification through replacing goods in kind with a 'cash nexus'.

As local government administration strengthened in the early nineteenth century, the shift to cash estimation of worth was furthered by rate assessments for different kinds of property. It continued with developments as diverse as converting probate appraisals into monetary values, and the abolition of truck payments in kind to work people – the latter being a particular concern of both humanitarians and political economists. The mechanisms of conversion helped to create a range of new skills including surveying and map making, accountancy, auctioneering and valuing, in both town and countryside. Other developments favoured the financial specialities of accountancy and the sale of securities. The early nineteenth century was the period when securities were listed under official prices, when provincial stock exchanges, including Birmingham's, were established, and when public auditing of accounts for entities such as the railway companies became accepted. All these mechanisms pointed towards lifting the burden of trust from personal behaviour to more remote institutional-ized forms while at the same time creating a corps of experts further removed from the amateur and closing ranks against the untrained working-class man or the woman of any background.

In a similar vein, the late eighteenth century was also the period when insurance against fire risk began to be widely used. Insurance plaques on buildings became something of a status symbol in local areas as well as an identifier for the fire company's engines. In order to calculate the cost of replacement for fire damage – itself an exercise in quantification – premises had to be classified more precisely. What was a hazard or a nuisance, what was productive plant, what was waste? The concept of life assurance also began to be accepted towards the third quarter of the eighteenth century. Life policies were recognized as a form of security to be used as yet another type of liquid property. The need to estimate and measure the life span, to separate the fit from the unfit, involved medical men as well as actuaries, experts in just such evaluations.[42] In order to calculate charges for annuities as well as life policies, it was necessary to have a more precise definition of an individual's chronological age. Exact age was a concept also promoted by the early statistical bodies and those bringing pressure to create a national census, culminating in civil registration of births, deaths and marriages in 1837. Finally, a more apparent and direct source of quantitative and rational thought lay with the expansion of science, in particular its application to technology which was a central concern of Birmingham manufacturers from the 1740s.[43] The success of some products depended not just on scientific innovation but on precision gained from standardized measurement which permitted the creation of interchangeable parts. For example, part of the Ransome family's successful Ipswich iron foundry depended on standar-dized, easily replaceable plough shares.[44]

The valuation of actions and materials in monetary terms was regarded as a quintessentially masculine skill and prerogative. Such expertise was an essential part of the middle-class challenge to the aristocratic male whose skills lay with gambling, duelling, sporting and sexual prowess. The accomplishments of middle-class men were primarily sedentary and literate, the manipulation of the pen and the ruler rather than the sword and gun. They implied a cerebral control of the world but were no less effective in yielding economic rewards which could lead to wealth and power.

Land and capital

It was not so much the ownership of land *per se* which ran counter to this orientation, but the way land was regarded and used. Male heads of landed families thought in dynastic terms, believing the intact estate to be the basis of power and status. Like all property owners, the aristocracy and gentry felt tension between their desire to hand on an unbroken patrimony and to support a variety of dependants, usually but not only, members of their family. Since land is finite, primogeniture was the usual form of aristocratic inheritance, strengthened through the device of entail which limited the heir's ability to sell or give away part of the estate. Nevertheless, there were constant pressures to break entail precisely to provide such support.

The increasing liquidity of capital freed from land, which was so central to the economic fortunes of the middle class, thus represents at least a partial solution to this dilemma.[45] The middle class favoured partible inheritance, a roughly equal division of property between all dependants. The difference in the two patterns is strikingly illustrated by the change in inheritance practices of men in the judiciary. As Duman has shown, as the social background and identification of this elite group shifted away from the gentry and towards a more codified legal profession, so they began to leave their substantial properties away from a single heir, usually the eldest son, to their wives and children equally, with a growing minority even turning over initial control of the whole to the wife.[46]

An important consequence of the middle-class pattern of partible inheritance, however, was that great wealth was necessary before it would be possible to free all sons from the necessity to work. John Hanson, a City merchant who moved into rural Essex to farm and play the country gentleman, realized that it would be better to bring up his fourteen children, all of whom survived, in London where the boys would be groomed 'for business, Merchants or Bankers or what they have a turn for and therefore if taken entirely out from the Scene of Business and brought up in the Gayer Scene' it might be an 'arduous task to make them relish business', as his mother wrote to him.[47]

Partnership introduced a flexibility for middle-class undertakings lacking among the aristocracy where only inheritance, purchase or marriage could increase land holdings. Partnership meant that new personnel, new skills and resources could be brought into the enterprise without the necessity of marriage, although marriage was often used to cement an already existing partnership.[48] It can be argued that primogeniture was less necessary because partnership and other adaptable features kept most significant capital in liquid form among the middle class. Partible inheritance, too, encouraged a positive view of active economic life for men.

The absence of primogeniture was striking in our analysis of 622 wills from the two areas. There was clear evidence of partible inheritance from 55 per cent of lower middle-class wills and 48 per cent from the upper middle class. Some evidence of partible inheritance appears in 79 per cent of cases and if one child, usually a son or son-in-law, received stock or tools, the other children had either already been provided for or received cash equivalents. Even those successful merchants and manufacturers who were closely connected with the local gentry seemed to have held to a version of partible inheritance. Samuel Galton, a wealthy Birmingham banker who, by the time of his death in 1832 was a considerable landowner, divided his land as well as liquid capital between his three sons. His daughters were left equally lucrative trusts to provide an income.[49] This pattern emerges as a model for the upper reaches of the middle class. On the whole sons and daughters are treated as if they had a right to inherit equally in terms of values even if they inherited different *kinds* of property.

It is also important to keep in mind that a business, farm or professional practice had to be potentially lucrative to make it attractive to a successor as a going concern. Many businesses were on too small a scale to make this possible.[50] It is not surprising, therefore, that in 30 per cent of the wills examined there were explicit directions to convert real to liquid assets through sale and to divide the proceeds between the various legatees often with the injunction to 'share and share alike'. Even prestige houses such as the ornamental villas built on the outskirts of provincial towns were often not regarded as family homes in the sense of 'a county seat', but at death would also be sold to raise capital.[51] From various evidence, including the wills, it appears that through the lifetime of the children (and dependent others) lump sums, apprenticeship premiums, partnership capital and other transfers were being made as pre-mortem arrangements. This would provide for children sequentially as their needs arose, for example at marriage, and also as the enterprise fortunes rose and fell. These inheritance patterns and economic strategies were in keeping with a general outlook which did not stress continuity in the enterprise. It was common for a man to be involved in several different partnerships or to shift from one type of business into another. Nor does there seem to have been concern with giving the enterprise a strong identity. Such casualness was related to the absence of corporate forms previously discussed, and after mid century there does appear to be a stronger family identification with a specific 'business house', more closely related to the private company than the simple partnership or single entrepreneur.

The relative fluidity of many businesses is also related to the place which business activity took in middle-class life. Contrary to some ideas about entrepreneurship, business and economic pursuits did not always dominate men's consciousness.[52] It has been noted that many religiously committed men feared that business concerns were usurping their energies and attentions. A Congregational Suffolk brewer, active in politics and other local affairs, felt that 'it is a very grevious evil when a man suffers his business to become his master and he begins to serve it as if he were a slave'.[53] Even the Essex Unitarian, George Courtauld, when his son as a young man was dithering about what trade to enter, sharply remarked that 'the aim of business is to provide for wants and comforts in the world' and rag picking would be better than chemistry if it paid better in order to support family and social obligations to the community.[54]

Enterprise finance

It was as well that many took such a relaxed view, for throughout the period there remained a dearth of trustworthy institutions for raising capital or in which to invest. The problems of the banking system were only the most well known. Smaller country banks, in particular, failed continuously. The sixty which collapsed in the terrible winter of 1825–6 were the most dramatic casualties of a general insecurity 'stemming from the volatility of both business and the money market'.[55] A detailed study of the Essex village of Witham during this period reveals a number of bankruptcies. Under unlimited liability this could have disastrous effects on the individuals and families concerned, the twists of fortune which became the stuff of Victorian novels. But within a small community the effects rippled far beyond the individual family. A leading attorney, steward for Tollesbury Manor, property owner, and pillar of the established church, Jacob Howell Pattisson went spectacularly bankrupt in the 1850s. He and his wife, daughter of local gentry, together with their sixteen children, had to leave the town. But Pattisson was also trustee and general financial factotum and men like Jesse Owers, yeoman, had named Pattisson and his father (and partner) as executor and handed over his fortune of £360 to them to invest in public funds to produce an income for his widow.[56] One family's tragedy, however, could be another's opportunity. When Matthew Harvey went bankrupt in Witham and had to sell all his property, the shopkeeping family of Butler moved in to buy up the leavings and build on Harvey land. Thus fortunes rose and fell at every level.

Given such uncertainty and the fact that credit arrangements remained essentially local or at the most regional, personal reputation became a key to survival. The behaviour of the entrepreneur, his family and household as well as their material setting, were tangible indications of financial as well as moral probity. The couplet coined for the late eighteenth-century gentleman farmer could have equally applied to any family enterprise:

> Keep up appearances, there lies the test
> The World will give thee Credit for the Rest.[57]

As most economic historians have long recognized, capital and credit were mainly raised from personal sources. Even in manufacture, most capital was needed for transport, labour, and rental of premises rather than heavy plant or machinery. Credit was necessary for short-term purposes such as buying stock or bridging the gap between buying raw materials and producing and/or selling goods, between sowing and harvest. 'Cash-flow' was the most serious problem even for professional men made vulnerable by long periods of waiting for bills to be settled.[58]

Church or chapel membership was particularly effective in displaying integrity. Local voluntary society membership also provided local knowledge about creditworthiness as well as more general business contacts. The establishment of such a base was undoubtedly one of the attractions of groups such as the Freemasons which flourished in this period. Active Freemasons, as with church or chapel, could gain a fair idea of a man's personal capacities and resources. Fellow members of such organizations would be more willing, not just to make loans or investments under such circumstances, but to give guarantees and stand surety for various posts from postmaster to bank manager. Other important but less tangible assets gained from local knowledge included good will and the reputation of a business or professional practice. Finally, many routine financial transactions demanded a certain amount of personal trust. Private banks used their own issue of bank notes, and local shops continued the practice of trade tokens (issued as their own currency). The heart of commercial operations was the Bill of Exchange and the Promissary Note, both of which rested on assumptions of others' creditworthiness.[59]

Of all the mechanisms which were being developed by the middle class to solve their problems of capital needs, credit and the balance between patrimony and dependency, probably the most significant was the way men and women's property was handled. The devices developed to retain the use of women's property while at the same time ensuring their support, meant that the marriage of daughters or sisters was not necessarily a drain on resources; indeed such marriage might enlarge the field of partners, contacts and sources of finance as will be seen.

Thus the Galton sons of Birmingham inherited land and cash and were expected to manage and use their assets while the daughters were given income in trust. There was no expectation that women would be active economic agents or even care for their own property which, as in the Galton case, was left in the hands of six male trustees. The idea of 'provision' for women as dependants derived from aristocratic arrangements but took new forms within middle-class property. The provision was made in such a way that male trustees had access to the women's capital to use in the pursuit of their own economic interests.[60]

The personal trust (as separate from the charitable trust) was based in equity, and had been created to preserve landed property intact while ensuring protection for daughters after marriage. In particular it was meant to guarantee that sons of daughters would receive a share of their grandfather's estate. The trust form was appropriated on a large scale by the middle class since it could be divided between income for support and capital as described above and had the subsidiary advantage of keeping part of the family assets safe from creditors even under unlimited liability.

The increasing use of trust-like arrangements was part of a move away from the common law right of widows to traditional dower (or thirds – a fixed part of their husband's estate). With formal repeal of dower in 1833, wives lost the absolute right to inherit. Only in cases where provision had been made by trust (or its equivalent) the widow might 'enjoy the use of her own property'.[61] The move was not an unequivocal gain for wives. Rather it represents part of a gradual shift to flexibility of property arrangements while at the same time increasing the personal dependence of women on their male protectors, especially as many a trustee was, in fact, the husband. Even before the act, in the wills, several testators specifically break dower, often in return for the widow's limited rights to support, usually withdrawn on remarriage.

The essence of any trust, charitable or personal, centred on the separation of legal ownership, vested in one or more trustees, from the rights of the beneficiary to specified proceeds from the property.[62] The trustees were allowed to act upon the property, to sell or rent the legal title, to make contracts on it. As long as the beneficiary continued to receive the proceeds, a great deal was left to the trustees' discretion. Indeed just under two-thirds of all the trustees named in the wills were male friends and 35 per cent male relatives. As long as trustees were primarily kin and 'friends', the trust was intermediate between a family dominated inheritance system and state dictated rules.[63]

The use of trusts on marriage or death can be taken as a rough indicator of high income and status since it shows sufficient resources to release widows and children from self-support. In the sample of wills from both areas, trusts were made for wives in one-third of cases; in just over one-quarter among the lower middle class and 55 per cent in the upper middle class. 71 per cent of men of independent means left their widows property in trust; 35 per cent (about the average) of merchants, tradesmen and manufacturers, but only 15 per cent of professionals, an indication that their resources were in skills and income rather than property.

Under common law, all of a woman's liquid property, unlike land, became her husband's at marriage. Unless there had been a trust, the whole of the family's resources were open to seizure for debt. Furthermore, daughters and widows became possible targets for fortune hunters, even at modest levels.[64] Thus the desire to protect vulnerable female property was integral to middle-class practice at the same time as the concept of female dependency was being elevated in political and social thought. The growing use of trusts by the upper middle class was one device for control over women's assets, but even where trusts were not specifically made, executors were often instructed to convert property through sale. For example, John Long, yeoman of Witham, in 1811 directed that his friend William Potts was to sell his lands and buildings in order to provide £20 to the testator's sister after which his wife was to have the remaining money.

Another common practice primarily among the lower middle class was to direct the wives to carry on the business as a holding operation until children were old enough to take over. Abraham Garrard, tanner of Witham, in 1801 appointed a fellow tanner and a farmer as trustees and guardians to his children. His wife was to 'carry on my Business of a Tanner's at my now Dwelling House and Tan Office', and the trustees would help her to do so until the eldest son reached 21. Even where a wife inherited and controlled all property during her lifetime, she would often have no say over it at her death since her husband would have given directions for its disposal in his will. In addition there were often specific directions laid down about living arrangements for widows and their children. In the sample of wills only 15 per cent of the upper middle class left their wives completely free of all control and direction either of the property or the way they were to run their lives. There is also some evidence from the wills that testamentary control over women's property increased over the period.[65]

A similar combination of support and control characterizes the provision made for children, nieces, nephews and grandchildren. In those cases where children were present, about one-third of inheritance was in trust form, reaching 48 per cent in the upper middle class. The difference in the two groups is less, however, than in the case of wives for it involved young children incapable of self-support. Of those with independent means (including women), 55 per cent left property to their children in trust; 46 per cent of those in trade and, in contrast to their behaviour with wives, professionals 43 per cent. Small masters and farmers only did so in about 25 per cent of cases which indicates that they were using other strategies. The control of children's fate including directions for apprenticeship and for living arrangements was completely absent in 47 per cent of the lower middle-class and 29 per cent of the upper middle-class sample.

In those cases where children were differentiated by sex, it is significant that sons were *more* often directed than daughters. No detailed instructions were given to daughters in 46 per cent of cases, but only 28 per cent of sons were free to do what they wished with their inherited property. This indicates that while daughters were often provided for financially by trust-like arrangements they were at least then left to carry on their lives, while sons, who more often inherited premises, tools and stock were given more explicit directions.[66]

Providing for dependants

Part of the middle-class masculine role was to manipulate and control property in order to support dependants. Trusteeship, both formal and informal, was an extension and formal recognition of that role. Only 9 per cent of trustees in the sample were women, almost entirely widows holding property in trust for their children. They were never trustees for other people's property. Armaretta Argent, widow of a Witham farmer, was a trustee as well as guardian of her children. However, she shared her trusteeship with her husband's two brothers, also farmers. Although she inherited the stock of horses, cattle and implements of husbandry, the trustees were instructed to sell all the rest and divide it between the seven children. Her share, even of household goods, was not to exceed £100. She remained a joint trustee and guardian 'so long as she continue my widow and no longer', a set of terms which gave little of the usual trustee's discretionary powers. Wives, however, were often called upon to act as executrix. Of wills with an identifiable executor, 28 per cent were wives, 30 per cent male friends and 19 per cent male kin. An executor could act in a similar way to a trustee directing property according to the wishes of the testator but the arrangement was less formal and, more important, short term. Once the property had been disposed of or redirected, the task was over, unlike a trusteeship which was on-going, even beyond the life of the trustee and beneficiary.

It was noted that a smaller proportion of professional men seem to have used trust devices in providing for their widows. This points to an important group whose property was mainly in the form of income based on fees for services, small investments, pensions, annuities, subscriptions, rents or mortgages rather than urban land, buildings, stocks or machinery and tools.[67] A nineteenth-century expert on banking practice declared that clergyman, naval or military officers, professional men and salaried officials of every degree, along with annuitants of all kinds, unless they had other property which extended beyond their life incomes were, 'manifestly ineligible' to borrow from banks, or, indeed, to stand surety for others.[68]

Women as investors are not even mentioned, yet their investments were important in supplying mortgages for town expansion; they made up 20 per cent of loan capital traded in late eighteenth-century towns.[69] Female capital supported the joint stock companies behind municipal utilities and railways.[70] Widows and spinsters were the core of those investors requiring a steady income without administrative worries. As the 'ardent saving section of the community', they favoured safe investments like annuities.[71] Indeed the annuity may be seen as the classic form of income provision for the dependant: female kin, 'friends' and ex-servants. An annuity was the purchase of an income out of capital for a fixed, regular sum to be paid to a beneficiary.[72] Annuities could be perpetual, even a type of property to be inherited, but were often for life or a fixed period with conditions attached, for example with a prohibition on remarriage, or to take care of the testator's children. Estates were often sold to facilitate the creation of annuities. Annuities were a reasonably secure source of income although not always foolproof. In the 1800s, an Essex doctor's sister had an annuity from the income of a farm. When the property was sold, the new owner queried whether he was still responsible for paying and it took a local lawyer (the woman's nephew) several years to enforce its provisions.[73] The annuity was a type of income even more carefully controlled by the donor and his representatives since, unlike the trust, the recipient did not have a claim on the capital but solely on the income.

This type of income was closely related to a pension, still often regarded as the spoils of office and sometimes even available for purchase. Arthur Ryland, a first generation Birmingham solicitor, despite considerable kin support and local patronage, was only making a modest living in the 1840s. In 1844 the Treasury awarded him an annuity of £94 a year as compensation for a Commissionership of Bankruptcy which he had lost. 'This is a most agreeable thing', he confided to his diary, 'I have often thought with some anxiety of the possibility of my being laid up with illness – this will keep us from want.'[74] One of the groups beginning to set the social tone in provincial towns, particularly after the war, was military officers, who since the mid eighteenth century had enjoyed the option of retiring on half-pay as well as having pensions provided for their widows and orphans.[75] The families of retired service personnel were an important part of the local middle class in Essex and Suffolk.

In addition to these steadier sources of income, the subscription was often used as a reward for talent, for special functions or a claim on those in a position to grant such funds, in some cases bordering on the giving of charity. The recipient could solicit subscriptions as when Mary Ann Hedge, a Colchester clock manufacturer's daughter, raised a local subscription for the publication of her books. Since subscribers' names were published in the preface of such volumes or in the local press, they gained status for helping to support a worthy person and setting an example to the community. Bernard Barton was only a bank clerk in Woodbridge, Suffolk who received a small salary. Yet he had a national reputation as a writer. When he lost his small investments in a business failure, local friends were joined by national figures such as Southey and Lamb to raise a subscription which provided him and his daughter with an income for life.[76]

There were thus a variety of sources and types of income, including rents, which provided a living to those who wished for a 'genteel competence' not requiring active intervention. These resources were used by both men and women, but there is no doubt that the latter depended on them more heavily. In the census sample from the two areas, 63 per cent of all middle-class female household heads were 'independent' as an occupational classification (and 70 per cent of those so designated could be regarded as lower middle class).

These various sources of support for dependants often had to be cobbled together to make provision by precisely those men who the banker saw as poor credit risks, those without property behind them. The idea of clubbing together to form mutual societies to insure against contingencies had begun in the early eighteenth century, but within the middle class the idea of individual responsibility for wives and children transformed such schemes into the purchase of life assurance policies, a by-product of which, once again, was to produce collateral to be used to raise capital. The most obvious appeal was to the professional man who, even with an income of £1000 a year, could leave his family destitute[77] and it is no surprise to find that civil servants, medical men and the clergy were the leaders in the field of life assurance. Although the Rev. Richard Cobbold had built his own rectory in a Suffolk village in 1827 he bemoaned the fact that he could not leave his wife a 'residence of an independent kind' when she was a widow, for, as he remarked, 'few people suffer more severely from change of circumstances than clergymen's widows'.[78] This sentiment was echoed by the Congregational minister in Essex who pointed out to his congregation that the minister, unlike his tradesmen and farming parishioners, had nothing to fall back on if deprived of his post as they were threatening him.[79]

In no other economic form does the concept of female and childhood dependence show more clearly than in the concept of life assurance, the epitome of masculine responsibility. The Birmingham Victorian Benefit Building Society in 1850 summed up the message in promoting life assurance: 'it assures the *only certain means*' by which provision can be made in the event of death for those dependent on the exertion of others: 'the desire and power to make provision for others, to secure competency and comfort to those from whom death has removed their natural protector, which is the first object of Life Assurance, is a privilege, as it is one of the first duties of civilized man'.[80]

The provision of life assurance could also be good for a professional image. A Medical Benevolent Society was established in Birmingham in 1821 whose object was to assist indigent practitioners and their widows and orphans. The trustees and officers were well established medical men in the town and, quite apart from humane motives, it was not in their interests to have their profession reduced in the public eye by being associated with destitution. All registered medical practitioners were eligible and the emphasis on registration was significant. One of the major preoccupations of the medical profession at this time was to exclude men regarded as not properly qualified. There were quarterly meetings of the Court of Directors of the Society to deal with claims on the funds. The annual subscription was 1 gn. which, presumably, was within the means of all but the most poverty stricken doctors. One of the rules of the society stipulated that if widows remarried they could no longer claim benefits, making clear it was the woman's status as a dependant which was at issue; 'on remarriage' meant she became the responsibility of another man.[81]

Lurking fears that such forward rational planning might show a lack of faith in God's will had to be dispelled. As one proponent of life assurance wrote in 1804, 'I do not intend to speak against a manly [sic] and religious dependence on the Author of our being',[82] while an article on 'life assurance' in a family magazine (found in the attic of an Essex farmhouse) neatly solved the issue by closing the piece with a stress on the need for 'insurance for blessedness' through religion.[83] Although the idea of life assurance was widely propagated, it was slow to take root and only grew with the rise of salaried white-collar occupations in the second half of the nineteenth century. It is estimated that by 1845 only about 100,000 people carried individual assurance.[84] Among the 158 wills examined for Witham, only one person, significantly a solicitor's clerk, Daniel Till, specifically mentions life assurance.

This range of financial organizations gave middle-class men access to resources and built up their expertise. In controlling their own family's destinies, these men were gaining skills and contacts which were vital to their running of local affairs, a pattern nowhere more evident than in the office of trustee. As the period progressed men with some legal or financial training or at least business experience, began to specialize as trustees and executors. In Witham several legal partnerships of father and son appear in such capacities in a great number of wills as well as the previously mentioned solicitor's clerk, Daniel Till. As would be expected, these were the solicitors like Jacob Pattisson who were also entrusted with sums of money to invest for their clients. Trustees and executors were customarily left small sums for their pains, which in the case of such specialists could build up into a tidy sum. But it was probably the inside knowledge of local affairs, particularly property transactions, which was the greatest advantage of being a trustee. A variety of local records reveals that certain men constantly appear in similar semi-public positions, not only as trustees for individuals but for town and religious charities, the almshouses, distributions to the poor and school foundations as well as the chapel. In Witham, the Barwell family of farmer/butchers and the farmer/builder Beadels – father and son, brothers, uncle and nephews – over the years formed a pool of 'community brokers'. Their subsequent purchase and turnover of property shows how their scope of operations was enhanced by information they had picked up. Their reputation as men of business as well as their own fortunes flourished.[85]

The Essex and Suffolk Equitable Insurance Society was started in Colchester in 1803. It provided fire insurance to the surrounding region and was run as a corporate trust. In its first years, local businessmen, professional men and farmers, as directors, themselves took much of the responsibility which later devolved on to a paid official. The directors accepted or rejected proposals, adjudicated on every claim however small, looked into the standing of every applicant for a sub-agency, personally made whatever survey was considered necessary, signed and examined all policies and endorsement of policies. 'Neither they nor their secretary had any previous training in insurance business, no statistics and very little other information was available to them, and *it was necessary therefore, for them to feel their way very carefully*' (our emphasis).[86] Such an experience must have been not only invaluable in teaching business skills, but the involvement of the bankers, grocers, merchants, millers, brewers and others in the overlooking of such claims must have produced valuable insights into local affairs; the movement of markets, land transactions, building plans, and the rise and fall of individuals and their families.

It was through such experience that middle-class men gradually built up the personal competence in business affairs which was part of a masculine persona. This model was often put forward as being natural to men in the same way that homemaking, wife and motherhood were seen as natural to women. This competence, however, was clearly a product of experience, of the creation of economic, legal and social forms which reinforced masculine responsibility and authority in the expanding economic sphere.

The interdependence of enterprise, family and friends

The particular characteristic of middle-class property was its flexibility. Material assets were supplemented by and could be converted into personal skills and expertise in a variety of ways. But this personal element in the use of middle-class property was set in a network of kinship, 'friendship' and community. The thrusting individual entrepreneur whose only aim was profit maximization is rare in the local records. There are innumerable examples of the way personal ties entered into business and commercial affairs, not only the trust and partnership but many a less formal guise. Richard Garrett who expanded his father's Suffolk forge to lay the foundations for an agricultural machinery business married the daughter of a man who invented an early threshing machine. Although there was never a formal partnership between them, such a contact provided a vital source of technological expertise.[87] An Essex estate agent had established an agency which 'could never have thrived so well or made so few mistakes had it not been for his father and elder brother who were solicitors in Chelmsford'. His son married into a Devonshire silk merchant's family having met his wife through his friendship with her brother at boarding school. He then went on to borrow a substantial sum from his father-in-law to buy a partnership in a Chelmsford bank, which increased the scope of his business.[88]

Kinship ties provided London or even overseas outlets for provincial enterprises. Merchants, farmers and manufacturers, and especially bankers, depended on London facilities and, with trusted kin in such positions, the wheels of business turned more smoothly. Even at a more local level, kinship and friendship often provided the paths along which goods and services travelled. The farming family of Cordy benefited from the marriage of three daughters to Ipswich shopkeepers. Kinship ensured a reliable outlet for farm produce; the shops were assured supplies from fresh stock.[89] Relations, friends or co-religionists were used to stand surety, to raise a loan, to guarantee a post for an agency or for a clerkship. Relations as creditors might delay or ease the repayment of debt. Samuel Walker who had wavered between unsuccessful business ventures and whose real commitment was to the ministry, had borrowed over £500 from his maternal uncle, an Essex wool merchant. Walker could only repay the debt in small regular instalments and these payments formed the basis of regular visits between the two families.[90]

Kin and friends connected to a business could be counted on not to engage in industrial sabotage or the leaking of trade secrets. They were an ideal source of new skills and personnel for the enterprise, especially younger members of the family and children of friends. Sons were sometimes sent out to be trained by other relatives and friends. An Evangelical vicar in Ipswich coached the son of his friend, a country parish priest, and guided the young man through his entry to a church living.[91] An Independent minister, similarly, coached the son of a local doctor who was a deacon in the chapel for a career in the ministry in return for free medical services to the minister and his family.[92]

The group with the greatest overlap between kinship, friendship and religious community were the Quakers, as their use of the terms 'cousin' and 'Friend' testify. Since their ministry was entirely made up of laymen (and women), they often combined religious missions with commercial travelling. Entry into a town or village Meeting and to local Quaker homes was used as an opportunity to make loans, buy supplies, show samples of goods and even acquire marriage partners. This enabled Quakers to build up networks of wholesale and retail, supplier and buyer, debtor and creditor, of the utmost trustworthiness, networks which could usually carry an enterprise over financial difficulty. John Perry, an Ipswich draper, was twice declared bankrupt in the hard times of the 1820s and 1830s. He was supported by the powerful and wealthy members of his local Quaker congregation; in particular, his wife's niece's husband, Robert Ransome, a partner in a large iron manufacturing business. The Elders gave advice, made loans and backed his efforts at collecting debts. Ransome, as Perry's landlord, also arranged to rent him a smaller shop.[93]

While the immediate family was important for certain tasks, such as the raising of infants and small children, the boundaries of kinship were fluid, the definitions of kinship and friendship malleable. This flexibility provided a range of material and economic resources which gave personal ties a depth based on mutual welfare. Such interchange does not have to be seen in terms of altruism *or* instrumentality. For instance, since there were few safe outlets for investment, surplus capital could be directed along personal lines at commercial rates of return while at the same time building up reciprocal relationships. A young man surplus to the immediate family enterprise could be sent off for training, and could contribute labour to a like-minded family. Parents could be confident that their son's general conduct would be overlooked and his welcome secure.

The above arrangements did not always, however, lead to unequivocal felicity. There were sometimes contradictory pulls on individuals committed to both a business and personal mode. For example, decisions to give financial aid and services could be pressed because of friendship or kinship obligations when it might not be in the best interests of the business. Provincial bankers in particular were forced into such a position without being able to shelter behind more impersonal mechanisms such as formal securities against loans.

Some kin and friends who were not successful in a worldly sense could become a burden on the better off. John Harriott who had retired from the Navy had a brief partnership in the wine trade with his father-in-law. He soon pulled out to farm in Essex and the business deteriorated until the older man was being threatened with gaol for debt. Harriott assumed responsibility for paying this off, protecting his father-in-law's honour and business credit even after his wife's death and his subsequent remarriage.[94] Elizabeth Gibbins, daughter of a prosperous Birmingham Quaker banking family, married a man with no established family business and his lack of success was a source of constant worry to the family. For a time he found work as a commercial traveller in the iron trade and his wife then hoped this would 'give him an opportunity to support his family respectably' but ten years later he was unemployed again. It was rare for such a case to be abandoned by family or friends and Elizabeth was fortunate in being able to partially depend on them for support for herself and her children.[95]

Family and friends could give poor advice, fail to provide efficient services, even refuse aid. Archibald Kenrick set up in business as a buckle manufacturer in late eighteenth-century Birmingham with the help of his parents. He was soon in need of money to bolster his credit and paid the older couple a visit hoping to arrange a loan. He recorded in his diary that his mother had refused as they 'had but little income and a necessity of making a provision for my sisters'. However, his father consented to a loan of £100 which would be deducted from his inheritance. 'Mother consented unwillingly as she had saved it for my sisters.' Archibald then pointed out that it was hard for him to begin 'without any foundation and very discouraging' and admitted that he may have 'spoke rather too warm'. His parents then reminded him that they did what they could for all their children and that 'they lived closer than any of us. . . .'.[96]

The combination of material, social and emotional ties could become explosive. Family and friendship quarrels could have disruptive effects on business, while business failure, or even success, could quickly sour personal relations. In the next generation of the Kenricks, Samuel had been taken on as a partner by his uncle Archibald in 1812. However, a disagreement led Samuel to leave and go into direct competition. Not surprisingly this produced difficult and complicated feelings for all those concerned. This was particularly acute for Samuel's cousin Marianne Kenrick, daughter and sister of his previous partners, who Samuel had married shortly after entering the business. Marianne was torn between her husband on the one hand, and her father and brothers on the other. Samuel began to be subject to paranoid feelings, cut off from the people he had lived and worked with for so long. Rebecca Kenrick, Marianne's sister, commented on the situation in a letter. She found herself wishing that Samuel had a male friend he could talk to, but his friends up to then had, of course, been precisely those cousins (and brothers-in-law) with whom he was now at loggerheads. Unfortunately, she went on, 'he has no one but Marianne to talk over business with. It is much better he should open his mind to her than keep it all to himself. But still it is wearing on her. He so often thinks one or other looks cold or sly on him and is so surprised Marianne cannot see it'. Rebecca went on to say that she herself made a point of not talking to either side.[97]

Nowhere were the ties of kinship, friendship and business more evident than in the way partnership functioned. By far the most common form of partnership was father and son(s), brothers, uncle and nephew. Sisters married their brothers' partners and sisters' husbands often became partners after marriage thus binding two families into the fortunes of the enterprise. Arthur Albright, a manufacturing chemist in Birmingham, took into partnership his sister's husband Edmund Sturge and Edmund's brother Joseph Sturge. When that partnership was dissolved he turned to another brother-in-law.[98] Since one of the main problems of the partnership form was continuity of personnel, these personal ties helped to counteract the potentially disruptive winding up of the business or search for new partners at the death or withdrawal of the old. When both sons of a Colchester paint merchant died young, he turned to his son-in-law, a draper in the town. This young man switched to the paint business and moved his family over the shop. Significantly, he had been a keen member of the same Congregational chapel as his wife's family.[99]

Partnership and the analogous less formal arrangements characteristic of the lower middle class throw light on the somewhat puzzling combination of deep, often affectionate, connections between relatives and what appears to be strict, even harsh business arrangements. In joining a partnership, the pattern seems often to have been for the father or senior relative to provide a sum for the son to buy into the enterprise, which the junior would then be required to pay back with interest out of his share of the profits. This might be true even when the son was in partnership with his father and the profits came from the family firm.[100] Such an arrangement can be regarded as a type of pre-mortem inheritance but timed to be of maximum use and to minimize the drain on family resources. Corresponding strategies were used at a less prosperous level. An aging farmer sold his stock to his sons after he had permission from the landlord to turn over the lease of the farm to them. He used the interest from this sale, duly extracted from the sons, to buy milk back from them to use in a milk round he set up to support his old age.[101]

Similar patterns can be discerned with post-mortem inheritance. Sons (or nephews) would be given an option to buy back into the enterprise often with resources left to them. This gave the legatees some flexibility if they chose not to take up the option, but there would have to be strong inducement not to do so. A Witham farmer left his wife his stock and tools, but his two brothers-in-law who were also farmers were willed the lease, the implication being that they were to farm the property until the eldest son, John, reached 21. At that time, John was to pay his uncles the value of the lease plus stock. If he died or refused to do so, the three other sons in turn were to be given a similar option. These young men would be expected to pay for their opportunity to work the farm out of the proceeds of their father's estate residue left to them.[102]

These arrangements are almost always found among male kin. The daughters of the Witham farmer received an equal share of the estate but with neither obligation nor opportunity to re-enter the family business and, of course, daughters or nieces were not expected to enter into partnerships. As we have seen in the sample of wills, daughters were more often than sons left legacies free from controls or directions for future use. The expectation of a commercial debt/credit relationship between the male generations and its absence for women draws attention to a central feature of gender and property relations. A son or younger man was 'loaned' capital and other resources on condition that he repay when he was in a position to do so. A daughter was regarded as being a permanently *personal* dependant of her father (or brothers) unless and until she married and became dependent on her husband. She 'owed' personal service to the male head of the household, including being sent to assist in the households of her brothers or other kin, since she could never pay back her support or inheritance financially or in services to the working enterprise. Rebecca Kenrick's brother entered into partnership with his father, with all the trappings of formal financial arrangements and a growing share of the profits. Her father had settled a steady income of around £300 a year from the business for her use. Rebecca kept house for one of her brothers, took care of her elderly mother and spent much time staying in the homes of her other brothers when their wives were producing the numerous Kenrick off-spring.[103]

These inter-generational arrangements reflect the flexibility of middle-class property. They also are evidence of the key role of active male and passive female forms of that property. Such flexibility was also a feature of the pool of kinship, friendship and community relationships which could be called upon at various times and which helped to counteract the potentially disruptive or competing claims of several adult children on one family enterprise. Surplus sons could be diverted to other enterprises while daughters could add husbands as partners or subtract themselves to other establishments as wives of male entrepreneurs.

The role of marriage in the enterprise

This process was encouraged by the free choice of marriage partners. 'Free choice' was, however, set in a carefully controlled context of mutual values and religious concerns. Within the lower middle class, spouses were found through local kinship, friendship and religious communities. The more prosperous the family and the wider its sphere of operations, the likelier the chance of marriage outside the local area, although not outside the 'community'. Quaker marriages are an example of a group spread very thinly geographically but highly integrated in a network extending within regions, over the whole British Isles and occasionally even overseas. Since a period of training in the household of kin or friends was one of the most common experiences of young men in a variety of occupations, it is not surprising that often a future wife was met there. Among numerous other examples, this was the way that the Kenrick ménage had reached the uncomfortable position of familial divisions. The originator of the buckle business, Archibald Kenrick, had taken his nephew Samuel into the business in the period when his own sons were too young to help. In 1811, Samuel was offered a choice between becoming a salaried clerk or a partner. He opted for the partnership and cemented the relationship by marrying his cousin, Marianne, who was, of course, also his senior partner's daughter.

The records for both local areas reveal a minority pattern of sibling and cousin marriages. In the former, two brothers from one family would marry two sisters from another or brother and sister marry sister and brother.

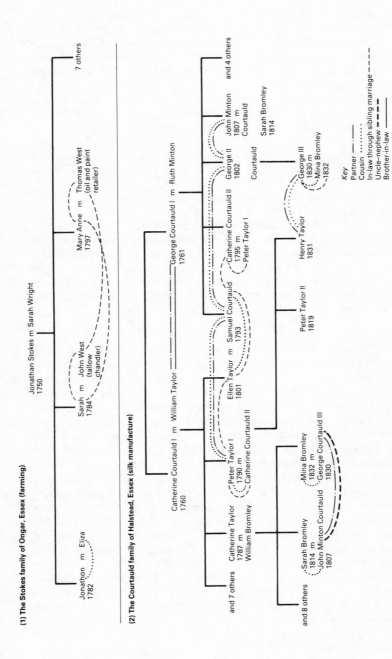

(1) The Stokes family of Ongar, Essex (farming)

(2) The Courtauld family of Halstead, Essex (silk manufacture)

Figure 3 *Sibling, cousin and partnership marriage*

Sources: M. Karr and M. Humphrey, *Out on a Limb: An Outline of a Branch of the Stokes Family*, 1945–76, privately printed 1976; S. L. Courtauld, *The Huguenot Family of Courtauld*, privately printed 1975; D. C. Coleman, *Courtaulds: An Economic and Social History*, Oxford 1969.

The resulting alliances may or may not have been formalized by partnership. With sibling marriages, the next generation produced 'double' first cousins and it was not unknown for these cousins to subsequently marry each other. As in any such alliances, the connections were not only bound up in the two people involved but their parents, as in-laws, would be related to each other twice over and thus they would have a double interest in nieces, nephews and any grandchildren. These marriage alliances do not seem to have been peculiar to any one religion, occupation or geographical area, but were integral to the general combination of personal and economic linkages.[104] Intermarriage also sealed relationships of friendship. Rebecca Solly, a Unitarian from Essex, deeply desired that her best friend would become her 'sister' which she eventually did by marrying one of Rebecca's elder brothers.[105] Men, too, prized friendship which they confirmed by marriage. George Gardner married the sister of his childhood playmate and adult friend, James Soanes, despite her malformed spine. Their second son was named Soanes Gardner, giving permanent recognition of the friendship between the two families.[106]

Sibling and cousin marriage served to counteract the centrifugal tendencies of partible inheritance. In a sense it was an alternative to elaborate marriage settlements. It may be argued that free choice marriage controlled in this way provided a form of security in binding together members of the middle class in local, regional and national networks, a guarantee of congenial views as well as trustworthiness in economic and financial affairs.

The crucial role of marriage in business affairs permeates the lives of the middle class in this period. One example among innumerable others of the particular way a marriage could change the fortunes of an individual and an enterprise is the case of Isaac Reckitt, son of a Quaker farmer from Lincolnshire, who stumbled from farming to a failing milling venture with his brother. His luck turned when he married within the Quaker community. His wife was one of the six lively Coleby sisters whose widowed mother had supported them and their only brother by running a boarding school in Essex. Reckitt was able to raise capital from his mother-in-law, but equally important, he had access to the expertise, advice and credit of five powerful brothers-in-law: Sarah Coleby's husband was Robert Ransome from the Ipswich firm of iron manufacturers, Mary had married a prosperous Essex farmer, Hannah a London accountant and Jane a London merchant. His own wife, Anne Coleby, as well as their daughter, helped in the early days of Isaac's latest venture, a starch mill, until success was assured by the publicity gained at the Great Exhibition and having starched whitened linen became a mark of respectability, making 'Reckitt's Starch' one of the earliest named household products to reach the mass market.[107]

Even second marriages, with their potential conflict between the children of the first and second alliance, could widen contacts and increase resources since relationships were often maintained with the relatives of the dead spouse. After his remarriage, William Bentall continued to do business with as well as visit socially his first wife's parents, known as Father and Mother Foster (sic).[108] Matthew Boulton, the Birmingham iron master, married two sisters sequentially and so gained the bulk of the property which his parents-in-law had in their gift.[109]

The place of marriage alliance in the business enterprise was explicitly recognized in middle-class culture. One form of such recognition was in naming patterns. Although, in keeping with patrilineal convention, the eldest son was often given his father's first name, one of the later sons would be called by a first (or middle) name taken from a female maiden surname, usually either his mother's or grandmother's. Thus, the Suffolk iron manufacturer Richard Garrett named his third son Newson, his wife's family of Newson having held the farm whose forge had laid the foundations of the business. All types of economic activity and religious grouping used this naming convention: the Birmingham doctors, Bowyer Vaux and Peyton Blakistone, the Ipswich attorney, Eddowes Sparrow, the Witham miller Hoffgaard Shoobridge, the Suffolk farmer Woolnough Gross, a Suffolk vicar, Rev. Tighe Gregory, a Colchester confectioner, Chigwell Wire. Gentry families also occasionally used this device but more often would drop the paternal surname altogether. For them, adopting the female surname was often a prerequisite to inheriting land. Such substitution has not been found in a single case among the middle class. Rather the female line was voluntarily recognized, but in a subordinate place as a first or middle name for a second or subsequent son.

In a different but no less effective mode, the interconnection of business with the web of personal relations was given recognition in the way the language of commerce was used. This is illustrated, for example, in a poem which a Midlands commercial traveller in hardware quoted in an 1811 letter to his fiancée, daughter of a Rochdale draper who he had met at her chapel while he was on his selling travels:

> If the stock of our bliss is in stranger's hands rested
> The fund ill-secured oft in bankruptcy ends
> But the heart is given bills, which are never protested
> When drawn on the firm of Wife, Children and Friends.[110]

Training for the enterprise

The close connection between partnership and marriage is further indicated by their coincidence in the lifecycle of young men. This pattern was often reinforced by living arrangements where the junior partner moved into premises located in or next to the business, freeing the senior partner to withdraw to a separate residence. James Ransome became a partner in the Ipswich iron foundry in 1829, the year that he married, having spent several years as an agent selling agricultural machinery for the firm in the surrounding region.[111]

One result was that the average age of marriage seems to have been later than for the population as a whole: from the cases with usable data from both areas, the average age of marriage was 29 for men and 26.5 for women, several years older than the averages which have been estimated for the general population of that period.[112] Late age at marriage seems to have been associated with building up a business position rather than a strategy for family limitation, for in the local areas we have found the demographically unusual combination of late marriage with large families. Unless the age of marriage of the wife was such as to make more than a few children possible and leaving aside childless marriages, of the eighty-three families for both areas for which we have information, the average number of children was 7.4 with birth intervals of from fourteen to twenty months.[113]

The boys born into these families had schooling up to the age of about 14, followed by training in a position, either formal or informal apprenticeship. Even where sons followed fathers, there seems to have been some effort to give the young man experience of another household and enterprise. Here the networks of kin and friendship were heavily used. Except for formal arrangements where premiums were paid, general experience of business methods and habits was the most important part of the training, and although many sons did follow fathers, it was by no means inevitable. In any case for many enterprises it was impossible to absorb the large number of sons.

Men could not expect to have sons to follow them in business. For a start they may have had only daughters or no children at all. Childlessness was regretted and provided for by the informal 'adoption' of a nephew or a 'friend's' son in childhood. Joseph Phipson was taken in by his childless uncle and aunt with prospects of joining their Birmingham manufacturing business. However, his aunt died when Joseph was still young. This was not only an emotional loss because, on his uncle's remarriage, he was eased out of his place in both household and business.[114] Some childless families would also take in a niece, particularly where her own family was large and with few resources, but her function would be as companion and household help where the arrangements were less formal and might well go unrecorded. The twenty-one co-resident nephews over age 16 in the census sample would be only the residue of those not titled apprentice, shopman, manager or some other occupational designation within the family enterprise. There was less need felt to categorize the fifty-four nieces.

Even when there were sons, they might not be able to fit into the business. The Essex miller and cornfactor, Golding Constable, had an eldest son who was mentally backward and barely managed to support himself as a gamekeeper, while his second son John, as is well known, resisted entering the business and insisted on training as an artist in London. There was a long wait for the youngest son Abram, seven years John's junior. The possibility of using the three daughters to fill the breach was never considered since the Constables had some notions of gentility. Abram Constable never married and the business was sold in his lifetime.[115]

The dearth of sons could be made up not only from nephews, but by using the labour of younger brothers and brothers-in-law. This pattern served the purpose of cementing ties between the families of husband and wife. The supply of younger siblings was assured by the large numbers of children in each family, and the experience of living away from home under the watchful eye of an older brother or sister removed many an adolescent from tensions with his or her own parents. William Gardner was an Essex brewer and wine merchant who never got along with his oldest son. By his late teens the young man had created a local scandal by getting the squire's daughter pregnant. Gardner's wife had been his first cousin, the eldest of twelve children of a well-off London innkeeper. Her youngest brother was only a year or two older than the scapegrace son. This George Gardner was well known to his country relatives since he had lived with them for a time during his school days. At the time of the eldest son's disgrace, the second son was only 11, the three intervening children being girls. William Gardner thus called for George, his young brother-in-law *and* his first cousin, who was delighted to return to Essex and became a right hand man in the business. George was soon in line for a partnership when he was recalled to London to join his elder brothers in a hay merchants' business. William Gardner's second son died at 21 and he had to wait until the reliable third son eventually took over the business.[116] Sometimes even more informal arrangements combined training with the use of youthful labour. Tom Heyes was in his teens when he paid long visits to his married sister on a nearby farm where he spent much time with his brother-in-law in his varied tasks, particularly the harvest. He accompanied him to market, went fishing with him, helped him to follow up a stolen mare. Tom's sister, too, spent time on the farm helping her elder sister with the children.[117] In some cases an older brother or brother-in-law might be persuaded to take on a younger brother in return for parental investment in his undertaking.

The experience of the Shaen family of Hatfield Peverel in Essex illustrates many of these points. Samuel Shaen was a Unitarian, trained as an attorney but devoting most of his time to farming. The eldest of his nine children, also Samuel, was sent to a school in Hove run by a Unitarian minister related by marriage to the Essex Unitarian Courtauld/Taylor connection. At 16 the boy was put into the London law office of his paternal uncle, for in 1820 Ann Shaen had married a metropolitan attorney. With great trepidation and many parental warnings, Sam was sent off to lodge in the City with his *mother's* sister who had married her cousin, a timber merchant. The middle sons of the Shaen family were not so easy to place as the family expenses grew and the post war agricultural slump bit into the Essex economy. Benjamin emigrated to Australia at 16 and his younger brother William would have followed had he not been sponsored by a gentleman who paid for his schooling and apprenticeship in the law. William seems to have made long visits to his sponsor's family to whom his relationship must have been much like that of Jane Austen's brother whose Navy career was similarly underwritten. Within this single family can be seen the socialization and settling of young men through two sets of aunts and uncles, one maternal and one paternal, a religious network contact and an older style of patronage-cum-adoption, not forgetting the safety valve of the colonies, familiar to readers of Victorian fiction.[118]

The patterns described above should make it evident that the large numbers of children born and raised, far from being considered a drain on individual families, were the key to maintaining the web of personal relationships which supported economic institutions. This is not to say that disjunctions between needs and resources, or conflicts between individuals and households never occurred. Nevertheless, the interchange between kinship, friendship and partnership often made it possible to overcome these. If the focus shifts from individual nuclear families to the group as a whole, then it becomes evident how such patterns contributed to the survival and enhancement of the middle class, given the uncertain, even hostile economic and demographic environment.

Young men living in and around the workplace were given an early and easy familiarity with the everyday minutia of business life. George Holyoake, as a child in the 1820s, helped with such tasks as running errands in his mother's horn button business which was in a workshop attached to the house in central Birmingham.[119] Nor in the early part of the period were girls exempt from such experience. In her poem, 'The Old Foundry' written in late middle age, Jane Ransome, daughter of the founder of the Ipswich iron works, recalled the early days of the business which 'proved how industry may tread, a height proud indolence never claimed'. She indicates that she knew the foundry 'long and well' before it moved out of the town centre to the dock area by the river. The poem goes on to describe the workmen who she had watched pouring the 'ploughshare glittering in the sand'.[120] Even where the household was not as close to a productive premise, the frequent boarding of apprentices, young assistants and pupils provided models for boys (as well as possible future husbands for girls) and at least ensured that children were conversant with business and professional themes from an early age.

The lifecycle pattern here described gave young men ample time to learn, even to experiment with various occupations. The fact that changes in their business and professional lives tended to coincide with marriage or other familial events reinforces the point that creating and maintaining an 'establishment', was seen as an integrated step. Marriage and the expectation of a large family to support directed the mind to the necessity for making a livelihood in a respectable way. Marriage and a family life above all created an atmosphere of domesticity which was the basis for a moral and religious life and which it was the main aim of business to support. The rewards of doing so, in turn, gave colour and meaning to the drab and irksome parts of business life.

Retirement from the enterprise

Once the effort of raising, educating and placing their numerous offspring was well underway, many middle-class men seem to have either withdrawn from active business or professional practice to take up a different occupation, to take part in political, scientific or voluntary affairs or to give more attention to serious religious concerns. Any or none of these might be combined with simply enjoying their homes and gardens. Whatever their motivation, such withdrawal gave scope to the younger men in the enterprise to take over greater responsibility. Archibald Kenrick's nephew John wrote to him when the older man was considering changing the partnership agreements in order to gradually withdraw from the firm:

The prospect of such a season of leisure towards the decline of life, is one of the strongest motives to a man to go steadily on year after year with the drudgery of business; indeed without it, the complete absorption of many men's minds in the affairs of the world in the early and middle part of life would be hardly justifiable.[121]

For the serious Christian, the 'season of leisure' was a time to devote to family life and his own soul. For others, the mixture of motives for leaving active involvement in the enterprise can illustrate the complex relationship of the middle class with gentry culture. The Galton banking family of Birmingham had wealth and rank enough to encourage country house living and even intermarriage on the margins of the gentry, yet Samuel Tertius Galton did not see himself as emulating a gentry lifestyle. He seems to have left the bank in sheer 'commercial wearyness' in 1831, following the particularly stressful decade of bank failures and commercial unrest.[122] Such motives seem to fit the pattern and timing of partnership and investment observed in many enterprises at the upper end of the scale. R. J. Morris has shown in a detailed study of a Leeds' attorney's financial affairs how some transfer of capital into less active forms of investment such as railway companies deliberately allowed a man to wind down in early middle age if he had the financial capacity to withdraw.[123] This type of retirement should not imply that the older man necessarily severed all connection with the firm, only that it had less of his concentrated attention. It was a pattern which allowed the transfer of authority to younger men without the grim battles characteristic of the later Victorian period when the simple partnership and more ephemeral enterprise had hardened into the business house or private company. As evidence from the wills suggests, it was more a general guidance of family welfare which the senior male figure wished to have in his hands.

Another argument against the idea that middle-class families were trying to imitate the gentry in turning their backs on active business life is evidence that the pattern of early retirement goes down the social and economic scale to levels where such emulation would have been out of the question either in terms of resources or cultural background. For those much less well endowed than bankers like the Galtons, full domesticity could still be a primary objective of a working life as we have seen with James Luckcock's entry into 'domestic bliss' in Edgbaston. In 1850, two-thirds of all households headed by men who had retired under 55 years old were located in Edgbaston, although Edgbaston male households for all occupations only made up 47 per cent of the whole census sample.

It may be significant that a turning to domesticity freed from the cares of business was sought in late middle age when the senior man could literally leave the cares of business behind him by moving his home away from the enterprise. In a town like Colchester, such a move might have been from the dock area to Church Street in the town centre where retired families might mix with professionals, who themselves if they could might retire to a villa on the outskirts of the town. Farmers' retirement might be associated with a move *into* the town centre, and retired farmers are a distinct presence in country towns and villages in the census sample. Running a rural industry could also mean that at retirement, the senior partner might choose to move into the heart of the town to escape the rush and excitement of business life.[124]

Enterprises could cease to exist for a variety of reasons besides the central figure's unwillingness to carry on. There were bankruptcies, failure to find successors, illness or early death, not only of the head but others in the family and friendship network. A father's death might mean that young sons were forced to take on responsibility, while at other times the duty might devolve on the widow. But death could also bring with it release from the necessity to join the enterprise if a handsome legacy was involved, the latter being the experience of young Francis Galton.[125] The unacknowledged importance of women to the smooth running of a business can be sensed in the severe problems which arose at their death. When Candia Cadbury died in early middle age, John grew so depressed and uninterested in the business that profits from the shop fell drastically and the Cadbury sons had to salvage the family finances.

Whatever the reason, there was certainly no stigma attached to a man's abandoning his occupation as long as the establishment could be maintained at a sufficient level. It may have been that other members of the family or kinship circle were now contributing income, or investment property, legacies and marriage portions had become available on a large enough scale to release a man from business pursuits if he so wished. Positive virtue, not idleness, was associated with a domesticated life devoted to family and friends, home, garden, philanthropy, science, politics, as well as religion. In this special sense, status honour was awarded to 'not working', that is not being actively engaged in business, although some features of this retirement may have been allied to gentry culture.

Whatever the motivation, independent and retired heads of households made up 23 per cent, or almost one-quarter, of the total middle-class sample in 1851. As is to be expected this distribution reduces to 11 per cent among households headed by men. In Witham, George Edwards, at age 53 was a non-practising surgeon who, with his wife and unmarried sister – a fundholder – and two domestic servants, lived at the end of the town where the elite families clustered. It usually would take a good part of a lifetime to achieve such a position. The average age of independent household heads was 59.4. Even then, not many men reached this goal. The Witham nonpractising doctor was one out of only four independent households headed by a man, the other eighteen being female. In all areas, 72 per cent of independent household heads were women, a high proportion of whom were elderly widows.[126]

The argument has been made that the aim of the establishment was primarily the survival and well being of the family in its widest sense. Not only did men see their business and family life as one, they often regarded the former simply as the building blocks for the latter. For most, the domestic setting remained their ideal. Even if it entailed a move to the countryside, this was a stronger motive than the wish to control rolling acres or seek gentry approbation. Thomas Webb, a Birmingham manufacturer (and Jane Webb Loudon's father), bought a small country house about 7 miles from the town after the coincidence of his bankruptcy and his wife's death in 1821. He celebrated his move in a poem which does credit to Cowper's view of domestic retirement:

> When business, oft by profit led,
> Employ'd my lab'ring hands and head
> A cot, I hop'd on rising ground,

Would at some distant day be found,
Where I might view in humble pride,
The vast expanse of nature wide;

There know what sweets, away from strife,
Attend upon a well spent life,
To Heaven, I bend the grateful knee
For in this place the whole I see.[127]

5 'A man must act': men and the enterprise

Moderate clothing, moderate houses, the power of receiving friends, the power of purchasing books and particularly the power of supporting a family, will always remain objects of rational desire among the majority of mankind.

Thomas Malthus, 1798

The economic, legal and customary form of the middle-class enterprise has been surveyed. It had its origins in a combination of landed estate practice and merchant commercial experience, but it was middle-class men who built on these origins, expanding and moulding devices such as the trust to their purposes and needs. Their calling to do so was not in doubt, for their identity depended on their ability to operate as economic agents. To become adult men within their own terms they must provide a livelihood which made possible a domestic establishment where they and their dependants could live a rational and morally sanctioned life.

The masculine persona which emerged within this group was organized around a man's determination and skill in manipulating the economic environment, always within an abiding belief in a world shaped by religious forces. His puny strength was also pitted against the stern course of a more novel destiny, the market. The contrast between such intense self-generated activity and the awfulness of these necessities could undermine even the bravest confidence. Far from carrying the blustering certainty of the late Victorian paterfamilias, early nineteenth-century masculine identity was fragile, still in the process of being forged and always measured against the background of condescension from the gentry as well as the long tradition of artisan pride. The mood in which middle-class men faced their world was well expressed by a seed merchant, a self-made man in the best middle-class tradition. He had personally experienced business fluctuations to the point where, once or twice, he had been unable to meet his creditors; as he bitterly remarked: 'I may be a man one day and a mouse the next.'[1]

The equation of masculine identity with occupation was by no means complete. Perhaps the most striking feature of economic life was that tasks which are now specialized and seen to be only properly performed by experts, were then still vaguely defined. The task or function was the focus, not a full occupational identity. People moved between activities and used a variety of ways to support their livelihood. Work to be done came in uneven batches, an obvious example being the harvest when almost everyone capable had to lend a hand. This allowed for slack times when social life could be carried on. Buying and selling were intermingled with much tea or beer drinking and the exchange of local news both in homes and public houses. Many tasks were subcontracted so that production took place outside the entrepreneur's premises, leaving merchant/manufacturer simply as co-ordinators. People with quite small amounts of property would still be involved in market relations at the borderline where artisanal production merged with trade.

Both men and women had to balance their time and energy between a wide range of duties. Moves towards masculine identification with occupation, however, can be discerned in official documentation such as trade directories, where gentry status continued to be designated by labels 'gentleman' and 'lady'. Significantly, 'widow' remained a category which overrode any specific occupation even when it is clear from other evidence that such women were following a trade. By mid century, middle-class men were beginning to be marked out by an occupational title which grew more precise and sophisticated.

The evolution of the census follows a similar pattern. The early census, from 1801 to 1821, roughly categorized families as agricultural or in 'trade manufacture'. By 1831, families were abandoned and adult males were divided into nine major occupational groups.[2] There was some uneasiness about the whole procedure, as the official report noted. The census:

had entirely failed, from the impossibility of deciding whether females of the family, children and servants were to be classed as if of no occupation or of the occupation of the adult males of the family. . . . But the often recurring and unanswerable doubt, as to what is to be deemed a family? – had caused a further alteration. . . .[3]

The 'alteration' was to concentrate on the occupation of adult males. By 1851, the accepted sexual division of labour had become permanently enshrined in the census which itself contributed to the equation of masculine identity with an occupation.

In the course of the nineteenth century, tasks and functions began to be more firmly associated with certain titles, with tightening up of training and entry requirements. Large-scale and extra-familial institutions had grown up, and these became the setting of specific occupations: barracks, hospitals, workhouses, asylums, prisons, large schools. Whether run by the state or private organizations, such establishments spawned bureaucratic managements with salaried staffs. Men of the middle class who reached maturity in the mid nineteenth century would, then, see themselves as oriented to a career in a more systematic way than their grandfathers. Their masculine self would be more deeply implicated in what they did rather than in who they were in terms of kinship or religious loyalties. The discussion which follows, catches middle-class men during this period of transition. The very exercise of dividing up the group into occupational categories is somewhat artificial. While the discussion may serve to bring out variations between social groups, the movement of individuals within and between these categories must always be kept in mind.

Middle-class men and occupations

The census sample at mid century divides as 31 per cent of household heads in the higher echelons and 69 per cent in the lower (34 per cent and 66 per cent respectively if only male household heads are taken). This division cut across every occupational group, although proportions varied from the salaried, mainly made up of less wealthy and influential families, to those with independent incomes who were more prosperous and had greater local status and potential power. The lower middle-class enterprises tended to be smaller, have less plant and less complicated hierarchies of management.[4]

The distribution between upper and lower ranks varied both within and between the two sample areas. In the market town of Colchester the middle class may be estimated as 18 per cent of the total population, divided between 3 per cent of larger merchants, millers, brewers, wealthy medical men and attorneys, retired farmers and those living on independent incomes and 15 per cent in the lower ranks: the general practitioners, clerks, tradesmen, actuaries, agents, apothecaries, innkeepers and small masters possibly employing one or more assistants, and many, although by no means all, also employing a general female servant.[5]

A large village such as Witham, with a population of 3300 at mid century, had approximately 4 per cent of the higher classes, made up of a handful of resident gentry, clergymen, retired military officers, farmers whose land averaged over 300 to 400 acres and who, as a group, employed over 200 men, an extremely wealthy attorney and the one large manufacturer (of brushes). The 13 per cent making up the lower middle class included fourteen innkeepers, the smaller farmers and baliffs, two millers, varied shopkeepers and small masters as well as school proprietors and teachers and the newer white-collar, state and railway non-manual employees.[6]

In the smaller villages, there was a greater gap between the majority of agricultural labourers and handful of artisans on the one hand, and the minor gentry, large farmers and usually the vicar who made up the elite. In an 'open' village, with a population of about 360, this group made up 8 per cent of the population, while the innkeeper, schoolmaster, farm bailiff and shopkeepers made up another 10 per cent of households.[7] However, in a tiny 'closed' village in Suffolk, population 156, the upper strata included the squire as well as large farmers together with the vicar making up 12 per cent of village households, while the intermediate group was almost entirely made up of servants of the large houses: groom, coachman, gamekeeper, farm steward and their kind made up 26 per cent of households, so that in this village almost 40 per cent were differentiated from the labouring population in a more traditionally hierarchical pattern.[8]

Birmingham in 1851 had a population of 250,000. Here there were still clusters of professional, salaried and commercial middle-class families in the town centre. In the most well-to-do shopping streets, few of the proprietors had moved out and a majority of the premises were occupied by families with living in assistants, apprentices and servants. On the other hand, the larger manufacturers and certain professional groups, such as lawyers, had already moved further out, with a fringe of lower middle-class families on the edges of Edgbaston, Birmingham's foremost suburb. Edgbaston's population was mainly middle class in composition. Within it one-half of male household heads and one-third of female were in the upper strata of the middle class, by far the largest single concentration of the elite in our study.[9] Their massed presence in one geographical area was a novel feature of mid century middle-class experience.

The separation of work from home, implied by a suburban development like Edgbaston, was not uniform nor was it by any means solely based on technology or size of plant. Some manufacturers chose to continue living next to their works. However, the increasing division between manufacture, wholesale and retail trade meant that in the case of the former two categories, it was easier to move away from the counting house or factory. In Birmingham, by mid century, many attorneys had moved their homes to Edgbaston, while medical men maintained their town centre location. However, in the market towns, lawyers continued to live above or next to their offices, despite the fact that in both areas law was practised in a similar way.[10] The decision for a family to live separately from their enterprise, therefore, depended on a variety of factors: material, economic, social and cultural.

The construction of purpose-built 'offices' was a slow process, the first in both areas being put up by voluntary bodies like insurance companies and the proud municipal corporations. In early nineteenth-century terminology, 'office' still usually referred to kitchens and outbuildings, the working part of an estate or large house. These would have included a harness room, the stables and the room where accounts were kept, labourers paid, travellers interviewed. For merchants, the 'counting house' was a room adjacent to the dwelling place. The separation of an office can often be traced in ground plans showing doors originally opening into the parlour or even bedrooms as well as domestic furniture transformed into office desks and chairs.[11]

The balance of groups within the middle class shifted over the period and varied between the areas. Nevertheless, it is possible to draw a picture of the position by the end of the period using a snap-shot drawn from the 1851 census. In the sample taken as a whole, and considering households by the stated occupation of their male head, trade was the largest single group with 28 per cent, followed by professionals of all types at 21 per cent, and the salaried, 13 per cent. In the rural areas, farmers made up 10 per cent, balanced in the urban areas by manufacturers at 12 per cent and in both innkeepers at 4 per cent. The retired and those of independent means made up the remaining 11 per cent. Some activities had a wider range than others, for example trade and commerce varied from the wealthy merchant to the small village shop. In the census sample, a higher proportion of male household heads could be classified as upper middle class in manufacturing and the older professions of the church, law and medicine as well as the expected households with independent means whereas only 6 per cent of salaried and 2 per cent of innkeepers could be so designated.[12]

Table 4 *Proportion of male household heads in socio-economic class by occupation (total sample) percentages*

	Trade	Manu-facture	Farmer/ miller	Clergy	Law	Medicine	Prof.	Salaried	Inn-keeper
Lower middle	62	52	70	48	42	44	71	94	98
Upper middle	38	48	30	52	58	56	29	6	2
Total	100	100	100	100	100	100	100	100	100

	Independent	Retired under 55	Retired over 55	Total
Lower middle	56	38	70	66
Upper middle	44	62	30	34
Total	100	100	100	100

Note: N = 1143
Source: 1851 Census sample

Men who attained the status of household head tended to be older in the upper middle class; 82 per cent were over 35 years old in contrast to 72 per cent in the lower middle class and 64 per cent in the working class. One-quarter of these high-status men were over 55 years old. Furthermore, 31 per cent of them were more than 5 years older than their wives compared to 17 per cent in the lower middle class. This age gap indicates a position of authority and the means to obtain it within the family as well as the enterprise. Certain occupational groups, too, favoured older household heads, manufacturing and the older professions in particular, while the salaried had only 64 per cent of household heads over 35 years old. Some of these occupations were associated with late marriage and higher rates of celibacy, reflected in the age gap shown above. For example, almost a quarter of all attorneys who were household heads were both single and over 35. Of those who did marry, 35 per cent were more than five years older than their wives.

Extended training and the need to accumulate capital characterize the occupations which had a higher proportion falling into the upper middle class. Men in these groups had to wait longer to attain the position of household head and to marry. A high standard of living and the accompanying status can be regarded as much as a lifecycle stage as a static place in the social structure. Both successful manufacture and the higher reaches of the professions implied a delay in achieving an elite position. However, they differed in that the former focused on the accumulation of property as part of daily activity. Occupations which rested on income derived from individual skill and training did not centre around profit-making to the same extent, a difference in emphasis which might have consequences for men's outlook on life.[13]

A closely related distinction was the necessity for some enterprises to deal with a workforce, large or small. Others mainly dealt with clientele. Manufacturers were seen to be at the forefront as employers of wage labour, although farmers in the arable regions had been facing this issue since the mid eighteenth century as had merchant/manufacturers who had dealt with outworkers. For many professionals, their external relations were with clients rather than employees, but these could range from the working class to their own peers to the gentry and aristocracy. The social level of person who they serviced had a direct connection with their own income and status.

The search for a 'sound commercial education'

Specialized occupational identities linked with specific skills inevitably led to a concern over the preparation of middle-class boys for their future position. Discussions around this subject also attracted advocates of religious and scientific training in early youth, part of the general advocacy of mastery over self as well as the external world. Historians have drawn attention to the imposition of new forms of labour discipline among the working classes, but what is less often considered is that such habits had also to be learnt by employers. As Isaac Taylor said in his handbook for youth, *Self Cultivation Recommended*, 'men do not play like children'.

Plate 16   King Edward VI's Grammar School, Birmingham, a boys' school under Anglican aegis and patronized by the established middle class

Regularity was the life of business and the regularity of school helped create the willingness to undergo dull routine, to produce steady application to a task. Above all, the education necessary to train a youth to 'act rightly' would lead him to attain the 'emulated epithet' of *manly*: 'a man must act, whether to earn his living or even if not, yet he must act'. His education should rest on 'self-instruction, self-command and self-acting energy'.[14]

The end of the eighteenth century and beginning of the nineteenth can be understood as a transition between a system built around informal training of children by the family, kin and community to one which relied on institutions created specifically for educational or professional training. Boys tended to be taught to read along with tasks such as doing up their buttons and the rudiments of basic hygiene by their mothers and other women. They were taught in dame schools or mixed groups at home until the age of about 7. From then to 14 some schooling was becoming important, followed by formal or informal apprenticeships.

The educational institutions for boys that emerged at this time were not yet set to meritocratic standards. Both staff and pupils were often appointed through patronage, kinship or friendship. However, the transition was well under way by the late eighteenth century, hastened by nonconformist concern over their children's place in a society dominated by the state church. Dissenting groups had led the way with the establishment of academies in the eighteenth century and the Dissenting Schoolmasters Relief Act of 1779 formalized recognition of their rights to do so. The nonconformist academies modified the heavily classical curriculum of an education dominated by the Church of England, developed to produce priests, gentlemen and attorneys.[15] They emphasized science and practical skills, and were the focus of groups like the Birmingham Lunar Society in the late eighteenth century whose members included men of business like Matthew Boulton and James Watt as well as scientists like Erasmus Darwin. The Lunar Society and its Midlands circle took an intense interest in educational debates. They had been influenced by Rousseau's ideas about children, reinterpreted by their fellow members Thomas Day, Richard Edgeworth and his daughter Maria.[16]

These educational reformers stressed the relation between teaching and experience and the encouragement of scientific attitudes among children; an emphasis on *useful knowledge* was echoed in Utilitarian debates on education.[17] By the early decades of the new century the establishment of new schools was putting these ideas in practice. As apprenticeship waned, special schools for military, naval, engineering and commercial training were being set up, often as a family business by men with experience in these fields.[18] On more general lines, Matthew and Rowland Hill acknowledged the influence of the Edgeworths in a description of the school they planned for their native Birmingham. It was to be an institution for the 'liberal instruction of boys in large numbers'. Their venture, Hazelwood, caught the attention of the outstanding Utilitarian theorist, Jeremy Bentham.[19]

The reform of boys' education was in the air from several quarters. Public school foundations were under scrutiny, culminating in Arnold's celebrated campaign.[20] A series of investigations in the 1830s by the Charity

Commissioners revealed the appalling state of many endowed local foundations all over the country, including the sixteenth-century schools of King Edward's in Birmingham and Colchester's Royal Grammar School, the latter nothing but an educational sham.[21] Such schools were facing competition from large numbers of private academies and proprietary schools which were becoming a common form of family enterprise. Only a tiny handful of the more wealthy and cultured sent their sons to public school or substantial boarding schools, the latter more common in the rural areas where day schools were less available. Many families still taught their boys at home or sent them to study with a clergyman, either by the day or as boarders.[22]

In 1848, the Birmingham Statistical Society, in a survey of the town's education, estimated that there were ninety-seven superior private and boarding schools in the town catering for over 2000 pupils (just over one-half being girls).[23] Many of these were aligned with specific religious communities which continued to operate the most common form of patronage well into the Victorian period. In 1832, the Warwickshire Quaker Quarterly Meeting decided to establish a boys' school in Birmingham so that their sons would not have to be sent away to board. William and Hannah Lean who were invited to run the school were entrusted with what was as much a religious as an educational task.[24]

A detailed examination of the three major Birmingham schools for boys brings out the sectional variations within the local middle class as well as the changing aims of educational practice. The forms taken by the schools – a charitable trust, a family partnership and a joint stock company – illustrate the developments discussed in the previous chapter. As with most grammar schools, King Edward's had been founded as a charitable trust and run by a group of trustees and governors dominated by the Anglican and Tory interest. It had become something of a reserve for the more elite families, its classical curriculum appealing to merchants, large-scale manufacturers and upper professionals, although a small number of Dissenters served as governors and attended as pupils. The controversy which surrounded the school in the early nineteenth century made it an issue in the political life of the town and contributed to forging an articulate middle-class consciousness. Rising land values had given the school's endowment a much increased revenue. The use of this wealth was contested; some pressing for enlargement of the classical side and others wishing to encourage the provision of a more commercial curriculum which had grown up on the 'English' side, mainly located in the eight small subsidiary schools scattered over the town. It was proposed that these should be consolidated and expanded, a by-product of the scheme being the uncontested closing of the existing limited provision for girls.[25]

Among causes of complaint were the heavy emphasis on the classics and the favouring of boarders – mainly the sons of clergy, medical men and lawyers – for scholarships to Oxbridge over the day boys from manufacturing and commercial backgrounds.[26] These objections were linked to an attack on the old closed Corporation and peaked over the issue of Dissenter representation among the governors. In the 1830s the death of several staff, including the head who had reigned for forty years, allowed a new breed to take over. They, while defending the classics as the basis of all education, conceded that 'this is a manufacturing town',[27] and that after a 'fair proportion of Latin and Greek' had been offered, it was certainly very desirable that the system of education should be extended. Mathematics, which had not been taught, was recognized as an important part of education.[28] The rebuilding and relocation of the classical school, too, became contentious. Those opposing its removal to the edge of the town stressed that the school was a public trust and should be accessible to the 'INHABITANTS OF BIRMINGHAM'.[29] Proponents of removal objected that the present central New Street site exposed the genteely raised boys to moral dangers: the nearby prostitutes and the possibility of 'hearing constantly the slang of coachmen and to look upon scenes of vice and depravity'.[30] A series of compromise reforms were carried out to stem the criticism of King Edward's and counter the competition from schools such as Hazelwood. The classical school, however, remained a high status establishment with upper middle-class pupils. Plans for three tiers, the second to be for the sons of tradesmen and lesser professionals and the third for 'mechanics' were dropped, and the 'English School' catered mainly for Birmingham's solid lower middle class: the sons of upholsterers, commercial travellers, victuallers, jewellers, tobacconists, brass founders and retailers.[31]

One of the dissatisfactions over the running of the grammar school had been poor teaching and lack of discipline, combined with frequent and sometimes brutal use of the cane. In the spring term of 1833 there had been a riot and the police had to be called in. Simple rules of order such as establishing a roll call were instituted by the new regime, although many of the reforms were honoured more in theory than in practice, according to Francis Galton who regretted his time as a pupil at King Edward's in the late 1830s. The atmosphere remained pugnacious among boys and masters alike and he was denied instruction in 'mathematics and solid science'.[32] Parents of boys like Francis Galton were in a dilemma given this situation in Birmingham's most prestigious school. Undoubtedly, the nonconformists, particularly at Hazelwood, had provided the most 'useful' and enlightened education in the town up to the time of its removal to London in the 1830s.

Hazelwood was run as the Hill family business by father and sons in partnership. The Hill family were connected with other Birmingham Unitarians such as Joseph Parkes, the radical attorney, and Hazelwood was marked by a nonconformist and radical political allegiance.[33] The men of the Hill family had been publicly committed to the reforming cause since the 1790s, and had been associated with radical organizations from the Hampden Club to the Birmingham Political Union in the 1830s culminating in Matthew Hill's election as Radical MP.[34] As Unitarians, their religious and political beliefs meshed with their Utilitarian conception of the world.

Hazelwood drew its clientele from local manufacturing and commercial families, most but not all, nonconformist, who sought an education to equip their sons for public life as well as private business. In keeping with their ideals of autonomy and self-government, discipline in the school was left as much as possible to the boys on the grounds that self-regulation and representation were the key to the proper functioning of a community. A judiciary was appointed for lapses of discipline and corporal punishment was forbidden. Societies were formed for charitable ventures and for purchase of books and repair of equipment in order to give practical experience in running 'public business'.

The emphasis on practicality was part of the Hills' strong commitment to Utilitarian principles and attracted parents keen for semi-vocational training for their sons. Orderly habits, so necessary for business, were to be instilled. The organization of the school day was strictly routinized and every change marked by the bell. Punctuality was mandatory and a monitor had to ring the bell or make other signals more than sixty times a day. The Hills regretted the length of the holidays since it allowed the boys to break with all their regular habits. Three times daily there was a general assembly to check that everyone was present and the boys marched in to the sound of bell, drum and band. Rowland was able to write in 1820 with apparent complacency:

The school is now a very perfect machine . . . we are able to appropriate every minute of the day to its respective use. The bells ring, the classes assemble, break up, take their meals etc. with such clock-like regularity that it has the appearance of almost magic. . . .[35]

Efforts to introduce rational and comparable time standards reached even the domestic side. While Matthew Hill appreciated his mother's efforts in running the household numbering over 150, she resisted planning her work to scientific standards. She had complained:

it was impossible to have the dinner at the exact time and a large leg of mutton required more time to roast than a smaller one. I said no doubt it must have more time but the cook must begin earlier. She gave in on my earnestly desiring it.

Even Matthew's sister, Caroline, was active in checking that each of the boarders was neat and tidy in the morning.[36]

When the Hills moved their school to London in the 1830s, nonconformists and Anglicans joined forces to set up a new venture more suited to a settled and enlarged middle class. The Edgbaston Proprietory School which opened in 1838 was a joint stock company with trustees and a committee made up mainly of men who were active in the Birmingham business world. The families which patronized the school represented the backbone of the local middle class: merchants, manufacturers, well-to-do surgeons, many of whom were already living in Edgbaston. They expected their sons to have to make their way in the world and wanted an education to fit them for commercial and civic life. In so far as the pupils went on to higher education it tended to be London University rather than Oxbridge. The school's modified classical curriculum and genteel tone was non-controversial and concentrated on grooming a generation of 'fit and proper persons' who would take Birmingham into the second half of the nineteenth century.[37]

It was well recognized among the senior generation that education did not end with the mid-teens when the average boy entered a business. Birmingham had several academies and training centres for specialized subjects, including medical colleges. Samuel Lines and his sons established a successful Drawing Academy which not only taught standard subjects such as water colour painting, but also offered design as an adjunct to the manufacture of metal products. Lines had been advised that there was a 'great want of teaching in Birmingham' among engineers, die sinkers, japanners and others whose employment depended upon their knowledge of ornamental art. He offered classes for these young men at 5.00 a.m. before their day's work began.[38]

The schools which have been discussed were large and well established. But much education at this time was more casual and less expensive, parents entering or withdrawing their sons as family resources and demands allowed. Some parents sent their sons to day or boarding schools run by relatives, not only for their congenial atmosphere but to get reductions in fees. The small school run as a family enterprise was exposed to the vagaries of trade prosperity in the local area as well as incapacity or death of its limited staff. Boys' schools covered a wide range of fees and the average school proprietor or master was more akin to John Beckett, the Birmingham schoolmaster whose will was proved for under £20 in the 1780s.

Many young men, including the Hill brothers, essentially educated themselves and a plethora of clubs, institutes and other organizations were created both for and by them for this purpose. Book Clubs, Debating Societies, the Mechanics Institutes, Literary and Philosophic Societies, the People's Hall, the Society of Arts, the Atheneum and Brotherly Societies rose and fell, catering to every strata and interest, a few even open to the ranks of the respectable artisan. Whatever social level they reached, the same mixture was used. Classes, lectures, exhibitions, books and newspapers were available for an admission fee and annual subscription, the cost determining the social level of the clientele. At a minimum, there was a warm room where congenial fellows could meet in an informal atmosphere. In the early days, the premises would most likely be a back room in a public house, but later purpose-built buildings mushroomed. An important latent function of these organizations was to provide experience in holding office, public speaking, keeping accounts and minutes – all useful in business.

Many of these organizations were associated with the various religious persuasions in the area. By mid century, one-third of the 183 Essex parishes had some provision for adult education among Anglicans, while nonconformists also had classes, libraries, debating societies and public lectures connected to their chapels.[39] Perhaps the most pervasive fellowship for self-education was the Sunday school and its influence on the lives of men from both the rural and urban area was marked. Sunday school study and teaching was often supplemented by individual reading and informal discussion among friends. This contributed to the sense of belonging to a community of like-minded men, further consolidating friendship networks and giving meaning to what was for many a new and radically different view of their world.

The studies undertaken in self-improvement programmes included basic skills of reading, writing and ciphering as well as technical subjects, of special importance in a town like Birmingham. Apprentices and shopmen often formed the core of discussion groups, even those formed for philanthropic or religious purposes such as Birmingham's Brotherly and Young Mens' Societies.[40] Quaker and nonconformist tradesmen are known to have started discussion groups for the apprentices and shop assistants of Ipswich, Yarmouth and Colchester.[41] Young men's opportunities for self-improvement were legion by the second and third decades of the nineteenth century and undoubtedly provided some avenues for mobility. From Norfolk, Suffolk and Essex, men who later made national reputations as diverse as the radical Unitarian minister W. J. Fox, the linguist George Borrow and the evangelical divine, Charles Spurgeon, were partially the products of self-teaching. However, the existence of both formal and informal organizations whose purpose was self-development, must draw attention to the way such efforts were embedded in a type of communal effort. In contrast to the Smilesian portrait of the scholar burning his lonely midnight candle, the future man of public and business affairs was more likely to be found in enthusiastic discussion of subjects ranging from the French Revolution to the existence of the Trinity or local geology with half a dozen youths over a pint at the Rose and Crown or their master's back parlour.[42]

Commerce and trade

Commercial pursuits were the largest single livelihood throughout the period, making up one-quarter to one-third of male household heads in the census sample. Commercial development was encouraged by the rapid growth of population as well as by changes in lifestyles. In Suffolk, a contemporary noted that 'the number of farm tradesmen (sic) must be trebled and thus other trades have increased'.[43] Labourers, now paid in wages rather than boarded by the farmer, had to purchase supplies through retail outlets. It was estimated that one family in twenty-one in Essex had some connection with retail business, although not all were full time and Birmingham's trading population also burgeoned.[44]

The larger the town, the more variety in type of trade.[45] Improved local and regional transport by road, canal and, later, railways, aided growth and specialization. Slowly the hand manufacture of goods for sale on the premises shifted to separate retail shops. For example, at the end of the eighteenth century some Colchester craftsmen were producing cheap long case clocks, mostly to be sold to farmers. They also introduced batch production of moving parts to sell to smaller local watchmakers, while doing a thriving retail trade in clocks, watches, jewellery and other goods.[46] Retail trade was often combined with farming. Butchers' shops were an obvious outlet since butchers almost always slaughtered their own meat; farming families would have one brother who ran the shop and another on the farm. Within retail trade, there were variations in the amount of capital and plant needed to start up and maintain services. Fresh produce was the easiest and cheapest to establish while stationery, drapery, bookselling and ironmongery required more credit with slower turnover. Retail sales of some products increased in the eighteenth century, for example drapery and haberdashery, since the machine production of textiles, combined with efficient transport, could supply retailers all over the country. Others, like foodstuffs, remained closer to local suppliers, even continuing to deal in exchange of produce and services as well as cash.[47] It was mainly at this less formal and less costly end of retail trade that women could play a more independent part.

Except for specialists in millinery and dressmaking, larger more prosperous trades were run by men. In the central district of Colchester, the large tailors, watchmakers, booksellers, jewellers, upholsterers, chemists and drapers shops were all headed by men in establishments employing domestic servants as well as living in apprentices and assistants. At the further end of the High Street were courtyards with mainly working-class households where the shops were small; greengrocers, tailoring or dressmaking establishments staffed by a woman, often a widow, on her own or with one assistant.[48] The type of product sold affected the sexual division of labour even when the business was on quite a large scale. While Birmingham traders as a whole were the group most likely to allow their wives to directly inherit their businesses (85 per cent), the sub-group of victuallers followed this pattern in almost every case. For example, a victualler, Joseph Lyndon, left an estate of approximately £2000 and yet specified that his wife should carry on the business.[49]

The most important changes in retailing over the period were in the location and procedures used. Before the transformation of buildings into shops, where stock was displayed as well as sold, the main forms of sale had been fairs, markets and itinerant traders. Mass manufacture of some 'fancy goods' – Birmingham 'toys' being one of the most important – actually increased opportunities for travelling packmen, pedlars and fairs, but in the long run led to specialized shops with fixed and marked prices. Gradually fairs became either centres of wholesale trade such as the great lamb fair at Ipswich (where upwards of 100,000 beasts were sold in a few days) or primarily social occasions.[50]

Markets were not so much replaced by shops as changing in both products and premises. Weekly markets for foodstuffs tended to remain local until after mid century. Early nineteenth-century Essex had at least eighteen large markets and Suffolk upwards of twenty-six. However, markets in the larger towns began to be provided with a stable site. In 1809 Ipswich had a New Market built which covered over an acre, while in Colchester a mid town pub garden was converted into a butter, poultry and vegetable market.[51] At the same time in more remote rural areas itinerant pedlars continued to be important sources of goods as well as news. A farmer's wife met a packman while out walking from whom she bought a trinket for her son and later that month recorded that 'the Jew brought my salt spoons this evening, cost 1s 1d'.[52]

Newspaper advertisements and diaries point to sales of house contents at a death or bankruptcy as important sources of furniture, books, pictures, plate, linen and china. Beyond the local markets and even regional fairs, the better-off could make journeys to London to buy more fashionable goods, a practice much facilitated by the railway. Even in coaching days, an Essex farmer or doctor made occasional forays to the capital, partly to see the sights but also to buy surgical instruments, a coat, some silver spoons.[53] Shops used devices such as advertising exhibitions of goods associated with London fashion, holding special inspection days for new acquisitions. By the second quarter of the century, Chelmsford's shops were 'well stocked', with 'handsome plate glass windows'.[54] An 1820s commentator on Birmingham wrote: 'We are now in the high tide of retail trade . . . the shops of the higher degrees are very handsomely fitted up; the form and sweep of the windows and the style of the decorations, emulating those of the Metropolis.'[55]

The premises for retail trade were usually rented and almost invariably part of the building where the family lived. In a remote Suffolk village, the main shopkeeper had a bakehouse and also sold groceries, haberdashery, farthing cakes and penny bindings. The kitchen of the bakery house was next door to the shop with a brick, uncarpeted floor but a warm chimney corner for the master's chair.[56] In the centres of large towns, lock-up shops where the family lived off the premises did not become common until after mid century. Even more than most middle-class livelihoods, commerce was flexible and could be entered and exited as family circumstances dictated. A rural grocer raised his nine children at the shop, at one stage moving to his mother-in-law's farm but eventually retiring back to the High Street, moving the family as the balance of resources and demands dictated.[57]

Since premises were rented, most capital was used for stock and equipment. A country shop could be started with a £75 legacy, but capital requirements could range above £500 and £1000 was not unknown for a top quality business.[58] Training in trade was often picked up by children from parents or relatives, although formal apprenticeships existed in higher branches. An Essex youth was apprenticed for a premium of £500 to a wholesale linen draper around 1800, a sum which matched the most expensive legal or medical training. However, a commercial background might mean movement between trades. A boy trained as a chemist could adapt to the wine trade, a draper to the oil and paint trade.[59] Basic education topped up with a few commercial subjects plus the experience of taking some responsibility and learning 'the habits of business' – to keep simple books and deal with customers and suppliers – seem to have been the decisive qualifications.

The family remained the most important source of labour for the small retailer. Food for sale was baked and preserved in the family kitchen if not also grown and gathered by the household. As an Essex grocer recalled, the shopkeepers made candles, cut up loaf sugar and weighed it out into bags, they prepared raisins and currants (the grocer's 'Christmas nightmare'), tasks which could be incorporated into household routine.[60] Larger retail shops and wholesale counting houses depended on living-in assistants and apprentices. Most of these employees were young, their relationship to master and mistress much like personal service. Serious Christian households would usually try to employ co-religionists and family harmony was stressed. The wealthy Ipswich draper, John Talwin Shewell, was also a Quaker minister. Junior members of the Ipswich meeting, together with Shewell's apprentices, gathered at his house to read and discuss his friend John Joseph Gurney's evangelical tract, *On the Peculiarity of Friends*, with their master/minister. Later several of his apprentices became ministers themselves.[61] Labour in such a setting was usually inexpensive and docile; master and mistress were also often kin. Young people living in often had no option but to stay where they had been placed, and discipline included the still legitimate use of force. Such cheap labour helped to keep costs down and freed what capital was available to tide the enterprise over bad spells or allow expansion.

In status terms, shopkeeping as an occupation represented something of a new element, especially in rural areas. In the isolated Suffolk village of Wortham, an outsider became postmaster and general grocer in the 1840s. He bought up old weaver's cottages and let them at what local opinion saw as excessive rents. The rector, who saw himself as a parson with paternalistic responsibilities for his flock, regarded this man as an interloper, not even a Dissenter like many rural shopkeepers, but a 'freethinker' and 'phreno-logist'. The rector's resentment was understandable given that his family bought about £70 worth of groceries annually, yet the shopkeeper never contributed to the Reverend's school nor, reading between the lines, acknowledged the cleric's rightful place in the social hierarchy.[62] Many urban traders had been drawn from the ranks of former upper domestic servants and both groups had close ties with small farmers. In status terms, the element of personal service demanded by retail trade was considered demeaning and tainted the calling with an opprobrium escaped by the merchant. Local literature hints at special sensitivity to the status of retail trade. A Birmingham Unitarian minister reminded his congregation that there was nothing inherently dishonourable about retail trade. He eulogized younger sons of the local gentry who had recouped family capital in a town shop, and recommended such action more generally. These men, 'though they stood behind their counter, had a quiet gentlemanly dignity of bearing, very different from the obsequiousness of their modern representatives'.[63]

The appeal to the dignity and trust of co-religionists was an effective way of conferring local reputation and promoting local trade. In both town and countryside a ready-made clientele existed in the religious community. The building and supplying of hospitals, workhouses and schools in the early nineteenth century also provided large-scale opportunity for local trades-men, and religious as well as political affiliation often determined contracts. Selective trading, however, could be a two-edged weapon. The tradesmen of Colchester were heavily dependent on farmers and landowners in the surrounding countryside for their custom. Town retailers' support for nonconformist issues was muted in the face of this economic reality. It was one thing for the wealthy Quaker brewer who was secretary of the Colch-ester Anti-Corn Law League and well known for his radical views to harangue his fellow tradesmen to stand up for themselves, but their liveli-hoods depended on a discretion, sometimes interpreted as servility.[64]

The rank of even a merchant's family within a local area depended not just on the product or size of the enterprise but on the community itself. A wholesale operation such as the malting and shipowning concern started by Newson Garrett in a small Suffolk coastal town where there was no immediate gentry, gave the family social precedence only matched by the widow of an East India tea planter and the clergy, even though the Garretts had started life in a pawnbroker's shop in London's East End.[65] In a larger community, merchants had marked their status by moving away from the dockside or warehouse district. By 1850, of the twenty-five merchants operating from Colchester's dock area, nine lived elsewhere, several in the town centre alongside professional men and large shopkeepers but a few in surrounding villages and one or two in the town's first suburban street.[66] Birmingham commercial families rose and fell with the metal trades, those of Essex and Suffolk with agriculture, and it is understandable why Ipswich shopkeepers walked out to the fields of a summer evening anxiously watching the state of the harvest. The Napoleonic War brought thousands of troops to Essex and Suffolk to be quartered and fed, laying the foundations for several trading fortunes. A cynical Suffolk doctor saw the local barrack master as a sinister figure building local patronage but most of the local middle class welcomed the trade he represented, and Colchester's leading families readily accepted the elaborate entertainments provided by a family whose affluence derived from military tailoring.[67]

In the eastern region, both the former predominance of the wool trade and the presence of retired merchants from the City of London had produced a local elite accustomed to an influx of commercial wealth. In Birmingham, the concentration of nonconformists in commerce gave them access to prestigious and powerful social circles in the town. Nevertheless, it was seldom possible for the first generation, in retail trade in particular, to gain full social acceptance.[68] Many commercial fortunes were used to send sons into the professions thus enhancing the family's status and providing the enterprise with useful skills and contacts. The Pattisson family had been based in the Witham area since the seventeenth century, steadily accumulating a fortune from shopkeeping and land dealing until they were a powerful force on the local scene. The generation of the late eighteenth century broke tradition and entered the professions. William Henry Pattisson became a local attorney and sent his son, Jacob Howells Pattisson, to Cambridge before bringing him into legal partnership. Jacob completed the rise by marrying a member of a local gentry family. In the Witham of the early nineteenth century, both the wealth and contacts acquired in trade were distinct assets in this social climb when they had been smoothed over by education and a professional practice.[69]

Not all shopkeepers aspired to such heights. Particularly those with strong religious commitments were content to use trade as a respectable means of making a living. The gradual division between the production of goods on the premises and their sale over a counter contributed to the separation from eighteenth-century artisan culture. The forge at the back of the ironmongers' premises on the High Street of market towns was closed down as mass production sent a stream of commercial travellers out of Birmingham with a variety of small iron ware, while agencies were established for the larger items such as the Ransome plough. Retailers claimed expertise in the packaging and sales of these more finished goods, although many items in, for example, grocery still required final preparation by the purchaser. Both family labour and living-in assistants continued to be heavily used and the small shop has remained the place where family labour was most common to the present day.[70]

Banks and banking

In the provinces, 'banks' dealing only with money transactions had slowly evolved out of general commercial activities. Before they became full-time bankers the Gibsons of Saffron Walden had been brewers, the Twinings of Colchester in tea and grocery, the Oakes of Bury St Edmunds, wool merchants. In Birmingham, the Lloyds had been iron masters, the Galtons gun manufacturers and the Gibbins in the metal trades. Men could be partners in a bank and continue actively in another enterprise. Into the 1830s, many solicitors and tradesmen, as well as some manufacturers, clergymen and even doctors continued to perform banking functions, even if it was simply holding and investing the savings of a labourer who did not trust those new inventions, banks.[71]

Nevertheless, during this period the establishment of country banks flourished, and in a town like Birmingham were acknowledged to be the most important source of capital outside kinship networks. In Essex and Suffolk, where there appear to have been only five banks in the whole region in the 1780s, by the 1820s there was a network of several important banking firms, each 'drawing upon' some leading London firm and having branches or agencies in adjacent smaller towns.[72] In 1814 Birmingham had six banks, and 1827 saw the opening of a Birmingham branch of the Bank of England, the first of many new banks during the next decade. Despite the dominant position of London and the Bank of England, there was a need for local intermediaries to handle a variety of transactions such as tax collection, the payment of soldiers and the provision of cash; with the war scare of 1797 to 1818 the Bank of England ceased issuing cash payments, a boost to country banks.[73] Until the Bank Charter Act of 1818, banks within a radius of 56 miles from London were not allowed to have more than six partners and only relatively modest sums were needed to start operations. This made it more important than ever for those performing banking functions to be impeccable in financial matters and have an intimate knowledge of the affairs of the locality. Many men moved into banking as a way of raising capital for their own ventures and there is no doubt that fortunes could be made, although the risks were great under unlimited liability.

For the most part, bankers supported projects with short-term returns, particularly in the earlier part of the period. This made them reluctant to invest in land or mortgages and turned bankers' attention to urban land or industry. Local builders and farmers mainly had to continue to rely on kinship for capital. There also was a close association between banking and insurance, partly because bankers wanted to see their investments protected against fire risk. Colchester bankers were among the first directors of the Essex and Suffolk Equitable Insurance Society, and James Oakes was a Director of a Suffolk and General Insurance Company.[74] It is possible that the involvement of bankers with urban building rather than land reinforced their search for alternative sources of displaying wealth and status, including philanthropic activities. Solid respectability was also demonstrated in their lifestyle and homes. Banks usually operated from the bank house, often a room on the ground floor with the family of the banker or manager occupying the rest of the house. Such buildings became imposing structures in the town landscape. When James Oakes turned from wool stapling to become a full-time banker in the 1790s, he employed Sir John Soane, the London architect, to remodel his home in the centre of Bury St Edmunds. Soane designed a dignified building with the banking rooms to the left of the vaulted hallway.[75]

When a provincial bank expanded, it tended to be through the establishment of regional branches or agencies with kin occupying these posts. Several networks laced Birmingham and the eastern regions. For example, the Quaker Alexanders and the Anglican Oakes seem to have operated amicably in eastern Suffolk, but there were rivalries among many others. In the periodic bank failures, the weaker would be cannibalized. James Oakes reflected the fears of many bankers that 'evil persons' might spread rumours about the soundness of a bank's credit, a serious threat as it could precipitate a 'run' on the bank's resources.[76]

The educational background and training of bankers varied. An established family might send second generation sons from the isolated countryside to boarding schools where they could mix with the sons of gentry and top professionals. Birmingham bankers would have been more likely to attend either local private academies or the grammar school. Many would have gained experience in other kinds of establishments and some training in the bank, whether formal apprenticeship or not, became necessary. There was a definite social divide between those destined to be bankers and staff. A Birmingham banker's wife worried that her son, in training at the bank, was mixing too freely with the clerks while his father was away on business.[77] While such a spell in management might be useful experience for bankers' young kinsmen, a manager did not necessarily move on to become a partner since substantial capital was required. Even to gain the manager's position required guarantors to give fairly large sums as sureties.[78] However, bank managers and even agents had a position of status and an assured salary and gained access to knowledge of local opportunities. As a small town bank manager wrote, he needed to combine 'the inscrutability of the Sphinx with the impeccable reputation of Caesar's wife'.[79] The need for trustworthiness is reflected in the over representation of Quakers among the banking personnel from the local areas.[80] The banker was one of the most wealthy and powerful people in the community and this often led to links with local gentry. The Rounds of Colchester had made their money in publishing in London and moved to Essex to purchase a small estate about 6 miles from the town. The second generation started a bank, while another branch produced the Rev. James Round, Evangelical vicar of St James. A Round sister married the son of a wealthy City merchant who had also bought up an Essex country house. Banking interests undoubtedly helped to integrate the Rounds into the highest Anglican and Tory interests of the town and its surrounding region.[81]

Although the rewards could be abundant, provincial banking created particular problems for its practitioners. Each customer's standing in the community had to be intimately known by the banker, yet he must not be seen to openly favour any one 'connection'. Given the frequent face-to-face confrontations in church or chapel and the regular social mixing in homes, it became difficult for a local banker to refuse transactions with, or cast doubt on the financial position of, his local clients. The most frequent reason for the failure of private banks was helping out businesses from motives of private friendship. The problem was particularly serious because, in a local region, the bank tended to be tied to the fortunes of the main industry. Many bankers in Essex and Suffolk got their fingers burned after lending to farmers during the war boom, only to be caught in the agricultural depression of the 1820s.

Another problem stemmed from the direct dependence of provincial banks on London, a dependence unlike that of most other local enterprises. A solid base of local confidence combined with direct, preferably personal, links with the main London banks were the only defence which could supply credit and cash to tide a provincial bank over periodic crises. The Oakes used both in the dreadful December of 1826 when the banking system of the whole country seemed to be collapsing. On Sunday, 18 December, Orbell Oakes took his own chaise and, together with his wife Betsy and the local squire, drove from Bury St Edmunds to London to raise all the gold and Bank of England notes they could and have them in Bury by Monday afternoon. In fact, Orbell arrived back in the early hours of Tuesday morning, 'most amply supplied . . . and saved the day'.[82] On the same fateful Sunday, the Moilliet banking family of Birmingham arrived back from Geneva and were met by young James Moilliet who had collected all the gold that could be raised from London contacts. Together they hastened back to Birmingham, Amelia Moilliet transferring part of the precious cache in her personal travelling bag. Again the bank was saved.[83]

The families of bankers were intimately concerned with the fortunes of the bank. Their lifestyle was under particular scrutiny by the local community and their female members would be expected to take a leading part in local affairs. Mrs Round, of the Colchester banking family, was particularly active in Sunday school affairs, lending the grounds of the house for annual tea parties.[84] At a more humble level, the wives of bank managers were responsible for keeping the bank premises clean and tidy, answering queries and helping out behind the scenes. Although full-time bankers were few (only eighteen in Birmingham and thirty in Essex in 1851), the local power and influence of the banking enterprise was great. As one of the few active careers taken up by the gentry its status was also high. Nevertheless, bankers from middle-class backgrounds were committed to many of the values of their group; in serious religion, in a recognition of domesticity, and in particular a world view which stressed order and accountability. They ardently supported the need to quantify and measure the social world for, after all, one of the main functions of the banker was to convert a 'man's worth' into monetary terms.

Manufacture

Since the eighteenth century, manufacture had been seen as the moving force in English development, the engine of Victorian progress. The iconography of a town like Birmingham was dominated by metal manufacture, and by 1836 Birmingham was specifically named as a 'manufacturing town',[85] a new designation distinguishing it, along with the better known Manchester, from those centres such as Liverpool dominated by mercantile enterprise. Nevertheless, even at mid century, in the census sample, manufacturers made up only about one-fifth of the town's middle class and in the whole census sample household heads in manufacture were 10 per cent. In the Essex and Suffolk countryside, a handful of isolated brewers, millers and tanners were joined by newer iron foundries, or fertilizer plants. In rural towns, there was a sprinkling of coach builders, distilleries, and some strawplaiting, but the only genuine factories were the silk mills of southeast Essex.[86]

Opportunities for engaging in more than one pursuit were less in manufacturing than, for example, in trade. Even so, there are cases such as the farmer or publicans who ran brick kilns, a few turning to larger-scale manufacture of clay pipes and tiles. In Birmingham, however, most manufacturers kept within the various branches of metal production. Birmingham 'toys' had been well known since the eighteenth century, primarily items made by hand in small workshops. Over the next fifty years, the production of buttons, and papier mâché ware was expanded widely. By 1866, Samuel Timmins was able to claim that 'within a radius of thirty miles of Birmingham, nearly the whole hardware wants of the world are practically supplied'.[87] The development of the brass trade and the invention of new processes such as the stamp and die method made articles not only cheaper but with a superior finish. From the eighteenth century, Birmingham manufacturers were also exploring new marketing techniques. 'Baskerville' japanned his surname on his carriage with a different design on each panel, a dramatic way of displaying the process, while Alfred Bird, the inventor of 'Bird's custard', pinned up a sign in his workshop:

> Early to bed. Early to rise
> Stick to your work . . . And Advertise.[88]

'Wherever the view of profit opens', wrote William Hutton, Birmingham's first historian, and himself a tradesman and manufacturer, 'the eyes of a Birmingham man are open to see'. The town was renowned for its freedom from restrictions and its innovative character.[89]

Over the period, selling tended to separate from manufacture. In the eighteenth century the merchant/manufacturer had collected and marketed goods made in small out-work shops or the small master had sold his product direct. Now larger manufacturers started to use commercial travellers to take samples to wholesalers and retailers. Some used junior members of the family and prospective partners for this task. Recent historians of Birmingham have queried the assumption that small workshop production remained the major organization in the metal trades.[90] Such workshops may have still dominated numerically in the 1840s, but there had been a shift to steam power which required larger premises and outlay of capital.[91] A number of firms had emerged which aimed at low cost per unit of output. Small masters, who predominated in metal finishing, could no longer compete and became dependent on outsiders for finance and supplies or they subcontracted themselves. Unlike commercial operations, the tendency in manufacture was towards interdependent and hierarchical chains of long-term credit.

The scale of the enterprise did not necessarily have to do with complicated machinery or even steam power. Soho (Boulton and Watt's great works) was larger because of the reorganization which had taken place in management, not because of its machinery.[92] Hand tools were still extensively used in large metal manufacturing works, employing the workman's skill, his 'experience of head, hand and eye'.[93] Conversely, the glass industry required heavy capital investment in fixed plants, yet many modest manufactories managed to survive. The Chance glass works was operated on a large scale although production remained heavily dependent on skilled workmen using hand processes, and Chance Brothers has been seen as a prime example of the uneven development of manufacture.[94]

Technological and design improvements also played their part in manufacturing expansion. Such techniques as 'japanning' on papier mâché, utilizing steel for small items such as pens and experiments in chemicals show technology producing new or improved commodities. The importance of science to the Birmingham scene had been promoted by Priestley and the Lunar Society in the eighteenth century, and James Keir's chemical experiments were vital to his glass factory which was the first after Soho to use steam power.[95] That great achievement of Birmingham's early industrial expertise, the Boulton and Watt works at Soho, had used the mixture of 'Mechanism and Chymistry' with 'taste and elegance' in other words, technology and design.[96]

For the sons of these manufacturers, growing up in such an atmosphere promoted similar careers. James Watt, whose father had been a teacher of mathematics as well as a shipwright, picked up skills at the home-based workbench.[97] Alfred Bird developed his interest in chemistry from his father who was an astronomer and his grandfather, an instrument maker.[98] Unfamiliar demands produced opportunities to be grasped by enterprising men. Although apprenticeship continued to be used as basic training, because of novelty in many processes there were few established guilds to control entry or conditions.[99] Placing young men with family and kin for training was widely used. Arthur Albright, who was to become a well-known Birmingham manufacturing chemist in the 1850s, was apprenticed to his uncle, a Bristol chemist, who had no children, while the young Samuel Courtauld was sent to an uncle in London to settle him into more business-like ways before returning to the Essex silk mill.[100] Neither Boulton nor Watt's sons were apprenticed but they were given an education designed for the business, including James Watt junior spending time at Wilkinson's iron works, being trained in drawing and carpentry. There were already marriage connections between the two enterprises and the relationship to young Watt was semi-familial.[101]

It may well have been the absence of apprenticeship specific to manufacture which made formal scientific and commercial education for boys so important to the Birmingham middle class. Some manufacturers were particularly keen to promote schools of design. James Bisset, son of a modest Scottish landowning family whose financial circumstances suddenly worsened, abandoned his classical education and started to learn arithmetic and other subjects which he hoped would qualify him for a trade. He cultivated his knack for drawing and design, went to Birmingham to join a brother with an established business and started work in japanning where design skills were valued. He attended one of the new design schools in the town, an investment in time and money which later paid off handsomely in his thriving japanning business.[102]

The next stage for the hopeful young manufacturer was usually a partnership. The variety of skills and amounts of capital needed meant that of all the middle-class enterprises, manufacturers depended most heavily on partnerships. The joint stock company was only permitted for public utilities and metal extraction. There had been some local attempts to set up such companies to ensure supplies of raw materials. On a smaller scale, Birmingham's 'capital clubs', a form of voluntary society, provided one possible means to enable small producers to set up on their own account. None of these schemes could meet the needs for capital and personnel and partnership continued to be the major source for both. Men often entered more than one partnership to suit their varied interests. Boulton was partner with Watt for steam engines, the latter contributing mechanical knowledge, while at the same time being in partnership with Fothergill for the manufacture of 'toys'.[103]

It was only when a partner could not be found through kin or friends that managers would sometimes be employed. Occasionally managers were failed owners. Thomas Clark employed the ex-owner of a greenhouse factory as his manager.[104] But more often managerial posts were filled by younger men on the way to establishing themselves, and being groomed as future partners.

As with partnerships, it was kinship and family which provided the most reliable source of finance, both initial capital and credit facilities. It was Archibald Kenrick's marriage in 1793, which brought him £500 and an additional £500 the next year when his wife turned 21, that allowed him to establish a new hollow-ware concern following the crisis in the Birmingham buckle trades. Loans from other parts of the family were later decisive for this enterprise. Archibald's eldest son, also Archibald, married Anne Paget in 1825 and received £2000 in trust for her. His father-in-law was called upon more than once to help out with a loan at times of acute financial embarrassment.[105]

Early nineteenth-century manufacture may have been more specialized and heavily capitalized than commercial ventures but family labour was still extensively used, not only in partnership and managerial capacities but in supplementary forms. This is indicated in the numerous cases of, at least small manufacturers leaving the business to their wives in their wills; on average 80 per cent. This pattern partly depended on the type of manufacture since certain processes and products were strongly associated with men or women, the former requiring training and special skills, the latter gaining their experience informally, through family membership. A Birmingham chaser and huckster left his stock-in-trade for the chasing business to his son while his wife inherited that of huckstering which she was instructed to pass on to her daughter. To be a chaser required particular skills and training; there were few female chasers in Birmingham.[106] Many manufacturing processes were still being done in and around the home, involving wives and children. Wives helped out with simple home manufacture, such as that of steel pen making. At rush time they could be called on to help wrap and label goods, write letters and keep the books. In one enterprise, experiments in paper manufacture were made by boiling rags on the kitchen stove where the household could hardly help being involved.[107]

Manufacturing enterprises of any size presented particular problems in the management and control of employees increasingly gathered in one work place. An important minority of these units could be very large, such as Ransomes' iron manufacturing business at Ipswich which expanded by producing iron goods for the railway to a workforce of over 1000 by mid century.[108] In isolated rural districts with first generation waged labourers, a strict but benevolent paternalism could be invoked. Pensions for long-term workers and gifts such as the Christmas leg of pork were balanced with casual blows from the master's stick for poor workmanship and steep fines for stepping out of line.[109] Where the workforce was primarily female, women of the family might be brought in to act as overseers as when George Courtauld employed his four daughters in his first Essex mill.[110] Such direct contact caused social unease. Even middle-class men were seeking to separate themselves from such close involvement in manual work and contact with workmen. In the days of the smaller workshop in Birmingham, the brass master might spend his day with his workmen, and he, 'not unfrequently begirt with apron, examined the work, tied it up, made out the invoice and sent out the finished work', but this 'primitive state of things' was not to last.[111]

The nub of the change was the economic and social meaning attached to manual and craft work as opposed to management of labour, materials and markets. When young Samuel Courtauld was havering over joining the family silk mill and hinted that he might take up engraving, his father crisply remarked:

. . . how is it you seem to forget that mere manual labour – though of the higher class – is very rarely indeed so valuable as a business – as those modes of trade or manufacture which allow us a profit from the labour of many persons?[112]

The gradual move of manufacturers to suburban areas seems to have been both cause and effect of the gradual separation of the family home from the works. In the census sample, 25 per cent of male household heads in Edgbaston were in manufacture, the largest single group next to those living on independent means. Some men followed an intermediate pattern before making the break complete. James Watt continued to work at home while the factory was a short distance away, his assistants coming to his house.[113] Similarly James Keir, when he was running the Tipton glass works and living some distance away, had a counting house at home where his clerks worked.[114] The development of a suburb like Edgbaston seems to have completed the separation for many, especially the better off. Only in isolated rural areas did a man like William Bentall specifically design his new home within the industrial complex of his enlarged agricultural machinery works.[115]

Undoubtedly, being able to live away from the noise and clutter of production and the intrusion of socially inferior work people partially motivated these moves. Ryland, the Birmingham plate manufacturer, suffered the ignominy of having to move from his pleasant Edgbaston home back to quarters at the workplace when his business was at a low ebb. His son recalled: 'It was an awful come-down to my father who had always been a foremost man in the town.'[116] Manufacturers were relieved to be able to move away from a dangerous proximity to the labouring poor, particularly during the politically uneasy years of the 1840s. There were some Birmingham manufacturers whose wealth permitted them to move into the surrounding countryside but often the motive was to farm as a business. One of the town's successful manufacturers established himself as an 'improving farmer' at Elmdon Hall which had long been a seat of the Warwickshire gentry. There he was visited by the Witham doctor, Henry Dixon, himself a keen agriculturalist where they undoubtedly exchanged views about Dixon's friend and neighbour, Mechi, inventor of the 'magic razor', who had poured the money from manufacturing his invention into his experimental farm. After the visit Dixon remarked that 'these trading citizens make the best farmers'.[117]

In status terms, Birmingham was a relatively self-contained society with its strong nonconformist presence and many manufacturers were content to remain within the local system. Education aided those who did wish to enhance a position based on manufacturing wealth, at least for the second generation. James Keir, who had come from a landowning background into chemical manufacture, was anxious to establish chemistry as a genteel pursuit. In writing a textbook for his daughter he made a distinction between two branches of the subject. In the book she inquires why the man who keeps a shop with red and blue bottles in the windows is also called a chemist like her papa:

That man is a *trading chemist*, and his trade is to make Spirit of Hartshorn and such things as he can sell and he probably knows the part of Chemistry which is necessary for his purposes and little more. . . . [The other] may be distinguished by the name of *Philosophical Chemist*, for he studies and makes experiments, not to make things to sell, but to acquire more knowledge of the properties of bodies.[118]

Some manufacturers, however, were more concerned to challenge traditional gentry values, whether on religious grounds as in the case of committed Quakers or in terms of a more general claim for their contribution to society. James Watt wrote feelingly of the distinction between inherited wealth and active invention and manufacture:

The Squire's land has not been so much of his own making as the condensing engine has been of mine. He has only passively inherited his property, while this invention has been the product of my own labour and of God knows how much anguish of mind and body.[119]

Few manufacturers had a condensing engine to their credit, but Watt here states part of the essential difference in orientation between the middle class and the eighteenth-century gentry just as in his commitment to home life, he expressed another.

Farming

In the arable regions of the south and east, mid eighteenth-century agriculture had evolved into the uniquely English 'three tier' system. Most land was owned in the form of large estates by the aristocracy and gentry, the remainder belonging to institutions like the church or colleges or to attorneys, shopkeepers and bankers of the market towns. Farming tenants rented the land with farmhouse, and outbuildings, land which they worked with their families supplemented by waged labour.[120] The flexibility of the system was furthered by the availability of 'off-hand' lands which could be rented away from the farm so that the tenant could respond to shifts in the market as well as family circumstances.

Customary provisions for working the land required the landlord to supply materials, buildings and facilities such as drainage and hedging while the tenant added stock, seed and tools. By the latter part of the eighteenth century, farmers in the eastern region were described as the 'active capitalists of English agriculture'.[121] While the proportion of families in the whole country engaged in agriculture fell to just over a quarter, in Essex it held steady at about one-half. Essex, in particular, had the advantage of having much of its land already enclosed, and the average farm was already conducive to this type of production. Improved coastal, canal and road transport linked grain growing areas to their primary markets of London and the Midlands. Some farmers and not a few landowners had previously been in the wool trade or even City merchants, so that their general business orientation easily took to grain production for the market.[122] The blockcades of the Napoleonic War period which gave the final blow to the dying wool trade also guaranteed the agriculturalists a buoyant market. Despite the fact that wartime taxation bore heavily on farmers, their profits shot up, aided by low rents on pre-war tenancies. During the war, an Essex farmer with a modest acreage sold supplies to the Colchester barrack master, carted military stores and rented extra land to increase production.[123] New farms, significantly named 'Trafalgar' or 'Waterloo', were built on marginal lands and there was a virtual rush of people like journalists, shopkeepers, even army officers 'running helter skelter' to be farmers.[124]

It was well that arable farming experienced the golden years of 1790 to 1818. With the peace, the bottom dropped out of the market and those with little experience or capital went to the wall. Larger farmers, particularly those with other economic interests, were better able to survive, but the gulf between large and small farmers increased. Even before the slump, the range of farming operations had been pronounced; the acreages worked by 'cottage farmers' were barely more than smallholdings.[125] As he travelled the eastern counties for the Board of Agriculture in the 1800s, Arthur Young noted that houses of small farmers 'are frequently wretched hovels, not better, if so good, as decent cottages'.[126]

At the other end of the scale were farmers living in converted manor houses, families such as the Hutleys of Powers Hall in Witham, who farmed over 1500 acres and represented a power in the local community. In the earlier part of the period, not only had agriculture supplied all food stuffs but also most of the raw materials of industries such as brewing, milling, textiles, even chemicals so that chains of supplier to consumer remained local. By the 1850s, a much expanded 'farming industry' was using inorganic raw materials and even importing some food such as cheese. Farmers themselves began to 'consume' industrial products like bone meal and fertilizer.[127] It was the large farmer who could take the full advantage of this shift from a largely extractive to a manufacturing process.

Unlike manufacture, however, farming enterprises were constantly combined with other activities. Arthur Young, describing Witham, noted that, 'most of the farmers had lucrative businesses as well and included local clothiers, tanners and even the clergy and a lawyer'.[128] The census portrait of Witham a half century later confirms this, with a third of the town's middle class having some farming connection.[129] The Suffolk banker, James Oakes still turned out to see his harvest in, while an Essex physician was as concerned about the state of his corn as of his patients.[130] Shopkeepers in the market towns grew much of their own produce, while small farms were often combined with public houses, a brick kiln, blacksmithy, pottery or carting business. Clergymen and doctors farmed on the side, while attorneys, surveyors and estate agents were often also substantial farmers, thus keeping in close touch with their primary clients.

Because farming was so often a family enterprise, these activities could be undertaken by more than one member as well as by the male household head. Nevertheless, most farms and farmhouses were rented by a single family, and formal partnership between farmers was rare. Young adult sons might stay on the farm to help their fathers or elder brothers while they gained experience but they would leave on marriage and take up their own farm. Many of the widows heading a farm household were farming with a young son, often as a holding operation until he was old enough to take over the tenancy. The leasing system could work to the advantage of either landowner or farmer. Pressure could be brought to evict tenants but they might also move on to better their position leaving the landlord tenanted by the incompetent or bankrupt. Short tenancies gave control to the landlord but reduced farmers' motivation to make improvements, and this period saw much conflict over definition of tenants' rights. The fortunes of many farming families as 'tenants at will' (that is with no formal agreements) rested on trust between farmer and owner.[131] The support of a local kinship, friendship or religious network could be an important element in gaining and keeping the tenancy of a good farm. Orderly habits not only on the farm but in domestic life supported an image of trustworthiness.

Farm leases could be inherited but, unlike other property, it was difficult to convert them to cash. A more common pattern was to take on extra land with a second or third farmhouse for adult sons to farm. The eldest son would move to the subsidiary farm leaving one of the younger sons to assist the older couple and eventually take over the farm when they retired or died. Kinship contacts, including the female line, were central to this system. Thomas Seabrook, son of a prosperous farming couple in Boreham, Essex, as a young man took over the farm and lands of his mother's parents in a village about 20 miles to the east, since she had been an only child. Two younger brothers also went to the village to another farm and butcher's shop belonging to the maternal grandparents. Three of the five Seabrook sons were thus provided for from this source. The fourth brother ran the butcher's shop connected with the farm in Boreham still worked by his parents. The lease for this farm originally had been inherited by Thomas senior's mother so that in this family the use of women's property and resources can be traced over three generations.[132]

Although fathers and sons did not often go into partnership, they frequently farmed within the same or nearby communities; they hunted together, attended markets and dined in the same clubs. Robert Bretnall of Witham, whose son started farming in the next village, not only gave the young man sums of money but paid his rent, insured his stock, arranged with his landlord for renovations, sent over extra hay and one of his own men to help with the barley harvest.[133] Bretnall, like many others, also liberally gave advice. Another farming father wrote in a letter that his son 'is very industrious and you may imagine frequently requires his father's assistance. . . . It adds much to our comfort having him so near'.[134]

There is evidence that some farmers followed the general pattern of withdrawal from active work in late middle age. Then either a son or male relative might take over the farm or the farmer would simply let the lease fall in. The system encouraged turnover, and attachment to a particular farmstead does not seem to have been widespread. An Essex farmer, fifty years tenant of the paternalistic Lord Howard, was offered the chance to stay on in the farmhouse but chose retirement into the nearby town.[135] This business-like attitude to transfers of property extended to arrangements within farming families, part of the farmers' increasing implication in longer credit chains and the power of middle men or 'factors'. A small Essex farmer sold corn to London buyers through the Corn Exchange, but he also sold butter to the local blacksmith, butter, cream and poultry directly to the squire, cheese to a local gent, a cock to the doctor, wheat to the local baker, eggs to Colchester market, turnips and sheep feed to his neighbour as well as some barter for services such as medical care in return for fresh produce.[136]

The implication of farmers in the market economy was a prime factor in their taking on more managerial tasks and less manual work alongside their men. In 1807, from January to August, an Essex farmer made forty-four journeys away from home excluding going to chapel. Most of these forays were attendance at markets in neighbouring towns.[137] The more prosperous farmers, using the improved road network, could now keep a riding horse as well as a light wheeled vehicle in addition to the farm cart. The gig became particularly associated with prosperous farmers, a group sometimes disdainfully dubbed the 'gigocracy'.

Market towns have been described as nodes of ideas for progressive farming.[138] Here working farmers gathered on market day and had their meal provided by the local inn, the 'ordinary' (at a fixed price high enough to deter labourers). The more enterprising also began to join Farmers' Clubs, all-male assemblies meeting in local public houses. These clubs were less prestigious but more practical than the Agricultural Societies patronized by the gentry landlords. Whereas in 1804 there had been only one Agricultural Society in Suffolk, by 1846 there were five, as well as twelve Farmers' Clubs.[139] One of the earliest was formed by James Allen Ransome, grandson of the founder of the Ipswich agricultural machinery firm. As a young man, he had been sent to a neighbouring rural area, part of his job being to call upon smiths, builders, wheelwrights and farmers. He combined these duties with the Quaker ministry and in 1837 became secretary to the nascent Yoxford Farmers' Club, where, for ten years, he was its driving force.[140]

Much of the 'progressive farming' promoted by the clubs was concerned with orderly methods of work and the conversion of time and labour to cash equivalents in an attempt to estimate profitability. For example, in 1845 the Yoxford Farmers' Club took the decision that all payment in truck to agricultural labourers should be converted to money wages so that the men could go to market and purchase 'what they pleased'.[141] The widespread replacement of sundials by clocks in farm kitchens in the eighteenth century was followed by the adoption of thermometers and barometers in farmhouse halls and parlours. In 1813, a local vicar remarked on the latter innovations as 'a most useful instrument for the husbandman . . . and a striking instance of the intelligence of this period'.[142]

Spatial arrangements on the farm also began to reflect the more orderly approach. The recycling and storage of manure fitted in with general views of classifying materials and separating functions. More expensive tools and tackle needed a separate room, valuable stock had to be housed under cover in purpose-built buildings. Agents, middle men and bankers provided much of the drive for rational methods, pressure they could back up with financial sanctions. Of course in everyday life, many farmers, especially those on smaller holdings, had neither the interest nor resources to attempt such rationality. In fact, the less well-off farmers might have good reason to resist rational farming with its explicit accountability. When an ex-naval officer took on a marshland farm on the remote Essex coast in the 1790s, he tried to get his fellow farmers to use his recently published *Tables for the Improvement of Landed Estates*.[143] Their hostile reaction stemmed from the fear that, if improvements were made, rents might be raised. The very act of publishing objective standards and production goals could be used to make invidious comparisons based purely on economic criteria.

A further stumbling block to rationalization of farming was the close connection between production for market and family use, the continued mixture of sources of farming income. Rather than the lure of pure profit maximization or economic rationality, it was the external pressure from the market economy combined with a serious Christian cast of mind that seems to have produced a general shift in farming practice. Farmers aimed for more control over their working as well as non-working lives as they became more vulnerable to new market forces, as well as their old adversaries, weather and climate.

The most significant change brought about by specialization in arable production was the substitution of waged labour for living-in farm servants. In 1851, the twenty-four farmers of Coggeshall, Essex, employed 250 labourers or just under ten men to every employer. This coincides with Saville's ratio of employer to men of 1:8.4 for Essex compared to 1:4.7 for the country as a whole and 1:2.5 for Cumberland, an upland area of family farms.[144] Since these estimates are averages, some farms had much larger workforces, making them comparable in size with manufacturing enterprises. A medium to large farm of between 200 and 400 acres would have to employ up to two dozen men, a number almost impossible to board in the old way, even in the largest establishment. During the war, too, with the high price of food, cost conscious farmers increasingly forsook boarding farm servants, especially since this prevented labourers from then claiming rights of parish settlement.

Whatever the economic considerations, growing social differences meant that farmers' families wanted more privacy and farmers' female relatives, like their men, wanted some release from arduous physical work. The changes came gradually with farm servants put to eat at separate tables in the common kitchen, then a 'keeping room' or parlour for the family was introduced with the labourers taking a midday meal only in the back kitchen (locally the 'back house' or 'bak-hus'). The tradition of the Harvest Supper (in Suffolk, the Horkey) with its special ales, songs and rituals slowly changed from the lavish spread in the common 'house place', with master and mistress at the head of the table taking their part, to a separate meal provided in the kitchen where the farmer and his wife would put in an appearance only for the final toasts. Later still, the local publican might be paid to provide the whole affair with much heavy drinking and women seldom present.[145] When some of these rituals were reintroduced in an effort to rekindle 'organic community' they were usually held either out of doors or in the barn. By 1846, a prosperous Witham farmer paid his harvest labourers a lump sum, a pair of gloves and six pints of beer a day, noting in his diary that 'I did not promise them any Victuals or ending.'[146]

The gains made by farmers and landowners from the high price of corn during the war increased distress among labourers now forced to purchase their own provisions. Their resentment at such practices inflamed existing anger at the new Poor Law and fear of displacement by new methods of farming, particularly with the introduction of threshing machinery. Periodic riots and incendiarism wracked the farming community, with larger farmers and the clergy as particular targets while some smaller farmers sympathized with the labourers. The blazing ricks and barns which could be seen from Colchester town centre or which lit the night sky over Witham were reminders of the problem of order.[147] Farmers responded with a combination of paternalistic schemes of reward for loyalty and harsh punishments, possibly administered on the spot by the master's own hand.[148] In 1839, Witham's most powerful farmer, and a formidable Poor Law overseer, William Hutley, advocated stopping all out relief for three months after an outbreak of incendiarism in opposition to the more tender-hearted vicar.[149] Concern over these issues focused on the shift to wage labour, for farmers and their wives had largely given up control over the young, single servant (of both sexes). Working-class labourers were urged by middle-class commentators to adopt a pattern of domesticity and become responsible for the support of their wives and children. However, this raised fears among farmers that they would indirectly be supporting the labourer's dependants through higher wages. Marriage and his own 'home' might steady the male labourer but it was reassuring to know that women and children would have to still earn their own keep.[150]

The new wealth of farmers and their increased literacy and power at the local level was also a challenge to the local gentry.[151] A particularly sensitive area was education and general culture. Modern farming required increased literacy and numeracy. This led to the establishment of private schools such as Ongar Academy, founded in 1811 by the son of an Essex farmer whose brothers also became farmers near by.[152] In a survey of Suffolk, the complaint was made that smaller farmers could not afford the £40–50 annual fees for the grammar school and 'owing to the advantages of the free and parochial schools now spread through the county, our labourers' children will be better taught than our own'.[153] Farmers and their families were taking part in book clubs, reading newspapers and some had small libraries. Retired farmers, their widows and spinster daughters made their homes in market towns near their relatives and friends who were often shopkeepers. Even when still actively farming, those with a serious Christian connection mixed with their more urban counterparts through regular church and chapel visits.

Both men and women in farming families highly valued the religious home, the training of children and a respectable, if not genteel, lifestyle. These ideals were expressed in the commemorative meeting of an Essex family. On 1 December 1840, Ann and Thomas Seabrook, with their eleven surviving children and thirty grandchildren gathered to celebrate family life and hand on to their posterity a memorial. 'Conjugal affection and happiness' was their aim, 'industry and frugality' their custom, 'not with a view to heap up riches, but to enable them to hand down to their Children the means to appear respectable', above all that they, as 'Stewards of Christ' might ensure for themselves *everlasting life*'.[154] Within this framework, the standard of living and social aspiration of the more prosperous part of the farming community had risen visibly. In the words of a contemporary, late eighteenth-century farmers had 'lived in the midst of their enlightened neighbours like beings of another order; in their personal labour they were indefatigable; in their fare hard, in their dress homely, in their manners rude. We ne'er shall look upon their like again'.[155]

Despite the savage fall in farm incomes in the post-war period, aspirations remained. The reduction in food prices did not bring back the boarding of farm servants. The Select Committee on the Depressed State of Agriculture in 1833 investigated the belief that farmers were extravagant and spoiled by high war profits. An informed opinion was that although expenditure may have had to be retracted, 'I cannot say that they have returned to their former habits of farmers because they could not have kept their *grade* in society.'[156] Raised aspirations backed by worldly resources stirred up fear that farmers would become too independent of traditional control by gentry, landowner and clergy. In many areas, farmers had been resident longer than the clergy who were coming into rural parishes as part of sweeping church reforms. Clerical incomes could not always match expectations of social and cultural leadership, not to speak of the vexed issue of tithes particularly for the nonconformist farming community.

The wide range of farming operations and incomes and the lack of a clear demarcation within farming, such as that which divided retail and wholesale trade, contributed to this unease. Not all wealthy farmers who had the resources to do so necessarily wanted to take up a gentrified existence.

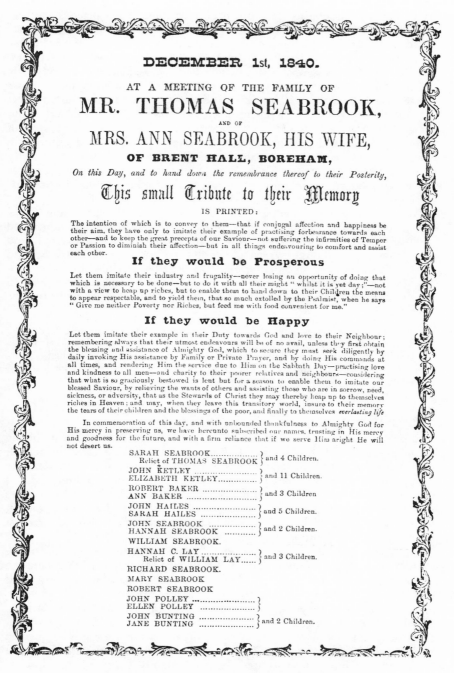

DECEMBER 1st, 1840.

AT A MEETING OF THE FAMILY OF

MR. THOMAS SEABROOK,

AND OF

MRS. ANN SEABROOK, HIS WIFE,

OF BRENT HALL, BOREHAM,

On this Day, and to hand down the remembrance thereof to their Posterity,

𝔗his small 𝔗ribute to their 𝔐emory

IS PRINTED:

The intention of which is to convey to them—that if conjugal affection and happiness be their aim, they have only to imitate their example of practising forbearance towards each other—and to keep the great precepts of our Saviour—not suffering the infirmities of Temper or Passion to diminish their affection—but in all things endeavouring to comfort and assist each other.

If they would be Prosperous

Let them imitate their industry and frugality—never losing an opportunity of doing that which is necessary to be done—but to do it with all their might "whilst it is yet day;"—not with a view to heap up riches, but to enable them to hand down to their Children the means to appear respectable, and to yield them, that so much extolled by the Psalmist, when he says "Give me neither Poverty nor Riches, but feed me with food convenient for me."

If they would be Happy

Let them imitate their example in their Duty towards God and love to their Neighbour; remembering always that their utmost endeavours will be of no avail, unless they first obtain the blessing and assistance of Almighty God, which to secure they must seek diligently by daily invoking His assistance by Family or Private Prayer, and by doing His commands at all times, and rendering Him the service due to Him on the Sabbath Day—practising love and kindness to all men—and charity to their poorer relatives and neighbours—considering that what is so graciously bestowed is lent but for a season to enable them to imitate our blessed Saviour, by relieving the wants of others and assisting those who are in sorrow, need, sickness, or adversity, that as the Stewards of Christ they may thereby heap up to themselves riches in Heaven; and may, when they leave this transitory world, insure to their memory the tears of their children and the blessings of the poor, and finally to themselves *everlasting life*

In commemoration of this day, and with unbounded thankfulness to Almighty God for His mercy in preserving us, we have hereunto subscribed our names, trusting in His mercy and goodness for the future, and with a firm reliance that if we serve Him aright He will not desert us.

SARAH SEABROOK.................. ⎫
  Relict of THOMAS SEABROOK ⎬ and 4 Children.

JOHN KETLEY .... ⎫
ELIZABETH KETLEY............... ⎬ and 11 Children.

ROBERT BAKER .... ⎫
ANN BAKER .... ⎬ and 3 Children

JOHN HAILES .... ⎫
SARAH HAILES .... ⎬ and 5 Children.

JOHN SEABROOK .... ⎫
HANNAH SEABROOK .... ⎬ and 2 Children.

WILLIAM SEABROOK.

HANNAH C. LAY .... ⎫
  Relict of WILLIAM LAY...... ⎬ and 3 Children.

RICHARD SEABROOK.

MARY SEABROOK

ROBERT SEABROOK

JOHN POLLEY .... ⎫
ELLEN POLLEY .... ⎬

JOHN BUNTING .... ⎫
JANE BUNTING .... ⎬ and 2 Children.

Plate 17   Memento from the Seabrook family, farmers in Boreham, Essex

Overt rejection of gentry values may have rankled and gentlemen would try to put these nouveaux riche of the countryside in their place. A Suffolk vicar noted with malice when the 'over-educated' children of farmers squandered their fortunes.[157] Another used ridicule, calling local 'yeomen' backward in their use of dialect, a 'type of dissenter'.[157] Unlike manufacturers, farmers represented a way of life which had a long history, and nostalgia for their old simplicity and frugality contributed to resentment by those above and below them. The Suffolk poets George Crabbe and Robert Bloomfield grieved over the change, while Cobbett, a political radical but social conservative, was venomous towards a lifestyle he saw as the result simply of greed and pretentiousness.[159] Farmers' wives and daughters, in particular, came to embody the new values. Their education was not directly linked to farming practice as in the case of men. They appeared as the prime movers in modern consumption patterns, to desire the piano in the parlour, or the new styles of dress.

Farmers had represented a type of homely, heavily masculine virtue associated with the world of horses, dogs and fields; 'John Bull' continued to wear the dress of an eighteenth-century farmer. The new customs and new money were thought to lead to effeminate and expensive habits. And as so often happened, women carried the negative qualities of the group. The greed and expensive habits of farmers' wives and daughters were blamed for the farmers' search for high profits, often at the expense of labourers. Such women:

usurped the honest and manly simplicity of manners which has so long dignified the British character . . . the very farmer's daughter has laid aside her stuffs for muslins, her handkerchief for the meretitous display of naked charms, her diffidence for coquetry and the bloom of virtuous industry for the harlotry of paint.[160]

The professions

The professions entailed the sale of services, particularly those involving the manipulation of words, visual forms and abstract ideas. Over the period, they became more formal and efforts were made to establish them as closed groups with their own entry requirements, period of training, code of conduct, fixed scale of fees and even certification. These features were particularly true of the older professions of the church, law and medicine, which required a background in the classics, effectively excluding most working-class men and all women.

By 1851, professional male household heads made up 21 per cent of the middle-class census sample. Within this group, roughly one-half were the older professions of the church, the law and medicine, while the other half were mainly teachers plus a scattering of newer professions such as engineers, architects, surveyors, estate agents, naturalists, authors and artists. The latter group grew with the prosperity of the middle class as a whole, some with developments such as the railroads, others directly connected with manufacture or farming. The older professions also expanded to meet increased and more sophisticated demands mainly from the middle class itself.

At this time, the medical profession was divided into three groups. There were the higher status physicians, some of whom were Oxbridge or Edinburgh graduates, and most of whom practised in London. In 1843, Birmingham listed only fourteen physicians out of 200 medical men. The second tier were surgeons, whose position rose during the period, and finally there were the apothecaries. Although status differentials remained, the trend was to merge these categories into 'general practice'.[161] These doctors were now leaving the making up and sale of drugs to the retail chemist, and routine physical care of patients largely in the hands of women.[162] Charging fees for their time rather than medicine raised their status. Wealthy Birmingham middle-class families patronized both physicians and surgeons, while most of the middle range looked for general skills at moderate charges. Only in the rural areas were some small farmers and tradesmen still consulting lay 'wise' men and women, although female midwives might be more widely used.

By 1828, the series of lectures started as self-education by a few Birmingham doctors had become a Medical College followed by several other medical schools in the town.[163] The training such schools could offer depended partly on the establishment of hospitals and dispensaries, most of which were for working-class patients and an important part of philanthropic middle-class effort. Between 1797 and mid century, eight hospitals were opened in Birmingham while the Essex and Colchester Hospital, started in 1820, was a leader in the region soon followed by several others.[164] Doctors sought positions in hospitals, although unpaid, as aids to building a reputation, with the chance of further income from teaching. Training and entry in medicine had long been a mixture of apprenticeship and formal education, although the trend was towards the latter. Practising doctors charged premiums as high as £200 with pupils living in. Medical men were found as leaders in scientific and cultural societies in both towns and rural areas. They were less evident in political or economic organizations, more heavily patronized by the legal profession.

Lawyers as a profession differed from medicine in that they had never had a gild organization. They were directly attached to courts with a division between attorneys and solicitors. By an early eighteenth-century ruling, every candidate for admission to a court had to have been articled to an attorney or a solicitor for five years. With the creation of a Law Society a more professional identity began to emerge although there remained several less formal routes to practising law. Birmingham, like most provincial towns, had no court of its own and therefore no resident barristers. Solicitors were the backbone of the profession and the more active would represent clients at Warwick Quarter Sessions or in London, often through an agent or other contact.[165]

Provincial attorneys combined a great variety of tasks. A late eighteenth-century Birmingham lawyer might sort out land titles, draw up building leases, organize the lending of money, making of bonds, the administration of trusts, witness apprenticeship agreements and wills and visit properties to be sold. In the countryside, attorneys did estate work, even acting as auctioneers, so that there was considerable rivalry between the emerging professions of estate agent, surveyor and attorney. Lawyers in market towns were in a position to acquire land for themselves, and included men like William Mason of Colchester whose clients were mostly farmers, some of them wealthy. Mason managed to raise £41,000 in mortgages between 1786 and 1800.[166] Like Jacob Howell Pattisson of Witham or George Josselyn of Ipswich, these wealthy lawyers and property owners were a power in the local community, helping to bind together the commercial, trading, manufacturing and farming interests and many were active in local politics.[167]

By the early nineteenth century, provincial lawyers were pressing for a more regulated profession. Birmingham was one of the earliest to form a Law Society;

for the purpose of promoting and encouraging a correct and liberal course of practice in the Profession; and of discountencing and opposing all practices that may have a tendency to bring it into discredit or to lessen its respectability. . . .[168]

The society particularly disapproved of the less orthodox methods of slipping into the law such as serving for a few years as a clerk to a recognized attorney and then applying for admission to the Law Lists. The celebrated case of the Birmingham radical, George Edmonds, who had started as a schoolmaster and subsequently taken up the law, ran on from the 1820s to the late 1840s, keeping the issue in the public eye.[169] Like most professional societies of the period, the Law Society acted as a social and dining club and included honorary retired members. When the vice-president of the Birmingham society died in 1837, his son took his place and, with the other members, attended the funeral. In the eulogy to the deceased, it was stressed how he had fully lived up to the ideal of the profession, helping to 'exclude from it all that might contaminate or lower its standards . . . especially by the pattern of individual conduct'.[170]

In the early modern period it was the gentry who, together with the clergy, had been the only literate sections of the population. By the eighteenth century, paid professionals had taken over many functions from gentlemen, such as acting as 'stewards' for greater lords. In the nineteenth century these activities began to peel away into separate professions. In the 1830s, Nathaniel Lea of Birmingham, originally trained as a surveyor, was involved in more and more brokering work as well as estate agency and auctioneering. He began to specialize as a broker working from his own home with minimal overhead costs, only later taking on a clerk.[171] In comparison to other occupations, professional practice, which rested on the ability to sell one's self, needed little capital. The main costs were in education and initial training plus the postponement of earning capacity. The older professions, in particular, dealt with the intimate affairs of their mainly middle-class clientele: their property, their bodies and souls. Trust between practitioner and client played a large part in their relationship. Hence patronage by community leaders was an important element in both training and building up a clientele. Birmingham's Quaker community had its own doctors and dentists. Witham's Anglican and nonconformist circles tended to use their own practitioners, although the Congregational (with Whig sympathies) Dr Dixon chose an Anglican (Tory) as a partner which widened the scope of his practice.[172] We have seen how Charles Boutflower, a leading Colchester medical man and strong Evangelical, named his second son William Marsh Boutflower, in recognition of his beloved vicar at St Peter's church who was also a director of the hospital where Boutflower had an appointment.[173]

By its nature, a profession emphasized individual training, skills, personality and sponsorship. Partnerships were used but were not as important as in other occupations and were legally prohibited among the clergy. Partnerships, where they existed, tended to be between father and son, or uncle and nephew, and were a way of handing on clients and the 'good will' of the practice rather than lateral expansion through brothers or brothers-in-law.

The location and mobility of professional practices varied. Medical men often went from their homes to visit patients, and most of the men so occupied seem to have travelled a good deal. An Essex estate agent spent much of his time 'in the saddle', once travelling 150 miles in four days on horseback, in his own light carriage and by coach.[174] Attorneys, who often employed clerks, seem to have moved their homes away from their offices in Birmingham, although in the market towns of the eastern counties they often remained in the town centre if in active practice.[175] Of the twenty-seven solicitors practising in Colchester at mid century, thirteen lived in the same house as their office, eleven either next door or within a few minutes walk. Almost all these were located within the town walls and only three had moved to the nascent suburb of Lexden.[176]

Kinship and family played a key part in successful professional establishments. General cultural training from early childhood was important while kinship resources both bought and endorsed respectability. William Withering had a father and uncle who were physicians in Warwickshire. His father was able to give him a classical education under a neighbouring clergyman and send him to Edinburgh followed by a short time in London and Paris hospitals. Withering settled in Stafford and, although not wealthy, enjoyed the 'best society' including marriage to an elite attorney's daughter and friendship with the celebrated Erasmus Darwin. Darwin recommended the young man to a Birmingham practice on the death of its holder. The move increased Withering's £100 a year income tenfold and he soon became a leading Birmingham figure, a member of the Lunar Society and able to rent Edgbaston Hall at £237 a year.[177]

It was possible, but much more difficult, to enter provincial professions without such backing, if alternative sources of support could be found. A Birmingham doctor who became surgeon to the Town Infirmary and Workhouse as a poor student had asked for a loan from one of the earliest banks, Taylor and Lloyds. Mr Taylor 'lent him the money, [but] the annual interest on this debt together with the premium for the Life Assurance which he was obliged to take as security was a drag upon him for years'.[178] Henry Dixon, the Witham doctor, was son of a small farmer from an isolated part of Essex. He began casual work for a local farmer who dabbled in medicine and decided to train further, his reading having been guided by his master's self-taught son. Dixon had saved £95 of the £200 needed for London training and a fellow member of the Independent chapel loaned him the remainder. An elderly woman patient on her death bed 'loaned' him the 100 gns necessary to buy a vacant practice. Through his enthusiasm for shooting, Dixon began to mix with local notables although his main entrée into practice was through the Congregational chapel.[179]

The female relatives of professional men serviced living-in apprentices and pupils, took messages, helped make up drugs, keep books and write letters although it was more difficult for them to make a direct contribution than in other forms of enterprise. On the other hand, the domestic establishment of the professional man, as well as the property and contacts brought to the household, could make the difference between a limited practice and access to higher circles, both socially and professionally. A Birmingham physician who married a daughter of the wealthy banking Galton family gained £8000 in trust from his wife's inheritance in addition to the money from her grandfather's estate settled on her at marriage. With the security of the second inheritance, the couple bought a small house for £600 in Edgbaston's professional 'ghetto'. Lord Calthorpe, the ground landlord, insisted on £300 being spent on outbuildings and they also planned a servant's hall, housekeeper's room, a man's servant's room and a laundry. Adèle Galton Booth wrote to her brother: 'You will, I think consider our piccolo Palazzo a degree in beauty beyond Temple Row' (their Birmingham centre home). Adèle's husband repaid this family support by recommending his nephew, Francis Galton, as a pupil at the Birmingham Hospital.[180]

Professional families, particularly in the upper strata, were dependent on the exertions and skill of the male practitioners to a greater extent than in other middle-class occupations. We have seen that professional men were at the forefront in developing mutual benevolent and assurance societies. They were less concerned with controlling the property which they left to their wives and bankers often regarded them as poor financial risks, since their income from a practice ceased at death. Professional men named their wives as executrix in 90 per cent of their wills in comparison to 60 per cent of manufacturers and farmers.

Many professionals dealt primarily with the middle class and gentry. Mastering new machinery and processes or dealing with working-class employees were not part of their daily experience; their wives and children could be kept unsullied from proximity with the working world. Lawyers, teachers, doctors, and above all the clergy and writers spent their lives manipulating words, explaining the middle class to itself. As a legal writer claimed at mid century:

The importance of the professions and the professional classes can hardly be overrated, they form the head of the great English middle class, keep up to the mark its standard of morality, and direct its intelligence.[181]

Within this group were found some of the most prominent in exhorting their peers about appropriate roles for men and women. A lawyer using the trust mechanism, a doctor advising a woman against any worldly or intellectual excitement, the vicar's sermon on family life, the schoolmaster's talk on manliness and work, as much as the artist's or writer's portrayal of idealized ringleted maidens and stalwart youths, contributed to the creation of middle-class values.

The professions covered a wide spectrum of wealth and status. At one end were the powerful property-owning attorneys mixing with bankers, wealthy farmers and manufacturers or even the gentry. Lawyers bought or rented large villas on the edges of the town as did J. W. Whately at Edgbaston Hall.[182] One of the first large suburban homes on the outskirts of Colchester was the gothic 'Turrets' (sometimes known as the 'Villa Franca') built by the attorney and town clerk, Francis Smythies, in 1818.[183] Wealth filtered through the law was one of the surest ways of enabling a family to move into positions of power and influence as well as being socially acceptable to gentry echelons and metropolitan circles. Law was the platform where the middle class and the upper class might meet. We have seen how Daniel Harvey Whittle, attorney and scion of a Witham shopkeeping family, through a combination of contacts and personal dynamism rose through a colourful career in local and eventually national politics, becoming MP for Colchester in the 1820s.[184]

Nevertheless, the professions also contained a large section of families living in a more modest style. In 1851, George Street on the fringe of Edgbaston housed younger or less successful solicitors, surgeons and other professionals clustered in houses rated at about £40 a year, where one or at most two domestic servants were employed.[185] Such positions were sometimes the goal of men from modest beginnings; the sons of small farmers, retail traders and small masters who were now benefiting from the reformed grammar schools and recently founded academies. A first generation Witham solicitor, Joseph Howell Blood, was clerk to the powerful attorney Jacob Howell Pattisson, related through his mother's side. By the 1840s, Blood had become clerk of the workhouse, clerk of the JP's bench and chairman of the Board of Guardians, the kind of post that would not have existed in the eighteenth century. By the 1850s he had set up his own legal practice in the town, later joined by his eldest son. His younger son, using a combination of family money and connections, emerged as the Rev. Howell Pattisson Blood.[186]

Many of the less prestigious professions had difficulty in closing ranks against unrecognized practitioners; it was well into the nineteenth century that Chartered Surveyors were able to streamline their organization.[187] This was nowhere more true than in teaching, the largest of the sub-professions. The accepted gender divisions decreed that girls and young boys should be taught by women so that teaching was never able to close ranks or require the esoteric and expensive training of the older professions. The threat of women entering a more highly structured teaching profession that emerged after 1850 came to be a central issue in the later nineteenth century.

The salaried

During the nineteenth century, a group of positions emerged which were innovative, not just in the tasks performed but in the form of reward, location of work, the relationship to authority and a reliance on continual daily application to tasks. These clerical and administrative posts grew from the increased scale and complexity of economic, political and social institutions and the sheer volume of business they produced. These functions had originated in the church and its traditional methods of governance.

Many were honorary and part time, offering little direct payment but carrying opportunities for influence and profits from office. The positions of church warden, parish clerk, vestryman, clerk of the market, town sergeant and water baliff are some examples from the local records. Other positions demanding some literacy and the ability to keep records had been filled by confidential servants of the gentry or the great merchant houses. Scriveners, stewards and baliffs were posts requiring personal loyalty to the master. The salaried positions which evolved, retained some of the characteristics of privilege through patronage, but also implied a lack of independence characteristic of domestic service. Even in the nineteenth century, the line between salaried staff and male personal servant was not always strictly drawn.

By the 1830s, the larger scale of business, the growth of local and national government, especially the Poor Law, the explosion of voluntary society activity, all produced a demand for clerical competence, bookkeeping and letter writing. Anderson has maintained that previous studies have 'underestimated the number of clerical workers already present in the mid-nineteenth century'.[188] Certainly, one of the largest categories in this group, salaried school teaching, was beginning its exponential growth well before compulsory education of the 1870s. The wills from Birmingham had only one salaried testator in 1780, a schoolmaster who had nothing to leave his wife but £20. By 1858, in contrast, a considerable proportion of the sample were salaried. In the census sample of the two areas, salaried positions made up 11 per cent of male household heads, although the number of salaried employees was probably considerably greater since many were not household heads. In Birmingham, in 1841, clerks were one out of the seven categories employing over 1000 people in the town.[189] In the countryside, salaried and white-collar occupations were a thin peppering, mainly in the market towns and coastal ports.

Like the professions, salaried positions depended on individual attributes. Decent clothing, cleanliness, manners and basic education all demanded some family resources to start a young man's career. Many men found their way to permanent salaried posts through church or chapel, in activities like Sunday school teaching or other cultural interests, gaining experience and confidence as they come to the notice of older, more prosperous sponsors. George Holyoake was originally trained as a whitesmith in Birmingham's Eagle Foundry where his father was employed. During the 1830s, he became involved with the Mechanics' Institute and when his tutor at the institute died in 1839, Holyoake took over some of his classes. He survived on part-time teaching and secretarial work until he found a position at the Hall of Science in Worcester.[190]

Kin, friends or patrons continued as important to gaining a salaried post partly because some financial guarantee, often substantial, was usually required. For the newly created post of governor in an Essex workhouse a householder willing to put up a bond of £100 had to be found.[191] One source of guarantors, significantly, seems to have been contacts gained through upper domestic service. In the early nineteenth century, patrons would expect to press for their candidates. Far from this procedure being regarded as 'nepotism', it was seen as normal. After the Ipswich draper,

John Perry, had gone bankrupt, he was temporarily employed as Clerk to the Election Committee. He then tried unsuccessfully for a position as Clerk to the Board of Guardians in a nearby Union recently formed under the new Poor Law legislation. He also applied for the office of accountant in the new Ipswich wet docks. He was beaten for this post by a man who, Perry claimed, had known about the position for much longer and therefore was 'able to canvass as many months as I had days'. Perry ended up acting as a 'writer' in London, copying the registers for the Friends Society, work which he obtained through his Quaker connections.[192]

Towards mid century, clerical positions were being incorporated into bureaucracies, particularly in local administration. More onus was placed on the character and education of the individual and less on his connections. Salaried positions came closer to the definitions of an 'occupation' than almost any other nineteenth-century economic activity. The masculine connotation of occupation is confirmed by the fact that incumbents of salaried posts were almost all male with the important exception of school teachers. In 1841, only five of Birmingham's 1369 clerks were women.[193] Conditions of service assumed clerical workers would take on support of wife and children even if, in reality, many 'dependants' of these men had to contribute to family income.

In the earlier part of the period, men in clerical or managerial positions were often expected to live above or behind the office, guarding the premises as well as being available around the clock. Their wives would be responsible for cleaning and running the buildings and often prepared the midday meal for the senior partners. In the 1830s, the Birmingham Law Society used the rooms of their librarian for an evening debating society. These were eventually stopped as he protested about meetings interfering with his domestic arrangements.[194] A similar unease over mixing domestic life with a salaried position may have been behind the difficulty of both the Essex and Colchester Hospital and the Essex and Equitable Insurance Office in keeping their resident apothecaries and secretaries respectively, despite the provision for the latter of a £200 salary plus rooms, taxes, coal and candles.[195]

As the century progressed, the growing salaried workforce began to live in separate domestic dwellings. In Witham, Jacob Howell Pattisson bought land in the centre of the town in the 1840s and created a new street of modest houses on which he oversaw and heavily contributed to a new gothic-style Anglican church, a National School, the Savings Bank and the police station. By 1851, the residents included an auctioneer and estate agent, the relieving officer of Witham Union, the assistant actuary of the Savings Bank, the superintendent of the police, the clerk curate of Witham, an infant schoolmistress and the national schoolmistress. The majority of these houses had a rateable value of £12–14 a year, which roughly marks the lowest level of middle-class housing.[196] On the margins of Edgbaston there was a similar development on a larger scale in the quiet streets which were becoming havens for clerks, commercial travellers, rate collectors and schoolmasters.

The type of dwelling and the area where the salaried lived indicates both their relatively low status and their youthfulness. While the upper middle class for the whole census sample was roughly one-third, among the salaried section it was only 6 per cent. 36 per cent of the male household heads of the salaried group were under 35 compared with 23 per cent of the clergy, 18 per cent of medical men and 33 per cent of the total sample. This age distribution was taken as a snapshot at mid century and indicates that either men in such positions might, in middle age, move into partnerships or become independent entrepreneurs and professionals or, that at least some, might represent a new generation of lifetime white-collar salaried occupations.[197]

Many of these positions were in a transitional stage between personal service and/or a small family enterprise in a salaried occupation, if not career. Certainly the total exclusion of the wives of such men was not always expected, as indicated in the domestic role they played in the positions of residential clerks and secretaries. T. H. Finigan was employed by a Birmingham philanthropic society as a town missionary in the late 1830s. Much of his work was with prostitutes in the notorious, heavily Irish district, known as the Gullet. Finigan relied on his wife to help him in this work, in keeping with the expected orthodoxy that men should work with men and 'ladies' with 'women', particularly if home visiting was required. In training another agent he warned:

not to meddle with female cases at all, such as I meet with abundance in my district. . . . I advised him in all female cases – sick or abandoned – or otherwise, to submit them to me as the Senior Agent; and then, that my wife and I, as we usually do, would go to them – and as, almost in all female cases, an experienced Matron is best calculated for domiciliary visits my wife would gladly visit on such occasions and read, and exhort, and pray with them. . . .[198]

Mrs Finigan also visited sick women and the couple took repentent prostitutes into their own home while waiting to enter them into the Magdalen. In estimating his hours of work week by week, Finigan commented that if his wife's time had been counted he would have clocked up at least fifteen hours more. He also started to take his son with him and occasionally sent him to meetings in his place. Finigan was influenced by a variety of ideas in organizing his work. In the traditional mode he assumed that his family would be included, his wife's contribution in keeping with the duties of the wives of the clergy. On the other hand, he was a salaried worker, appointed by a lay committee to whom he was responsible. There was as yet no specific training nor much job security. Like the clergy, he had no family enterprise or property to fall back on; unlike them his foothold in a middle-class occupation was precarious. His status was symbolized when he was offered a ride home from a temperance meeting; the president of the Temperance Institute sat inside the carriage with Finigan perching outside with the coachman. A man like Finigan depended for livelihood on doing his work in what was judged to be an acceptable and appropriate way by his superiors. In fact he was dismissed in 1838 after some disagreement with the committee.[199]

It was difficult for men in salaried positions to build up a 'patrimony' for their dependants. They were vulnerable to illness or death and lacked even the stock and tools of the artisan/craftsman. Unlike the professional they had little goodwill of customers or clients to bequeath. Most of the clerks in the sample of wills left everything to their wives, but this amounted to small bits of property, mainly liquid capital, unsupported by the means of continuing to make a living. Salaried positions put men into the hands of their employers and patrons. The price of their secure posts was that they were often regarded as servants of the partners, directors or committees of management, despite relatively high salaries. The range of tasks they carried out was wide while their reliability and discretion had to be absolute. The Oakes banking family entrusted one of their clerks to bring £7000 of cash from London and another to collect all the rates from eastern Suffolk from another bank. At times the clerks from the Oakes Bank seem to have doubled as personal servants to the family and on days when the bank was particularly busy would stay on to dine and drink tea in the evening, although separately from the family.[200]

It was to the advantage of salaried men to remain in the good offices of their employers and superiors. Clerical workers and school teachers tended to be seen as the shock troops of voluntary societies, as well as in paid positions such as the town missionary described above. They were called in to man the ranks of Bible distributors, to keep the books and collect subscriptions, significantly tasks also sometimes undertaken by the wives and daughters of higher ranking professional men. Some men, if they had talent and forceful personality could rise through such avocations to positions of local influence if not wealth although the route was never easy.

Sponsors and patrons of the correct religious or political complexion were a necessity. The combination of lack of property and lack of independence, characteristic of salaried posts, lowered their status often further than their incomes would warrant, a position superbly illustrated by Dickens's character, the clerk Uriah Heep. As a result there were particular ambiguities about the masculine associations of their jobs, despite the fact that almost all such posts were filled only by men. Clean hands, polite speech, neat clothing, high standards of literacy, the indoor, sedentary nature of their work also acted as marks of distinction from the working class but ran against the grain of a masculinity allied to physical prowess and manual skills. Independent artisans, small masters, and small farmers often regarded such men, together with those in domestic service, as 'flunkeys'. The continued twentieth-century image of clerical work as 'this very unmasculine calling', of those 'born to be men and condemned to be clerks' stems from these origins.[201]

It is understandable that clerks, schoolmasters and other salaried workers felt called upon to mark their masculine imprint in terms of upholding the façade if not the substance of domesticity. Their particular dilemma was that often their incomes did not permit foregoing their wives' and daughters' earnings. Because of the individual nature of their own work, it was not easy to integrate family labour into their own efforts as, for example, shopkeepers could. Wives and daughters of these men in the local areas were found to be running shops, teaching school and similar activities in their own right. Nevertheless, this sector of the middle class seems to have been equally receptive to the notions of domesticity.

William Austin was a salaried worker, probably a clerk, in a Birmingham manufactory in the later part of the period. He was also a Baptist lay preacher who aspired to become a town missionary. In the journal he kept in 1851–2, shortly after his marriage, his attitude to his wife, and the division of labour within the family is in accordance with the most advanced concepts of 'separate spheres'. His wife was not in paid employment and seems to have found it lonely at home all day. The couple lived quite far from his workplace so that it was early evening before he got home. He would then often settle down to study or do Sunday school or chapel work. One evening he was disconcerted to find on coming home at 8.30 that his wife was out at a neighbours and he upbraided her for neglect of domestic duties. He sought the Lord's help in making her a contented dependant, as he confided to his diary:

My beloved wife is all to me that I could require in most respects – in other respects she is improving. Bless the Lord. This evening I returned home, found my wife under the influence of a little temptation – rather dissatisfied and unhappy through having been alone all day. But I talked, we read and bowed at the Family Alter, the Lord broke her heart and humbled her before him so that we were greatly blessed.[202]

From the early nineteenth century, the image of the middle class has been the manufacturer, the 'Manchester Man' which so caught contemporary imagination. In one of the most enduring texts from that period, Mrs Gaskell's *North and South*, published in 1854, the active character of the manufacturer hero is represented by 'an expression of resolution and power . . . sagacious and strong'. The heroine makes the mistake of describing him as a 'great tradesman' and is rebuked for confusing manufacture with trade. As a clergyman's daughter brought up in the uncomprehending southern shires, she replies that she applies the word to 'all who have something tangible to sell' as opposed to her clerical father and her suitor, a London-based attorney.

The strong, dark, straight-browed textile manufacturer of humble origins is here contrasted with the pale hesitant clergyman, his face 'soft and wavering . . . showing every emotion'.[203] Like all stereotypes these are clichés which are built on a faint basis in reality. The bedrock of manufacturing and commercial fortunes was the tangible production and sale of things. Manufacturers and tradesmen moved among physical objects in that production. Along with large-scale farmers, they disciplined and dealt directly with the growing body of wage paid labourers, the most feared and least understood social phenomenon of late eighteenth- and early nineteenth-century English society. Professional men dealt more with abstractions, symbols and ideas; they sold services not goods. They could more easily keep their hands and clothes clean. They faced only clients or at most clerical salaried employees.

Yet underlying these distinctions, it was recognized that production was the force on which all profit and wealth was ultimately based. The novelty of manufacture, its dirt and drama held a special fascination. The incomes of many professional and salaried men ceased when they stopped practice, but the plant and property created by manufacture endured. In penning the literature, delivering the lectures and sermons, staffing the voluntary societies of the provincial middle class, professional men might be the more vocal, but it was the manufacturer, banker and merchant who usually paid the bills.[204]

The images of middle-class men, both at the time and those we hold now, vary in kaleidoscopic patterns, helping to define the boundaries of that entity called the middle class and guiding both the beliefs and actions of men. What all have in common, however, is the masculine penumbra of these activities. What men did was defined as man's work; because they did it, they were men.

6 'The hidden investment': women and the enterprise

> ... 'tis evident that men can be their own advisers and their own directors, and know how to work themselves out of difficulties and into business better than women.
>
> Daniel Defoe, *Moll Flanders*, 1722

Women's identification with the domestic and moral sphere implied that they would only become active economic agents when forced by necessity. As the nineteenth century progressed, it was increasingly assumed that a woman engaged in business was a woman without either an income of her own or a man to support her. She already shared with the men of her class the spiritual stumbling blocks to active pursuit of business. But unlike a man whose family status and self-worth rose through his economic exertions, a woman who did likewise risked opprobrium for herself and possible shame for those around her. Structured inequality made it exceedingly difficult for a woman to support herself on her own, much less take on dependants. But beyond the negative effects on women who openly operated in the market, the construction of domestic ideology and the lure of new patterns of consumption offered attractive alternatives.

At a time when the concept of occupation was becoming the core element in masculine identity, any position for women other than in relation to men was anomalous. In the 1851 census, the Registrar General introduced a new fifth class, exclusively made up of women:

The 5th class comprises large numbers of the population that have hitherto been held to have no occupation; but it requires no argument to prove that the *wife*, the *mother*, the *mistress* of an *English family* – fills offices and discharges duties of no ordinary importance; or that children are or should be occupied in filial or household duties, and in the task of education, either at home or at school.[1]

This conception had been developing over a long period. In the late seventeenth century, for example, trade tokens used by local shopkeepers and small masters carried the initials of the man and woman's first name and the couple's surname, but by the late eighteenth century only the initials of the man were retained.[2] This serves to confirm a contemporary's view (born 1790) that whereas his mother had confidently joined in the family auctioneering business, the increased division of the sexes had seen the withdrawal of women from business life within his own lifetime.[3]

The resulting picture of what middle-class women were actually doing and how they survived is fragmentary. Local records inevitably favour men's role in both enterprise and market relations. While in both the urban and rural areas women made up just over 50 per cent of the middle-class population, they were only 28 per cent of testators leaving wills and 20 per cent of household heads in the census sample. Information on women's occupations where they were not a household head is so unreliable as to be almost useless, and, by definition, married women were not considered heads of households. In the census sample, 69 per cent of female household heads were widows and 21 per cent single women, and by default the discussion of women's occupations must centre mainly on these groups. For women, marriage was indeed a 'trade' and as economic actors they appear as shadows behind the scenes of the family enterprise.

Alice Clark for the seventeenth and Ivy Pinchbeck for the eighteenth and early nineteenth centuries have outlined the slow shift from women's active participation in commerce, farming and other business pursuits. From their work it is clear that the consolidation of textile production in the market, the first sector to be so organized, had already had a strong impact on women's by-employments such as spinning which had been carried on in even quite prosperous families.[4] The loss of opportunities to earn increased the dominance of marriage as the only survival route for middle-class women as illustrated by the metamorphosis of the term 'spinster', from one who spins to an unmarried woman. By the nineteenth century, the courtesy title, *Mrs* (shortened from mistress), which included single women who had reached middle age, fell into disuse. 'Spinsters' were given this somewhat pejorative label throughout their lives. By the second half of the nineteenth century, a woman's own first name came to be used only when she was single or widowed, while the convention of designating a married woman by both her *husband's* first and surname, prefixed by Mrs, became the common practice and was seen as a form of respect paid to middle-class rather than working-class women.

A number of developments fostered the contradiction between women's perceived and actual relation to the economy. One of the most important was the growth of scale, creating divisions between larger and smaller operations. The 26 per cent of Suffolk farms where only family labour was employed would be a vastly different setting for the farmer's wife and female relatives than for a woman like Jane Ransome Biddell whose husband farmed over 1000 acres, and where numerous servants including a housekeeper were employed, releasing her to take part in the cultural and intellectual life of nearby Ipswich.[5] In manufacturing, the cannibalizing of modest independent workshops by larger, better financed concerns, spelt the doom for many female entrepreneurs. As such enterprises were drawn more heavily into the regional or even national market, the tendency was to specialize, to produce for agents or middle men who would consolidate products. The shift to arable farming, for example, meant that in Essex and Suffolk subsidiary activities like dairying sharply declined, precisely the area of farm work which had been traditionally women's work. Cheese making, which had taken place on almost every farm over a certain size, where the farmer's wife used her own labour augmented by her daughters, nieces, sisters or living-in dairymaids, shifted to centralized production in other parts of the country. By 1843, when the Royal Commission on Women and Children in Agriculture made its investigation, it was announced that the patience, skill and strength needed to produce cheese made this work unsuitable for women.[6] The preferred activities of corn growing and cattle fattening 'give but little trouble to the housewives of the present generations' according to an Essex commentator.[7]

The general trend to supersede craft training and experience was particularly disadvantageous for women, compounded by their exclusion from a more scientific culture. In farming, for example, the introduction of both hand and steam powered machinery, and the use of chemistry for fertilizers increased impediments for women farmers.[8] Larger units of production with more rational work flows implied a larger workforce increasingly made up of day labourers, most of whom no longer had a chance of becoming independent producers, thus destined to remain social inferiors. There was a growing feeling that genteel women, particularly the young and unmarried, should be removed from contact with such a workforce both by physical separation and psychological barriers. With a predominantly male workforce, it was even more difficult for women to wield authority. This is sharply illustrated by changes in farming practice. For a variety of reasons, since the mid eighteenth century, there had been a gradual displacement of female labour from the fields, except for casual seasonal tasks.[9] The suitability of field work, indeed any outdoor work for women, was almost always discussed in moral terms, thus turning attention from the practical questions of directing labour. According to a Suffolk social commentator,

Our inquiries have convinced us that it (field labour) is a bad school of morals for girls and that the mixing up with men on whom poverty and ignorance have encrusted coarse and vulgar habits, tends to greatly uncivilise and demoralize women of maturer years; single women whose characters for chastity are blemished, work in the fields, the topics of conversation and the language that is used amongst the men and women are described as coarse and filthy.[10]

Such attitudes multiplied the problems already faced by farmer's wives who no longer acted as house-mistress overseeing the men's domestic life. Supervision of field work on far-flung acreages meant riding horseback, often alone, to deal with the labourers. While this may have given added status and authority to male farmers, thus 'elevated above their work force',[11] it ran contrary to notions of feminine propriety.

These factors bore particularly heavily on women operating in their own right. As long as their economic contribution remained within the family they could continue to be active. It was external relations which raised more acute difficulties. In addition to dealing with a wage labour force, there were also clients, bankers, solicitors and agents. These would be men with increasingly fixed expectations of appropriate feminine behaviour. Many of these men, while willing to act as protectors and intermediaries for dependent women, would neither expect nor countenance their independent economic action.

Within this pattern, certain activities became more closely associated with one or the other gender. Some of these connections stemmed from previous male monopolies through the gild system, even where it had faded to a remnant. The exclusion of women from the ranks of the building trades – joinery, wheelwrights and smiths – had serious consequences since it was from these crafts that engineering, surveying and architecture developed. Other gender typing was of more recent origin. The equation of outdoor activity with men, and the indoors as the setting for respectable femininity affected the division of labour in a myriad of ways from farming, as above, to the expectation that within an enterprise women could do preparation of products and services or finance as long as these activities were kept out of sight.

An effort was made to have certain tasks performed by the expected gender. If a family failed to produce the requisite boy or girl, man or woman, the wider kinship or friendship network could be tapped to make up the deficiency. Among the better off, hired labour of the correct age and sex could be substituted. In lesser establishments, tasks usually assigned to one gender might have to be undertaken by the other, at least behind closed doors. This crossing of such a significant boundary, if made visible, could be taken as a sign of social inferiority when social status was crucial to building a picture of creditworthiness. The equation of women with domesticity came to be one of the fixed points of middle-class status. Yet the development of the market did offer some enticements for women to use their skills if not their capital. It may, indeed, be argued that the concerted attack on any display of female *sexual* independence may have much to do with fears about new opportunities for their *economic* activity.

Women and property

As Ann Whitehead has succinctly argued, property forms indicate relationships between people mediated by the disposition and control of things.[12] The middle class in this period, far from taking the opportunities afforded by the move away from land as the main form of property, continued to build on the principles of patrilineality, and patriarchy. Middle-class women continued to be on 'the margins of ownership' in a manner analogous to the restraints often imposed on working-class women (particularly when married) who had to or wished to sell their labour power within artisan culture.[13] Intense fears surrounded the 'impertinent' independent mill girl who refused the paternalistic discipline of domestic service or even the oversight of the parental home, and who might also, it was felt, refuse to fit the role of respectable working-man's wife. A similar if less often expressed alarm surrounded the idea of middle-class women using their skills or property to establish independent careers. It could, in fact, be argued that much of the concern about women working in mines and fields expressed in the 1840s was a transplanted discussion of deep seated uneasiness about the middle class itself. Although he was proud of his daughter who ran a successful school, a Quaker farmer solemnly warned her that she would never marry if she was known 'only as a School Mistress'.[14]

The relationship of women to property had never been made explicit. While John Locke had directly linked the concept of property ownership to independence, both he and Thomas Hobbes did not clarify how women's control of property and their expected subordination within the family could be reconciled.[15] In legal and practical terms, if anything, women's position had deteriorated from the seventeenth century. As landowners in their own right, women were vastly underrepresented. They made up only 4 per cent of the 404 landowners in Suffolk at mid century and almost all their land was in small parcels.[16] In the gentry, at least freehold land – real property – had been returned to a woman's control after her husband's death. Middle-class property was, as has been seen, mainly in other forms: leasehold and copyhold land, buildings, investments and effects, which had foregone even this limited right. With the ending of customary rights of dower, a development recognized by law in 1833, marriage virtually turned legal control of a woman's property permanently over to her husband.

The control of women's 'testamentary capacity' extended beyond their male relatives' lifetime. The preponderance of men's over women's wills in the sample (72 per cent men and 28 per cent women) was not only because testators were confined to widows and spinsters by the rules of coverture, but also because many widows were never able to exercise that right. Sometimes the limits are explicitly stated in the wills. Many wives inherited the use of the property only until their children reached majority, while others were allowed its benefit 'as long as she remain my widow and no longer'. A Birmingham artist who died in 1840 left approximately £200 to his wife in the form of a pub and nine houses, but only during her life and even then with conditions. If she were to remarry or to break up the household and stop giving the son a comfortable home, then the young man was to get 7 shillings a week from the property towards his maintenance and no future husband of the widow was to have any rights over the inheritance. At his wife's death the property was to go to his son and his wife's son by a former marriage, the shares carefully spelled out.[17] In an analysis of Colchester wills for the lower sector of the middle class, D'Cruze found a decline of widows given a major control of the property from 42 per cent before 1805 to 27 per cent after that date and those who were left a life interest only almost doubled.[18] Our own sample of wills for both areas shows a 12 per cent increase in men who controlled all aspects of legacies left to widows.

The disabilities which women faced in consolidating property are also indicated by the fact that they more often specified multiple legacies in distributing their own property. One-third of women named more than five legatees but only one-fifth of men, a pattern even more marked in the lower middle class. Furthermore, women tended to leave personal effects and small parcels of money to named individuals, many of them wider kin or friends, a pattern which emphasizes both the dispersion and the personal nature of their property.[19] Finally, a father or uncle had the option in leaving an inheritance to instruct for the breaking of coverture, found in eighteen wills. Whatever a man's motives for this step – concern over keeping property in his line intact for a grandson or to protect his daughter's interests – the fact remained that unless he had made this particular stipulation a woman's inheritance passed to the legal control and use of her husband. In many cases, women undoubtedly used this property, even becoming the moving force in many a commercial undertaking, but the concept of dependence was nevertheless enshrined in such practices.

Patterns of ownership were closely related to patterns of control. It was primarily women who were the beneficiaries of 'passive' property yielding income only: trusts, annuities, subscriptions and insurance. Under the terms of a trust, the needs and wishes of the beneficiary were supposed to be fulfilled but interpretations could vary. Dr Dixon of Witham being called to act as a trustee noted in his diary that 'Miss Cox's present views are of entire indifference to me'.[20] The situation was particularly serious for an Essex woman who wanted to separate from her husband who had already borrowed money against her marriage settlement. Her only other source of income was an uncle's legacy for which her brother was a trustee. She finally managed to wrest control of her own property but only after much struggle.[21] The problem was that trustees were overwhelmingly male kin or friends of the family as we have seen in the sample of wills. In fact one of the most commonly named trustees was a son-in-law, in other words the husband of the woman whose property was in trust.

Even in those cases where women had a direct financial stake in the family enterprise, their legal status prevented them from active partnership. Their investment was often in the form of loans where the maximum they could receive was about 5 per cent in interest rather than sharing in the profits – and the risks – of partnerships.[22] The resulting economic vulnerability was enhanced for special groups of women. Evidence has already been presented concerning the anxiety of professional and salaried men whose incomes ended with their death. This lacunae was noted by the friends of an Essex professional man who had suddenly died leaving a widow with several small children and a capital of only about £50. They set about raising a subscription 'for the purpose of setting up Mrs Martin in some establishment, possibly a school, by which she may be enabled to educate and support her children respectably'. Mrs Martin did not even know of these efforts and was not consulted in any way. Her fate was completely in the hands of male well-wishers. Fortunately for her, the instigator of the subscription emphasized that Mrs Martin had 'conducted herself creditably through this trying time' and thus her proper behaviour was rewarded by male intervention on her behalf.[23]

A separated wife was in an even more unfavourable position. An Essex man who had been accused of a homosexual relationship fled the country to avoid arrest. Despite the fact that she had five young children, his wife was ostracized by her father and brother, who refused to even stand security for payment of the husband's debts. At last a local friend intervened noting with approval that the wife was known as the most active party within the business. His help enabled her to carry on the business, thus keeping both house and income intact. The friend had to intervene again when the husband returned demanding funds from his wife, money which was his by legal right.[24]

The characteristics of women's property reinforced their propensity to turn attention away from economic activity. A clergyman's widow living on the rent from an Essex farm, when pressed to make improvements in the buildings, replied that as she only had the benefit of the income during her lifetime, she should not be expected to bear the costs. Such a realistic assessment of her position partly explains her concern with maintaining a genteel lifestyle. Her sole aim was to extract maximum rent promptly paid from the property and she grumbled at requests for rent abatements in the hard times of the 1820s. Unlike the model ladies of the tracts, she cared little that her tenant had a large family or lacked sufficient capital to farm efficiently. A man might well have taken charge of this situation himself but the widow confessed to being too ignorant in such matters for her opinion to count. She had neither experience, education nor, above all, motivation to expand her property even if she could have been taken seriously in the world of market operations. In fact, she was unable to even stem the decline of prosperity in her little property and had placed herself completely in the hands of a somewhat shady but powerful Colchester attorney.[25]

It is not surprising that women were regarded as poor credit risks given their legal disabilities, dependence on male intervention and good will, and the short-term nature of their business ventures. It was more common for a woman to inherit or raise a lump sum than establish a viable credit chain to support an on-going enterprise. Banks remained wary of lending to women so that their sources of capital and credit continued to be mainly kin and friends well into the period when men were turning to other institutional sources. This general lack of commercial credibility was an important factor in the limited scale of women's business operations.

This is not to say that the *aggregate* of small investments held by women was not an important source of capital in early commercial and industrial development. Quite the contrary; economic historians have begun to recognize that women could make up a substantial proportion of those with financial resources.[26] When an Essex village vestry wanted to build a workhouse school they raised a loan by selling annuities, one-third of which were bought by women.[27] The portfolio of Mrs Henstridge Cobbold (*sic*) from the Ipswich brewing family included bonds in the local canal, rail road and insurance companies as well as the Ipswich Gas Light Company;[28] the last investment was also held by her friend Jane Ransome Biddell whose farmer husband acted as Mrs Cobbold's financial agent.[29] Nor should the above discussion give the impression that some women, at least, did not take an active interest in their own financial affairs; women such as the personal clients of Birmingham's earliest stockbroker, Nathaniel Lea.[30]

Nevertheless women's property, so closely tied to their lifecycle status of daughter, wife and widow, only allowed at most a semi-independence. This limitation was compounded by problems of maintaining their own and their family's status precisely by *not* being openly involved in market activities. Once these overlapping forces are understood, it becomes more understandable why it was so difficult for women to form groups based on mutual interest which also relied on mutual control and manipulation of funds or property. The formation of such groups was a commonplace for middle-class men. Men created and ran societies and organizations grounded on corporate property not only to conduct business but for political, cultural, intellectual and even social life. The bonds forged on the basis of communal control of funds contributed to group loyalties even if only a 'kitty' built up for an annual convivial evening at a local inn. There seem to be no female equivalents to these informal or semi-formal groups.

Women could only operate property through kinship networks which, by definition, included both sexes. There is some evidence from the wills and census sample that sisters, and to a lesser extent, aunts and nieces, shared property as well as ways of making a livelihood in all-female households, but this was a mainly unmarried minority. The limitations on women's control of property, then, had not only serious implications for individuals but more generally for the ties of women to each other and the possibility of creating any but the most ephemeral alliances to support their mutual interests.[31]

Women's contribution to the enterprise

In the earlier part of the period when household and enterprise were so intermingled there was only a narrow line between the prohibition on married women acting in a business capacity and their encouragement to pledge their husband's credit as a housekeeper. As the nineteenth century progressed, however, the view hardened that female relatives were and should be dependants. The move to separate family affairs from business was a potent expression of these changes. The same forces which favoured the rise of the private company and ultimately the business corporation, the development of public accountability and more formal financial procedures also shifted the world of women ever further from the power of the active market.

Within this context, it is not surprising that the transformation of honorary positions into salaried posts which has been observed for men is scarcely discernible for women. There was no precedent for female access to a post such as parish clerk, for example, which became secularized in the nineteenth century. The parish clerk had derived from the clerical assistant to the priest, described in an Essex parish as 'a man who is able to make a will or write a letter for anyone in the parish . . . the universal father to give away brides, and the standing god-father to all new born bantlings'.[32] Women had to wait until the late nineteenth-century establishment of bureaucratic positions based on meritocratic principles for which they could prepare themselves and to which they could appeal.

A second consequence of economic dependency has been the overshadowing of women's contribution to the enterprise. Recent sociological studies have had to rediscover the vital part played by wives in small businesses and the support systems they provided for many male occupations, the recognition of women as a 'hidden investment'.[33] But in the nineteenth century female involvement in the enterprise was widespread, not just wives but also daughters, sisters, nieces, mothers, aunts, cousins and occasionally unrelated female 'friends'. First, there is abundant evidence for the direct contribution of women's capital to the family enterprise. The son of an Essex farmer whose brothers had all become farmers was able to combine his self-education with £800 brought by his wife at marriage to start a successful boys' school. When her father died leaving £600 the school was expanded into purpose-built premises.[34] Among the lower middle class, women were constantly used as sources of small sums to start off a business or as credit. In 1831, an Ipswich baker, facing a series of heavy financial demands, borrowed £4 from two of his sisters-in-law to pay off his flour supplier.[35]

This is a story repeated many times over. George Courtauld borrowed lump sums from his sister and a female friend in the early days of the Essex silk mill. When he married, he and his new bride, Ruth Minton, used her marriage portion to live on so that all profits could be re-invested in the mill. She saw this as part of her contribution along with keeping house. She wrote to a friend: 'I am no longer that useless, unconnected being who lived only for herself, a burden to her Friends.' When George later went to America leaving their eldest son, Samuel, in charge, Ruth Courtauld gave up her house which was mortgaged so that Samuel could start free of debt. She went to live with him at the Mill House paying £30 into the household expenses as well as acting as his housekeeper. Samuel acknow-ledged that this aid in money and kind carried the business through a critical period. In return, his mother gained both a home and livelihood, although at a lower standard. She also felt she had played an active role in the family establishment.[36]

The combination of women contributing resources and gaining a place was common. Dorothy Wordsworth when in her early 20s, lived as a 'mother's help' with her elder brother, a Suffolk vicar. After she had inherited her share of the family property (£1800 invested at 4 per cent), she and her brother William were able to set up housekeeping and later she helped care for William's children.[37] There was a variety of ways in which women made financial contributions to the enterprise. A sister asked no interest on a loan of £150 for the first three years of a manufacturing enterprise as well as keeping house and helping in the business.[38]

The skills and contacts women brought could enrich male careers. In food manufacturing businesses it was the recipe provided by a sister or a wife which became the secret of success.[39] Some women who had been in domestic service had access to employers' good will. A quondam master might stand guarantor or even give a legacy. A Birmingham bookseller's prosperous business was based on the batch of books given to his sister when she left service.[40] Service gave young women wider horizons and specialized skills. An Essex woman, having been an upper servant in a town family, returned to marry a man from a farming family who had descended to being a wage-paid team man. Marriage to this 'remarkable woman' who was able to do dressmaking as well as help run the farm, restored the family to independent farming.[41] Women like these sometimes provided one of the leading elements in commercial success, literacy. A contemporary who admired the wealth and position of an illiterate Birmingham auctioneer noted that:

Providence had given him a help-meet who conducted his correspondence, superintended his books, graced his hospitable board, and otherwise, by the ease and unaffected politeness of her demeanour, and the use of good, sound common sense, had contrived to make his name respected and his acquaintance deserved by men of all grades and people of all denominations.[42]

It has been recognized that personal contacts played a central role in the functioning of both household and enterprise. Men took a keen interest in these affairs, their letters and diaries are filled with gossip about family and friends and their attendance at social gatherings. Nevertheless, women held a special place in building and maintaining relationships. Sisters, aunts, grandmothers and female cousins were ardent matchmakers. They arranged visits for their offspring and themselves paid long visits to relatives. They gave and received gifts. It was the farmer's wife who provided the Christmas goose to be dispensed to patrons and kin. A mill owner's wife admitted that she wrote letters more often than her husband for 'he considered it more my province to keep up a correspondence with our distant relatives and friends'.[43] The fact that women more often designated people by name when leaving their small properties at death – a locket to a niece, a petticoat to a sister – emphasizes the importance of personal contacts in their lives.

Women's contribution to the enterprise was centred above all in the creation of its personnel. The marriage of sisters and daughters was a prime source of partners. But beyond this, women bore and raised the next generation of sons and nephews, the future partners and entrepreneurs. This task must, indeed, have consumed much time and energy for mothers and the other women involved, particularly as the physical and moral care of children had become a serious and self-conscious issue. The average of seven plus children borne to a family absorbed the married woman's life span from her late 20s (average age at birth of first child was 27.3) to her 40s (average age at birth of last child was 40.6), with birth intervals of fourteen to twenty months.[44] Aunts and older sisters also played a prominent part in raising children. They, like mothers, provided the orderly, disciplined framework which was the basis of the serious Christian household. These women saw moral and religious training as the core of their educational function. They also recognized the importance of understanding the natural world, often seen as an adjunct of the Creator's great design. Even the youngest children were started on the path to habits of self-discipline, fitting for both a commercial and religious future. The daughter of a farmer married to a bank manager looked back in late middle age on the problems of child-rearing. She emphasized the need to arrange the day in a regular pattern of activities with time periods allotted to each. Even for a toddler sitting at a table stringing beads, 'there should be a degree of perfectness and even something approaching to business habits encouraged and expected even in these little amusements to give a worth and interest to them. Perfect play is the anticipation of perfect work'.[45]

In later childhood, boys were encouraged in their exposure to a working environment. An Essex woman ensured that her eldest son was taught the family foundry business from the bottom up, overseeing his instruction by a foreman and applauding his first efforts at casting a plough.[46] For girls, it was more a question of informal apprenticeships in the duties and skills of the household, although at times these overlapped with work for the enterprise. Primarily, however, their efforts were directed to servicing the household and manpower of the enterprise. Women trained not only their own daughters but nieces and other female relatives and friends. In the 1800s, a farming household took in the 15-year-old daughter of a distant relative, also a farmer, whose wife had just died leaving a family of younger children. The girl was taught to run a farmhouse so that she could bake and generally take over the household for her father.[47]

Women played an important role in caring for pupils, shop men, apprentices as well as nephews, nieces and their younger siblings or those of their husbands who might be resident in the household. In addition to providing meals, clean linen and tidy rooms, women were responsible for the moral and emotional development of these young people. An advertisement for an apprentice in a local Birmingham paper assured its readers that the successful applicant would be treated as one of the family.[48] How much provision of either a material or psychological kind was actually given depended on the resources of the family and the personality of the women in charge. Memoirs do indicate, however, that a young aunt, a schoolmaster's wife and others in similar positions could have a strong influence on some boys in their commercial, intellectual or religious development.

Next to wives, daughters and sisters were the most important group in providing these services to households. They took over the care of children left motherless through death in childbirth; they followed their brothers to other towns or villages when they went to set up a new business. In 1822, a corn merchant who had been supporting his mother and seven younger siblings since he was a very young man come to Birmingham, accompanied by his sister as housekeeper. She remained with him in this capacity since his wife died within a year. It was only after his sister's marriage in 1846 that he married again.[49] The organizing and running of these households could reach the proportions of many commercial establishments. A Witham grocer's household included eight children and five male assistants, while establishments of up to a dozen were not unknown.[50] Clergymen who took in pupils or ran small schools regularly catered for from half a dozen to twenty pupils, the average number of resident boys in schools in the two areas being fifteen.[51]

Even unrelated women friends or female relatives not living in the household could play a part in middle-class youths' development. Henry Crabb Robinson, who later became a well-known man of letters in London, was the son of a Bury St Edmunds tanner. His education and general cultural development was taken in hand by Catherine Buck a woman friend of the family, half-a-dozen years his senior. Her own intellectual accomplishments must have been of a high order since she later became the close friend of Dorothy and William Wordsworth and the wife of Thomas Clarkson, philanthropist and anti-slavery advocate. She was instrumental in introducing Crabb Robinson to the London literary world, although she remains unpublished and unknown.[52]

These instances may support the contention that, in a broad sense, women contributed cultural as well as monetary capital to the economic life of the middle class. Both these forms, however, were more indirect than the use of women's labour. Where property and educational resources were more limited, there is abundant evidence that women were working at a wide variety of tasks within the family enterprise. Their general usefulness was recognized in the advice given to young Samuel Courtauld by a business associate of his father: 'if a good wife fell in your way I would take her as an assistant even though she may not be rich in the World's wealth'.[53]

Occasional or even continuous use of wives', daughters' or sisters' labour was easier when living quarters were near or in the working space. As late as 1854, a letter from the wife of an Essex tradesman assumed the combination of household and commercial tasks: 'In settling into my new home and duties here in the business-house, I have earnestly desired to fill my situation rightly, to be enabled to walk before our household in the fear of the Lord.'[54] In some cases, the wife would run a business next door to and often related to that of her husband, thus in the directories are found husband and wife teams of a clockmaker and tea dealer, a grocer and pork butcher. In villages, the wife or daughter/sister of a farmer might use the front room as a small shop. At a more elevated level, James Bisset, who was a Birmingham manufacturer of some standing, enjoyed a hobby of collecting to the point where he turned his house into a commercial museum run by his wife.[55]

Some enterprises were premised on the steady use of female family labour. Schools were jointly run not only because women serviced the boarding pupils, but because they also taught, if only knitting and needlework to the girls. Many salaried positions for men encouraged or even required a female adjunct. Under the terms of an Essex charity, the schoolmaster was paid £32 a year to teach thirty poor boys while his wife, unpaid, was responsible for the forty girls.[56] Retail trade, in particular, enabled women of the household not only to help out but often to be the de facto means of providing a livelihood. A Quaker who inherited his uncle's drapery shop 'depended much on his young wife for its effective management'. Her involvement in the shop was recalled by a family story that, when suddenly called away to a customer, she popped the then baby (there were nine children) into an open drawer and forgot where she had put it.[57]

Within the family business there were diverse roles women could play. Emma Gibbins held dinner parties for the partners after meetings of the Digbeth Battery Works conveniently located next door to the house.[58] The wives and daughters of several Witham solicitors regularly witnessed wills, which implies that they may also have copied documents and performed other clerical tasks. An Essex estate agent was proud of his daughter's business ability as she copied all her father's large correspondence.[59] A draper's wife represented her husband at an important funeral – an unusual step for a women – when he was 'all alone in the shop' and could not go.[60] Women might step in when husband, father or brother were ill or absent. They took messages, fended off importunate clients or creditors and ordered supplies. During harvest, if not raking hay or stacking corn, women provided the extra baking and brewing for the field workers. Even the rather flighty 17-year-old whose mid century diary is filled with genteel visiting and hints at attachments with young men, breaks off in June to record that she and her two sisters 'have been working at hay making in the Mill Fields' which prevents her visiting but, 'I don't dislike it half as much as I thought'.[61] Female family labour was called in to cope with specific problems or crises in the enterprise, and many such a success story must have resembled the coach proprietor who built up a business from a small beginning through 'downright industry and a systematic application to business in which the female members of the family were called to assist'.[62] The implication is that once a modest level of prosperity had been reached, the female members could withdraw.

The extreme case of women's labour used to make up for the absence of male support was widowhood. The pattern of widows as temporary incumbents of an enterprise discerned in the wills is confirmed from more qualitative sources. Frequently the sequence followed the story of the Woodcock family of High Street, Colchester. William Woodcock had run a watch, clockmaking, goldsmiths and jewellers business. When he became ill, his wife, Ann, added an agency for the East India tea company. He died soon afterwards and she carried on the business with the aid of a journeyman. In 1828, her son married and took over the business which his mother had been holding for him and she retired, now aged 51, to a cottage at the rear of the shop with her three unmarried daughters.[63] It was not unknown for the widows of bankers, merchants and other highly placed families to play a similar part. The widow of Samuel Alexander directed the influential Ipswich bank during the interim before her son took over, while Boulton and Watt of Birmingham continued to deal with the widow of their London banker for many years.[64]

Some young men benefited from this arrangement where their mother (step-mother, aunt) provided an enhanced patrimony by the time they came of age. Maria Savill, the young widow of an Essex builder, despite her responsibility for ten children and two step-children, built up the family business as a spring board for her son to become a successful architect and surveyor and founder of a family firm prominent among Chartered Surveyors for the rest of the century.[65] Nevertheless, the social and business climate made it difficult for a widow to do more than hold her own economically, and many must have either chosen or been forced to settle for small incomes supplemented by traditional women's expedients such as taking in lodgers. Their children would almost certainly lose out in the economic stakes.

Women were expected to move in and out of positions directly supporting the family enterprise. They were accustomed to earning small sums of money in the interstices of household management. Farmer's wives and other female relatives were kept busy smoking, pickling and preserving food as well as daily cooking and baking. Not only did these finishing processes feed the household but 'keeping a good table' was part of their claim to respect in the rural community. It was possible to combine these activities with selling a few goods or services, although records tell us very little about the extent and variety of such income. How much, in fact, did the wife of an Essex farmer benefit from her cow keeping as reported in her husband's diary: 'Total amount for the two Alderney's made in the Year, £50=6=6. My wife took for her hard labour in managing the two cows £5=0=0 and I received £45=6=6 like all other lazy persons for doing nothing.' He also paid his daughter-in-law small sums for rearing puppies for him and his married sister one penny each for ducks she had raised.[66]

Dressmaking, plain sewing and other tasks related to domestic needs would be the most obvious ways of making extra cash, but writing and teaching were also commonly fitted into a household routine. There were more unusual possibilities: Ann Constable, John's eldest sister, bred dogs.[67]

Such sidelines provided goods for the household, brought in a little extra cash or in some cases were a pastime for the women of the family. The common factor in many women's activities in households at all levels, however, was that they were seldom paid as individuals. A sister working in her brother's shop, daughters working for their parents, wives with their husbands, seldom had a regular or fixed wage. A woman who had entered a clergyman's household as a religious disciple and unpaid mother's help began to supplement the family income by teaching in the evening, but found that her pupils' parents paid the minister for her services.[68]

As long as the household was able to support its members, the lack of individualized income was not serious. It should be kept in mind that an individual wage did not yet have the symbolic identification with personal worth which it acquired in the twentieth century. But when women were left without support, often also without a home and social place, they might be particularly vulnerable. Often they were left with partial income such as an annuity, too low to support a respectable lifestyle no matter how circumscribed. Such women were forced to move from one relative or friend to another, caring for children, nursing the sick, giving a hand in the shop, acting as companion to an elderly aunt or uncle. The suspicion that even married women might be contributing more than their share to the household establishment and selling short their own interests was seldom voiced. But the wife of a businessman who had retired at 60 with barely enough to maintain a respectable lifestyle and nothing much to occupy his time did have reservations. She had married him to escape the drudgery of school teaching and despite a devout commitment to the values of domesticity she had a sharp eye for women's position. 'The wasted hours of most men would do almost half the work of women', she wrote to a like-minded friend.[69]

In 1809, the *Ipswich Journal* ran an advertisement for a schoolmistress whose most important skills included good manners and correct conduct: 'Any lady of reduced fortune possessing the above accomplishments and being less desirous of a salary than of obtaining an eligible situation, will meet with kind and liberal treatment from the principal of the school.'[70] Such a proposition reveals that women, with some education and culture, were regarded as being able to enhance the reputation or at least give a tone of respectability to an establishment, whether a school or their own household. The appearance and behaviour of the mistress, especially when on display at church or chapel or at public events, proclaimed the reputability of the enterprise as clearly as her bonnets or dresses indicated its spending power. An Essex agent for many large estates noted in his diary how pressure from many landlords favoured Anglican communicants. He also noted that wives were almost always consulted about leases; their sobriety, sense and experience could make a difference as to whether leases would be granted, the terms and renewals.[71]

In their capacity as status bearers for their households, adult women faced a number of contradictory pressures. They were expected to be seen at specified public functions and often had to go from home to pay visits, if not buy household supplies or do errands for the family business. But over the period there was increasing social derogation for women who openly walked or rode horseback except for non-utilitarian recreational or health reasons. In the eighteenth century, a prosperous farmer and brewer's wife thought nothing of riding on horseback the 20 odd miles from her village to the market town to transact her business.[72] But with the growing emphasis on the protection of women, light-wheeled vehicles came to be their acceptable mode of transport, although more expensive to maintain than riding horses. Lack of access to means of mobility and the risks of losing status by being seen in many public places, particularly alone, was a serious disadvantage to a woman doing business.

Such obstacles to physical and social mobility were part of the way status considerations encouraged women to play down selling themselves or their products. Three sisters left in a precarious financial position by the bankruptcy and death of their father, manager for a Suffolk shipping company, turned to writing popular history books. Despite the urging of their guardian and trustee, they often refused payment for their work.[73] For farmers, the various corn, cattle and produce markets were their club where 'gossip of the countryside could be exchanged', particularly information about prices, turnover of farms and new farming practices. Not only were such markets off limits for women with pretensions to gentility, but their adjunct, the public house market day 'ordinary' was hardly a venue for women. By the 1830s, a Suffolk man commented on the notoriety of a female cattle dealer who sat with other dealers at The Swan, drinking and smoking a pipe and locally known as 'The Duchess', by that date considered an eccentric.[74] The change to formal marketing with its male ambience, from the financing by boards of trustees to the convivial dinners held in their spacious halls, was a serious disincentive to women.

The contributions to the enterprise through women's labour were contradicted by her role in displaying rank through the appearance of a non-working lifestyle. This contradiction was related to the more general conflict between achieving a commodious lifestyle and the more religious or cultural emphasis on education and learning, despite protestations that a religious commitment was compatible with a comfortable home life. This latent controversy was often played out by women who were particularly associated with setting the tone of the family lifestyle. Those groups whose claims were solidly based on property – the manufacturers, tradesmen and farmers – were able to build their material 'plant' in a way which was often hard to match for the spokesmen of middle-class values, the clergy. In the countryside, where farmers and clergy formed the backbone of the middle class undiluted by other groups, farmers' female relatives came in for particular criticism for their status pretensions. The wives and daughters of clergymen had seen themselves as leaders of refinement, but nevertheless looked uneasily over their shoulders as wartime prosperity raised the position of their uncultivated neighbours. There was less friction where farmers' families found themselves in areas without resident clergy and playing a leading role against superstition, folk belief and what was viewed as rural ignorance and apathy. Against this they pitted both their intense conversionist religion, commitment to scientific modes of thought and conceptions of respectable behaviour. The less educated or well travelled among the farming group might take an intermediate position on issues such as beliefs in ghosts but on the whole they enthusiastically supported more modern ideals. In the early nineteenth century, a Quaker farmer's wife, recently moved to an extremely remote area in Suffolk and acting as the sole 'lady' of the village, took on such a role when she deliberately exposed her young children to smallpox after having them vaccinated to demonstrate the efficacy of the new frightening procedure to the villagers.[75]

While all groups were deeply committed to the concept of domesticity and women's sphere within it, the explicit statement of these values seems to have been somewhat greater among the households of professional men: army officers, medical men and above all the clergy. It may have been that they were more frequently left without means of support than among those whose livelihood stemmed from more solid property. Their education and background emphasized literacy and, furthermore, their direct contribution to the professional man's earning capacity was more problematic.[76] Mary Ann Hedge, a committed spinster parishioner of the Evangelical William Marsh's church of St Peter's Colchester, wrote books for children, moral tales and novels. In one of these, her heroine was of high degree but her husband had been 'reduced' to acting as land agent to an earl. This female paragon not only does all the household cooking but draws and paints so that when her husband falls ill, she pleads to finish some sketches due for his employer. Mary Ann Hedge's approval is echoed in the husband's acknowledgement that 'the World has admired *as mine* works which were the effort of conjugal affection'.[77] This view effectually conceals the actual economic position of women within the household by presenting the wife's actions in terms of affection and moral duty. Hedge's notion of a wife's role is expressed in language suitable to a scion of a clock manufacturer's family: a wife is to be 'the grand-spring that sets in motion all the machinery of domestic comfort in regular and harmonious motion'.[78] Similar pressures were brought to bear on daughters. For example, the preparation of goods for sale could take place in back premises where the daughter with aspirations to gentility could be shielded from being seen in public but their labour might also be needed to serve customers. The balance between helping out the family enterprise by cheerfully undertaking such duties and an anxiety about maintaining the family's social standing is a constant theme in the literature aimed at young women as we have seen in Jane Taylor's novel, *Display*.

Nowhere were the contradictions and their consequences for individual women more evident than in the attitudes towards widows and their livelihood. Having proved their feminine commitment through marriage, widows were given legal and customary sanctions to enter the market. Indeed, they were often expected to be able to support themselves and their dependent children in a reversal of their acknowledged dependency within marriage, a position sometimes brutally thrust upon them. However, they were not expected to aspire beyond self-support. At a time when the unrestrained pursuit of business by men was still a questionable virtue, it was abhorrent in a woman. The Suffolk poet, George Crabbe, celebrated the wife and mother who died young, her place in the garden, the fireside chair, the church pew were hallowed by reverent memories. She is contrasted with the surviving widow, her head full of accounts, ruling her household with a rod of iron, whose sons long for her death.[79] Few widows had the option of remaining in active business with high incomes. Realistically a widow's chances of operating near that level were remote and above all such ambition ran against the grain of feminine propriety. The bankers, solicitors and agents as well as fellow (sic) traders, merchants, farmers or manufacturers with whom she would have to deal would have been men with firm ideas of proper feminine behaviour. For those widows who could, it was easier to retire on to a fixed income. In the 1790s, Matthew Boulton wrote to his partner about the sale of an iron manufactory, reporting that the 'assigned reason for selling is that many of the company are females, who do not find it convenient to carry on such extensive concerns'.[80] By mid century inconvenience had changed to social catastrophy.

Widows faced a range of difficulties. For example, as farming became more rationalized and profit oriented, those landowners who had invested heavily in improvements sought tenants who would be 'intelligent and enterprising',[81] not the received stereotype of a widow. George Eliot, an estate steward's daughter, described a fictional case of the farmer's widow whose husband's dying wish had been for her to carry on the farm. When she goes to plead her case with the landlord she is dismissed in just these terms of an appeal to both the supposed capacities and right conduct of femininity. 'You are about as able to carry on a farm as your best milch cow. You'll be obliged to have some managing man, who will either cheat you out of your money, or wheedle you into marrying him.' The landlord goes on to predict that the farm will run down and she will get in arrears with the rent. She argues back that she knows 'a deal o'farming an' was brought up i' the thick on it' and that her husband's great-aunt managed a farm for twenty years and left legacies to her 'nephys an' nieces. Phsa! a woman six feet high with a squint and sharp elbows, I daresay – a man in petticoats; not a rosy cheeked widow like you'. This widow knows that once all the stock have been sold and debts paid she will have hardly anything to live on. Since this is fiction, the secretly benevolent landlord arranges to have a cottage let to her at low rent with a plot for a cow and some pigs where she will be able to live in suitable retirement.[82]

However, landlords in the real world, while subscribing to a similar view of women's place, were not as helpful or were often unable to be as liberal. John Oxley-Parker, the agent for a large number of landowners in mid Essex in the 1830s, was called in to negotiate the lease of a widow who had kept on a farm after her husband's death. Along with her neighbouring farmers and her brother-in-law, he urged her to give up the attempt. He noted in his diary in connection with this case how important it was for tenants to have both character and capital. The questions he asked himself about a prospective tenant were: 'Was he an energetic farmer? Did he know his job and use his initiative in doing it?' Oxley-Parker finally urged the widow to throw herself on the mercy of the landlord, a member of a wealthy Colchester banking and farming family, but to no avail and she had to leave the farm with no compensation.[83]

For many women, however, a release from the drudgery and anxiety of economic activity was a realistic ambition, not to be dismissed simply as status striving. The prosperous farmer dressed in white buckskin trousers and beaver hat riding over his acres, directing his men, attending market was 'working' but very much in a managerial capacity. So too the farmer's wife aspired to be freed from heavy manual tasks. A farmer's daughter who remembered the work involved in the hot dinners with boiled beef and, at Harvest, special cakes and home brewed beer, was not surprised that 'farmer's wifes were glad when the men boarded themselves and all their wage was paid in money' although it 'snapped some of the ties which bound the servant and master as fellow creatures'.[84]

The majority of women knew that they would have to work within the household if not the enterprise. It was rather the way their contribution was defined which was significant. The evolution of the concept of work in relation to women's activities is suggestive here. Catherine Marsh, Rev. William Marsh's daughter, growing up first in Colchester and then Birmingham as part of an Evangelical household, was held up as a model of feminine behaviour as she helped her father in his ministerial duties. She wrote letters, saw callers and ran the house after her mother's death. Her friend and biographer recalls that Catherine was always busy, always 'working'. She defined this term: 'Fine needlework in young days and when there was a later fashion for crochet bonnets she quickly made 27 for her friends.'[85] 'Berlin wool work' first made its appearance in Colchester in 1796 and was seen as initiating the vogue for amateur needlework and 'useless' crafts, characteristic of nineteenth-century middle-class women's definition of work.[86]

Women, then, did not necessarily conceive of themselves as 'working', but they did have a stern conception of duty, the moral imperatives which made them ever ready family aids. They expected and were expected by others to be on call to help family and friends. After his wife's death, the childless shopkeeper, John Perry, made constant calls on the support of his relatives. Among others, his unmarried niece came to stay to help him 'in the department of looking over my linen'.[87] Yet some of the more prescient seemed to have been aware of their vulnerable position. The daughters of a silk merchant tried to educate themselves, partly for enjoyment but also, as one wrote, they had 'early seen how precarious was the tenure of wealth derived from business with its incessant fluctuations'.[88]

The education of women and its effects

Like men, women's first duty was to train themselves for a religious life. But for women this could also be the central aim of education. When Jane Taylor, as editor of a religious youth's magazine, was consulted about a young lady's education she answered: 'The grand end which we ought to propose to ourselves in every intellectual study is *moral* improvement' (her emphasis).[89] Learning was to be used in the service of others. The young sister of a Colchester Independent minister struggled against ill health to 'gain more knowledge to enable me to become an agreeable and suitable companion' to her beloved elder brother.[90] But in addition, since women were regarded as central to the image of family status, their training was directed to that end. The arts, drawing, piano playing, knowledge of French which became the staple, and much derided, fare of female

accomplishments, were deliberately paraded as being the opposite of business duties. A tradesman's daughter whose experience had been in teaching
young boys tried to obtain a position as a schoolmistress. She could offer
a sound grounding in grammar, geography and arithmetic but every advertisement, even for farmer's families in the country required music, French
and the various accomplishments of what was called a 'genteel education'.[91]
Catherine Hutton recalled in later years that when she was growing up in
the Birmingham of the 1770s there were no boarding schools for girls. The
day school she went to provided an education limited to spelling and reading
from the Bible plus a little needlework.[92]

Given these restricted facilities, what went on in the family was central
to girls' development. Some more progressive parents like the members of
Birmingham's Lunar Society taught their daughters in the same mode as
their sons. One of the society, Erasmus Darwin, published *A Plan for the
Conduct of Female Education in Boarding Schools* in 1797, a most
enlightened document. Not only did he argue for the importance of girls
being educated at school rather than at home, he also wanted science and
mathematics in the curriculum.[93] A modest Birmingham manufacturer was
ready to sacrifice his dining room furniture for the education of his children,
both his sons and daughters.[94] Thus a minority of middle-class girls,
especially those from professional families, were exposed to a general liberal
education. The aims of that education, however, were specifically non-
vocational. Unlike their brothers, such young women were not expected
to add vocational training. Even the occasional high standards achieved in
painting, music or languages were contained within an amateur framework.[95] In 1805 a girl from a Unitarian Essex family, who had been taught
Latin by her father, carefully copied a maxim attributed to Arthur Young
into her commonplace book:

The conversation of men not engaged in trifling pursuits is the best school for
the education of women.[96]

Undoubtedly where there was an intellectually inquiring atmosphere in the
home and men were committed to the education of their daughters and
sisters, young women had a better chance of a broad exposure to a variety
of subjects than in the confines of girls' schools. Home education was also
preferred since girls' moral and physical development could be more closely
supervised and the centrality of the family enhanced.

Most middle-class girls were excluded from the staple fare of the reformed
grammar schools as well as the new boys' academies. The original foundation of many grammar schools had been for the respectable poor of both
sexes, but had long been appropriated for middle-class boys. Of the 593
adult males in an Essex village at the turn of the century, fifty-six had had
a free education at the local grammar school, almost all sons of farmers and
tradesmen but also a few 'mechanics'. A handful of these boys, including
the two sons of the vicar, took up the annual free place at Christ Church,
Cambridge offered through the grammar school.[97] None of these opportunities would have been possible for local girls. Basic Latin and Greek, the
ticket for entry into law, medicine and the Anglican clergy, were effectively
closed to girls as well as the newer commercial and scientific subjects,

although the latter were sometimes offered in a watered down version. Botany, for example, was rewritten for young women with the sexual classification of plants expurgated.[98] Natural history subjects were offered for their moral and religious analogies as much as scientific potential. 'The study of nature leads us to nature's God' wrote Mary Ann Hedge, in a book on the training of girls.[99]

Parents, making a realistic expectation of economic returns from their children's education, invested more heavily for boys. Girls were expected to make do with the teaching of unpaid kin and friends. It was at the margins that these decisions were especially significant, as when a small farmer sent his sons to school but refused to let his daughters go since they needed only to milk, sew, cook and bear children.[100] When girls attended school, their commitment might be less than their brothers. A newly opened seminary for Young Ladies and Gentlemen in Ipswich in 1809 offered reduced prices for 'Young Ladies whose other engagements allow them to attend only half days.'[101] Girls could expect their schooling to last only a year or two or to be interrupted by family demands. The daughter of the manager of a small town gas works was brought back from boarding school to help in the house since no servant was kept.[102] Boys, too, would be recalled to enter the family business, if necessary, but the disjunction between the content and form of their education and their subsequent business life was not as great. Home education could be even more easily set aside if parents or older siblings who were teaching had other demands on their time. The regime of the governess and visiting master was only employed by the wealthiest already committed to a general education for their daughters. For the others, their lessons often had to be fitted in around general household schedules and the distractions of the family business.

Emily Shore was the daughter of a rural clergyman who also boarded half a dozen pupils. A bright child, she was taught Latin and Greek by her father and English and history by her mother. Even at an early age she was teaching her younger siblings. In 1831, at age 13, she wrote a sketch, 'The Interruptions', illustrating the impossibility of reading an extract of history to her mother as the housemaid, cook and nursemaid wanted directions, callers came to the door, a thimble was lost and the younger children wanted attention. Emily Shore's routine included afternoon calls with her mother, visits to the poor and Sunday school teaching, all regarded as equally if not more important than her intellectual development. Un-directed, she veered between a passionate, and somewhat guilty love of poetry and a self-imposed heroic programme of reading and rote learning complete with wall charts, a not unusual combination for girls with such tastes. Such an agenda had no aims and no end, either in its own terms or in recognition from external bodies or in leading to an occupation. Often such preoccupations looked odd if not selfish or even immoral. In her mid teens, Emily experienced a breakdown which she interpreted as having 'overtaxed my strength with study' and turned to learning housekeeping which she had previously despised but which now made her feel useful.[103]

Girls from wealthy and cultured homes, such as the Galton and Moilliet banking families of Birmingham, were educated by mothers who themselves were freed from involvement in the enterprise and who had enough help in the household to take their daughters' training seriously. This was supplemented by special teachers coming in for music, languages and dancing plus the odd year at boarding school.[104] In homes with a good library and encouragement to use it, some women in the upper echelons were able to reach high levels of literary and even scholarly achievement. These young women were also likely to be offered at least a limited form of travel within Great Britain if not abroad, a favourite theme in their travels being literary excursions, as, for example, the visit of an Ipswich girl to the setting of Scott's novels.[105] These were the young women who also benefited from long visits to the homes of relatives and friends which widened their horizons. Jane Ransome Biddell, born 1782, was the Quaker daughter of a wealthy Ipswich manufacturer. Both before and after her marriage to an equally wealthy Anglican farmer, through her education and cultural activities she had entry into the upper echelons of the town. She was an admiring friend of local elite families like the Cobbolds, owners of a local brewing firm who themselves had produced a group of clergymen and women who helped to set the tone of Ipswich society. A woman like Jane Ransome Biddell had a housekeeper to aid her management of the household of nine children. She might well have had more time for cultural pursuits than her busy husband who was immersed in the farm and surveying business. She wrote poetry, some of which was published in local newspapers.[106]

Continued self-education was permitted to women like Jane Biddell. It was rather the women in the middle and lower ranks who were culturally most disadvantaged. Their sole avenue of mental cultivation was the Sunday school. There were no facilities beyond the lending libraries which often gave limited access to women. The Mechanics Institutes and Literary and Philosophical Societies which were so important for their male equivalents were usually closed to young women. They might only be admitted to selected public functions or borrow books to read at home; occasionally to use the reading rooms at prescribed times. The Colchester Literary Society only allowed women to use the rooms after 5 p.m. in the later nineteenth century when subscriptions were falling.[107] In most cases, women were excluded from both regular meetings and discussion groups or managing committees. Lower subscriptions and admission fees for women reflect both their secondary status and less ready access to cash. At the Ipswich Mechanics Institute in the 1840s, the novelty of a woman lecturing on women's issues received full press coverage but little local support.[108] The Book Clubs, Debating Societies, and Natural History Field Clubs which were heavily used by apprentices and shopmen were for the most part off limits to young women. Only Quaker and some nonconformist circles encouraged semi-formal outlets for both 'youths and maidens'.

The effect of such a regime on the lives of young women, particularly among those not elevated enough to benefit from a liberal education or lowly enough to take a full part in making a living, was to promote a concept of respectability which began to close off knowledge of the world outside family, friends and co-religionists. Bowdlerized reading matter and lack of experience combined to create a real need for male protection, not least in financial affairs. An exclusive interest in the home, either as the site of a status-enhancing lifestyle or a religious commitment for themselves and their children, reinforced the disinterest in business affairs being put forward in the prescriptive literature. Undoubtedly there were many discrepancies between the aphorisms and ideals copied into girls' commonplace books and the circumstances of their own lives. But to underestimate the effect of such literature would be foolhardy, particularly when it was combined with property forms which reinforced dependence. The preponderance of historical records from men and the shadowy forms of many women's lives makes the interpretation of this problem even more acute. It is almost impossible to know how a woman like Elizabeth Gardner, wife of a brewer and wine merchant in a small Essex town, was regarded or how she saw herself in relation to the family business. The firm was run by her husband from an office in the house next door to the brewery. In the 1840s their income was enough to employ a nurse and two maids to help with the six children, leaving Mrs Gardner free for local philanthropic ventures such as penny readings as well as a social life including friendship with the vicar. She was, however, also intimately connected to the brewery to the point where she was able to take over when her husband died and the business became known as E. Gardner and Son.[109]

Women as teachers

Official sources only allow a detailed knowledge of the occupations of widows and spinsters. By far the largest group of these women, 63 per cent, were listed as 'independent'. Of women in active occupations, the category of professional was most common; undoubtedly mostly school-mistresses either owning their own schools or employed by others. Professionals were followed by trade and then by innkeeping and farming. In part, the occupations of women, as of men, depended on the area. In 1851, female headed households in farming predominated in the villages, for example, while the highest proportion of salaried female heads were found in central Birmingham.[110] In all areas, however, when women were called upon to contribute income or become the sole support of a house-hold, as Mrs Gaskell's little Miss Matty knew, 'teaching was, of course, the first thing that suggested itself'.[111] As the period neared mid century, teaching became the only occupation in which middle-class women could preserve something of their status. By 1851, women made up 64 per cent of the teaching force in Essex and 79 per cent in Birmingham.[112]

A variety of factors attracted women to teaching in addition to its rela-tively high status. Teaching was seen as an extension of childrearing which was being given special emphasis within serious Christianity. It needed few resources and little training to enter. Changes in the location and methods of instructing the young were making teaching into a more recognized activity, less casual and more formal but not to the point where women were forced out. As with many other activities, to be a schoolmaster or mistress was not necessarily a fixed occupation, although there were moves in that direction. Teaching could be taken up as a by-employment by women running households or engaged in a different family business.[113]

Like other enterprises, too, schools were embedded in the local economy, the commodity of 'education' to be exchanged for other goods and services. An advertisement in a Birmingham paper of 1820 states:

A genteel school in the vicinity of Birmingham, has now a vacancy for three young ladies as scholars, where their religious and moral education will be strictly attended to. As the Establishment has neither a Miller, Draper, nor Grocer's daughter, the Advertiser would be glad to receive either, as their consumption in each article is very considerable.[114]

Women, as much as men, used religious networks to gain pupils, their membership of a church or chapel would gain them credibility and draw pupils to their school. The close association between religion and teaching meant that when choosing a mistress for a working-class school, religious connections could be the key to a salaried post.

For school proprietors, formal partnerships were not as common as in other business since capital requirements were less. There were arrangements falling between outright ownership of a school and salaried teaching, such as subcontracting to take pupils for a capitation fee. Working partnerships between husband and wife were common, although officially the husband usually owned the school. Elizabeth Fry in her correspondence described William and Hannah Lean's Quaker school in Birmingham as theirs but in the directory it is listed in his name only.[115] Rowland Hill was partner with his father after a long period of serving in the family run boys' school, Hazelwood, in Birmingham. After his father's retirement, new articles of partnership were drawn up between those brothers still involved with the school. Mrs Hill, who had been instrumental in the early days of the foundation, and the two Hill sisters were no longer even included in the business meetings; there was no question of them being legally incorporated in either ownership or management.[116]

One reason for their exclusion was that Hazelwood was a school for older boys. There was no way that young women could take a position of authority in such a setting, even if they had had the necessary classical education. Mary Carpenter who had been educated alongside the boys in her father's academy had also helped with teaching. In 1826 when her father, Lant Carpenter, collapsed with acute depression, an ex-student, James Martineau, was called in to take his place in school and chapel while Mary was sent as governess to a family. In 1829 the boys' school was closed down and Mrs Carpenter, running the domestic side, and Mary doing the teaching, opened a girls' school to support the family. Mary was bored with having to teach a young ladies' curriculum but there was no way she could have maintained the boys' school.[117] By convention, women were confined as both school proprietors and teachers to girls' schools and schools for both sexes under about the age of 7.

A large proportion of the early nineteenth-century educational effort was undoubtedly aimed at the middle class. In the 1840 Birmingham survey, at least one-third of the children between 5 and 15 who were getting some education were at the 'superior schools' and home tuition would raise this figure. Rewards for teachers varied and profits were by no means great except for the largest and therefore almost always, boys' schools. Staff in schools like Birmingham's King Edward's Grammar, where teachers were almost entirely ordained clergymen, had incomes in the £200 to £400 a year range which were then doubled by capitation fees.[118] These positions, in fact, were part of the route to clerical preferment, an option completely closed to women. The income and social standing of the pupils' parents determined the profit, income or status of the teacher. At one end were tiny village schools, such as the one in Suffolk started by the vicar in a former bricklayer's cottage. An ex-farmer and his wife were paid 10 shillings a week plus free housing and the pence they could collect from the children. The wife was expected to teach the girls and see to the cleaning of the building.[119] Even more lowly, the dame school was usually little more than child-minding for the youngest children, often of working mothers. Nevertheless, occasionally the women who ran such schools were able to give more than basic reading and at least they were able to pick up a little income from such ventures. From the census sample, it would appear that many schoolmistresses were on the fringes of the middle class, particularly in the National or British and Foreign schools. Their male relations included agricultural labourers, small holders, auctioneers, a hostler and a coal carter. Female school teaching undoubtedly reached deeper into the working class than its masculine counterpart. This contributed to the low social standing of a woman in teaching, as Dora Pattison found when, as a vicar's daughter at mid century, she took the schoolmistresses' route to independence.[120]

The differential in salaries for men and women continued down the scale. The Witham National School in 1840 was offering £55 a year for a master and £35 for a mistress.[121] The higher amount paid to men was justified on the grounds that they would have a family to support and would be expected to teach extra, more highly valued subjects such as arithmetic and bookeeping in the lower grade school and classics in the higher. Men were also more often better qualified. Many men and women in this period owed their own education and recruitment to teaching to the Sunday school movement. But for many women this remained their only experience. No girl would have had access to the university training which permitted a well-known minister to set up a school where fees of £100 a year could be charged.[122]

As a family enterprise, schools for boys and girls differed in their structure as well as aims and curriculum. There was no role for a man in most girls' schools since only the most prestigious and expensive schools provided masters in specialist subjects. Yet an adult female was almost an imperative in boys' and girls' schools alike, preferably a relative: wife, sister, mother, aunt. Her essential tasks were overseeing the domestic side, managing the servants, organizing food and linen, caring for children who were ill and generally supplying a home-like atmosphere. Even a small boarding establishment like the Leans' Birmingham Quaker school, with its six children of the family, added up to seventeen people for meals without the day boys. In 1817, when Hazelwood School had become a substantial establishment, Rowland Hill acknowledged that his mother was 'possessed of courage and spirit, and well adapted to the situation she occupies as manager of a large household'.[123] Girls' schools and the co-educational schools for younger children also used family labour, but it was almost entirely female on both the domestic management and teaching side. Often there was no formal agreement, but younger kin would act as an assistant, although partnerships between sisters, aunt and niece were not unknown.

In the census sample at mid century there were twenty-five schools with women heads and twelve with men. Two-thirds of the women running schools were single, the rest widowed compared to only 15 per cent of men, the remaining 85 per cent being married. However, the 'family atmosphere' felt as desirable for girls was evident in the relative sizes of school households. The average number of boarders in girls' schools was five pupils, compared to fifteen for boys. Taken all together, these schools housed twenty-three adult female relatives and visitors (excluding wives of married schoolmasters), most of whom would be involved in running the school. Of these, ten were sisters of the household head (see Table 10, Appendix 3). Furthermore, women were more often found running small, day schools. In 1848, in Colchester, women headed ten day and four boarding schools, while men managed five day but six boarding establishments.[124]

Before the impact of domestic ideology had made women's sphere more synonymous with unpaid labour, there are more examples of married women running schools, especially if the family income was insecure. Mrs Ann Morgan married the Rev. Thomas Morgan, a Baptist minister, in 1803, a year after he had come to Birmingham's Cannon Street chapel where her father had been a deacon. From 1809, her husband's health deteriorated and he resigned in 1811. His stipend had been £100 since Cannon Street was a prosperous church. How was the family now to survive with four young children to support? As one of her sons later wrote, 'Then was the character of the wife and mother tested. On her seemed to be cast the burden of being the chief provider, for a time, for the support of their young family during that crisis of their lives, and she applied herself to undertake the duty.' Mrs Morgan set up a school and in 1813 was able to utilize the money from her marriage settlement, together with 'such other means and help as Mr Morgan could command', to buy a house in Moseley, a village 2 miles from Birmingham, then in countryside. The extra land provided a farming interest for Mr Morgan to the benefit of his health and the family's standard of living. Mrs Morgan managed to educate her own daughters in the school and make enough money to provide for her sons, educating them herself when young, later sending them away to school and further training. By 1820, Mr Morgan recovered sufficiently to take a co-pastorship and, by 1825, the family income was such and the children sufficiently launched for Ann Morgan to retire.[125]

This pattern is characteristic of most schools run by women. Necessity forced women to take on these responsibilities; with prosperity they withdrew. Therefore, there was usually little interest in handing on a school to the next generation. Most girls' schools closed down with changed circumstances of their originators and few records survive. Those that have are the successful and longer lived, the exceptional. Nevertheless, their story may give some insight into one of the few areas where women were able to survive economically on their own and even gain a modicum of independence.

Mary Ann Phipson started her school in Birmingham in the wake of a crisis in the family button business. Up to that time she had suffered from hypochondria and depression and the necessity to open the school was, therefore, acknowledged to have acted as 'the outward call to a vocation for which previously there had been an incipient desire and a personal adaptation'. She started by recruiting four pupils through her contacts with Carrs Lane chapel where her father had acted as deacon to John Angell James, his cousin by marriage. Mary Ann Phipson already had a reputation at the chapel as a responsible Sunday school teacher. At first she despaired of being self-supporting and considered emigrating to Australia. However, slowly the number of pupils grew, sent to her by friends and neighbours.[126] One such neighbour, Thomas Southall, a Quaker chemist, sent his daughters to her school and when Miss Phipson was looking for larger premises in the 1840s he became her landlord.[127] From the beginning her sister Rosalinda helped her, later joined by another sister, Sarah. By 1851, Mary Ann Phipson was living in a large house in a Birmingham suburb with a paid assistant, twenty-three girl pupils aged between 10 and 22, a cook and two housemaids.[128] Throughout their lives, the Phipson sisters had been profoundly influenced by their clerical kinsman and pastor, John Angell James. By 1853, when the school had moved yet again to purpose-built premises in Edgbaston, James himself presided over evening gatherings round the 'domestic circle' encouraged at the school. There he exhorted the girls on their mission and their sphere.[129]

Sarah Bache, too, used a male support group in running her successful Birmingham school for girls. Her father had died young and her mother ran a small school, but Sarah's own education was minimal and she was apprenticed to a mantua maker. She had, however, taught in the New Meeting Sunday school and there came under Priestley's spell. Through this Unitarian connection, she was able to build up her own school which she ran in partnership with her sister until the latter's marriage and then with her half-sister, Phoebe.[130] Later she was joined by a niece who she herself had educated. Through their membership of the New Meeting and association with the group of men around Priestley, Sarah Bache and Phoebe Penn developed close friendships with three men who were themselves friends, and who helped the young women with their business affairs. One of these was Thomas Hill, also running Hazelwood School. Hill was, in turn, helped by Miss Bache and Miss Penn in 1820 when a fire ravaged Hazelwood's buildings and the girls' school provided stockings for the boys and food for breakfasts. Phoebe Penn's brother-in-law, Lant Carpenter, himself running a school, advised her on advertisements and on the history curriculum, the last a real aid to women with weak academic backgrounds. He lent her money in 1825 when the school moved to a larger house and his wife, Phoebe's sister, was asked to suggest menus for the girls' meals since she had a long experience of feeding a house full of pupils.

Sarah Bache was a competent and intelligent woman who built up a successful school from almost nothing. Unlike many women in this position, she enjoyed her autonomy. She wrote to her sister, Bessy, who came to help her with the domestic side of the school:

Come then! dear, dear sister; come and share the happiness (for most frequently does happiness inhabit this apartment), of your Sarah, with independent spirits.

Let us take our homely but wholesome meal together; enjoying, at once, those two delightful sensations of independence, because we eat the bread we have fairly earned, and of grateful thankfulness to the Being who has put this independence in our power.[131]

Despite her delight in the control of her own life and the freedom this gave her, Sarah Bache was inevitably constrained to educate the girls in her school primarily to be wives and mothers. In 1808 she had consciously resisted making the school more genteel when it had become popular with over sixty pupils and raised fees to discourage further inquiries. 'We do not wish people to think that we shall make it more of a genteel school', she explained to her brother-in-law, 'I shall still continue to be so vulgar as to teach what is useful and not what is fashionable'. The useful programme including reading, needlework, geography and the use of the globes and grammar for 17s. 6d a quarter. Extra was charged for writing and accounts, ancient geography and drawing maps. By 1810, French was introduced and by 1816, when the school moved to its new Edgbaston premises in the elegant house formerly occupied by a banker, the announcement of the opening struck a distinctly fashionable note. Miss Bache and Miss Penn hoped that 'their present plan will enable them to unite with Mental and Moral Culture, a greater Attention to elegant Accomplishments, and that the Salubrity of the Situation be beneficial to their own Health and that of their Pupils'.

Sarah Bache retired and sold the school in 1838 when she was 68. She was unfortunate enough to lose most of her savings two years later when her investments failed. Her former pupils rallied and presented her with £200, proving themselves true 'friends'. In her thanks, she shows how far her attitudes to women had changed since the 1800s. 'I gratefully acknowledge', she told them, 'and most truly enjoy, the pecuniary advantages your purse . . . will afford me, but be assured that which constitutes my highest gratification . . . is the well grounded hope, that you are rising up faithfully to fulfill "Woman's Mission", by becoming truly Christian Daughters, − wives −, and Mothers'.[132]

The schools of Miss Phipson and Miss Bache were larger and lasted longer than the average concern. A young girl from Birmingham was sent to a more ordinary establishment which offered:

a limited number of young ladies for Board and Education, on the plan which they have successfully adopted for many years, combining the personal comforts of a private family, from the advantages derived from association in study with eligible companions. . . .[133]

Neither Miss Bache nor Miss Phipson had any training in the classics nor, of course, the chance of a clerical career which gave prestige and profit to the larger boys' schools. Only the girls' finishing schools of spa and seaside towns or the Metropolis could charge high fees and their emphasis was almost entirely on social skills and contacts. Keeping these provincial schools on a 'family scale' made the tasks undertaken by the staff seem less like work and more as if the women were carrying on their usual domestic duties.

There was a thin line between being in business and simply catering for and instructing a few extra children. Some of the establishments, indeed, could hardly be called schools – they were simply extensions of a normal household. In this way, such female headed 'educational households' were analogous to those where lodgers were taken to supplement or replace other income sources, a device used mainly by the working class but not unknown higher up the social scale.[134] Taking in lodgers seems to have been a strategy particularly used by female household heads in salaried posts. These households were prominent in central Birmingham in the lower middle-class urban setting, whereas girls' schools flourished in a more suburban context. In the census sample there were six schools run by women in Edgbaston but none in central Birmingham. However, the underlying economic and social motivations were similar.

Women as innkeepers

Servicing lodgers as an extension of women's caring functions was carried out on a larger scale in inns, although the lines between private home, lodging house, public house and inn were sometimes difficult to draw. (Certain categories partly depended on the granting of a liquor licence.) Women were undoubtedly running inns: 6 per cent of female household heads in the census sample. All areas had some public houses and in certain towns along main transport routes, such as Witham in Essex, innkeeping became an important sector of the local economy. Every male innkeeper who made a will in Witham left his business unconditionally to his wife as did most of those in Birmingham, some of these being substantial properties. 71 per cent of the widows of innkeepers were given complete control in contrast to 50 per cent of the whole sample of wills. In 1851 in Witham, Sarah Nunn was still at the Spread Eagle thirteen years after being widowed, while Eleanor Tanner ran the King's Head as a widow from 1847 until her own death in 1853.[135]

These legacies were an important resource for women. In the late eighteenth and early nineteenth centuries, inns and public houses were the centre of several subsidiary activities – the coaching business and provision of short haul vehicles such as the post chaise, being the most important. Innkeepers often doubled as owners of coaches and controlled their own routes since horses had to be stabled and travellers boarded at frequent intervals. Women were able to take advantage of their position within inns to become involved in the transport side. In the 1790s, Deborah Gooding ran the Chelmsford Machine Fly on a lucrative Essex to London route, a journey which often terminated at the Bull, Aldgate.[136] This large City inn was also run by a widow, 'the all powerful Ann Nelson who had found means of making her name known on almost every road out of London'.[137] Although women such as these could find a foothold in the transport business through their management of inns, they faced competition from men who started with capital resources and business experience – men such as Thomas Hedge the younger son of the Colchester clock manufacturing family, who snapped up coaching routes and purchased inns and livery stables to build up a profitable local transport empire.[138]

Other agencies were also based in public houses, which offered a central location and storage facilities as well as a guaranteed clientele. Tools for sale or hire were provided from pub yards and therefore could be managed by women such as the Essex area agent, Mrs Warren dealing in black-smithing equipment and Mrs Sergeant, a 'machinist' who contracted to rent threshing machines.[139] Women would sometimes run the pub while male relatives farmed or worked in other occupations – a Suffolk publican's husband was a vet, for example. Like the school, the inn or pub was based in the building which housed the family. Much of the brewing was done on the premises and the publican sold his or her own brew in a front room. Even from the outside, a *public* house looked exactly like a *private* house, except for the sign hanging over the door.[140]

However, within this industry changes were also taking place which tended to push women to the margins. In the seventeenth century the slow exclusion of women from beer making had begun, and by the early eighteenth century they had been confined mainly to domestic brewing, this in an industry which was the biggest industrial undertaking at that time. By 1800, more and more public houses were themselves being bought up by breweries turning the publican into a retailer.[141] The usual consequences of the larger-scale, more rationalized, centralized marketing which followed, produced the crop of male managers, clerks and agents, under whose authority many public houses were run.

Internally, the informality of the early pub also changed. The introduction of a counter began to place a 'bar' between the customer and publican. Legislation of the 1830s which created a category of unlicensed beer shops did provide opportunities for women to earn, but at the lowest end of a trade that was increasingly being differentiated by the social rank of its clientele. The Evangelical onslaught on drinking and its association with public disorder, including political disaffection, gave public houses a bad reputation. A farmer who was a churchwarden and right-hand man to the vicar felt rather out of place in the free and easy atmosphere of his local village pub, yet he often went there to attend sales, always held in pubs, for 'as an inhabitant of the district he felt a need to know the values and ownership of lands and houses'.[142] By the 1850s, public drinking places had become specialized and stratified by class, to the point where Brian Harrison has claimed that 'no respectable urban Englishman entered an ordinary public house'.[143] If these reservations held for men, then they were doubly effective in making public houses anathema to genteel or even respectable femininity.

This association proved a serious constraint on women's business activities, and presented a dilemma for the women who owned, managed or worked in public houses. The Woolpack, a Birmingham public house in the 1840s, was regarded by the new owners as having a somewhat objectionable class of customers. The landlord therefore divided the pub into several areas ranging from dining rooms for drovers to a commercial room for businessmen to a smoking room for casual or ordinary visitors and the 'snuggery' behind the bar into which none but a privileged few were allowed to enter. Here the landlady and her daughters also sat. 'The fun occasionally was fast and furious, but no breach of decorum was permitted' and a box was supplied for hospital charity donations levied as 'fines' for bad language.[144]

The most lucrative part of the hostelry trade faded quickly in the 1830s and 1840s with the coming of the railways. Railway building and management were closely associated with engineering, organized on a large scale as private companies and often staffed on military lines, all characteristics uncongenial to women. The heavily male ambience of the railway system has not often been commented on but was a significant factor in the economy of the second quarter of the nineteenth century. Only the less profitable small inns and public houses which continued to supply chaises and other light vehicles for connecting journeys to railways terminals remained allied to transport. A few women did run such businesses, but the livery stables which evolved from these centred on the masculine monopoly of horse culture and women's direct connection with transport was effectively broken by mid century.

On the other hand, the fact that inns and public houses were increasingly rented from breweries and thus could be taken up without much capital meant that women continued on the food, drink and lodging side. Undoubtedly this option remained an important part of the lower middle-class service trades in particular where women were employed as family members. Indeed, women might be deliberately sought as employees in their capacity to provide a home-like atmosphere and control disorderly behaviour. By mid century most of the women independently operating public houses were widows, and only 7 per cent of inns and taverns and 10 per cent of beershops in Ipswich were listed in women's names as opposed to 47 per cent of lodging houses, a smaller scale, less formal alternative.[145] Significantly, the printed census at the same date does, however, list innkeeper's *wives* as a separate category.

Even before the changes which eased women out of the more lucrative parts of the trade, there were limits to what they could make of their position. A landlord might take advantage of the contacts he made in the course of activities as diverse as billeting soldiers, housing itinerant traders, running a post office, swearing in constables, playing host to vestry and other local government meetings, social and political clubs. Freemasons met in public houses and even a chapel was not averse to holding a debate in such a setting. There was nothing to stop a female innkeeper providing any of these services, but their presence on her premises seldom led to other kinds of business activity. A male publican, on the other hand, could evolve into a corn factor or make a more general use of his position. Jonathan Bull, an Essex village publican, worked the small holding surrounding the pub in addition to being an overseer to the Poor Law guardians, helped to raise troops during the war and generally acted as an opinion leader with an interest in any local business going on.[146] He has no known female counterpart.

Women in trade

The largest single occupation of middle-class women earning their livelihood in their own right as well as assisting their male relatives, was in trade.

Plate 18 Illustration from Jane Taylor's story for children in which she urged girls not to be too proud to help in the family shop

Most of this was at the less capitalized, less formal end of the commercial spectrum with quick turnover and short credit chains. The general shop-keeper, especially in the village, was more often than not a widow taking advantage of the general move to fixed retail distribution.[147] Millinery and dressmaking, catering to an all-female clientele, were the main exceptions to male dominance of the higher reaches of retailing. In Witham, by far the most prominent female establishment was the millinery shop at the socially select end of Newland Street. It was run by two sisters employing six living-in assistants and their mother living on an annuity.[148] Training for the higher branches of these trades required apprenticeships with premiums as high as £50 and starting capital of double that amount.[149] Journeywomen milliners in Colchester earned about 6 shillings a week in 1800, well paid for women's work. In the late eighteenth century, women dominated the retail women's clothing trades: out of nineteen retailers in the town, sixteen were women. Wealthier Colchester milliners travelled to London during the fashionable spring season to purchase up-to-date stock. Some specialized: Mrs Courtney made muffs, Mary Waynman mended fans, Ann Wilder starched muslin, lawn, gauze and lace. Women like these acted independently, taking apprentices, making out bills in their own name, even when married. For example, Mary Boyle charged the Colchester MP 1 shilling each for twelve favours used in an election campaign. In this period, some remained in business throughout their married life and widowhood and left real estate as well as cash legacies. Yet many milliners, too, withdrew on marriage or other changed circumstances. Even this skilled trade lacked a monopoly; apprenticeship might be an advantage but was by no means compulsory. Rather 'judgement of changing fashions, a genteel manner and a network of local contacts and credit' was more significant.[150]

As with teaching and purveying food, drink and lodging, the range of women offering dressmaking and millinery was wide, and because every girl was taught to sew, there was always the possibility of using unpaid family services. The local records only show a handful of women professionally engaged in these trades in the later part of the period. The daughter of a master baker in Ipswich served an apprenticeship as a dressmaker and went into partnership with her master in the 1830s.[151] The publicity surrounding a fire uncovered a woman running a chemist shop with a living-in apprentice.[152] Two sisters ran the bookselling and publishing business they inherited from their father.[153] There is no indication from either these odd examples or the local directories that any of these enterprises ever expanded to any size or became known for specialized products.

Anxiety about the status of retail trade was particularly acute for women, as is shown by the ambivalence towards the wife of a grocer expressed in a poem by Jane Taylor. Her fictional portrait was based on a real couple who had retired from a grocer's shop to a newly built imposing brick house from which the husband had served as Mayor of Colchester. Here Taylor is ostensibly attacking the prejudices of the 'little gentry of our narrow sphere'.

> The powder'd matron, who for many a year
> Has held her mimic routs and parties here,
> (Exchanging just the counter, scales and till
> For cups of coffee, scandal and quadrille)
> Could boast nor range of thought nor views of life,
> Much more extended than our grocer's wife.

The mayor's wife:

> Her thoughts unused to take a longer flight
> Than from the left hand counter to the right

is portrayed as vulgar, and incapable of refinement, although true religion will make palatable even the ultimate social humiliation of having served behind a counter.[154]

Jane Taylor was acutely aware of the nuances of status between Anglicans and nonconformists as well as within the various nonconformist communities within the town. The connection of retail trade with nonconformity was strong. Twenty-one out of the twenty-four families (88 per cent) who were in trade in the two areas were nonconformists of some variety (see Tables 1 and 2). Women were more visibly active in retail trade than almost any other family enterprise. They also had a greater part to play in the affairs of the local chapel than in the hierarchically organized Anglican church. It is possible that a combination of these factors contributed to the special concern over the status of women in trade. Whatever the reasons, owning or working in a shop, which might have been the height of ambition for the working-class woman, could represent the depths of degradation from the perspective of the upper middle class.

The marginal place of women in the economy

Women had been active in the early days of manufacturing enterprises when the scale was small and linked to direct sales. Birmingham women in the eighteenth century were known to be manufacturing in workshops, sometimes with male relatives or, as widows, on their own. George Holyoake's father had moved from being an independent bucklemaker to working as a skilled engineer in a foundry. His mother continued the button workshop she had started, before her marriage; the marital home fronting on the shop where she employed several work people. As her son recalled:

She received the orders; made the purchases of materials; superintended the making
of the goods; made out the accounts; and received the money besides taking
care of her growing family. There were no 'Rights of Women' thought of in her
day, but she was an entirely self-acting, managing mistress. The button business
died out while I was young, and from the remarks which came from merchants,
I learnt that my mother was the last maker of that kind of button in the town.[155]

Respectable married women did start their own small businesses, for example Mrs Clark who went into the Birmingham fancy trade. However, when her husband prospered through his invention of a machine for winding cotton, she withdrew into domestic exclusion in Ladywood, not necessarily losing caste for her excursion into the business world at this date.[156]

But even without the enticement of domesticity or the possible loss of status entailed in having run a business, women were increasingly hampered by the growth in scale of manufacturing enterprises. They faced the increased problem of maintaining authority over a larger, more distanced workforce, the need to take a more active part in the formal market, the requirement for heavier capital input and for scientific and technical knowledge. As in farming, women in manufacturing and retail families took on a diversity of semi-employments, some of which were directly absorbed in the enterprise such as the jam made for sale by a grocer's wife and daughters. The Mrs John Bright, who acted as agent for Bright's custard powder in an Essex town in 1845, is representative of the women who acted as agents for a variety of goods and services,[157] as much as the refined spinster who took in convalescent patients and ran a high-class home for the genteel mentally disturbed.[158] Women whose main resource was some education, turned to writing popular books for children, moral tales and tracts and also history, biography and science with titles such as *The*

Observing Eye or *What is a Bird* produced by a farmer's daughter.[159] The daughter of a clergyman living on the outlying Essex coast, like her brothers, gained a certain reputation as a composer of hymns. She was not unusual for a considerable proportion of nineteenth-century hymns were written, translated and composed by women (classics such as 'Nearer my God to Thee' and 'All Things Bright and Beautiful' among many others).[160] A Suffolk Independent minister based his successful second career as a choir master on a system of notation invented by a female Sunday school teacher, who, with her sister, had perfected a system of training choirs.[161]

From cases like the above, a pattern emerges of women able to take part in, even to make money from, activities which were seen as primarily part of a family-based avocation, skills which were sometimes used as the basis of a family business. Not without reason did Isaac Taylor call his collective memoir, *The Family Pen*. Within such an enterprise, women were able to establish a niche in the less public part of a field. They etched the engravings and hand tinted the prints, rather than creating the originals. It was more acceptable to them as well as to others to translate than to write under their own names, particularly outside the more acceptable areas of children's literature, religious works and fiction. Catherine Winkworth, related by marriage to the Shaen family in Essex, and a friend of Mrs Gaskell and James Martineau, made fairly substantial sums by her translations from the German for which she has gained a lasting reputation. However she was doubtful about the suggestion that she write her own material:

You can see with half an eye that that would be a very different affair from simply translating a work all ready to hand. The latter would only require a competent knowledge of German and some fluency and taste in English composition, but the former would require *judgement*, literary and historical, and an immense amount of information.[162]

In addition to these subsidiary activities, women contributed to family welfare by acting as part of a team. They entered the salaried positions available to men, some of these resulting from the growth of state and voluntary institutions. However, within these posts, women's position almost invariably reproduced their domestic role. An Essex parish which had to staff its new workhouse required the governor to 'write a good hand and be something of an accomptant' as well as supervising the male inmates. His wife, as governess, in addition to supervising the females, was to attend the sick and organize lodging, food and clothing. A family enterprise then emerged as the daughter became a teacher in the girls' school attached to the workhouse which was subsequently run by an aunt while the son became master at the boys' school.[163]

With most residential posts, the major difference between a man and a woman was that the former brought his family with him, often to supply domestic help, while the latter was mainly in charge of domestic arrangements for the institution no matter what her subsidiary duties. In these positions, women were often forbidden to bring dependants. A Birmingham Unitarian foundation, the Protestant Dissenting Charity School, advertised in 1836 for a governess who 'must be a single woman or a widow without a family, and about the middle age'. One applicant was refused since she wished to bring an adopted child. The spinster who was appointed later was allowed to have her widowed mother living with her but only after a meeting of the ladies' committee had considered her long service and provided that the arrangement in no way interfered with her duties and there was no financial loss to the school.[164]

The Essex and Colchester Hospital, founded 1820, made a sharp contrast between the men and women in their employ. The trustees, a committee of management and physicians (non-stipendary) were all male and drew up the conditions of service. The resident apothecary was required to be over 35 years of age and trained to dispense drugs. It was his duty to supervise the male patients, including leading their prayers morning and evening. He was provided with board and lodging without restrictions on any family and a salary of £50 a year. The matron was the only woman at staff level. She, too, had to be over 35, but was also required to be a spinster or widow with no dependent children. In addition to supervising and praying with the female patients, she took charge of household goods, kept accounts of provisions and overlooked the wards for cleanliness and order as well as organizing the female nurses and maids. Her rewards in kind were the same as the apothecary but the salary was £30. The nurses, maids, and male orderlies and groundsmen were 'to be to the Apothecary as their master and the Matron as their Mistress', thus reproducing a family model with a sexual division of labour.[165]

In the local records Mary Merryweather was one of the few women in a salaried white-collar post. She had been imported from London to help in Courtaulds' mill where she acted as social worker and disciplinarian for the predominantly female workforce. Her title in the 1851 census is 'Moral Missionary Amongst Factory Hands' and the fact that she boarded nine factory girls in her home shows how closely her position stressed the feminine type of duty.[166] There are examples of less highly placed women adding to family income and sometimes also receiving housing by acting as a gaoler (although this was forbidden by law in the 1830s), and librarians for small private or voluntary societies which were springing up in provincial towns. The Castle Library in Colchester paid its librarian (who was wife of the town gaoler), 11 gns a year or 4s. 6d a week, not enough to survive on even at the lowest middle-class level.[167] On closer inspection many librarians were more involved in keeping the premises clean, lighting fires and providing refreshment at the meetings of the male subscribers, than dealing with books.

A comparison of the activities of a farmer's wife in the late eighteenth century and one in the 1820s illustrates the shift. Both women were married with children but the woman in the earlier period spent her time helping to manage the farm and work people, travelling extensively on horseback to markets and the provincial town to shop, visit the theatre or consult her lawyer. She speaks of 'doing my brewing' and records drawing bills of credit and the sale of 'my turnips'.[168] The woman of the later period is caught up in renovations in the farmhouse, including new kitchen equipment and adding a parlour. Her world is confined to church going, social visits, a little church related philanthropy and family affairs, subjects which the earlier diary certainly does not overlook but which form only a part of its interests.[169]

The same forces which relegated women's economic activity to these shadowy areas, have affected the historical sources. When family status could be tarnished by acknowledging that its womenfolk worked for an income, it is likely that much went unrecorded. Women's marginalization increased as the economy itself became defined as part of the public domain. A sample from the directories for Birmingham, for example, does not list a single female merchant after 1800, yet as late as the 1830s evidence from only a sample of wills produces a bone, timber and marble merchant who left instructions for their wives to take over the business. The pattern is well defined by the field of medicine. Much eighteenth- and early nineteenth-century health care, particularly in the countryside, was still in the hands of women who gathered and grew the herbs which were the basis of most remedies. With enclosure of common lands, sources of supplies were cut back. At the same time, male apothecaries began to make drugs, while the increasing manufacture and sale of commercial cosmetics tended to be run by men. Professional medicine with its specialized training and scientific rationale was closed to women, both in its earlier form based on a knowledge of the classics and the later development of experimental method. But women were not excluded from health *care*. On the contrary, middle-class wives and mothers were seen to have an important, if sharply circumscribed, role as responsible for the fitness of their family through the provision of a healthy home and diet, and careful home nursing in illness. The Birmingham doctor, Pye Henry Chevasse, made this division of labour explicit in his popular books, *Advice to Wives on the Management of Themselves during the Period of Pregnancy, Labour and Suckling* and *Advice to Mothers on the Management of Offspring*; works which increased both his purse and his reputation, locally and nationally.[170]

Some women continued to practise herbal medicine at least for their poorer neighbours, but middle-class taste was turning to the more expensive and prestigious male doctors favoured by the women in both local studies. The struggle over medical territory was particularly centred around childbirth and childcare. The Suffolk poet, George Crabbe, himself trained as a doctor, portrayed the change in the fate of the village midwife, originally recipient of respect from both rich and poor until a young farmer married a townswoman who called in a doctor for her confinement.

> Fame (now his friend) fear, novelty and whim,
> And fashion, sent the varying sex to him. . . .

The doctor gained the custom of the rich, leaving the poor to the midwife:

> 'Nay', said the Doctor, 'dare you trust your wives,
> The joy, the pride, the solace of your lives,
> To one who acts and knows no reason why,
> But trusts, poor hag! to luck for an ally?–
> Who, on experience, can her claims advance,
> And own the powers of accident and chance?

A whining dame, who prays in danger's view,
(A proof she knows not what beside to do;)
What's her experience? In the time that's gone,
Blundering she wrought, and still she blunders on:–
And what is Nature? One who acts in aid
Of gossips half asleep, and half afraid.
With such allies I scorn my fame to blend,
Skill is my luck and courage is my friend;
No slave to Nature, 'tis my chief delight
To win my way and act in her despite:–'[171]

Women, men and occupational identity

Medicine is a striking instance of the general way men's occupations have been shaped by the structure of sexual inequality. This point is often overlooked by studies which concentrate only on women's work, and ignored in general studies of work which usually focus on men without explicitly saying so. It is instructive to look at a range of activities from the local records which encompass both masculine and feminine experience especially in the earlier stages of a person's career. It should also be remembered that young men, too, were at times constrained into positions which were uncongenial to their tastes. Such a young man had to be reconciled to his duty by being reminded of his 'natural' destiny. If he proved restive, these expectations would be made explicit in the sermons he heard, in the moral tales he read and most effectively by his loving relatives and friends. Young Samuel Courtauld was not too eager to join his father in the silk mill for he longed to play the violin and at one point toyed with the idea of entering the Unitarian ministry. His mother wrote to him in 1809:

Consider, dear boy, that the comfort of your old mother and young brothers and sisters may yet depend on your care and industry. I assume this Idea will act as a sufficient stimulus. . . .[172]

It did, and Samuel threw himself into mill management with some enthusiasm.

Middle-class men were expected to be active economically, they had access to patronage, education, training, contacts, experience and legal forms which enhanced these expectations in varying degrees.[173] In the expanding opportunities of the early nineteenth century, some men were able to build careers on previous training and skills. A young man who had been apprenticed to a miller found little difficulty in being taken on to the management of an engineering business, having picked up relevant skills while acting as a millwright.[174] Others started in the related crafts of carpenter and wheelwright. From such a base, virtually a male monopoly, large-scale building operations were mounted where sons or grandsons in several local families became surveyors, estate agents or architects.[175] Through their building interests, these men were also in a position to acquire property and become a powerful presence in the local community, sealing their arrival by marriage into high status families.[176]

One reason why women found it so difficult to operate in these areas was the prohibition on manual skills (outside the domestic) which was so closely tied to their feminine status. The 'common-sense' attention to tools and materials which created an area of mutual interest for many men, from skilled artisans to highly educated scientists, had no female counterpart. Nowhere was this more evident than in the subject of horse culture, a rapidly expanding field. In the eighteenth century, the care and use of horses was steeped in tradition, often allied to the knowledge of 'cunning men' and 'wise women' and it remained so in some isolated rural areas.[177] But with the development of new stock breeding and more valuable animals, the trade of 'farrier' came to be a masculine specialism which in the second quarter of the nineteenth century was evolving into veterinary science.[178] In a small village on the Essex/Cambridge border, a family of labourers who began to specialize as horsemen produced one member who, through informal training and knowledge, set up as a veterinary surgeon. His sons became, respectively, a doctor and a professor of physiology at Cambridge.[179] Occupations connected to the sea provided another sphere of opportunities for middle-class men. Women occasionally were found as merchants or managing wharfing facilities. However, they could never move back and forth between these functions and going to sea themselves, either as a ship's officer, or to carve out a career in the Royal Navy (more open to talent than the Army at this period).

The occupations so far surveyed were based on activities traditionally closed to women. But there were areas from which women had not been excluded. Middle-class girls were positively encouraged to draw and paint and, where resources permitted, were given training in developing their artistic talents. Some reached high standards, even exhibiting locally and nationally. Like their brothers, some of the more accomplished had been trained in the studios and workshops of their fathers. Unlike their brothers, however, what these women could not do, except in the most unusual circumstances, was to become professional artists with a commercial reputation in their own right.[180] High art implied a free floating individualism which ran counter to the modesty and willingness to divert energies to others, demands which were so central to femininity.

The opportunity to turn a knack for drawing into a livelihood was more important for the ordinary young person. In a town like Birmingham, designing for the metal trades might be combined with teaching, as with a man who set up a flourishing Drawing Academy, later run by his son.[181] A Suffolk artisan's son was making £200 a year by mapmaking and surveying at the height of his practice.[182] Birmingham and the market towns of Essex and Suffolk boasted several painters making a living producing portraits and decorative art for a middle-class clientele. A Colchester engraver of 'humble parentage' who had been apprenticed to a local printer, left his provincial origins and pursued his career in the metropolis, where he used his rural background to specialize in landscapes.[183] Many women did engraving, colouring and illustrating but they did so as part of a family. An artistic talent might set them to teaching the neighbourhood daughters or be an aid in obtaining more regular school teaching. However, many must have remained like the young Quaker woman who helped run the house at the farm and brewery of her parents and who did her flower painting on silk by getting up before the household was awake. Her brother became a professional artist.[184]

Middle-class men and women both had become keenly interested in gardening as well as the more theoretical branches of horticulture and botany. Humphrey Repton, who lived most of his life in Essex, had been apprenticed to a wool merchant but had a passion for botanical studies. As a young man he made a deliberate decision to turn this into a profession, using the term *landscape gardening* and passing on the speciality to his son.[185] Opportunities for such professional work were increasing with the creation of scientific bodies and specialist gardens.[186] Commercial nurseries were also an expanding sector for men with more practical gardening experience, and several seed firms such as Thompson and Morgan of Ipswich which were founded in this period have survived into the twentieth century. While undoubtedly many women were vital to the development of a family horticultural business, as a group they had lost their previous prerogative of the farmer and cottager's wife supplying seeds and propagating plants. Women's interest in both gardening and botany was rather guided into a hobby or to act as a healthful 'restorative'.

The lack of opportunity to exchange scientific and practical information, as well as the absence of public recognition for their work, was a special stumbling block for women with interests in botanical subjects as well as horticulture and gardening. Most botanical societies did not admit women, at least not to full membership. The papers they had written might be read out for them by a male member, but women remained isolated from the informal support so vital to building a professional image and expertise.[187] The young men who gathered to search for and study specimen plants and animals in the Natural History Field Clubs were often apothecaries' apprentices or shop men, some of whom later turned their hobby into employment. By the 1840s, the class composition of these associations covered a wide range from artisans to upper middle-class men, but no women were admitted to these clubs.[188] A few women from the local areas wrote and published on botany, natural history and horticulture, often for a juvenile audience. It was clearly more acceptable to express these interests in print from the confines of their own homes.

The experience of a set of twins from a wealthy Suffolk timber merchant's family well illustrates the differing expectations for young men and women. In his late teens, Samuel Scott entered the family business as junior to his uncle. His twin sister, Charlotte, after her education as a young lady was complete, returned to live at home where she developed an interest in botany. When she was about 19, her uncle, head of the family as well as her guardian, indulgently noted that Charlotte's botanical collection and greenhouse occupations 'seem at this time to occupy her greatest share of attention'. Two years later, Samuel had become established as a partner in the business with the prospect of eventually taking charge, while Charlotte's interests had become centred in a mysterious illness, a nervous complaint which gained her uncle's deep concern but which fixed her firmly in a career as an invalid and her botanical interests dwindled.[189] Not all middle-class women with such talents became invalids, of course. Charlotte Scott may have been especially disadvantaged by living in a remote village. Nevertheless, the trivializing of a genuine enthusiasm seems to have been at least as common as the flowering of upper middle-class women in the guise of recognized amateurs of distinction.

It is difficult to judge how women like Charlotte Scott reacted to their situation. Despite the blandness of the sources, there are hints that conflicts over resources within the family were not unknown, particularly between brothers and sisters. It has been seen how both Archibald Kenrick in Birmingham and Samuel Courtauld in Essex as young men starting out in business demanded a lion's share of the family property for their ventures in opposition to their mothers who specifically wished to protect their daughters' interests. The female family members had a difficult case to sustain, for as Samuel somewhat ingenuously explained: 'It is proposed that this money should be actively employed for the more immediate advantage of one individual [himself] but in a general view of the family collectively.' Although he admitted that the property would be 'somewhat endangered' if invested in the mill, like young Kenrick, he won his point since his sisters had in mind to open a school which would only have served for their own short-term support. As soon as the mill was solvent, Samuel gave his sister Sophia a larger allowance so that she could give up going out as a governess and be spared 'all the mortifications' of that position.[190]

When family resources were stretched, it was expected that sisters would assist in educating brothers, if necessary to earn income to enable them to train and to generally underwrite the young men's economic ventures. A widow would often run a school with her daughters in order to give her sons a rudimentary education and have the means for their further training. As one brother later wrote to his sister: 'How you girls toiled that we boys might be well prepared for later life; for which I am ever grateful to you.'[191] The expectation was that when the young man had reached his goal, he would support the mother, aunt or sister who had thus invested in his future. However, this did not invariably follow and some men felt uneasy about admitting that they had been dependent on a woman's work to support them. There exist a few bitter denunciations by sisters who gave support – financial, emotional and in doing all household tasks – only to later find that the brother despised them as ungenteel when he had reached his professional or commercial goal.[192] Others had to stand by and watch a brother lose the common patrimony through mismanagement or personal failure. The notion of female influence must have had an ironic flavour for the wife of a failed shopkeeper whose constant moves of living quarters along with the shop had made her ill with anxiety. Her husband feared losing her: 'so tenderly loved, despite little differences in worldly affairs' when she tried, 'I am sure to be my good Counsellor.'[193]

The restrictions on middle-class women were made up of a combination of forces, including subtle associations of places, activities and images which strongly defined femininity and masculinity. The association of men with the dynamic engine of the industrial age, manufacture, was particularly vivid and, for a variety of reasons already discussed, women's part in a manufacturing enterprise was usually limited. A woman manufacturer in her own right was regarded as an anomaly. The unmarried farmer's daughter who successfully ran a brick and tile kiln on a commercial scale was 6 feet

3 inches tall and had waived all claims to a customary feminine identity; she appears as an oddity in the family chronicle.[194] From childhood play with drawings, tools and bits of machinery indulged in by a boy, the association of masculinity with production persisted. Even where a girl showed an aptitude in that direction it was difficult to sustain. A Birmingham iron master who had made his fortune by improving an iron puddling process, had an eldest daughter with a gift for practical invention. According to a memoir by her son, she turned this to solving household problems. Having noted the wastefulness of the open fire place, from her own templates she cut a piece of iron and mounted it on bricks so reducing draughts and saving coal. As her son commented, 'she anticipated the slow combustion grate'.[195] What he did not add was that she did not turn this invention into a mass produced product which might have made another fortune.

Practical mechanical skills, the heart of the Birmingham metal industry, were clearly outside the rubric of the feminine sphere. But for women the canons of scientific thought were also limited to private affairs and, ultimately, to non-utilitarian ends. The solid education and training in science and rational thought which was given to the daughters of men in groups such as Birmingham's Lunar Society, could be used only within the confines of the household or in female philanthropic ventures. Two grandsons of Lunar Society members were the cousins, Francis Galton and Charles Darwin who both carried the tradition of ordering and classifying their world into their scientific work and through which they gained world-wide recognition in the later nineteenth century. One of Francis Galton's aunts had been raised in a similar atmosphere but lived out a quiet domesticated existence in Birmingham. She applied a systematic world view closer to home. She is recorded as possessing:

a triple inkstand with three coloured inks, triple penwipers and pens; every conceivable apparatus for writing; printed envelopes for her various banks and business correspondents; printed questions for her grooms, 'Has the mare had her corn' etc; a dozen or more cash boxes, elaborately arranged to receive in square labelled compartments each kind of coin from each type of her property. The apparatus for the instruction and relief of the poor – tracts, ounces of tea and sugar, worsted stockings, bundles for mothers' aid etc. etc. were arranged in separate indexed presses, with records of all transactions relating thereto. The crockery ware of the store-room and housekeepers' room was all lettered and all metal articles, pans and pots were duly labelled, as were the garden tools, and there were corresponding labels on the pegs on which they were hung. As many as 100 painted labels have been counted in a flower bed of hers of 12 square feet.[196]

How did women survive?

In both rural and urban areas and over the whole period, women made up between 5 and 15 per cent of the economically active population listed in the directories. However, by mid century the range of their activities had noticeably narrowed. In the 1790s their occupations included gaoler, whitesmith, plumber, butcher, farmer, seedsman (sic), tailor, saddler. Even in the first decades of the new century, male curtain ring, pipe, gun and varnish manufacturers specifically instructed in their wills that their wives should carry on the business. By the 1850s, dressmaking, millinery and teaching were by far the main occupational groupings listed for middle-class women.[197]

The result was a predictable massive overcrowding, and low wages symbolized by the fate of the governess in both fact and fiction. The presence of unpaid family female labour primed with just these skills and waiting in the wings to take over if income did not run to paying for professional services was a constant threat to any attempt at monopoly which women in these occupational groups could muster. In that most egalitarian group, the Quakers, the women of the 1780s and 1790s had run shops and schools and roamed the countryside as lay ministers, but by the next generation they were transmuted into respectable domesticity. Lucy Greenwood, born in the 1820s, had a mother active in the Quaker ministry who aided the wholesale/retail business that laid the foundations of her son's successful business career. Lucy, however, took no part in such activities but spent her life voluntarily organizing and running the Halstead Industrial School for girls. She never married and lived on the school premises, where for over thirty years she was as absorbed in its daily life as any owner of a proprietary school, but far from making a living from her work, she spent her patrimony lavishly in its service.[198]

By mid century, whenever family finances would permit, the energy, organizational skill and sense of commitment which middle-class women had put into economic activity were deflected into domestic affairs. They managed a set of servants or themselves undertook domestic tasks and organization which set a standard of personal services unknown before (or since). Occasionally women were able to turn these formidable skills and energy into publicly recognized philanthropy using organizing techniques and business routines picked up from their close association with the family business and various male relatives and friends. The scale of charity affairs, like bazaars organized and run by women, gives a glimpse of this hidden world. As their chronicler, Prochaska, has written, 'philanthropic enterprise was, in a sense, *laissez-faire* capitalism turned in on itself'.[199]

From this study, the appropriate question to be asked may not be what occupations were held by middle-class women in this period, but rather how were these women surviving? The brief answer must be: as part of a family or household enterprise, whether working entirely on the domestic side, contributing behind the scenes, engaged in part-time paid work, living on and contributing investment income or more likely a combination of any of these options. Even a crude indicator like the 1851 census shows 109 daughters over age 30 living with parents compared to fifty-eight sons in the local areas. The census sample from both areas contained 296 widows, 200 or 68 per cent who were household heads. Of the remaining widows who were not in a position to head a household, 55 per cent were living either as mothers or mothers-in-law, that is with adult children. Just under a half of these dependent widows were in the homes of married men. Another 21 per cent were living with other widows who headed the house-hold, an example of female kin and friends pooling resources.

The women who were in occupations needing little capital and much energy included a high proportion of younger widows. 43 per cent of female household heads in trade were widows in the 25–55 age range. Of those in professional occupations (overwhelmingly teaching) almost all were in the same group and 60 per cent of these were widowed. Older widows predominated in occupations requiring some property; they were the majority in farming and innkeeping. Many of these widows would be holding the inn or farm for a son to take over. However, by far the largest group of female household heads in the census sample was of 'independent' means. Edgbaston was peppered with households such as number 16 Hagley Road where Sarah Green, age 75, lived on the rental of house properties and provided a home for four middle aged children, a sister and an unmarried nephew, all without occupations and in receipt of rents and annuities. At number 18 on the same road, were two spinster sisters in their late 60s, existing on a combination of landed property and investments. With a house at a rateable value of £23 a year and two female servants, they were comfortably off, but by no means had the resources to move in the highest Edgbaston circles.[200]

Two-thirds of female household heads living on 'independent means' were widows, but they were considerably older – 67 per cent were over 55 (and one-quarter actually over 70). This pattern was even more marked for upper middle-class women of independent means and, in any case, the upper middle class made up 83 per cent of all independent female household heads. In Edgbaston, virtually all the upper middle-class female household heads were over 40, as were almost all in the town centres of Essex and Suffolk. This contrasts with the position in central Birmingham where a large group of female household heads were in trade at a modest level, 25 per cent, and another 15 per cent were innkeepers mostly in the younger age band.

From the local studies it is evident that women's decision to enter the market depended on their control over family property. As the discussion has emphasized, the form of property – whether in land, building, investments, skill or individual income – was an important element. Professional men made up only 5 per cent and salaried men only 1 per cent of those even making a will, although they were 20 per cent and 13 per cent respectively of the middle class in the census sample.[201] The widows or orphaned daughters of these men, who had access to enough house room, could replace income by taking in pupils, lodgers or boarders. Another expedient was to let the home, with or without shop premises, and live at a more modest level using the rent as income, a course easier to follow if the house was owned but quite possible under sub-leasing.

These strategies confirm that the major identity of most middle-class women was undoubtedly familial rather than occupational, whatever *tasks* they were actually doing. Of the women over the age of 25 in the census sample who were not households heads, two-thirds were wives living with their husbands, and the other one-third were female relatives. Of these, the largest single group, as may be expected, was unmarried daughters followed by sisters (see Tables 6 and 7, Appendix 3). Prescriptive literature about the desirability of sisters being companions to their brothers who would support them is confirmed by numerous cases in the local records.

From the census sample, it appears that men took on the support of sisters-in-law and mothers-in-law in addition to adult daughters and their own sisters, while female headed households were more likely to contain mothers, aunts and nieces as well as sisters and daughters. In many of these cases, women contributed both labour and income, whatever the expected direction of support might have been. Helping with housekeeping and childcare or sick nursing was the preferred existence for a single woman or widow and might bring some of the authority and privileges of being mistress of a household. Many of the numerous female visitors found in middle-class households on census night could well have been acting in such a capacity for friends; a quarter of all widows who were not themselves household heads were listed as visitors. However, women's position in these households was vulnerable. Not only were they exposed to the same vicissitudes as men within the family enterprise, they were also ultimately dependent on the capacity and good will of relatives and friends, not to speak of the emotional and psychological dependency they might have built up over the years. A minority of women seem to have spread the risks by combining resources with other women. The chances of an adult unmarried woman living as a relative in a household headed by a woman were almost double what would have been expected if adult female relatives had been randomly distributed among all households in the census sample.[202]

For a middle-class woman of the early nineteenth century, gentility was coming to be defined by a special form of femininity which ran directly counter to acting as a visibly independent economic agent. Despite the fact that women could hold property, their marital status always pre-empted their economic personality. The ramifications of this fact for their social and economic position were profound. It can be argued that nineteenth-century middle-class women represent a classic case of Parkin's distinction between property as active capital and property as possession, in this case enforced by coverture. Absence of property as capital has been seen as the most powerful element in 'social closure', that is exclusion from control over one's own life chances.[203] This conception lay at the heart of women's sexual and political dependency, a situation recognized by early feminists whose first aim was reform of married women's property. While material circumstances differed widely, all strata within the middle class operated within the same legal and customary framework. The forms of property and inheritance they practised were not significantly different. The reading material offered, the sermons preached and, most of all, their own experiences, offered few alternatives to the conventional view of female respectability with all its contradictory consequences. Many of these contradictions flowed directly from the dominant upper middle-class conception. Mrs Ellis expressed this view with chilling finality:

gentlemen may employ their hours of business in almost any degrading occupation and, if they but have the means of supporting a respectable establishment at home, may be gentlemen still; while, if a lady but touch any article, no matter how delicate, in the way of trade, she loses caste, and ceases to be a lady.[204]

Part Three

Everyday Life: Gender in Action

Introduction to Part Three

In this period, the generations of the middling ranks were actively shaping their world. We have seen how they were reinterpreting their Christian heritage and building commercial and professional institutions from existing forms of property. A turn of the kaleidoscope brings into view further facets of their project: a range of organizations and behaviours helped contain the tension between intense application to business and religious goals. These focused on careful regulation of spatial, temporal and social categories. In finding a cosmic and mundane place for themselves, no task was greater than that of definition and demarcation: of people, places, time and matter. The content and boundaries of categories were delineated by constant discussion, trial and negotiation.

Of these categories, the distinction between the public world and the private arena was central. But this was by no means yet fixed, the shifting ambit of public and private was as much as territory of the mind as physical space. As time passed, these divisions became embodied in bricks and mortar, in carefully regulated social interaction and rules of etiquette. Even within the enclosed world of the home, however, some spaces, times and activities were more public than others. Only gradually did 'private' functions retreat to a hidden core. As the spatial and temporal quarantine between the public and the private grew, they were ever more identified with gender. A masculine penumbra surrounded that which was defined as public while women were increasingly engulfed by the private realm, bounded by physical, social and psychic partitions. Men, in their privileged position, moved between both sectors. These dichotomies and their association with gender identity, inevitably emphasized hierarchy, the fixing of individual social and sexual place.

Such massive reordering necessitated leaps in imagination interspersed with painstaking, minute, even trivial changes. This section concerns the living out of the categories created by the middle class. First we examine family relationships in all their contradictory richness. Increasingly these were played out in the private home, distanced from the market place. But the doors of these homes were not yet closed to a tide of informal visits for business and friendship. Taken together with children, visitors and other supernumeraries, these households were relatively large: 6.2 as an average for the group in 1851. As expected, this was higher in the upper middle class with 7.6 and 5.6 in the lower.[1] This compares with a range of 4.27 to 5.41 for the country as a whole in the same period.[2] The presence of non-kin, mainly apprentices and shopmen, shows up in the average of 7.1 for trade households, and the largest household size at 7.4 was among lower professionals where schools predominated. But the size of middle-class households also depended on whether a man or a woman was at the head. Twice as many female headed households had fewer than five members as those headed by men. In fact, the experience of life for two-thirds of individuals was in a household headed by a married man with over five members (and for 22 per cent over ten).[3]

Family and household relationships were framed by the physical setting which middle-class entrepreneurs as well as ideologues did so much to promote in homes and gardens. Many families, having increased incomes, were preoccupied with new patterns of consumption: what goods to buy, how much, how to display and care for them. Not only their houses and furnishings and gardens, but their bodies, personal habits, clothes and language had to be cast into new moulds. As always, gender and class categories were most clearly stated through the quotidian.

At the same time, the public sphere was being recast. Men were active in creating the framework of markets, voluntary societies and a nascent state organization. The study of the public sphere in the local communities brings out the affinity of these organizations both with each other and with the family enterprise. The story of upper middle-class men's leadership over subaltern ranks in the lower middle class and the shadowy but vital role of women in public, forms the substance of the last chapter.

7 'Our family is a little world': family structure and relationships

Marriage is generally the origin of the elementary community of which larger communities . . . and ultimately the nation are constituted and on the conjugal state of the population, its existence, increase and diffusion, as well as manners, character, happiness and freedom ultimately depend. . . .

Registrar General, Introduction to the Census, 1851

The idea of the family framed middle-class provincial life from the enterprise to the organization of consumption. Some families even created a formal 'family fund' to pool and redistribute individual incomes.[1] However, the definition of the family was never rigid, its boundaries were indistinct and shifting. Kin could go unrecognized while friends could be an intimate part of family life. Visiting, for longer or shorter periods, was widespread. In the local areas on census night, 1850, visitors made up 11 per cent of individuals over 25 (excluding household head). Family may have started at the biological core of parents and children but the social concept of marriage was its heart and this strengthened over the period. For example, the endorsement of illegitimate children waned. In wills, legacies for illegitimate offspring cluster in the earliest decades.

As in any kinship system, some relationships even when acknowledged were played down, others were privileged. A youngster would be told that he or she 'credited' (resembled in feature and personality) certain family adults. A mother urged her adult son living in London to wear mourning for an uncle.[2] One after the other, the daughters of Robert Martineau, the Birmingham brass manufacturer, were sent as companions to their aunt, Harriet, in much the way that an Essex girl paid a long visit to her father's spinster sisters after the death of their mother. She was rewarded by being told how she 'much endeared herself' to her aunts by her 'considerate and affectionate attention during their severe trial'.[3]

In the late eighteenth century, technical and organizational developments fostered family relationships. Increasing literacy, the introduction of the postal service, fast and relatively cheap travel by coach, steamer and later railway, all encouraged family and friends to keep in touch. In the 1770s it might take several weeks to hear news of death in the family, but by the early nineteenth century family members could be alerted to attend more distant funerals.

Inclusion of relationships further from the nuclear core helped to create the dense network which gave security to individuals. Large numbers within each family, combined with flexible boundaries, contributed to cohesion of the group as a whole, as well as defusing potential conflict from intense intra-family attachments. There was an element of choice in interpreting the concept of family.[4] But the same factors raised problems. The sheer size of many families created centrifugal forces which pulled interests apart. An Essex woman feared that the death of the widowed matriarch, who had raised fifteen children and already had over fifty grandchildren, would doom her family to dispersal.[5] A group this size was simply too large to hold together by the accretion of gossip, letter writing, gift giving, visiting and mutual services which formed the web of family life, while the division of the original couple's resources could cause dissension. Inevitably families waxed and waned as younger members broke away to create their own families. Without land or a great house, on the one hand, or a permanent business house, on the other, a family was almost certain to disintegrate through time. High mortality meant inevitable break-up of many marriages and that a large number of people were widowed in middle age.[6]

Although familial boundaries were flexible, the concept of family was framed by Judaic-Christian tradition and law, overlaid by custom which elevated a model of gender and age relations giving primacy to older men. The implications for men's power over women's life chances were not only accepted but applauded. Specific categories of age, gender and function were seen as necessary to staff a family. If these were not filled biologically, surrogates were found. In particular, men and women acted as educators, sponsors or even 'pro-parents' (taking over parental functions) to many youngsters beside or in addition to their own, partly because high mortality and morbidity constantly menaced family continuity.

Certain relationships were reinforced by both the needs of the enterprise and religious belief. Both arenas bolstered motherhood and the role of sisters. The emphasis on certain relationships and their close association with stereotyped gender characteristics provided a stable framework for individuals but, at the same time, could generate tensions. Subordinate, weak femininity and strong, dominating masculinity were belied in adult women's power over small boys, for example. Such contradictory situations inherent in family structure were compounded by personalities which ran counter to expectations. Within the gendered characteristics, too, there were contradictory elements. Idealized womanhood was asexual and chaste, yet the supreme goal for women was marriage and motherhood, conditions which publicly proclaimed sexuality. As always, people seemed to manage by picking their way through the discrepancies, often saying one thing and doing another. Tensions shimmer through letters, diaries and in the fantasy of fiction or poetry. Often accommodation gave way to sullen retreat but on rare occasion flared with spectacular violence.[7]

The role of marriage in family formation

Marriage was the economic and social building block for the middle class; it was the basis of a new family unit. On marriage men assumed economic and jural responsibility for their wives and the expected brood of children. With marriage, women assumed their full adult status. The process of courtship and marriage was a serious step for both men and women, not usually undertaken until their middle to late 20s. For active Christians, marriage was central to their deeply held beliefs about the family. An elder of a Quaker congregation wrote in the commonplace book of an Essex ironmonger who was about to be married:

I consider you now as entering the more arduous scenes of Life and filling more important Stations than during your single State and most earnestly desire you may now on your entrance into the arduous paths, be wisely directed, for much depends on this important crisis.[8]

The system of individual choice of partner under careful monitoring has been described. While compatibility was sought, romantic attraction was played down. A newly fledged Essex solicitor and committed Independent (like his fiancée whom he had met at chapel), wrote to a friend of his engagement: 'I have no visions of Felicity, I wish not the intenseness of pleasures, they will soon destroy, mine are the pursuits of comfort.'[9]

Both men and women expected to contribute to a marriage but not in the same way. The Puritan tradition of domesticity included the ideal of woman as helpmeet. While this gave her a central role within marriage, it in no way implied overturning man's superiority in public affairs. Indeed, it aided the view of women as home-centred by nature. An indication of the increasingly protective and authoritative role of men is seen in the age differentials between husband and wife. Until the seventeenth century, there was an idea that a man would do well to marry an older woman with property and skill, but by the end of the eighteenth century, this was increasingly viewed as distasteful. The young, dependent, almost child-like wife was portrayed as the ideal in fiction, etchings, songs and poetry. Such an image of fragility and helplessness enhanced the potency of the man who was to support and protect her. From the local records with usable information covering 1780 to 1850, 73 per cent of husbands were older than their wives by an average of 4.3 years.[10] In the census sample, 52 per cent of husbands were older than their wives but 23 per cent, or just under one-quarter, were more than 5 years older. As might be expected, the age gap was widest in the upper strata of the group. Among the upper middle class, 60 per cent of husbands were older than their wives and 31 per cent, or just under one-third, were more than five years older. By far the majority of remaining couples were of the same age and in only 12 per cent of cases were wives older (8 per cent in the upper middle class). For professional couples the gap was greater than the average, while among couples of independent means, three-quarters of husbands were older, with 37 per cent more than five years older.[11] Both these groups were at the forefront of promulgating domestic ideals.

For a man, settling into marriage often coincided with taking on new responsibilities in business or profession. It was also seen as a way of containing potentially distracting sexual adventures. John Howard Galton, the youngest of a Birmingham banking family and the darling of his mother, became involved in an affair at the age of 23 and was packed off to the continent as rumours circulated of an illegitimate baby born in Ireland. He returned to make a good marriage with the daughter of a leading manufacturer.[12] An Evangelical cleric in Suffolk saw marriage as 'the great civilizer'. The married state 'enables every man to rest secure in his enjoyments . . . with this security the mind is at liberty to expand and has leisure to look abroad and engage in the pursuits of knowledge, science and virtue'.[13] Birmingham's Joseph Priestley conveys what this meant in describing his marriage:

a happy connexion, my wife being a woman of an excellent understanding, much improved by reading, of great fortitude and strength of mind, and of a temper in the highest degree affectionate and generous; feeling strongly for others, and little for herself. Also greatly excelling in everything relating to household affairs, she entirely relieved me of all concern of that kind, which allowed me to give all my time to the prosecution of my studies, and the other duties of my station.[14]

Such benefits, both tangible and intangible, had to be paid for. As the period progressed, couples were less willing to start marriage without sufficient resources. Matthew Davenport Hill noted that his parents had married in 1701 with an income of 1 guinea a week which would have been intolerable in his own generation.[15] Bachelors saved towards marriage as did George Cadbury when the business was not doing too well. He walked everywhere and pared his personal expenses to £25 a year.[16] The first task after being accepted as a suitor was to work out the problem of 'how to keep a wife'.[17] A young clergyman with little property fell in love with the daughter of a Birmingham banker. The couple decided he should no longer visit as it was clear that they would not have enough to marry on. However, when her father died several years later, they discussed whether it would be prudent to marry on £500 to £600 a year. After much family consultation, they did so as soon as her share of the inheritance was paid.[18]

Nevertheless, families as well as young people themselves, were not enthusiastic about long engagements. They had already waited until their mid 20s before contemplating courtship, marriage was acknowledged as a safeguard to virtue, as James Luckcock reminded his audience of teachers from the Birmingham Old and New Meeting Sunday schools.[19] Men were expected to 'speak' in a courtship, although the process was still relatively informal with siblings often playing a part. A young Birmingham chemist in the throes of courtship half seriously regretted the passing of the 'patriarchal epoch' when fathers relieved their sons of 'this perplexing business' when a man has to 'satisfy all mental and sentient tastes . . . to secure a companion and helpmeet, neither soar too high or to descend too low, neither too nicely critical or too easily caught; not so easy to hit all this'.[20] Men had the advantage of being able to initiate a proposal, but they risked rejection. Archibald Kenrick, the Birmingham manufacturer, resolved to speak to the young lady of his choice, and then was devastated by her lack of interest.[21]

The significance of marriage for middle-class men cannot be overestimated. It profoundly affected their economic, social, spiritual and emotional life as well as everyday standard of comfort. This was demonstrated forcefully when a wife was away. A Birmingham manufacturer spoke of his wife's absence as 'something like the loss of a part of myself'.[22] When an Essex doctor's wife was sent to London for medical treatment, he wrote: 'I am now alone at home which is very dull and dreary. . . . I now know the value of my absent friend and the feelings connected to the married state.'[23] The death of a Suffolk manufacturer's wife in middle age left him feeling as if he had lost his 'dearest earthly treasure'.[24] The successive remarriages of men who had lost their wives (often in childbirth) were partially motivated by the need for someone to run their households and look after their children. An Essex farmer left with three young children explained that 'man was not born to live alone. Having experienced much comfort in the married state, and my children requiring some careful female to manage and bring them up, I soon determined to look out again'. This he did and married again not once but three times.[25]

If marriage was thus an 'important crisis' in a man's life, it could be the key to a woman's future. With the closing of respectable means of earning their own livelihood, some women felt forced into marriage by circumstances, unwilling to remain a burden on their family. A young Suffolk woman who had gone to teach in a school when her father's farm failed, admitted that she married to gain a home, although 'my heart had never been entangled and was not at all ready to put on chains'.[26] Several women complained of pressure to marry from well-meaning friends when they would have preferred to remain single. For some women marriage presented problems with its structured dependency and burden of children. A young married woman wrote to her mother with satisfaction that her husband generally let her have her own way and was generous with an allowance for clothes and pocket money. She felt she was fortunate, knowing 'how men can plague their wives if they have a mind'.[27] There are various hints of the contradictions surrounding marriage for women. The commonplace book of an Essex farmer's young daughter in the 1830s includes several entries by older siblings and brothers-in-law which stress the desirability of marriage. The 'Lament of the Single Girl' emphasizes the disadvantages of a single life. 'Lines on Marriage', which expresses women's doubts, has a young man answer:

> This independence which you prize so high?
> What is it? Solitude and Apathy!
> Like some dejected Vine near which is found
> No sheltering Elm to raise it from the ground.[28]

For those women who had a satisfactory home life with an assured income, such considerations weighed heavily. Rebecca Solly was at the younger end of a large family of prosperous Essex Unitarians. When she was still living at home, aged 27, she wrote in her diary: 'I cannot wish to conceal from myself a gradual alteration taking place in my character, a respect and love for the duties of a single life, a dread of the selfishness, the littleness, the increase of worldly cares which accompanie [sic] marriage.' She determined that she would never unite herself 'but to one I can esteem and respect and who will be my first and last friend in adversity'.[29] The expected difference in age and experience between husband and wife could have added to such apprehensions. Far from fleeing the stereotypical 'surplus woman' position, many of these women seem to have regarded the serious step of marriage as a not unmixed blessing.

The actual business of courtship presaged many of these dilemmas. Women had to wait on men to make the first move, although brothers, sisters or friends could be used to act as go-betweens and alert a young man to the woman's inclinations. The daughter of a Birmingham manufacturer had felt some interest in a young man from a similar background but then decided against him. He was delicately told that he should no longer call at the house but some months later she changed her mind. Utilizing a friend as an intermediary, she reinstated the young man as a suitor.[30] In courtship affairs, depending on a brother could be a two-edged weapon. Some exercised censorship, some whose sisters were acting as their housekeepers or who benefited financially from keeping their sisters single, could try to prevent a marriage, while others could try to forward a match for their own purposes. Rebecca Solly, at 29, was being urged into marriage to one of her brother's friends when inquiries by her mother into the man's character stopped the negotiations. Another brother then introduced Samuel Shaen, a fellow Unitarian and an attorney whom she later married. It was Samuel's attentions to her mother at dinner which first aroused her admiration and he asked her to sing that evening, events which kept her 'awake half the night'. But subsequent silence made her think she might be mistaken. Nevertheless, 'enquiring how large his Income was just passed through my mind' and later that month, Samuel wrote to her mother who answered as Rebecca dictated. The following week he rode over and for a short time they were alone together.

Perhaps in the corner of the room might Cupid have been seen laughing at my proud and fancied independence – So it was I believed myself as free when I left the library that day as when I entered it – however I will now acknowledge . . . my meditations were not very old maidish and I certainly wished that money at least might not conclude the Affair.[31]

The financial negotiations were not completed for another fortnight and it was only then that 'the first kiss of love was imprinted on parting'.

Samuel again came to dinner and some 'serious conversation . . . on religion concerning which I felt considerable anxiety' resolved that second most important issue. Rebecca Solly's following diary entries indicate that women as well as men were not indifferent to physical attraction:

That Evening and the next day love was not far distant but still I was not prepared for what passed at the Harpsichord at night – He read a copy of a letter my mother had written to his and his distress at its coldness was most agitating to me and unconsciously I said something expressing his power over my heart. Dear fellow, yes, I owe him not my beloved husband but my doting, my almost maddened lover's burning countenance.

Even as she wrote the entry describing the first kiss, she 'felt the blood rush into my cheeks and recall the feelings of that feverish moment'.[32]

Not all courtships ran as smoothly as that of Rebecca Solly and Samuel Shaen. Their eldest daughter fell in love with her cousin, son of Rebecca's brother with whom the Shaens had quarrelled bitterly. She was sent off to visit relatives in Germany and it was only when she seemed to be going into a decline that they relented.[33] A Suffolk merchant, acting as head of the family, was more successful in stopping the marriage of his niece by sending her off to the seaside. She had said she would die if not allowed to marry her chosen one, but she returned to a sanctioned match with a local doctor.[34] In this period, some of the contested choices of young women were in terms of religious commitment rather than erotic attachments. Worldly, unconverted parents sought a more business-like arrangement. William Marsh's first wife Maria had to reconcile filial duty with Evangelical fervour in uniting with the young clergyman. The opposition of her widowed mother meant a long period of waiting until the older woman relented and was herself converted.[35]

An older woman with her own income would be given more freedom of choice but even here, family pressure could be intense. Sophia Galton had remained at home to look after her elderly father while her siblings had all married. After his death, her life felt lonely and without purpose. To the shock and disapproval of her relatives, she married her father's trusted bank clerk, a match 'totally beneath her in every way' as a niece wrote, although she also admitted that her aunt always appeared happy.[36] However, the fact that Sophia had made no settlement of her property away from her husband and that the reputation of the family would be degraded was uppermost in the minds of her brothers, one of whom wrote to another: 'I suppose there is not a low beer shop in the district that has not canvassed the affair well over' and confessed that he had not shown his face in Birmingham for three weeks.[37] Sophia Galton felt hurt that her brothers seemed more concerned about these issues than her personal happiness.[38] However, the possibility of unscrupulous fortune hunters was one of the dangers which brothers felt called upon to prevent, no matter how heavy handed such protection could sometimes be.

The mother of a young woman who was to marry a Birmingham Quaker wrote to him about her daughter shortly before the wedding: 'I trust she will find a father, a brother and a friend all united in one of the tenderest and kindest of husbands.'[39] This description captures the ideal of an early nineteenth-century marriage where the more mature husband would care for, guide and advise his young wife. Love would be tender rather than passionately erotic. The dependent position of a wife was an opportunity for her to use moral and spiritual influence. Yet such marriage faced almost inevitable difficulties. A woman like Rebecca Solly had education, property, a similarity of tastes and outlook and an obvious sexual attraction. Even in such favourable circumstances, trouble arose for the Shaens over money matters, the upbringing of their nine children and loyalties to their respective kin. Samuel's career faltered with set-backs in the post-war Essex economy. Rebecca felt 'that my endeavours to sooth are sometimes ill-judged' and she resented his heavy handed jokes. She pondered on whether it was right to fail to sympathize with her husband or oppose his unrealistic habit of building 'castles in the air'.[40] Doubts about slavishly following the model of total subordinate are briefly hinted at even by writers like Mrs Ellis, although almost always because of the evil effects on men, turning them into monsters of selfishness.[41] Rebecca Solly Shaen was grateful that there were so few important differences between Samuel and herself, but how to handle those tensions that arose within the accepted wifely framework troubled her considerably.

The contradiction between the equality of Christian souls and the acceptance of structured inequality in the practice of marriage was at the heart of
this dilemma. James Luckcock deeply believed in the equality of his
marriage, yet so completely did he speak for his wife that at the time of a
severe illness when he thought he might be dying, *he* wrote a poem about
himself in her voice. Entitled 'My Husband' it catalogued his thoughtful
and caring qualities (see also Appendix 1):

> Who first inspired my virgin breast,
> With tumults not to be expressed,
> And gave to life unwonted zest?
> > My husband.
>
> Who told me that his gains were small,
> But that whatever might befal,
> To me he'd gladly yield them all?
> > My husband.
>
> Who shun'd the giddy town's turmoil,
> To share with me the garden's toil,
> And joy with labour reconcile?
> > My husband.
>
> Whose arduous struggles long maintain'd
> Adversity's cold hand restrain'd
> And competence at length attain'd?
> > My husband.[42]

Whatever the excesses of a Luckcock, this was a period when men were
still closely involved in domestic life, just as women were still often active
in the family enterprise. While the roles of father and mother were seen as
distinct, the responsibilities and pleasures of parenthood were common and
regarded as the most solemn of a lifetime. As the Rev. John Angell James
said: 'It is indeed an awful thing to be a parent.'[43] The large number of
children in each family has been noted from the local records. The frequent
remarriage of widowers who then started second or even third families
raised these figures. These numerous children were produced despite the
late age of marriage, a combination indicating more a need for youthful
labour and longer training than a conscious desire to reduce the total
number of births. There is little evidence from the local records that large
families were actively discouraged which would have been, in any case,
contrary to religious belief.

The unusual demographic constellation of late marriage and large families
produced certain significant family characteristics. The most immediately
obvious was the sheer numbers in many families despite the depredations
of infant and childhood mortality. Rebecca Solly Shaen was the youngest
of fifteen children. She married at 29 and had nine children in the next
thirteen years. Her sixth child who was born a week after her own mother's
death was that lady's fiftieth grandchild and this was by no means unique.[44]
A consequence of such large numbers was that even in the commodious

living quarters of the upper strata, families of mixed ages, sex and temperament lived in close proximity. No wonder discipline and the rituals of order
were seen as absolute necessities.

A second result was an inevitable gap between the oldest and youngest
siblings within a family. The elder group might well have children of their
own near in age to their young sisters and brothers. The ensuing *intermediate generation* would be compounded by second marriages with step
and half siblings.[45] The possibility of surviving grandparents for the younger
members of the family would be slight since their own parents would
have been in their 40s or more when they were born. Adults performing
'grandparent' functions would often be found instead among middle aged
aunts and uncles. Older siblings often took much responsibility for younger
where the parents were dead or incapable through illness or age. Men took
on the wardship of younger brothers, setting them up in apprenticeships
and acting as trustees; elder sisters frequently aided or substituted for a
mother's care. Younger unmarried siblings in their teens or early 20s, not
yet involved in their own family life, could be an important source of
emotional and material help to the children of their older brothers and
sisters, making welcome playmates and companions to their young nieces
and nephews. The household of James Ransome, the second generation
partner in the Ipswich engineering firm, contained his brother's teenage son
who was apprenticed to the firm as well as Mrs Ransome's young sister
who helped care for the ten children. When Mrs Ransome died leaving a
houseful of young children, her sister stayed on to become the stereotypical
beloved maiden aunt. These celibate young adults provided not only a pool
of labour for house and business, but could act as a buffer between parents
and children.[46]

Fatherhood

The recognized head of such households was the eldest male: the husband
and father or, in his absence, brother, brother-in-law, or eldest son. He
was the civil as well as religious representative. He exemplified external
authority and the Fatherhood of God; and he usually controlled economic
resources. There is scattered evidence that some men exercised their power
in a direct and domineering manner. But the local sources more often point
to an intense involvement of men with their families, and a loving interest
in their children's lives. In any case, the religious community would have
checked an openly harsh display of naked power and many of these households were still open to the coming and going of numerous visitors and
kin. A Colchester attorney took full charge of his seven children when his
wife was invalided with continuous childbearing. According to his son, 'the
realizing of a Utopian notion of family affection' was the mainspring of his
father's life. After the death of the eldest daughter and the eldest son's loss
at sea, the father became even more reluctant to see his other children
growing towards independence.[47] In situations like this, loving care could
extend paternal authority. A wool merchant, as a paragon of fatherhood,
often used to speak proudly of his family as a 'republic' but, as his daughter
later recalled, 'to which we, as children were inclined to add *sotto voce*,

with a dictator at its head'.[48] Such fathers effectively used love to control.
George Courtauld was both demanding and interfering and reminded his
adult children that he had loved them from the cradle. 'I have been a nursing
father [*sic*] to all of you.'[49]

Many of these men revelled in their role as fathers. According to their
religious convictions, children were given by Heaven as an obligation but
also a delight. A Birmingham bookseller confessed that 'my children are
my treasure and my happiness. I have ardently wished I might not be
separated from them. . . . The world would only exhibit a barren desert
without them'.[50] The nonconformist publisher, Josiah Conder, co-author
and friend of the Taylor sisters, was moved and excited by the birth of his
first child in 1815. He saw the event as a link with the past and the future.
His friend, the poet Southey, already a father himself, wrote to him in
congratulation: '. . . when they begin to know you, and you can handle
their soft frames without fear, they very soon lay fast hold upon a father's
heart'.[51] Such men had themselves grown up in large families and as boys
been familiar with babies and small children, often doing some informal
baby minding. A Quaker apprentice spending time with his older brother's
small children observed that 'most babies are interesting little things'. For
such a teenage boy whose religious principles and steady application to
work cut him off from many elements of play – dancing, music, rowdy
behaviour of various sorts – the company of young children must have
been refreshing.[52] There is ample evidence that into old age, uncles, fathers
and grandfathers played with the numerous children who filled their houses
and gardens.

It can be surmised that while the regular care of very young infants was
in the hands of women, men were at least occasionally left responsible for
children, although often with the aid of a female servant. When Ruth
Courtauld went to visit her own family in Ireland, George was left in Essex
for months at a time with several of the children. In a letter she inquires if
the 2 year old 'still sleeps with Papa'.[53] When a Birmingham banker's wife
was away in 1824, her husband sent a report about daily life at home:

Bosco and myself exhibit a picture of domestic happiness, for we discourse not
wrangle, whilst the weighty subjects which we discuss are rather relieved than
interrupted by the prattle of Rosabel serving as a kind of *burden* to the music of
our discussions. We are all very good too. I have been to church with Bosco,
and after that I have gathered acorns with Rosabel. So there is nothing among us
but love and health and happiness and peace.[54]

Fathers seem to have been especially concerned during the frequent
illnesses of their children. The deeply religious found the threatening
illnesses of young children a test of belief; fathers hovered over convalescing
daughters and sons. Some fathers were actively involved with nursing,
including sitting up at nights with the patient. Archibald Kenrick's wife
wrote in a letter about her young son's severe fall: 'I am so thankful that
Archibald was at home to foment him himself, for he says it was done
thoroughly and we know he manages it so much better than anybody else
can.'[55]

It was the death of a child which brought out paternal feelings most strongly. In the case of sons, the father's role as protector and guide included starting the boy in a career, the budding young life which had been the 'strongest root which fastened a man to the world' in the words of a father who had lost his only son.[56] For daughters there was rather the loss of companionship and service. The sentiments expressed by a Birmingham banker at the death of his daughter both demonstrate the depths of his grief and document the psychic benefits derived by a father from her feminine attentions:

I am so overwhelmed with the sudden loss of my precious child, that I scarcely know how to write. The dear girl just entering a time of life – She was so serviceable and attentive to the little things that concerned us, as well as the more important ones. She is constantly before me in every movement I take, remembering how joyfully she met me on my return from Town in the omnibus, was the first to open the door, and come to meet me – indeed it seemed to her a pleasure in every way to anticipate my wishes, that I cannot express the sorrow it has brought over my mind.[57]

The intensity of feeling between a father and his children must of necessity be attenuated when the family was numerous. This is recognized in a poem copied by a Suffolk farmer's wife, 'The Youngling of the Flock'. The poet pleads a place for 'another claimant . . . though my heart be crowded close'. The cry of this frail baby stirs the 'father's heart to do and dare' in order to make the 'sojourn fair', but above all, this youngling will be his 'prop, his blessing and his pride' in old age, an expectation which makes up for the burden of support.[58] The ambivalence suggested by this poem and echoed in several family records was more directly expressed in the diary of a Colchester farmer who laconically recorded in 1835: 'An additional calamity in the shape of another son born today' and twenty months later, 'A dreadful calamity in the birth of a 4th son today.'[59]

Fathers came into their own as companions and teachers to older children. They are found taking children on holiday outings, going for walks with them, and teaching them skills, especially outdoor activities. A Quaker tanner from an Essex village played imaginative games with his nine children and 'shone brightly' in their company. He taught his daughters to ride and his sons to swim.[60] Fathers told stories and were favourites to read aloud while the women were busy with needlework. James Ransome, who was heavily involved in the public affairs of Ipswich as well as the family iron foundry, was a much loved father of ten children who found time to take them for walks on Sundays and weekday evenings to the shipping docks and occasionally to the works. In the garden he made a 'quiet little bower' in an oak tree with an entrance of rustic steps.[61]

Paternal duties also included the enforcing of discipline and instruction in serious subjects such as handling money. Samuel Tertius Galton insisted that his son at boarding school keep strict accounts. He wrote advice on study habits in language befitting a banker: 'Every hour is precious. Let it produce its effect and lay the foundation of habits of energy and application and furnish you with a rich fund of morality and information – this will be your stock in trade in future.'[62] Fathers led family prayers which named wrong doers and praised the virtuous before the gathered household. They made the ultimate decisions on schooling, apprenticeships, careers and approval of marriage partners, although undoubtedly heavily influenced by wives and other relatives. It was fathers who were often detailed to warn teenage sons about worldly vices, particularly in sexual matters.

Not unexpectedly, there is some evidence of clashes between fathers and growing sons. A Suffolk merchant and an Essex estate agent both took a new departure in sending sons to university. Both had to delicately indicate in letters that debt and the sowing of even mild wild oats were not befitting the homes or future prospects of these young men. In both cases much love and respect existed between fathers and the sons who voluntarily joined the family businesses.[63] Further down the social scale similar readjustments took place between an Ipswich baker and his teenage son who rebelled by staying out all night, followed by a row, 'the worst we ever had'. Two weeks later the youth was away from home at Soham fair for eight days. After this outburst, he too seems to have settled down to work with his father.[64]

If a father did not take his son into his own business, he felt a responsibility to settle him elsewhere. When a younger son of a Birmingham banker was about to finish his apprenticeship, his father planned to confer with him about staying in the line of business in which he had trained or being placed in another situation. 'These are cares that as a father I am desirous of doing right in, and the best in my power for all my children' he wrote to another son.[65] Some sons were groomed for public affairs. Evidence from membership lists and the local press indicates that fathers and adult sons spent time together in voluntary societies, male dining groups and sporting activities.

Fathers do not seem to have felt the same kind of responsibility for girls. 'Daughters neither require nor admit of the same tuition', one father wrote to another,[66] the basic need being to provide for them financially. Nonconformist and more rationally oriented men did take seriously the general education of their daughters, some adding unconventional subjects like science. The educational tradition of Birmingham's Unitarian community was a powerful element in the later development of girls' opportunities, and the influence of a father like the Suffolk maltster, Newson Garrett, on his daughters' future feminist careers has been acknowledged.[67] Much of a father's influence on his daughters was informal. He visited his daughters away at school and chaperoned them to their destinations or he took them as travelling companions. As young single women, daughters were more available than the busy wife and mother. Their role as attentive listener made them a welcome audience and they could be counted on as a loving aide in illness or old age.

Early training in docility and their potentially weaker economic position meant that daughters did not arouse as much anxiety as sons. A Birmingham clergyman agonized over his children in a letter in 1838:

I can truely say, that the older my children grow, the more difficulty do I find in the discharge of parental duties. The best mode of attempting the formation of character occupies much of my thoughts. With respect to the girls, the path appears to me comparatively clear; but the boys, who must eventually mix with a variety of characters, occasion me much anxiety. They must be exposed to vice;

how, in dependence on the divine blessing, they may be most effectually prepared to encounter it, is a deeply important question.[68]

The father's authority over all his children remained while they lived under his roof and depended on him for income, an authority reinforced for daughters through the structure of inheritance. Given the late age at marriage, a father might well be in his late 60s or into his 70s when the youngest children were in their 20s. Such a father felt it quite within his province to order young women to bed, to forbid visits or suitors. It should, however, not be assumed that paternal power was always exercised harshly. Many of these fathers were adored so that the bonds of love and duty made children's claims to independence even more difficult. At the death of their father, the Galton children were bereft. He had been 'their friend, their companion, their everything. . . . In all troubles he was our adviser and sympathiser. We felt left alone in the world'.[69] Mothers and other female relatives gave sanction to and reinforced both the authority and benevolent image of the father. Maria Marsh constantly stressed to her children what a model of perfection was the Rev. William. She wrote to her daughter away at school: 'I hope that you will more and more rejoice that you are blessed with such a father, whose piety, cheerfulness and affection render our family circle a scene of peace, harmony and love.'[70]

Men's close involvement in domestic life became more difficult as the home was separated from the enterprise and public affairs. By the 1830s fathers were being urged to devote an hour or two in the evening to be with and teach their children or to walk out with them in the morning. Even where the family business was combined with the home, fathers might be hard pressed. The Hill brothers understood the pressures on their father in the early days of Hazelwood school and appreciated his efforts to pay them attention, their understanding furthered by their own involvement in the enterprise from an early age.[71] The daughters of a Birmingham chemist recollected that while their father had no time to take an active part in their education, he was interested in their progress and helped them prepare lessons, despite 'close attention to business, he found time to enter our little cares and pleasures'.[72] It was particularly painful when religious duty conflicted with a man's family. A Birmingham clergyman was torn between his vocation to the ministry and his role as a responsible parent when he was offered a more valuable living. As he wrote to a friend: 'As a father of a family, with two sons to be provided for, two or three hundred a year additional income ought not to be hastily rejected', but as a minister it would not have been the right decision.[73] Other men had to balance active fatherhood with the attractions of public duties, private hobbies and social life. The more worldly models of politics, the 'dandy' and the sportsman all presented viable alternative models of masculinity. The fact that so much literature stressed the benefits and enjoyments of fatherhood hints that other venues might have been equally attractive. The childless Dr Dixon of Witham, after attending a dinner in Fishmonger's Hall in London, piously noted in his diary: 'Clubs and Companies estrange men from domestic and social life and thus leave mother and child too much unprotected.'[74]

Clergymen, writers and publishers were particularly likely to be working at home and thus expound the pleasures of domestic life. In fact, their wives and children might not always find their father's continual presence an unmixed blessing and had to learn early the 'virtues of silence and low voices' while papa was at work.[75] Isaac Taylor was a passionate adherent of domestic life whose workshop was part of the household. As a proponent of scientific study he gave lectures on astronomy to young people in the town as well as teaching it to his own family. When they were beginning to leave home, he instituted a tradition that at the time of each full moon – the dates of which he calculated and sent to each member of the family – at precisely 9 p.m. each one would look up at the sky, knowing that at that moment every absent loved one would be in the thoughts of the others.[76]

Not all children proved amenable to regimes of benevolent rule. The sons of James Luckcock dashed his dreams of continuing the family business he had so carefully built up, and to his great discomfiture he was forced to install a manager.[77] Daughters, in particular, practised a form of passive resistance by falling ill or becoming so intensely religious as to effectively withdraw from family affairs. Louisa Courtauld in her early 20s and having been thwarted in her scheme of setting up a school, was sent with the other Courtauld children to travel to America with their father. She jumped ship at Gravesend and took a post as governess in Scotland.[78]

While a man's own children had a clear claim on his protection and support, the concept of fatherhood was by no means limited to biological offspring. Masters stood as fathers to their apprentices and pupils, a position which was reinforced if they were also uncle or elder brother (or brother-in-law). The resources of fatherhood could merge into trusteeship and the general control of minors, as when Dr Dixon acted as protector and 'banker' for the illegitimate children of an acquaintance.[79] An entry in a local commonplace book entitled 'The Last Behest', expects the eldest son to take the dying father's place:

> My son! my eldest son approach – To you my charge is great
> For thou alone of all the flock – hast wrought to mans estate
> O look thou on my children, with a brothers watchful eye
> And lead them up in holiness – O promise ere I die!

The son is charged with protecting his sister's name for 'remember son – thou art her father now' and with supporting his mother's 'falling years'.[80]

In this romanticized version, the father can no longer discharge his duties through death. But real fathers also went bankrupt or failed in other ways to support their children. Since expectations of such support were the main strand in defining the good father, economic failure was often seen as personal failure entailing a loss of respect and thus manhood in a man's own as well as his children's eyes. The struggles and reproaches of children, especially daughters, whose fathers had failed or left debts must have poisoned family relationships, particularly in the latter part of the period when women were less likely to be able to gain their own income and had less understanding of the economic world and its inherent risks. Dickens, for example, became lyrical in creating forgiving daughters who continue to adore failed and flawed fathers, the more base and unattractive the father, the more self-sacrificing and redeeming become the daughters in his fiction.[81]

Fathers in the local records most certainly desired to become the progenitors of a family, to beget and rear children and to form them according to ideas of a good life. These goals were not necessarily aimed at forming a family dynasty in the gentry mould. Rather fatherhood was a responsibility and an enjoyment, both part of a moral destiny.

Motherhood

Expectations for mothers differed from the father's role in significant ways. Mothers were to be relied upon for personal care and emotional rather than economic support. While for fathers involvement with their children's lives was a matter of choice, it was regarded as natural for women to take up the whole duty of motherhood and there was scorn for the aristocratic habit of leaving children in the care of nursemaids and servants. Nevertheless, this natural aptitude could always be improved; reason and principle could strengthen maternal love. Even the local press carried articles on the overriding importance of a mother's part in the first six years of child life.[82] Conversely, it was expected that all women, whether biological mothers or not, had a maternal instinct.

The central place given to the mother was not unique to this group or this historical period. But in the provincial middle class, mothers bore and reared the next generation of manpower for the family enterprise and the household, while the emphasis on family life in evangelical religion gave a central place to the mother in creating a home. If a mother failed in the task of raising healthy, seriously minded and well trained children, she sent forth 'damaged material'.[83] Ann Taylor composed the poem, 'My Mother' in 1802 when she was just 20. It quickly gained a national and international reputation and remained in print well into the twentieth century (see Appendix 1).[84] Richard Cadbury, the Quaker cocoa manufacturer, while not given to flights of fancy, wrote a poem about his mother including the lines:

> Can Heaven bestow a warmer glow
> Of sunshine from above,
> A purer, holier pledge below
> Than in a mother's love.[85]

In fulfilling these ideals, women first had to face the physical and emotional demands of childbearing and infant care through a good portion of their adult lives. The combination of late marriage and large families gave an average age of 27.3 at the birth of the first child and 40.6 at the birth of the last, that is thirteen years of continuous physical mothering.[86] The pattern is best seen in a few exceptionally detailed local records. At age 31, Robert Brightwen, a Quaker corn merchant in Essex, married in 1798. His wife Mary was 25. Starting within a year of marriage, ten children were born, of whom four eventually died. The average interval for the first seven

births was twenty-three months when the children had survived more than two years, but fell to eleven months after a baby had died. Following Dorothy McLaren's findings for the previous period, this pattern strongly suggests that breastfeeding was being practised, with the natural contraception effect of lactation being suddenly withdrawn at infant death. For the Brightwens, also, the penultimate and ultimate birth intervals of thirty-one and thirty-nine months follow a generally recognized pattern.[87] It is impossible to know whether this usual configuration of longer intervals for later births was due to sterility of husband or wife as they grew older, more miscarriages as the mother aged, decreased intercourse or a deliberate attempt to limit family size – or more likely a combination of these factors.[88]

Another detailed record from an Essex Anglican, iron founder's family of the same period is less conclusive, but reconstruction of birth intervals

Plate 20   Rebecca Shaen, aged 6, daughter of Rebecca Solly and Samuel Shaen, painted *c.* 1818. Rebecca later married her cousin Henry Solly

and infant deaths suggests breastfeeding for the first eight children and wet nursing for the last four, understandable given the wife's declining health.[89] Ann Martin Taylor bore eleven children in the sixteen years between 1782 and 1798 (of whom six lived). This represents, on average, a birth every nineteen months, which drops to fifteen months if the last three births are discounted as above (see genealogy, p. 60). Here we do know that all were wet nursed. The last Taylor child was put to nurse for about two years in a hamlet on the edge of Colchester and after service every Sunday, the whole family walked down to see 'baby', which suggests that wet nursing in this case was due to physical problems, an interpretation which fits with Ann Taylor's known commitment to motherhood.[90] Ann Martin Taylor was bearing children from the age of 25 to 41, which means that during this period she was pregnant for over half her time. Mary Brightwen's ten children occupied her from age 26 to 45, making her pregnant for a third of those years. If she breastfed each child for only one year (slightly less when an infant died), she would have been pregnant and nursing 85 per cent of that time, and if breastfeeding is more realistically estimated at fifteen months, this would rise to 95 per cent.

Similar childbearing patterns appear in all strata of the local groups. Martha Gibbins, wife of the wealthy Birmingham banker Joseph Gibbins, married when she was only 20 and bore seventeen children in twenty-seven years, eleven of whom survived to adulthood. Of her last four children, one was stillborn and the others died within a year of birth; tragedies which were compounded by her own ill health. Her eldest children were marrying and starting their own families when she was still immersed in pregnancy and the care of small children. A mother like Martha Gibbins would simultaneously face the whole range of maternal concerns from the demands of infant feeding and illness to placing sons in apprenticeships and the courtship of youths and maidens.[91] Motherhood under these conditions was a rigorous and time consuming business. Nevertheless, childlessness could be a disappointment, although opportunities for mothering the children of relatives and friends were legion and childless women would be expected to be available for childcare. In the census sample, female headed households had more than double the proportion of young children unrelated to the head than in male headed households.

The progression to a model of full-time motherhood as a central part of middle-class gentility can be traced in many of the local families whether the aims were primarily religious or more worldly. Archibald Kenrick came to Birmingham in the 1780s to establish a buckle business. His mother was familiar with business arrangements and he could record in his diary: 'Stayed with Mother all the rest of the day talking over past transactions and money matters.' Despite the fact that after his marriage he lived close to the foundry he had established, his wife played no part in the business and occupied herself completely with home and children.[92] However, it would be simplistic to expect a straightforward development from eighteenth-century business woman to nineteenth-century full-time mother. The separation, both physical and psychic, between workplace and home was long and uneven; the grounds often contested.

A shift in ideals, manners and behaviour of this magnitude was bound to make some distinction between generations of mothers and daughters. Vulgar or simple, old fashioned mothers being upbraided by more sophisticated daughters were the stock in trade of fiction. Sometimes the conflict could take the form of a daughter's commitment to serious Christianity in opposition to what she saw as a mother's frivolity or crude worldliness. But the high status of motherhood and the stress on filial duty created difficulties for the pious daughter.[93]

The daily life of the women who coped with large families and mixed households in the context of a precarious income created a spectrum of problems of which living up to ideals of gentility was only one. The large numbers and close spacing of babies meant that it was difficult to give individual attention to each child, a watchfulness which was felt to be particularly necessary for spiritual and moral development. Maria Marsh was pleased when occasionally only one child was at home as focus of her exclusive attention.[94] One way to lighten the burden of daily care was to use servants. The upper strata did employ nursemaids at this time and there seems to have been general participation by other servants in childcare. This would have been a necessity given the high standards of cleanliness, clothing and control being demanded. Ten young children meant twenty stockings to buy, if not make, to keep clean and mended as well as to daily supervise putting on to little feet. Mothers had to oversee the development of a middle-class moral code as well as the acquisition of correct speech and behaviour. Since many servants were recruited from the countryside, their superstitious beliefs and coarse expressions were particularly suspect. It was all very well to be advised to let 'Baby be master of the household for the first year of life' if you had help in seeing to the toddlers and other tasks, but the pressures must have been intense, often augmented by the mother's fatigue and ill health, especially where she was also helping in the enterprise.

A further strain was imposed by the inevitable and realistic fear about a child's death. Gorham has argued that such fears were behind the anxious tones of manuals on childcare by mid century.[95] The fact that these women bore so many children seems to have done nothing to lessen the grief at their loss. Amelia Moilliet, wife of a wealthy Birmingham banker, was close to all seven of her surviving children (born between 1802 and 1812). The eighth and youngest, Albert, was born after an interval of five years and his mother could spend more time with him. He had always been delicate and despite employing several servants, Amelia took him with her when travelling. On a visit to friends when he was 2 she 'carried my beloved in my arms during all the day'. The first separation from him and his illnesses were times of greatest anxiety. (Albert Moilliet died aged 12.)[96] The poignant passage in the memoirs of an Essex shopkeeper's wife faced with the mortal illness of her infant son shows the depth of attachment:

I have often found it difficult on awakening in the morning to fix my whole heart in meditation on my God and my duty, as I had been much favoured to do in time past. But thou, Oh Lord! knowest when the feelings of nature were awakened in viewing the dear child's sufferings, and anticipating the separation which would probably soon take place – how often I was enabled to say in sincerity, 'Not my will, but thine be done'.[97]

Even when children did not die, illness was rife – there were the usual childhood diseases in addition to fevers, accidents and the dreaded consumption. The wife of a brewer had fourteen children, including five stillbirths. All the children were vaccinated, a procedure widely practised in this group but itself requiring some nursing care. The eldest three had whooping cough when they were 5, 3 and a few months old, the next three had it five years later when they were 3, 2 and 1. All six of these children had both chicken pox and measles as did four of the later ones and the remainder had one disease or the other. Frequently, therefore, as well as being both pregnant and caring for a small baby the mother had to deal with several ill children.[98] It is understandable why the cause of scientific medicine flourished in such situations. As with childbirth, the medical man was becoming an adviser to the wife and mother in the business of health, just as the lawyer acted for her husband in the business of property. During this period manuals and advice books based on common ideas and herbal remedies which could be made up by the women themselves were giving way to directions from the expert, formally trained, male doctor. Many of these productions were consolidating changes that had already taken place. By the 1830s and 1840s writers on domestic duties such as Mrs Ellis approved this development and gave credence to women's dependence on medical expertise. The popular Birmingham doctor, Pye Chevasse, whose books were aimed specifically at middle-class mothers, deplored the common practice of 'disobeying a medical man's orders or only adopting half his measures', and the threat of 'the untimely grave' for the child which Chevasse held out for such disobedience was only too real.[99]

The anxiety about a child's health was increased for Christian mothers who feared for their children's souls and the ultimate devastation of never meeting with them again in Heaven if they died unprepared. Maria Marsh, like so many of these mothers, took the moral and spiritual training of her children as her most sacred duty. She wrote to her daughter on her twelfth birthday: 'Oh my sweet child, could you know my anxious desire to see you a real Christian, I think your love to me would stir you up to seek the mercy and grace of God.'[100] The religious framework, preying on a sense of guilt, aided discipline among such large numbers of children. When the Marsh children were disobedient, their mother would take the offender into her own room and point out the sin committed: 'how grievous it was in the sight of God and how painful to her'. They then would kneel and pray together.[101] A Quaker mother of nine expressed the general feeling: 'A mother would have hard work indeed if not for a throne of grace to which she may resort.'[102]

Spiritual training began in infancy, and mothers (or their substitutes) were expected to give or at least overlook the first lessons, including reading, writing and spelling. Many mothers kept records of their children's progress, making little distinction between formal skills and general development. Few boys were taught at home after the age of 6, but mothers continued to supervise the education and training of daughters. Mothers were instrumental in inculcating general standards and behaviour, coincidentally emphasizing differential roles for boys and girls. A woman like Amelia Moilliet believed that she had been 'endowed by nature with a remarkably quick insight into the minds of my children' which she thought gave her special knowledge of their characters and the evils to which they would be exposed because of these traits: 'This almost prophetic spirit, strengthened by maternal love often caused me intense anxiety.'[103] These mothers turned to each other for support and practical advice. Letters between mothers and daughters, sisters and other female kin and friends are full of concerns about daily life with children, their minor illnesses, sleep patterns, stages of walking and talking. A Birmingham chemist's wife wrote to her sister-in-law describing the newest baby: 'She takes a good deal of notice and smiles so very prettily making a little cooing noise, the other children continue to be fond of her, the little girls stand by me when I am dressing her and reach the different things as I want them.'[104]

Mothers were especially concerned over sons when they began to leave their daily care, first for school and later for work. Writers like Mrs Ellis and Ann Martin Taylor recognized the special need for a mother to keep her son's respect, yet both writers warned that sons would inevitably take their own way to a greater extent than daughters. Rebecca Solly Shaen fretted over young Samuel's departure for his legal apprenticeship in London despite the fact that he was to lodge with her own sister whose husband was also their cousin, and so 'comparatively speaking' he was 'most eligibly situated', but:

when I think how young he is, not 16, how unformed in every sense of the word, how my Motherly heart yearns for him. In putting up books of Instruction or amusement and consulting him he says, 'you know best'. . . . How great the responsibility – if I urge upon him grave instruction prematurely I may disgust and make impressions sadly the worse of what I intend, the happy word and the happy moment will no longer be in my power. Have I said it whilst I had the opportunity? . . .[105]

Mothers bore the added disadvantage of themselves often being ignorant of some aspects of the 'world' and were further constrained by feminine delicacy from discussing sexual matters. William Pattisson's mother was anxious when he left Witham for his legal training in London in 1820. She wrote to an old family friend, in oblique terms, asking him to reassure William's anxieties about purity. Mrs Pattisson apologised for her maternal disquiet which had prompted the letter and 'has cost me many tears and no little repugnance have I overcome'.[106] Contrary to the uplifting literature, some mothers seemed to feel that their helplessness denied them their son's respect, and feared being neglected in old age or widowhood.

The relationship between mothers and their growing daughters was less often broken. Except for a possible year or two of boarding school and visits to relatives, a daughter could expect to remain living with her mother until (and if) she married. Undoubtedly there were strains in some of these relationships. More ambitious and intellectual daughters chafed against the placid domesticity of their mothers, while some mothers dominated and used daughters as unpaid domestic aides. However, many of these women shared a common religious outlook and devotion to domestic affairs, particularly after daughters had married and had children and were better able to appreciate their mothers' lives. The daughter of a Birmingham bookseller felt that she would never recover from the death of her mother, an affection which she maintained could not be compared even to the love of a husband and duty of a child.[107] Rebecca Solly Shaen experienced the death of her mother as 'a very bitter grief . . . with every feeling gratified as a Wife and Mother, I have felt most keenly that I was also a daughter'. By the time Rebecca was in her 60s and her own nine children were grown up and dispersed, she herself felt the strain of keeping the family together. 'Really, my old head and heart has felt quite bewildered with all these scattered children.'[108]

In addition to their own children, women often helped to bring up nieces, nephews and younger siblings and cousins who lived in their household and were responsible as well for the 'dear young men that surround our table' as a Colchester shopkeeper's wife described the residential assistants.[109] Elder daughters and unmarried sisters were aides and deputies for mothers. In a few wealthy families poor relatives or paid dependants might perform some of these functions. The Galtons had brought up the daughter of their gardener who, as somewhat older than their own children, became a confidant, trusted friend and mother's helper.[110]

With assistance, enough material resources and robust health, mothers seem to have derived enjoyment and a sense of purpose from their maternal role. A woman as a mother, as Mrs Ellis wrote, 'has now an object peculiarly her own'.[111] The strains and difficulties within the maternal role were many, however. There was ambiguity about the aims of mothers for their children. Salvation was a central duty, but worldly claims had to be recognized and steering adolescent children between the two gave many uneasy moments. Mothers themselves often had other commitments – to husbands, the enterprise or to other relatives – which resulted in calls on their time and energy which could conflict with maternal duty. The elevation of motherhood within pious families could turn attention away from the mother's own religious quest through prayer and self-examination.[112]

Inevitably, a mother had to cope with a different relationship to her adult children as she moved into old age, often weak in health and sometimes dependent for material support. Despite the fact that widows and even wives were expected to support dependent children if necessary, there was no guarantee that they would make a return. Their reciprocal duties were less clear than the formal partnership between father and son and rested more heavily on personal affection backed by moral sanction. There are some glimmerings of restiveness on the part of mothers, particularly about the lack of time, energy and opportunity for a woman to develop her sense of self separate from domestic identities. Mary Wright Sewell declared that she had 'no ambition to get upon the world's platform and fight for its prizes. . . . I would rather train up a little child to love and serve God and be a blessing to his country than do anything else'. Yet as she only had two children, she extended her crusade for motherhood, setting up mothers' meetings and writing best-selling tracts.[113] The son of a woman who had run her own workshop in Birmingham while rearing eleven children later came to realize 'how much better it would have been for her – how much more enjoyment, peace, repose and freedom from anxiety would have fallen to her – had her family been limited to three or four children'.[114]

Even a woman as well placed as Jane Ransome Biddell, whose inheritance and husband's income allowed her to hire a housekeeper, virtually stopped writing poetry from age 31 when her first child was born to the birth of her tenth and last when she was 44 (including twins). A poem on the Muse four years later reflects how domestic demands prevented creativity but gave other pleasures:

> Ideal forms no longer glide
> In dreaming mood before my view
> As nesting round my own fire side
> I see a little laughing crew. . . .
>
> But not a muse my call attends,

> They shun the dear domestic hearth
> And inspiration still descends
> On spirits more detached from earth.[115]

In Maria Marsh's words, motherhood was, indeed, a 'world of business to those who are in a small measure desirous of doing their duty'.[116]

Children

From the early part of the eighteenth century, children had begun to be identified as a group with their own interests and needs. They were allowed more freedom in a less harsh and authoritarian context and gained their own literature, toys and pastimes.[117] By the end of that century, the elevation of innocence, the unspoiled and the natural within romanticism, furthered the special place of children. Foreign commentators were struck by the way children of the English middle classes, in contrast to those of the aristocracy, were treated as loved companions by their parents.

Evangelical and Enlightenment traditions, despite their differences, focused on children's character as the basis for reforming society. Birmingham's Unitarians practised rational childrearing at Hazelwood School, and in homes like the Galtons where their eldest daughter was brought up on texts like Thomas Day's (of the Lunar Society) *Sandford and Merton*. Yet Cowper's *The Task* was also read aloud in the Galton family circle.[118] While parents like the Galtons distrusted feeling and stressed practical duties, evangelicals believed in childhood innocence and hoped for conversion. In the course of a family walk, a Utilitarian parent gave practical lessons on botany while the evangelical called attention to God's handiwork. Both believed that understanding the value of time was indispensable and laid down set schedules which kept order with seemingly little resort to physical punishment. The threat of being denied parental – and God's – love was a powerful disciplinary measure which some sensitive children found hard to bear. Jane and Ann Taylor's verses express the technique forcibly:

> And when you're good and do not cry,
> Nor into angry passions fly
> You can't think how Papa and I
> > Love Baby

> And when you saw me pale and thin
> By grieving for my baby's sin
> I think you'd wish that you had been
> > A better Baby.[119]

The size of these households, plus neighbourhood kin, meant that normally there would always be companionship for children. The son of an Essex shopkeeper recalled that, while not allowed to mix with the village children, their happy family circle made up for the restriction.[120] Within a predominantly working-class area in Birmingham town centre, the young

Gibbins relied on the extensive family network across town to provide cousins as playmates.[121]

With all the loving care, boys still had to learn that they were made of sterner stuff and prepare to enter a wider world. Very small children were dressed and treated more alike but by the age of 5 or 6, boys were taken out of petticoats in the ritual of breeching, the first step towards manhood. The youngest son in an Essex brewer's family who was dressed in this way until he was 7, deliberately muddied his petticoats in order to be properly breeched.[122] Girls, who remained in petticoats, were not expected to be as adventurous. While boys were given hoops, balls and other toys associated with physical activities, girls played with dolls, dolls houses, needlebooks and miniature work baskets. Both sexes took part in activities such as keeping pets and tending small gardens, but the range of boys' pets was wider, including kites and owls as well as the more familiar rabbits, cats and dogs. Girls' gardens concentrated on flowers, while boys might plant trees and ferns. Boys were taught to swim and dive, activities not often encouraged for girls. Rebecca Kenrick played with her older brother until by the time she was 6 her mother worried that she was becoming 'rude' and a 'compleat tomboy'. She was sent off to stay with a childless aunt who groomed her in more appropriate feminine behaviour.[123] Boys were expected to be physically tougher than girls, naturally tolerant of dirt and personal untidiness.

As cleanliness and order became central parts of middle-class culture, girls had to develop a shame about dirt and slovenly behaviour as part of their femininity – being called a 'hoyden' was something of a disgrace – whereas boys had to negotiate a course between these elements of gentility and virile indifference to such petty matters. A Suffolk merchant's son, aged 13, was invited to dine with the local rector regularly each Sunday. When once he had put off going because of a rainstorm his host quizzed him: 'Are you made of sugar or salt that you thought the rain would destroy you?' The young man never again missed an appointment because of the weather.[124] Education and early work experience followed gender divisions. The census sample suggests that in households supported by trade, slightly more sons under 16 than daughters were kept at home – either at school or helping in the enterprise or both. However, among professional families, more than twice as many daughters were resident in the under 16 age group, indicating that their brothers were being educated away from home.

The greatest distinction came in later adolescence when the boys began to be seriously groomed for work in the outside world. As long as the enterprise was integral to the children's home, both sexes could help with light tasks. However, suburban living meant that boys had to be formally initiated into business. This step, taken in the middle teens, often coincided with first communion in the Anglican church or being made a full member of a nonconformist congregation. For girls, too, these religious ceremonies marked their progress to adult status and may have been accompanied by somewhat more responsibility at home. They could not, however, have had the impact that the first work experience did for their brothers. Family rituals also emphasized different destinies. A paper manufacturer's two young sons were chosen to lay the first bricks of the new steam mill,[125] whereas James Luckcock had his daughter lay the stone for his Edgbaston home, 'the green pastures of domestic comfort'.[126]

Coming from an affectionate home atmosphere, boys would often suffer greatly when sent away to school or, at a later age, to apprenticeships. Severing close home ties was part of the hardening process of becoming a man. When they left at marriage, daughters, too, felt the wrench. The very closeness and concern of parents and other adults could make the establishment of an individual identity particularly difficult for teenage girls. Ann Martin Taylor's acerbic comments on adolescence are undoubtedly based on her experience of raising six children. The surprisingly modern tone is explicable given the combination of intense love, manipulation of guilt and high expectations which have similarities to the middle-class family of the present. She notes that the 'sweet simplicity of childhood' was often succeeded by a most troublesome period:

There is an indefinite carriage and conduct in some young persons towards their parents which, although not decidedly hostile, is sufficient to deter a by-stander from coveting *such* a heritage. . . . Their *manner* rather than *matter* of what they say – as though they were addressing not merely different ages but different species.[127]

Most adolescents seemed to pass through this stage and established amicable relationships with parents. Constant rounds of visits, exchange of gifts and services reinforced these ties. It has been seen, for example, how farmers who were seldom in formal partnerships were often close to their sons in both a working and social environment. Parents with resources to spare were generous to children starting out in marriage and distance was becoming less of a barrier in maintaining these relationships. By the 1840s, a Suffolk farmer and his wife regularly visited their daughter in London by using the steam packet from Yarmouth. They brought country produce up and took grandchildren back for country air. The mother was also able to rush to London during her daughter's severe illness by using the new 'penny-a-mile' rail service.[128]

Children also owed parents services and support. Sons were expected to be ready to take over as head of the family if necessary. The practice of early withdrawal from the enterprise reduced potential conflict between fathers and sons, yet certain fears remained. Some parents were reduced to living on the bounty of their sons, as happened to a Suffolk man whose venture into steam boats literally blew up his capital.[129] An Essex diary recounts the cautionary tale of a man reduced to begging after giving up his £1000 business and house to his son only to be turned out of doors. The diarist completes the entry by thanking the Lord for her dutiful children.[130] Such anxieties underscored the injunctions to filial duty in poems such as Ann Taylor's most popular poem 'My Mother'.[131]

From the local records, many sons appear to have been not only dutiful but loving towards their middle-aged parents. The young Witham lawyer, William Henry Pattisson, himself cooked custards when both his parents were ill, although he admitted he was especially eager to reconcile them to the choice of his fiancée.[132] An Essex brewer living at home with his parents also made special dishes for his invalid mother since both his sisters had died.[133] The Ipswich draper John Perry was particularly close to his father who lived near by. With deep sorrow he watched the older man's progressive decline. When he was finally bedridden, Perry sat by his bed and helped him to wash and dress: 'Poor dear man. How very weak and childlike he is, quite unable to help himself', and the son agonized over the coming loss.[134]

However, it was daughters who were expected to perform such nursing duties as a matter of course. An adult daughter with few prospects of her own income had little choice, even without religious admonition. Young Amy Camps tending her dying mother needed the 'exercise of my more passive graces' and invoked the Lord's aid in her task.[135] Nursing was only a part of general daughterly duties. Jane Webb Loudon, John Claudius's wife, was the only daughter of a Birmingham businessman and lost her mother at an early age. She felt special responsibility for her father, and at 12 wrote a poem for his birthday which ended:

> Thou dearest father! hear my prayer!
> That long succeeding years may show
> Your welfare is my dearest care,
> My all of happiness below. . . .[136]

Jane Webb did not marry until after her father's death, a not uncommon pattern especially for only or youngest daughters.

There were several factors which gave such father–daughter relationships a special intensity in this group, particularly where the mother was dead, incapacitated or absent and where a daughter was substituted as surrogate mother or housekeeper. We have seen how expectation of personal services to the family household in reciprocation for support was inherent in the structure of the enterprise and the form of female property. The cultural norm of child-like innocence as the attractive mode for adult women was confirmed by the practice of men marrying younger women. The higher the status and resources and, presumably, the possibility of choice by the man, the greater the disparity in age. (In the census sample, within the upper middle class, thirteen men were twenty or more years older than their wives – probably second marriages.) Second and subsequent marriages, where the wife could be of an age with a man's elder daughters, accentuated this pattern. Finally, the elevation of the father–daughter relationship as an ideal went some way to solving the inherent contradiction between idealized feminine purity and the sexual realities of childbearing which was at the core of motherhood.[137]

Some local material gives intimations of particularly intense ties between fathers and daughters. Clergymen, in particular, exercised the fascination of fatherhood from the nursery to the Sunday pulpit and clerical daughters seem to have been among those with closest ties to their fathers. When Maria Marsh died, the three teenage daughters of the Rev. William took over the running of the household and their mother's parish duties. The two elder married but Catherine assumed the special role of her father's companion. On her seventeenth birthday he had written: 'My darling Kate

– I loved you as a babe, I have delighted in your youth and you will be a comfort to me in advancing years.' After her second sister's marriage when her father was threatened with blindness, she wrote to him: 'I bless God many times in the day that I have formed no sort of link which can prevent me living for you.' When William protested that he ought not to stand in the way of her marrying, she replied that she would rather spend a short time with him 'a thousand times than have a long life of happiness with anyone else in the whole world'. Catherine later had to come to terms with the Rev. Marsh's two subsequent marriages. The day of her father's return from his second wedding trip, she forced herself to rejoice: 'Oh life is very full of blessed interest whilst we can speak to perishing sinners of a living Saviour. It makes even my widowed heart [sic] sing for joy.'[138]

A father would sometimes prepare a motherless daughter to run his home for him as soon as she was old enough, often in her middle teens. One of Bernard Barton's most popular poems was 'To a Little Housekeeper', undoubtedly based on his only daughter Lucy who did take over her widowed father's menage.[139] Such a position had attractions since a young girl gained responsibility, respect and affection without a break from familiar surroundings and the necessity to cope with a new, sexual relationship. If there were younger siblings to care for, she gained experience and the credit of mothering. Such a daughter could become the emotional focus for her father, and motherless girls were even urged to fulfil these duties in order to prevent the ill-considered remarriage of their widowed father.[140]

It is not difficult to understand why, in these circumstances, erotic overtones sometimes seep into these father–daughter relationships. The daughter of a banker was delighted to reassert her position after the death of her step-mother. Her father's relationship to his children had been typical: 'We were exceedingly fond of our father. At the same time *his word was law*. It never entered our minds, I believe, to openly disobey him.' Her response to his return after an absence is significant. 'He clambered down [from the carriage] into my arms, and our first *long* kiss was much too overpowering, for me to be able to describe the sensation!' In the days after his return her father was 'much alone with *me* . . . and I am delighted to find him able to be thoroughly intimate with me and throwing a great deal into my hands'. She found that 'Papa was most generous to me. My situation at home is delightful, and its importance suits my natural disposition. Both the dear gentlemen [her brother was living at home] depend much upon me and I am to take the mistress-ship in a few weeks.'[141] The displacement of erotic attachment on to a daughter figure is confirmed in the case of a country clergyman whose beloved daughter had died of consumption at age 19. His other daughters had married or made lives of their own and his wife withdrew into invalidism. In his late 40s, he befriended the neighbouring family of a retired army officer, also a widower with three unmarried daughters. The clergyman increasingly singled out the one of these who was the closest in age to his dead daughter and bore her name, Emily. He became the love and centre of her life for twenty years, and tried to make her his mistress.[142]

These may appear as extreme cases of replacement of wives by daughters. Yet the literature of the period, particularly from the 1840s onwards, is replete with family tales where the mother figure is shadowy or absent. Charles Dickens, in his life as well as his writing, continually returns to the attractions of young girls, starting with his two teenage sisters-in-law who successively lived in his household. He had a close semi-flirtatious relationship with his own daughters, the eldest devoting her life to hagiography of her father, capped by his later infatuation with a 17-year-old actress. For Dickens the combination of childishness and womanliness of a Dora Copperfield, complete with miniature work box and doll-like house-wifery, seems to have been a powerful, even titillating image as it was to many early Victorian readers.[143]

The discussion of a single father–daughter bond brings out only one important dimension within family relationships. In such large families, the burden of support and care could be spread over several siblings; a widower's daughters often splitting up the wife's duties. Yet women felt conflicting loyalties to fathers, husbands and children. The only daughter of James Keir, a member of Birmingham's Lunar Society, had married the banker, J. L. Moilliet. When her father became old and senile she was torn between her duty to care for him or accompanying her husband to Switzerland where he had banking business. She was fortunate in being able to compromise since she had trustworthy servants to nurse her father.[144] The spinster sister of a Witham solicitor's clerk had no such option. Her brother left her a cottage and a small insurance policy if she would care for his four motherless children. In his will, he states that this legacy of *both* support and burden of care would come into effect if and when she became free of obligation to live with and care for their father.[145]

Brothers and sisters

The expectation that a brother left in such a situation would turn to his sister was rooted in both experience and values. The brother–sister tie was idealized in literature and had a strong basis in everyday life. Brothers and sisters shared economic resources as well as family origins. They were often later joined through partnership of a man with his sister's husband or through 'sibling marriage'. The relationship gained in intensity from the nostalgia surrounding common childhood experience when that stage in life was held as the key to innocence and happiness. The late age at marriage meant that brothers and sisters could continue their shared life as young adults for as long as fifteen years. During this period they had lived through family crises and were often implicated in each others' courtship and career adventures. As with fathers and daughters, brothers and sisters approached the model masculine–feminine relationship without the explicit sexuality of marriage.[146] Emphasizing the innocence of childish love was partly a way of protecting these deep emotional attachments.

In the idealized model, the brother was always older than the sister. Their attachment and treatment of each other was explicitly meant to prefigure that of marriage and through it they were to learn appropriate gender behaviour. George Eliot adored her older brother and has given a powerful portrait of their relationship in *Mill on the Floss*. In a retrospective poem she notes how the brother and sister's 'self-same world' was enlarged for each by the 'loving difference' of boy and girl; how the elder, stronger, wiser brother learned a noble mastery over impulse in protecting and guiding the footsteps of his little sister – a 'like unlike, a Self that self restrains'.[147] Mary Ann Hedge, the only daughter among seven sons of a Colchester clockmaker, wrote a long essay on the reciprocal duties of brother and sister which she prefaced with the verse:

> That tender union, all combin'd
> Of Nature's holiest sympathies;
> 'Tis Friendship in its loveliest dress
> 'Tis Love's most perfect tenderness

And she compares the love of brother and sister as second only to the conjugal union. Like other domestic ties, that between siblings was seen as natural yet it had to be explained and proclaimed at length. For Hedge, the respect due to moral superiority and sense of weakness by the sister should be combined with the consciousness of power, protection and support by the brother. The brother acts as an 'indulgent monitor' to mould his sister into correct femininity. The sister influences him by passive example and expectation, never direct criticism or suggestion.[148] This division of behaviour represents an exaggerated prescription of what was found in many families where young men's involvement with the world of work and public affairs was relayed back to their sisters for whom they often became a window on that world. In 1809, when the two younger brothers next in age to Jane Taylor left Colchester for London apprenticeships, she composed the verse:

> A sister's affections, the hopes and the fears
> That flutter in turns in her heart
> When a Brother sets out on his stormy career
> What magic of words can impart?[149]

Brothers who were older by many years acted as mentors to younger sisters left at home. They were trustees and business advisers for their sisters and sisters sought refuge in the homes of brothers when widowed (or abandoned), even if several brothers had to club together to make up an income. In return, sisters were expected to give personal service to brothers; a service which was regarded as a good in itself but also as the best preparation for learning wifely duties. The literature stressed a sister's religious and moral influence on more worldly brothers and there is some evidence that young women were often the first in a family to be converted. George Eliot, among others, tried to attract her brother to her fervent evangelical faith when she was a young woman. She had to give up the attempt and found that her importuning simply widened the rift between them, much as another sister who finally admitted that if all brothers were successfully converted, business might suffer.[150] Most sisterly duties were more mundane, from mending stockings, carrying messages and nursing in illness to acting as companion and listener. Just as a daughter was assured that she could prevent a father's reckless remarriage, a sister who fulfilled the humblest tasks was told she could keep her brother from making a rash marriage – or worse – by making his home cheerful and comfortable. The making of a home for a brother as an 'occupation' for unmarried women has been surveyed. A bachelor or widowed brother would expect a single or widowed sister to become his housekeeper and care for his children unless she had the most pressing of claims on her.

Whether the particular roles allocated to brothers and sisters were felt as obligation or opportunity depended on circumstance and resource as much as personal inclination. There is no doubt that the lives of brothers and sisters remained closely interwoven and seemed to have had a special salience, often displaying a depth of warm affection on both sides. Samuel Shaen, the Essex attorney, was friend and adviser to his two spinster sisters who lived in Witham with their mother, about 4 miles from his home. He was 'shocked and saddened' by the death of 'Sister Louisa' and regarded himself as 'chief comforter' to 'Sister Hepzibah'.[151]

The longevity and intensity of these relationships could also make conflict explosive when it came. It has been seen with the Kenrick family how this was exacerbated by the mingling of business and family interests. In the case of unmarried siblings living together, brothers usually controlled more resources and options. A sister keeping his house was always in danger of losing both livelihood and home if her brother married. A sister in this position is reputed to have intercepted a letter her brother had written asking their parents' permission to marry.[152] Even where sisters had income of their own and the home remained intact, the loss of a brother's company could be keenly felt. In a close family of adult siblings when the favourite brother became engaged, one of the sisters took every opportunity to decry his fiancée's vulgarity and refused to kiss the bride at the wedding. She described the final parting with her brother: 'He held me in his arms, embracing me as he never, I fear, will do again.'[153]

While the lived relationship of brother and sister had some affinity with the model, inevitably it was more complicated. In the first place, large families meant that the single pair of fiction or prescription was open to wider choice and undoubtedly some sibling pairs were closer than others.[154] When Mary Constable was 30, she was detailed to spend the winter in London keeping her brother John company. She was living with her younger brother, Abram, who was coping with taking over the milling business in Essex. Abram felt it would do them both good to be away from each other for a while. After their parents' death, Mary kept house for Abram. Within a year they had parted and she ended up as companion to a nephew although Abram never married.[155]

A multitude of siblings could mean squabbles over resources in which their spouses joined. After a dispute over their parents' property, Rebecca Solly Shaen never crossed her brother's threshold until he was on his death bed.[156] A brother who was relied on for advice and support might turn out to be mistaken or uninterested or even, as has been seen, take money from his sisters and give little in return. The idealized strong elder brother and adoring younger sister was often in reality reversed by temperament, and age. A formidable eldest sister – virtual head of the family since her parents' death – had to stand by while her younger brother, barely in his 20s, took over running the family bank during a crisis.[157] In such a situation, the young man would have to stand on all the power and privilege of his masculine prerogative to overcome the disparity. Deep jealousies and griev-ances from childhood also carried over into siblings' adult years. Dickens may have idealized younger sister figures in his fiction yet he never forgave his removal from school and forced employment in the blacking factory when his next elder sister was encouraged in her musical career.[158]

Right behaviour of elder siblings was encouraged as an example to younger children, while parents helped to promote the role of brother and sister in their growing children. When young Samuel Shaen took his first legal post in Leeds, Rebecca sent one of his sisters to keep house: 'She is now with Sam, may she be of service to him.' When Rebecca was musing on the death of her own brother, Tom, she was struck by how much her son, Ben, seemed to resemble him in temperament. As a girl, she had tried to help Tom with his lessons as she now helped her 'own dear boy'. A sister was expected to grow up and serve as wife and mother; the brother to enjoy the privileges and responsibilities of husband and father.[159]

The closeness of the brother–sister tie has inevitably raised speculation about its erotic content. In fiction, for example, the pure sexless sister and loose, often working-class, woman of the world are contrasted stereotypes. And much speculation has surrounded the relationships of well-known figures such as William and Dorothy Wordsworth. But the Wordsworths were in no way unusual and exhibit all the standard features of innumerable other adult brothers and sisters.[160] The latent element of power, the strong emotions aroused, the differing expectations for men and women, gave a fierce edge to fraternal ties. A woman such as Harriet Martineau experienced the estrangement from her cherished brother, James, so deeply that she would never write about the circumstances of the rift. The attachment she had felt for this younger brother was 'the strongest passion I have ever entertained', and a mixture of envy and love comes through her statement that 'brothers are to sisters what sisters can never be to brothers as objects of engrossing and devoted affection'.[161] Sometimes the young sister-in-law – that is the wife's younger sister who often lived with a couple – became like a real sister, and yet also like a wife. The legal prohibition against the marriage to a deceased wife's sister which was passionately debated from the 1830s to its abolition in the early twentieth century, suggests similar deep-seated tensions.[162] The erotic overtones between brother and sister have an affinity to the pattern observed between father and daughter. Most of the fictional accounts are from a male voice. It has been pointed out that for Dickens, fantasizing about younger sisters (or sisters-in-law) was central to his 'fondest forbidden game', sexual attraction to young girls.[163]

The merging of the wife with her sisters is not far fetched. Of all relation-ships in this period, sisters may well have been the closest to each other. Sisters had lived together through childhood and adolescence without the periods of absence almost inevitable for a brother. Only marriage could remove a young woman permanently from her parental home, leaving, as one sister wrote, 'a chasm' in the family circle.[164] The loss was felt most acutely at the death of a sister. Jane Ransome Biddell was especially affected by the death of her elder and only sister since they had earlier lost their mother. It was 'a sister's love sincere, taught me to dry the filial tear'. It was her sister who had kept her from straying from God and 'who would nurse her in illness now?'[165]

Our study of business enterprises has shown how single or widowed sisters could pool their resources to establish a home, with or without taking in pupils or boarders. Some of these all-female households instituted a rough division of labour which imitated more conventional families. Three Quaker sisters were able to live on the modest income left by their brewer father. The eldest, who was highly educated, a minister and active in philanthropy, played the male role taking care of the finances and disciplining her sisters' emotional excesses. The youngest sister managed the domestic side 'and was as the hands and feet' of that of which the eldest was the head, a division of labour echoed in the menage of Hannah More and her sisters.[166]

Sisters-in-law could be close, for marriage to a friend's brother turned friendship into sisterhood, the match sometimes having been fostered by the two women to that end. In cases of brother–sister marriage to sister–brother such ties were compounded. The menage of William, Dorothy and William's wife, Mary Wordsworth (and often the visiting Sarah, Mary's sister) is familiar. Dorothy and Sarah's share in raising William and Mary's children was also a common experience. Sisters and sisters-in-law together undertook the care of elderly parents, and had a general concern with the adolescents of the family. As in modern families, sisters were instrumental in keeping members together and sisterhood became the prototype of female relationships.[167]

Brothers and brothers-in-law were more often directly linked through the enterprise. Brothers were not only partners but were often in related occupations where services, customers, goods, expertise and credit were constantly exchanged. Brothers were the favoured trustee for a man's widow and children. These business arrangements did not preclude deep emotional attachment between many adult brothers. Abram Constable was living at home when John, his elder by seven years, was in training as an artist in London. Abram had freed John by taking his place in the corn business and interceded with their father for more finance for the struggling artist. Abram wrote that he 'would have died for his brother John'.[168] In fiction, it was the father's brother who was often portrayed as the kindly figure who steps in to save the orphaned family by placing the sons in situations, buying back the family home or providing one himself. The husband's brother becomes almost his reincarnation, although the sexual tensions in the wife's sister relationship are nowhere given the same attention partly because the widow with children was not seen as a sexually desirable object. There seems no suggestion of legally prohibiting such a marriage (which is, in fact, encouraged in the Old Testament). The fictional role played by the husband's brother is matched in the local records, although more often it is the wife's brothers who took action in her interests. The Yarmouth draper whose elder brother had twice given him disastrous advice in business affairs, sought the aid of his wife's brother who bought back some of their furniture after the bankruptcy.[169]

Deep friendships lasting a lifetime were made between in-laws. In the

1780s, an Essex man wrote to his recently married sister how much he missed her and his 'brother Savill' and added, 'but I have at last uniformly concluded that we are separated only by a few miles. . . . Make my kindest Love to my Brother'.[170] The nomenclature here is significant. The prefix 'Brother' or 'Sister', followed by the surname was used for both own siblings and in-laws. Brothers and sisters and their spouses became uncles and aunts to the children of the next generation. Nephews were the favoured partners after sons and brothers; nieces the favoured companion and house-hold help after sisters or daughters. Information from the wills sustains the expectation that aunts and uncles were regarded as surrogate parents. Of the 166 female testators, 36 per cent took siblings or siblings' children as their 'primary legatee'; sisters being 11 per cent and nieces 8 per cent. As would be expected, the proportion of siblings and siblings' children who were primary legatees of male testators was lower since they often had widows and their own children as first responsibility. Nevertheless, even then, brothers and sisters, nieces and nephews accounted for 10 per cent, and of these sisters were half again as likely to be named as brothers as primary legatees for men.[171]

The role of wider kin

Uncles and aunts provided an important resource even when the parents were alive and capable. Several local families sent children away to schools run by parents' siblings or used their homes to board. They were particu-larly useful in starting off a young person's career. The ten adult siblings of an Essex farming family had a complicated exchange arrangement among their children. Two nephews from different branches were sent to the academy run by their uncle. Two others were apprenticed to uncles in urban trades. The maiden aunt who ran a stationers shop took in a niece as informal apprentice who, in turn, set up in a bake shop with the help of a niece from the third generation.[172] Even spending a month in the hive of Evangelicalism at the rectory affected the Rev. Marsh's three nieces who went home to start a household Bible Association. (Marsh himself admits that he was converted by an aunt in his boyhood.)[173] Where pairs of siblings had intermarried, they became double uncle and aunt to the same children. Interest in the younger generation was also strong where cousins had married and aunts and uncles thus became mothers and fathers-in-law and grandparents twice over. It was not unknown for the children of sibling marriages to marry each other as double cousins thus producing a singularly dense family web (see Figure 3, p. 220).

Cousins were favoured as close friends. Because of the large numbers and wide age range, there was a greater choice than with siblings. Female cousins could act as surrogate sisters and female pairs of cousins were often as close as sisters. The fact that cousins could marry, however, could make the relationship of male–female cousins problematic.[174] A Quaker apprentice was particularly close to his cousin Sophia since his sisters closest in age to him had died. He sent Sophia volumes of Cowper and other gifts including a framed portrait of himself, while she mended his stockings. After Sophia's marriage when he himself was courting, his prospective bride's parents wished to know the extent of his previous attachment, whereupon he answered:

Thou knowest the regard I have for Sophy, thou knowest too, how intimate we were for I have told thee all, and though some suspected more than friendship, it was only because they knew not how to reconcile such brotherly and sisterly attachment to a relationship not nearer than cousin.[175]

Male cousins could be called upon to perform general masculine functions of advice and protection, if not support. A young Essex attorney found himself taking over the business and financial affairs for his somewhat tiresome cousins living in London on the proceeds of an Essex property. However, there were some compensations for while rural Bocking sent a turkey to Hampstead at Christmas, Hampstead regularly sent fish to Bocking.[176]

Grandparents when they were alive also provided aid and support. A City merchant living in Essex who had had fourteen children took in two widowed daughters and their young families (one whose husband had been killed in the Peninsular campaign) as well as the daughter and her children whose merchant husband was frequently abroad. At that time, his own youngest child was under 3 so that provision for childcare was readily available.[177] In the census sample, grandsons under 16 were more frequently to be found in less well off households where their labour would be welcomed. Girls living with their grandmothers (who were household heads) made up a quarter of all forty-three resident grandchildren.[178] As often as not, while grandparents provided the home and material support, it was the young aunts – the daughters at home – who gave actual care. The intervention of this intermediate generation could help soften disparities between the elderly grandparent and young children.

It has been observed how marriage ties bound together not only the couple but their siblings and siblings' children. A similar strong bond can be traced between married people and their spouses' parents – again reinforced in the case of sibling marriage. These relationships were recognized in business dealings which survived the death of a spouse. But it could also include affection and mutual concern over grandchildren. William Bentall, an Essex farmer, was on cordial visiting terms with the parents of his first wife, Susanna Foster, who had left two young children. After William's remarriage the elder couple continued their childcare, and from the tone of William's diary he was still attached to 'Father' and 'Mother' Foster to the extent of attending a funeral in the Foster family.[179]

Familial reciprocity at the margins of cousins and in-laws merged into friendship. The Essex farmer, John Bunting, had a daughter and a son who married respectively, the son and daughter of the near-by farming family of Seabrook. When John Bunting died in 1858, his will named Richard and Robert Seabrook as executors, describing them simply as 'my friends'. However, from other evidence we know that they were also his daughter's husband's brothers as well as his son's wife's brothers and uncles as well as fathers to his two sets of grandchildren.[180] The ramifications of such overlapping relationships were further complicated when remarriage and step-kin were involved. The expectations and responsibilities surrounding all family relationships were to some extent mutable. They were most strongly enforced within the inner core of husband and wife, parents and children and siblings, radiating outwards to aunts and uncles, nieces and nephews, grandparents and cousins.

There was, however, a small minority of people, voluntarily or not, left with only meagre family resources. The former were almost always men who were socially and geographically mobile and had chosen to cut themselves adrift from their family of origin. Instead they attached themselves to sponsors, as in the case of the impecunious but ambitious Dr Dixon in Witham who relied on a woman patient and fellow chapel members.[181] A few individuals were without family through demographic accident. Henry Crabb Robinson, the son of a Suffolk tanner who became a well-known man of letters, had only two brothers and did not marry himself. His eldest brother lost his wife after the birth of two children who died young. The two surviving children of his other brother became high Anglicans and Tories and had fallen out with their uncle. Robinson had been articled to a Colchester lawyer along with a fellow Independent, William Henry Pattisson, from Witham. He made the Pattissons into a substitute family, spending his holidays with them, supplying Mrs Pattisson with books and following the progress of their children. William's wife wrote to Robinson saying: 'Your claims, my boys and my own, on the regard of William, are so distinct, yet so strong that I trust they will never be disregarded or undervalued.'[182]

The Robinson family had always been sickly and vulnerable to consumption. The Hedge family of Colchester, on the other hand, were usually long lived, but they were not immune from the epidemics which decimated even middle-class homes. By the time she was 30, Mary Ann Hedge, lifelong spinster, had lost all seven of her brothers. In 1815, she also lost her mother and four nephews and nieces within three months. By the age of 40, she had only one nephew left in the Colchester area. In late middle age she wrote a 'Fireside Reverie' which dwelt on being 'the only remaining link in the golden chain which bound in sweetest, firmest union the charities of parent, child and brother'. The 'Family Fireside' which she regarded as the 'sublime of human life' was now cold and empty and she was left feeling 'void of soul', her only comfort being her fervent belief in the after life when all would be united in the Heavenly Home.[183]

Mary Ann Hedge was one of the women who turned the quest for the 'golden chain' of happy families into a quasi-profession. But there can be no doubt that family life was a positive experience for many people and, perhaps most important of all, they made a point of perceiving it in this way. But inevitably, the burdens and rewards of family life were unevenly spread, producing conflicts of interest between branches and individuals. The expectation built up for family support and love could turn endemic tension into flaming and bitter rows, almost predictable where property and emotional attachment were so closely linked. The dispute over the inheritance of Rebecca Shaen resulted in the break off of relations between brothers and sisters. Although ultimately her children's claims were won, she feared that they would be more injured by family divisions than benefited by pecuniary advantages gained. For herself, 'I once had a very large circle to love and by whom I was beloved – but this subject is too much for me' and her diary then remains silent on this matter.[184]

Tensions over loyalties between the natal and marital family frequently surface even in small matters such as where the adult children would spend Christmas or family celebrations. It has been seen how each spouse's family and their own children could struggle for the services of a woman or the material support of a man. At times these intra-familial conflicts were exacerbated by differences in status and resources. When one branch of a family had made its way up the social ladder, poor or vulgar relations could be a handicap. Yet there are numerous examples of more prosperous or educated relatives giving kin a helping hand. Many of the rituals instituted or expanded by the middle class not only celebrated family life but brought straying sheep back into the fold. Birthday gatherings, funerals and Christmas were occasions when the junior branches were expected to attend or at least send representatives.[185]

Personal inclination and ability could often run counter to standard rules and expected characteristics, making some women and even men restive. While all male and female roles were seen to partake of clear cut gender characteristics, only one – husband and wife – embraced legitimate sexuality. The underlying erotic associations were, however, found wherever there was the constellation of male power through age, experience, material and cultural resources. Large families which created an intermediate generation helped to spread these tensions, but could also blur boundaries. Since the family was set up as a model of peace, harmony and purity it was difficult for such tensions to be expressed. It could be argued, for example, that the concern of the middle class with working-class familial disorder and incest may have had as much to do with their own preoccupations.[186] It is interesting that despite the emphasis on motherhood in the prescriptive material, the depiction of mother–son relationships is somewhat thin, if overly idealized. In contra-distinction to fathers and daughters, or brothers and sisters, in local fiction, only one writer alludes to this relationship. A widowed mother finds the joy of a husband and child's love 'exaltedly combin'd in her belov'd first born son'.[187] The depth of anxiety aroused by admitting an erotic cast to the mother–son, or older woman–younger man relationship may have been simply too great. Sons (younger brothers or nephews) had the task of breaking away from an intense but *dependent* relationship with their mother (or substitute female care taker), who combined love for the child with firm moral sense, pressing upon the boy's feelings of guilt, sin and duty. Under such emotional pressure the transition to dominant masculinity might well have been uneasy. The ensuing splitting between pure asexual and idealized mother/sister figures and the forbidden territories of prostitution familiar to the psyche of mid and late Victorian men become more understandable.[188]

But for all of those where economic survival as well as social, personal and sexual identity depended on defining a place within a family, emotions ran deep. Most men and women of the provincial middle class would have agreed with Rebecca Solly Shaen, looking back in old age at mid century, that, indeed, 'Our Family is a little World.'[189]

8 'My own fireside': the creation of the middle-class home

Twas a home for a Poet, Philosopher, Sage,
Twas a cradle for youth, an asylum for age;
Where the world's burning cares and its sorrows might cease
For all was humility, comfort and peace.

Anon, quoted in the commonplace book of Jane Seabrook, Essex 1832

On a rainy afternoon in August 1832, a 12-year-old vicar's daughter recorded in her diary that, while walking near the rural parsonage, she had seen 'a poor miserable woman in a tent by the roadside . . . she has a bad drunken husband who has quite starved her; and now that they cannot pay their rent they have been turned out of their house. To add to her miseries, she is very ill, having just given birth to a child. Mama has been once or twice to see her and given her broth'. A few weeks later, she saw a figure lying by the roadside who she assumed was sleeping but later discovered was dead from cholera.[1]

The recording of such incidents by a young, delicately raised girl brings home the concrete threats which surrounded many middle-class families. Along with continuing political unrest, the exigencies of poverty, brutality, pressing sexuality, disease and death were all too familiar. Against these, people struggled to control their destiny through religious grace and the bulwark of family property and resources. These shields took practical as well as symbolic form in middle-class homes and gardens and in the organization of the immediate environment through behaviour, speech and dress. The sense that individuals, with God's help, were captains of their fate, was daily confronted by material conditions and recalcitrant human beings. Great effort went into creating a life programme which would at once guide their own aims and behaviour while proclaiming status and spreading influence to others.

What was a home?

The building of a separate space where this programme could be carried out was their achievement. But the form of housing, the shell within which that space, 'a home', was to be made, was neither fully thought out nor secure. Most middle-class housing was rented; much of it was still attached to the enterprise. Landlords might be reluctant to introduce expensive alterations and so block or delay innovation; on the other hand, rental

Plate 21 The interior of an Essex farmhouse from an amateur painting. The farmer's widow is surrounded by paraphernalia of the middle-class home: barometer, paintings, patterned wallpaper, brass fender and carpets

meant relative ease in moving to better quarters. In the early part of the period, 'home' was as much a social construct and state of mind as a reality of bricks and mortar. When a purpose-built or renovated home was constructed it was highly prized. Catherine Marsh, the 14-year-old daughter of the Rev. William, wrote of her delight in returning to her Edgbaston home after a visit: ' "Home", the very name, how sweet it is and what a sense of comfort and happiness it does convey.'[2] One of the greatest hardships of the comparatively poor members of the middle class was to go into lodgings, in other people's houses. As a middle-aged Colchester spinster noted bitterly, living in lodgings meant never being able to impress a personality on surroundings, intrusions of privacy, restrictions on hospitality and sudden notices to quit.[3]

Both the desire for efficiency and moral purpose had elevated the ordering and separation of time, tasks and space to a central place in middle-class life. This was as true for women as for men, for domestic affairs and housing space as for business. In 1821, when she was 16, the daughter of an Essex Independent wool merchant–farmer, was given a commonplace book, printed with divided sections for various entries complete with instructions. The title page exhorted: 'The improvement of our time is the first consideration in human life, for on time depends eternity . . . let no hour or minute be without its use.'[4]

The search for segregated living patterns and housing was in two stages. Productive work first had to be banished from the domestic area. Within this space, cooking, eating, washing, sleeping and other 'back stage' functions then began to be separated from polite social intercourse and eventually to have special places for each function. In the 1793 renovations of the Taylor's house in Lavenham, the parlour had a sliding panel 'for convenient communication with the kitchen'.[5] This informal proximity was soon phased out of middle-class homes and not reintroduced until the 1930s.

The second separation was epitomized by the suburban villa: physically, financially and socially removed from the enterprise, the strong tide of segregation noted by F. M. L. Thompson and taken up in Cannadine's discussion of Birmingham housing.[6] While the aristocracy and gentry had segregated some functions and spaces since the seventeenth century, their leisured lifestyle incorporated both estate management and honorific legal and political duties in the design of country seats.[7] At the other extreme, wage labourers, whether in factories or on the land, daily experienced a disjunction between the small space where they slept and ate and the employers' premises where their work-filled days were spent, with streets, open spaces and taverns serving their brief leisure. It was the middle ranks who erected the strictest boundaries between private and public space, a novelty which struck many early nineteenth-century travellers in England.

Within that space, both the worldly and the religious followed routines which emphasized their commitment to the family. Twice daily family prayers, an innovation often cited in the local records, stressed the allocation of roles among family members, while underlining the whole. Family occasions were marked by ritual. In 1813, when Isaac and Ann Martin Taylor's eldest son, also Isaac, turned 21 the family made a special ramble into the countryside, ending with a festive meal. There 'the day was passed as happily, perhaps, as if a host of tenants had been regaled in front of the Ancestral Hall'.[8] The New Year was a time to take stock, while Christmas was becoming the time for family gathering and pledging of loyalties. A Quaker woman's Christmas recollection of an Essex farm expressed the 'living presence of the Lord when we gather around the board for meals, around the hearth, soft accents, glances of love and friendship' and the yearning it strengthened to meeting friends in Heaven.[9]

Family time was also important for secular pursuits in such practices as recreation on Sundays and summer holidays. In Essex and Suffolk, a week or two in lodgings on the coast promoted the development of seaside resorts like Southend and Walton-on-Naze. From Birmingham, the wealthier might go further afield to the Isle of Wight, while Aberystwyth became a favoured holiday spot. During these breaks from the routine of business, the father could renew his place in the family. Botanizing or looking for shells, the pursuit of science and taste, could be combined with wonder at God's handiwork by old and young together.

Such preoccupations and routines grew from an indigenous middle-class provincial culture. However, there were tensions between this culture and the aristocratic leadership which stressed lavish expenditure on clothes, food, furnishing, equipages and entertainments, part of the traditional trappings of leadership. There were also contradictory elements within middle-class culture. An Italian, reflecting on his visit to England in the 1820s, declared that 'comfort is in the mouth of every Englishman at every moment' and that 'family' took the place of continental 'society'; even the English national song seemed to be 'Home Sweet Home'. Yet he was perplexed that the Englishman was also obsessed with working.[10] In standards of housing, furniture, food, service, dress and behaviour, there was always a tug between demonstrating worldly status – and creditworthiness – and a religious, moral rejection of the material world. Too much success could spill into extravagance and incur debt. 'If I cannot raise my means to my wishes, I bring my wishes to my means' was the received wisdom handed down in a Unitarian Essex family.[11] And yet, maintaining a certain material level was necessary to moral worth. In middle-class eyes to be poor was to be vulgar despite special pleading: 'It is an idle, a mistaken, an unmanly [sic] fear, that a reduction in the way of life is disgraceful.'[12] Rural surroundings were promoted not only as more conducive to religion but also for simpler living. Where wealth and space permitted, some of these tensions could be reduced by using more public rooms for display and keeping 'family' rooms for everyday use and religious practices, the segregation itself being a sign of a well ordered life. Where a 'double set of apartments' was not possible, the divisions had to be marked by a firm segregation of tasks, time and personnel.[13]

Women were mainly responsible for creating and maintaining the house, its contents and its human constituents. To this end, they had first to order themselves. Those born in the mid eighteenth century had a simpler lifestyle and were cruder in manner and speech. Their children and grandchildren's generations were often shocked by their more relaxed elders. A commentator has noted the difference in an Independent Witham family, where the eighteenth-century woman with her earthy good sense and informal power within her community gave way to the equally intelligent and strong character of her daughters-in-law, better educated but 'ladies at the mercy of the etiquette necessary to an enlarged urban society'.[14] Not all women made the transition with good grace. Some who had grown up heavily involved in the enterprise refused to move into segregated housing, a type illustrated by the mill owner Robert Thornton's mother, in Mrs Gaskell's *North and South*. Some women chose religious retirement, some more worldly advancement. But whatever the route, the genteel household was becoming the focus of most women's lives.

Exactly what level of consumption denoted gentility was a perpetual problem. By the 1790s, a range of comforts and even luxuries was becoming available to a larger proportion of the population. In the following decades, war and inflation again shifted the boundaries of the desirable and the possible. James Luckcock, the Birmingham jeweller, in his *Hints for Practical Economy in the Management of Household Affairs*, impressed upon his readers the absolute necessity for accurate knowledge of both income and expenditure. Luckcock aimed his exhortations at those in the income range £50 to £400 (the same lower limit at which income tax began and maximum over which full rate was charged after its introduction in 1802). For Luckcock, under an income of 1 gn a week (at least twice a labourer's wage), life seemed to verge on privation.[15]

Burnett estimates that in the early nineteenth century, food and servants took up one-half of a typical middle-class income, a proportion roughly confirmed in the local records, with rents and rates accounting for between one-eighth and one-fifth more. Extra lump sum expenditure then had to be found for furniture, special clothes, a son's partnership or a daughter's wedding, often such large items waiting on investment income, windfalls or sales of assets.[16] Serious Christians added regular amounts for subscriptions to voluntary societies and charities, an important form of religious and moral consumption. Eligibility for local office and voting rights also depended on the rateable value of property, and seating position in church or chapel depended on what pew rent could be afforded.

Expenditure had to be balanced by the numbers in the household, their needs and contributions. The definition of family and household, however, was fluid. According to the Registrar General, by the mid nineteenth century, the family consisted of a head and dependent members, preferably including servants, living within the same dwelling.[17] Over the period, the idea had developed that such a dwelling should be a space enclosed from the intrusion of all who were not 'family and friends'. A mid century Suffolk commentator wrote approvingly of local housing which allowed even the artisan a 'separate tenement secure from vulgar curiosity and mischievous meddling'.[18] Here a political radical echoes Loudon's view that space between dwellings made practical piety and good domestic habits easier to maintain.[19] Similarly, lodging within other people's houses had been standard practice at least for eighteenth-century urban dwellers; for example, Archibald Kenrick first went to Birmingham to set up as a bucklemaker and settled into lodgings. But in the nineteenth century lodging became associated with a stage for the young, or an expedient only for the genteel poor.

A similar desire for privacy marked property boundaries with gates, drives, hedges and walls around house and garden. Humphrey Repton strikingly demonstrated the effect in his paper model of the space in front of his Essex 'cottage' where the view of shops, road and passing public was cut off by fencing, shrubbery and trees; a strong contrast to the communal squares and terraces of Georgian styles.[20] The novel device of the semi-detached house, combining the privacy and economy of a smaller house with the appearance of one twice the size, was peculiar to suburban development.[21] The inherent anti-urbanism of middle-class culture was reflected in the quintessential image of early nineteenth-century desirable housing, the *white cottage* with thatched roof and porch embowered with honeysuckle and roses. 'The White Cottage' in the commonplace book of an Essex farmer's daughter is the place where 'the world's cares and sorrows might cease, for all was humility, comfort and peace'.[22] But middle-class housing had to provide more than just a haven for family withdrawal for the home was also a stage for social ritual and outward manifestation of status in the community.

Undoubtedly, some details in housing and furnishing came from gentry emulation. For example, there are hints that visiting professional men, the local attorney calling to draw up a document and stopping for a glass of wine or the doctor attending a prestigious patient, noted and imitated the accoutrements of upper-class style. The homes of local gentry were regularly opened to a select public, providing a glimpse of taste to be followed even if it was electroplate rather than solid silver which graced middle-class sideboards. But the middle classes used and transformed gentry settings for their own purposes. Their type of housing, its distribution in towns and villages, its gardens and surroundings were part of the bid for independence from traditional aristocratic dictates. Neither was this pattern in direct line with the eighteenth-century mansions of merchants built next to counting houses and packing sheds or of professionals inhabitating eighteenth-century terraces and squares.

Part of the need for more segregated living space came from new activities made possible through time and labour freed from subsistence needs: reading, writing, music, fancy needlework, pursuit of scientific hobbies and the entertainment of friends. The capacity to create and beautify this type of home was becoming an expectation of natural feminine identity. A farmer prayed that God would permit his family 'the great gift of a new or restored, more commodious dwelling' that 'my Lizzie will have more scope for her tasteful devices. She understands the adornment of a home'. This contrasted with his childhood, for he found a great change towards a 'loftier and more refined civilization hallowing our dwellings', which he identified with women's influence.[23]

The demand for middle-class housing had built up over the latter half of the eighteenth century and blossomed in the boom of the first two decades of the nineteenth.[24] All levels, from the residences of gentlemen to the refitting of modest shops, were affected by the new ideals. Much of this early development was in-filling along main roads or parcelling up of large gardens within the old town centres.[25] In late eighteenth-century Colchester, for example, manufacturing, professional and banking families had imposing residences on the main streets leading out through crumbling town gates. Such homes, near huddled courts of small artisans or tenements of the poor, emphasized status through architectural devices in house fronts, windows and doorways. With population growth and the escalation in building, parts of the town became differentiated into docking facilities, warehouses, manufacturing workshops and markets. Professional offices and retail outlets clustered in certain areas, albeit still housing the living quarters of the family.[26]

In late eighteenth-century Birmingham, attempts were made to create small enclaves for the well-to-do, such as Old Square with its communal gardens, trim walks and iron palisadoes.[27] A slightly later select development, the Crescent, planned to compete with Bath, was never completed for, like Old Square, it had the inconveniences but not the advantages of

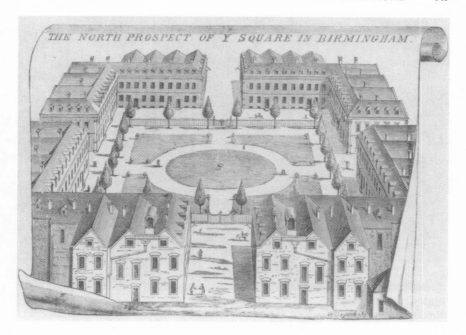

Plate 22 Old Square, Birmingham. A late eighteenth-century housing development for the middle class

town or country and was marred by the 'near neighbourhood of the canal-wharf, with all the concomitant noises, and a superabundance of vulgar language . . . detrimental to the eligibility of the place of a domestic residence'.[28] Only limited new building had spread to the outer edges, the genteel residences of Birmingham's Moseley and Balsall Heath in the 1780s.

Building promotion also depended on whether large landowners were willing to release blocks of land. The Colmores and Gooches who provided most of the early examples in Birmingham were matched on a smaller scale by the Mildmays of Chelmsford and the Fonnereaus of Ipswich. However, many of these early projects suffered the fate of a Birmingham bucklemaker, immortalized in popular song, who built himself a country house only to find that:

> The town itself has walked up hill,
> Now he lives beside a smokey mill,
> In the middle of the streets of Brummagem.[29]

The only sure way of escape was to build or rent a country house well beyond the town boundaries. By 1818, the country round the town was 'studded with houses belonging to the opulent inhabitants of Birmingham . . . or of those who have retired from busy scenes of life'.[30] Gradually these were added to by purpose-built 'ornamental villas', often put up or

Plate 23 Digbeth House, the home of Thomas Gibbins, manager and co-owner of a Birmingham metalware company, and his wife Emma Cadbury Gibbins from 1837–50. The house was next door to the works

rented by wealthy bankers and attorneys on the edge of towns, as much for investment as a family seat in the gentry sense.[31]

In villages close to coaching lines, improved coastal, canal and river traffic or later railways, there was also much new building and remodelling. Farm out-buildings in the high street were replaced by homes and shops. Even purely agricultural small villages had their complement of middle-class families in addition to the clergy.[32] In Rochford, Essex, in the 1820s, a solicitor, who also acted as auctioneer and land agent, moved to the newly refurbished 'Connaught House' just off the main square when he married the daughter of the bank director. His brother, also a solicitor, lived in the square at 'The Lavenders', later a boarding school. Opposite was a druggist shop with living space above. A corner house across from the bank house was used by a farmer for general dealing and agricultural machinery, and was his home from which he farmed.[33]

The separation of home from work

The expansion of middle-class housing, whether though the conversion of existing buildings or the building of new structures, provided a source of lucrative investment and made fortunes for local families. These homes were designed to enhance privacy and respectability even when next to or part of the enterprise. At first there was some ambivalence about the desirability of separation. Families moved between premises near the works at the town centre and villas on the outskirts as the prosperity of the business waxed and waned. It is significant that in a moral tale by a Suffolk clergyman, 'A

Plate 24   Blue Mill, Witham, Essex, and the adjacent home of the miller's family

Merchant's Wife', the young husband's desire to move away from rooms over the counting house is portrayed as striving for status and due to 'false shame'. His more modest Christian wife does not mind 'living above'. She argues: 'you have no fatiguing walk, now, after a wearisome day; and while the counting house is so near me, I have more of your society'. Proximity and interest in the business allows her to save them from bankruptcy by her opportune intervention.[34] Yet such proximity ran counter to valued privacy and protection from public gaze. In 1819, two young ladies visiting Birmingham's Galton and James Bank complained: 'Called . . . on Mr and Mrs James, the only unpleasant part of which was, the being ushered as usual through the Bank.'[35]

Since for merchants goods were processed in workers' cottages, the business had only contained the counting house and space for storing raw materials and packing finished goods. For generations, spaces for these activities had been part of residential premises. In Birmingham and Colchester sumptuous houses were adjoined by such offices and could, for example, include 'tenting grounds' for cloth, although hedges, walls and shrubbery might be used to screen productive activities from the living quarters.[36]

Manufacture such as brewing, where success depended on the entrepreneur's supervision, kept brew houses sited next door to the works, not a great inconvenience since brewing had to ensure ingredients free from smoke and smuts. But even where a process was noisy and dirty, the family might still live beside or near even such noisome works as a tannery. An Essex farmer, William Bentall, turned to manufacture after his successful invention of a special plough. In 1817 he moved to take advantage of the new Blackwater canal, and accommodated the numerous household of his three marriages in a house within the foundry complex where the family stayed into the 1870s.[37] Millers continued to live in mill houses close to or contiguous with tidal or river mills. Where the entrepreneur and his family did move away, often a son, younger partner or manager moved in, a pattern followed in the Constable family when Golding built a new house in the village just before the artist, John's, birth leaving a manager in the mill house.[38] Similarly, Matthew Boulton's large new warehouse by Birmingham's canal was designed with a side entrance giving access to the manager's house next door.[39]

Into the nineteenth century, banking operations were usually carried on in the front room of the bank house partly as a security measure when specie was kept in cash boxes or chests.[40] In one such bank house even the privileged youngest daughter was banned from entering the sanctum of the 'Bank Parlour'.[41] Similarly, accommodation for schoolmasters usually adjoined the school if not below or above the single school room. Birmingham's King Edward VIth School, built in the 1830s, was typical, with a centre and two wings on three sides of a small quadrangle with a dwelling-house for the headmaster, three school rooms and a library and behind it a smaller house for the second master.[42]

Professional men had little practical motivation to separate family life from those business premises which were neither dirty, nor noisy and which did not involve the social threat of a large workforce. In market towns, most doctors and attorneys remained in the centre, although they were beginning to cluster in more genteel streets. The Pattissons, whose legal practice and land holdings made them one of Witham's wealthiest families, lived in a large, double-fronted brick house in a central position on the main street. It was connected to the building used for law offices by a gangway between the first floors.[43] Doctors saw patients and mixed drugs in their front rooms and boarded their apprentice assistants in the house. In the main street of an Essex village, an early nineteenth-century surgeon occupied a handsome house with 'three parlours, three elegant bedrooms and a coach house'.[44] Even when Birmingham's prominent physician, Withering, a member of the Lunar Society, made the decision to rent Edgbaston Hall, he was assured that such a residence 'near Birmingham would be equally well adapted for his professional employment'.[45]

The separation of functions in shops took the form of removing preparation processes from rooms used for eating and sleeping. An eighteenth-century Ipswich butcher kept his chopping block and 'cliver' in the backroom/kitchen, the front room being used for living and sleeping and, significantly, still housing a spinning wheel. By the early nineteenth century, the hall as a place for living and sleeping had dwindled to an entry while the two main rooms became dining room and parlour. The shop was now a separate room holding stock and/or tools.[46] By the 1820s, shops in a town like Chelmsford were 'well stocked', and some of them had 'handsome plate glass windows', while Birmingham reached 'the high tide of retail trade . . . the shops of the higher degrees are very handsomely fitted up; the form and sweep of the windows and the style of the decorations emulating those of the Metropolis', including a 40 foot show room with cut glass decor and Doric columns.[47]

The growth of fire insurance had necessitated a clearer definition of a shop as opposed to living premises. The Housing Act of 1827, in setting penalties for burglary, stated: 'that no Building although within the same Curtilage [courtyard] with the Dwelling House . . . shall be deemed Part of such Dwelling House . . . unless there shall be a Communication between [them] either immediate or by means of an enclosed Passage'.[48] Inns, hotels and public houses gradually yielded separate rooms for the family. By the 1830s, 'the drinking place became less like a home and more like a shop', while privacy for the drink seller, as we have seen, was ensured by the introduction of 'the bar' marking his (or her) domain.[49]

Farms presented the greatest challenge to the separation of domestic life from production. Yet by the early nineteenth century, there had been extensive alterations to existing farms and much effort went into planning new ones. Novel farming methods tidied many functions into barns and sheds; manure was cleared from farmyards for use as fertilizer. The older pattern had been a square of utilitarian buildings with the farmhouse making up the fourth side, no garden but an entrance through a mucky yard.[50] This 'casual chaos' changed with the 'more planned and purposeful lay-out of the new order'.[51] Farmhouses, too, had additions of brick fronts, sash windows and door lintels covering their muddle of elevations, hiding mud and wattle exteriors. By siting the kitchen and working places at the back and presenting such a front to the road, 'farmhouses could approximate to mere . . . residences that could just as well have appeared in town'.[52] By the 1840s, 'Essex farmhouses and buildings are for the most part substantial and ornamental with neat gardens and choice evergreens',[53] thus fulfilling Loudon's dictum that the common operations of the yard should not be seen from or interfere with the approaches to the house. Indeed, he had maintained that the distinguishing feature between the country residence and the rude farm was the appearance of house, garden and grounds.[54]

The semi-circular drive past the doors with gates marked the genteel dwelling. Another was the addition of back premises to act as 'offices', kitchens and stables, for example, where the manual work was performed (foreshadowing the evolution of the modern meaning of 'office'). These features figured prominently in renovations undertaken by the Anglican clergy who particularly benefited from housing reform, even though the rectory or vicarage was still next door to the church. In the countryside, agricultural prosperity increased tithe income, while everywhere a government act, 'Queen Ann's Bounty', had promoted the residence of parochial clergy by matching funds for modernizing residences. In 1828, a Suffolk vicar raised £1000 on Glebe tithes, matched by the fund, to erect new outbuildings and remodel the rectory with dining and breakfast rooms, butler's pantry, servants' hall, kitchen and back kitchen and the luxury of an indoor water closet.[55] An Essex coastal village in the 1820s saw both the old hall and vicarage remodelled, the latter with a new well, storage rooms for vegetables, harness room and stable, privy and circular lawn – cost to the hall £3500, to the vicarage £1434.[56]

In the eighteenth century, most houses in the Essex countryside had been timber framed with lath and plaster walls and thatched roofs.[57] But by the 1830s, modest manors, large farmhouses, and rectories had changed to a comparable lay-out and physical appearance. Both market towns and villages experienced a rash of brick fronting, the installation of sash windows, doorways with carved lintels or doric columned porticos. Slate roofs were replacing thatch, giving both a handsome appearance and protection against rodents and insects. Yet these improvements were also recognized as claims to social standing. The vicar of Witham fulminated against what he saw as sham: 'every dwelling needs put on a new brick front as though lath and plaster were a disgrace'. His disgust may partly have been because the vicarage had been encased in a brick shell leaving the roof on its old supports with 'room for a man between the timber frame and outside wall', supporting nothing, but collecting rain water.[58]

In a manufacturing town the size of Birmingham, demand for specialized middle-class enclaves grew, as large tracts of working-class housing jostled commercial development in the town centre. The Rev. William Marsh, when in Colchester, lived in the vicarage on the High Street around the corner from his church of St Peter's and next door to the Corn Market. In 1829 when he was called to the town centre church of St Thomas's Birmingham, the family chose to live in the recently developed suburb of Edgbaston over a mile away.[59]

Edgbaston represented the largest, most exclusive suburb in the town:

> See Edgbaston, the bed of prosperous trade,
> Where they recline who have their fortunes made;
> Strong in their wealth, no matter how possessed,
> There fashion calls, and there at ease they rest,
> The beauteous suburb swells with lofty pride;
> The vulgar poor are there forbid to hide.
> With longing eye, the favoured of the day
> Towards the loved purlieu make their eager way;
> And as their broughams by our dwellings wheel,
> We think how nice it is to be genteel.[60]

Clergy and professionals were some of Edgbaston's most enthusiastic residents as befitting their espousal of domestic ideals. By the 1850s, twenty-one clergymen (including John Angell James) lived in the suburb although there were only three local churches.[61] Such as area also appealed to those on independent incomes or retired, for although totally separated from the town's overcrowded courts, it was within 10 minutes' carriage drive or a brisk half hour's walk from the centre. According to a contemporary, the soil, the air and elevation overlooking the open country, the 'exclusion of manufactories and small houses render Edgbaston a favourite place of domestic retreat'.[62] Yet the still active businessman could feel comfortably free from the social exclusion he might experience in villages dominated by gentry.

Unlike earlier developments, Edgbaston maintained its momentum through increased demand and the dominance of the landowner, Lord Calthorpe, with his far-sighted agent. Calthorpe was an Evangelical and for such Christians who favoured the provision of aids to morality, improved housing was a moral duty as well as an attractive long-term investment. Through careful control of leases and aid for amenities such as the Botanical and Horticultural Society, he ensured that the suburb remained residentially segregated despite the variety of its housing.[63] Edgbaston prided itself on its rural ambience; the old church and Edgbaston Hall helped maintain the aura of village life. The roads were bordered with trees and hedges securing privacy from the public gaze so that 'few points in England exhibit such an assemblage of architectural beauty amidst a landscape of so strictly a rural character', according to the local guide.[64]

Calthorpe's firm control protected the rewards of industry and success embodied in Edgbaston's homes:

> Glorious suburbs! long
> May you remain to bless the ancient town
> Whose crown ye are, rewarded of the cares
> Of those who toil amid the din and smoke
> Or iron-ribbed and hardy Birmingham,
> And may ye long *be* suburbs, keeping still
> Business at distance from your green retreats
> And the tall chimneys of the Millocrat
> Outside your smiling border.[65]

Undoubtedly Edgbaston was vital in keeping middle-class families within Birmingham's boundaries. An early historian of the town had observed how wealthy manufacturers celebrated their success by moving beyond its boundaries.[66] Now they remained and identified themselves as the town elite. Edgbaston's population rose from just over 1000 in 1801 to around 16,500 in 1841, and by 1850, twenty-nine roads had been laid out and uninterrupted growth assumed.[67] Previously those who had succeeded in business retired into the deeper countryside or genteel areas like Leamington, as did the japanner, James Bisset.[68] But now the typical family progression was like the Southalls, retail chemists who moved from the shop area in Bull Street to the modest development in Balsall Heath, finally arriving in Edgbaston.[69]

Agreement between ground landlord and tenants meant constant improvement in properties. A Quaker chemist was able to use the wealth from manufacturing phosphorous in the 1840s to remodel his modest Edgbaston home, gradually adding rooms and amenities as succeeding children were born.[70] Despite the control exercised by Calthorpe, house design in Edgbaston was typical of the middle-class villa style, allowing for much individual taste and moving away from Georgian uniformity.[71] The final effect was variation within a basic pattern, as with the Rev. Swann's 'family residence' in 1830's Edgbaston: 'an elegant veranda standing at an agreeable distance from the road, shielded by neat shrubbery with a garden entrance for servants and tradesmen and a large well cultivated garden', while inside were two parlours, five bedrooms plus kitchen and all the now expected offices.[72]

The meaning of the garden

In both image and practice the garden setting of the villa proclaimed the values of privacy, order, taste, and appreciation of nature in a controlled environment. Gardens were now seen as an extension of the home, a conceit enhanced by the introduction of glass doors ('French windows') opening from parlour or dining room. Smaller, non-utilitarian gardens surrounding a separate house became an integral part of the romantic, anti-urban individualism of the middle class.[73] The eighteenth-century gentry had enthusiastically supported estate improvement through landscape gardening. John Loudon, Robert Kerr and other nineteenth-century experts argued that a miniature version was within the means of all. But the broad sweep of grass and trees, the lack of ornamentation and muted colours recommended by Capability Brown or Humphrey Repton needed modification for middle-class taste. Nor were the eighteenth-century urban models more appealing with their communal squares and the terrace house with its narrow strip of yard at the back. By mid century, the individual villa garden had become the triumphantly dominant design.[74]

A larger effect was provided by pooling resources to create parks and botanic gardens, usually financed by subscription or floated as private companies. Their lay-out and acquisition of exotic and scientific plants imitated the grounds of the country estate but were open to a select public, regulated by graduated fees for admission. Like private gardens, they introduced new varieties brought from the empire and created by plant breeding. The Birmingham dahlia show was a well advertised but respectable annual event, while a public house in Colchester held flower shows in the yard which were expressly open 'not to all the meaner sort of people, but only to such of them as love flowers, can behave civilly and come without dogs'.[75]

Improvements in cast iron and the removal of the tax on glass had encouraged the growing of exotics in the conservatories of the wealthy, a fashion now followed in the modest middle-class greenhouse.[76] Thomas Clark, the Birmingham manufacturer of greenhouses, promoted Loudon's hope that the greenhouse 'would be an appendage to every villa, and to many town residences a mark of elegance and refined enjoyment'.[77] The family of a prosperous bucklemaker who had moved into a more salubrious part of Birmingham in 1811 soon established 'a nice greenhouse with grapes and flowers as well as peaches, apricots and nectarines in the open air'.[78] The local records suggest that grapes grown under glass had become the equivalent to the aristocratic pineapple, a high status gift. A Suffolk farmer gave bunches of them to business associates and friends he wished to mark with special favour.[79] By the 1830s, the lower middle class, especially the town dweller, was making do with the 'Ward case' full of ferns.[80]

The main feature of the middle-class garden was the lawn. The eighteenth-century lawn had been a 'great plain in a Park adjoining a Noble seat' (*OED*), cropped by sheep or laboriously by hand scythe. In the nineteenth century, it evolved into the suburban green carpet kept in trim by the iron lawn mower, first manufactured in 1830 by the Ransomes of Ipswich. The lawn was bordered by shrubberies, flower beds, fruit trees and vegetable beds, if there was no separate kitchen garden. For flowers, James Luckcock, in Edgbaston, had deliberately chosen the 'humble cowslip and unpretending fox glove, the meek snowdrop as well as the chaste and elegant lily or the magnificent Piony' (*sic*)[81] in keeping with his radicalism, for in this period certain flowers such as pinks and carnations were associated with artisans, others like dahlias were more genteel – and expensive.[82]

These innovations had reached even the countryside, for while in eighteenth-century Essex, 'gardens were few or were thought hardly worth valuing for probate',[83] by the 1800s when Arthur Young surveyed the country, he found farms improved into genteel residences with lawns, pleasure grounds and gardens.[84] In promoting gardening rural clerical families were leaders, for they commanded both leisure and the ideals to direct garden design. The Independent minister, Isaac Taylor, created gardens for himself and his neighbours wherever he found himself, be it a converted cloth merchant's house in the centre of Colchester or an Essex farmhouse. There, according to his daughter, the garden 'soon became a charming spot, with shrubbery, walks, terraced paths, rustic seats and flint-paved grottoes'. These standard accoutrements of garden design were installed by farmers, manufacturers and shopkeepers in the local areas. The prospect of the garden provided strong visual confirmation of the middle-class ideal. Ann Taylor recalled her father's completed rural idyll:

The house, newly white-washed, looked exceedingly pretty among the trees, covered with vine, which clings round the porch and surrounded by a large countryfied garden, laid out by father's unconquerable contrivance, in the prettiest rural style. There is an arched gateway over the wicket entrance, a fine row of poplars on one side and fruit and flowers in abundance.[85]

James Luckcock gave a similar picture of his Edgbaston garden. The house was sited in a corner of his one-third acre plot. Along the back, a terrace joined a sloping lawn for about one-fifth of the garden. Down one side was a raised bed with evergreen shrubs and his flower collection. 'Serpentine' walks led to arbors, seats, and urns bearing suitable inscriptions and a nearly life-size statue of Ceres made of plaster of Paris and dusted with sand to look like stone. He planted one chestnut and one mountain ash, 'as I always considered a few venerable and majestic Trees essential to the character of a respectable country mansion', in typical Luckcock hyperbole.[86] Beside a trellis twined with creeping roses shading the window 'with their odorous Luxuriance' he had placed a rustic seat bearing the inscription:

> I'll not repine though fate shut out,
> The gaudy World's tumultuous din
> He reck's not of the World without
> Who calm, enjoys the World within. . . .

Below the terrace, an archway with small wicket gate led to his neighbour, the school proprietor Sarah Bache, allowing the 'friendly intercourse' between equals, so much part of Edgbaston's attraction. As the final illusion, another seat at the bottom of the garden gave a view of the canal,

Plate 25   Three advertisements for an early lawnmower showing how aids were developed to allow middle-class men to cut the grass in their gardens without losing status

but the towing path was carefully concealed by a hedge which screened the 'intrusive notice of the Boatman and gives to the water the complete appearance of a River'. In toto, Luckcock's miniature estate measured approximately 55 by 90 feet.[87]

The creation of the middle-class garden required a range of new products from building materials and tools, gardening books, to seeds and plants.[88] Business opportunities flourished for local nurserymen and specialists, such as the seed merchants, William Thompson of Ipswich, many of whom began to produce printed catalogues.[89] But the garden was also an idea. From Cowper's *The Task* onwards, the moral force of the garden is a theme in middle-class writing. The garden was paradise, but required constant diligence; it represented both Nature's growth and God's design, sentiments expressed by the Suffolk bank clerk and poet, Bernard Barton in 'On a Garden':

> Enough of Nature's wealth is there
> Lost Eden to recall
> Enough of human toil and care
> To tell man's helpless fall. . . .[90]

Gardens were used as teaching devices. Children were given small plots to inculcate patience, care, tenderness, and reverence along with practical science lessons. Hannah More, too, had extolled the virtues of gardening for the young. In 1809, a young woman, on first reading *Coelebs*, remarked how the author echoed her mother's sentiments in declaring that not all the costly indulgences for youth can compare with 'an amusement so pure, so natural, so cheap, so rational, so healthful, I had almost said so religious, as that unbought pleasure connected with a garden'.[91] When young Douglas Galton was away at school his mother wrote with details of his little plot.[92] The banking Galtons had been brought up with gardens for several generations, but for a struggling farmer, a garden for children was a novel idea. He had noticed that his young daughter seemed fond of flowers and purchased the book *Mary's Garden* to help her start the little plot he had cleared of chickens:

I had not realised a flower garden as constituting a playground for children. . . .
I suppose it will teach the little gardeners to play their task and create a little paradise of flowers with their own hands.[93]

Children *as* gardens was a favourite metaphor for writers on domesticity. Morality had to be sown, cultivated and deeply rooted against the winds of adversity and the weeds of vice eradicated, as a clergyman wrote in the juvenile magazine edited by Jane Taylor.[94] The flower garden, in particular, was encouraged for girls. While all the Cadbury children had gardens, the boys experimented with trees and ferns, the girls, flowers.[95] For adults, too, the garden had different connotations for men and women. The active man of business found solace and peace coming home in the evening to water his plants or, like Luckcock, to make an absorbing rational activity for retirement. Here men could do physical work without losing cast, as Cowper demonstrated. They might cut the grass using the new lawn mower or prune trees and vines. A keen gardening doctor from Prittlewell in Essex spent all of 18 March 1826 in his garden, trimming hedges and sowing seeds garnered from Versailles and the Bois de Boulogne.[96] Men could also care for and nurture tender plants, revel in colour and design, in contrast to the aggressive competitiveness of masculine pursuits in the outside world.

Women's relationship to the garden was otherwise. In the eighteenth century their domain of medicinal and vegetable plants had been eroded. As market penetration grew, they were relegated to consumption or amateur gardening. Within garden imagery women were increasingly associated with flowers, their brilliant colouring, fragility, fragrance and existence for decorative purposes only. Jane Webb Loudon, daughter of a Birmingham businessman and John's wife, was premier writer on gardening for ladies. She maintained that 'whatever doubts may be entertained as to the practicability of a lady attending to the culture of culinary vegetables and fruit trees, none can exist respecting her management of the flower-garden as that is pre-eminently a woman's department'.[97] As a Colchester brewer wrote in his long poem on his native town, 'In every woman's soul there dwells pre-eminently a natural fond affinity for flowers.'[98]

In this period 'the language of flowers', originating in France, had been taken up and forwarded by romantic and nature poets and is reflected in commonplace books from the local areas. Women became responsible for decorating mantles and tables with flowers, a practice introduced in the 1820s, overcoming earlier superstitions about bad luck caused by bringing living or wild things into the house.[99] A paraphernalia of stands and containers, plus many books of expert advice accompanied this 'naturally' feminine occupation. Gardens were laid out with dry gravel, walks kept private with shrubberies for ladies' exercise and colourful parterres for their enjoyment.

But women might also work in the garden themselves. In 1824 Elizabeth Cadbury wrote to her daughter: 'I have spent sometime this morning changing my plants from one pot to another, a job, thou knows, I like best to do myself', and Maria Cadbury recollected the delight of being with her mother when she was gardening, looking over the rockery 'which needed her own watchful care' to flourish.[100] However, what garden work women could do was problematic given its association with manual tasks, soil and manure. In 1815, a Quaker wrote to her sister urging her to take regular exercise, and what better than gardening 'as the ladies do here' (in Devon), 'there is one . . . we see digging and hammering away. She is rather a masculine woman, but looks in a good state of preservation'.[101] Jane Loudon tried to counteract this image in her best selling *Gardening for Ladies*, while admitting that 'digging appears at first sight a very laborious employment and one peculiarly unfitted to small, delicately formed hands and feet'. (Here she assumes a biological sign of genteel femininity.) She assures her readers that with the aid of her book, gloves, a light wheelbarrow augmented by the services of an old man, a woman or a boy, she can do 'all her own work'.[102] Behind walls and hedges, genteel women could legitimately engage in brisk physical activity and even display some aggression against pests and weeds. Whatever the details of gender connotation, the garden was becoming an important extension of the middle-class domain where men and women could meet in 'complementary tranquility'.[103]

The lay-out of the home

In turning living quarters into a home, the first change was in the lay-out of the buildings. When James Oakes renovated his house and made the bank parlour, he also pulled down the back to make way for a new wash house, brew house, scullery and 'offices'.[104] When possible, rooms were being set aside for children, to be called 'nurseries' as Loudon instructed his readers in 1838.[105] These arrangements were promoted by the rationalization of domestic tasks, the more manual being increasingly taken over by servants who were doing less work connected to the enterprise. As more servants became available, family members were released for more cultural and social activities, now carried on in rooms kept for that purpose.[106]

Creating and maintaining these surroundings was always difficult given the insecurity of middle-class incomes. Even with sufficient resources, there were snares in steering a course between profligacy and parsimony. It was all very well for Hannah More to dictate that: 'Proportion and Propriety are among the best secrets of domestic wisdom', but by whose standards?[107] James Luckcock berated the effort to keep up 'our dress, our establishments and in those observances of fashion and etiquette which the "exclusives", that is the London Bon Ton world, assumed as their sole test of respectability and rank'.[108] Yet the opposite stance, of constant concern with making ends meet was neither genteel nor ultimately conducive to a religious outlook. George Crabbe, the Suffolk doctor/cleric, wrote approvingly of the modest farming family which practised:

> The wise frugality that does not give
> A life to saving, but that spends to live.[109]

By the 1830s, a range of modifications and additions had unquestionably added both comfort and gentility. The early nineteenth-century taste which favoured lightness and space was giving way to the heavy upholstered cluttered effect of the mid and late Victorians. Cowper's sparse domesticity, the sofa, shutters and tea urn, had now burgeoned with carpets, curtains, redesigned grates, mahogany furniture, wallpaper, chintz covers and bedsteads.

Where possible, eating now took place in a separate dining room with linen tablecloths, napkins, pottery and china and, at least, silver plate. Everyday goods were separated from best, which were used to mark the Sabbath and family rituals like Christmas or, more rarely, for formal entertaining. Arthur Biddell, the bluff Suffolk farmer who prided himself on his simplicity despite a substantial income, maintained: 'Gay Plates require Silver Spoons, Glasses instead of Black and White Mugs – a clean cloth and nice knives and forks and all this necessitates food and wine to match the plates; real China Tea things, a silver Cream Jug and Plated Pot.'[110] There was the apparatus of a more literate culture: books and bookcases, desks,

Plate 26 The interior of the drawing room at Crix, the Shaen family home in Essex. From
a watercolour by one of the Shaen daughters, *c.* 1835. The furnishings are comfortable
but still relatively light and simple

music stands and instruments, a proliferation of cabinets and tables for
sewing and embroidery, games and scientific collections.

These changes came slowly. Household needs and resources varied and
many had to make do with older-styled premises. Families inherited furniture and household goods or bought from sales and auctions for few could
afford to start housekeeping with completely new stock. The result was
often a mixture, for example, an early nineteenth-century farmhouse
retained the living kitchen with flagged floor and open hearth turf fire. Yet
the sitting room had a carpet with Chippendale chairs and tables, a 'register'
grate and high mantlepiece, some Wedgwood, a few books and toys,
although the walls were wainscotted, not papered.[111]

The aristocracy and gentry had begun adding halls and corridors in the seventeenth century to give more privacy and mark the family from the public domain, and by the 1770s, servants had been banished to back premises to be summoned by bell pulls.[112] But in smaller houses, the most important late eighteenth-century innovation was setting aside one room specifically for social intercourse: the middle-class equivalent to the (with) drawing room was the parlour (parler, to speak). In the 1790s, a Suffolk village family who ran a bakery-cum-haberdashery spent their time in the brick-floored kitchen with the master's wooden chair in the warm chimney corner and doors opening to the shop and garden. Only at Christmas was the parlour with its spinnet used for family gatherings.[113] Birmingham in the same period was no different. A family who operated a profitable print works lived in the kitchen, the liveliness of that room being 'a great point . . . for there they received their company and there were we entertained with chocolate and coffee'.[114]

By the 1830s, the parlour was coming into more regular use. An Ipswich town house, functioning as a genteel residence for a shopkeeper's family in 1827, included a vestibule, dining room and parlour with separate kitchen, backhouse and laundry.[115] Experts like Loudon made it a cardinal principle that the parlour or drawing room should have better fittings and furniture with a superior appearance. In everyday life, the dining room with more homely furnishings and large central table, fire and lamps was more often used, doubling as library, study, sewing room and general gathering place.

The use of rooms partly depended on the formality of social circles but more obviously on the size and composition of the household. When Isaac and Ann Taylor first moved to Suffolk, they rented a farmhouse in the centre of a village. They could not afford extensive furniture so the children used empty rooms as indoor play space.[116] When John Cadbury and his family moved to Edgbaston from living over the shop in Birmingham town centre, their home had an 'almost cottage like appearance' and needed extensive alterations. The kitchen was turned into a children's room first for play and later a school room, and two new kitchens were built. As the children grew up this room, with large windows overlooking the newly laid out garden, became 'our prettiest sitting room'. Later three more bedrooms and back staircase were added as servant numbers increased.[117]

Given the large numbers of children, it was usual to share beds as well as rooms. Even substantial residences might have only three bedrooms to house parents, children, relatives, visitors and servants. The privilege of an individual bedroom was unusual. A vicar's eldest daughter gained her own 'dear little room' when in her teens, a 'true delight . . . which was quite my property, and I feel completely independent'. She glowingly described its large proportion, two white curtained windows, four posted bed, handsome carved chimney piece, bookshelves, wash stand, bonnet press, dressing table, mahogany chest of drawers and writing table.[118]

Perhaps the most striking example of changes wrought by the separation of functions and the desire for privacy was on the farm, where the house remained part of the working complex. During the phasing out of farm service, labourers were segregated at their own table in the living kitchen, or fed a midday meal in the back kitchen or 'bakhus' (Suffolk), while the family ate separately and sat in a parlour.[119] A door to the parlour avoided entrance through the kitchen, keeping family and hands apart. In a small Essex farmhouse the best parlour remained a 'houseplace' where 'the men were admitted to regale themselves – master and man together after their daily labour unless there was company', a pattern already considered old-fashioned by the 1800s.[120] Maids and daughters no longer shared bedrooms reached through the parents' room. Parents and children now had separate premises opening off an upstairs hall.[121]

Furnishings of farmhouses began to express a more rational lifestyle as when the ornamental 'weather house' gave way to modern instruments.[122] The diary of a farmer's wife in 1823 covers extensive alterations including grates and a chimney converted to an overmantel, redecoration with wallpaper, the addition of a parlour with carpets and curtains, the purchase of pictures and, significantly, bell pulls.[123] George Crabbe was struck that a Suffolk farmer's house – estimating his income at about £600 a year – with its big stair case and spacious hall, had 'nothing at first sight to remind one of the farm'.[124]

Local sources reveal a clear rise in the standard of furnishings for all occupational groups. Inventories taken after the destruction of homes of prominent Birmingham nonconformist families in the Priestley Riots of 1791 show living rooms without carpets and only a few pieces of mahogany furniture. Priestley himself had a mahogany sofa covered with material to match his curtains, impressively affluent for that period.[125] In 1806, a small Essex farmer proudly listed two tables and six chairs made locally for £4 'out of my own tree in my yard'.[126] By the 1830s and 1840s, inventories for William Marsh in Edgbaston, a Birmingham lawyer, and Bernard Barton, a bank clerk, all reveal a collection of Brussels and Axminster carpets, a variety of sofas, settees, stools, tables, cabinets, sideboards (the furniture mostly of mahogany), together with smaller pieces for special functions: sewing boxes, a medicine case and umbrella stand.[127]

Living rooms blossomed with decorative additions: 'Rich china ornaments' on the new mantlepieces, and paintings, both amateur and professional. In 1811, Henry Crabb Robinson persuaded his close friend and fellow attorney, William Henry Pattisson of Witham, to have his sons' portrait painted by Thomas Lawrence, the rising artist of Robinson's London circle. The portrait, later sold as an engraving entitled 'Rural Amusements', shows the boys dressed in velvet suits in Byronesque pose against a background of stormy skies. The Pattissons, whose wealth derived from several generations of Witham shopkeeping, had already begun to collect paintings, and saw nothing incongruous in presenting their progeny (who later became, respectively, a physician and a lawyer), in such a romantic image.[128]

The newer style was often adopted when a couple married and started an establishment. Luckcock urged that it was necessary to start with a year's income, one half to spend on furnishing.[129] The bride might bring glass, silver or linen as well as cash as part of her settlement. An Essex Quaker shopkeeper was fortunate when, around 1800, he married a woman from a neighbouring Meeting who brought £1000. His mother, who had kept house for him, moved to a cottage at the bottom of the garden and alter-

Plate 27 'Rural Amusements' painting by Thomas Lawrence of William Henry and Jacob Howell Pattisson, sons of the Witham attorney, 1811

ations were made: 'the sitting room with its nicely sanded floor, was converted into a carpeted parlour', and the house furnished 'according to more modern notions'.[130]

In the next generation, a Birmingham broker was married in 1836 and his first child was born in 1837. By 1841, the family had moved to Edgbaston, each event involving financial outlay. The wedding meant clothes and wedding expenses as well as new glassware, tablemats, iron bedsteads, a new clock and a sofa. The arrival of the baby meant special nursery furniture, linen and blankets. The removal to Edgbaston involved equipping the house with new locks, hooks and screws, a kitchen grate had to be overhauled and the garden had to be laid out with privet hedge and asparagus bed. Five more children necessitated further outlay, and from household account books it took several years to build up a comfortable home.[131] A marriage was often a time for home improvements, as with the young Cadburys who had moved into the house that went with the shop when their seniors retired to Edgbaston and found the house was so 'metamorphosed with flowers, a sideboard and curtains that it was almost difficult to recognise the old family mansion'.[132]

Others might remodel and refurnish with a sudden increase in wealth.

The family rows in the 1820s over Rebecca Solly Shaen's inheritance must have ended in her favour since almost a third of the Shaen's house near Witham was pulled down and £1800 spent on making it more 'convenient and the grounds more beautified'. This included moving the kitchen from the basement to an addition built at the back and installing two water closets at a cost of £45; a marble fireplace for the dining room cost £22. A London upholsterer was engaged, there were grained mahogany doors, brass curtain rods (no doubt made in Birmingham), 64 yards of silk for the drawing room curtains with tassels and fringes, pier glasses, a rosewood table and a set of mahogany dining room chairs with green morrocco chair seats. Even the family pew in the parish church was renovated, although it was only used by the chapel-going Shaen's Anglican servants. The Shaen home became as elegant as a small country seat, and an appropriate setting for the neighbourhood's first nonconformist JP. Rebecca Shaen fretted about the cost and often disagreed with Samuel who regarded as necessities what she felt were luxuries. She worried about creating unreal expectations in their children, while Samuel's attitude was that they might as well enjoy it now rather than inherit it later. Rebecca gave in, for as she ruminated, the renovations were an 'investment' in family life: 'as property our residence is more than as much more valuable than merely bringing back the money spent'.[133]

Running the home

Within the middle-class rubric, maintaining privacy and the hallmark of respectability presented logistical problems when households were large, especially with numerous young children. In the census sample, children under 16 (whether or not related to the household head) made up 27 per cent of the household population, 15 per cent being children under 10. Shared beds as well as sleeping quarters were the rule; space for eating, washing, or just sitting was cramped by later standards. Regimented procedures for the minutiae of behaviour were the only way of keeping order under such conditions and entailed a strict distribution of both objects and activities. 'A place for everything and everything in its place' was, for good reason, an often quoted maxim.

Yet within this general framework, visual images could be more important than the functional use of labour and materials. Polished surfaces and mirrors reflected candle (later oil) light; warm colours and textures gave a domestic cosiness and rich feeling, physical warmth was provided by open coal fires, shutters, heavy curtains, carpets and upholstered furniture.[134] The resources needed for a sitting room fire separate from cooking operations partly explain why the parlour was seldom used in less well off households. Nevertheless, the availability of cheap coal, combined with the imagery of the open fire and hearth, meant that the continental style 'close stove' was never popular. Ruskin was only one of the powerful coterie who saw the domestic hearth as the apogee of the domestic temple, the image which easily overrode arguments for efficiency in use of fuel or labour.[135] There was only a gradual acceptance of the kitchen range where most cooking was done, yet enthusiasts like Rumford had invented efficient

Plate 28   Advertisement for T. Ryland and Son's Silverplate

versions as early as the third quarter of the eighteenth century. Despite
constant improvement to flues and fireplaces which furthered the separation
of cooking and heating, few were quickly adopted and the smokey chimney
with a wasteful fire remained the norm, not least because of jurisdictional
struggles over installation between landlord and tenant. The necessary
substitution of baking for roasting facilities since 'baked meats' had been
associated with the food of the poor caused further reluctance to close in
the kitchen fireplace. The elderly slavery reformer, Thomas Clarkson, who
retired to Playford Hall just outside Ipswich, refused to modernize the
large, high-ceilinged stone-floored kitchen where meat was roasted on a
spit before the open fire.[136]

Technical changes in lighting made a longer day for leisure or business,
for time spent with the family together after dark. The poor might struggle
on with rush lights and inferior tallow candles; a benefit of higher income
was wax tapers and, by the 1830s, oil for lamps.[137] The gleam of silver (or
plate) on polished wood gave the impression of good housekeeping, evoking
the time and energy spent rubbing with beeswax. In fact, carpets, curtains,
canopied beds and soft chairs could harbour more dirt and dust than sanded

stone flags and sparse wooden furniture. Large towns presented special problems in keeping a house really clean; housewives had to battle with coal smoke, smuts and waste products like wet rubbish which in the country had been recycled on the land.[138] Concern with dirt and disorder drew new boundaries between what was valuable and what was waste and in the process, moral or social criteria were often used rather than the hygienic standards of the twentieth century based on a germ theory of disease.

Cleanliness was also associated with individual behaviour. Arthur Young, travelling in late eighteenth-century France, was impressed with the refined table manners, that each person kept his own glass at the dinner table and had clean napkins and linen.[139] Changes in hygienic practice partly took this personal form because water supplies sufficient for standards of modern household cleanliness depended not on moral oversight, but communal action and large-scale capital investment which neither households nor local organizations were willing to undertake until after mid century. Many villages remained dependent on brooks and fetid ponds. Even in small towns pumps were only slowly erected, and often depended on philanthropy or were run for profit, while middle-class homes had to ensure their supplies with wells which often ran dry.[140] In larger towns, even when piped water had been brought into the back premises of wealthier homes, supplies were intermittent and cheap servant labour delayed efforts for raising water above ground level. In any case, personal cleanliness was directed to washing hands and faces rather than overall bathing, so that wash stands with ewer and basin (another lucrative item for pottery manufacturers) were becoming standard bedroom furniture. Women now had to carry up water and empty slops, either themselves or overseeing servants.

If the provision of water supplies suffered from the vagaries of local politics and desire for profit, waste disposal lagged even further behind and most houses made do with ash pits and outdoor earth closets. Well into the late nineteenth century outdoor privies for men and servants reserved the one indoor facility for the modesty of ladies.[141] Keeping up even an appearance of cleanliness in town centres must have been daunting. In 1819, two young Quaker women visiting Birmingham were impressed with the neat appearance of their co-religionists' houses, given the grime and smoke of the town. Clean steps, doors, and window ledges, gleaming brass knockers, and starched white curtains dramatically demonstrated the break between private rectitude and public squalor.[142]

Moving to the leafy purlieus of Edgbaston did not necessarily solve the problem. A report to the Public Health Authorities covering Hagley Road (with villas renting from £60 to £180 per annum and the home of Rev. John Angell James) stated that, even in the 1840s, there was no drainage and that open ditches on each side of the road were 'full of green and fetid matter' where water closets were discharged. Many premises had cess pools which overflowed into local wells. R. T. Cadbury complained in his evidence that ditches surrounding his Edgbaston home were 'in a most putrid state, reeking with the content of water closets in the finest neighbourhood of Birmingham'.[143] Without the means for proper washing, bugs, nits and other insect pests remained a plague, on which mistress and maid waged constant time and energy consuming attacks. Yet even then, moral and social concern often superseded physical health. Mid century Ipswich was particularly backward in water supply and drainage. A local commentator – and political radical – denounced the fact that one 'out office' (euphemism for privy) had to serve for several houses: 'Are not these circumstances sufficient to destroy all modesty, to blight the beauty of the female character and to banish all feelings of self-respect from the human mind?'[144]

It was often the offensive smell, signifying both health and moral hazards which concerned middle-class people. According to scientific ideas of the time, diseases were spread by 'myasmic contagion', signified by smell.[145] For example, at a time when the middle ranks were using soap for laundry, many labourer's families still used urine. Given their resources, the gap in personal hygiene between the habits of poor and moderately well off was widening. The importance of odour in maintaining social hierarchy, which remained until the mid twentieth century, derives from the way smells represent the object in a particularly powerful way.[146] When Rebecca Solly Shaen was in her teens, she went on a tour of the north with her sister and mother. In Hull, away from the refinements of Essex, their carriage was surrounded by sailors making them glad to escape to the local inn, 'tho it was but exchanging one evil for another; the stench in the house was almost suffocating'. Further north was worse. When they encountered a papered room they were delighted by 'the charms of cleanliness, having been in so many dirty stinking holes'. Finally, arriving on the Isle of Mull, they found the laird living in a mud-floored house, his sister a 'dirty, smart trollope'.[147]

Ideas about the nature of cleanliness and order directly affected the lay-out of middle-class housing. Segregating the mess and smell of food preparation from the social ritual of eating became an important hallmark of respectability and meant that the kitchen became ideally as remote as possible from the living rooms, no matter the cost in servants, or wife's time and labour. The English obsession with fresh air also stems from this period. Light and air let in from the enlarged sash windows allowed that 'ventilation and mitigation of smell', which Newman claimed 'helped to make a population moral and happy'.[148] Maintaining and running such homes required greater investments of time and energy as well as money. For example, closed ranges had to be cleaned with blacking and brushed liberally with 'elbow grease'. Oil lamps needed careful cleaning and trimming if the wicks were to burn brightly, fires had to be lit laboriously from a tinder box until the invention of matches in the 1830s.

The religious household with its fixed times for prayer and consciousness of the value of time was particularly well suited to organizing more elaborate programmes. Those first-generation converts, Isaac and Ann Martin Taylor, with their rigid timetable of praying, eating, working, walking and recreation, were not under pressure from business demands, since Isaac's work was freelance. Rather religious precept provided the template. 'Let everything be done decently and in order' was a maxim that Ann Martin Taylor advocated, extending from 'religious concerns to all affairs of life'.[149]

At the same time, the importance of household management grew as more consumption passed through the cash nexus. More elaborate accounts were kept where there was a housekeeper. For example, a farm household charged for milk, eggs and other products from the farm in cash terms, although interestingly, this degree of economistic thinking mainly seems to appear where hired personnel ran the household.[150] In almost all households, some clothing was bought ready made as well as much food, including bread. Local records list purchases of bread, potatoes, meat, fish and beer as well as tea, sugar, paper, sealing wax, gun powder, brushes and brooms, children's clothes, newspapers, musical instruments, pills, paintings, coal and candles. Households paid to have knives sharpened, clocks cleaned, hair cut and beards shaven, children educated, shoes mended, for coach and rail fares, for sending letters and parcels.

Growing dependence on the market increased vulnerability to irregular or insecure income and heightened the values of deferred gratification, avoidance of debt and strict budgeting. Keeping track of income and expenditure was provided for in cheap, easily available accounting books, part of the stock-in-trade of expanding publishers. A typical example described in a Birmingham advertisement provided: 'an easy concise and complete Method of keeping an exact Account of every article made use of in a Family throughout the Year', together with marketing tables, receipts, correct stamps for bills, and all the equipment for the business of housekeeping.[151] It was for the wife, as 'faithful steward of your Husband's income' (a concept with religious overtones), to keep account of the income which it was his 'duty as it will be his pleasure to provide'.[152] To this end, James Luckcock urged teaching girls arithmetic, not so that the 'fair students could later be placed at the counting house desk to the neglect of household duties' but to enable them to understand income and expenses. Such understanding would enable the wife to feel an interest in their *joint* prosperity, now missing in her segregation within the home. 'What assistance she has given in saving, she will consider as her proper share in the management and the part she can play in helping to raise the family in the "scale of society".'[153] An extreme example of this mentality appears in the records of a merchant's family who moved from the City of London to Walthamstow in Essex in the 1840s. The husband allowed a certain amount of housekeeping for which the wife kept full accounts. She also kept records of her eight children's progress, their illnesses and innoculations. In addition there were ruled account books with column entries for gifts and letters received and given, evenings spent at home whether with friends or alone, calls paid and received – a kind of profit and loss ledger of family and social life.[154]

Evidence from the local areas does show women beginning to rely on order and self-discipline to organize formidable work loads, often incorporating work for the enterprise. In the 1830s, Louisa Garrett (mother of Elizabeth Garrett Anderson, Millicent Garrett Fawcett and eight other children), living near the family maltings on the Suffolk coast, was the mainspring of the household. She led family prayers, kept strict accounts and wrote business letters for her almost illiterate husband. She also washed and fed the children, supervised cooking and baking, as well as the annual pig killing, the laundry, dairy and cleaning.[155]

The drive for segregating ceremonial and cultural life from the underside of material existence began to affect methods of housekeeping, shaping the division of labour within the home as deliberately as in the enterprise. Girls helped their mothers with multiple duties, although they also read, wrote letters, went visiting and for walks, fitting the various activities into a structured day or week but not yet caught up in the formal etiquette of later Victorian society. In 1833, the Agricultural Select Committee was informed that farmers' daughters seldom worked in the dairy but they did help with housework.[156]

Both the timing and form of meals changed during this perod. Ale and small beer as the main beverage had given way to tea in the late eighteenth century except in remote rural areas, and less beer was brewed at home. The noon dinner followed by substantial tea or supper, often preceded by small beer, was changing.[157] By the 1820s and 1830s, the family dining hour was 3 to 4 p.m., and by mid century it had moved to early evening in a town like Birmingham. Wealthy provincial families began to mount special dinner parties for guests rather than the constant round of informal dropping in. Larger establishments might give several such performances a month with about a dozen guests seated in the refurbished dining room and waited on by servants, although, significantly, some banks, merchant houses and manufactories also kept a room with facilities for cooking for formal entertaining. Such affairs were a far cry from the eighteenth-century rural practice of cooking outside on the 'house green' in summer with all sitting round the cooking fire through the evening.

Cooking was now banished to the kitchen except for a tiny hob where the lady of the house might make tea, or in less elevated households, pancakes or drop scones over the parlour fire. A good portion of the enhanced middle-class income was being spent on more elaborate food. Eighteenth-century innovations of tea, sugar and chocolate were augmented by more 'made up dishes', coffee and wines. A Colchester wine merchant, supplying the garrison during the war, later flourished by delivering to professional and farming families, his horse and cart emblazoned with his name proclaimed his custom as it stood at their doors.[158] The earlier pattern of dining set out sweets and savouries together in several courses, making visible the plentitude on offer. A Birmingham banker's daughter recalled dinner parties of her youth in the 1820s, with 'soup and fish, next [to] a joint at the bottom, Calf's head or veal at the top, Fowles on one side, Ham on the other and four entrees at the corners of vegetables with all the dishes on the table at once'. The second course was game and seven or eight sweet dishes.[159] In the next decades this gave way to the more sophisticated dinner 'a la Russe', with courses following on one another, clear boundaries marked between sweet and savoury dishes which now had to be handed round by servants, although the master might still carve.[160]

Overseeing the buying in of provisions was an important part of a mistress's role. At this period, most still did their own marketing but the stigma of being seen in public carrying parcels was growing. Fiction picked up these sensitive areas. In the early 1800s, Jane Austen ridiculed Mrs Bennet's preening herself that her daughters had nothing to do with the kitchen.[161] By the 1830s, Harriet Martineau has one of her pretentious characters urge the heroine not to let down her family's social position by carrying a basket through the town with the small end of a carrot peeping

from under the lid.[162] Town grocers began to solve the dilemma by
delivering for those who could not send servants, although undoubtedly
many women and children continued to shop for themselves, particularly
in the countryside, and the breadwinners of Edgbaston were not above
stopping at the butcher's or grocer's on their way home from town.

Another major task for women was laundry work. This had grown
since the eighteenth century when more frequent changes of the recently
introduced cotton clothing became desirable. Sheets, towels, the linen
napkins admired by Arthur Young, not only had to be purchased and
hemmed, but laundered, along with white linen around the neck and wrists
for men, aprons, kerchiefs and nightwear for women and a variety of
children's clothing. New habits of hygiene and also signs of morality were
displayed by such fashions. For example, the spotless starched headgear of
Quaker women was remarked upon favourably in local records. By the
1840s, we find an array of tea cloths, tray napkins, cheese tray cloths,
oyster cloths and dusters besides the ordinary linen, all to be laundered in
a merchant's Essex household.[163] The early eighteenth-century orgies of
washing once or twice a year were no longer sufficient for the higher
standards of cleanliness and amount or variety of linen – local records
indicate washing days at about monthly intervals.

The wash house with a pump in the yard which was added to remodelled
residences implies that washing was now done on the premises, and no
longer taken to the nearest brook; thus it was part of the individual household, and no longer a communal activity. A commentator on early
nineteenth-century Essex disapprovingly described how, on the road out
of Saffron Walden, 'busy bustling housewives of the town send forth their
household linen to be blown about'; the desire to be distinguished by
their well bleached washing is the motive in its exposure to 'universal
observation'.[164] The better-off could now launder with bought soap,
replacing lye from wood ash or urine. The monthly wash day now meant
routine upheaval for the household. All lent a hand; women of the family,
servants and extra washerwomen. In a bank manager's menage, coloured
clothes, whites and muslins were soaked separately for several days and
simmered on the stove, put out to bleach, then washed and, in bad weather,
dried on stretchers before the fire (whites had first to be blued).[165] Men,
officially at least, took no part in washing. Bernard Barton, lodging with
two women who also ran a school, doubted if the letter he was writing was
intelligible, 'for all hands are busy round me to clap, to starch, to iron, to
plait – in plain English, 'tis washing day, and I am writing close to a table
in which is a bason [sic] of starch, caps, kerchiefs etc. and busy hands and
tongues round it'.[166] The literary-minded daughters of a Quaker
businessman who were passionate devotees of Byron and other poetry read
while they 'clapped' their clear starching, reading and clapping alternately
and 'all the time our souls were not on this earth'.[167]

The finishing processes of starching and ironing made linen look clean
for longer and strengthened the image of order and purity, but they were
heavy consumers of female energy, using weighty ember-filled irons
constantly in danger of scorching or marking the linen with soot. Women's
caps and children's clothes had ruffles and frills necessitating special

goffering irons and elaborate starching, and steaming.[168] Entrepreneurs once again benefited. In the 1840s, the Reckitts, relatives of several Essex families, built a fortune on producing commercial starch and blueing.[169] In 1808, Archibald Kenrick's West Bromwich firm had produced a handful of irons, by 1836 they offered twenty-seven varieties.[170]

Women were responsible for overseeing the appearance of all household members. In addition to laundering, they bought, made and mended all clothing. Although written evidence is scarce, one of the great silences about women's lives was undoubtedly filled with needlework. From the long flat-fell seaming of sheets to the embroidered chair cushions, from making up boys' suits to exquisitely worked velvet slippers for papa at Christmas, middle-class women were constantly sewing, and their daughters were taught to do so from the age when they could grasp a needle. The 'work' boxes and sewing chests listed in local inventories, and the samplers, quilts and other surviving artefacts speak forcefully for what is seldom said in words.

However, men also took an active part in setting up the home. It has been seen how they often planned and maintained the garden, or at least the masculine sections of it. Men were responsible for buying certain items: wine, books, pictures, musical instruments and wheeled vehicles. They accompanied their wives to buy furniture and carpets, while both men and women painted and papered rooms. In the 1820s, a civil engineer in a West Midlands ironworks made drawings for alterations to the house, shopped with his wife for furnishings in Birmingham and carpets in Kidderminster and papered the rooms.[171] A commercial traveller in the same decade also shopped for a carpet while in Kidderminster, and he constantly wrote details about servants and household affairs to his wife while away from home.[172]

Who actually did what also depended on how elaborate the establishment was, how much servant help was available and how involved the home was in the enterprise. Better-off women needed to understand housekeeping but not necessarily how to carry out specific tasks. The reminiscences of a Quaker household of the 1830s, run on liberal and plentiful lines, show how girls were incorporated into domestic matters. As soon as they were tall enough, they made their own beds, helped wash up, fetched laundry from the garden and folded it. As they grew older they regularly made the 'extra delicacies required for company, and though it sometimes took us away from our drawing and other favourite pursuits, it was on the whole a pleasure and interest to us'.[173] As in this Birmingham household, such recollections are often ambivalent and seem to be justifying girls' work in the house. The floor scrubbing, pan washing, window cleaning, nappy changing and heavy laundry were increasingly felt to be demeaning and distracting from higher duties. Either they were done by the family behind closed doors or working-class women were brought in, but necessity meant daughters filled the gap. In a Suffolk Quaker family where the widowed head became manager of a new gas works, no servant was kept for three years and during that time one of his daughters was 'much engaged in household duties'.[174] Even in the more opulent Shaen household, turnover of servants in the 1830s meant that the two youngest daughters in their teens had to pitch in, although only doing lighter tasks.[175]

The question of servants

By mid century, genteel women in the wealthiest households would only have arranged flowers, done fancy embroidery, possibly being able to distil flower essence and make special confections. But the majority of middle-class women did a substantial portion of housework and childcare to reach the new standards, despite an increase in domestic servants. Although some of these servants were still partly employed in the enterprise, the distinction was muted in many establishments.[176] In the early nineteenth century, *domestic* service began to be seen as a separate category, marked by the gradual preponderance of females as men moved into day labour or white-collar positions.

By mid century, 82 per cent of servants in middle-class households in the local areas were female, and a third of these were under the age of 20. Whether or not a household employed residential domestic servants depended on a *combination* of needs and resources. A third of lower middle-class households had no residential servants compared to 15 per cent of the better-off. Only 6 per cent in the lower middle class had three or more servants, but almost half the upper middle class were so served. But these figures obscure the several reasons which promoted servant keeping. Some types of households demanded more servant labour than others. For example, only half as many farm households were without any servants as the average. Despite the fact that the census excluded servants wholly engaged in farm work, it is probable that young women listed as domestic servants on farms were helping in the yard and dairy as well as doing household chores.

More households headed by single people and more headed by women were likely to do without any servants: they tended to be less well off, but also might have fewer people to service. At the other extreme, male headed households were twice as likely to have three or more servants than those headed by women. From both qualitative and quantitative sources it appears that professional households, in their special concern with domesticity, employed more than the average number of servants. Clergy families in particular, possibly living up to the expectation that they should help to train young girls, were well served with three times the average percentage of four or more servants; half the upper middle-class clergy ran this full complement.[177]

Advice on servant keeping and the level of expenditure at which more than one specialized servant could be afforded multiplied. In reality, this pattern would vary over the lifecycle, rising with the heavy demands of numerous young children, and falling with the availability of older daughters or female relatives. Illness or death of the wife and mistress could, if necessary, be made good by a general servant or housekeeper when no female relative could be found.

Finding and employing trustworthy servants was often a perplexing and time consuming task. Once found and settled in the household, keeping servants was a source of constant anxiety. The high turnover of servants was a feature of the period, and created potential and actual upheaval. In 1846 Sarah Cadbury wrote to her sister that their servant 'will have been with us seven years, is not that a long time and we are going to have a treat'.[178] Servants left, either to better themselves or to marry. Since marriage was so highly valued, it was difficult for employers to object but there was much private disgruntlement, as when a Birmingham widow wrote to her son that her cook wanted to marry: 'We see there is not much consideration nor gratitude in servants; she must know how I have been circumstanced and still am, and I should wish to be so off that I could leave home any time with ease.'[179]

This issue highlights the social gap fostered and the difficulty in acknowledging claims of servants' own family and friends. Ann Martin Taylor assumed that 'a master can hardly appear to them other than a being of a different species'.[180] Families did not wish their careful homes to be invaded by disruptive, alien standards, and feared theft. Some employers tried to impose a 'no followers' ban, excluding a servant's personal network; others only allowed selected relatives: mother, siblings or an acknowledged suitor. But many were helpless to stop servants going out and meeting friends. One of the latent consequences of order and strict routine was to prevent servants slipping away at odd hours.

If servants had been recruited from long distances, they were forced to cut ties with their own community; hence the preference for country girls. In 1826, a Birmingham iron manufacturer wrote to his absent mother about replacing their manservant, John:

I have thought whether John might not be someways objectionable to us from the circumstance of his family and friends living on our side of Birmingham. . . . It would not do at all to have them coming over to see him, nor for him to expect frequent absence to go to see them.[181]

The larger and more aristocratic the household, the further afield servants were recruited, but among the provincial middle class, recruitment was more local.[182] In Colchester in 1851, three-quarters of servants had been born within a radius of 10 miles of the town; the furthest distance it was possible to walk in a day off to visit family.[183]

Tensions were endemic to the master (and mistress) servant relationship, but when service or apprenticeship had been an acknowledged step towards adulthood, when kin often doubled as servants and when lifestyle distinctions were less pronounced, these were easier to contain. The children of small farmers, particularly during times of agricultural distress, had often spent some time as servants, part of the way urban culture spread to rural areas.[184] By mid century this was less likely, and servants were increasingly recruited from the young women of labourers' families now surplus to agricultural employment.[185]

By mid century, as we have seen, three-quarters of middle-class households in the areas had at least one servant living in. As household members, their appearance, behaviour and language reflected on its image. However, too close imitation of middle-class lifestyle could threaten fragile middle-class status. Where resources permitted, servants could be incorporated yet kept at a distance in separate parts of the house. It was one-servant house-holds (just under one-half of all servant keeping households) that might be explosive. On the other hand, multiple servant households had their prob-lems and demanded careful supervision. Several servants persisted in not keeping to their own tasks, in borrowing each others' equipment. They *would* use the apple peeling knife for other purposes, or forget to change from kitchen to parlour aprons. There were often jurisdictional disputes, which left one young mistress unable to get the back passage floor washed at all.[186] The longer chain of command meant that orders could be muddled or deliberately ignored, while separate kitchen meals increased possibilities for wasted time and materials, raising costs. The sheer scale could be daunting. When Mrs Gaskell visited the Shaens in Essex in 1847, the ten in the parlour 'were supplemented by thirty two in the kitchen' necessitating a 40 lb sirloin of beef and two turkeys to be served for dinner.[187]

Contradictions between familial forms and market relations crystallized in domestic service.[188] Rumblings had appeared in the eighteenth century in struggles over vails (tipping) which were phased out of private houses but not, significantly, of pubs or inns. Gradually, payment in kind for beer, tea and sugar was transmuted into cash while struggles continued over 'perquisites' (perks) such as dripping, rabbit skins or cast off clothing, part of the transition from personal patronage to cash. The highly 'rationalized' household of an Essex merchant in the 1830s put time schedules, duties and rewards in writing in an attempt to forestall conflict, although many employers had to turn a blind eye.[189]

Both rewards and punishments often remained personal and arbitrary. For example, legal and moral pressure to care for servants in illness was part of the relationship, but difficult to implement in small, hard pressed households. A Birmingham banker could afford to call in the family surgeon for the gardener's injury and the town's highest paid physician for their old housekeeper, and Maria Marsh hired a young girl to attend her elderly servant when ill, but both families had wealth and space as well as religious commitment.[190] Such actions hovered between family inclusion and charity.

There was the related tension between a growing ideal of expertise, of hiring – and firing – the best person for the job, and personal familial loyalties of long service. A servant who was genuinely part of the family could become crotchety and less efficient as she grew older and capable of manipulating the household through intimate knowledge of personal weaknesses. The Cadbury's servant of over fifty years moved with them from the shop accommodation to Edgbaston where she reigned as upper housemaid, resenting interference from grown up daughters, 'considering no one could clean the plate as she did or wait on the family' who gathered on Sundays.[191]

All employers potentially faced such problems. But the gender of both employer and servant coloured the relationship. For example, men who had no female kin to act as mistress, were vulnerable to sexual innuendo in respect to female servants. In the late eighteenth century, Julius Hardy, a Birmingham buttonmaker, as a bachelor, had a workman and his wife living with him, the wife doing the cooking. In addition, there was a servant girl. After the workman was sacked, Hardy had to decide whether to marry: 'what step shall I make to obtain a continuance of even, orderly management or good government in the little concerns of my house?' He felt this 'momentous affair' needed 'much deep and long consideration' but discovered to his horror that the maid was pregnant. Fearing he would be blamed, he dismissed her. While Hardy looked around for a wife, an older married woman was called in to superintend the new servant girl.[192] A handful of men solved the conundrum by marrying their servant to the consternation of more genteel relatives.

The master was responsible to his servants as to his children and other dependants. Men who took this seriously faced the hostility and humiliation of having to dismiss servants if business failed. But servants, unlike children, could try and protect themselves by not becoming too involved with the family, leading to a detachment deplored by employers. Men were legally responsible for hiring and firing servants. As long as the servant had also been part of the enterprise, jurisdiction between master and mistress was not a particular problem. But when the household became solely the woman's domain, men retained ultimate authority and, except in female headed households, the mistress acted only as deputy. In this role she had both gained and lost power. Her association with non-productive, more decorative activities cut her off from the validation of the external world even while religious, educational and moral experts extolled her new role.

There was particular confusion over manual work in the household. We have seen how, in the enterprise, the master was becoming responsible for management, external affairs of buying and selling, and was not expected to take a direct part in the production process. But it was uncertain how far the housewife should delegate, particularly in critical areas like cooking and childcare. A farmer's wife in the 1820s who took no part in farm work, where servants were employed and a parlour kept, nevertheless was up at 6 a.m. to make puddings and other solid fare for visitors.[193] Yet spending time on food preparation, hardening white hands with blisters and burns, was likely to be judged ungenteel in many circles. In the 1840s, the unmarried daughters of a retired army officer regarded their sister-in-law as vulgar, her mother no more than an upper servant, and one who 'prefers the society of those with whom she can talk of butter and eggs and the price of flour and milk'.[194]

With the move to suburbs like Edgbaston, women had less opportunity to meet working-class people face to face except their servants whom they came to regard as representatives of that class. Even more than men, they alternated between Christian charity or patronage and draconian justice, especially at times of general political unrest. Further problems arose because servants misunderstood many of the newer middle-class rituals. Insistence on external symbols of order as well as separation of tasks seemed unnecessary and often implied more and harder work. Instructions which implied that hard work had moral value, 'the polish produced by rubbing being superior to French polish or any other', must have had a hollow ring to those doing the rubbing.[195]

The generation of young women growing up in the 1820s and 1830s was apt to have less experience of domestic tasks than their mothers and grandmothers. This increased their ineptitude when starting housekeeping,

made them more dependent on their servants and undermined the respect
based on skill. On the other hand, younger women had to learn from
reliable older servants. When Candia Cadbury moved to Birmingham at
her marriage and was separated from her mother, she was 'glad to have a
good steady body who understands the order and routine of things to
depend upon – it renders the task much less difficult for me'.[196]

Middle-class women did, however, usually have the advantage of better
education. Some felt it their duty to teach servants to read and write,
partly as a religious gesture as well as making them more useful. An Essex
shopkeeper's wife having so taught her maid, claimed that the girl told her:
'I never thought much about these things till I learnt to read and have been
read to so much.'[197] Yet there was constant unease that 'literary domestics'
might be tempted beyond their station.[198] Female servants' dress created
special difficulties since one of their perks was cast off clothing and they
did not wear uniforms until after mid century. Yet maids were expected to
be neat, clean and respectable. One Essex mistress warned in writing: 'Each
female servant's is expected to dress as plain as possible – no white gowns,
Flowers, Feathers or any Finery allowed whatsoever.'[199]

The day-to-day management of servants was becoming a central part of
middle-class women's role, and was seen as analogous to men's place in
business. Progressive men as in the Birmingham Unitarian Hill family could
relax authority. Both Frederick and Arthur Hill 'felt repugnance to see
women employed in heavy bodily work, and each in his own house assisted
the female servants in such acts among others as carrying up the filled coal
scuttles'.[200] The mistress, trying to establish authority, could not often risk
such spontaneous acts. Mrs Ellis might blandly assure that 'kindness
blended with dignity' would invariably be repaid with a 'double share of
affectionate and faithful service', but the reality of conflicting interests and
high turnover was not encouraging.[201]

While 'influence' proved to be a vapid concept in practice, appeals to
religious belief were more effective and evangelicals often hired only
religious servants. Servants were not equal in worldly rank, but they were
naturally equal in the sight of God, as John Angell James maintained. For
him, the household was 'intended to be a seminary of virtue and piety, of
which master and mistress are the teachers, and the servants as well as the
children, are the pupils'.[202] James's imagery is revealing. By regarding
servants as children, women could justify their personal control, and could
rule by granting or withholding food, praise, abuse and even physical
punishment.

Under these pressures, as we have seen, that many mistresses welcomed
strict routine as a way of controlling large households of both children and
servants. When rules could be externalized, whether through dictates of
religion or on the basis of rational, business-like or scientific ideas (or both),
some order could be brought out of potential chaos. Not that the older,
rule of thumb relaxed atmosphere was necessarily more egalitarian. Servants
as well as children and young adults in some eighteenth-century households
had lived in fear of the master's (or mistress's) temper and strong arm. But
in nineteenth-century households, the status hierarchy had widened, and
formal controls strengthened. When meals were expected to be punctual to

the minute, or weekly cleaning routines held to the force of ritual, the mistress's burden of constant and personal intervention was lessened.

There are indications from the records that women found it particularly difficult to deal with adult male servants. The middle-class mistress lacked the aura of the born lady to counteract expected female inferiority and men servants spent more of their working lives outside, away from her direct supervision. The Essex merchant's wife determined to run a rationally organized household, required express permission for a servant's absence, except for Sunday church, and kept a running record of such absences. Some servants, for example the children's nurse, had only one or two days off a year throughout the 1830s. However, the footman simply took time off when he felt like it without asking. 'Johnson away again' frequently appears in the record, but there was little that could be done to curb such masculine independence short of sacking him.[203]

Age and experience aided the mistress of domestic staff but religious belief supplied the conviction. In 1798, the wife of an Essex shopkeeper dealt imperturbably with her male servant in her persona as Quaker minister:

This evening I submitted to what appeared a duty, in speaking to our man-servant on the subject of profane swearing. . . . I warned him of the danger of such a practice and cautioned him against passion, which he alleged in excuse for his crime. True peace resulted from his little act of obedience.[204]

The ability to give favours or rewards was certainly more effective than the nebulous influence of example. Larger, wealthier establishments could not only offer better pay and conditions, but also dispense patronage especially to upper servants who tended to stay longer with a family. The Marsh's governess was found employment as matron of a fever hospital, Maria Marsh believing that her advanced age would keep her from infection and 'God protects those who do their duty'.[205] Clerical families, in particular, had access to such patronage for posts or helping servants' families to receive respectable charities.

Clergy families, too, took the training and placing of young servants as part of their philanthropic duty. The Marsh's daughter, Catherine, befriended a young Irish girl who was placed in a training school for servants for four years and then joined the Marsh rectory as under housemaid before rising to become cook–housekeeper where she 'proved herself to be not only a clever and faithful servant but also attached and grateful friend to all the family'.[206] Lady visitors to organizations such as the Birmingham Protestant Dissenting Charity School could recruit a chosen pupil into their service.[207] Such sponsorship enforced discipline, as did dependence on a 'character', or reference, for further employment. Nevertheless, any or all of these devices were fallible in imposing a familial model on servants or attempting to control their personal life. There is an irony in Hannah More's situation in the 1830s when in old age and alone she was left at the mercy of her servants who held revels in the kitchen, laying waste to her patrimony while she was bedridden upstairs.[208]

Given these constant tensions, why did middle-class families strive to include servants in their well-regulated homes? If wives and daughters had

had to scrub the floors, wash all the household linen, produce meals for large households as well as care for five or six young children, they would have become exhausted drudges, incapable of much cultural or religious activity. Middle-class women had no more taste for grinding toil than the men who preferred the ledger and the pen to the plough, anvil or loom. Servants resident in the home provided round the clock help and fitted the familial model. Despite constant warnings about leaving children with servants, their help with childcare seems to have been normal practice, given other demands on the mistress. In the Colchester census sample, by far the largest category of second servant was nurse to young children and general servants would also spend time on this task. Only with ample resources and few children was it practical for the mother to take full charge.

The Cadbury children stayed with the servants in the country house when their parents were working in the Bull Street shop. After the older daughters had finished their schooling, they sometimes went to town to help their mother, and the maid was left to care for young Emma whose dinner she would keep warm in the oven if she, in turn had to go out.[209] An old servant like the Galton's 'Patty' (Miss Paterson), daughter of a gardener who had been brought up and educated by Mrs Galton, acted as a 'second mother'. When the Galton boys first went away to school she wrote to protect them when they angered their father. The nature of her relationship comes through her letters: 'I will write to you as often as you like but I cannot, my dear love, come and see you so often as you or I should like . . . your Mama in consequence of your Papa's being from home is much engaged with company and therefore requests me without fail to write for her to little darling. . . .'[210]

In some ways this kind of informal arrangement protected children from the excesses of more specialist nursery staff who were coming into fashion in mid century suburban homes. A later branch of the Cadbury family suffered from a nurse who had seemed on the surface a model, 'beautifully neat and clever with our dress and nursery'. It was only when the mother heard screaming one day that she investigated, and found Maria in a cupboard, her finger caught in the door. The nurse also held her hand over the children's mouths when she struck them to prevent their cries being heard as she had been expressly instructed not to strike them.[211] Yet it was these specially chosen upper servants who were sought, for it was particularly the fear of cultural contamination from 'ignorant domestics' which prompted mothers to protect their children from the superstition and vulgarity of lower-class culture, including sexual knowledge.

Prohibitions aside, many children found excitement, entertainment and affection with servants. Those servants still connected to the enterprise often were able to introduce suburban children to its mysteries.[212] Intensely religious servants could have a profound effect on youngsters as when Charles Spurgeon, the Colchester evangelical, was guided through his teenage doubts by the servant in the schoolmaster's house where he boarded.[213] Those children in homes totally separated from the enterprise now found a microcosm of the outside world within their own households through domestic servants. The often strict instructions to treat these inferiors with respect only emphasized social distance and here, too, children learned the patronage of charity. In a Suffolk village the full force of social hierarchy was brought home to the 5 year old who witnessed the conviction of one of his father's servants for a theft of £20 from the house, including the death sentence passed on the servant's friend.[214] Children could observe that the division of labour in service also followed strict gender lines: women did indoor work, men gardening and stable tasks. The highest ranks of ceremonial service continued as masculine preserves, by mid century many men's growing distaste for personal subordination, often interpreted as 'effeminancy', turned them from service altogether.

Middle-class women were at the centre of the master–servant (sic) relationship. Personally and daily, they experienced the contradictions of operating across class lines in a family setting. This task was added to the upbringing of their own children and any young people attached to the enterprise. For both offices they needed every scrap of authority they could muster. Elizabeth Galton recalled her Birmingham childhood around 1810 when 'every woman when she married, let her be ever so young, wore caps' not only because they were becoming but which 'made them look matronly and mistress of their home'.[215]

If a woman ran the household efficiently and took firm control, she had to do so through force of personality combined with strict routine. She had to be firm and business-like, yet these qualities were the opposite of that feminine softness, gentleness, and submission of self which constituted the claim to feminine influence. Relationships with servants were a special, indeed a crucial, case of the more general dilemma. Rebecca Solly Shaen, as wife of a prominent Essex attorney and farmer, sensed the disparity between professed axiom and daily practice. In her late 60s she was fretted by the demands of a large establishment with several unmarried children at home and a reduced income. In her diary she confessed the difficulty of attempting to 'do good, to your children, your servants, your poor neighbours. . .'

in knowing when to stand up to those you are trying to help, to bring out the good and eradicate the bad, to devote head and heart without a thought of self, and then bear suspicion, the calumny, the opposition of those for whom one has laboured.[216]

Women had traditionally organized the feeding of the household and care of young children, and they took most responsibility for either doing or overseeing enlarged domestic tasks. These were incorporated into general moral and religious duties, part of personal service to the master of the household as symbol of love and subservience, and ultimately a central part of feminine identity. In 1809, Hannah More had expounded the managerial aspects of housekeeping in Coelebs:

Now all these arrangements of life, these divisions of time and these selections and appropriations of the business of the hour, come within the department of the lady. And how much will the cares of a man of sense be relieved, if he chuse a wife who can do all this for him.[217]

By the 1840s, this 'household business' had enlarged to a wide range of duties requiring skill, diplomacy and the ability to absorb contradictory demands.

9 'Lofty pine and slender vine': living with gender in the middle class

Man is the rugged lofty pine
That frowns on many a wavebeat shore;
Woman the graceful slender vine
Whose curling tendrils round it twine,
And deck its rough bark sweetly o'er. . . .

Anon. from the commonplace book of Mary Young
Walthamstow, Essex 1828

A well ordered, well appointed home went some way to counteract the precariousness of middle-class life. But lack of communal services such as paved roads, water supplies and sanitation, focused attention on personal behaviour. Against existing fatalism, here was an opportunity for individuals and families to mould their own destiny, supported by evangelical habits of self-scrutiny. And every day there were opportunities for comparisons with the vulgar conduct of the ranks below. By mid century, the correct use of a handkerchief could connote both inward grace and social status.[1] The core of this refined behaviour was common to men and women, but in every nuance, observing appropriate gender definitions was crucial to gentility.

Manners and gentility

In the mid 1840s, Robert Bretnall of Witham, born 1775, was in his early 70s, describing himself variously as a miller or a landed gentleman proprietor. In fact his income came from a combination of active farming, rents (mainly from cottages) and an annuity from his trusteeship of a local brewery estate, giving him enough wealth to keep a carriage and man servant. He mixed with the local Witham elite of doctors, solicitors and large farmers and dabbled in Whig politics. He and his wife attended the Anglican church and cultural affairs such as concerts at the Witham Institution. One of his favourite pursuits was outings to London, now accessible by train, to shop or just browse. At age 73, in the Metropolis, he bought velveteen to make himself a shooting jacket and breeches, he bought pipes, shirts, socks and pearl buttons as well as tea and coffee. When he sold shares in the local railway, he went up to town and bought silver plate: a Britannia metal dish cover, a plated liquour stand for £5/10s, luxuries by any definition. On 17 June 1846, he and his wife went up (first class) to deposit £500 in a City bank and bought a 'gown piece' for her and returned to Witham by a late train, according to his diary, both 'drunk as Lords'.

Other evidence illustrates that Robert and Sarah Bretnall were aware of changed standards of propriety but, at their age, did not always comply. Robert spent much time hunting, eating and drinking in inns, and gossiping at markets, fishing for eels or shooting rats in the barn. His and Sarah's two children were illegitimate, the couple only having married when the younger was 12. Robert's spelling and vocabulary were shaky; he read little beside a newspaper. He showed signs of having a hasty temper, engaging in frequent fights with neighbours over fishing rights and a dung hill. One row had simmered for eighteen years, and when Bretnall was shooting hares in the wood, his enemy appeared flanked by two grown sons, one of whom looked 'black as Hell', whereupon Robert left a 'charm' to do him damage. In 1847, he records shooting a partridge 'altho it was Sunday', and in 1848 in another altercation with a neighbour over a rabbit, 'flew into a most violent passion and made use of a most dreadful expression viz: "God damn your eyes" '. His candid diary reflects the blend of older forms of uncontrolled behaviour and new seriousness:

June 21, 1846: Before we went to church I walked into my home field and was suddenly taken short before I could get my trouses [sic] down. I shit myself most tremendously from shoulder to flank, cleaned myself with some grass as well as I could went to Church with my wife and returned God thanks for all his merciful benefits bestowed on me.[2]

Robert Bretnall was literate, wealthy and keen to adopt the outward trappings of gentility which meant some restraints on his conduct. In practice, the habits of a lifetime were not easily shed, although this did not prevent him from being accepted socially. His social power stemmed from his ownership of property, farming activities, local business and charitable activity as trustee, witness or governor.

Middle-class women had no such power. The minutiae of everyday life, their personal behaviour, dress and language became their arena to judge and be judged. In 1847, the young daughters of a retired army officer expressed scorn at their prospective sister-in-law. Her men folk did not 'dress for dinner' and only two weeks after the wedding she allowed her husband entry to her room when she was dressed only in her stays.[3] These young women, born almost half a century after Bretnall, were the inheritors of gentility, the code coloured by the Christian tint which had touched the late middle age of the Bretnalls. This canon covered every aspect of an individual's life and its enforcement was central to women, both for themselves and in ordering the behaviour of men. Refusing to countenance dirty fingernails, coarse speech, or muddy boots sprawling on the new carpets was the material counterpart of influence, particularly effective when wielded by older women over their young male 'family and friends'. Since boy nature was taken to be dirty and rough, it needed the restraining hand and softening influence of a mother or sister. Girls were presumed naturally clean, dainty and quiet. Much childhood propaganda went into creating these putative natural characteristics which were the hidden texts of dozens of stories, poems and tracts for early nineteenth-century children, Jane and Ann Taylor's productions included. Bretnall's friend, the doctor Henry Dixon, as a young man had been taken in hand by a local clergyman's widow who groomed the poor farmer's son who up to then had 'no acquaintance or knowledge of the manners of a real gentleman; they were scarce in our rural population'.[4]

Training started in childhood along with the teaching of religion, the Puritan connection between cleanliness and godliness made manifest. This included modesty, keeping the body covered, refusing to directly name its parts and functions, and keeping limbs and voice under control. However, there was some confusion over what was to be so controlled and hidden. For example, breastfeeding was being promoted on both medical and religious grounds, the supreme act of motherhood, yet modesty made its performance indelicate. Suckling in public became increasingly associated with working-class practice. The solution was for a mother to keep herself and her babies within the seclusion of the home wherever possible.

Adult women acted as gatekeepers for admissible behaviour. Their personal failure to maintain standards was doubly grievous, as illustrated in a piece of Essex village street theatre in 1825. During the acrimonious split between an Independent minister and his congregation, the latter accused his most powerful deacon, a wealthy local farmer, of courting popularity with chapel members. The deacon had deliberately walked arm in arm down the village street with the local outcast, 'a woman remarkable above anyone I ever saw at Coggeshall for *filth*, not', he hastened tò add, 'that I despise poverty but the most indigent may be neat and clean'. The final clerical insult maintained that the woman was 'half covered in *virmin*' (sic), at which the minister apologized to his readers for using such a coarse expression (emphasis in original).[5]

Next to personal cleanliness and modesty, table manners were a test of status, not surprising when so much business as well as social life was transacted over meals. The paraphernalia of the table encouraged higher standards. Wedgwood's mass produced crockery meant separate clean dishes for each type of food, while a Birmingham manufacturer of electroplate extolled the benefits of forks. 'They create a higher degree of taste, refined taste improved manners, improved manners imply a loftier state of moral feelings.' So while profits rolled in, 'the tone of society is improved'.[6] In popular mythology, small farmers often embodied backward vulgarity. In 1816 a local paper reported that an Essex farmer accidentally cut off a gentleman's finger in trying to carve the wing of a fowl, the incident 'occasioned by the eagerness of the company who all had their hands in the dish at the same time'.[7]

Table manners could mark social inclusion. Henry Dixon observed the Witham curate's annual dinner for gentry, professional men and farmers: 'The tenant farmers are a louty lot in such company. I saw one of them slily appropriate an apple and pocket the same. Forks in such company were in jeopardy.' He queried whether the 'experiment' would succeed. 'Neither party were at ease', his medical self excepted.[8] Increased refinement in dining was extended to women leaving the table at the end of the meal when men could then smoke, drink more heavily and discuss topics no longer suitable for the fair sex – business, politics and worldly (sexual) subjects in a more earthy idiom. This custom was by no means adopted widely before mid century but the standard was set.

One reason for excluding women was the heavy drinking which still went on despite evangelical efforts. Eighteenth-century society had assumed a certain level of hard drinking. In the 1770s a brewer/farmer's wife recorded the launching of a new wherry in their river when a mixed company came to celebrate, starting in the afternoon and 'the Gentlemen staid til past 12 o'clock and were very drunk'.[9] Beer and spirits had been traditionally associated with health, muscular energy and virility and were ubiquitous at a time when water supplies were poor. Contracts were sealed with a drink; ale and spirits flowed in officers' quarters, Oxbridge colleges, local clubs, political dinners and hunting outings. The ability to drink one's neighbour under the table was a sign of masculine prowess, while stout and oysters were popularly believed to be an aphrodisiac (to the benefit of the Colchester oyster trade). It often took the willpower of religious conviction to break through the masculine identification with heavy drinking. Local freemasons and tradesmen's clubs partly owed their success to peer pressure which allowed male conviviality without excess. But the most powerful sanctions were familial. Two Essex brothers, born in the 1780s, deliberately rejected the heavy drinking of their ship's captain father while a 20-year-old banker's son, alight with a conversion experience, proclaimed in 1820: 'This day I wrote to my Father on Drunkeness, he having the day before got very drunk.'[10] Intoxication was doubly castigated in women, both in itself and as leading to uncontrolled, immodest behaviour. Tea, from being regarded as a harmful intoxicant, became a beverage identified with women and afternoon tea gradually a feminine light meal. Women were expected to take the lead in more refined social activities. A retired naval officer who took up farming on the remote marshlands of Essex in the 1800s, felt that genteel women had suffered from a lack of cultivated recreations for the 'convivial meetings of men, either at home or abroad, consisted chiefly in trying whose head was hardest at drinking flip or punch, sitting all the time enveloped in a thick atmosphere of tobacco smoke'.[11]

However it was accomplished, all were agreed that drunkenness in the middle ranks had fallen markedly by the 1840s, further distinguishing them from the loutishness of those below and debauchery above.[12] The use of tobacco was also being curtailed. In particular, chewing tobacco and spitting were denigrated; travellers to the continent noting that there this 'horrible beastly custom' continued unchecked.[13] Middle-class men continued to take snuff (although the associated dirt was making this less popular) and to smoke pipes. But refined women, except in the most remote rural areas, no longer touched tobacco in any form and often banished men's smoking to the kitchen, outhouse or garden.

Robert Bretnall not only occasionally drank to excess, he swore oaths, yet was uneasy when he did so. Another farmer, as a churchwarden and dressed in his Sunday best, would accompany his sisters to church. Yet if on his way he spied blackbirds in his fields, he would shake his fists, wave his arms and shout rude expressions to the embarrassment of his genteel female relatives.[14] Evangelicals, in particular, looked with horror on using the Lord's name in vain and strong language by women was becoming even less acceptable. Harriet Martineau recalled the 'odd and striking' spinster sisters, born in the eighteenth century, who were friends of her family in Norwich, with their false hair, rouged cheeks and racy language. Once when their carriage door stuck one of them called out in a voice loud enough to be heard in the house, 'My God, I can't get out.'[15] Swearing not only mocked religion, but was associated with backwardness ignorant proverbs and rustic beliefs in charms. Yet men, in their business and sporting life, had to understand more uncouth terms, and too much refinement in language, as in general behaviour, implied a flight from masculinity. They, therefore, had special problems in proving robust manliness within refinement.

Language and speech, like other parts of middle-class culture, were becoming more formal, more differentiated and more careful of gender connotations. A merchant recalled that in his father's mid eighteenth-century generation, men had simple, homey names like Jack, Billy and Jimmy, the women Polly, Molly and Kitty. In his times more pretentious names were becoming popular.[16] A Birmingham woman also noticed that by the 1820s, wives were calling their husbands by their full name or surname.[17] Following Lucinda, the heroine of More's *Coelebs*, women began to develop their own linguistic styles, which stressed refinement and purity but avoided showing excessive learning. The 'strong-minded' daughter of a Birmingham manufacturer who published novels and numerous articles declared in 1788 that she had firmly decided 'never to enter a dispute' since she thought this 'unaimiable in a woman'.[18] Young women were developing their own idiom around symbols of femininity: the 'language of flowers', exchanges of hair to be worn in lockets and brooches, the play with gloves and ribbons.

Changing attitudes to sexuality

Women cultivated the language of friendship and love in which sexual passion had no part. (Thomas Bowdler's expurgated *Family Shakespeare* was published in 1818.) By the early nineteenth century, there had been a gradual shift from the earlier view of women as sexually voracious towards the innocence and passivity of Victorian sensibility. Yet at mid century a nonconformist minister still warned the young country youth to beware becoming embroiled with his master's wife, the older married woman seen as a particular snare. True manhood was not to be gained through sexual adventure but by self-control through religious commitment which was the strongest guard for a young man.[19]

Jacob Unwin, son of an Essex brewer, was just such a youth, apprenticed to a London printer about 1814. On returning from chapel one Sunday evening, he struck up a conversation with a 'very genteel young female'. and offered her his arm, this contact being made without introduction of family, friends or chapel membership. His reason for this presumption, he said, was a fear that the young woman was going on 'the road to destruction' as she acknowledged that she disliked church-going. He entreated her to 'seek pardon through the blood of the Lamb', but to no avail. Later he admitted to his diary that he was 'rather taken with her person; my passions strove within me, and I bless God that I was prevented from offering any liberties to her which I am sure she would have accepted'.[20] It was better to keep young men from sexual knowledge and guard their sensibilities. In 1808, at an inquest on a fire in Chelmsford an older man was substituted for the young unmarried gentleman coroner who would have had to view the 'mutilated remains of two young ladies . . . naked at the time of the fire'.[21]

Yet, at least in the earlier part of the period, the products of sexual irregularities were often accepted, particularly if, as with Bretnall's children, the couple subsequently married. Another Essex farming family accepted that the eldest son's bride was pregnant at marriage.[22] But seduction and adultery, the speciality of the debauched gentry, were severely censured.[23] A special sermon, directed at young men and women, was preached at St Peter's, Colchester's Evangelical church, on the day William Corder was hanged for the seduction and murder of Maria Martin in the notorious Red Barn case, just across the Suffolk border. The vicar, who claimed to have witnessed Corder's repentance in the death cell, stressed how small sins starting with disobedience to parents, unchaste association and prostitution led to Corder's 'horrid paths of wickedness and vice'.[24]

It was the open recognition of sexuality which was suppressed along with other vulgarities. Male sexual passion was to be contained and hidden, women's to be ignored if not denied. As a result, most of the records are silent on such subjects. Only when discussing the poor and ignorant are there hints at an understanding by both men and women. The ex-naval officer and farmer who tried to bring religion and scientific enlightenment to the wilds of the Essex coast, described the visit of an old woman and her daughter who complained that she was accused of being a witch. The villagers alleged that she had teats in her armpits to suckle imps and she begged him to examine her to falsify the stigma. Both he and his family – who were present – laughed at her simple beliefs and he records that the rosy cheeked daughter had 'bewitching powers I thought strong enough to induce an examination if she chose to solicit it'.[25]

On the other hand, the few references to homosexuality were no laughing matter. Emotional warmth between brothers, cousins and male friends was strong, but sexual acts between men were regarded with outraged horror. The same improving farmer was called upon to help family friends when the husband was accused of a homosexual connection. The young wife, with several children, was abandoned by father, brother and friends and feared her husband would be hanged. The farmer hesitated for he felt that if the crime had been robbery or even murder it would have been easier, but such 'infamous' behaviour might soil the reputation of anyone who tried to help.[26]

Female friendships flourished and were freely referred to in passionate terms. They often were formed under religious influence as when a vicar's teenage daughter regarded her pious older friend with 'childlike reverence and loverlike attachment'.[27] There is no way of speculating the exact emotional, much less physical meaning of such relationships. Warm, loving attachments were frequent between siblings, parents and children, proto-kin and friends. Thus, despite the long period of youthful celibacy, sexuality was firmly directed to procreation within marriage, the high birth rate and short intervals between births indicating its active pursuit.

Mobility and gender

Provincial middle-class culture at this time seemed as much concerned with strengthening ties within the family and controlling women's independent behaviour as with sexuality. Growing constraints on the physical and social mobility of women, especially young girls, is a motif across a range of activities. Into the early nineteenth century, a great deal of enjoyment was still gained through walking, often combined with dropping in to chat with neighbours or relatives. In the countryside, which even in Birmingham was within easy reach, this might be combined with berry picking, gathering mushrooms and other ways of using the products of fields and hedgerows. Meals eaten out of doors were popular and still relatively informal. A day out at the local beauty spots of Hagley or the Leasowes was the equivalent for Birmingham tradesmen of the more affluent and minor gentry's visits to stately homes.[28] For those with access to horses, riding for pleasure and exercise was widespread for both men and women.

Walking and riding as forms of transport were, however, beginning to segregate the sexes. It was assumed that men would learn to ride and the city-bred clerk was somewhat derided as effeminate for not being able to do so. Horses were considerably cheaper and more convenient to hire than wheeled vehicles. Some occupations such as auctioneers, estate agents, doctors and farmers depended on being mobile, mainly on horseback. An Essex agent's success was partly attributed to his capacity to spend whole days in the saddle.[29] But horses and the stables were eminently masculine affairs; buying, selling (and betting) on horses was a central part of masculine culture and women now mainly rode for exercise. One of the reasons why many widows and daughters migrated to town centres and suburbs was the difficulty of obtaining personal transport.

In the eighteenth century, versatile small vehicles were few. A wealthy Birmingham doctor, abroad for his health in 1787, gave approval of his wife's move from Edgbaston Hall to their town house for the winter; the only location 'for women without a carriage is to be found in town'.[30] The next thirty years saw marked improvements in road construction and maintenance and the rapid growth of public stage and mail coach transport, one of the main forces incorporating the middle ranks in a wider culture.[31] It also witnessed the invention and perfecting of a wide range of both open and closed wheeled vehicles, from the humble gig used by farmers to the stately landau and barouche, or the small light self-driven phaeton or Stanhope suitable for ladies. In towns many of these could be hired for short periods or leased on five year contracts (including maintenance), or they could be bought, built to order, ready made or second hand.[32] Coach builders flourished, some establishing substantial businesses such as the Perry family of Witham, with spin offs in such items as upholstery, lamps and special clothing.[33] Livery stables for the hire of riding horses, horse and vehicle or horses for the family carriage were another growth area, often, as we have seen, connected to pubs and inns.

The difference such mobility made, especially in rural areas, was dramatic. On the Essex coast, it was remarked that whereas in the 1760s there were only eight single horse chaises in the whole parish, by the early 1800s even 'farmers of 200 acres' almost all kept some form of chaise and some even four wheeled carriages.[34] One reason for using these vehicles was to allow women mobility. A Birmingham commentator noted that ladies did not sit outside on public coaches, but a Birmingham banker's daughter felt it was 'infra dig' for ladies to travel in a stage coach at all. Posting, which meant hiring a chaise with a postboy, was expensive, as the same young lady noted, at least 1 shilling and 9 pence per mile with tips and turnpike tolls extra.[35] Riding horseback for serious travel was difficult to arrange and placed modesty in question; it was suitable only for the most backward farmers' wives.

But in higher circles walking could also present problems for women, as Elizabeth Bennet in *Pride and Prejudice* discovered when she arrived with muddy shoes and skirt at her genteel neighbours.[36] Elizabeth Head Cadbury was happy to walk back from the shop in Bull Street to the country house in Edgbaston with her husband at night; later generations would have regarded this as decidedly odd behaviour.[37] The new wife of the Unitarian minister at the New Meeting astonished members of the congregation by walking 4 miles to pay a wedding visit.[38] Women were becoming constrained by canons of respectability which added considerably to the cost of their physical mobility. By the 1830s, the change to more restrictive clothing, layers of heavy petticoats and larger, trailing dress lengths contributed to their containment.[39] The desire to keep a carriage, or at least a chaise of some kind, was not just snobbery but crucial in counteracting isolation.

In addition to difficulties with availability and expense, middle-class young women had to be shielded from possible exposure to the hazards of public travel, including sexual and social advances, by being accompanied by a man or an older woman. It is instructive to compare the practical instructions for travel given to the young son of a Birmingham banker with the timidity of a Colchester girl in her mid-teens, proud of her ability to find a protected upstairs room in the London inn where she was to await her brother.[40] By the 1830s Rebecca Shaen's daughter, although in her 20s, was handed over by her mother to her aunt in London for the journey to Brighton and thus had 'safe conveyance'.[41]

For more distant journeys women's problems did not end with travel. Finding quarters suitable for ladies was often an obstacle, as one of the Galton daughters discovered on a journey from Birmingham to Cheltenham where the only hotel 'respectable for ladies' was of an inferior grade. In Cheltenham,

They all go into lodgings which makes it much less desirable for us than Leamington, as domestic society is our great object.[42]

For the middle-class women, even more than men, the railroad solved many of these dilemmas, although there were early suspicions of its acceptability on the same grounds as the stage coach, the public setting open to all. However, with seating divided into classes and 'ladies only' carriages, the railroad did make travel easier even for delicate ladies. The railroad made travel formal, rational, punctual and relatively cheap. As Dr Dixon commented in 1843 when he was able to travel by train with his invalid wife from Witham to London, the punctuality and certainty which the railroad engendered

will have a very sound influence upon some of the troublesome uncertain people which we meet with. Habits of punctuality are important in all conditions of society and these railroads wait for nobody.[43]

Nevertheless women were mainly still restricted to shorter journeys, part of the general constraints on their physical mobility. Young men were expected to roam, to seek adventure, to go out from as well as return to the home. When the young son of a Suffolk timber merchant was visiting Lowestoft, in the evening he walked by the seashore by moonlight, revelling in being alone to think through his decision whether to enter the church.[44] Henry Crabb Robinson, just free of his attorney's apprenticeship in Colchester, took his small patrimony and set off to walk alone across Germany, where he visited Goethe and initiated his role as interpreter of German romanticism to the English, an unthinkable course of action for a feminine counterpart.[45] Some earlier generations of young women had a certain freedom, their elders confident about their religious training and social milieu of family and friends. In the early 1800s, the daughters of a Colchester doctor enjoyed sitting on the ruins of the town walls reciting Byron's poetry by moonlight with their friends Jane and Ann Taylor. But solitary ramblings, much less longer journeys, came to be out of the question and girls were increasingly closely guarded.[46] The issue of the desirability of respectable women moving freely about alone focused on concern over unmarried girls. Joseph Gibbins's youngest daughter Martha, who was born in 1798 and brought up in central Birmingham, was walking across the town to school by herself when she was 9 years old. In a letter to her brother William she described the following incident:

I am become so much of a woman as to go to school by myself. One day, as I was returning from school, a boy was so rude as to offer to *kiss* me, and he called another boy to do the same, so I went into a reputable looking shop and asked the man if he would be so kind as to speak to those boys, for they had been behaving rude to me, and I told him I was Joseph Gibbins' little girl. He came out, sent them away, and I got home without being interrupted again.[47]

It is difficult to imagine the daughters of Edgbaston moving around Birmingham with the freedom of Martha Gibbins; the point of living in the suburb was to try and ensure that such incidents did not take place.

Gender and the social occasion

Accompanied by men, there were still some rural pleasures which women could enjoy. Fishing continued to be a popular pastime and a number of women, from Quakers to worldly Anglicans, mention the pleasures of fishing in company with brothers, fathers and husbands. However, hunting and shooting remained the central feature of rural life. Foxhunting was the traditional mixing place for the three tiers of the English countryside, for even labourers followed the hunt on foot, and hunting was often claimed to be the social cement which bound the classes together. But hunting was becoming an all-male preserve. By the late eighteenth century the chase was more formal with subscription packs replacing private arrangements, giving women less opportunity to participate. The wildness of the hunt, the 'blooding' with the fox's tail, those elements which made it a 'manly exercise and sport', were inimical to feminine decorum. The costume of pink coat and breeches, evolved from uniforms worn during the war, was not for ladies whose long skirts when perched on a side-saddle were further disincentives to hard riding.

An emphasis on masculine chivalry, the need to protect women through any supposed difficulty and to retain a ceremonious intercourse between the sexes, meant that men felt they would not be able to push ahead when women were in the chase. R. S. Surtees, the great hunting journalist, described hunting as displaying 'all the excitement of war with only half its danger'. He maintained that

women are as much in their place at the meet watching and cheering the men on as they are out of it tearing across the country

and added that their presence as spectators could help to raise the moral tone.[48] Hunting thus provided an ideal form of male bonding for all classes, the

strongest preservation of that natural spirit . . . for a life of active energy, independence and freedom . . . and corrective to effeminacy

in the words of a foxhunting MP.[49] Meanwhile, the women, whose men had organized the Suffolk hunt, for example,

played the harpsichord and the new forte-piano, paid visits to each other, organized balls and made up theatre parties.[50]

The behaviour and presence of women at other public events such as horse racing also came under scrutiny. Racing became more organized, with more regularized rules for types of entry, distances to be run and the provision of prize money. Often races were combined with agricultural shows which provided a more protected environment at which ladies could have appropriate accommodation as with Chelmsford's self-consciously genteel efforts in the 1820s with the Galleywood Races. Farmers' womenfolk might be assigned to a second rank enclosure or a chosen inn where they gathered, between the exclusiveness of the gentry and upper status professional elites and the promiscuousness of rural labourers. Together with town tradesmen, often literally their kin, they were visibly a middle group. Here the clothes, demeanour and accent of their female members were on public display.[51]

A similar development was affecting fairs. The growth of retail shops in the towns and pedlars in the countryside meant that fairs were separating between wholesale business, and those mostly for entertainment. The latter were especially abhorred by evangelicals as when the local rector attacked

Chelmsford Fair as 'an abode of moral darkness', and Essex magistrates joined with Wilberforce's anti-vice campaign to close many local fairs.[52] The refined wife of a Birmingham banker writing to her brother-in-law in 1807 about the Birmingham Fair commented,

> I hear the market is full of shews – wild beast, puppets, dwarfs and giants – besides many other wonders – are now exhibiting themselves to the delight and amazement of all the Country Bumpkins who are come from far and near to see them.[53]

While this attitude was growing among those with pretensions to gentility, there were many who were not averse to gingerbread from the fair, were fascinated by the 'feats of dexterity and magical skill' and would vary select concerts and assemblies with performances such as the 'Great Wizard of the North' who visited the Birmingham Society of Arts in 1840.[54] In the rural areas the attraction of the fair lingered on, too, but was increasingly associated with children and childish things.

The tensions of class and gender alliance are exemplified in traditional Guy Fawkes celebrations. By the end of the eighteenth century, these had been curtailed in the general clamp down on crowd activity. Leadership of the revels had shifted to young men from artisan and trade families, the 'bonfire boys'. Here a cross-class, all-male coalition took a non-political form, although local issues and potentates were often 'guyed'. In Chelmsford and Witham, local gentry and militia officers attempted to control the affair, giving money and supplying the venue. Secrecy maintained by the guy masks allowed clerks and sons of respectable townsfolk to take part, often leaving their seniors to turn a blind eye to the proceedings.[55] What is significant, however, is that whatever the class make-up of the Guy Fawkes crowd, its leadership if not membership, was male. Mixed gatherings could continue but only in a proper domestic setting. Birmingham's serious middle class held private family parties to celebrate the Guy. On 7 November, a young Quaker went to one co-religionist to help make fireworks, on 8 November to another to help make the Guy and on 9 November to the Cadbury's for tea and a bonfire.[56]

Markets, too, were becoming specialized and enclosed; ladies might do their shopping in certain parts only. In the early years of the nineteenth century the place for sheep on Birmingham's market day was the Free Grammar School while the pig market was held at the Old Crown. An old lady recalled that in the 1780s

> all respectable females who traversed the street on market days had to turn into the middle of it to preserve their cleanliness, the footpaths being reserved for the special accommodation of the superior animal to whom the spot was devoted.[57]

Small wonder that the building of the town's Doric Market Hall in 1834 was greeted with pride.

The hunting field, race course, fairground and market were public arenas where all gradations of society might congregate. But the provincial middle class had their own semi-public gatherings. As might be expected the ceremonials connected with the family stood out as occasions for the gathering and reinforcing of kinship and friendship ties. Weddings were marked by church services and followed, where possible, by a meal, often a break-fast. For example, when Mary Ann Galton was married in Birmingham, the large wedding party was entertained at her grandparents' country home.[58] Some wealthy middle-class families used weddings as an occasion for paternalism, particularly in rural communities. In 1820s Suffolk, the bachelor uncle, head of the family firm, gave a wedding feast for his niece described in the *Bury Gazette*. With church bells ringing and guns firing groaning tables were spread by the river and 500 villagers were welcomed to this 'truly noble sight'. The couple, who breakfasted with a select party of friends, set off for their wedding trip

amidst the blessing of the poor, to whom this amiable young lady was most dear, for her heart, was 'open as the day to melting charity'.[59]

Funerals were also used to mark the influence of powerful local leaders; clergymen, like John Angell James as we have seen, but also men like William Henry Pattisson, the Witham attorney, at whose death the town's shops all closed. However, most middle-class funerals were occasions for family, friends and co-religionists. Cousins and other family members were urged to send a representative to the ceremony even over quite long distances. These requests were almost always to men, despite their business commitments. Over the period the records suggest that women began to stay away from the burial service and the graveside ritual although they might be present at the meal afterwards. In the 1770s all the family, including the young children, of a wealthy farmer/brewer attended the funeral of the wife's father, but by the 1840s this was much less common.[60] A modest Ipswich draper attended his father's funeral without his wife, although a devoted female servant was there.[61] Female friends or more distant relatives might be present, but not daughters and widows, displaying their grief in public. Robert Bretnall's daughter-in-law's mother did not attend her husband's funeral and diarists made a point of remarking when women in the family *were* there.[62] Women were beginning to be considered too delicate to bear the public rituals of death. If they did go, they were advised to follow the practices of the nobility and gentry and remain in the church while the actual burial was taking place outside.[63] A scene from Mrs Gaskell's *North and South*, published in 1854, confirms that refined women were believed too sensitive to sustain public displays of grief. The strong, although thoroughly feminine, heroine who has sustained her father during her mother's terminal illness pleads to go to the funeral in lieu of his seeking a male friend. Her father answers that,

'My dear, women do not generally go'
'No' [responds the heroine] 'because they can't control themselves. Women of our class don't go, because they have no power over their emotions, and yet are ashamed of showing them.'[64]

This convention contrasts with the business-like account of the funeral of an Ipswich master baker's mother-in-law. His wife paid £2-2-0d towards the expenses, presumably from money of her own. She and her husband went to the 'funral' together with three other couples from the family, returning to the house-cum-shop, to take tea and settel the business comfortable . . . agreeball to the wich of all present,

including paying the bills.[65]

Meanwhile, the more genteel were moving away from the bustle of an undifferentiated public even in death. The Dissenting wish not to be buried in Anglican churchyards aggravated a growing concern at the overcrowded and insanitary nature of the churchyards. It was reported of Ipswich, for example, that,

Several of our graveyards are situated in the midst of thoroughfares, where it is impossible that the last offices for the dead can be performed with that degree of solemnity and impressiveness that is desired.[66]

The ubiquitous John Claudius Loudon was in the forefront of providing a solution to this problem; properly designed cemeteries which would dispose of the dead in such a way that their decomposition would not be injurious to the living. Furthermore, a well designed cemetery ought to improve both moral sentiments and general taste. A cemetery properly kept, he argued,

might become a school of instruction in architecture, sculpture, landscape gardening, arboriculture, botany, and in those important parts of general gardening, neatness, order and high keeping.[67]

Cemetery companies were established according to joint stock principles. Birmingham boasted three by mid century, one of which was exclusively for Dissenters and one for Anglicans, while smaller towns such as Ipswich made do with one but allotted space for two chapels, one Church of England, the other nonconformist. Those who could afford it could now rely on seclusion from the undifferentiated public in death as well as in life.[68]

Those left behind, too, carried the message of social demarcation. Both men and women wore mourning at the death of kin and friends as a way of recognizing, or denying, important social relationships. Women's dress had always played the major role in mourning ritual and it was women whose clothes and accessories were elaborated into what became the Victorian cult of mourning. The Essex silk manufacturing family of Cour-tauld built a fortune on the production of black silk crepe, which became the epitome of genteel mourning in women's dress, caps and veils.[69] The period of mourning, at least among the higher ranks, prevented women being seen in public, but was not too burdensome as long as social life was informal with family and friends. But even in the 1820s, Amelia Moilliet wore mourning for her father for two years.[70] Wearing mourning implied withdrawal from the world and became a heavier responsibility for women as the importance of men's public activities grew.

Middle-class men's and women's part in rituals of various kinds and appearances in various places was being plotted and codified áccording to developing notions of gentility and respectability. Sometimes common masculine interests overrode class divisions; at other times men and women appeared together in class solidarity. Nor should we expect these boundaries to be fixed, or consistent. For example, it should come as no surprise that even wealthy genteel women enjoyed swimming in the privacy of their own gardens or grounds. Likewise, while lady-like sensibilities may have been too fragile to sustain public display of emotion at funerals, the local records hint that some women enjoyed the drama of public courtrooms and relished a good trial. Of course many men regularly attended court proceedings as magistrates, lawyers, jurymen and spectators witnessing the law being enacted. But the public spectacle of the criminal trial carried a moral message and the mere presence of genteel women might raise the tone of the proceedings. For women admitted to few other forms of public entertainment, the colour and drama must have been irresistible. Among other provincial ladies, Sarah Bretnall, Robert's wife, seems to have made few excursions from Witham and then almost always in his company. On 8 March 1847, however, while her husband and son were fishing, she and her daughter-in-law enjoyed a day's outing at Chelmsford Assizes to hear a murder trial.[71]

Gender as appearance

The everyday appearance of individuals was also transformed by central concerns with status and gender. The change for men was, perhaps, even more striking than for women. From a concern with physical virility or at least its appearance, male selfhood increasingly depended on occupation, and public activity. This was reflected in a dramatic change in men's clothing. By the 1840s, the success of the middle-class challenge to aristocratic leadership was as clear in standard masculine appearance as it was in the repeal of the Corn Laws.[72] Eighteenth-century men's clothes had expressed their position – the leather breeches and paper cap of the artisan, the linen smock of the farm labourer. Aristocracy and gentry sported outfits of ruffles, lace, silk and satin in bright and pastel colours for dress wear. Their heads were powdered, faces rouged and bodies scented, while satin breeches, silk hose and dainty pumps revealed the line of their hips, legs and feet, and hinted at sexual display. Except for sporting clothes, simplicity in colour and line was still associated with Puritanism and only nonconformist sectarians maintained drab dark colours and sober textures. Merchants and professional men followed a version of aristocratic costume modified to their circumstances. A young Birmingham manufacturer, on his first visit to London in the early 1780s, proudly recalled every detail of his outfit. His hair was dressed in a high toupe, handsomely frizzed with open curls and profusely powdered. He wore a light blue coat, white cashmere waistcoat, shirt with deep laced frill and lace ruffles (made by his sister), stock with brilliant stock buckle, white silk stockings and shoes with silver buckles (a prime item of Birmingham manufacture). His hat was a three-square cock, and, young as he was, he had his cane with a gold head, a present from an elder brother.[73]

Men actively engaged in the enterprise would wear working clothes during the week but appear in similar finery on Sunday. An early nineteenth-century farmer retained the smock frock in the country, but on Sundays and for journeys to London wore top boots, knee breeches, a frock coat and beaver hat bought in the Metropolis. It was his wife's task to care for this outfit, carefully kept in a special dresser.[74] By the early

Plate 29 An image of youthful femininity found in the scrapbook of Jane Seabrook, an Essex farmer's daughter, *c.* 1830

nineteenth century the division between working and Sunday clothes was encouraged by the religious revival, but, in general, simplicity in clothing was urged, particularly for men. As John Angell James expostulated, 'cleanness and neatness border upon virtue, as excessive foppery and expensiveness do upon vice. It is unworthy of a female to be inordinately fond of dress, but for a *man* to love finery is despicable indeed'.[75]

Religious conviction on its own would not have been sufficient to effect such alteration without the commitment to productive work. Arthur Young, Suffolk farmer and civil servant, was an Evangelical convert but also adherent of scientific rationality, his days filled with duties for the Board of Agriculture. In a visit to France in 1797, he chafed against donning full masculine dress at midday:

What is a man good for after his silk breeches and stockings are on, his hat under his arm, and his head *bien pourdre*? Can he botonize in a watered meadow? Can he clamber the rocks to mineralize? Can he farm with the peasant and the ploughman? He is in order for the conversation of ladies which to be sure . . . is an excellent employment; but it is an employment that never relishes better than after a day spent in active toil and animated pursuit.[76]

The change came piecemeal. Swords were transformed into walking sticks, the tax on flour for hair powder during the war accelerated its decline, the drive for clean linen made ruffles and laces prohibitive and they interfered with activity. However, the most contentious change was from breeches and stockings to trousers, a transformation accomplished in about thirty years. Early in the century, a Suffolk gentleman commented on Wellington's introduction of such garments during the Peninsular campaign as a convenience, which met with resistance from the soldiers. Trousers were also suspect among the elite; his son reported back from Cambridge in 1809 that students appearing in chapel or hall wearing trousers were being marked absent.[77]

The transition began with full length tight fitting pantaloons, that is breeches and stocking in one piece. Pantaloons, like knee breeches, showed off men's limbs and sexual parts, making them conscious of the way they stood. The final change to trousers in the late 1830s and 1840s, disguised all exposure in uniform, shapeless dark serviceable cloth (with disastrous consequences for the hosiery industry). Younger men first adopted the style, widening the gap between old-fashioned and new. An Ipswich draper was in his late 50s in 1838 when he wore trousers for the first time but he 'soon parted from them'.[78] But a wine merchant ten years his junior living now in London regularly wore trousers, only buying knee breeches for his wedding and immediately reselling them to his tailor.[79] The older style continued to be worn for such ceremonial occasions, balls and evening wear. Older men who refused to adopt the new costume appeared increasingly eccentric.

By the 1830s, the only touches of colour that remained were in, for example, the waistcoat, often embroidered by female relatives. High starched collars and gloves gave young men a chance for small vanities, but the effect, promoted as assiduously by Brummell and the Dandies as serious Christians, was restrained. Along with bright or pastel colours, silk and satin became primarily feminine materials, men only being allowed to indulge in velvet for special occasions (Bretnall's shooting jacket) or touches such as the green velvet collar on the wedding coat of a Birmingham manufacturer in 1836.[80] Gradually, other male adornments were stripped down: the wearing of corsets, cosmetics and perfumes was abandoned, jewellery and flowers were reduced and then only for ceremony. Only the utilitarian watch remained, carried in a special trouser pocket attached to a broad silk ribbon – gold for the rich – with seals and insignia of office or society membership displayed on the watch chain.

By the 1850s, the change was almost complete. The interim romantic youthful image, often termed Byronesque, suited to pantaloons and the cravat with locks curling over the collar, had given way to stiff, dark, heavy materials, shapeless nether garments, and narrow black tie. Heavy whiskers, topped by the black 'stove pipe' completed the picture, associated with Victorian patriarchal authority, carrying a strong masculine identity but now devoid of overtly personal sexual attraction. Even radicals who had worn distinctive colours, hats and other marks of their political commitment well into the nineteenth century, began to dress like all middle- and upper-class men in the ubiquitous trousers and coat. The 'gorgeous plumage' of the eighteenth century only remained in ornamental livery of male servants (livery was originally a pledge of aristocratic service) or in the ceremonial dress of the armed services. Social status for men was now expressed in the nuances of the cut and material of the suit, or the quality of the shirt, which could still be expensive. A bank manager turned down promotion on the grounds that the extra expense in clothes and washing to present a proper appearance would cost more than the rise in salary.[81]

The new masculine image spanned the range from gentry to clerk, their common masculinity overriding occupational differences. As we have seen, boys were kept in petticoats until about age 3 or 4, when they were breeched, often at a family ceremony. From 4 to about 7 they were put in 'skeleton suits' of tight trousers buttoned to a little jacket, a neat costume allowing plenty of movement. Girls remained in petticoats, for centuries a symbol of their continued dependent position.[82]

But in any case changes in women's dress, while significant, were not as dramatic as for men and received less comment in local records. The thin clinging material, vertical lines and loose limbs of the war period gave way in the 1820s to more confined and modest coverings. By mid century with the crinoline, 'knickers' or underclothes were introduced for the first time.[83] A Birmingham woman remembered her girlhood in that period with stiff boned stays which had to be laced every morning from behind. Stays and petticoats had shoulder straps so that it was difficult to raise the arms.[84] The sloping shoulders and tight sleeves, too, made large gestures or heavy work difficult, and dresses buttoned behind so that a woman could not dress herself. Ringlets, soft colours, sandals laced with ribbons, increasingly full skirts, small waists and large bonnets favoured a petite, dainty, almost child-like image and must have been trying to well built active women, but the style was a deliberate foil to the new masculine archetype. Between 1810 and 1820, hanging pockets in women's skirts began to give way to the dainty reticule (or ridicule) carried over a wrist which prevented carrying anything else.[85] Indoors, caps were worn, usually adopted at marriage, although older single women had a version and a widow's status was marked by a special cap.

Provincial outlets for women's fashions were making an impact, as cited in local descriptions of shopping expeditions. The use of 'Flanders babies' (fashion dolls) for display had reached rural Suffolk by the end of the eighteenth century. London styles were reported in detail in local newspapers, often the only item specifically addressed to the 'fair sex'. Haberdashers and milliners regularly offered inspection days for new stock, opportunities taken up by farmers' wives and daughters as well as their urban counterparts. In May 1823, Miss Pitty invited the ladies of Hadleigh in Suffolk to inspect her 'neat and fashionable selection of Millinery, Straw, Leghorn Bonnets, Silks, Satins, Lutestrings, Norwich Crapes, Bombasins, Lustres, Muslin Dresses, Stays, Laces, Edgings, Gloves, Trimmings'.[86] Women now carried the bright colours and luxurious materials. Silk, always costly, and once only worn by the aristocracy, became closely associated with feminine gentility, the silk gown a symbol of affluence but with erotic overtones. Young innocent girls were kept in cottons and muslins for silks belonged to the mature and sexually experienced.

Evangelical spokesmen constantly warned young girls about the lure of dress. A preoccupation with personal adornment is not surprising since it was one of the few arenas for women's creativity and standards of women's dress were important in demonstrating family position. When she was 19, Amy Camps, one of Rev. Marsh's devout parishioners recorded in her New

Year review of her soul how she was beset by vain and foolish thoughts
on dress, an anxiety echoed by a Quaker mother about her pride in dressing
her children.[87] One of Jane Taylor's didactic tales for girls, significantly
entitled 'I Can Do Without It', portrays a 14 year old having to learn how
to spend her first dress allowance. At the 'capital hatter's in the town' – a
thinly disguised Colchester – there is a tempting display of fashionable
beaver hats trimmed with satin, loaded with plumes and most becoming
pink satin linings, embossed bands and dangling tassels which 'caught the
eye of the fair passenger'. She had to decide how much to lay out on what
kind of dress appropriate to her station.[88]

The contrast between the straight lines, practical materials and business-
like images of men's clothes and the soft, flowing curved lines, the rich
colours and textures, elaborate detail and constricting shape of women's
clothes was becoming a powerful part of gender segregation. The connections between beauty, taste and morality going back to Burke and drawn
on by practical men like Loudon as well as by poets and novelists, centred
on feminine form, appearance and behaviour. Ruggedness of features, a
certain disdain for appearances, even brusqueness, were signs of manliness.
Perhaps it was underlying doubts about the masculinity of their calling that
prompted particular concern with the manly image of the clergy. Samuel
Newton, the influential Congregational minister in Witham, had the advantage of being a big man whose irregular features were seen as 'endearing',
and implying sincerity as with John Newton, the Evangelical vicar who
had inspired Cowper.[89] Such physical presence 'bespoke honest endeavor',
the opposite of metropolitan foppishness. Thomas Binney, the bookseller's
son, ministering amid the silk and lavenders of a wealthy merchant congregation, according to contemporaries, had a countenance 'from whence
determination, resolution and passion have swept away all indications of
smoother amenities . . . the importance of possessing a frontish piece of
ugliness, of outrements with a view to obtaining command over audiences',
and Binney used indignation and scorn to rouse his congregation. His
'noble manliness' was manifested in 'daring independence', in being 'rough
and rugged', even moody.[90] The Taylor sisters' friend and co-author, Josiah
Conder, described Binney as being particularly 'masculine and impressive'
in the pulpit.[91]

The diametrically opposite feminine ideal was symbolized by the wood
anemone or rosebud, so often applied to the young queen. Mary Ann
Hedge, the Evangelical Colchester writer, summed up the contrasted image
in one of her stories where the young woman was 'delicately blooming,
with cheeks tinted with a blush, bright as the rosebud which adorned her
bosom', while her brother was 'dark and ruddy, of manly stature and
evidently of great muscular vigour with a penetrating fire in his eye'.[92] She
drove home her point in a handbook for girls which declared that anger,
allied to pride, was a 'frightful passion', violent anger in women being
almost as disagreeable as drunkenness.[93] Henry Crabb Robinson
commented unfavourably on the unladylike and 'hoydenish' conduct of a
girl acquaintance seen running in the streets of his native Bury St Edmunds.
Robinson was a friend of William Cowper and later the Wordsworths, but
he kept a circle of relatives and close friends in Essex and Suffolk. His

writing displays a fear and distaste of independent behaviour in women, expressed by disparaging their attractiveness. Ann Plumtree was a highly educated contemporary of Mary Wollstonecraft who moved in radical circles. Crabb Robinson was shocked when one of her books was recommended to some 'delicately brought up' young friends of his. He had looked it over but never finished it, it was so 'extremely obscene'. He delighted in telling the story of relaying the news of Ann Plumtree's death to Charles Lamb who replied: 'What an ugly ghost she'll make.'[94]

Maintaining firm boundaries between masculine and feminine appearance and behaviour both helped to uphold men's position of dominance and ensure that they would carry out their masculine functions. But these distinctions were also seen as paramount in the struggle against endemic disorder. Emma Cadbury, who had married Thomas Gibbins and lived next door to his Battery Company in Birmingham town centre, witnessed the Chartist demonstration of 1839. The crowd passed in front of their premises and as it was one of the largest houses in the neighbourhood, the Gibbins feared they might be attacked. As the family watched the procession behind closed Venetian blinds, Emma Gibbins was struck most by 'the very coarse hard-featured women'. The demonstration and a strike soon afterwards had a profound effect on her and the family later removed to Edgbaston.[95]

The wealthy farmer's wife with her illegitimate children, her silk gowns and occasional drink too many, the genteel town manufacturer's wife watching the grim Chartist women marching past her house, and even the radical female author's ghost all played their part in the theatre of class and gender.

10 'Improving times': men, women and the public sphere

The noblest men that dignify our age,
The brightest names that live on history's page. . . .

H. H. Horton on the men who made Birmingham 'Birmingham', 1851.

Middle-class men's claims for new forms of manliness found one of their most powerful expressions in formal associations. The informal, convivial culture of eighteenth-century merchants, traders and farmers was gradually superseded by an age of societies. Men organized themselves in myriad ways, promoting their economic interests, providing soup kitchens for the poor, cultivating the arts, reaching into populated urban areas and rural outposts. This network of association redefined civil society, creating new arenas of social power and constructing a formidable base for middle-class men. Their societies provided opportunities for the public demonstration of middle-class weight and responsibility; the newspaper reports of their events, the public rituals and ceremonials designed for their occasions, the new forms of public architecture linked to their causes. The experience of such associations increased the confidence of middle-class men and contributed to their claims for political power, as heads of households, representing their wives, children, servants and other dependants. This public world was consistently organized in gendered ways and had little space for women. Indeed, middle-class feminists in the second half of the nineteenth century focused many of their efforts on attempting to conquer the bastions of this public world, a world which had been created by their fathers and grandfathers.

James Bisset of Birmingham

In 1776 James Bisset, the 16-year-old son of a Scottish merchant who had failed in business, arrived in Birmingham where one of his brothers was living, hoping to make his fortune.[1] Bisset was soon apprenticed to a japanner for he liked painting. Being, by his own account, a very sociable fellow, he quickly established friendships and social connections. He had expected to find Birmingham a 'black and dismal town, smoky and unhealthy', but was delighted to discover that it had many fine streets, good brick buildings and one of the most handsome churches he had ever seen.[2] His interest in drawing meant he was soon giving lessons to fellow apprentices to whom he was willing to lend his books and favourite *Gentle-*

man's Magazine. To celebrate the end of his apprenticeship he gave a supper and dance for his friends, the food provided by the widow of his brother's partner and the wines by his ex-master. Having no capital, his prospects were uncertain, but he was lucky enough to invent 'Imperial', a new process whereby convex glasses could be painted on the inside, which brought him employment.

Bisset loved the theatre and was involved in the establishment of the first Birmingham Amateur Theatrical Club. He enjoyed dancing, playing games of bowls, quoits or fives, he was a good singer and poet and constantly in demand with his friends. Most of his evenings he spent in a tavern, though not a drinking man himself; he was a regular member of Freeth's Circle, the group who met in Freeth's Coffee House to enjoy company and talk, and often joined in a debating society or some activity associated with the Freemasons. In retrospect he insisted that he was never a party man but he was on the edges of the Radical circles of Birmingham in the 1780s and 1790s.[3]

To keep his wife company, for he had married in 1787, he attended St Paul's church and particularly enjoyed the musical voluntaries which were not allowed in the stricter Scottish Presbyterian church. An active member of the business community, he joined with a group of other men in his neighbourhood concerned about robberies to establish a protection system; this involved a group's dining together and then patrolling the area. Every Wednesday he attended a social club at Vauxhall, a 'recreative lounge' which had been established for the 'Respectable Families' of Birmingham with a bowling green, tavern, well laid out gardens and an orchestra. On the edge of the town lay Vauxhall,

> A rural spot, where tradesmen oft repair
> For relaxation, and to breathe fresh air.[4]

There Bisset would meet his male friends: manufacturers, doctors, lawyers and clergy. From about three in the afternoon to mid evening they would play bowls, indulge in a game of whist and drink, whether tea or something stronger.

Meanwhile, Bisset's wife, Dolly, was completely occupied at home, a home which was also a workshop:

> Domestic affairs seldom trouble my head,
> (My partner, for life, in all those takes the lead;)

wrote her husband in 1800.[5] 'All her cares and her attentions', he later recorded, 'were fixed and most fully employed in her little nursery, which happily came on delightfully, and yielded her extreme satisfaction'.[6] Bearing ten children, of whom only four survived, her health was not good, but she was busy at home especially after they acquired a larger house and opened a museum in it, the repository of the paintings, curios and birds which James, like so many of his contemporaries, collected and admired. Bisset found his wife's domestic disposition the perfect complement to his lively and sociable self. Having established the new house, however, Bisset decided to break with his old habits and stay within his own domestic circle. 'I was always of a most cheerful disposition', he later wrote of his convivial days,

I sung a lively song and generally sung those of my own composition. My company was eagerly sought after, and in most parties, I am sorry now to say it, I chiefly played the first fiddle. Many an evening have I stayed out late (aye, and *early* too), leaving one of the best wives in the world sitting up by herself, after putting the young ones to rest, whilst I was roaring myself almost hoarse at the tavern, amusing many that I cared very little about.[7]

He then abandoned the regular evenings at the pub and spent them instead at home.

In 1813 the family moved to Leamington, the spa town which provided an outlet for the successful of Birmingham, and there Bisset established a museum and picture gallery. He wrote a guide to Leamington and became one of its most established townsmen, eventually owning property. Dolly meanwhile ran the museum. Bisset still visited Birmingham, enjoying the new entertainments of the early nineteenth century, and in 1829 attended the series of 'conversazione' held by the Society of Fine Arts.

> These CONVERSAZIONE's held,
> (By tickets freely sent),
> To every *Party* did a scene
> Of *Novelty* present;
> A species of amusement rare,
> Did pleasures yield in store –
> That such, in no *provincial* town,
> Were ever known before.

The conversazione provided opportunities for 'rational social intercourse' and discussion, combined with viewing the pictures and sculptures which were on exhibition.

> Nothing can equal the joy of my heart
> To see the advancement of *Science* and *Art*

wrote Bisset, and he felt compelled to add,

> 'thinks I to myself' as around I was moving
> The TOY SHOP OF EUROPE is daily improving.[8]

The conversazione were held in new rooms built for the purpose in Temple Row, one of the town's most prestigious professional streets. There were 600 pictures on exhibition, shown off to advantage in the evening with gas lighting. Many of the paintings were by local artists, for one of the purposes of such societies was to foster local talent, so essential to the commercial and manufacturing prosperity of Birmingham's decorated ware. Others were old masters, lent by neighbouring gentry and local patrons. It was a select company who attended (indeed the following year the Countess of

Dartmouth was there) for cards of admission were required and tickets were only 'freely sent' to those who were associated with the society.[9]

Events such as this mark the distance which had been travelled between the 1790s and the 1820s. Bisset's social and cultural life had been pre-eminently organized around the pub and was mainly associated with a group of male friends. This easy, male, club-based conviviality, captured in the painting by Eckstein of Bisset and his friends with their pipes and their pots, so characteristic of late eighteenth-century culture, was gradually changing. Club and pub life was slowly giving way, in middle-class circles, to more formal methods of association. These societies, with their rules and constitutions, inaugurated a new era in public life which offered very different opportunities to middle-class men and women. How were relations between the sexes organized in the more formal public sphere as it developed in the late eighteenth and early nineteenth centuries, and in what ways did this connect with the gathering of the middle ranks into a more coherent class?

Voluntary associations

The public sphere, meaning the realm of life in which public opinion can be formed, was increasingly significant in eighteenth-century England. It was a part of civil society, independent of the state, yet able to influence that state through the organization and mediation of public opinion.[10] Private individuals meeting in clubs or coffee houses could join together into public bodies, or exert their influence through journals and newspapers, and make claims that were heard by government. Merchants, farmers and manufacturers increasingly wished to have a voice in this public life. Bisset's membership of the regular (male) circle at Freeth's Coffee House, his readership of the *Gentleman's Magazine*, that journal which together with *The Spectator* aimed to educate and improve the middling ranks, his place at town dinners, his role as town poet and songster all signal him as belonging to the public sphere, able to play his part in the formation of public opinion and its communication to those in power.

The demand for independence from aristocratic patronage and a client economy by the 'middling sort' was not to be conferred by the gentry; it had to be won. Collective action, through clubs, lodges and societies was one way of doing so; it provided economic support as well as political debate and discussion. As Brewer notes, many of the clubs were proud that they united Anglicans and Dissenters, men from different trades, merchants and gentlemen, Whigs and Tories, in a common association, promoting 'unanimity and harmony' instead of conflict.[11] 'Unanimity and harmony' enabled the middle classes to speak effectively.

But the clubs and informal groupings were gradually replaced by more formal organizations, relying less on networks of family, friendship and religious and business association. The public character of such societies made them open and visible to all and indeed *public* accountability was one of their principles.[12] Meetings announced in newspapers, formal constitutions with named patrons and committees, accounts which were published; these were the hall-marks of the new societies. Some were public

Plate 30 'Freeth and his circle', J. Eckstein, 1792. James Bisset, the japanner, is fourth from the right

also in their efforts to create a national network and such societies mushroomed from the late eighteenth century.

These voluntary associations or societies divide into four overlapping categories. First were the philanthropic societies, which usually had some religious inspiration though they frequently operated on an interdenominational basis. These were the Sunday schools, charity schools, infant schools and other enterprises which aimed to educate the poor. There were societies which hoped to alleviate poverty and illness, through the provision of food in times of acute distress to blankets for lying-in mothers, hospitals for the poor and support for the respectable aged. There were associations for dealing with specific problems: the deaf and dumb, the blind, conversion of the Jews, as well as a plethora of organizations aiming to bring religion to the labouring people.

The second category were those societies which aimed to provide for the cultural, scientific and educational needs of the middle classes themselves. These ranged from committees which set up assembly rooms, libraries, book clubs, reading rooms and 'private' concerts open to subscribers only, to botanical and horticultural societies, literary and philosophical societies (known as the Lit. and Phils.), societies of arts and schools for the sons of the middle class. The third category were those which related to business and property: farmers' clubs and agricultural societies, the Association of Ironmasters, Chambers of Manufacturers which became Chambers of Commerce, doctors' and lawyers' organizations and associations to protect property. The last category were the more overtly political, the anti-slavery societies, political unions and the Anti-Corn Law League.

These societies were all established and organized on roughly the same lines. First a group of men would meet together informally to express interest. They would then call a public meeting which would be announced in the press and at this meeting a committee would be set up, officers elected and subscribers invited. A financial arrangement would be instituted and regular meetings established. In the late eighteenth century these were usually at midday, but as business became more regularized they tended to take place in the afternoon or evening, thus not interrupting the working day. An annual general meeting was usually held, a ritualistic occasion when the committee presented its accounts to the public and reviewed its accomplishments, a procedure echoing both the casting up of accounts to God by the religious, and the principle of subscriber democracy so dear to the hearts of middle-class men.

Subscriber democracy, the 'characteristic institutional form of the societies', was a form which allowed for finely graded hierarchies.[13] The way in which the societies were established, the origins on which they were built and the forms of organization which emerged all contributed to the maintenance of existing divisions between men and women. But the associations of the rapidly growing public sphere not only reflected and confirmed the patterns of relations between the sexes on other sites, such as churches and chapels, they directly assisted in the construction and dissemination of particular practices in relation to men and women of the middle class.

Take the foundation of the Birmingham Infant School Society in 1825. In July 1825 there was a meeting of gentlemen at the town's Public Office, attended by clergy, lawyers, manufacturers, traders, bankers and medical men from different denominations. The location of the meeting, in the denominationally neutral Public Office, stressed the unified nature of the call.[14] Their aim was to provide education for the infants and small children who were currently roaming the streets because their parents were working, part of a wider movement aiming to tackle this problem.[15] The gentlemen established a provisional committee with a clergyman in the chair and invited subscribers. The provisional committee soon published a public address arguing the need for such a project, emphasizing Christian fears of the disease, idleness, moral depravity and criminal experience lying in wait for these 'multitudes of children'.

The school they hoped to establish would teach habits of 'cleanliness and decorum', provide 'activity and amusement', 'intellectual improvement and moral discipline'. As one of their early annual reports remarked,

At a period of public agitation like the present, it is especially needful to strengthen every link which connects the different classes of society, and there exists no link so binding as the interchange of benevolent feeling – as the kindness on the one hand, and the gratitude on the other, called forth by the communication and the reception of good.[16]

It was both Christian and expedient to improve the labouring poor, morally and physically.

Several committee meetings were held, followed by a public meeting at the Royal Hotel. There, Lord Calthorpe, the local Evangelical peer, was invited to be a patron of the new society. The prestigious presence of the aristocracy was of great symbolic value to the middle-class elite, even though the position of patron involved little real power. Calthorpe's name would appear, his financial support be requested, but it was the big battalions of the middle class who would run the society, with their subaltern supporters. The local bankers, Taylors and Lloyds, agreed to be treasurers, utilizing their professional skills to assist charitable ventures while simultaneously demonstrating their own status and probity. A permanent committee was established, made up of physicians, clergy, lawyers, bankers, manufacturers and retailers. There were Anglicans, Quakers, Congregationalists and Unitarians, Whigs, Tories and even those sympathetic to Radicalism. A subscription system was set up whereby the amount donated carried its own rewards. Subscribers had the right to exercise their patronage by recommending a child to the school. The more they gave the more patronage they could command, thus reproducing within the formal membership the wider distinctions in the ranks of the middle class, while at the same time uniting them around common aims.

At the Royal Hotel meeting it was decided that since the school would be mixed it would be essential to have lady visitors to deal with the day-to-day workings and supervision of the girls' section. The co-operation of the ladies of Birmingham was, therefore, 'respectfully and earnestly solicited'.[17] By now the gentlemen had been meeting for several months, had established the rules and regulations and devised the system of organization. Women had no professional skills to offer, they were not bankers or lawyers, nor were they appealed to publicly. Rather, the committee privately solicited their wives, daughters, relatives and friends to form a ladies' committee and to take on the work of visiting. Subsequently, as was usually the case with such arrangements, the men's committee held all formal power but the ladies dealt with many practical arrangements concerning the girls. Any formal matters had, however, to be referred to the men. Clearly much of the negotiation in such cases was done informally. A wife on the ladies' committee would mention to her husband on the gentlemen's committee some matter arising, and he would attend to it.

The relative positioning of men and women in middle-class associations can also be seen in Birmingham's Botanical and Horticultural Society. Established in 1829 with both the Earl of Dartmouth and Lord Calthorpe as patrons and with the elite of the Edgbaston bourgeoisie on its committee, the society was organized as a joint stock company with shareholders. Earlier societies were usually established as trusts, a form which was especially used to provide for female dependants. Not surprisingly the trustees appointed were always men, for it was assumed that they would take financial responsibility in voluntary associations, as in the rest of the economic world. Furthermore, the trustees were usually the most substantial men associated with the venture and the two Botanical and Horticultural Society trustees (still given that title despite the joint stock form) were blessed with the epithet of 'Esquire'.[18] The novel idea behind such joint stock companies was that money invested would bring dividends in the improved happiness and morality of the beneficiaries. There was no investment so truly profitable, argued a Birmingham manufacturer, as the 'Joint Stock Bank of Benevolence'. Here was compound interest 'without risk, trouble, jealousy or alarm'.[19] But the shift to the joint stock principle led to no increased responsibility for women. Women could certainly become shareholders, although an early listing of the Botanical and Horticultural Society names eight women among some 250 men.[20] These male shareholders exhibited their wealth and prestige by having their names printed in the local paper, a by-product of the public giving of money, whatever the cause. Even in the rare societies where there were female officers, the treasurer was usually a man. Some ladies' committees even stipulated in their rules that the gentlemen should audit their accounts, write their reports and approve their minutes.[21] This was no doubt to avoid the kind of problem which a West Bromwich manufacturer described in a letter to his sister in 1834:

The longest job on which Rebecca has employed me has been the writing from her dictation the Annual Report of the Provident and Dorcas Society. . . . Poor Mrs Hood the Treasurer could not make her cash accounts right, she tried at it all one evening but could not unravel the mystery, she went to bed late, but could not get a wink of sleep, the General Meeting was to be held next day so she got up at two o'clock in the morning and remained up puzzling at her accounts till eight when Mr Hood got up and took the matter in hand, after some time he found that Mrs Hood had entered 15 shillings as fifteen pounds.

This same manufacturer went on to describe a charitable meeting at which both men and women voted. A disagreement led to one woman protesting that she would follow the dictates of her own conscience in her own district at which she was firmly reprimanded by the chairman who assured her that 'amongst men the Minority always submit to the Majority'.[22]

The men's committee which gradually established the rules and regulations of the Botanical and Horticultural Society held shared assumptions as to women's dependent status. Shareholders were allowed to take in a certain number of ladies according to the number of shares held. This was a new privilege granted in 1833 when the admission of ladies by payment was considered. Shareholders were already allowed to take in one member of their family providing they were 'residing with him'. Now this was to be extended. In this way the thorny problem of allowing in ladies who were not spoken for was avoided since all admitted were guaranteed 'either personally or by written order'.[23] In 1836, faced with financial problems, there were discussions as to whether subscribers of 1 guinea annually, a relatively modest contribution, should be allowed the privilege of taking in one 'female member' of their family, an issue which took some time to sort out.[24]

Ideas as to the proper relations of the sexes also permeated discussions of working-class entry to the gardens. As the select committee on public walks had declared:

A man walking out with his family among his neighbours of different ranks, will naturally be desirous to be properly clothed, and that his Wife and Children should be so also; but this desire duly directed and controlled, is found by experience to be of the most powerful effect in promoting Civilization, and exciting Industry . . . what inducement can be more powerful to anyone, than the desire of improving the condition and comfort of his family?[25]

Some officers of the Botanical and Horticultural Society were anxious to utilize the gardens in this way, but others were concerned at the potential damage to the property. Initially workers were allowed in on Mondays and Tuesdays and the presence of two policemen was requested in case of trouble. After a year of the experiment it was reported at the AGM that 'upon the whole they have conducted themselves in the most satisfactory manner'.[26] But the society continued to be wracked by debate as to who should and should not be allowed access. Like many similar societies it had contradictory aims, seeking to provide exclusive facilities for the middle classes (sited as it was in the heart of Edgbaston), and at the same time to extend that 'Joint Bank of Benevolence' to others in the name of self-improvement.

Furthermore, it was difficult financially to run the gardens on a very exclusive basis since this meant relying on shares and subscribers rather than entry fees. (The committee were shocked to discover at one point that some members of the middle classes had been taking advantage of the 1 penny entrance for the working class, and were leaving their carriages at the corner.) In 1846 such debates came to a head and a large number of resignations followed the decision to liberalize entry procedures, a policy which proved financially successful. This tension between exclusivity and financial solvency was a perennial problem for such ventures. The dancing assemblies in the town's Royal Hotel in 1825, for example, were bedevilled by the difficulty of sustaining numbers at a sufficiently genteel level.[27]

Protection societies, already well established in the late eighteenth century, aimed to provide physical protection for members' property. Not surprisingly they, too, were predominantly male organized. James Bisset had taken turns walking the streets of Birmingham with his friends, on the look out for robbers and thieves, and Birmingham jewellers and metal manufacturers, concerned for their valuable stocks, co-operated in the defence of their properties.[28] Rural organizations aimed to control crimes against property by offering rewards for information and helping constables apprehend suspects. Even here, when patrolling was not necessarily a regular part of the activity, women were in a tiny minority. Of sixty-five Essex Protection Societies, only 6 per cent of the 737 members were women. Many of the positions held in the societies were inherited with land and the differential meaning of property holding is reflected in the non take-up of such offices when they fell to women.[29] In towns, the atmosphere was no more congenial to genteel femininity. The Colchester Association for the Protection of Property and Prosecution of Housebreakers and Thieves met at the town's Castle Inn in 1834. A distiller was in the chair and a banker acted as treasurer. The meeting was followed by a convivial evening with an 'excellent dinner' served by the landlady, at least twenty-five toasts and songs provided by various members.[30]

Similarly, when the issue was defence of the realm rather than private property it was men who were called upon. The raising of volunteer troops relied on local office holders such as clergymen and overseers and marked a coming together of local gentry and middle-class men. At a meeting in Witham in 1798, carpenters, builders, architects and land surveyors pledged to serve under an 'Esquire', to exercise at least three times per week and to be ready for call up in the face of invasion. Each man was to provide his own uniform and to bear all his own expenses, bar arms and ammunition.[31] The popular pastime of watching the exercising of the Volunteers must have provided a potent reminder of the divisions between men and women.

Many voluntary associations catered for the needs of particular occupational groups. The West Midlands all-male ironmasters met regularly in Birmingham, Birmingham lawyers founded their own Law Society, farmers organized farmers' clubs which excluded women and met in local public houses. Suffolk in 1804 had one prestigious Agricultural Society, by 1846 there were five, as well as ten farmers' clubs.[32] The pursuit of agricultural improvement was often linked with scientific knowledge and again this presented problems for women, excluded as they usually were from scientific education.[33] Many small specialist clubs dealt with the study of natural history, a branch of learning which was especially important to apothecaries and chemists, who used field studies of medicinal plants as part of their programme for training apprentices. No women were members of such clubs.[34]

Furthermore, men could use the skills they acquired through their occupations to offer particular services to voluntary associations, services which brought with them increasing status both in the voluntary and state sectors. Doctors might be appointed to distinguished honorary positions in charitable hospitals. Such appointments might bring the opportunity to meet potential clients, the chance to give evidence to a Public Health Inquiry, or receive an appointment as district coroner. A Birmingham lawyer was instrumental in a change in the law which exempted scientific societies from tax and was honoured for this.[35] Men's occupations thus gave them skills which were not confined to the pursuit of private profit; the clergyman who gave the opening address, the banker who acted as treasurer, the lawyer who acted as secretary all translated their expertise in other arenas into developing the societies.

Particular male occupations also encouraged certain kinds of activity in the public sphere; the Birmingham traders who were enthusiastic in establishing a new market hall, built to a Doric design, not only improved their commercial organization but demonstrated themselves to be public spirited individuals.[36] Similarly, those farmers, clergy and local shipowners who erected the corn and cattle market in the Suffolk town of Framlingham proved both their business acumen and their civic worth.[37] Public recognition for entrepreneurial activity reinforced men's professional identities, as when the salesmen and butchers of Witham gave a presentation dinner to a local fellmonger in recognition of his economic contribution. It was held at the White Hart in Chelmsford and provided 'a scene of conviviality and friendship tempered with the utmost order and decorum'.[38] An equivalent occasion for Witham's foremost milliner, Miss Robinson, for example, was almost unthinkable.

One of the most influential and wide-ranging of the masculine

associations was the Freemasons. The lodges had their origins in the medieval gilds and had always emphasized brotherhood in skill. From the beginning of the eighteenth century, gentlemen interested in architecture and
geometry as part of a 'gentle' education had begun to enter, leading a slow
shift away from the stress on craft. In the early days, widows had access
to the lodges if they maintained their husband's trade but this died out,
and the new value given to scientific education completed their exclusion.
By 1740 Freemasonry was an accepted feature of English life, one of the
eighteenth-century all-male convivial societies, in which dining, drinking,
toasts and ritual proceedings all played a part.[39] Often clergymen acted as
supervisors in the rigidly hierarchical structure headed by God, the 'Master
Architect'. Initially the meetings were usually in taverns, providing

a convenient opportunity for that compound of refreshment, smoking and
conversation, in circumstances of ease rather than elegance and undisturbed by
the society of women in which many men can take a rational pleasure.[40]

With their local and national organization the Freemasons provided a bridge
between town and country as well as between aristocracy and the middling
ranks. They celebrated many of the eighteenth-century Dissenting values
in a non-denominational context; charity, trust and honour intertwined
with rationality, science, tolerance and latitudinarianism. Yet for them,
science encompassed an interest in mystery and their symbolism and ritual
celebrated virtues of manliness. The level, the compass, the plumb-line and
the Pillars of the Temple were evocative of 'solidarity, rectitude, directness
and good craftsmanship', echoing Loudon's binary imagery, evoking an
essential masculinity.[41] The membership of Colchester's Angel Lodge, in
1835, included a sprinkling of gentlemen but the majority were farmers,
shopkeepers, merchants, professionals, innkeepers, clerks, some artisans, a
dancing master and an army officer. The influx of the latter during the war
led to the establishment of several new lodges in the region which, like those
examined for Birmingham, provided both business and social contacts.[42]

   In 1723 the newly created Grand Lodge issued the first written *Book of
Constitutions* which expressly stipulated that no women were to be
members. This shift from oral tradition to written rules, as was so often
the case, made explicit the latent and customary exclusion of women. At
the same time Masons were strongly in favour of the recognition of familial
responsibilities. Freemasonry helped to give location to young men who
could not yet marry and set up on their own and, 'as a single-sex organization with a strong moral code, it served as a protection against disastrous
liaison and premature marriage'.[43] Indeed, it provided a hearth for those
who did not have a home.

   But Masons were expected to marry and the initiation ceremony included
gifts and a party for the Masons' wives together with the promise of charity
for their widows and children. Belonging to a lodge gave a man protection
similar to that provided commercially by life insurance, but with the added
assurance of friendship and care, the brother Masons taking the place of
lost husband or father.[44] We have no record as to what James Bisset's wife,
Dolly, thought of her husband's extensive Masonic activities, but it was
said that women were pleased when their men-folk were part of such a

sober and serious organization, which discouraged rowdy drunkenness while praising responsibility to dependants. Women's involvement with Freemasonry followed the standard practice of observer and audience. In Colchester, several ladies

honoured the company with their presence at a public breakfast, and were permitted to see the regalia and form of the Lodge . . . and after the ladies had withdrawn, the brethren proceeded in open lodge, with the great lights, Bible, Book of Constitutions etc. carried by the proper brethren to St Peter's Church where . . . an excellent sermon was preached.[45]

Freemasons, both from Colchester and Ipswich, were present as a body at civic functions; the laying of foundation stones for the Essex and Colchester Hospital in 1819, St Botolph's Church in 1836 and the Town Hall in 1843.[46] Masonic funerals were occasions to emphasize the masculine virtues of loyalty to the community, probity in business and responsibility for dependants. Freemasonry provided an attractive arena for the expression of masculine independence. No man in personal service was allowed to become a member; that dependent status too closely resembled a woman's familial position.[47]

An Essex small farmer exemplifies the activities of many men of his class and period. A member of Colchester's Angel Lodge of Masons, busy with war efforts providing carts and gunpowder, a member of the vestry and a local cricketer he also belonged to a club which met at the riverside quay pub in Wivenhoe, the Rose and Crown.[48] Hostelries such as the Rose and Crown were central to the social activities of middle-class men in the late eighteenth century and the early decades of the nineteenth century. 'Almost every man had his tavern where he regularly spent a portion of each day', wrote one Birmingham antiquarian, and the pub was the exchange and newsroom, the place where men would gather with their pipes and drinks for that quintessentially masculine occasion, a convivial evening.[49] The son of a Birmingham miller, born in 1779, commented critically in later years on his father's attachment to the pub,

My father, who though an upright respectable man, and whose example was always the farthest from anything unworthy, was nevertheless too taken up with his worldly affairs, and too apt to leave his children wholly under the care of servants – it being at that time the fashion with even the best and most correct men to pass the greater part of their evenings at a tavern.[50]

Eliezer Edwards gives a vivid description of the kind of 'semi-familial' character of these taverns which were often used as postal addresses. There the landlord

soon drew around him a 'company' who looked upon his house as a second home and assembled there day after day and year after year, each man occupying, with solemn regularity, the same chair, and drinking from the same cup or tankard for perhaps half a life time.

At Birmingham's early nineteenth-century Red Lion there was an 'ordinary' which became very popular with the well-to-do, here described by one of its habitues:

I dined there for about 15 years. Mr and Mrs Birch sat at the top and bottom of

the table. . . . Mrs Birch was a virulent Tory and Mr Brich was a thorough-
going Radical. They never disputed nor had any controversy but would join in
any political discussions that were going on, thus balancing political matters
much to the amusement of the guests. Great order was preserved at table; I do
not recollect a word being said that could give pain or annoyance to the most
modest female. The table was well supplied with fish, roast and boiled beef or
mutton, pastry, cheese and salad, for 1s 3d each. There were generally from
twenty to thirty diners. . . .[51]

In this case they were definitely all male apart from the overseeing landlady,
helping to keep order and tone.

Particular pubs were noted for their politics or their music, while others
kept special rooms for clubs. Colchester had its Pitt Club, the Freeman's
Loyal True Blue Club, the ultra-Tory Brunswick Club, each associated
with a pub: the Red Lion for reformists, The George more exclusive, The
Three Cups being Tory headquarters.[52] The Union in Birmingham had one
room for The Order of the Bucks, a club devoted to good fellowship,
conversation and innocent mirth, and one for the Staffordshire ironmasters
who met regularly from the late eighteenth century to defend their common
interests and promote their trade.[53] In a time when there were few public
buildings, the pub, with its combination of social and business activities,
was an obvious setting for all manner of male associations but this choice
of location inevitably acted as another form of restriction on women's
involvement.[54]

Meanwhile, the Bucks, the Beefsteak Club, the Masons, the Whigs and
Tories, the protection societies and the book clubs gathered in their
favourite taverns, mixing business and benevolence with their beverages.
Dining and drinking together were integral to sales of goods, contracts of
service, electioneering and many other activities, and were an accepted part
of early nineteenth-century public affairs, for men. Women joined at the
margins; young boys learned their future role by watching. In 1806, a
Suffolk town corporation put on a typical Portreeves Feast. Schoolboys
went at 2 p.m. to the King's Head and had tea with about fifty ladies until
later in the evening when the men had risen from dinner and created much
noise and confusion on their entry being 'mostly intoxicated'. Women and
boys left about 10.30 p.m., the gentlemen stayed on until next morning.[55]

The new scientific, philosophical and philanthropic societies often started
by meeting in pubs but moved to building their own premises where
possible. Some book clubs closed because of too much wine drinking, and
the more formal literary and philosophical institutions with their purpose-
built lecture rooms and newsrooms began to replace the easy informality
of the pub. In rural areas, where there were neither the resources nor the
personnel for such enterprises as a Lit. and Phil., the informal settings in
pub and home remained and seem to have occasionally been used by women
and children.[56]

The architecture of the new public buildings associated with voluntary
activity maintained the sexual divisions already fixed in pub culture. Lady
subscribers to the Birmingham Philosophical Institution, for example, were
allowed into the lecture room, museum and library but not to that male
sanctum, the newsroom.[57] There men could smoke and talk freely, discuss

the price of corn, the partnerships dissolved, the bankruptcies declared, property for sale, all items prominently displayed in the local press and assumed to be masculine perogatives. As Jane Taylor commented in *Display*, how disagreeable the sight of a newspaper was to a young girl who was regularly required to read about such subjects to her father.[58]

Assumptions as to the proper separation between the sexes also underpinned the design and use of philanthropic buildings. The Evangelically inspired Essex and Colchester Hospital, for example, built in 1821, had separate wards for men and women. Even prayers were read separately, Matron officiating for the women morning and evening, the male apothecary, who also acted as secretary, for the men. By 1827 the men had to be transferred to an upper floor and the women kept on a lower in an effort to control patients' improper behaviour.[59] New schools and Sunday schools as they were built made separate provision for boys and girls, the Witham New Union Workhouse in 1835 adapted the previous building to ensure separation of the sexes.[60] Even the Birmingham Prison, as early as 1800, was approvingly described as having

The cells of the male and female inmates [are] entirely unconnected and the yard provided for exercise by day, is also, for the same purpose of separation, divided into two parts by a high wall.[61]

Here ideologies about separate spheres combined with philanthropic imperatives to produce distinct physical locations for men and women.

Philanthropic societies

Some divisions between men and women were enshrined in bricks and mortar, some in custom and practice and others in association rules and regulations, but none were so set as not to be open to contestation and negotiation. Strict divisions between men and women were least sustained in philanthropic societies for there women were needed to deal with female cases. Indeed, they could claim on the highest Evangelical authority that 'charity is the calling of a lady; the care of the poor is her profession'.[62] Hannah More's language is revealing here for she combines the older religious idiom of 'the calling' with the new idea of 'the profession', something which requires training and expertise and which More sees as being a vital part of the moral and practical education of girls. No serious Christian would have disputed the need for women's charitable endeavours, but there were, as has been seen, serious disagreements both among the Evangelicals themselves and other religious groupings as to the proper nature and extent of women's philanthropic work. William Wilberforce was adamantly opposed to Ladies' Anti-Slavery Associations and grounded his objections on St Paul.

All private exertions for such an object become their character, but for ladies to meet, to go from house to house stirring up petitions – these appear to me proceedings unsuited to the female character as delineated in Scripture.

His main fear was that women would become caught up in the 'warfare of political life'.[63] The Quaker, Elizabeth Fry, was strong in her insistence that the most powerful justification for ladies to enter even such dangerous places as prisons was that only they could effect the necessary work of moral reform with women. Her acceptance of the different spheres of men and women allowed her the claim that females had their own vocation with their own sex.[64]

For many of the serious middle class 'Sunday and Weekly Schools, Bible Associations and other Benevolent undertakings' were the proper occupations of both men and women, young and old.[65] Spiritual equality between the sexes had wrenched open a space for women in the extended activities of church and chapel but the extent of that space was constantly subject to discussion. 'Women must be careful', argued Colchester's Mary Ann Hedge,

even how they follow a virtuous impulse; they must calculate the consequences that may arise even from benevolence itself, and study to combine goodness of heart, with propriety of manners, and the duties imposed upon them by society.[66]

Moralists from More to John Angell James and Mrs Ellis would have had no difficulty in agreeing with this. The problem was, how to combine womanly duties and modesty with woman's spiritual mission. For some, the solution was to confine feminine benevolence to the informal and the private. Reaching out from one's own home to that of another in distress was entirely acceptable.[67] But many were prepared to justify some involvement in the wider world, provided it was undertaken with modesty and care. John Angell James drew the line at door-to-door collections. 'Nothing can be more repugnant to my sense of propriety', he thundered,

than for young women to be sent out with what are called 'collecting cards', to wander over a town knocking on the doors of anybody and everybody for the purpose of begging money, and sometimes entering into counting-houses and assailing even young men with their importunities.[68]

'Collecting cards' seem to be representing here sexual immodesty and a break-down of propriety. Perhaps the scurrilous *Birmingham Monthly Argus and Public Censor* may have had James in mind when they made fun of the pious ladies who, sent out by the 'man they all love' disguised their husband hunting with collecting cards.

We hope the 'dear man' did not set up the 'Collecting Carriage', and appoint an engaging 'Collecting Committee' for the purpose of entrapping the *unwarned young men*. We are aware that he is a very methodical kind of gentleman and perhaps this new plan may be a 'little bit' of private policy of his own to obtain husbands for the dear creatures who look so charmingly pious when he is preaching about the vanity of the wicked world etc.[69]

Malicious attacks such as this remind us that the serious Christian world had no monopoly on public discourse and that many were not won to this particular version of the improving endeavour. On a kinder note in 1842 the middle-aged Witham doctor, Henry Dixon, grumbled at the intemperate activities of young women with their philantrhopic imperatives. 'These are bagging affairs', he complained in his diary, and 'are put into the hands of young ladies who run about with little bags and books. (Walking is quite out of the fashion) and at present are very successful in their vocation'.[70]

Such complaints reflect a view of women which refused to take seriously any preoccupation other than the familial.

In this context, the life of a woman such as Colchester's Amy Camps, who gained her sense of herself in large part from her evangelizing mission, must be read as a triumph in the face of adversity.[71] Compare her struggles even to be allowed as a hospital visitor with the possibilities for a man like her contemporary, the Quaker James Ransome, who started in business as agent for the family firm in the Suffolk countryside. During his six years there he was involved in an allotment society, helped to form a farmer's club and was active in the East Suffolk Agricultural Association until his Dissenting politics made it advisable to keep a low profile. In 1839 he returned to Ipswich and became the honorary secretary of the Ipswich Mechanics Mental Improvement Society. The preliminary meetings of the Young Men's Association were held at his home; Freemasonry, Ipswich politics, Ragged Schools, Mutual Benefit Societies, a Working Men's College, village clubs and reading rooms all jostled for his attention.[72] Such a range of activities was impossible for a woman since they were barred from farmer's clubs, all but social affairs of the agricultural associations, many mechanics institutes, Freemasonry, borough politics and some reading rooms. Small wonder that philanthropy came to occupy the status of profession for some women.

By the 1840s with changes in economic organization and the tightening of ideological boundaries, it no longer took the campaigning vigour of an Amy Camps to see philanthropy as a way of life. The upper middle-class daughters of a well-to-do gentleman farmer, whose brothers were being trained for the professions, knew that they had to acquire resources and accomplishments to make themselves useful, although they could not contemplate gainful employment. If they remained single, their father assured them, they would find a place for themselves for,

What would become of schools, clothing clubs and charitable institutions of every kind, if they had to depend on chance moments spared by busy mothers?[73]

The alternative to a useful life as a single woman, as indicated by the attack on charitable work as a cover for flirtation, was the search for a husband requiring quasi 'political' strategies, coalitions and competition. 'Making a hit', as leading a man to propose was called in some circles, was the major organizational satisfaction to be derived from this female culture.[74]

Given this lack of alternatives, kindly fathers, particularly in the upper middle class, would often be prepared to support their daughters' philanthropic efforts substantially. The daughters of a Birmingham banker set up a Sunday school at the back of their house. When the family moved to Leamington on the father's retirement from active business, the Sunday school became a day school, partly in the interests of the daughter, Adele, who was a semi-invalid:

my father allowed us to have a little school for poor children, chiefly for Adele's pleasure, as she could enter into so few amusements. He built a room for it next door to our stables and we took forty little girls. . . . We taught reading, writing and arithmetic, sewing, mending, marking and cutting out. We also taught them to plait straw and make their own bonnets. When old enough to go into service,

my Mother allowed us to have the girls in the house for a fortnight, to learn
under our maids, who took great pride in their pupils and turned them out tidy
little servants.[75]

The scale of women's philanthropic enterprise is impossible to quantify
since official representation clearly does not reflect their informal activities.
An examination of the extant subscription lists and reports of the Birmingham societies between 1780–1850 suggests that at most women constituted 10 per cent of the subscribers and only a fraction of the committee
members and officers.[76] But men frequently subscribed to societies as the
head of a family, their contributions 'covering' their wives and children just
as the wife was defined legally as 'covered' by her husband. The charity of
the wife must have been hidden in the public benevolence of her husband.
John Angell James strongly opposed this practice, believing that women
should be able to decide on their own charitable gifts without having to
'beg first' of their husbands.[77] Clearly some Birmingham men agreed with
him. The daughter of a retailer marrying a manufacturer in 1837 received
a present from her father of 100 golden sovereigns in a silver chain purse.
Her new husband stipulated that any money which came to her from her
parents should be at her disposal for personal or charitable use.[78] But the
wife of a Birmingham merchant banker had no such independent fund and
was grateful that her husband allowed her to contribute annually to a young
girl's education.[79]

Inevitably, much of the philanthropic work done by women had no
public face. Female activities in support of such a delicate area as Magdalen
Asylums emerge only through letters and diaries, and the clergy dominate
the official records of such institutions.[80] Beyond these hidden contributions
there was a vast amount of private benevolence and informal charity. Such
ventures were particularly important in the countryside for although even
small towns often had a range of philanthropic societies, villages were
unlikely to aim so high. Furthermore, in closed villages especially, the
control of the gentry remained extensive and there were fewer opportunities
for middle-class association. In these circumstances, forms of philanthropy
long associated with gentry paternalism were more prevalent. Rent
collecting by women property owners could merge into moral visiting.[81]

The mustard manufacturing enterprise of the Colmans, in rural Norfolk,
gave each workman at Christmas a piece of pork. The weight depended on
the size of the family (all part of the mistress's useful knowledge) and the
pork was given out from the scullery door of the millhouse where the
Colmans lived. A traditional Christmas dinner was laid on for the men and
their families, organized by Jeremiah Colman and his wife, with Jeremiah
taking the men into one room in the millhouse, his wife conducting the
women to another. Mrs Colman regularly visited the village school and on
Valentines Day gave each child a penny and a bun while they sang hymns
for her. In addition Mrs Colman ran a clothing club, buying fabric and
selling it at cost price. In this she was helped by an unmarried female cousin
of her husband's who was with her at the sales, 'presenting each member
with tickets to show their credit and checking their purchases'. In time a
school room was built for the talks and the club which previously had

taken place in the outbuildings of the millhouse.[82] Similarly, the wife of an Essex rural ironmaster,

would comfort the families of sick women with gifts of soup, fruit and jelly and often warm clothing.[83]

Personal dependence was here closely linked to the family of the employer, while in towns formal associations struggled to reconstruct relations between classes, built on dependence and gratitude, but no longer tied to the workplace. Many urban employers, particularly serious Christians, continued with paternalistic practices similar to those of the countryside, but the new organizations were a recognition of the inadequacy of such individual enterprise in the fast moving urban world.[84]

Gender differences were explicit in the segregated benevolence of Jeremiah Colman and his wife. Such practices accorded with custom and propriety. But in the new world of the formal association, the commitment to public democratic forms and proper constitutions meant that rules, regulations and voting procedures were spelt out, the gentlemen granted privileges not offered to the ladies. Gentlemen committee members, ladies voting by proxy – these were the hallmarks of the early philanthropic societies.

Yet as respectable public buildings gradually replaced public houses as the venues for meetings, and as hotels became more demarcated according to class, so such formal occasions as annual general meetings gradually became more accessible to women. At the national level women could not attend the AGM of the Church Missionary Society until 1813 and they had to wait until 1831 to be admitted to the Bible Society's annual gathering, a striking example of the way men could from the start build on their local contacts in a way that was much more difficult for women.[85] The Birmingham Association of the British and Foreign Bible Society for their anniversary in 1821 announced that 'seats will be reserved for the ladies as usual', but a dinner was held afterwards for the gentlemen at the Stork Hotel.[86]

Anti-slavery was recognized almost from the beginning as a peculiarly feminine concern, dealing as it did with such questions as dependence, children, marriage and family life. The organizers of a public meeting on slavery which was to be held at Birmingham's principal hotel in 1833 announced beforehand that 'proper arrangements' would be made for the ladies. However, the argument that developed between radical critics and anti-slavery supporters became so fierce that 'many of the ladies hastily retired in considerable alarm', and eventually 'to such a height did the interruption rise, that the few ladies who still remained precipitately left the room'.[87] Ladies' anti-slavery groups were some of the first to meet and organize separately from men: Birmingham's Female Society for the Relief of British Negro Slaves, established in 1828, met in private homes, an indication of their difference from the parent organization.[88] Female anti-slave societies appealed to women as consumers not to buy slave-grown sugar, a campaign backed up as in Birmingham with house-to-house visiting.[89] No national organization sprang from such groups as with the equivalent male societies and a hallmark of much of women's philanthropic work was that it remained at the local and small-scale level.

Dealing with the problems of other women and children was the likely aim of most women's groups, such as the Female Benevolent Society, established in Birmingham in 1802 to relieve 'indigent married women when ill or confined'. Lady visitors examined the applications while a Mrs Dickinson of Summer Hill was ready to receive subscriptions.[90] These were modest ventures in which men had little or no part; often not presuming to publish reports or make appeals through the newspapers. Lying-in charities and blanket clubs were a favourite focus for women, since modesty precluded male involvement. Colchester's Lying-In Charity was administered by the wives of the town's leading political figures. In the 1830s and 1840s it was dealing with approximately 250 cases a year, a considerable contribution in a market town. This charity, one supporter claimed, 'like a ministering angel, steps in and supplies what is more valuable than gold'.[91] These 'ministering angels' provided not only financial support but also attention, care and no doubt some nursing skills.

The more prestigious, public and formal associations were started and run by men, though in cases of female clientage they would often welcome the ladies' support. Birmingham General Hospital, for example, one of the town's longest established charities with aristocratic patronage, admitted no lady visitors and no female committee members were appointed until after 1900.[92] Ladies' fundraising activities were welcomed, however. The wives of the governors and committee of the Essex and Colchester Hospital were particularly energetic and in 1827, a 'magnificent bazaar and dejeurner' was held in the garden of a prominent Colchester banker, mainly organized by his wife and raising £700 for the hospital. Such bazaars took many months of organization together with the preparation of the articles of 'lady manufacture' so essential to such occasions.[93] Ipswich enjoyed a bazaar in its Assembly Rooms in 1823 and an 'elegant collection of WORKS of GENIUS, TASTE AND INDUSTRY' was sold for the benefit of a variety of public and private charities. The ladies' committee organizing the event had, on the previous day, collected up the items for sale, adding inventories and prices.[94] In such ways women made their considerable financial contribution to philanthropy.[95]

Institutions such as the Birmingham General and the Essex and Colchester Hospital reflected the capacity of prominent citizens to deal with sickness and ill-health and were thus vital to their prestige. The opening of the Essex Hospital was an impressive ceremonial occasion with a parade from St Peter's through the town led by the Evangelical Marsh, together with fellow Anglican and nonconformist clerics, backed up by other local worthies, the Freemasons and the Volunteers' Band.[96] The smaller efforts of earlier and more remote hospitals, as in Bury St Edmunds, could elect two widows to their committee, reflecting variation in practice particularly where able and willing men might have been less available.[97]

But the male and female philanthropic worlds remained substantively different and when women moved in it was usually because men were moving out into new concerns. This is illustrated by the Kenrick family of West Bromwich. Archibald Kenrick had spent the 1790s building up the family business but he was also active in promoting Sunday schools and organized a provident association among his own workmen.[98] In 1790 he had married Rebecca Smith and she was kept busy with her six children, born between 1798 and 1807, and keeping in touch with her many relations and friends. When the weather was good the family regularly attended Birmingham's New Meeting, but Rebecca died two years after her last child was born and never had time for activities beyond the family.[99]

Her daughter, also Rebecca, born in 1799, provides a sharp contrast. She never married and her life was spent travelling between family and friends, giving help where it was needed, whether to her step-mother, or as she got older, her sister Marianne who was subject to nervous illnesses, or her brothers' growing families. She had a small income provided for her by her father and brothers from the family business and her main interest became philanthropy. She took an active part in temperance work, becoming a total abstainer in 1840, as well as visiting the poor, organizing Sunday school tea parties and distributing tracts. As she confided to her diary in 1841, her philanthropic work gave her 'outdoor' satisfactions,

I enjoyed my home after my summer's wandering particularly. . . . Out of door occupations were gardening and visiting the poor.

In 1842 she recorded

At Easter the girls school was established at Bromwich and shortly before Xmas the boys school – Two fresh objects of interest for which I have to be grateful.

Spending time with her various relations meant that she could pass from one set of summer treats to another,

The fine summer gave an opportunity for many rural entertainments – we had the factory school to tea at Springfields – Boys Sunday School and Graham St Schools to tea at Handsworth, and several Gypsy parties.[100]

Rebecca Kenrick's activities were noticeably different from those of her brothers Archibald, Timothy and George. She worked behind the scenes, visited and provided tea. Her brothers took on the public positions of leadership and provided the financial backing. 'Archibald promised to act on the committee and be treasurer', recorded Rebecca, when planning with her neighbours, the daughters of a glass manufacturer, how to develop their temperance work, and she added, 'which is very important aid to us indeed without him we could make no way'.[101] George had earlier established a *Temperance Gazette* in the town, an activity which it would have been impossible for a middle-class woman to sponsor, and the work of the Temperance Mission established by the Kenricks and their allies was an extension of this enterprise. Archibald was both president and treasurer of the mission and instrumental in setting up a library, reading room, conversation and class room. He guaranteed the rent and donated George's library to the mission after his untimely death. His business and philanthropic efforts made him one of the most respected leaders in the area.[102]

Rebecca's nieces enjoyed a different kind of life from their grandmother or aunt. Their fathers, Archibald and Timothy, benefiting from increased prosperity, moved from living near the works in West Bromwich to Edgbaston.[103] Rebecca's niece Caroline, whose sister Harriet was Joseph

Chamberlain's first wife, kept a journal between 1854–9. She was fully integrated into the upper middle-class social world of the neighbourhood with visiting, parties, concerts, dinners and balls. She helped to organize a library but kept no record of visiting the poor, reminding us that a life centred around philanthropic work was a minority choice among middle-class women.[104]

For those women who did get involved, on whatever scale, the effects were varied. Philanthropic societies offered women opportunities, both to work with men and on their own. They might learn to administer, to organize, to deal with money beyond household expenses, to speak at least in small meetings, to move around the town distributing tracts and visiting the poor, to write, to find new friends. Their efforts always rested on their special claim to moral authority and influence. Not surprisingly, philanthropic work also provided one of the few public sites for the direct expression of sexual antagonism between middle-class men and women.

Some women deduced from this, as did the Chelmsford Quaker, Anne Knight, that feminism offered women's rights the best hopes, others heeded the words of More and Ellis and maintained their faith in separate spheres.[105] The latter response was by far the most common. The Independent publisher's wife (co-author with Jane and Ann Taylor), Eliza Conder, described the 'vulgar clamour' at the International Anti-Slavery Convention in London in 1840, when there was an attempt to introduce female delegates as part of the representation from the United States:

And all this in the presence of the 'ladies' themselves, several of whom were most untidily arrayed in creased and limp dresses, tumbled and soiled collars, coffee-coloured cambric handkerchiefs, hair anything but neat, and nails which served as hieroglyphics for 'unwashen hands'. I believe too, the object of the 'fair visitors' is, in part, to waken the ladies of England to a sense of their 'rights', and the maintenance of the same. If we are thus to start out of our spheres, who is to take our place? Who, as 'keepers at home' are to 'guide the house', and train up children? Are the gentlemen kindly to officiate for us?[106]

But while Mrs Conder, from her view in the ladies' gallery, may have believed that the boundaries of male and female spheres were clearly defined, she and thousands of women like her were engaged in stretching and shifting those boundaries by dint of their philanthropic work, while providing thousands of hours of unpaid social work. Women may not have been exerting real social power and engineering major social change through their associations, but nor were they simply taking as given the boundaries of female social action.[107]

Leisure and pleasure

Formal associations changed the nature of leisure and pleasure for the middling ranks, as well as their more serious endeavours. Public balls, assemblies and 'routs' were favourite entertainments of the eighteenth-century gentry, merchants and professionals, often timed to coincide with the agricultural, judicial or political calendars and held in purpose-built Assembly Rooms, and organized by committees of gentlemen. By the early nineteenth century, the serious banned all dancing and the more worldly were becoming suspicious of public balls. In the 1820s Amelia Moilliet allowed her daughters to go to one Birmingham ball but decided not to do so again.[108] As the formal dances like the minuet were replaced by the romantic waltz necessitating couples holding each other on the dance floor, it became increasingly necessary for careful mothers to know exactly who their daughters' partners would be. A 17-year-old vicar's daughter thought the new dances, the waltz, cocquette and bourgette, which she saw on a visit to her aunt and uncle 'highly objectionable' in public but acceptable in private.[109] Dancing, as with so many aspects of life in this period for the provincial middle ranks, was a mixture of formal and informal. Drinking tea together, playing cards, backgammon, chess, shuttlecock, quoits, bowling, cricket, walking and dropping in on family and friends, impromptu dances and music making vied with more formal functions depending on rank, wealth, location and inclination.

Private entertainments became increasingly important as the respectability and propriety of some public leisure pursuits were questioned. A Birmingham manufacturer reminisced in the 1880s about his grandfather's love of the theatre at the turn of the century. He had attended most nights and was a close friend of the theatre manager. By far the greater number of well-to-do people lived in or close to the town centre and, he recalled, 'there being very few chances of getting entertainment, and the theatre being open only for a season, and that not a very long one, it was generally pretty well attended'.[110] In those days, theatre going raised few moral doubts and some of Birmingham's leading citizens planned a new, grander building in 1774, more suited to the growing social and economic importance of the town and with the potential to 'improve the morals, the manners or taste of the people'.[111] To prove their point, a portico was constructed and a coffee room added. Theatre performances were usually sponsored by an individual or group whose name would be prominently displayed on programmes and posters, yet another means of proclaiming status. Freemasons, local schools, army units, professional and social clubs as well as individuals were found as sponsors in the local areas, giving such groups control of what was performed and patronage of local managements and individual actors. Benefit performances were also favoured for local charities. Here women could play a role as individual sponsors and organizers.

Evangelical fears about worldly attractions were aroused particularly by imaginative and emotional forms of entertainment, the novel and the theatre. Hannah More had been an enthusiastic theatre-goer, and playwright, counting the great actor, David Garrick, as one of her closest friends, until her conversion led her to question the whole institution of the theatre. William Marsh ran a losing campaign in the Colchester press against the theatre company from Norwich which had proposed a theatre building for Queen Street in 1812, partly to provide entertainment for army personnel.[112] John Angell James also made a public stand against theatregoing, sparking off a lively public debate in 1824 when he preached a sermon attacking the theatre as an agent of young men's destruction, answered by the manager of the Theatre Royal supported by Joseph Parkes, the Utilitarian lawyer.[113] These onslaughts against the bright lights, false gaieties and inflamed passions of the theatre world, heralded a period when few

of the respectable provincial community would attend. In particular, the
connections with drink and prostitution were too close. Women as spectators, but particularly as sponsors, playwrights, managers and actresses
tended to lose an arena of action under this decline.

Birmingham's Theatre Royal had its worst decades between about 1808
and the late 1830s, when a combination of middle-class disapproval and
working-class poverty meant poor audiences. An attempt by the manager
in 1813 to create a fashionable evening when all those going would be
'surrounded by those they might be pleased to meet' was doomed to
failure.[114] Even amateur and home dramatics suffered as Jane Austen
reminds us in *Mansfield Park* where the intended production of a morally
dubious play 'Lover's Vows' in the absence of the patriarch Sir Thomas
stands for all that is rotten in the moral economy of the Bertram
household.[115]

The town of Romford in Essex was not unusual in its attempt to maintain
a small private theatre, the moving force being a local apothecary. It was
sponsored by the Romford Philanthropic Society, but as a contemporary
noted, even amateur actors could acquire a loose reputation, particularly
amateur women. Indeed, the ladies of Romford seem to have been 'loathe
to risk their reputations, even for charity' and the manager was constrained
to resort to hiring professional actresses.[116] It was not until the 1840s that
the fortunes of the Royal in Birmingham looked up, with segregated seating
arrangements allowing the middle classes to separate themselves from the
masses in the pit. Friday night was particularly fashionable since most
artisans had not been paid, and it was possible to hope for a more select
audience.[117] A respectable and successful Birmingham manufacturer, well
known for his patronage of the arts and his care for his workforce, could
go back to the patterns of a previous generation and spend all his evenings
in the theatre without any slur on his good name.[118]

With public concerts, much depended on the type available and it was
easier to develop exclusive occasions in large towns than small. The early
nineteenth century saw the emergence of a new high status musical public,
relying on a combination of pricing and reserved seating to ensure a properly
lofty tone.[119] Such eminences were achieved from modest origins. The
Birmingham Triennial Music Festival, a major occasion for the West
Midlands, had its beginnings in a mid eighteenth-century apparently male
'Musical and Amicable Society' which met in a pub, The Cherry Orchard,
and combined its singing activities with acting as a friendly society. Its
printed code of rules included this paean to the powers of music to combat
potential conflict when combined with ale.

> To our Musical Club here's Long Life and Prosperity
> May it flourish with us, and so on to posterity
> May Concord and Harmony always abound
> And Divisions here only in Music be found.
> May the Catch and the Glass go about and about
> And another succeed to the Bottle that's out.[120]

A clerk to an ironfounder, a leading member of this society, proposed that a choral society should be established from the club. This choral society did some charity performances and it was decided to try and raise money for the town's general hospital, the building of which had been started but was slow due to lack of funds.[121] The first festival was held in 1768, with bankers and physicians well represented on the organizing committee, and after being held irregularly for the first twenty years settled down to a three yearly cycle from the mid 1790s.

From the beginning the festivals aimed high, with aristocratic patronage, an organizing committee including the elite of the town, and plentiful clerical support with the churches often being used for performances of sacred music. The occasion offered 'a solemn public ritual'

at which the people of Birmingham could affirm their own high calling in the lofty themes of sacred oratoria.[122]

The Messiah was established at the first festival as the central work and retained its pride of place, expressing some of the dynamism and climactic optimism of the town's middle class while holding as its central message the knowledge that 'my Redeemer Liveth'. An apotheosis was reached when Mendelsohn conducted the first performance of *Elijah* in the Town Hall in 1846. The festival became *the* event of the Birmingham season on those years it was held. Preparations took months with the programme to be organized, the performers engaged, the venues sorted out and publicity arranged. Meanwhile, there was extra business for the milliners and tailors, with those attending wanting new clothes. Grocers and butchers could rely on special orders as friends flocked in to stay and hotels and private lodgings filled up. Extra hairdressers would come in for the week itself, extra servants be taken on and coach masters could guarantee good business. 'The oratorios' argued *Aris's Gazette* hopefully in 1790, 'will probably be superior to any yet performed out of London'.[123]

The assemblage . . . is of the very first degree for throng and for fashionable display

wrote a commentator admiringly as he described the crowded lines of carriages waiting outside St Phillip's for their genteel occupants and a Birmingham banker's daughter sneered at the manufacturer who paid £100 so that he could sit with the nobility at a performance of *The Messiah*.[124]

In the early days much of the festival was held at the Theatre Royal and it was the festival committee which decided to rebuild it after a fire in 1820, thus ensuring its free use for their events. 'So high a treat has never before been offered to the public of Birmingham' said *The Gazette* when the new theatre opened just in time for the festival of 1820.[125] Such hyperbole was more than matched by the boundless admiration for the new classical Town Hall, modelled on the Temple of Castor and Pollux in the Roman Forum, and completed in 1825, which became the site for the major festival events. Indeed, the town hall organ, said to be the most powerful in Europe and in some points surpassing every other organ in existence, was initially financed by the General Hospital particularly for the festival and cost £3000.[126] During the festival week countless other entertainments were laid on – public and private balls, dinners and outings, art exhibitions and

Plate 31 A grand banquet at the Birmingham Town Hall, 1845

lectures. It was the week when Birmingham showed that it aimed beyond brass, claiming the cultural leadership of the West Midlands.

But the festivals were not only an expression of civic pride, an assertion of the town's right to act as a 'cultivator and successful promoter of the musical art in its highest developments'.[127] It was also a moment for Birmingham men to express their pride. From the humble beginnings in the Cherry Orchard they had created a week of refinement and renown. Men were the organizers and initiators of these events, women were present as performers and consumers. Those ladies who attended in their new finery, publicly displayed their husband's capacity not only to pay their hairdressers, milliners, haberdashers and maids, but also to provide a week's entertainment to kin and out of town friends, squashing them in even to the point of sleeping in the attic.[128] Only the strictest would argue against attendance. 'Concord and Harmony' did reign between Anglicans and Dissenters, Tories and Radicals, aristocracy, gentry and the middling ranks. Men could feel confident in taking their wives and daughters to events which had become family occasions, for a new phenomenon in the musical world was not only reserved seating which ensured segregated audiences but 'family tickets'.[129] Musical publishers also now catered for familial tastes, offering sacred music for sale adapted to their use.[130]

The festival was the apogee of Birmingham's musical life, but many of the ongoing events reiterated these civic and familial themes. Men-only occasions did not disappear as in the Harmonic meetings held at the Town Hall Tavern in the 1840s, a meeting 'of conviviality, fine ales and splendid cigars' with a professional gentleman at the piano.[131] But such functions were outmatched by the concert seasons in the Town Hall, the Assembly Rooms and other such venues, where every attention was paid to the comfort of the ladies. Private concert seasons were also still being held, with attendance confined to subscribers who had to ballot for membership and the great and the good of the Birmingham elite acting as stewards and organizers. On arrival at these occasions 'persons' were appointed 'to open and shut the doors of carriages, and announce them to the company as they draw up'.[132] Being seen, and being seen to be seen, was of the essence of the event.

Those 'fit and proper persons' who acted as stewards for the private concerts, men who were well-known doctors and lawyers, merchants, bankers and clergymen, were performing one of the important tasks for such middle-class associations. Concerts and balls had their stewards as did card and dancing assemblies. Election meetings and 'chairings', race meetings and many other public events also appointed these men whose brief was to organize, to decide who was to be admitted to both the inner and outer circles, to act as masters of ceremony and even as bouncers. On 2 January 1835, there was a ball in Chelmsford, part of the holiday season festivities to raise money for the charity school. 'The stewards will be the principal gentlemen in the town and neighbourhood' announced the *Essex County Standard* and their later report on the ball, after dwelling on the decorations and the 200 who had attended in their finery, added that the affair 'did great credit to the gentlemen entrusted with its management'.[133] Often in such a report the stewards were named, thus publicly demonstrating their right to inclusion within the elite, whether at its highest levels, Birmingham's Music Festivals, or the somewhat more lowly level of The Harmonic Society. Indeed stewarding could be one of the ways in which young men learnt their public roles. In 1815 a crowd of 8000 attended the end of the war celebrations in the Suffolk coastal town of Yarmouth. Genteel women and girls watched from their windows as did Mary Sewell, her mother and sisters, while her father and future father-in-law, her brother and her future husband, acted as stewards.[134]

The Birmingham manufacturer who attended the theatre every night in the late eighteenth century, in part because there was little else to do, would have been astounded by the range of entertainments in town and countryside by the mid nineteenth century. Concerts had multiplied and private dances were always available for those who thought the public too promiscuous. The diary of the son of a Quaker manufacturer in Birmingham gives a good indication of the pleasures available even in a religious household. The young man enjoyed playing chess, attending his Young Men's Reading Society (where the assembled group played Blind Man's Buff after discussing the text), playing charades, twenty questions, bagatelle and dominoes not to speak of football, cricket and iceskating (all of which could be exclusively enjoyed in Edgbaston). He had holidays in Wales, that favourite spot for the Birmingham bourgeoisie, days out in Sutton Park, attended the Flower Show at the Town Hall, went to the baths, the essay meetings, the Panorama in New Street, to concerts in the Town Hall, celebrated 5 November with other Quaker families, read *Punch* and the *Home Companion* and educated himself at the Philosophical Institution.[135]

Lit. and Phils., it has been argued, specialized in the 'social legitimation of marginal men', since 'natural knowledge' provided a distinct and novel base on which such men could build a separate philosophy and cultural system.[136] The Birmingham Philosophical Institution, with its origins in a small scientific discussion group, was founded in 1813 and had its own premises. It was organized in the normal way with a president, two vice-presidents, treasurer and secretary, committee of sixteen gentlemen, plus (male) fellows and associates who were elected in recognition of contributions they had made. Even the proprietors were all men, although at subscriber level there was a sprinkling of women. They were, however, not expected to attend special general meetings which included a dinner.[137]

The Unitarian influence in the society was extensive, though not exclusive, reflecting the strong Unitarian commitment to science and rationality. 'The social millennium', as Joseph Priestley had written to Burke,

will be brought about by the influence of the commercial spirit aided by Christianity and true philosophy. . . . Public money no longer wasted [on war] will be spent on public libraries and public laboratories. The empire of reason will ever be the reign of peace.[138]

This 'empire of reason' was promoted through the pursuit of science, literature and the arts. The society aimed to discuss natural history, physics, chemistry, literature, political economy, the arts and philosophy. It excluded religion and politics, those divisive subjects, and would have no practical medicine. The premises included a newsroom for the men, a lecture room, library and museum. The museum, which in time necessitated the appointment of a curator (another of the new kinds of employment available to men), provided rich opportunities for that 'collecting, possessing, displaying' so beloved by middle-class men, indeed, as R. J. Morris has written,

the barbaric joy of a class of men just beginning to feel their power in the success of war and industry.[139]

That joy in finding new objects, labelling and classifying them, was shared by many nineteenth-century men whether their concern was with plants, fossils, or art erotica. For women, these 'barbaric joys' were limited to collecting for their own homes and gardens. It was linen, furniture, clothes, hats and caps, together with flowers or shells, which preoccupied them rather than the wilder penumbra of nature.[140]

The major feature of the Philosophical Institutions' season was its lectures, almost always given by men and particularly revered by those who, influenced by Bentham, regarded it as the best method of teaching. Public lecturing was yet another new career for men, often utilized as an extra source of income by penurious Unitarian ministers. On many occasions they were attended by women, unless the subject was deemed unsuitable.[141] The audience was often 'numerous and rather brilliant' and those lecturers who provided illustrations, specimens and practical experimentation were particularly popular.[142] Thomas Wright Hill was proud to provide such a lecture in Birmingham, relying on his sons to help him with the presentation of the visual material, harking back to his childhood game of pretending to be a preacher and standing up on a box to declaim his message.[143] After the lectures, tea would be provided, a social as well as educational element and in 1818 dinners were instituted in the 'philosophers' houses' on Monday evenings. The same year after a successful trip along the canal it was decided to institute an annual outing.[144]

While men could hope for new opportunities from their Lit. and Phils., at the level of learning, remuneration and companionability, women's expectations had to be more limited. Much the same pattern is found in the range of similar institutions established for the middle classes in this period, Birmingham's Athaneum and Polytechnic Institutes, for example. In Mechanics Institutes, however, founded in 1833 in Colchester

for the promulgation of useful knowledge among all persons but more especially the working classes

the exclusion of women was sometimes less complete. From 1835 members in Colchester were encouraged to bring female friends with them to the lectures in order to swell the audience while the rival Anglican Literary Institute allowed no women as members until 1888 and even then required them to leave the premises at 5.00 p.m. One-third of the members of the Chelmsford Mechanics Institute, founded in 1833, were women in 1852.[145] In Ipswich they were so bold as to bring in a woman lecturer, particularly striking in a rural area where self-improvement societies were less well developed.[146] While Birmingham's Philosophical Institution had been content with a male lecturer 'On the social condition of women in different periods of history', Ipswich produced Mrs C. L. Balfour to speak on 'The Moral and Intellectual Influence of Women in Society'. The *Suffolk Chronicle* reported this as a topic of great importance but noted that some of the usual patrons

thought proper in a fit of prudery to keep aloof from knowledge imparted by a female.

Mrs Balfour called for 'a larger extension of action for her sex' but entirely disassociated herself from the dangerous 'dogmas of the Wolstencraft [*sic*] school'.[147]

Such advances towards women's public participation in scientific and intellectual life were sometimes possible in the improving strongholds of the progressive and Dissenting middle class, especially when they were concerned to create opportunities for working men and women rather than their own wives and daughters. Societies of arts, however, continued with the now familiar pattern of active membership for men combined with passive consumption for women. The Birmingham Society of Arts, founded in 1821, was the result of the coming together of professional artists, who had been organizing together for some time, and local manufacturers, lawyers, bankers and clergymen, even the ubiquitous John Angell James, who hoped to afford

the means of forming and correcting the taste of the rising generation, and contribute essentially to the improvement of all those branches of manufacture which are most susceptible of decoration.[148]

On the first exhibition of Birmingham artists in 1814, the daughter of Birmingham's historian William Hutton (who had no love for the town after the attack on the family property in the riots of 1791), remarked acidly that she thought the 'genius of the artists of Birmingham . . . more calculated to paint tea boards than pictures', but a recent study of the Society of Arts has stressed the primacy of the improving motif, the desire to refine the taste of the town, rather than its commercial imperatives.[149] The regulations of the new society stipulated the usual hierarchies with patrons (particularly vital when exhibitions depended in large part on the loan of works from local collectors), proprietors, governors and trustees. 'Every Member' it was specified in rule ten,

shall have admission for himself to the Institution, and the power of admitting any number of individuals of his family to view the Works of Art, and to draw and model there. . . .

While rule eleven made it clear that all lady members would vote by proxy.[150]

The full meaning of such regulations can only be understood with a knowledge of contemporary artistic practices. Fine art, design and the teaching of art were all developing in this period as new fields for men. Professional art practice demanded skills beyond those taught at the amateur level which it was hard for women to acquire unless they were working in artistic families where studio space, skills and materials were available. Propriety excluded women from life drawing and from the large scale and ambitious.[151] A major debate within the Birmingham Society of Arts was that between male artists and gentlemen as to who should make decisions; for example, what kinds of exhibitions should be mounted? The gentlemen wanted to improve taste with exhibitions of old masters, the artists wanted to exhibit and sell their own work, and this became an argument which simmered and erupted over several decades.[152] Women artists were necessarily marginal to such disputes, so that as new professional opportunities arose, such as training through the new schools of design, an absence of female representation in the formulation of such plans meant that they were never promulgated with women's needs in mind. Similarly, as consumers, women were locked into taking what was on offer rather than making and shaping possibilities themselves. As in all other efforts outside of philanthropy narrowly defined, the differential opportunities for men and women in the cultural institutions of the middle classes were firmly set.

Men, women and citizenship

Women's marginality was even more pronounced in the world of politics and civic life. They could attend the assizes as spectators, but they could never hope to play any part in the administration of the law or share in its majestic spectacle. The assizes were regularly preceded by a grand procession, attended by judges, lawyers, clergy and other public figures, and designed to display not only the power of the legislature but also the public place of its local protagonists. Henry Clay, for example, successful japanner and in 1790 the High Sheriff of Warwickshire, led a cavalcade from his house in the centre of Birmingham to the Warwick Assizes (the town did not have its own county court until 1847, another of the symbolic moments in the achievement of full civic status). As a local poet rhapsodized:

> The day was delightful and brilliant the train,
> Twas harmony all, and may harmony reign,
> Nor DISCORD her BANNERS display.[153]

Such harmonious sentiments may have been somewhat wishful thinking in the year before the Priestley Riots but the belief in the potential of the local elite to improve the times, quell discord and build peace and prosperity on the basis of commercial and financial progress was a powerful one.

Provincial middle-class men were able to use their enterprise, their business and professional acumen to make new claims for themselves to be public 'somebodies', men who were known in their own local communities and some of whom came to be known nationally.[154] But the claim to be a public man no longer rested, as it had done in the eighteenth century, on the ideal of the 'disinterested gentleman', removed from the base activity of making money and able to philosophize independently from the security of property.[155] Now men were arguing from the claims of their religious seriousness, combined with their belief in the dignity of work.[156] It was as a captain of industry that Matthew Boulton came to take an active part in securing economic policies favourable to West Midland manufacturers, and to speak on these issues at the highest level.[157] It was a Birmingham banker, proud of his knowledge of currency matters, who led the Birmingham Political Union to victory in 1832.[158] These were the men who were lauded in the annals of the town,

The noblest men that dignify our age
The brightest names that live on history's page.[159]

Often it was membership of a professional association which built up the confidence and created the rationale for local men to make claims for political representation and power, as with the Birmingham ironmasters. In many of these associations, the membership was drawn from a range of practitioners so that, as with Freemasons, men learned to converse, argue, communicate ideas and knowledge with social inferiors and superiors, drawn together for a common purpose. Wives and daughters might be assisting in these business enterprises but they had no access either to the education and training gradually devised for such societies as they became national and regulatory bodies, nor to the exchange of ideas which took place at the dining and drinking sessions. Within local communities membership of such bodies was one of the routes to public visibility and prominence. Men learned to speak for their interest group and later for their community or class.

As property owners, some middle-class men claimed rights and responsibilities and learnt something of local office holding. As freemen of a town (on the basis of birth, purchase or apprenticeship), they had the right to vote long before 1832. Freemen, for example, would travel to Colchester to exercise that vote, legitimately tasting political privilege and being involved in the hurly burly of elections.[160] As employers, middle-class men had responsibilities, whether in relation to the Poor Law or vouching for their employees in courts of justice. Lower middle-class men might forge a public identity through lesser offices, whether as bailiff or town clerk, as vestryman church warden, Poor Law guardians, members of improvement commissions, highway surveyors.[161] Some women, particularly in the countryside, managed to exercise rights that went with their property, like the female surveyor of highways in Solihull in 1838, but they were the exception. Over the period it was increasingly difficult for women to exercise those rights on the grounds of propriety.[162] Meanwhile, men were not only encouraged to do so but used such small opportunities as the basis for further demands and when legislation freed nonconformist men to seek public office, their womenfolk remained excluded.

The Ipswich baker, Jeremiah Howgego, learnt how to operate in public, if on a small scale, through his membership of The Wellington Club, a Tory group particularly concerned with the rights of the freemen of Ipswich. Sometimes he chaired their meetings, and was on the committee. In January 1834 a meeting took place at which about 200 men were present, plenty of 'Welch Rabbets' were consumed and the issue of reform was discussed. Under reform, freemen might lose their vote, as they did in Colchester, and twenty-four members subsequently met to form a 'Resalation' which was to be sent to the House of Commons. Through his club, Howgego learnt about elections and voting procedures: as he records in August 1832,

Club Night: 3 Candetits for the Warter Ballief . . . and the Men Pold in the Club Room, the Club Promesed to support that Man got the Most Voats.

Later that year he was involved with a disputed election and supported a Tory candidate not loved by the majority at the Wellington. He met with three others to consider 'the Best Moade of Sarving Mr M. on a Commety in is Elliction'. The rest of the committee found him 'all wrong in thare minds for voating for Mr Mackinnon' but he himselt was 'settesfide' having been publicly called a fool and risking expulsion for his views. Howgego's diary indicates his insecurity with the political process but also the way in which he learns to stand up for himself in public, how to 'voat', how to work on a 'commety', how to manipulate patronage, how to become in a modest way a public man. [163]

It was activities such as these, in professional association, in the chambers of manufacturers, in political clubs and, of course, in religious, philanthropic, and cultural associations which allowed men the right to speak for their communities, to attend such events as the proclamation of accession of William IV in Birmingham in 1830, when the public authorities, the clergy, the Dissenting ministers and between 200 and 300 of the most respectable tradesmen of the town gathered to celebrate. [164] It was men who organized the range of new public buildings which transformed Birmingham from a 'black place' of 'no taste' to

a town of spacious, wide and well-paved streets, abounding in public buildings, in the offices of large trading companies, and in private undertakings, exhibiting generally a highly advanced state of architectural decorations, and a general air of substantial wealth and industry. [165]

It was men in Colchester and Ipswich as well as Birmingham who were responsible for the gas lighting which made it possible to traverse the town more safely after dark. [166] It was men who led the demand for parliamentary representation for the town and for borough status. Men built, men planned, men organized, men acted. Meanwhile, what did women do?

Women's place in the public world of politics is aptly illustrated by an account in *Aris's Birmingham Gazette* of the visit of the Duchess of Kent and Princess Victoria to the town in 1830. The royals were greeted by a deputation of six gentlemen including the high and low bailiffs and members of the Society of Arts and were taken on a tour of some of the town's most famous manufactories. At their departure, the considerate manager of the Royal Hotel, where the royalty had stayed, allowed the ladies of Birmingham to line the passage of the hotel so that they were able 'in safety and convenience' to gratify their curiosity and show their attachment. [167] Similarly, at the great civic events such as the Incorporation Dinner of 1839, the banquet of 1845 or the dinner to welcome Prince Albert to the town in 1855, magnificent occasions held in the highly decorated and well-lit classical styled Town Hall, the ladies sat in the galleries, excluded from both the dining and the drinking, there only as spectators, even then only gaining a clear view of the proceedings after mounting a protest at being put behind pillars. [168]

Such a positioning of men and women was by no means confined to the great new industrial and urban centres. Women *as consumers* in both town and country might express political affiliation by selective trading. They might lobby informally for favoured candidates.[169] The Tory ladies of Colchester showed their appreciation of their local MP in 1843 not by public addresses printed in the local newspaper, nor by celebratory dinners held at local hostelries. Rather, 100 of them presented him with an elaborate embroidered screen, an effort in 'co-operative sewing', in appreciation of his activities for the locality.[170]

Such placing cut across party allegiances: Liberal dinners, Tory tokens of support, Whig election triumphs all manifest the same patterns. The Whig victory in Ipswich in 1820 was taken as the opportunity for a grand fete, at the centre of which was the procession with the successful candidates. The hustings in the centre of the market place accommodated about 400 ladies who were admitted by ticket and every window was thronged with 'lovely women' waving their handkerchiefs as the cavalcade went by. An ironmonger had a balcony perfect for

the convenience of the numerous ladies who were accommodated at his house to witness the ceremonies of the day.

'Much praise is due', lauded the *Ipswich Journal*

to the committee for. . . . The courtesy and liberality with which they provided for the accommodation of the ladies, who by their presence gave life and animation to the festive scene.

The hustings were bedecked with flowers, 'the Goddess flora had contributed her fragrant treasures', and 'other emblems of beauty, purity and innocence' further impressed the admiring spectators.[171]

The cavalcade itself was led by a horseman in armour, part of the appeal to chivalry and honour which was a powerful element in masculinity at this time.[172] The young men of the town had raised a special subscription to hire the armour, in keeping with the dignity of the occasion. Behind him came marshalls and trumpeters, seventy gentlemen all on grey horses, the Whig committee in carriages, the two successful candidates with their families all of whom were followed by further horsemen and more carriages. Finally there were the sedan carriers chairing as their centrepiece and pinnacle a 'beautiful cast of Britannia', the nation portrayed as a female, and with busts of royalty and favoured heroes – Fox, Nelson and Wellington representing England's military heritage; Shakespeare, Milton and, that provincial favourite, William Cowper, representing her literary glory.

All classes greeted the candidates, the *Journal* reported,

with enthusiastic expressions of popular regard. In this expression of feeling the ladies seemed to emulate the men, and by their fascinating smiles to give a still more hearty welcome to the highly favoured idols of the day.

As one of the candidates said in his speech, the ladies had 'added grace to the splendour of our victory' and no doubt that night, at the dinner for 400 men which followed the afternoon's excitement, the customary toast was made to 'the ladies'.[173]

This scene was 1820, the year of Queen Caroline. Her protagonists, too, had led processions in her support in full chivalric regalia, reminding themselves that men must look to the affairs of state and protect their dependent women and children. Such was the claim of the new middle-class public man.

Epilogue

Childhood — own entity

Through the stories of individuals and families, *Family Fortunes* argues that the men and women of the provincial middle class adopted distinctively different class identities, that the language of class formation was gendered. For them, as for us, the acquisition of gendered subjectivity was a process which continued throughout the lifecycle. Manliness and femininity were not fixed categories acquired in childhood but were constantly being tested, challenged and reworked both in imagination and in the encounters of daily life. In this process, linguistic, cultural and symbolic representations of sexual difference played a vital part, as did social organization. For all social institutions were gendered, from family and kinship systems to chapels and corn markets. The relations between the sexes were structured by property forms as well as direct ideological imperatives.

From the late eighteenth century, serious middle-class people increasingly claimed moral power for themselves, a claim fuelled by religious belief and the 'proud pretensions' of those who relied on heavenly approbation rather than earthly spoils. Their rejection of landed wealth as the source of honour and insistence on the primacy of the inner spirit brought with it a preoccupation with the domestic as a necessary basis for a good Christian life. Evangelical categorizations of the proper spheres of men and women provided the basis for many subsequent formulations and shaped the common sense of the nineteenth-century social world. Men were to be active in the world as citizens and entrepreneurs, women were to be dependent, as wives and mothers. In the pantheon of the serious middle class, feckless aristocrats and atheistic artisans had no place. They celebrated the converted, carefully placing them in a social hierarchy of the saved; the damned were execrated. The moral order which they attempted to impose had lasting effects, not only on relations between the sexes but also in definitions of who was properly part of the English nation. The 'teeming poor', the Irish, the gypsies, the unclean, all were consigned to the category of 'other'.[1]

But this common sense was riven with contradictions, both within these sets of beliefs and between ideology and the practical constraints of daily life. It was these contradictions which prevented closure and ensured continual shifts both in discourse and practice. Serious Christian men were caught between the desire for a religious life and the need for success in the commercial and public world if they were to adequately provide for and represent their dependants. That success was supposedly based on their individual efforts, but inevitably men relied heavily on wives, family and friends. The early emphasis on manly emotion faded and the development of a rational outlook increasingly restricted the expression of men's feelings. Some men were growing to fear the latent power of domesticated women, yet there was also concern that domesticity was too important to be left in the hands of weak subordinates.[2] The Anglo-Catholic movement of the 1840s, for example, can be interpreted as a search for a male-bonded culture which recovered the richness, colour and music increasingly denied to men while placing women firmly in separate sisterhoods as men recreated the religious world of ritual without female interference.[3] The elevation of purity for middle-class women locked into domesticity, and the expectation of their weak dependency, increasingly contrasted with the easy virtue and excitement of 'women of the streets'. This division between duty and pleasure could create psychic torment for many middle-class men.[4]

Women also faced contradictions. Their religion recognized their spiritual equality yet defended social and sexual subordination. Their class applauded self-assertion yet the feminine ideal was selflessness. Their supposed dependence and fragility was continually stressed yet they were expected to manage the 'business' of motherhood and the efficient organization of the household. Many women contributed directly to the family enterprise throughout their lives, yet received no public, or indeed, economic recognition.

Despite the balance between male power and female influence, men felt the need to systematically contain women and limit their potential. A society increasingly based on new forms of property, on liquid capital, could no longer depend on traditional forms of male dominance embedded in the traces of a feudal military system which had been inherent in land ownership.[5] New forms of capital required novel methods of restraining women. It was never the laws of property alone which prevented the myriad middle-class women who owned capital from using it actively. Rather, it was the ways in which the laws of inheritance and the forms of economic organization (the trust, the partnership, the family enterprise) intersected with definitions of femininity. The active generation of lasting wealth was virtually impossible for women.[6]

Apprehensions on the part of men were not linked only to women's economic potential. General unease about women's independence, both sexual and intellectual, was often close to the surface. Underlying the insistence on female modesty, was the anxiety about the 'floodgate' which might open if that modesty were not held firmly in place,[7] thus women would continue to have no voice in the body politic. As a Suffolk clergyman reminded his female audience in 1848, Adam came first and *named* the orders of the world.[8] Women's independent action was denounced as 'unwomanly', 'unsexed' or 'strongminded', epithets designed to undermine core feminine identity.

Marriage became both symbol and institution of women's containment. It was marriage which would safely domesticate the burgeoning garden flower into an indoor pot plant; the beautiful object potentially open to all men's gaze became the possession of one man when kept within the house like a picture fixed to the wall. Many women were aware of the constraints of marriage as well as the support and protection it might offer. Would not marriage, a poem in one young Essex woman's commonplace book asks, destroy the freedom of women? Indeed no, answers the young man, since Cupid's dart would ensure that the 'free flying bird, ambitious to roam' would become 'a very canary', rejoicing in her 'cage as a home'.[9] Another poem of the period, painstakingly copied out by several young women (in the local study), put it:

> Man's the Lord of creation, the head and the boast
> But woman's a Cipher, a cipher at most.

It was only when woman was placed beside man that she could 'make sense' and her husband achieve his full manhood for

> A Cipher when placed at the right hand just so
> Makes a figure just ten times the value, you know.[10]

Such was the currency of daily life which women had to attempt to remould for themselves.

Many of the key actors in the story of the middle class were born in the 1780s and reached adulthood during the decades of revolution, war, and industrial expansion. A small minority joined with artisans to denounce society in a Utopian socialist vision, deeply imbued with religious fervour. As Barbara Taylor has shown, this voice had special appeal to a handful of women from the middle class to whom the promises of domesticity were hollow.[11] It was the Quaker daughter of a wholesale grocer from Essex, Anne Knight (b. 1786), who summoned the first formal woman's suffrage meeting in 1851; her appeal, significantly, was to northern Chartist women, possibly survivors from an Owenite group. Anne Knight, unmarried and living on a small income from her father, spent almost all her life in Chelmsford and never spoke in public. She had grown up through various philanthropic causes, moulded by a fiery devotion to anti-slavery. Her radical feminism grew from her adherence to the extreme wing of the abolition movement and was forged at the anti-slavery convention when American women delegates had been excluded.[12]

By the late 1840s, Anne Knight was urging Ann Taylor Gilbert to join the cause of women's rights, particularly the franchise.[13] As we have seen, Ann Taylor and her sister Jane (b. 1782 and 1783) came from a similar nonconformist background. Like many of their generation, they were passionate supporters of anti-slavery and religious liberty. But in common with a more socially and politically conservative view, they joined William Cowper and Hannah More on the question of men and women's roles.

Ann Taylor's reply to Anne Knight in February 1849 stated what was to become the classic later nineteenth-century anti-suffrage position. Women were already represented by men. They had neither the voice nor the courage to speak in the public sphere and were far too busy in the private, 'inside the home' and in benevolent and religious societies which should be the 'boundary' of a woman's 'outdoor business'. Her defence, however, was based not on the use of scripture but on 'scientific' demonstration that a division of labour was a benefit to progress.[14] For Ann Taylor, women's ennoblement came not from rights but enlargement of mind through an education complementary to men's, through the 'brilliant star' of knowledge raising the 'dark night' of women's oppression.[15]

For all Ann Taylor's defence of women's relegation to the 'smaller but more perfect circle' of the private (here she quotes Hannah More), both she and her sister, Jane, betray an unease. Jane Taylor argued that women could take pleasure in both 'making a curious pudding' and 'reading a fine poem'. She speculated that the reason so few men, even among the intelligent, would not encourage the mental cultivation of women was that they 'trembled for their stomachs', fearing that a woman who could taste the pleasures of poetry would never descend to pay due attention to the mundanities which were so 'gratifying to philosophical palates'.[16]

As with the 'star of Knowledge', both sisters repeatedly use the metaphor of the heavens as a realm beyond the constraints of genteel femininity; the 'bright spark' in their most lasting poem for children, 'Twinkle, Twinkle Little Star'. In a story by Jane, the more serious girl turns from the chatter of a hat trimming session to watch the stars, where thoughts can range 'fair and free'. The 'various bars' of genteel poverty and womanhood cannot prevent the mind 'revelling mid the stars' and imagination 'ranging through the sky . . . with untold delight' to 'watch the changing splendours of the night'. For 'while thought is free, how'er enslaved the wretch, he has a circuit where no arm can stretch'.[17]

The daughters and granddaughters of the Taylors' and Anne Knight's generation found a world more rigidly divided into separate spheres for men and women. The tensions were deeper, the opportunities less. These generations of women spoke with a somewhat different, but no less contradictory voice. The Evangelical Anglican and Tory, Catherine Marsh, daughter of Maria and the Rev. William, was born in St Peter's Vicarage, Colchester in 1818, and brought up in Edgbaston. She was more genteel and intensely conservative on almost every issue, yet in her personal life she objected to being treated 'as if the world should be peopled with men and a set of breathing automatons politely called women'. In 1848, excoriating the 'ruffian outrages' of Chartists and striking colliers, she bewailed the lack of sympathy and compassion for women, the poor shirtmakers who were left in 'hopeless penury . . . socialism and infidelity sink women to a slave'.[18]

By the 1850s and with the publication of statistical details available for the first time in the 1851 census, public debate centred on what came to be defined as 'surplus' or redundant women. The simple expedient of shipping middle-class women to the colonies in proportion to men as a solution was countered by feminists who argued that if women were allowed to freely enter all occupations 'suited to their strength', they would cease to be superfluous.[19]

Thus as the women of Catherine Marsh's generation were reaching adulthood, the 'woman question' had crystallized around the issue of economic support and employment. The attention to that liminal figure, *the governess*, in fact and fiction, underscores the weight being given to the issue of middle-class women's crossing the now more clearly drawn public/private divide by working for wages even within a familial setting.[20] It is no accident that two of the earliest feminist efforts were directed to extending women's property rights and gaining recognized entry into employment.[21]

The mid century common-sense division into a public world of politics
and market activity assigned to men and the private sphere now contained
in the suburban villa set the framework for the feminism of John Stuart
Mill. His programme was based on individual rights of self-determination
and equal considerations of justice and his conviction that women's inferior
position was culturally, not naturally, determined. Yet this did not undermine his belief in a natural division of labour and of spheres.[22]

This book has been set in the period between Mary Wollstonecraft's
Vindication of the Rights of Women (1792) and John Stuart Mill and Harriet
Taylor's 'The Enfranchisement of Women' (1851).[23] It was a time when
middle-class feminism has been taken as quiescent or nonexistent. It may
well have been a time when there was more co-operation between articulate
middle-class men and women, involved as they were in building up the
material, social and religious base of their identity, battling as a proselytizing
minority for their place in the world and the rightness of their view of that
world.

As in all such aspirations, a dream sustained them, the dream of domestic
felicity expressed in Candia Cadbury's insistence on the affectionate feelings
of the Cadbury family for each other, their existence as 'a family of love'.[24]
The women of the early nineteenth-century provincial middle class caught
hold of that dream, but when it became a full reality they found their
sphere isolated, trivialized and often unable to give the support it had
promised.[25] It was in the experience of their daughters and granddaughters
later in the century that the inequalities, the lack of power and resources
for control over their own lives, came to be exposed and expressed.

In this book, we have tried to understand the lineaments and under-
pinnings of that dream and its consequences. In doing so we have highlighted one set of voices from the men and women who struggled to shape
and define the ongoing question of relations between the classes and the
sexes.

APPENDIX 1 Three poems by local authors

1 Ann Taylor Gilbert, 'Remonstrance', in J. Conder (ed.), *Associate Minstrels*, 1812.

2 Ann Taylor Gilbert, 'My Mother', in A. and J. Taylor, *Original Poems for Infant Minds*, 1805.

3 James Luckcock, 'My Husband', in J. Luckcock, *Sequel to Memoirs in Humble Life*, Birmingham, 1825.

Remonstrance

'Women in their course of action describe a smaller circle than men; but the perfection of a circle consists, not in its dimensions, but in its correctness.' (*Coelebs in Search of a Wife*)

> ******* Why this hopeless feud?
> This worse than civil strife,
> Which long, with poison'd darts, hath strew'd
> The vale of social life?
>
> To each, an helpmate each was made,
> Congenial, but diverse:
> The rougher path was *his* to tread;
> The mild domestic, *hers*.
>
> His iron arm was braced for toil,
> Or danger's ruder shock;
> To win the curs'd, reluctant soil,
> Or fence the cavern'd rock.
>
> The watchful eye, the pliant hand,
> To gentler duties led:
> By *her* the rural rite was planned,
> The simple table spread.
>
> Composed, retiring, modest, *she*;
> Impetuous, *he*, and brave; –
> His passions, boisterous as the sea;
> Hers, oil upon the wave.
>
> Wearied in far-extended chase,
> His ready meal she drest;
> With smiles illumed his dwelling place,
> With kindness soothed his breast.
>
> Thus, in the days of ancient man,
> Th' harmonious friendship grew,
> Ere yet those hostile names began,
> The tyrant and the shrew.

'Twas Nature's will that each obey'd;
    Nor envious question rose:
They felt for mutual service made;
    For friends, and not for foes.

But tired of Nature's wise controul,
    Immediate war began:
He had the power, and, proud of soul,
    Became the tyrant, Man.

Too feeble to sustain her part,
    She fell a sullen prey,
Content by influence and art
    To counteract his sway.

Degenerate, with degenerate time,
    Still wider breach was seen:
His was the bold, ferocious crime;
    Hers, petulant and mean.

Strange! thus to mar the plan of Heaven,
    Ingeniously perverse!
To turn the solace it had given,
    A blessing, to a curse.

Sure 'twas a cold unmanly pride
    The harmony that broke:
Why should the oak the lily chide,
    Because she's not an oak?

If all were lilies, where's the use,
    Or strength, the forest yields?
If óaks, the fragrancy we lose,
    And beauty of the fields.

Through following ages, dark and drear,
    Th' unnatural contest ran;
Nor generous feeling stole a tear
    From hard, obdurate Man!

Woman, his haughty will consigned
    In joyless paths to run:
No beam of day-light reached her mind,
And sages said she'd none.

At length, the brilliant western star
    Of Knowledge 'gan to rise;
The mists of ignorance afar
    Rolled sullen from the skies.

Neglected woman, from the night
    Of dark oppression raised,
Caught the fair dawn of mental light,
    And blest it as she gazed.

One champion, hardy, and alone,
    Stood forth her cause to plead:
But no; the weapons we disown
    That ask a martial deed.[1]

Enlightened feeling shall subdue,
  Or may we still endure;
Nor brave a combat, though we knew
  That victory were sure.

Triumph were only bright defeat;
  Disgrace, the laurel crown: –
OUR conquest is composed retreat;
  Concealment our renown.

The right that Nature gave, we claim, –
  Just honours of our kind:
We envy not the manly frame
  Of body, or of mind.

Man, in *his* way, perfection knows;
  And we as much in ours:
The violet is not the rose,
  Yet both alike are flowers.

Thus Venus round a narrow sphere
  Conducts her silver car;
Nor aims, nor seems, to interfere
  With Jove's imperial star.

Athwart the dark and deep'ning gloom
  Their blending rays unite,
And with commingled beams illume
  The drear expanse of night.

Boyle, Locke, and Newton, deep in lore,
  Man's lofty records trace;
Edgeworth, and Hamilton, and More,
  Our living annals grace.[2]

His soul is thoughtful and profound;
  Hers, brilliant and acute; –
Plants cultured, each, in different ground
  And bearing different fruit.

Among the social duties led,
  Where each excels in part,
Man's proudest glory is his head,
  A Woman's, is her heart.

Unwearied in the toilsome course,
  He climbs the hill of fame;
Takes immortality by force,
  And wins a mighty name.

Along a cool sequestered way,
  Her quiet walk she winds;
Sheds milder sunshine on his day,
  His brow with flowers binds.

Of art intuitive possest,
  Her infant train she rears;
To virtue by her smiles carest,
  Or chastened by her tears:

Beside the flitting midnight lamp,
    With fond and wakeful eye,
Wipes gently off the dying damp,
    Or sooths the parting sigh: –

'Tis here that Woman brightest shines
    (Though bright in other spheres):
Her name is drawn in fairest lines,
    When written by her tears.

Yet not the weak, the puny thing,
    Subdued to silly woe;
The firmest dignity may spring,
    Where softest feelings grow.

With you in mental fields to stray,
    She has not ill assumed;
And follows in the lucid way
    Your studies have illumed.

Then why, *****, why controul
    That dictate of the heart,
Which could not feel itself a whole
    Till Woman shared a part?

Why look with hard, unkindly view,
    On Woman's frailer part,
As if the weeds of folly grew
    But in a female heart?

In sorrow and in sin combined,
    Both sentenced to the tomb,
'Twould better speak a chastened mind,
    To cheer each other's doom.

Sweet were the pilgrimage of those
    Who hand in hand to heaven,
Would learn the cynic eye to close,
    Forgiving and forgiven.

Eve fled for refuge from her shame,
    Her grief, to Adam's breast;
The ruined hero felt the claim,
    Nor generous love represt.

Then, still let generous love beguile
    The weary walk of life;
Nor waste a sigh, nor lose a smile,
    In jealousy and strife.

Ann Taylor Gilbert
August 1807

Notes

1 A possible reference to Mary Wollstonecraft.
2 Maria Edgeworth, Hannah More and Elizabeth Hamilton, the latter a Scots writer on
    domesticity.

My Mother

Who fed me from her gentle breast
And hush'd me in her arms to rest
And on my cheek sweet kisses prest?
My Mother.

When sleep forsook my open eye,
Who was it sung sweet hushaby
And rock'd me that I should not cry?
My Mother.

Who sat and watch'd my infant head
When sleeping on my cradle bed
And tears of sweet affection shed?
My Mother.

When pain and sickness made me cry
Who gaz'd upon my heavy eye
And wept, for fear that I should die?
My Mother.

Who drest my doll in clothes so gay
And taught me *pretty* how to play
And minded all I had to say?
My Mother.

Who ran to help me when I fell
And would some pretty story tell
Or kiss the place to make it well?
My Mother.

Who taught my infant lips to pray
And love God's holy book and day
And walk in wisdom's pleasant way?
My Mother.

And can I ever cease to be
Affectionate and kind to thee
Who wast so very kind to me
My Mother.

Ah! no, the thought I cannot bear,
And if God please my life to spare
I hope I shall reward thy care
My Mother.

When thou art feeble, old, and grey
My healthy arm shall be thy stay
And I will soothe thy pains away
My Mother.

And when I see thee hang thy head
'Twill be my turn to watch *thy* bed
And tears of sweet affection shed
My Mother.

For God, who lives above the skies,
Would look with vengeance in His eyes
If I should ever dare despise
My Mother.

Ann Taylor Gilbert

My Husband

WHO first inspir'd my virgin breast,
With tumults not to be express'd,
And gave to life unwonted zest?
                    My Husband.

Whose manly conduct and good sense,
From fickleness my sure defence,
Encourag'd boundless confidence?
                    My Husband's.

Who told me that his gains were small,
But that whatever might befal,
To me he'd gladly yield them all?
                    My Husband.

Who fear'd the nuptial knot to tie,
Lest fortune should her gifts deny,
And thus delay'd the promis'd joy?
                    My Husband.

But who when fairer prospects beam'd,
Reluctant then no longer seem'd,
But eagerly his pledge redeem'd?
                    My Husband.

Who all my recent pains beguil'd,
And hail'd me as he fondly smil'd,
The mother of his first born child?
                    My Husband.

And when the sad bereaving blow,
Had laid a future darling low,
Who sooth'd my agonizing woe?
                    My Husband.

Who since by long experience try'd,
With tranquil pleasures never cloy'd,
Spent all his leisure at my side?
                    My Husband.

The rural walk who anxious sought,
By nature's simple precept taught,
To prize her most belov'd resort?
                    My Husband.

Who shun'd the giddy town's turmoil,
To share with me the garden's toil,
And joy with labour reconcile?
                    My Husband.

And when by winter's power subdued,
Whose presence could the hours delude,
And banish gloom from solitude?
                    My Husband's.

Who precept with example join'd,
To form his children's heart and mind,
And virtue's lovely path defin'd?
                    My Husband.

Who to his country gave his vows,
Would freedom's sacred cause espouse,
And every patriot feeling rouse?
                    My Husband.

Who strove with unremitting zeal,
The discords of the world to heal,
And benefit the commonweal?
                    My Husband.

Whose arduous struggles long maintain'd,
Adversity's cold hand restrain'd,
And competence at length attain'd?
                    My Husband's.

Who with me holds the doubtful scale,
Now downward pacing through the vale,
To finish life's eventful tale?
                    My Husband.

For such a kind propitious fate,
To thee my heart I dedicate,
Most faithful and affectionate,
                    My Husband.

Thou Power Supreme! – thee I implore,
Whate'er the bliss for us in store,
Unite with me for evermore,
                    My Husband.

                    James Luckcock

APPENDIX 2   Sources for the local study

The local area files

The four area files (Birmingham, Essex, Suffolk and Witham) were constructed around individuals, families and organizations. The sources used were: diaries, letters, family records, business records, local maps, rate books, some marriage registers, wills, the census of 1841 and 1851, newspaper reports, local histories, relevant B.A., M.A. and Ph.D. theses, records of local organizations, interviews with descendants of local families and national biographical collections. Eighteen directories for Birmingham from 1767 to 1855 and six from Essex and Suffolk from 1787 to 1850 were consulted.

It should be noted that for these purposes, both wills and the manuscript census schedules were used for information on named individuals, households, families and organizations as well as sources for aggregate data as described below. We were also able to do some record linkage through names and addresses using rate books, directories and the census.

From these varied sources, lists of over 500 named people and 120 family enterprises were built up, roughly half from Birmingham and half from the eastern region. A further list of eighty organizations from Birmingham was matched by a smaller organizational listing for Essex and Suffolk, again concentrating on Colchester and Witham. The listings of people, family enterprises and organizations were kept separate for consultation and analysis but were also cross referenced to be used as general files for the areas.

The wills sample

A sample of 622 wills was drawn, consisting of 392 from Birmingham and seventy-two from Edgbaston (at five yearly intervals from 1780 to 1855) plus 158 from Witham, that is virtually all from that period. These wills were taken from local deposits, thus avoiding too heavy concentration on the wealthiest strata whose wills would more likely have been proved nationally. [1](Wills for some named individuals located in central sources were used where appropriate for the area files.) Details from the sample of wills were then coded and analysed in SPSS format.

The main characteristics of testators in the sample were as follows (percentages):

Marital status		Sex		Class	
Single	16	Men	72	Lower middle	69
Married	49	Women	28	Upper middle	31
Widowed	35				
	100		100		100

The census sample, 1851

The sample from the manuscript census was made up of, first, twenty-nine 'clusters' from Anderson's machine readable sample of the national census which fell within the boundaries of Birmingham, Essex and Suffolk. These covered town centres and large and small villages. (Anderson's cluster is roughly equivalent to the original enumerator's district.)[2] We then added a substantial group of Birmingham middle-class households, and eight Edgbaston districts, almost the whole of that suburb except for the rural margins. The eastern region clusters were augmented by four districts from Witham, again covering the whole of that town, and two extra central Colchester districts. All new clusters were handled identically to Anderson's material. With the exception of the large central Birmingham group, all areas included working-class households, making 5811 households of all types in the full sample, but the analysis has concentrated on the 1413 middle-class households unless otherwise specified.

The information for each household was put on tape, including names and addresses, following Anderson's practice. Thus a print out was created which could be consulted 'by eye' as well as for computer use. The aggregate information was then transformed into SPSS and analysed in full, with the exception of data on birthplace which was only used for the area files on named individuals and families. The full sample was then redivided into four sub-areas: Essex and Suffolk villages, Essex and Suffolk towns, Birmingham centre and Edgbaston.

Thus, the census material was not randomly drawn. It was not even, strictly speaking, a sample, but was constructed to provide a quantitative base for the more qualitative material. However, for convenience, we have referred to it as a sample throughout the text.

For the analysis, we used Anderson's procedures with the exception of his occupational dictionary which was not then readily available. Therefore we constructed our own socio-economic and occupational codes as follows:

Class

| Lower middle class | Upper middle class |

Occupation

Trade	Professional other
Manufacture	Salaried
Farm/miller	Innkeeper/hotelkeeper
Clergy	Independent
Lawyers	Retired under 55
Doctors	Retired over 55

It should be noted that we used an identical code in the analysis of the wills which helped to give coherence to the source material.

The 1413 middle-class households were made up of 8766 individuals, of whom 2171 or 25 per cent were servants, thus giving an average household size of 6.2. 27 per cent or just over a quarter of individuals were under 16 years of age and 9 per cent over 55 (4 per cent were over 65).

Men headed 1123 or 79 per cent of the households and women 290, or 21 per cent. The sample divided into 970 or 69 per cent in the lower middle class and 443 or 31 per cent in the higher strata. But among households headed by men, there were 66 per cent in the lower and 34 per cent in the higher, while among women, 76 per cent were in the lower and 24 per cent in the higher strata.

Notes

1   Note that Vincent estimates that grants of probate were administered for roughly one-tenth of all men and one-fifth of women who died in Cambridgeshire from 1848 to 1857: see J. R. Vincent, *Pollbooks: How the Victorians Voted*, Cambridge, 1967.

2   M. Anderson, 'Preparation and analysis of a machine readable national sample from the enumerators books of the 1851 Census of Great Britain', Social Science Research Council Report, HR 2066, January 1980; W. A. Armstrong, 'The Census enumerators' books: a commentary', in R. Lawton, *The Census and Social Structure: An interpretative guide to nineteenth century censuses for England and Wales* (1978).

APPENDIX 3   Tables

1   Distribution of population in the two areas 1801 to 1851
    a   Numbers
    b   Percentage increase
2   Class of household head in sub-areas
    a   Men
    b   Women
3   Sex of household head in sub-areas
4   Marital status of household heads by social class
    a   Men
    b   Women
5   Sex of adult population in sub-areas
6   Adult women living as relatives in households headed by men by social class
7   Sisters and sisters-in-law resident in households headed by men by marital status of the head
8   Numbers of residential servants employed in households by social class of household head
9   Age differences between husband and wife by social class
10 Characteristics of schools in the local areas

Table 1 *Distribution of population in two areas, 1801 to 1851*
a   Numbers

Area	1801	1811	1821	1831	1841	1851
Birmingham	74,987	87,221	108,289	148,856	192,743	246,961
Essex	226,437	252,473	289,424	317,200	344,979	369,318
Colchester	11,522	12,644	14,016	16,167	17,790	19,433
Witham	2,186	2,352	2,578	2,735	3,158	3,303
Suffolk	210,431	234,211	270,542	296,000	315,073	337,215
Ipswich	11,336	13,918	17,475	20,454	25,384	32,914
Bury St Edmunds	7,655	7,986	9,999	11,436	12,538	13,900
England and Wales	10,578,956	12,050,000	14,181,000	16,364,000	18,658,000	20,959,000

b   Percentage increase

Area	1801	1811	1821	1831	1841	1851
Birmingham	—	16	24	38	29	28
Essex	—	11	15	10	9	7
Colchester	—	10	11	15	9	7
Witham	—	8	10	6	15	5
Suffolk	—	11	15	9	6	7
Ipswich	—	23	26	17	24	29
Bury St Edmunds	—	4	25	14	10	11
England and Wales	—	14	18	15	14	12

Source: Census of Great Britain.

Table 2a *Class of household heads in sub-areas: men (per cent)*

Area	Lower middle class	Upper middle class	Total
Essex and Suffolk villages	69	31	100
Essex and Suffolk towns	76	24	100
Birmingham centre	69	31	100
Edgbaston	56	44	100
Average for total sample	66	34	100

N = 1123 households
Source: Census Sample 1851 (sub-areas; middle-class households only).

Table 2b *Class of household heads in sub-areas: women (per cent)*

Area	Lower middle class	Upper middle class	Total
Essex and Suffolk villages	80	20	100
Essex and Suffolk towns	81	19	100
Birmingham centre	97	3	100
Edgbaston	69	31	100
Average for total sample	76	24	100

N = 290 households
Source: Census Sample 1851 (sub-areas; middle-class households only).

Table 3 *Sex of household head in sub-areas (per cent)*

Area	Male	Female	Total
Essex and Suffolk villages	91	9	100
Essex and Suffolk towns	79	21	100
Birmingham centre	88	12	100
Edgbaston	80	20	100
Average for total sample	79	21	100

N = 1413 households
Source: Census Sample 1851 (sub-areas; middle-class households only).

Table 4a *Marital status of household heads by social class: men*

Marital status	Working class		Lower middle class		Upper middle class		Total	
	Number	%	Number	%	Number	%	Number	%
Single	130	3	73	10	41	11	244	5
Married	3409	91	608	82	301	80	4318	88
Widowed	233	6	64	8	36	9	323	7
Total	3762	100	745	100	378	100	4885	100

Source: Census Sample 1851 (all areas; all class of households).

Table 4b   *Marital status of household heads by social class: women*

Marital status	Working class		Lower middle class		Upper middle class		Total	
	Number	%	Number	%	Number	%	Number	%
Single	104	16	76	34	22	34	202	22
Married	65	10	12	5	3	5	80	9
Widowed	463	73	137	61	40	61	640	69
Total	632	99	225	100	65	100	922	100

Source: Census Sample 1851 (all areas; all class of households).

Table 5   *Sex of adult population in sub-areas (including servants)*

Area	Men	Women	Number of adult women to each adult man
Essex and Suffolk villages	317	431	1.4
Essex and Suffolk towns	610	1123	1.8
Birmingham centre	488	643	1.3
Edgbaston	857	1944	2.3
Total	2272	4141	1.8

Source: Census Sample 1851 (sub-areas; middle-class households only).

Table 6   *Adult women living as relatives in households headed by men by social class*

Relationship	Lower middle class		Upper middle class		Total	
	Number	%	Number	%	Number	%
Wives	547	61	282	54	829	59
Mother, mother-in-law, aunt	34	4	14	3	48	3
Sister, sister-in-law	60	7	60	12	120	9
Daughters, nieces	250	28	161	31	411	29
Total	891	100	517	100	1408	100

Source: Census Sample 1851 (all areas; middle-class households only).

Table 7 *Sisters and sisters-in-law resident in households headed by men by marital status of the head*

Marital status of head	Lower middle class		Upper middle class	
	Number of sisters	%	Number of sisters	%
Single	29	48	21	35
Married	19	32	31	52
Widowed	12	20	8	13
Total	60	100	60	100

N = 120
Note: Households headed by men in the upper middle class were one-third of the total sample but contained one-half of the resident sisters and sisters-in-law.
Source: Census Sample 1851 (all areas; middle-class households only).

Table 8 *Number of residential servants employed in households by social class of household head (per cent)*

Number of servants in household	Working-class households	Lower middle-class households	Upper middle-class households	Total
0	87	30	15	26
1	9	47	13	35
2	3	17	27	20
3	⎫	4	22	10
4	1	1	12	2
5 plus	⎭	1	11	4
Total	100	100	100	100

N = 5811 households
Source: Census Sample 1851 (all areas; all class of households).

Table 9 *Age differences between husband and wife by social class (per cent)*

Age difference	Lower middle class	Upper middle class	Both classes
Wife 5 years and over older than husband	3	1	2
Wife up to 5 years older than husband	10	7	9
Same	38	32	36
Husband up to 5 years older than wife	29	29	29
Husband 5 to 10 years older than wife	13	20	16
Husband more than 10 years older than wife	7	11	8
Total	100	100	100

N = 827
Source: Census Sample 1851 (all areas; middle-class households only).

Table 10 *Characteristics of schools in the local areas**

| Area | Head of household running the school | | | | Sex of pupils by school | | | Schools having age range | | Average number of pupils per school | |
| | Male | | Female | | | | | | | Boys | Girls |
	Married	Single	Widowed	Single	Boys	Girls	Co-ed	6–11	12+	*Average number of pupils*	
Schools in Essex and Suffolk	5	1	3	4	6	4	3	7	5	20	7
Schools in Edgbaston†	5	1	2	4	5	5	1	2	6	9	3
Total schools in sample	10	2	5	8	11	9	4	9	11	15	5

*Please note: Figures are for numbers of schools except in the last section which refers to numbers of pupils.
†There were no schools in the central Birmingham sample. In all schools from the sample there were twenty-three adult female relatives and visitors, excluding the ten wives of married masters.
Of these twenty-three, ten were sisters of the household head.
Source: Census Sample 1851 (sub-areas).

Notes and references

Abbreviations

Newspapers

ABG	*Aris's Birmingham Gazette*
BC	*Birmingham Chronicle*
CC	*Chelmsford Chronicle*
ECS	*Essex County Standard*
IJ	*Ipswich Journal*

Location of sources

BRL	Birmingham Reference Library
BUL	Birmingham University Library
CBL	Colchester Branch Library of Essex County (Local Records Collection)
DWL	Doctor Williams Library, London
ERO	Essex Record Office, Chelmsford, Essex
FHL	Friends House Library, London
IRO	Ipswich Record Office, Suffolk
PRO	Public Record Office, London
WSRO	West Suffolk Record Office, Bury St Edmunds, Suffolk

Archives

DQB	Unpublished Dictionary of Quaker Biography held at Friends House Library, London and Haverford College, Philadelphia, Pennsylvania
DNB	*Dictionary of National Biography*

London is the place of publication unless otherwise stated. Citation is given in full the first time it is used in each chapter.

Prologue

1 See E. J. Hobsbawm's definition of the main characteristics of the bourgeoisie as a class in *The Age of Capital* (1977), p. 286.
2 The Luckcock material has been drawn from the following sources. Subsequently only direct quotes have been footnoted. J. Luckcock, 'My house and garden: Lime Grove, Edgbaston', BRL 375948; J. Luckcock, 'Narrative of proceedings relative to the erection of the Old Meeting Sunday Schools Birmingham and of various occurrences therewith connected', BRL 390807 C.1832; J. Luckcock, *Moral Culture* (1817); J. Luckcock, *Annual Address to the teachers of the Old and New Meeting Sunday Schools* (Birmingham, 1819); J. Luckcock, 'Thoughts on the means of employment and relief of the poor' (Birmingham, 1819); J. Luckcock, *Sequel to memoirs in humble life* (Birmingham, 1825); J. Luckcock, 'On the contemplated representation of Birmingham' (Birmingham, 1827); J. Luckcock, *Hints for Practical Economy in the Management of Household Affairs* (Birmingham, 1834); Birmingham Brotherly

Society, *Minutes* (Birmingham, 1835); T. Clark Junior, *A Biographical Tribute to the Memory of James Luckcock* (Birmingham, 1835).

3   Birmingham Brotherly Society, 'Minutes of the Meetings', vol. I (1796–1808) BRL 391175.

4   J. Luckcock, *Sequel*, appendix, p. 17.

5   J. Luckcock, *Sequel*, p. 54.

6   D. Defoe, *The Complete English Tradesman* (2 vols., 1726), vol. 1, p. 152. Thanks to Sally Alexander for drawing attention to this quotation.

7   J. Luckcock, *Sequel*, p. 28.

8   ibid., p. 51.

9   ibid., p. 81.

10 Contemporaries spoke of 'the middling ranks', the 'middling sort', or the 'middling strata' since the concept of 'class' was rudimentary in the eighteenth century and only became common parlance in the nineteenth. See Asa Briggs, 'The language of "class" in early nineteenth-century England', in A. Briggs and J. Saville (eds.), *Essays in Labour History* (1967). On the continuing problem of definitions, see G. Crossick, 'The petite bourgeoisie in 19th century Europe: problems and research', in K. Tenfelde (ed.), *Arbeiter und Arbeiterbewegung im Vergleich* (Munich, 1986).

11 C. Phythian-Adams, 'Rural culture', in G. Mingay (ed.), *The Victorian Countryside* (2 vols., 1980), vol. 2, p. 619.

12 C. Emsley, *British Society and the French Wars 1793–1815* (1979).

13 The work of R. J. Morris on Leeds gives a detailed analysis of the connections between Whigs and nonconformity, Tories and Anglicanism. He argues that the link is problematic rather than straightforward, *The Making of the British Middle Class* (forthcoming).

14 W. Marshall, *On the Landed Property of England* (1804), p. 335; quoted in J. Powis, *Aristocracy* (Oxford, 1984), p. 24.

15 M. Rose, 'Diversification of investment by the Greg family 1800–1914', *Business History*, **xxi** no. 1 (Jan. 1979); R. G. Wilson, *Gentlemen Merchants: The Merchant Community in Leeds 1700–1830* (Manchester, 1971).

16 A. O. Hirschman, *The Passions and the Interests: Political Argument for Capitalism before its Triumph* (Princeton, 1977). See also D. Sugarman and G. R. Rubin, 'Towards a new history of law and material society in England 1750–1914', in D. Sugarman and G. R. Rubin (eds.), *Law, Economy and Society, 1750–1914: Essays in the History of English Law* (Abingdon, Oxon, 1984).

17 E. Pickard, 'Some account of my own life', BRL 22/11.

18 P. Joyce, *Work, Society and Politics. The Culture of the Factory in Later Victorian England* (1982); P. Joyce, 'Labour, capital and compromise: a response to Richard Price', *Social History*, 9 no. 1 (Jan. 1984); David Roberts, *Paternalism in Early Victorian England* (1979).

19 E. Moers, *The Dandy: Brummell to Deerbohm* (1960); H. Cole, *Beau Brummell* (1977).

20 D. Andrews, 'The code of honour and its critics: the opposition to duelling in England 1700–1850', *Social History*, 5 no. 3 (Oct. 1980). The core of the new morality was contained in an argument against duelling in a favourite middle-class novel of the period, Thomas Holcroft's *Anna St Ives* (1970). See introduction by Peter Faulker, p. xiii.

21 L. Stone, *The Family, Sex and Marriage in England 1500–1800* (1977).

22 Claims for recognition almost always are given a moral basis. D. Lockwood 'Civic stratification', unpublished paper (April 1985). For the particulars of the English scene at this time see M. Butler, *Poets and Myths* (forthcoming). See also D. Landes, 'Religion and enterprise: the case of the French textile industry',

in E. C. Carter, R. Forster and J. Moody (eds.), *Enterprise and Entrepreneurs in 19th and 20th century France* (Baltimore, 1976).

23 See the comment of a unitarian attorney's wife that it seemed 'criminal' to lay-out plans many years ahead for posterity, as if 'gifted with omniscience'. Rebecca Solly Shaen, unpublished diary, Bodleian Library, John Johnson Collection 18 and 19, p. 225.

24 C. Binfield, *So Down to Prayers: Studies in English Nonconformity 1780–1920* (1977), p. 42.

25 W. Eastment, *Wanstead Through the Ages* (Letchworth, 1969).

26 K. D. M. Snell, *Annals of the Labouring Poor: Social Change and Agrarian England 1660–1900* (Cambridge, 1985), pp. 338–9.

27 W. Cobbett, *Rural Rides* (Harmondsworth, 1967), p. 199.

28 John Gillis, *For Better, for Worse: British Marriages, 1600 to the present* (Oxford, 1985), p. 135.

29 W. D. Rubinstein, 'The Victorian middle classes: wealth, occupation and geography', *Economic History Review*, **30** no. 4 (1977), p. 608.

30 J. Luckcock, *Hints for Practical Economy*; A. D. Harvey, *Britain in the Early Nineteenth Century* (1978).

31 J. Brewer, 'Commercialization and politics', in N. McKendrick, J. Brewer and J. H. Plumb (eds.), *The Birth of a Consumer Society: The Commercialization of Eighteenth-Century England* (1982), p. 24; R. J. Morris, 'The making of the British middle class', unpublished paper (1979); P. Corfield, 'The social and economic history of Norwich 1650–1850', unpublished Ph.D. thesis, University of London (1976), p. 568; J. Foster, *Class Struggle and the Industrial Revolution* (1974), p. 74; J. Burnett, *A History of the Cost of Living* (Harmondsworth, 1979), p. 77; D. E. C. Eversley, 'Industry and trade 1500–1800', in Victoria County History, *History of Warwick*, R. B. Pugh (ed.), 'The City of Birmingham', vol. VII (Oxford, 1964); 1851 census sample.

32 G. Crossick, 'Urban society and the petty bourgeoisie in nineteenth century Britain', in D. Fraser and A. Sutcliffe (eds.), *The Pursuit of Urban History* (1983).

33 J. Burnett; 1851 Census Sample; Birmingham and E. Anglia wills.

34 K. Lacey, 'Women and work in fourteenth and fifteenth century London', in L. Charles and L. Duffin (eds.), *Women and Work in Pre-industrial England* (1985); M. Prior, 'Women and the urban economy: Oxford 1500–1800', in M. Prior (ed.), *Women in English Society* (1985); A. Fraser, *The Weaker Vessel. Women's Lot in Seventeenth Century England* (1984); M. Berg, *The Age of Manufactures, Industry, Innovation and Work in Britain 1700–1820* (1985).

35 J. Obelkevich, *Religion and Rural Society: South Lindsey 1825–1875* (Oxford, 1976).

36 K. Thomas, *Man and the Natural World: Changing Attitudes in England 1500–1800* (1983).

37 C. Phythian-Adams, 'Rural culture'.

38 R. Porter, *English Society in the Eighteenth Century* (Harmondsworth, 1982), p. 167.

39 M. Jesup, *Extracts from the Memoranda and Letters of Maria Jesup, Late of Halstead in Essex* (York, n.d.), p. 10.

40 Official Directory of Ipswich. *James Allen Ransome: The Story of His Life* (1880); T. A. B. Corley, *Quaker Enterprise in Biscuits: Huntley and Palmers in Reading 1822–1972* (1972).

41 M. A. Hedge, *The Retreat or Sketches from Nature* (Colchester, 1820), p. 6. For a general discussion see K. Figlio and L. Jordanova, 'Myths of creation, knowledge of nature and the production of otherness', unpublished paper, Conference on History and Anthropology (February 1984).

42 William Burgess, 'Reciprocal duties of a minister and his people', sermon

preached at Thorpe-le-Soken, Essex (2 February 1823), *Essex Sermons* (Colchester, n.d.), CBL.

43   J. Obelkevitch, 'Proverbs and social history', in P. Burke and R. Porter (eds.), *Essays in the Social History of Language* (Cambridge, 1986).

44   Quoted in A. D. Harvey, *Britain in the Early Nineteenth Century* (1978), p. 316.

45   Count Pecchio, *Semi-serious Observations of an Italian Exile During His Residence in England* (1833), p. 41; E. M. Butler, *A Regency Visitor: the English Tour of Prince Puckler-Muskau. Described in his Letters 1826–1828* (1957).

46   H. Raynes, *A History of British Insurance* (1948); M. J. Cullen, *The Statistical Movement in Early Modern Britain* (Brighton, 1975). The construction of statistics was part of a political debate about social hierarchy and the role of the state. See P. Buck, 'People who counted: political arithmetic in the eighteenth century', *ISIS*, no. 73 (1982), pp. 42–3. Thanks to Ludmilla Jordanova for this reference.

47   Q. D. Leavis, introduction to Charlotte Bronte's *Jane Eyre* (Harmondsworth, 1973), p. 28; Note how these beliefs were deliberately ridiculed in middle-class literature by showing how the ghost turned out to be a creaking gate, a cow, a donkey. R. Bloomfield, 'The Fakenham Ghost', in Wm. Wickett, and N. David, *The Farmer's Boy: The Story of a Suffolk Poet: Robert Bloomfield, his Life and Poems, 1766–1823* (Lavenham, 1971). Jane and Ann Taylor, 'The Handpost', in *Original Poems for Infant Minds* (1865).

48   M. Weber, 'Religious ethics and the world: sexuality and art', in G. Roth and C. Wittich (eds.), *Economy and Society* (2 vols., Berkeley, 1978), vol. 1.

49   K. Thomas, *Man and the Natural World*, p. 43. M. Chamberlain, *Old Wives Tales: Their History, Remedies and Spells* (1981), ch. 4.

50   L. Davidoff, 'The rationalization of housework', D. Barker and S. Allen (eds.), *Dependency and Exploitation in Work and Marriage* (1976).

51   P. Brown and L. Jordanova, 'Oppressive dichotomies: the nature/culture debate', in Cambridge Women's Studies Group, *Women in Society: Interdisciplinary Essays* (1981).

52   M. Butler, *Romantics, Rebels and Reactionaries: English Literature and its Background* (Oxford, 1981).

53   M. Girouard, *The Return to Camelot: Chivalry and the English Gentleman* (1981).

54   L. Davidoff, J. L'Esperance and H. Newby, 'Landscape with figures: home and community in English society', in J. Mitchell and A. Oakley (eds.), *The Rights and Wrongs of Women* (Harmondsworth, 1976).

55   E. Burke, 'A philosophical inquiry into the origins of our ideas of the sublime and the beautiful' (1756), in F. and J. Rivington, *The Works and Correspondence of Rt. Hon. Edmund Burke* (2 vols., 1852), vol. 2.

56   For some effects of classical education see R. Jenkyns, *The Victorians and Ancient Greece* (Oxford, 1980); J. C. Reid, *Thomas Hood* (1963), p. 103.

57   On Gramsci's notion of 'common sense' see Q. Hoare and G. Nowell Smith (eds.), *Selections from the Prison Notebooks of Antonio Gramsci* (1971), especially 'State and civil society' and 'The philosophy of praxis'.

58   For the importance of dual categories see C. Whitbeck, 'Theories of sex difference', *Philosophical Form*, **5** no. 1 (1973–4); C. Whitbeck, 'A different reality: feminist ontology', in G. Gould (ed.), *Beyond Domination* (New York, 1983).

59   See, for example, J. Winship, 'Sexuality for sale', in S. Hall, D. Hobson, A. Lowe and P. Willis (eds.), *Culture, Media, Language* (1980); R. Coward, *Female Desire* (1984); J. Williamson, *Consuming Passions* (1986).

60   Status is here used as conceived by Max Weber: 'an effective claim to social esteem in terms of positive or negative privileges', in G. Roth and C. Wittich (eds.), vol. 1, p. 305. The importance of consumption in this historical period

has been described in N. McKendrick, 'Commercialization and the economy', in N. McKendrick, J. Brewer and J. H. Plumb (eds.).

61 E. P. Thompson, *The Making of the English Working Class* (1963). For a direct comment on Thompson's characterization of working-class culture see C. Hall, 'The Tale of Samuel and Jemima: gender and working class culture in early nineteenth century England', in T. Bennett, C. Mercer and J. Wollacott (eds.), *Popular Culture and Social Relations* (1986).

62 M. Ryan, *Cradle of the Middle Class: the Family in Oneida County, New York 1790–1865* (Cambridge, 1981).

63 See, for example, M. Darrow, 'French noblewomen and the New Domesticity 1750–1850', *Feminist Studies* (spring 1979); B. Smith, *Ladies of the Leisure Class: the Bourgeoises of Northern France in the Nineteenth Century* (Princeton, 1981); K. Hausen, 'Family and role-division: the polarisation of sexual stereotypes in the nineteenth century', in R. Evans (ed.), *The German Family* (1981). A recent study which takes a more comprehensive view is Suzanne Lebsock, *The Free Women of Petersburg: Status and Culture in a Southern Town 1784–1860* (New York, 1984).

64 M. Douglas, *Purity and Danger: An Analysis of Concepts of Pollution and Taboo* (Harmondsworth, 1966), p. 15.

65 S. Ortner and H. Whitehead, *Sexual Meanings: the Cultural Construction of Gender and Sexuality* (Cambridge, 1981), p. 12.

66 The importance of 'seeing' class and gender operating together is emphasized in J. Kelly, 'The doubled vision of feminist theory', in J. L. Newton, M. Ryan and J. Walkowitz (eds.), *Sex and Class in Women's History* (1983). The use of 'widow' as an occupational category in trade directories is a clear example of the ways in which women remained in a familial frame.

67 M. Chaytor, 'Household and kinship: Ryton in the late sixteenth and early seventeenth centuries', *History Workshop Journal*, no. 10 (autumn 1980), p. 29.

68 A. Kussmaul, *Servants in Husbandry in Early Modern England* (Cambridge, 1981), p. 7.

69 D. R. Bender, 'A refinement of the concept of household: families, co-residence and domestic functions', *American Anthropologist*, **69** (1979); O. Harris, 'Households as natural units', in K. Young, C. Wolkowitz, and R. McCullagh (eds.), *Of Marriage and the Market: Women's Subordination in International Perspective* (1981).

70 P. Bordieu, 'Marriage strategies as strategies of social reproduction', in R. Forster and O. Ranum (eds.), *Family and Society* (Baltimore, 1976).

71 R. Rapp, E. Ross and R. Bridenthal, 'Examining family history', in J. Newton *et al.* (eds.).

72 See, for example, H. Medick, 'The proto-industrial family economy: the structural function of household and family during the transition from peasant society to industrial capitalism', *Social History*, no. 3 (October 1976); N. Smelser, *Social Change in the Industrial Revolution* (1959); M. Anderson, *Family Structure in Nineteenth Century Lancashire* (Cambridge, 1971); T. Hareven, *Family Time and Industrial Time: Relations Between the Family and Work in a New England Industrial Community* (Cambridge, 1982). For a recent critique see D. H. J. Morgan, 'Family history', in *The Family, Politics and Social Theory* (1985).

73 T. S. Koditschek, 'Class formation and the Bradford bourgeoisie', unpublished Ph.D. thesis, University of Princeton (1981); A. Howe, *The Cotton Masters 1830–60* (Oxford, 1984).

74 D. Crozier, 'Kinship and occupational succession', *Sociological Review*, no. 13 (1965).

75 R. J. Morris, 'The middle class and the property cycle during the industrial revolution', in T. C. Smout (ed.), *The Search for Wealth and Stability* (1979).

76 The phrase is Esther Goody's quoted in H. Medick and D. Sabean, 'Interest and emotion in family and kinship studies: a critique of social history and anthropology', in H. Medick and D. Sabean (eds.), *Interest and Emotion: Essays on the Study of Family and Kinship* (Cambridge, 1984), p. 13.

77 Although this is not to argue that women's *property*, *income* and *labour* never entered the market. It was precisely the anomaly of their doing so which was seen as threatening.

78 E. Goody, *Parenthood, Social Reproduction and Occupational Roles in West Africa* (Cambridge, 1982), p. 15.

79 M. Strathern, 'The place of kinship: kin, class and village status in Elmdon', in A. P. Cohen (ed.), *Belonging: Identity and Social Organization in British Rural Culture* (Manchester, 1982).

80 C. Smith-Rosenberg, 'The female world of love and ritual: relations between women in nineteenth century America', *Signs*, 1 no. 1 (autumn 1975); N. Cott, *The Bonds of Womanhood. "Woman's Sphere" in New England 1780–1835* (Yale, 1977).

81 H. Perkin, *The Origins of Modern English Society 1780–1850* (1969), pp. 49–50. For a discussion of the variability of friendship, see R. Brain, *Friends and Lovers* (1977), pp. 12–20.

82 M. Strathern quoted in S. Ortner and H. Whitehead, p. 17.

83 J. Finch, *Married to the Job: Wives Incorporation in Men's Work* (1983). This view of work is a special case of the wider placing of women outside civil society. See J. Landes, *Women and the Public Sphere: A Study in the Representation of Gender Relations 1750–1850* (Indiana University Press, 1986).

84 See A. Yeatman, 'Gender and the differentiation of social life into public and domestic domains', *Social Analysis: Journal of Cultural and Social Practice*, no. 15 (August 1984).

85 We have used a modified version of the approach recommended in A. MacFarlane, *Reconstructing Historical Communities* (Cambridge, 1977).

86 W. A. Armstrong, 'Social structure from the early census returns', in E. A. Wrigley (ed.), *An Introduction to English Historical Demography* (1966).

Setting the scene

1 C. Dickens, *The Pickwick Papers* (Harmondsworth, 1972), p. 801.

2 J. Freeth, 'Birmingham tranquillity', in C. E. Scarse (ed.), *Birmingham 120 Years Ago* (Birmingham, 1876). For visitors reports see *Showells Dictionary of Birmingham* (Birmingham, 1885); C. Goede, *The Stranger in England* (1802); J. G. Kohl, *Ireland, Scotland and England* (1844).

3 W. Hutton, *History of Birmingham* (continued to the present by his daughter, Catherine Hutton) (1819), p. 141.

4 W. Hawkes Smith, *Birmingham and its vicinity as a manufacturing and commercial district* (Birmingham, 1836), preface.

5 J. G. Kohl, p. 11

6 For the economic history of Birmingham see C. Gill, *History of Birmingham* 'Manor and borough to 1865' (Oxford, 1952), vol. 1; Victoria County History, *History of Warwick*, R. B. Pugh (ed.), 'The City of Birmingham' (Oxford, 1964), vol. VII; S. Timmins (ed.), *The Resources, Products and Industrial History of Birmingham and the Midland Hardware District* (1866); G. C. Allen, *The Industrial History of Birmingham and the Black Country 1860–1927* (1929); M. Berg, *The Age of Manufacturers, Industry Innovation and Work in Britain 1700–1820* (1985); W. H. B. Court, *The Rise of Midland Industries 1600–1838*, 2 vols. (Oxford, 1953).

7 H. W. Dickinson, *Matthew Boulton 1728–1809* (Cambridge, 1937).

8 See, for example, W. Hutton and Thomas Carlyle quoted in *Showell's Dictionary of Birmingham*, p. 31.

9 D. E. C. Eversley, 'Industry and trade 1500–1880', in V.C.H., vol. VII; C. Behagg, 'Custom, class and change: the trade societies of Birmingham', in *Social History*, 4 no. 3 (1979); C. Behagg, 'Masters and manufacturers: social values and the smaller unit of production in Birmingham, 1800–1850', in G. Crossick and H. G. Haupt (eds.), *Shopkeepers and Master Artisans in Nineteenth Century Europe* (1984).

10 W. Hutton.

11 B. Little, *Birmingham Buildings: The Architectural Story of a Midland City* (Newton Abbot, 1971).

12 C. Gill.

13 See, for example, D. Cannadine, *Lords and Landlords: the aristocracy and the towns 1774–1967* (Leicester, 1980).

14 H. S. Pearson, 'New Street', in *Birmingham Archeological Society Transactions*, 40 (1914); H. H. Horton, *Birmingham: A Poem in Two Parts* (Birmingham, 1851); J. A. Langford, 'New Street a century ago', in *The Central Literary Magazine*, 2 nos. 1–2 (1875); E. Edwards, *The Hen and Chickens Hotel Birmingham* (Birmingham, 1878).

15 W. Hutton, p. 399.

16 D. E. H. Mole, 'The Church of England and society in Birmingham 1830–66', unpublished Ph.D. thesis, University of Cambridge (1961).

17 On the political history of Birmingham see J. T. Bunce, *The History of the Corporation of Birmingham* (Birmingham, 1878), vol. 1; R. B. Rose, 'Political history of Birmingham to 1832', in V.C.H.; C. Gill; E. P. Hennock, *Fit and Proper Persons: Ideal and Reality in 19th century urban government* (1973); D. Fraser, *Urban Politics in Victorian England* (Leicester, 1973); C. Flick, *The Birmingham Political Union and the Movements for Reform in Britain 1830–39* (Connecticut, 1978); J. Money, *Experience and Identity: Birmingham and the West Midlands 1760–1800* (Manchester, 1977).

18 C. Behagg, 'An alliance with the middle class: the Birmingham Political Union and early Chartism', in J. Epstein and D. Thompson (eds.), *The Chartist Experience: Studies in Working Class Radicalism and Culture 1830–60* (1982), p. 74.

19 W. White, *History, Gazetteer and Directory of the County of Essex* (Sheffield, 1848), pp. 13 and 49.

20 E. A. Wrigley, 'A simple model of London's importance in changing English society and economy, 1650–1750', in D. A. Burgh (ed.), *Aristocratic Government and Society in 18th Century England* (New York, 1975).

21 A. F. J. Brown, *Essex at Work* (Chelmsford, 1969).

22 A. C. Edwards, *A History of Essex* (1962).

23 A. F. J. Brown, *Witham in the 18th Century* (Witham, 1968).

24 H. Benham, *Some Essex Water Mills* (Colchester, 1976).

25 B. A. Holderness, '"Open" and "Close" parishes in England in the 18th and 19th centuries', *Agricultural History Review*, 20 (1922).

26 A. Young, *General View of the Agriculture of the County of Essex*, 2 vols. (1807), vol. 1.

27 North-west Suffolk, hillier and more wooded, retained dairy farming. A recent article challenges the view that small family-worked plots disappeared but, undoubtedly, larger commercial farms set the pace. M. Reed, 'The peasantry of nineteenth-century England: a neglected class?', *History Workshop Journal*, no. 18 (autumn 1984).

28 W. and H. Raynbird, *On the Agriculture of Suffolk* (1849).

29 J. Saville, 'Primitive accumulation and early industrialization in Britain', *Socialist Register* (1969).

30 J. Saville, p. 256.
31 *Essex Directory* (1791); *Essex Post Office Directory* (1850).
32 J. Booker, *Essex and the Industrial Revolution* (Chelmsford, 1974).
33 H. Benham, *Some Essex Water Mills.*
34 Census of Great Britain.
35 A. F. J. Brown, *Colchester 1815–1914* (Chelmsford, 1980).
36 B. Mason, *Clock and Watchmaking in Colchester* (1969).
37 J. Tuffs, *Essex Coaching Days* (Letchworth, n.d.).
38 A. F. J. Brown, *Essex People 1750–1900 from their Diaries, Memoirs and Letters* (Chelmsford, 1972).
39 A. F. J. Brown, *Essex at Work* (Chelmsford, 1969).
40 A. F. J. Brown, *Witham in the 18th Century* (Witham, 1969).
41 Janet Gyford, personal communication.
42 M. C. Wadhams, 'The development of buildings in Witham from 1500 to circa 1880', *Post-Medieval Archeology*, 6 (1972).
43 Witham File.
44 H. N. Dixon, 'Reminiscences of an Essex county practitioner a century ago', *Essex Review*, **xxiii** (1914), p. 92.
45 Witham Census 1851: thirty professionals were born outside Witham and of these, seventeen outside the county, while fifty-eight tradesmen were born outside the town and twenty-seven outside the county.
46 J. Player, *Sketches of Saffron Walden and its Vicinity* (Saffron Walden, 1845).
47 A. F. J. Brown, *Colchester 1815–1914* (Chelmsford, 1980).
48 M. Speight, 'Politics in the Borough of Colchester 1812–1847', unpublished Ph.D. thesis, University of London (1969).
49 Philip Hills, personal communication.
50 S. P. Watson, 'Nineteenth century Witham: the role of local government', unpublished B.A. project, Department of History, University of Essex (1978).
51 C. Brightwen Rowntree, *Saffron Walden – Then and Now* (Chelmsford, 1951).
52 A. F. J. Brown, *Colchester*, p. 78.
53 A. F. J. Brown, *The Chartist Movement in Essex and Suffolk* (University of Essex, 1979). For the role of Barmby and his wife in Owenite socialist and feminist causes see B. Taylor, *Eve and the New Jerusalem. Socialism and Feminism in the Nineteenth Century* (1983).
54 Essex and Suffolk File.
55 Between 1821 and 1831, Birmingham increased by 38 per cent; Essex and Suffolk by 13 per cent. Census of GB.
56 We did not compute birth place for the census sample but careful examination 'by eye' left the impression of many newcomers among the middle class. See also T. Kodischek, 'Class formation and the Bradford bourgeoisie', unpublished Ph.D. thesis, University of Princeton (1981).
57 J. Gyford, 'Men of bad character: property crime in Essex in the 1820s', unpublished M.A., University of Essex (1982); E. Hobsbawm and G. Rudé, *Captain Swing* (1969).
58 For example, a future Astronomer Royal, from Colchester Grammar School, son of a small farmer turned exciseman. W. Airy (ed.), *Autobiography of Sir George Biddell Airy* (Cambridge, 1896).
59 G. Cadbury quoted in A. G. Gardiner, *Life of George Cadbury* (1923), p. 17. All material on the Cadburys has been drawn from the Cadbury Collection and other Cadbury materials in the Birmingham Reference Library. The archive includes: 'Letters from Richard Tapper Cadbury and his wife Elizabeth to members of the family. 1806–55', BRL 466/300/1–21; 'Letters from Richard Tapper Cadbury to his wife Elizabeth (Head) Cadbury 1801–51', BRL 466/299/1–54; 'A collection of letters concerning the family of Benjamin and Candia Cadbury 1805–51', BRL 614280; 'Letters from John Cadbury mainly

to his parents Richard Tapper and Elizabeth Cadbury written during visits in Leeds. 6 May 1819–15 Sept. 1822', BRL 466/247; 'Collection of letters from John Cadbury addressed mainly to his wife Candia, written during John's visits in Ireland. 19 May 1842–8 June 1846', BRL 466/258; 'John Cadbury's account of his father Richard Tapper Cadbury', BRL 466/310/1–3; 'John Cadbury's notes on the death of his wife Candia Cadbury 3 March 1855', BRL 466/264/1–6; 'Candia Cadbury's Recipe Book', BRL 466/104; 'Letters from Candia to her daughter Maria, whilst at school 1853–54' BRL 466/102/1–6; 'Letters from Richard Cadbury to his sister Maria 28 March 1846–4 Nov. 1855', BRL 466/285/1–11; 'Letters from Henry Cadbury to his brothers, Richard and John 1849–56' 466/231/1–2; 'Letters from Henry Cadbury to his sister, Maria, 1852–54', BRL 466/232/1–5; 'Letters from Edward Cadbury to his sister, Maria, 1850–56', BRL 466/106/1–5; 'Letters from Richard Cadbury to his sister Maria 28 March 1846–4 Nov. 1855', BRL 466/285/ 1–11; 'Letters from Maria Cadbury to her parents whilst at Lewes School 23 March–9 November 1835', BRL 466/341/1–6; Maria Cadbury's Book of childhood reminiscences 'The Happy Days of our Childhood', BRL 466/344; 'Cadbury Family Book', BRL 466/445; The wills of Richard Tapper Cadbury (1860), Benjamin Head Cadbury (1880), Maria Cadbury (1887), Candia Cadbury (1888), John Cadbury (1889) are in the Probate Collection, BRL. Printed sources on the Cadburys include E. Gibbins, *Records of the Gibbins Family also a few reminiscences of Emma S. Gibbins and letters and papers relating to the Bevington Family* (Birmingham, 1911); H. C. Alexander, *Richard Cadbury* (1906); A. G. Gardiner and I. A. Williams, *The Firm of Cadbury 1831–1931* (1931); Barrows, *Barrows': A Store Record 1824–1949* (Birmingham, 1949); T. Insull, *John Cadbury 1801–89* (Birmingham, 1979).

60 J. Cadbury, 'On Richard Tapper Cadbury'.
61 E. Gibbins, appendix 1, p. 247.
62 J. Cadbury, 'On Richard Tapper Cadbury'.
63 M. Cadbury, 'The Happy Days of our Childhood'.
64 H. C. Alexander, p. 110.
65 A. G. Gardiner, p. 25.
66 Elizabeth Cadbury to Maria Cadbury and Sarah Barrow, 3 June 1828, 'Cadbury Family Letters'.
67 Candia Cadbury to Hannah Cadbury, n.d., 'A Collection of letters concerning the family of Benjamin and Candia Cadbury 1806–51'.
68 This section is based on the following sources:

Works about the Taylors:
D. M. Armitage, *The Taylors of Ongar: Portrait of an English Family in the 18th and 19th Centuries* (Cambridge, 1939); J. Bensusan-Butt, 'Jane and Ann Taylor as engravers', *Essex County Standard* (12 Jan. 1968); E. Blaikley, 'Four Isaac Taylors', *East Anglian Magazine*, 21 (1961–2), pp. 682–3; Colchester Library Bi-centenary Exhibit, Dec. 1983; L. Davidoff, *Life is Duty, Praise and Prayer: Some Contributions of the New Women's History* (1981); G. E. Harris, *Contributions Towards a Bibliography of the Taylors of Ongar and Stanford Rivers* (London, 1965); H. C. Knight, *Jane Taylor: Her Life and Letters* (1880); W. M. Letts, 'Ann Taylors Friend', Ms. WSRO HD 588/5/8; F. M. Savill, *Ann and Jane Taylor: A Colchester Reminiscence* (Colchester, c 1900); C. Stewart, *The Taylors of Ongar: An Analytical Bio-Bibliography*, 2 vols. (New York, 1975).

Works by the Taylors:
Rev. Isaac Taylor, *The Family Pen: Memorials, Biographical and Literary of the Taylor Family of Ongar* (1867); Jane Taylor, *Display* (1815); Jane Taylor,

Essays in Rhyme (1816); Jane Taylor, *Memoirs and Poetical Remains* (ed. Isaac Junior) (1831); Jane Taylor, *The Contributions of QQ* (1845) (Appearances in *Youth's Magazine of Evangelical Miscellany*); Ann Taylor Gilbert, *Sketches from a Youthful Circle* (1834); Ann Taylor Gilbert, *Autobiography and Other Memorials of Mrs Gilbert*, (ed. Josiah Gilbert), 2 vols. (1874); Ann and Jane Taylor, *Original Poems for Infant Minds* (1865); Ann and Jane Taylor, *Rural Scenes: or a Peep into the Country* (1848); Ann and Jane Taylor, *Rhymes for the Nursery* (1877); Jemima Taylor, unpublished recollections WSRO HD588/6/107; Josiah Conder (ed.), *The Associate Minstrels* (1813); Wills of Isaac Taylor (1829), PRO Prob 11/1764; Ann M. Taylor (1830), PRO Prob 11/1773 (for a full bibliography of Ann Martin Taylor's books see Chapter 3, note 114).

69 Ann Taylor Gilbert, *Autobiography*, vol. 1, p. 75.
70 Rev. Isaac Taylor, *The Family Pen*, vol. 1, p. 85.
71 H. Pinchback, *Ongar Congregational Church Essex* (1937).
72 Jane Taylor, *Memoirs*, p. 5.
73 Ann Taylor Gilbert, *Autobiography*, vol. 1, p. 105.
74 Jane Taylor, *Memoirs*, p. 95.
75 ibid., p. 107.
76 This book was dedicated to James Montgomery, a radical nonconformist who also wrote domestic poetry. One of Ann Taylor Gilbert's sons was James Montgomery Gilbert.
77 Jane Taylor, *Memoirs*, p. 72.
78 Since it was this 'dear little child' who edited the autobiography perhaps this should be taken with caution. Ann Taylor Gilbert, *Autobiography*, vol. 1, pp. 283 and 291.
79 Jane Taylor, *Memoirs*, p. 160.
80 Rev. Isaac Taylor, *The Family Pen*, vol. 1, p. 98.
81 Jane Taylor, *Memoirs*, p. 74.
82 Ann Taylor Gilbert, *Autobiography*, vol. 11, p. 19.

Introduction to Part One

1 J. Barrell, *English Literature in History 1730–80: An Equal Wide Survey* (1983).
2 T. W. Davids, 'Englands obligations to her pious men'. Sermon preached at Lion Walk Congregational church, Colchester, 9 April 1848, *Essex Sermons* (Colchester, n.d.), CBL.
3 Rev. C. B. Tayler, *Edward or Almost an Owenite* (1840).

Chapter 1 'The one thing needful': religion and the middle class

1 K. S. Inglis, *The Churches and the Working Classes in Victorian England* (1963).
2 R. A. Soloway, *Prelates and People: Ecclesiastical Social Thought in England 1783–1852* (1969); J. Obelkevich, *Religion and Rural Society: South Lindsey 1825–75* (Oxford, 1976); H. McLeod, *Religion and the People of Western Europe 1789–1970* (Oxford, 1981).
3 Quoted in H. McLeod, ibid., p. 107.
4 R. Bretnall, 'Unpublished Diary', ERO D/DBsF38, 24 July 1846. Thanks to Janet Gyford.
5 A. D. Gilbert, *Religion and Society in Industrial England. Church, Chapel and Social Change 1740–1914* (1976), p. 89.
6 M. Jesup, *Selections from the Writing of Mary Jesup: late of Halstead Essex* (1842), p. 24.

7   C. Binfield, *So Down to Prayers, Studies in English Nonconformity 1780–1920* (1977), p. 11.

8   C. Sturge, *Family Records* (1882), p. 107.

9   E. Gibbins, *Records of the Gibbins Family also a few reminiscences of Emma J. Gibbins and letters and papers relating to the Bevington Family* (Birmingham, 1911), p. 187.

10 The particular relation between Puritanism and the middling ranks in the seventeenth century has been the subject of a major historical debate. See particularly C. Hill, *Society and Puritanism in Pre-Revolutionary England* (1964). Defoe's Moll Flanders, by contrast, strikes a more secular eighteenth-century note.

11 F. K. Brown, *Fathers of the Victorians: The Age of Wilberforce* (Cambridge, 1961); A. D. Gilbert and T. W. Laqueur, *Religion and Respectability: Sunday Schools and Working Class Culture 1780–1850* (New Haven, 1976); F. E. Mineka, *The Dissidence of Dissent: the Monthly Repository 1806–38* (North Carolina, 1944).

12 H. N. Dixon, 'Reminiscences of an Essex county practitioner a century ago', *Essex Review*, **xxiii** (1914).

13 J. Walsh, 'The Anglican Evangelicals in the eighteenth century', quoted in T. W. Laqueur, p. 102.

14 W. Hutton, *History of Birmingham (continued to the present time by his daughter Catherine Hutton)* (1819).

15 Birmingham File.

16 C. P. Fox and J. Melville, 'Unpublished Diary of a Visit to Bingley Hall, Birmingham, 1819', BRL 669392, p. 16.

17 D. E. H. Mole, 'The Church of England and society in Birmingham 1830–66', unpublished Ph.D. thesis, University of Cambridge (1961).

18 D. E. H. Mole; H. McLeod, p. 84.

19 C. M. Marsh, *The Life of the Rev. William Marsh* (1868).

20 A. D. Gilbert, p. 121.

21 J. Glyde, *Suffolk in the 19th Century: Physical, Social, Moral Religious and Industrial* (1855), p. 263; K. S. Inglis, 'Patterns of religious worship in 1851', *The Journal of Ecclesiastical History*, **XI** no. 1 (April 1960).

22 K. S. Inglis, ibid.; D. E. H. Mole, 'Challenge to the church: Birmingham 1815–65' in H. J. Dyos and M. Wolff (eds.), *The Victorian City*, 2 vols. (1973), vol. 2.

23 M. Speight, 'Politics in the Borough of Colchester', unpublished Ph.D. thesis, University of London (1969), p. 250.

24 W. D. Balda, 'Spheres of influence: Simeon's Trust and its implications for Evangelical patronage', unpublished Ph.D. thesis, University of Cambridge (1981).

25 I. Bradley, *The Call to Seriousness: the Evangelical Impact on the Victorians* (1976); Birmingham and Essex and Suffolk Files.

26 A. D. Gilbert, p. 40; R. W. Ram, 'The social evolution of Five Dissenting communities', unpublished Ph.D. thesis, University of Birmingham (1972).

27 Rev. Bickersteth, quoted in O. Chadwick, *The Victorian Church*, 2 vols. (1966), vol. 1, p. 443.

28 Quoted in F. E. Mineka, p. 142.

29 W. Wilberforce, *A Practical View of the Prevailing Religious System of Professed Christians in the Higher and Middle Classes in this Country, Contrasted with real Christianity* (1797); R. I. and S. Wilberforce, *The Life of William Wilberforce*, 5 vols. (1838). There is an extensive secondary literature on the Evangelicals. See particularly, F. K. Brown; I. Bradley; W. D. Balda.

30   T. Gisborne, *An Enquiry into the Duties of Men in the Higher and Middle Classes of Society*, 2 vols. (1794).

31   W. D. Balda; C. M. Marsh.

32   Essex and Suffolk File.

33   D. Newsome, *The Parting of Friends* (1966), p. 8.

34   O. Chadwick.

35   D. E. H. Mole, 'The Church of England and society in Birmingham'.

36   D. E. H. Mole, ibid.; D. N. Cannadine, 'The aristocracy and the towns in the nineteenth century: a case study of the Calthorpes and Birmingham 1807–1910', unpublished D.Phil Thesis, Oxford (1975).

37   W. W. Stephens, *The Life and Letters of Walter Farquhar Hook 1798–1875*, 2 vols. (1878), vol. 2, p. 122; H. J. Everson, 'A Chronological History of Moseley, Balsall Heath, Kings Heath and King's Norton compiled from Aris's Birmingham Gazette', 5 vols. (1920–30), BRL 617940, vol. 5 (4 June 1827).

38   D. E. H. Mole, 'The Church of England and society in Birmingham'.

39   J. A. James, *Christian Fellowship or the Church Members' Guide* (Birmingham, 1822), p. 128.

40   C. Binfield, p. x.

41   ibid., p. 12.

42   R. W. Ram.

43   Quoted in J. Bennett, *The History of Dissenters from the Revolution to the year 1808*, 2 vols. (1833), vol. 1, p. 200.

44   E. D. Bebb, *Nonconformity and Social and Economic Life 1600–1800* (1935), p. 115.

45   R. W. Dale, *History of English Congregationalism* (1907), p. 482.

46   J. Bennett, vol. I, p. 169.

47   A. D. Gilbert, p. 36; E. Isichei, *Victorian Quakers* (Oxford, 1970).

48   M. Bayly, *The Life and Letters of Mrs Sewell* (1889), p. 68.

49   E. Isichei.

50   H. Allen, *A Beloved Mother. Life of Hannah S. Allen by her Daughter* (1884).

51   M. Jesup, p. 83.

52   See, for example, J. A. James, *Youthful Consecration; a Memorial of Rosalinda Phipson with an Introduction by John Angell James* (1844).

53   Rev. J. G. Breay, *A Memoir of the Rev. John George Breay, Minister of Christ Church Birmingham, with Correspondence and a Sermon* (Birmingham, 1840), pp. 79 and 393.

54   M. Jesup, *Extracts from the Memoranda and Letters of Maria Jesup, Late of Halstead, Essex* (York, n.d.), p. 10; A. Camps, *The Diary and Work of Mrs Amy Camps, with extracts from her Writing* (1893), p. 28.

55   Rev. C. Tayler, *Personal Recollections: With a Memoir*, Religious Tract Society (n.d.)

56   A. Camps, p. 83.

57   Biddell Collection, IRO HAq/D/2.

58   ibid.

59   M. Bayly, p. 78.

60   C. M. Marsh, preface.

61   H. Pinchback, *Ongar Congregational Church, Essex* (1937), p. 11.

62   See, for example, R. W. Evans, *The Rectory of Valehead* (1839).

63   *Christian Observer*, 19 no. 3 (1820).

64   M. Hennell, 'Edward Bickersteth', in *Sons of the Prophets: Evangelical Leaders of the Victorian Church* (1979).

65   Marsh children, *Memorials of a Beloved Mother by her children* (Birmingham, 1837).

66   Anon, unpublished diary of a farmer's wife on the Warwick/Leicester border (1823), 17 March 1823, BUL, Heslop Coll. Ms 10/iii/15.

67 John Perry, 'Unpublished Diary' 1818–42, 13 December 1838, FHL, Box T; H. N. Dixon, Unpublished Diary, 1841–50, November 1844. By permission of Dr Denholm and thanks to Janet Gyford.
68 Marsh children, p. 26.
69 M. Jesup, *Extracts*, p. 12.
70 J. Taylor, *Display* (1817), 6th edn, p. 184.
71 See for example H. Allen.
72 M. Jesup, *Selections*, p. 40.
73 R. I. and S. Wilberforce, *Life of William Wilberforce*, includes in vol. 1 copies of Wilberforce's weekly timetables.
74 H. C. Colman, *Jeremiah James Colman: A Memoir* (1905), p. 35.
75 G. H. Pike, *Charles Haddon Spurgeon: Preacher, Author and Philanthropist* (1886), p. 8.
76 E. Shewell, *Memoir of the late John Talwin Shewell* (Ipswich, 1870), pp. 54 and 62.
77 A. and J. Taylor, *The Poetical Works of Ann and Jane Taylor* (1877), p. 6.
78 J. A. James, *A Memoir of Mrs Elizabeth Bayley of Birmingham* (Birmingham, 1856), p. 60.
79 M. Priestman, *Cowper's "Task": Structure and Influence* (Cambridge, 1983), p. 7; J. Hopkins, *A Woman to Deliver her People: Joanna Southcott and English Milennarianism in an era of Revolution* (Austin, 1982).
80 Samuel Newton in file on Independent ministers, DWL; R. Winter, *The Character and Honour of the Approved Minister, A Sermon on the much lamented death of the Rev. Samuel Newton* (1822).
81 C. M. Marsh, p. 89.
82 ibid., p. 159.
83 G. R. Hamilton, 'Vicar of St. Peter's', in *James Hurnard: A Victorian Character* (Cambridge, 1946).
84 J. A. James, *The Crisis; or Hope and Fear Balanced*, a sermon delivered at Ebenezer chapel, 28 November 1819 (Birmingham, 1819), p. 27.
85 R. W. Dale (ed.), *Life and Letters of John Angell James including an unfinished autobiography* (1861), p. 339.
86 D. E. H. Mole, 'John Cale Miller: a Victorian Rector of Birmingham', *The Journal of Ecclesiastical History*, **XVII** no. 1 (1965).
87 J. P. Fitzgerald, *The Quiet Worker for Good, a Familiar Sketch of the Late John Charlesworth* (Ipswich, 1865), p. 43.
88 J. A. James, *The Crisis*.
89 For material on Owenism and Evangelicalism see B. Taylor, *Eve and the New Jerusalem: Socialism and Feminism in the Nineteenth Century* (1983).
90 E. P. Thompson, *The Making of the English Working Class* (1963), p. 827.
91 A. Briggs, 'The political history of Birmingham from 1832', in *VCH History of Warwick*, R. B. Pugh (ed.), 'The City of Birmingham', vol. VII; C. Flick, *The Birmingham Political Union and the Movement for Reform in Britain 1830–39* (Connecticut, 1978); C. M. Wakefield, *Life of Thomas Attwood* (1885).
92 J. A. James, in *Female Piety or the Young Woman's Friend and Guide through Life to Immortality*, 5th edn (1856), warned young women of the terrible dangers they faced from revolutionary politics if not under the protection of Christ.
93 Rev. C. Craven, *Church Extension or the Duty of the State in its Relation to the Church at the Present Period* (Birmingham, 1843), p. 16.
94 Rev. W. Marsh, *AntiChrist Detected* (Birmingham, 1841), p. 11.
95 Rev C. B. Tayler, *Edward, or almost an Owenite* (1840), p. 13 (his italics).
96 L. E. O'Rorke (ed.), *The Life and Friendships of Catherine Marsh* (1917), p. 290.

97   J. Seabrook, 'Faith without Works', unpublished Commonplace Book, Boreham, Essex (1829), by permission of Mary Mallawartarchi, Colchester, Essex.

98   Mrs W. Byng Kenrick (ed.), *Chronicles of a Nonconformist Family: The Kenricks of Wynne Hall, Exeter and Birmingham*, p. 217.

99   R. V. Holt, *The Unitarian Contribution to Social Progress in England* (1938); F. E. Mineka; R. W. Ram; J. Seed, 'The role of unitarianism in the formation of liberal culture 1775–1851', unpublished Ph.D. thesis, University of Hull (1981).

100 H. New, *Centenary of the Church of the Messiah Sunday School. Sketch of the History of the Schools from 1788 to the Present* (Birmingham, 1888); E. Bushrod, 'The history of Unitarianism in Birmingham from the mid eighteenth century to 1893', unpublished M.A. dissertation, University of Birmingham (1954); J. Money, *Experience and Identity: Birmingham and the West Midlands 1760–1800* (Manchester, 1977); M. Frost, 'The development of provided schooling for working class children in Birmingham 1781–1851', unpublished M.Litt. thesis, University of Birmingham (1978).

101 S. Madan, *The Principal Claims of the Dissenters Considered* (Birmingham, 1790); G. Croft, quoted in J. Money, *Experience and Identity*, p. 222.

102 Rev. Walter Birch, 'On infidelity and enthusiasm', sermon preached 28 July 1818 at St Peter's Colchester', *Colchester and Essex Sermons*, CBL, n.d., p. 8.

103 R. B. Rose, 'Political history of Birmingham to 1832', V.C.H., vol. 7; R. B. Rose, 'The Priestley Riots of 1791', *Past and Present*, no. 18 (Nov. 1960); E. P. Thompson.

104 See M. Russell, 'The Birmingham Riots, July 1791', BRL 486799; 'Journal of a tour to America, 1794–1795', BRL 660348; S. H. Jeyes, *The Russells of Birmingham in the French Revolution and in America, 1791–1814* (1911); W. Hutton, *The Life of William Hutton, Stationer of Birmingham and the History of his Family* (1816); Mrs C. H. Beale, *Reminiscences of a Gentlewoman of the Last Century* (Birmingham, 1891).

105 E. P. Thompson, p. 178.

106 D. M. Armitage, *The Taylors of Ongar: Portrait of an English Family of the 18th and 19th Centuries* (Cambridge, 1939).

107 See, for example, the Missionary movement in J. Walsh, 'Methodism at the end of the 18th century', in R. Davies, A. R. George and G. Rupp (eds.), *A History of the Methodist Church in Great Britain*, 2 vols. (1978), vol. 1.

108 G. F. A. Best, *Temporal Pillars. Queen Anne's Bounty, the Ecclesiastical Commissioners and the Church of England* (Cambridge, 1964); R. A. Soloway.

109 See for example, J. T. Bunce, *History of the Corporation of Birmingham*, 2 vols. (Birmingham, 1878), vol. I; C. Brightwen Rowntree, *Saffron Walden – Then and Now* (Chelmsford, 1951).

110 S. L. Courtauld, *The Hugnenot Family of Courtauld*, 3 vols. (Oxford, 1969), vol. I.

111 H. H. Horton, *Birmingham. A Poem in two parts dedicated to William Scholefield M.P.* (Birmingham, 1851); D. E. H. Mole, 'The Church of England and society in Birmingham'.

112 J. Kenrick, *Memoir of the Rev. John Kentish* (Birmingham, 1854); H. Hutton, *Gathered Leaves of Many Seasons* (1858).

113 King Edward Sixth School, Birmingham 'Governors order book, 1832–41'. By permission of Mr Walkington, Secretary to the Governors of King Edwards.

114 D. Newsome; M. Hill, 'The role of women in Victorian society: sisterhood, deaconesses and the growth of nursing', in M. Hill, *The Religious Order* (1973).

115 G. F. A. Best.

116 G. F. A. Best; J. Obelkevich.

117 I. Bradley.
118 J. Fletcher, *Christian Sanctity Exemplified and Rewarded* (Birmingham, 1819), p. 22. In this way, evangelical religion for the middle classes acted much as Methodism did for the working class, which substituted 'a frock coat for his posy jacket, hymns for his public-house ditties, prayer meetings for his pay night frolics', J. Walsh, p. 311.
119 D. R. Thomason, 'Journal of a visit to Birmingham during the Christmas vacation' (unpublished journal), BRL 822.
120 A. Camps.
121 A. Watkins, *Extracts from the Memoranda and Letters of Ann Watkins* (Ipswich, 1888).
122 Rev. J. Fielding, *A Series of Letters Addressed to the Church and Congregation Assembling at the Great Meeting, Coggeshall* (Coggeshall, 1815), p. 181.
123 E. Bushrod.
124 J. Howgego, 'Unpublished Diary, 1829–1834', by permission of V. Sheldrake.
125 H. C. Bentall, *A Merchant Adventurer: Being the biography of Leonard Hugh Bentall* (1936), p. 20.
126 C. C. Hankin (ed.), *Life of Mary Ann Schimmelpenninck* (1859); H. N. Dixon.
127 Essex and Suffolk File; J. Penfold, *The History of the Essex County Hospital, Colchester 1820–1948* (Colchester, 1984), p. 65. Mackintosh's wife had also been a member of the Taylor's youthful circle in the 1800s. Her sister was the 'original' on which Jane Taylor's *Display* was based.
128 S. Galton, 'Address to the Friends of the monthly meeting of Birmingham by Samuel Galton re his manufacturing arms' (1795), BRL Galton Family Papers, 194; W. A. Richards, 'The Birmingham gun manufactory of Farmer and Galton and the slave trade in the eighteenth century', unpublished M.A. dissertation, University of Birmingham (1972).
129 C. Bax, *Highways and Byways in Essex* (1939), p. 84.
130 W. Banks Austin, 'Unpublished Diary 1851–2', BRL 710101; R. W. Dale, *The Funeral Sermon for John Angell James* (Birmingham, 1859).
131 Essex and Suffolk File.
132 ABG, 10 and 24 April 1820.
133 W. H. Ryland (ed.), *Reminiscences of Thomas Henry Ryland* (Birmingham, 1904), p. 6.
134 Witham File.
135 See, for example, Jane Taylor's one novel, *Display* (1815) and E. Sewell, *Katherine Ashton* (1854).
136 A letter quoted in Witham Congregational church minutes 11 November 1848 (1822–49), ERO D/NC3/2.
137 J. Taylor, *Display* (1815).

Chapter 2 'Ye are all one in Christ Jesus': men, women and religion

1 On the seventeenth-century debate see particularly C. Hill, *The World Turned Upside Down* (1972). On the general trend towards the silencing of women preachers see H. McLeod, *Religion and the People of Western Europe 1789–1970* (Oxford, 1981), especially ch. 2.
2 J. Obelkevich, *Religion and Rural Society: South Lindsey 1825–75* (Oxford, 1976), p. 313.
3 H. McLeod.
4 *Family Prayers for Everyday of the Week: Culled from the Bible for Morning and Evening* (1824).
5 S. Meacham, *Henry Thornton of Clapham 1760–1815* (Cambridge, Mass., 1964).

6 On the seventeenth-century Puritan beliefs see particularly C. Hill, *Society and Puritanism in Pre-Revolutionary England* (1964), ch. 13.

7 E. M. Forster, *Marianne Thornton: A Domestic Biography 1797–1887* (1956), p. 20.

8 Corder Family, 'My Home and Friends' (1846), ERO TB/228/3.

9 G. S. Bull, *'Home' and How to Make it Happy* (Birmingham, 1854).

10 'Family Worship' in *Leisure Hour* (May 1852) found in the attic of an Essex farmhouse.

11 R. H. Inglis (ed.), *Family Prayers* compiled by Henry Thornton (1834); thirty-one editions had been published by 1854.

12 T. S. James (ed.), *The Works of John Angell James*, 17 vols. (Birmingham, 1860–4), vol. 12 *The Family Monitor, or a Help to Domestic Happiness*, p. 17.

13 Phipson Children, *A Tribute to a Father's Memory* (Birmingham, 1864).

14 Rev. J. G. Breay, *A Memoir of the Rev. John George Breay, Minister of Christ Church Birmingham, with correspondence and a sermon* (Birmingham, 1840).

15 C. M. Marsh, *The Life of the Rev. William Marsh* (1868), p. 2.

16 J. Glyde, 'The autobiography of a Suffolk farm labourer', *Suffolk Mercury* (1844).

17 C. M. Marsh, p. 2.

18 H. Groome, *Two Suffolk Friends* (1895), p. 13.

19 Rev. C. B. Tayler, 'The Holme Farm', in *May You Like It* (1823).

20 Quoted in P. Honan, *Matthew Arnold. A Life* (1981), p. 168.

21 T. Gisborne, *An Enquiry into the Duties of Men in the Higher and Middle Classes of Society*, 2 vols. (1794).

22 G. Thomas, *William Cowper and the 18th Century* (1948), p. 13.

23 W. Cowper, *The Task*, p. 541.

24 T. Clarkson, *A Portraiture of Quakerism*, 2 vols. (1807), p. 128.

25 R. Winter, *The Character and Honour of the Approved Minister: A sermon on the much lamented death of the Rev. Samuel Newton* (1822), p. 26.

26 J. A. James, 'The young man from home', in T. S. James, vol. 5, p. 422.

27 ibid., p. 468.

28 C. Hill; L. Stone, *The Family, Sex and Marriage 1500–1800* (1977); R. Trumbach, *The Rise of the Egalitarian Family. Aristocratic Kinship and Domestic Relations in Eighteenth-Century England* (New York, 1978).

29 J. A. James, 'Christian mercy explained and enforced', in T. S. James, vol. 1, p. 239.

30 Our underlining. ibid., 'The family monitor, or a help to domestic happiness', vol. 12, p. 78.

31 *The Christian Lady's Friend and Family Repository* (1832–3), p. 2.

32 ibid., p. 186.

33 Mrs E. Bayley, *A Memoir of Mrs Elizabeth Bayley of Birmingham with an Introduction and Reflections by John Angell James* (Birmingham, 1856), p. 187.

34 J. A. James, *Female Piety or the Young Woman's Friend and Guide through Life to Immortality* (5th edn, 1856), p. 63.

35 ibid., p. 63.

36 See, for example, C. C. Hankin (ed), *Life of Mary Ann Schimmelpenninck* (3rd edn, 1859), p. 105.

37 H. More, *Coelebs in Search of a Wife: Comprehending of Domestic Habits and Manners, Religious and Morals*, 2 vols. (9th edn, 1809).

38 Rev. T. Binney, 'Martha of Jerusalem or the Hebrew Wife', in *Mothers and Maidens or the Christian Spinster and the Hebrew Wife: A book for young women* (1850), p. 39; Rev. T. Binney, *Address on the Subject of Middle Class*

Female Education (Bishops Stortford, 1873), p. 64. H. Dixon, the Witham doctor, was one of the young men who 'sat under' Binney.

39   J. A. James, 'To young mothers', in *Female Piety*.
40   Rev. C. B. Tayler, 'The merchants' wife', *May You Like It* (1823), pp. 112 and 128.
41   W. Thackeray, *The Newcomes*, 2 vols. (1853), vol. I, pp. 20–1. The reality for Marianne Thornton, daughter of Henry Thornton, and at the heart of the Clapham Sect, was that the nearest she ever got to the family bank was to be entertained to dinner in the board room. E. M. Forster.
42   M. Ryan, *Cradle of the Middle Class. The Family in Oneida County, New York 1790–1865* (Cambridge, 1981), p. 87.
43   Rev. T. Binney, *Maidens and Mothers*, p. 57.
44   Rev. T. Davids, *England's Obligation to her Pious Men*. A sermon preached at Lion Walk, Colchester, 9 April 1840, *Essex Sermons* (Colchester, n.d.), p. 22, CBL.
45   A. J. Russell, 'A sociological analysis of the clergyman's role with special reference to its development in the early nineteenth century', unpublished D.Phil thesis, University of Oxford (1970); B. Heeney, *A Different Kind of Gentleman. Parish Clergy or Professional Men in Early and mid-Victorian England* (Connecticut, 1976); D. McClatchey, *Oxfordshire Clergy 1777–1869* (Oxford 1960); W. D. Balda, '"Spheres of Influence": Simeon's Trust and its implications for Evangelical patronage', unpublished Ph.D. thesis, University of Cambridge (1981); A. Haig. *The Victorian Clergy* (1984).
46   T. W. Hill, *Remains of the Late Thomas Wright Hill* (1859).
47   Essex File; Rev. William Burgess, *Reciprocal Duties of a Minister and His People*, Sermon preached at Thorpe-le-Soken, Essex, 2 February 1823.
48   C. M. Marsh.
49   L. C. Sier, *The Blomfields of Dedham and Colchester* (Colchester, 1924).
50   A. M. Deane, 'The church and her curates', quoted in A. Haig, demonstrates the importance of family connections in gaining a living.
51   Rev. John Savill, minister of Lion Walk church, Colchester, ERO D/Dcd.
52   Birmingham File; Birmingham Wills; Census of 1851, Edgbaston; Edgbaston Rate Book 1851, BRL.
53   Birmingham File; J. Priestley, 'Inventory of house and goods destroyed during the riots. 1791', BRL 174683.
54   D. McClatchey.
55   J. Seed, 'The role of Unitarianism in the formation of liberal culture 1775–1851', unpublished Ph.D. thesis, University of Hull (1981).
56   C. M. Marsh, pp. 103 and 104. A similar scene occurs in *John Halifax Gentleman* and is a demonstration of the esteem in which Halifax is held within the community. Dinah Maria Mulock (Mrs Craik) *John Halifax Gentleman* (1857).
57   L. Sier.
58   A. Camps, *The Diary and Work of Mrs Amy Camps* (1893), p. 39.
59   Anon. Diary of a farmer's wife, BUL, Heslop Coll. Ms 10/iii/15 1823, 18 July 1824.
60   A. Gilbert, *Autobiography and Other Memorials of Mrs Gilbert*, 2 vols. (1874), vol. I, p. 115. The ladies of the Unitarian Old Meeting, Birmingham, presented their two ministers with a handworked gown and cassock. E. Bushrod, 'The history of Unitarianism in Birmingham from the mid eighteenth century to 1893', unpublished M.A. thesis, University of Birmingham (1954).
61   J. P. Fitzgerald, *The Quiet Worker for Good, a familiar sketch of the late John Charlesworth* (Ipswich, 1865), p. 15.
62   Rev. J. Fielding, *A series of letters addressed to the Church and Congregation Assembling at the Great Meeting Coggeshall* (Coggeshall, 1815).

63 ibid.
64 M. A. Hedge, *My Own Fireside* (Colchester, 1832), p. 27.
65 Clergy, it was argued, should be married men with a healthy respect for and knowledge of domestic life. The practice of celibate priests taking confessions from married women was seen as particularly shocking. There was something unmanly, even unEnglish about the celibate Catholic clergy. See particularly Sir G. H. Smythe (Bart, MP), *Maynooth College: Justification of the term 'beastly' as applied to the Instruction at Maynooth College* (Colchester, 1841); G. F. A. Best, 'Popular protestation', in R. Robson (ed.), *Ideas and Institutions of Victorian Britain* (1967). Anti-Catholic feeling was widespread among evangelicals, see C. M. Marsh.
66 G. F. A. Best, *Temporal Pillars. Queen Anne's Bounty, the Ecclesiastical Commissioners and the Church of England* (Cambridge, 1964).
67 Quoted in D. McClatchey, p. 24.
68 J. P. Fitzgerald, p. 100.
69 H. More.
70 Birmingham, Essex and Suffolk Files.
71 Marsh children, *Memorials of a Beloved Mother by her Children* (Birmingham, 1837), p. 98.
72 C. M. Marsh, p. 88.
73 ibid., p. 101.
74 M. C. Marsh, p. 232.
75 For example, E. Sewell, *Autobiography* (1907), p. 15.
76 M. C. Marsh, p. 308.
77 L. E. O'Rorke (ed.), *The Life and Friendships of Catherine Marsh* (1917).
78 A. Haig. In the Thornton family Laura Thornton's marriage settlement stipulated that her husband, an Essex vicar, should take out a life insurance, the premiums for which would be paid out of Laura's settled income. E. M. Forster.
79 M. Hill, 'The role of women in Victorian society: sisterhood, deaconesses and the growth of nursing', in M. Hill, *The Religious Order* (1973); M. Vicinus, *Independent Women. Work and Community for Single Women 1850–1920* (1985).
80 Rev. J. G. Breay.
81 A. Douglas, *The Feminization of American Culture* (New York, 1978).
82 The section on James is drawn from the following sources: T. S. James; R. W. Dale (ed.), *Life and Letters of John Angell James*; Birmingham File; 'Church minute books 1838–48, 1849–56', BRL Carrs Lane Church Collection, nos. 5 and 6; A. H. Driver, *Carrs Lane 1748–1948* (Birmingham, 1948).
83 H. H. Horton, *Birmingham. A poem in two parts dedicated to William Scholefield M.P.* (Birmingham, 1851), p. 30.
84 E. Edwards, *Personal Recollections of Birmingham and Birmingham Men* (Birmingham, 1877), pp. 16–17.
85 C. J. Holyoake, *Sixty Years of an Agitator's Life* (1900).
86 Carrs Lane, 'Church Minute Book 1838–48'.
87 'Ministerial duties', in T. S. James, vol. 1, p. 258.
88 J. C. Miller, *Dying Pastors and the Undying Priest* (Birmingham, 1859).
89 J. A. James, *Christian Fellowship or the Church Members' Guide* (Birmingham, 1822), p. 47.
90 ibid., p. 107.
91 R. W. Dale, p. 91.
92 J. A. James, *Christian Fellowship*, p. 102.
93 ibid., pp. 102, 103.
94 J. A. James, 'Sermon on the death of Mrs Sherman', in T. S. James, vol. 2, p. 238.

95 R. W. Dale, p. 318.
96 J. A. James, *Christian Fellowship*, p. 19.
97 M. Rutherford, *The Revolution in Tanners' Lane*, 9th edn. (*c.* 1880), p. 375.
98 J. Knox, *The First Blast of the Trumpet against the Monstrous Regiment of Women* (Edinburgh, 1558).
99 J. A. James, *Christian Fellowship*, preface.
100 R. W. Dale; Birmingham File.
101 ibid.; 'Church minute books 1838–48, 1849–56'.
102 'Church book meeting and minutes 1783', BRL, Carr's Lane Church Collection, no. 4.
103 Corinthians I. 14 v. 34.
104 *Congregational Magazine*, 20, 3rd series I (1837).
105 J. A. James, *Christian Fellowship*, p. 170.
106 R. W. Dale; Women at Carrs Lane did not vote in deacons' elections until 1872. R. W. Ram, 'The social evolution of five dissenting communities in Birmingham 1750–1870', unpublished Ph.D. thesis, University of Birmingham (1972). Joseph Gilbert, the husband of Ann Taylor, when called to be minister at Hull, wrote and objected to the exclusion of the female votes at the time he had been unanimously elected. He accepted the call after consultation with John Angell James; A. Taylor, vol. 1, p. 316. It was common practice to have a group of male trustees who were responsible for the finances of the chapel. The Independent chapel at Whiting Street, Bury St Edmunds, had an inner circle of five trustees who were local businessmen with intimate knowledge of each others' worth and were related by marriage. R. G. Wilson, *Greene King: A Business and Family History* (1983). R. J. Morris has found that upper middle-class men tended to occupy the more significant positions in the chapel hierarchy with lower middle-class men as their subalterns – a finding which our research confirms. R. J. Morris, 'The making of the British middle class', unpublished paper (1979).
107 C. Binfield, 'Witham', in *So Down to Prayers: Studies in English Non-Conformity 1780–1920* (1977).
108 M. L. Smith, 'A brief history of Witham Congregational Church', mimeo (n.d.). We are grateful to Janet Gyford for this reference. In Mrs Oliphant's novel, *Salem Chapel* (1863) the women of the chapel are never happier than when 'hearing' the candidates.
109 New Meeting, 'Proceedings of the general meetings of the Congregation July 1771', BRL, Church of the Messiah Collection, 85; New Meeting, 'Minutes of the general meetings 1838–45', BRL Church of the Messiah Collection, 83. New Meeting, 'Vestry committee minutes 1813–25', BRL Church of the Messiah Collection, 126; New Meeting, 'Minutes of the committee of the New Meeting Sunday Schools 1834–42, 1843–52', BRL Church of the Messiah Collection, 98, 111; New Meeting, 'Report of the committee of the New Meeting Sunday Schools', in 'Church of the Messiah Sunday School Scrap Book 1791–1895', BRL Church of the Messiah Collection, 234; H. New, *The New Meeting and the Church of the Messiah, Birmingham. A Survey of their History* (Birmingham, 1912); E. Bushrod; R. W. Ram.
110 E. Bushrod, pp. 90–3.
111 J. Seed, 'The role of Unitarianism in the formation of liberal culture'; J. Seed, 'Theologies of power: Unitarianism and the social relations of religious discourse 1800–1850', in R. J. Morris (ed.), *Class, Power and Social Structure in British Nineteenth Century Towns* (Leicester, 1986).
112 Religious commitment could be substantial in financial terms for serious Christian households, especially nonconformist who were supporting a minister. See, for example, the accounts of an Essex wool merchant's family for 1821:

Sunday school	£2=2=0
Bible institution	£2=2=0
Charity school	£2=2=0
Missionary society	£1=0=0
Meeting and library	5s
Congregational mission	£1=0=0
Benevolent society	£11=4=0

£20=15=0

Savill Accounts, Bocking, ERO D/Dcd A5, 1821.

113 Birmingham Wills; Mrs C. Hutton Beale, *Memorials of the Old Meeting House and Burial Ground, Birmingham* (Birmingham, 1882); E. Bushrod; F. K. Prochaska, *Women and Philanthropy in Nineteenth Century England* (Oxford, 1980), especially part 1.

114 New Meeting, 'Proceedings at general meetings of the congregation July 1771–June 1868'; A. W. Matthews, *Life of Sarah Bache of Islington School Birmingham* (1900).

115 New Meeting, 'Proceedings at general meetings of the congregation July 1771–June 1868'; W. H. Ryland (ed.), *The Reminiscences of Thomas Henry Ryland* (Birmingham, 1904).

116 H. D. Budden, *The Story of Marsh St. Congregational Church Walthamstow* (Margate, 1923).

117 *Christian Observer*, 19 no. 225 (September 1820), p. 639.

118 E. Vaughan, *The Essex Village in Days Gone By* (Colchester, 1930).

119 Note the correspondent to the *Congregational Magazine*, 20, 3rd series I (1837) who knew of a Methodist woman preacher who had an illegitimate child, p. 576.

120 J. P. Fitzgerald, p. 15.

121 A. Klaiber, *The Story of the Suffolk Baptists* (1931).

122 H. Gurdon, 'The Methodist parish chest', *History Workshop Journal*, no. 3 (spring 1977), p. 75.

123 E. Isichei, *Victorian Quakers* (Oxford, 1970).

124 Quoted in D. E. Swift, *Joseph John Gurney, Banker, Reformer and Quaker* (Connecticut, 1962), p. 210.

125 E. Fry, *Memoir of the Life of Elizabeth Fry edited by two of her daughters*, 2 vols. (1847), vol. 1, p. 167. D. E. Swift, *Joseph John Gurney* has material on the criticisms of Fry within her own family.

126 Priscilla, Caroline and Eliza Ann Green daughters of Joseph Markes Green, Saffron Walden, DQB.

127 Sarah Lynes Grubb, minister for fifty-two years, DQB.

128 John Perry, unpublished diary, Box T, FHL.

129 Thomas Clarkson, *A Portraiture of Quakerism*, 3 vols. (1807), vol. III, p. 289.

130 Rev. C. B. Tayler, *Personal Recollections: with a memoir* (Religious Tract Society, n.d.), p. 30.

131 J. Bevan Braithwaite, *Memoirs of Anna Braithwaite* (1905), p. 59.

132 M. E. Fox, *Mary Pease* (1911), p. 23.

133 L. Barton, *Selections from the Poems and Letters of Bernard Barton* (Woodbridge, 1849), p. 24.

134 Quoted in E. Isichei, p. 109; L. H. Doncaster, *Quaker Organisations and Business Meetings* (1958).

135 R. Burls, 'Robert Dixon', in *A Brief Review of the Plan and Operation of the Essex Congregational Union* (1848); C. Binfield, section on 'Witham'.

136 On the 'age of societies', see J. Stephen, *Essays in Ecclesiastical Biography* (1848).

137 W. D. Balda, p. 111.
138 A. Camps.
139 Rev. J. Fielding.
140 Mary Ann Sims, for example, left the Rev. Robinson in Witham £100 and requested him to preach her funeral service; Will of Mary Ann Sims, ERO.
141 M. Ryan makes the point that women in the family were often the first converts, leading the men to join them. See *The Cradle of the Middle Class*.
142 Anon. Diary of a farmer's wife.
143 M. L. Smith, 'A brief history of Witham Congregational Church'. On women and philanthropy see F. K. Prochaska, *Women and Philanthropy in Nineteenth Century England*; A. Summers, 'A home from home: women's philanthropic work in the nineteenth century', in S. Burman (ed.), *Fit Work for Women* (1979).
144 J. A. James, *The Sunday School Teacher's Guide*, in T. S. James, vol. 16, p. 97.
145 J. A. James, *Female Piety*, p. 134; Carrs Lane, 'Minutes of Sabbath School 1812–45', BRL Carrs Lane Church Collection, no. 58; Church book meeting and minutes 1783–1810.
146 E. Shewell, *Memories of the late John Talwin Shewell* (Ipswich, 1870), p. 31.
147 A. Camps (December 1868).
148 S. Martin, *The Prison Visitor of Great Yarmouth* (1872).
149 Quoted in E. Bushrod, p. 176.
150 New Meeting, 'Church of the Messiah Sunday School Scrap Book 1791–1895'; 'Lists of Visitors to the Sunday Schools from 1824–30 and Minutes of the New Meeting, Sunday School Committee 1824–30', BRL Church of the Messiah Collection, no. 175; Minutes of the Committee of the New Meeting, Sunday Schools 1834–42, 1843–52; New Meeting 'Minutes of the Teachers Society 1834', BRL Church of the Messiah Collection.
151 John Perry (December 1838); Amy Camps (August 1865).
152 L. Maw, *A Memoir of Louisa Maw, daughter of Thomas and Lucy Maw of Needham Market, Suffolk* (1828), p. 49.
153 M. Bayly, *The Life and Letters of Mrs. Sewell* (1889); 'Mary Wright Sewell', DNB.
154 M. Charlesworth, *The Female Visitor to the Poor, by a Clergyman's Daughter* (1846), p. 129.

Chapter 3 'The nursery of virtue': domestic ideology and the middle class

1 Hazlitt, 'Commonplaces', no. 73 (15 November 1823), in P. Howe (ed.), *The Complete Works* (1934), quoted in T. W. Laqueur, 'The Queen Caroline affair: politics as art in the reign of George IV', *Journal of Modern History*, no. 54 (September 1982), p. 417. Laqueur's article is illuminating and our analysis has been much influenced by him. *Christian Observer*, 19 (1820), editor's preface.
2 Anon. 'Tale of a Royal Wanderer', in *A Political Lecture on Tails* (1820), p. 24.
3 Macauley quoted in J. Richardson, *The Disastrous Marriage* (1960), p. 192. For accounts of the Queen Caroline affair see R. Fulford, *The Trial of Queen Caroline* (1967); T. Holme, *Caroline* (1979).
4 T. W. Laqueur, p. 439; E. Halevy gives the classic account of the trial as a moment in radical history in *The Liberal Awakening 1815–30*, vol. 2, *History of the English People in the Nineteenth Century* (1961). A more recent version can be found in I. Prothero, *Artisans and Politics in Early Nineteenth Century London* (1979); A. J. Hone, *For the Cause of Truth – Radicalism in London 1796–1821* (Oxford, 1982). The DNB describes Caroline as dying, broken-

hearted. *The Concise Dictionary of National Biography* (Oxford, 1978), p. 207.

5 T. W. Laqueur, p. 466.

6 Quoted in R. Fulford, p. 243.

7 Anon, *The King's Treatment of the Queen, shortly stated to the people of England* (1820), pp. 4, 32.

8 C. Phillips, *The Queen's Case Stated* (1820), p. 27. As John Gillis points out the support which male radicals gave to Queen Caroline stemmed from their fear of libertinism and desire to defend the family – a constant theme for them throughout the early nineteenth century. J. Gillis, *For Better, For Worse: British Marriages 1600 to the Present* (Oxford, 1986), p. 223.

9 W. J. Fox, *A Funeral Sermon for Caroline, Queen of England* (1821); Burdett reported in *A Full Report of the Middlesex County Meeting* (1820), p. 13.

10 Anon. 'Queen Caroline', British Library Collection on Queen Caroline.

11 For example, *Address of the Female Inhabitants of Nottingham*, British Library 1852 b.9 (18). For the image of unprotected female see J. Evans, *A Sermon Occasioned by the Death of her Late Majesty Queen Caroline* (1821).

12 Quoted in R. Fulford, *The Trial of Queen Caroline*, p. 243.

13 John Bull (pseud.) 'Ode to George the IV and Caroline his wife' (1820).

14 J. H. Plumb, *The First Four Georges*, 16th edn. (1981).

15 Quoted in ibid., p. 148.

16 R. J. White, *Life in Regency England* (1963).

17 See, for example, the *Christian Observer* whose editorial line was to hope that a trial could be avoided, **19** (1820).

18 C. Rann Kennedy, *Poems: Original and Translated* (1857), p. 224.

19 *Christian Observer*, **19** (1820), editorials and correspondence.

20 Quoted in T. W. Laqueur, p. 427.

21 ABG (20 November 1820); S. L. Courtauld, *The Huguenot Family of Courtauld*, 3 vols. (1947), vol. III. Samuel Courtauld was later excluded from his local book club on account of his public association with the Queen's cause.

22 *A Full Report of the Middlesex County Meeting*; D. W. Harvey, Colchester's radical MP, was a staunch Caroline supporter, Essex File; Rev. C. B. Tayler, 'Mme de Stael', *Personal Recollections: with a Memoir*, Religious Tract Society (n.d.).

23 IJ (18 August 1821).

24 J. Seabrook, 'Commonplace Book' 1829–51, by permission of M. Mallawaratchi.

25 Rev. J. C. Barrett, *Sermon in Memory of Adelaide, Queen Dowager* (Birmingham, 1849), p. 11.

26 See, for example, Rev. G. S. Bull, *'Home' and How to Make it Happy* (Birmingham, 1854). On Victoria as the 'Rosebud of England' see N. Scourse, *The Victorians and their Flowers* (1983).

27 For an important discussion on the transformation of the eighteenth-century discourses on sexuality see M. Poovey, *The Proper Lady and the Woman Writer. Ideology as style in the works of Mary Wollstonecraft, Mary Shelley and Jane Austen* (Chicago, 1984).

28 L. Stone, *The Family, Sex and Marriage in England 1500–1800* (1977); R. Trumbach, *The Rise of the Egalitarian Family Aristocratic Kinship and Domestic Relations in Eighteenth Century England* (New York, 1978).

29 M. Wollstonecraft, *Vindication of the Rights of Woman* (Harmondsworth, 1975).

30 J. Luckcock, *Moral Culture* (1817); J. Luckcock, *Sequel to Memoirs in Humble Life Including the Period from 1809–25* (Birmingham, 1825).

31 Quoted in R. D. Altick, *The English Common Reader* (Chicago, 1963), p. 41.

32 I. Watt, *The Rise of the Novel* (Harmondsworth, 1963).

33 R. D. Altick, p. 64.
34 J. Barrell, *English Literature in History 1730–80: An Equal Wide Survey* (1983).
35 J. Money, *Experience and Identity: Birmingham and the West Midlands 1760–1800* (Manchester, 1977), especially ch. 6.
36 ABG (1 March 1790).
37 J. Money, p. 130.
38 Castle Library, Colchester, membership list, E. Simcoe, *A Short History of the Parish and Ancient Borough of Thaxted* (Saffron Walden, 1834); for Ipswich, T. Wright, *The Life of Edward Fitzgerald*, 2 vols. (1904), vol. I.
39 M. Butler, *Poets and Myths* (forthcoming).
40 W. Withering, *The Miscellaneous Tracts of William Withering* (1822).
41 J. Seabrook, 'The White Cottage', in 'Commonplace Book'.
42 M. Betham-Edwards (ed.), *The Autobiography of Arthur Young* (1898), p. 416.
43 J. Austen, *Sense and Sensibility* (Harmondsworth, 1969), p. 51.
44 M. C. Marsh, *Memorials of a Beloved Mother by her Children* (1837), p. 76.
45 T. Clark Junior, 'Leaflets, newspaper cuttings etc. relating to Thomas Clark Junior and Clark's metallic hothouse works. Birmingham 1813–63', BRL 520452.
46 J. Taylor, 'On visiting Cowper's garden and summer house at Olney', in *The Contributions of Q.Q.* (1845).
47 L. Barton, *Selections from the Poems and Letters of Bernard Barton* (Woodbridge, 1849).
48 C. C. Hankin (ed.), *Life of Mary Ann Schimmelpenninck*, 3rd edn. (1859).
49 Charlotte Brontë in *Shirley* (1849) makes the elderly aunt who reads Cowper sound faintly old fashioned but our evidence ranges from the 1780s to the 1850s. Birmingham and E. Anglia Files; C. Brontë, *Shirley* (Harmondsworth, 1974).
50 Birmingham File; A. T. Gilbert, *Autobiography*, 2 vols. (1874), vol. I, p. 202.
51 See, for example, J. A. James, *Female Piety or the Young Womans Friend and Guide Through Life to Immortality*, 5th edn. (1856).
52 M. C. Sturge, *Some Little Quakers in their Nursery* (1906).
53 H. Chorley, *Memorials of Mrs Hemans*, 2 vols. (1836).
54 J. P. Muirhead, *The Life of James Watt with Selections from His Correspondence*, 2nd edn. (1859); A. Galton, 'Letters to her brother John Howard 1805–33', BRL Galton Family Coll. 306, Letter no. 26; F. Hill, *An Autobiography of Fifty Years in Time of Reform* (1893).
55 C. C. Hankin (ed.), p. 105. Note, Scott was a favourite with the Ipswich Mechanics Institute; J. Glyde, *Suffolk in the 19th Century: Physical, Social, Moral, Religious and Industrial* (1855), p. 291.
56 Castle Book Club; Ethel Simcoe.
57 W. H. Ryland (ed.), *Reminiscences of Thomas Henry Ryland* (Birmingham, 1904).
58 R. W. Dixon, 'Reminiscences of the Old Dissent at Witham', *Transactions of the Congregational Society*, 5 (1911–12), p. 333.
59 Jane Ransome Biddell, 'Manuscript book of poems', IRO HA2/D/1.
60 C. Sturge, *Family Records* (1882); S. Chitty, *The Woman Who Wrote Black Beauty: A Life of Anna Sewell* (1971).
61 W. Beck, *Family Fragments Respecting the Ancestry, Acquaintance and Marriage of Richard Low Beck and Rachel Lucas* (Gloucester, 1897), p. 52.
62 A. M. Blackburn, *Poetic Gems: Partly Original but Chiefly Selected from the best authors designed to enrich the memories and form the taste of young persons* (Colchester, 1833). See also the books left by Ann Martin Taylor to her grandchildren in her will PRO 11/1773.

63 S. Galton, 'Letters to her brother John Howard 1805–33', BRL, Galton Family Coll. 307, Letter no. 21.

64 F. Hill. Frederick Hill married Martha Cowper who had written, *Parent's Cabinet of Amusement and Instruction*.

65 As, for example, Sarah Crompton in Birmingham, the author of several works. Birmingham File.

66 *Sale Catalogue of the Neat Household Furniture of the Late Bernard Barton* (Woodbridge, 26 July 1849).

67 E. V. Lucas, *Bernard Barton and His Friends: A Record of Quiet Lives* (1893).

68 G. E. Evans, *The Horse in the Furrow* (1960); H. Biddell, 'A short biography of Arthur Biddell', I.R.O. qs Playford 9.

69 Rev. C. B. Tayler, 'The Quaker Girl', in *May You Like It* (1823).

70 L. Barton, p. 276.

71 E. Moers, *Literary Women* (1978), p. 174. A Colchester surgeon, disciple of William Marsh was also deeply moved by reading 'Corinne'. J. B. Penfold, 'Charles Boutflower FRCS: Surgeon in Wellington's Army and Hon. Surgeon to the Essex and Colchester Hospital', *History of Medicine*, 7 no. 1/2 (spring/summer, 1976).

72 Note: Hemans' own marriage had broken up, a fact seldom publicized, DNB; H. Chorley, *Memoir of Mrs Hemans*, 2 vols. (1836), vol. 1, p. 304; F. Hemans, *The Poetical Works of Felicia Hemans* (Oxford, 1914), p. 478.

73 A. Moilliet, unpublished 'Memoranda', by permission of Mr J. L. Moilliet.

74 J. Taylor (ed.), *Memoirs, Correspondence and Poetical Remains* (1831), p. 294.

75 W. Hutton, *The Life of William Hutton, Stationer of Birmingham and the History of his Family* (1816), and Birmingham File.

76 W. Wilson, *The Life of George Dawson 1821–76* (Birmingham, 1905), and Birmingham File.

77 On the 'cultural marketplace' see M. Ryan, 'The empire of the mother. American writing about domesticity 1830–60', nos. 2/3 *Women and History* (1982).

78 A favourite day out for the Birmingham middle classes in this period was to 'The Leasowes', home of the poet William Shenstone (1714–63); Birmingham Directories.

79 For discussions of Cowper's life and work see G. Thomas, *William Cowper and the Eighteenth Century* (1948); B. Spiller, *Cowper: Prose and Poetry* (1968); M. Priestman, *Cowper's Task; Structure and Influence* (Cambridge, 1983).

80 J. Barrell.

81 W. Cowper, *The Task* book V, in *The Poetical Works of William Cowper* (Chandos edn, n.d.), p. 305.

82 W. Cowper, 'Retirement', ibid., p. 208.

83 W. Cowper, 'The Negro's Complaint', ibid., p. 407.

84 W. Cowper, *The Task*, book VI, ibid., p. 330.

85 G. Thomas, p. 13.

86 W. Cowper, 'Retirement', in *The Poetical Works*, pp. 194, 197, 207.

87 ibid., pp. 211, 194.

88 W. Cowper, *The Task*, books 3 and IV, *The Poetical Works*, pp. 271, 287.

89 ibid., book 3, p. 269; E. Shewell, *Memoir of the Late John Talwin Shewell* (Ipswich, 1870), p. 62.

90 ibid., book 4, pp. 274–7.

91 ibid., book 3, p. 262.

92 Quoted in Rev. George Betts, Commonplace Book IRO HD79/AF2/2/14; Dr Nathaniel Cotton came from a family of merchants. His sons and grandsons had typically evangelical connections with the East India Company and philanthropy. DNB.

93 On the 'entrepreneurial ideal' and the 'professional ideal' see H. Perkin, *The Origins of Modern English Society 1780–1880* (1969), especially ch. 7.

94 On Hannah More's life and work see, W. Roberts (ed.), *Memoirs of the Life and Correspondence of Mrs Hannah More*, 3 vols. (1834); H. Thompson, *The Life of Hannah More* (1838); M. A. Hopkins, *Hannah More and Her Circle 1745–1833* (1947); M. G. Jones, *Hannah More 1745–1833* (Cambridge, 1952).

95 H. Thompson, ibid., p. 247.

96 M. Syms, unpublished 'Letters and Reminiscences' (5 June 1810) by permission of the late Margaret Wilson.

97 Quoted in W. Roberts, vol. 3, p. 313.

98 M. A. Hopkins, p. 223.

99 M. Vitale, 'The domesticated heroine in Byron's Corsair and William Hone's prose adaptation', *Literature and History*, 10 no. 1 (spring 1984).

100 H. More, *Coelebs in Search of a Wife, Comprehending of Domestic Habits and Manners, Religion and Morals*, 2 vols., 9th edn (1809), p. 2.

101 H. More, *Strictures on the Modern System of Female Education*, 2 vols. (1799), vol. 2, pp. 186–7.

102 See, for example, G. J. Schochet, *Patriarchalism in Political Thought* (Oxford, 1975).

103 M. G. Jones describes *Village Politics* as 'Burke for beginners', p. 134.

104 H. More, *Essays Principally Designed for Young Ladies* (1777) pp. 2–3, 5. More was drawing on a tradition of Enlightenment thinking about sexual difference. See J. Rendall, *The Origins of Modern Feminism: Women in Britain, France and the United States 1780–1860* (1985); S. Tomaselli, 'The Englightenment debate on women', *History Workshop Journal*, no. 20 (autumn 1985).

105 H. More, *Strictures*, vol. 2, p. 27.

106 T. Gisborne, *An Enquiry into the Duties of the Female Sex* (1796), p. 286.

107 H. More, *Coelebs*, vol. 2, pp. 149–50.

108 See the discussion in M. Poovey, especially ch. 1.

109 H. More, *Strictures*, vol. 2, p. 179. Note Jane Taylor's novel whose title, *Display*, indicates concern with this theme.

110 H. More, *St. Paul*, 2 vols. (1815), vol. 2, pp. 268–9.

111 H. More, *Coelebs*, vol. 2, pp. 167–8, 180, 184.

112 R. Strachey, *The Cause: A Short History of the Women's Movement in Great Britain*, 2nd edn (1978), p. 13.

113 Q. Hoare and G. Nowell Smith (eds.), *Selections from Prison Notebooks of Antonio Gramsci* (1971), especially ch. 1.

114 This section on Ann Martin Taylor draws from: *Maternal Solicitude for a Daughter's Best Interests* (1814); *Practical Hints to Young Females on the Duties of a Wife, a Mother and a Mistress of a Family* (1815); *The Present of a Mistress to a Young Servant: Consisting of Friendly Advice and Real Histories* (1816); *Correspondence between a Mother and her Daughter at School* (1817); *Reciprocal Duties of Parents and Children* (1818); *The Family Mansion: a Tale* (1820); *The Itinerary of a Traveller in the Wilderness* (1825). The role of the publisher is indicated in that all were published by Taylor and Hessey.

115 A. Martin Taylor, *Maternal Solicitude*, p. 5.

116 ibid., p. 10.

117 A. Martin Taylor, *Reciprocal Duties*, p. 176.

118 A. Martin Taylor, *Practical Hints*, p. v.

119 ibid., p. 112.

120 ibid., p. 139.

121 ibid., p. 14.

122 ibid., p. 54.

123 A. Martin Taylor, *Reciprocal Duties*, p. 167.

124 ibid., p. 168.
125 See, for example, Mary Sewell who often used commercial language in writing about child rearing. M. Bayly, *The Life and Letters of Mrs Sewell* (1889).
126 A. Martin Taylor, *Practical Hints*, p. 27.
127 A. T. Gilbert, vol. I, p. 304.
128 ibid., p. 321.
129 J. Player, *Home: or the Months, a poem for domestic life* (1838).
130 P. Moon James, *Poems* (1821); J. Luckcock, 'My House and Garden: Lime Grove, Edgbaston', BRL 375948.
131 Jane Biddell, 'Home' in 'Manuscript poems' (1840), IRO HA 2/D/1.
132 L. Barton, p. 284.
133 See Florence Dombey's comment on the family house after the marriage of Edith and Mr Dombey. C. Dickens, *Dombey and Son* (New York, 1964), p. 530.
134 E. Conder, *Josiah Conder: A Memoir* (1857), p. 112.
135 M. A. Hedge, *My Own Fireside* (Colchester, 1832), p. 44.
136 H. Allen, *A Beloved Mother by her Daughter: the Life of Hannah S. Allen* (1884), p. 70.
137 J. P. Layer, p. 64.
138 J. Biddell.
139 See the anonymous and very popular poem 'Comparisons' quoted in Mary Young, 'Commonplace Book' (1828). Library of the London Museum.
140 L. Barton, p. 270. The caring, tender side of God's love was stressed, as resembling a mother's. See Rev. C. B. Tayler, preface to *May You Like It* (1823).
141 See Chapter 8, especially 1851 census data.
142 Mrs S. Stickney Ellis, *The Home Life and Letters of Mrs Ellis* (1893); M. Bayly; S. Chitty.
143 On J. A. James's attitude to Mrs Ellis, see, for example, *Female Piety*, p. 36.
144 H. Martineau, *Autobiography with Memorials by Maria Weston Chapman*, 3 vols. (1877); R. K. Webb, *Harriet Martineau. A Radical Victorian* (1960); V. K. Pichanick, *Harriet Martineau. The Woman and Her Work 1802–76* (Ann Arbor, 1980); Birmingham File.
145 Birmingham Botanical and Horticultural Society, 'Minute Book August 17, 1829–June 20, 1836', BUL 2/1/1/1, 4 April 1831; J. Gloag, *Mr Loudon's England* (Newcastle, 1970), p. 63; Colchester Castle Library.
146 Anon. 'Englishwomen of the seventeenth and nineteenth centuries', *English Review*, 12 (1847), p. 288. We are grateful to William Thompson for this reference.
147 Mrs Ellis's publishers had the inspired idea of re-issuing her *Wives of England* in a marriage-day edition bound in white morocco.
148 Mrs S. Stickney Ellis, *The Home Life and Letters*.
149 Anon. 'Englishwomen', p. 285.
150 A. W. Kinglake, 'The rights of women', *The Quarterly Review*, 75 (1844–5), p. 122.
151 Anon. review of *The Daughters of England* in *Congregational Magazine*, 25, 3rd series 6 (1842), p. 766.
152 Mrs S. Stickney Ellis, *The Women of England* (1839), p. 14.
153 ibid., p. 10.
154 Mrs S. Stickney Ellis, *The Daughters of England. Their Position in Society, Character and Responsibilities* (n.d.), p. 223.
155 Mrs S. Stickney Ellis, *Mothers of England, Their Influence and Responsibility* (n.d.), p. 27.
156 For a discussion of the feminist use of this concept see B. Taylor, *Eve and the New Jerusalem. Socialism and Feminism in the Nineteenth Century* (1983).

157 Mrs S. Stickney Ellis, *The Daughters*, p. 318.
158 Mrs S. Stickney Ellis, *Mothers*, p. 348.
159 Mrs S. Stickney Ellis, *The Women*, see the chapter on 'Marriage'.
160 Mrs S. Stickney Ellis, *The Home Life and Letters*, p. 94.
161 J. A. V. Chapple and A. Pollard (eds.), *The Letters of Mrs Gaskell* (Manchester, 1966).
162 Mrs S. Stickney Ellis, *The Daughters*, preface.
163 ibid., p. 373; Anon. 'Englishwomen', p. 288.
164 On the Christian tint see J. W. Croker quoted by H. McLeod, *Religion and the People of Western Europe* (Oxford, 1981), p. 107.
165 Mrs Ellis warned against the dangers of women becoming too selfless however. Mrs S. Stickney Ellis, *The Wives* and *The Women*; see also chapter 7.
166 H. Martineau, *Autobiography*; V. K. Pichanick, *Harriet Martineau*; F. E. Mineka, *The Dissidence of Dissent. The Monthly Repository 1806–38* (North Carolina, 1944).
167 H. Martineau, vol. I, p. 142.
168 On classical liberalism and its treatment of women see A. M. Jaggar, *Feminist Politics and Human Nature* (Brighton, 1984); R. W. Krouse, 'Patriarchal liberalism and beyond: from John Stuart Mill to Harriet Taylor', in J. B. Elshtain (ed.), *The Family in Political Thought* (Brighton, 1984).
169 J. Bentham, *An Introduction to the Principles of Morals and Legislation* (Oxford, 1839), especially pp. 58–9.
170 H. Martineau, vol. 1, p. 253.
171 ibid., vol. 1, p. 401.
172 ibid., vol. 2, p. 225.
173 J. S. Mill, *The Subjection of Women*, and H. Taylor Mill, *Enfranchisement of Women* (1983). See the helpful introduction by K. Soper to these two essays in the Virago edition.
174 H. Martineau, *Household Education* (1848), p. 241.
175 ibid., p. 244.
176 *The Magazine of Domestic Economy*, I, (1835–6), p. 66; 7 (1841–2), p. 271.
177 H. Martineau, 'The new school for wives', *Household Words*, no. 107 (April 1852); S. Crompton, *Evening Schools for the Education of Women* (Birmingham, 1852).
178 J. Loudon, 'An Account of the Life and Writings of John Claudius Loudon', in J. C. Loudon, *Self Instruction for Young Gardeners, Foresters, Bailiffs, Land Stewards and Farmers* (1845); J. Gloag, *Mr Loudon's England* (Newcastle, 1970).
179 J. Gloag, p. 61.
180 G. Taylor, *Some Nineteenth Century Gardeners* (1951), p. 39.
181 D. Allen, *The Victorian Fern Craze: A History of Pteridomania* (1969), p. 12.
182 J. C. Loudon, *The Suburban Gardener, and Villa Companion: Comprising the Choice of a Suburban or Villa Residence, or of a Situation on which to Form one; the Arrangement and Furnishing of the House; and the Laying out, Planting and General Management of the Garden and Grounds. Especially Intended for Those who Know Little About Gardening and Ladies* (1838), p. 2.
183 J. C. Loudon, *An Encyclopedia of Cottage, Farm, and Villa Architecture and Furniture* (1833), p. 1.
184 J. Gloag. Thanks to John Burnett for this reference.
185 J. C. Loudon, *The Suburban Gardener*, p. 88.
186 ibid., p. 8.
187 J. C. Loudon, *A Treatise on Forming, Improving and Managing Country Residences and the Choice of Situation Appropriate to Every Class of Purchaser*, 2 vols. (1806), vol. 2, pp. 4–5, 6, 9.

188 J. C. Loudon, *The Suburban Gardener*, p. 9.
189 ibid., p. 3.
190 Here he was echoing Humphrey Repton and Jane Taylor among many other didactic writers. Loudon was convinced that more privacy was also desirable for the lower classes.
191 J. C. Loudon, *Treatise*, vol. 2, p. 678.
192 J. C. Loudon, *The Suburban Gardener*.
193 J. C. Loudon, *The Greenhouse Companion*, pp. 1, 2.
194 An Essex Quaker woman in her early twenties of the shopkeeping class at home with her sister when both were dying from consumption wrote, 'Dear Martha and I seem now like a garden enclosed, kept from the many enjoyments which while in health I loved too well. From those things which were beginning to be fearful temptations, swallowing up the little seeds of good.' L. Jesup, *Extracts from the Papers and Letters of Lucy Jesup of Sudbury* (1858), p. 15.
195 J. C. Loudon, *Treatise*, vol. 1, p. 45.
196 ibid., vol. 2, p. 686.
197 ibid., vol. 1, pp. 38–9. The equation of beauty with morality is also a theme among local writers, for example expressed by a Colchester tailor and member of the Philosophical Society. J. Carter, *Two Lectures on Taste* (Colchester, 1834).
198 See N. F. Cott, 'Passionless: an interpretation of Victorian sexual ideology 1790–1850', *Signs*, **4** no. 2 (1978).

Introduction to Part Two

1 C. Feinstein, 'Capital accumulation and the industrial revolution', in R. Floud and D. McClosky (eds.), *The Economic History of Britain since 1700* (Cambridge, 1981), vol. I, 1700–1860, p. 137.
2 R. J. Morris, 'The making of the British middle class', unpublished paper, 1979.
3 D. R. Grace and D. C. Phillips, *Ransomes of Ipswich* (Reading, 1975); P. K. Kemp, *The Bentall Story: Commemorating 150 Years Service to Agriculture 1805–1955* (1955).
4 S. Timmins, 'The industrial history of Birmingham', in S. Timmins (ed.), *The Resources, Products and Industrial History of Birmingham and the Midland Hardware District* (1866), p. 222.
5 R. Gentle and R. Field, *English Domestic Brass 1680–1810 and the History of its Origins* (1975), p. 57.
6 ibid., p. 69.
7 John Pudney, 'Unpublished Diary 1757–1823', ERO, T/P 116/62.
8 C. W. Chalkin, *The Provincial Towns of Georgian England: A Study of the Building Process 1740–1820* (1974).
9 P. Unwin, *The Publishing Unwins* (1972); see also J. Evans, *Endless Webb: John Dickinson and Co. Ltd. 1804–1954* (1955).

Chapter 4   'A modest competency': men, women and property

1 L. Namier, quoted in C. Shrimpton, 'The landed society and the farming community of Essex in the late 18th and early 19th centuries', unpublished Ph.D. thesis, University of Cambridge (1966), p. 1.
2 R. S. Neale, 'The bourgeoisie, historically, has played a most revolutionary part', in E. Kamenka and R. S. Neale (eds.), *Feudalism, Capitalism and Beyond* (Whitstable, 1975), p. 98.
3 J. G. A. Pocock, 'Early modern capitalism: the Augustan perception', in E. Kamenka and R. S. Neale (eds.), p. 79.

4   J. Brewer, 'Commercialization and politics', in N. McKendrick, J. Brewer and J. H. Plumb (eds.), *The Birth of a Consumer Society: the Commercialization of 18th Century England* (1982), p. 199.

5   M. Ignatieff, 'Primitive accumulation revisited', in R. Samuel (ed.), *People's History and Socialist Theory* (1981).

6   E. P. Thompson, 'The moral economy of the English crowd in the 18th century', *Past and Present*, no. 50 (February 1971).

7   J. M. Roberts, *The Mythology of the Secret Societies* (1972).

8   'Patronage was the middle term between feudal homage and capitalist cash nexus', H. Perkin, *The Origins of Modern English Society 1780–1880* (1969), p. 49. See also his discussion of friendship, patronage and property, pp. 41–51.

9   F. M. L. Thompson, *Chartered Surveyors: The Growth of a Profession* (London, 1968), p. 64. Malthus, although he lived in the provinces, regularly attended several such gatherings in London including the King of Clubs. He helped to found the Political Economy Club in 1821 along with Ricardo, James Mill and Macaulay among others. P. James, *Population Malthus: His Life and Times* (1979).

10 P. Mathias, *The Brewing Industry in England 1700–1830* (Cambridge, 1959), p. 289.

11 Michael Lane, personal communication.

12 R. G. Wilson, *Gentlemen Merchants: The Merchant Community in Leeds 1700–1830* (Manchester, 1971).

13 The preamble to the Charitable Uses Act, 1601, limited trusts to educational, religious and relief of poverty uses. These trusts were not recognized in common law since the trust is a creature of equity. W. Holdsworth, *A History of English Law* (1966), 17 vols. (1966), vol. IV, p. 478.

14 B. C. Hunt, *The Development of the Business Corporation in England 1800–1867* (Cambridge, Mass., 1936), p. 9.

15 Unlike the trust, partnership came under common law which became more sophisticated in the early nineteenth century. J. Collyer, *A Practical Treatise on the Law of Partnership* (1832).

16 W. Holdsworth, vol. VIII, p. 192.

17 Significantly coverture was waived by custom in the City of London. J. Collyer, pp. 9–10, 72.

18 J. B. Saunders, *Words and Phrases Legally Defined*, 5 vols. (1969), vol. 1, p. 78. Matthew Boulton wrote in 1788: 'Partnerships ought to be founded on equitable principles and, like a pair of scales, to be balanced, either with money, time, knowledge, abilities in possessing a market.' Quoted in T. S. Ashton, *Iron and Steel in the Industrial Revolution* (Manchester, 1951), p. 60.

19 S. L. Courtauld, *The Huguenot Family of Courtauld*, 3 vols. (1957), vol. 2.

20 The move towards sleeping partners who only invested capital was linked to the development of limited liability in the late 1840s. J. Saville, 'Sleeping partnership and limited liability: 1850–1856', *Economic History Review*, Second series, **8** (1956).

21 Circular to bankers, 1838, quoted in B. C. Hunt, p. 86.

22 For a more technical discussion see: S. Pollard, *The Genesis of Modern Management* (1965), pp. 233–5.

23 B. C. Hunt, p. 20.

24 S. L. Courtauld, vol. 2.

25 L. S. Presnell, *Country Banking in the Industrial Revolution 1760–1830* (Oxford, 1956), p. 236.

26 J. Saville.

27 T. Blythe, 'Account books 1818–1826', ERO, D/Du 281: 4, 5 and 6; Samuel Webb Savill, 'Account books 1828'; ERO D/DcdF1.

28 H. Rayne, *A History of British Insurance* (1948), p. 175.

29　Among the effects of an Essex farmer was found a local adaptation of Hadon's account book for farmers published by Taylor of Colchester. It was presented as a *Farmer's Complete Account Book on a simple Plan, shewing at one view an exact account of workmen's names, labour and wages with the correct tables for entering every description of corn, seed, manure whether bought, sold or used for seed.* There were instructions for the valuation of live and dead stock and growing crops under distinct headings 'to enable the farmer to Balance his Accounts accurately at any time'. As is often the case, the farmer had begun to fill in the various accounts and forms but soon went back to using the book to scribble unconnected notes. Edmund Cook, farmer of Great Henny, Essex, ERO D/DU 441/54.

30　Significantly this view comes from an ex-paymaster in the Royal Navy: J. Munro, *A Guide to Farm Book-keeping, Founded Upon Practice and Upon New and Concise Principles* (Edinburgh, 1821), p. xi.

31　B. S. Yamey, 'Scientific bookkeeping and the rise of capitalism', *Economic History Review*, second series, 1 nos. 2 and 3 (1949), p. 100.

32　'At the close of every day, after casting up his accounts [i.e. writing in his diary] and humble and fervent prayer, the Lord . . . made it out that All was pardoned.' Quoted in W. Haller, *The Rise of Puritanism* (New York, 1957), p. 100.

33　E. A. Blaxill, *These Hundred Years 1838–1938: A Brief History of the Progress of Kent, Blaxill and Co. Ltd of Colchester* (Colchester, 1938), p. 13.

34　Rev. John Savill, 'Unpublished diary, 1823', ERO D/Dcd/F29.

35　Edward Gripper, farmer of Layer Breton, Essex, DQB; William Goodwin, 'Diaries 1791–1809', IRO HD 365/1–3.

36　E. P. Thompson.

37　James Ward, 'A tour to Cambridge, Norwich and Ipswich in the summer of 1815', unpublished manuscript, Bodleian Library, Top. gen. e. 72, p. 15.

38　E. Pickard, 'Some account of my life' (1839), BRL 22/11; C. Sturge, *Family Records* (1882).

39　A. Young, *General View of the Agriculture of the County of Essex*, 2 vols. (1807), vol. 2, p. 416.

40　C. Shrimpton, p. 331.

41　C. Emsley, *British Society in the French Wars 1793–1815* (1979).

42　H. A. L. Cockerill and E. Green, *The British Insurance Business 1547–1970: An Introduction and Guide to the Historical Records in the U.K.* (1976).

43　D. C. Eversley, 'Industry and trade 1500–1880', in *Victoria County History: History of Warwick*, R. B. Pugh (ed.), 'The City of Birmingham' (Oxford, 1964), vol. 7.

44　D. R. Grace and D. C. Phillips, *Ransomes of Ipswich: a History of the Firm and Guide to its Records* (Reading, 1975).

45　The increasing use of the strict settlement rather than the marriage settlement points towards a more middle-class solution. T. Murphy, 'Female shadow, male substance: women and property law in 19th century England', unpublished paper (1982), by permission of the author.

46　D. Duman, *The Judicial Bench in England 1727–1875: the Reshaping of a Professional Elite* (1982), ch. 6.

47　John Hanson, 'Unpublished memoirs', by permission of Jean Harding, Great Bromley, Essex.

48　Dobkin Hall sees partnership as a form of inter-vivos gift to keep capital intact but we would argue that in the early part of the period, at least, this was not an overriding concern. P. Dobkin Hall, 'Family structure and class consolidation among the Boston Brahmins', unpublished Ph.D. thesis, State University of New York at Stony Brook (1973), pp. 52–6.

49　Samuel Galton's will and other documents, BRL.

50   The question of sons following in their father's business is a related problem. Undoubtedly skills and contacts would favour such succession but the above discussion shows that it was a complicated issue and much more flexible than some historians have indicated. Preston notes very little pattern among what might be called 'middle-class' occupations, which he does not explain. B. Preston, *Occupations of Fathers and Sons in Mid-Victorian England* (Reading, 1977), Geographical Papers, no. 56.

51   T. R. Slater, 'Family, society and the ornamental villa on the fringes of English country towns', *Journal of Historical Geography*, **4** no. 2 (1978).

52   At the end of the eighteenth century the social commentator, Gisborne, tried to show how business opens the way for the progress of civilization, the diffusion of learning, the extension of science and, above all, the reception of Christianity. His strictures display much anxiety about the proper place of business in men's lives. T. Gisborne, *Enquiry into the Duties of Men in the Higher and Middle Classes of Society* (1974).

53   R. Wilson, *Greene King: A Business and Family History* (1983), p. 78.

54   S. L. Courtauld, vol. 2, p. 27.

55   J. Brewer, p. 216.

56   Witham File.

57   J. Trusler, *The Way to be Rich and Respectable* (1777), p. 11.

58   B. L. Anderson, 'Money and the structure of credit in the 18th century', *Business History*, **xii** no. 1 (January 1970).

59   BILLS OF EXCHANGE: a written request or order to one person to pay a certain sum of money to another without conditions. The first person was known as the 'drawee' and if the drawee accepted the bill he became the 'acceptor'. PROMISSORY NOTE: a promise to pay by the maker instead of a request to another to pay. The maker of the note guarantees to pay back the drawer.

60   R. J. Morris, 'Men, women and property: the reforms of the married women's property act, 1870', unpublished paper, University of Edinburgh (1982).

61   E. Spring, 'Law and the theory of the affective family', *Albion* (Appalachian State University, spring 1984), p. 13.

62   D. M. Walker, *Oxford Companion of Law* (Oxford, 1980), p. 1241.

63   By the eighteenth century, the trust had evolved into what Maitland once called 'a most powerful instrument of social experimentation', B. L. Anderson, 'Provincial aspects of the financial revolution of the 18th century', *Business History*, **xi** no. 1 (January 1969), p. 20; M. R. Chesterman, 'Family settlements on trust: landowners and the rising bourgeoisie', in D. Sugarman and G. R. Rubin (eds.), *Law, Economy and Society, 1750–1914: Essays in the History of English Law* (Abingdon, Oxon, 1974).

64   R. J. Morris, p. 4.

65   See also S. D'Cruze, 'The society now surrounding us: Colchester and its middling sort', unpublished M.A. thesis, University of Essex (1985), p. 56.

66   Here our findings differ from Morris's evidence from Yorkshire wills where 'male children usually received their portion free of any restraint'. This may be due to our emphasis on direction rather than control or restraint. R. J. Morris, p. 5.

67   This distinction is in line with Morris's argument about the role of professionals as opposed to proprietors in Leeds. R. J. Morris, 'Economic history of the Leeds middle class' (Conference on the Middle Class, Leeds, 1983).

68   G. Rae, *The Country Banker, His Clients, Cases and Work from an Experience of 40 Years* (first pub. 1886, 1976), p. 9.

69   C. W. Chalklin, *The Provincial Towns of Georgian England: A Study of the Building Process 1740–1820* (1974), p. 242.

70   R. J. Morris, p. 7.

71 B. L. Anderson, 'Provincial aspects of the financial revolution', p. 17.
72 J. Saunders, p. 91.
73 Samuel Webb Savill, correspondence with the Sayer Walker family, 1823–32, ERO, D/DU/cd/c6.
74 A. Ryland, notes from an unpublished journal 1844–50. By permission of Mrs R. Waterhouse.
75 M. Trustram, *Women of the Regiment: Marriage and the Victorian Family* (Cambridge, 1984).
76 L. Barton (ed.), *Selections from the Poems and Letters of Bernard Barton* (Woodbridge, 1849); Jane Loudon had her £100 Civil List pension (as widow of an eminent man), supplemented by the royalties from a friend's book dedicated to the memory of her husband. B. Howe, *Lady with Green Fingers: the Life of Jane Loudon* (1961).
77 'Life insurance', *The Leisure Hour: A Family Journal of Instruction and Recreation* (April 1852), p. 249.
78 R. Fletcher, *The Biography of a Victorian Village: Richard Cobbold's account of Wortham, Suffolk 1860* (1977), p. 70.
79 Rev. J. Fielding, *A Series of Letters Addressed to the Church and Congregation Assembling at the Great Meeting Coggeshall* (Coggeshall, 1815).
80 Birmingham Victorian Benefit Building Society, *Rules and Regulations* (Birmingham, 1850).
81 Medical Benevolent Society, *Rules* (Birmingham, 1897).
82 J. Ross, *A Few Loose Remarks on the Advantages of Friendly 'Societies', and also on a scheme for supporting the widows and orphans of teachers* (Edinburgh, 1804), p. 2.
83 'Life insurance', p. 249.
84 H. A. L. Cockerill and E. Green, p. 37.
85 Witham File. For the term 'community broker' we are indebted to S. D'Cruze, p. 72. The crucial role of the trustee is brought out in the controversy over Jacob Pattisson's handling of the family estate after his spectacular bankruptcy. See actions in Chancery, May 1861, ERO D/Dra E109.
86 B. Drew, *The Fire Office: Being the history of the Essex and Suffolk Equitable Insurance Society Ltd 1802–1952* (1952), p. 19.
87 V. Redstone, 'The Suffolk Garrets' (1916), IRO L92.
88 J. Oxley Parker, *The Oxley Parker Papers: From the letters and diaries of an Essex family of land agents in the 19th century* (Colchester, 1964), p. 91.
89 J. Thirsk and J. Imray, 'Suffolk farmers at home and abroad', in *Suffolk Farming in the Nineteenth Century* (1958).
90 Samuel Webb Savill, correspondence.
91 J. P. Fitzgerald, *The Quiet Worker for Good: a familiar sketch of the late John Charlesworth* (Ipswich, 1865).
92 Rev. J. Fielding.
93 J. Perry, 'Unpublished diary (1818–1842)'. FHL, Box T; DQB.
94 J. Harriott, *Struggles Through Life Exemplified*, 2 vols. (1807), vol. 1.
95 E. Gibbins, *Records of the Gibbins Family also a few reminiscences of Emma Gibbins and letters and papers relating to the Bevington Family* (Birmingham, 1911).
96 A. Kenrick, 'Unpublished diary (1787–89)', BRL 110/24.
97 R. Kenrick to L. Kenrick, July 1830 in R. Kenrick 'Letters from Mrs Archibald (Rebecca) Kenrick to her niece, Miss Lucy Kenrick: 1804–1858', BUL.
98 W. King, *Arthur Albright, Notes of His Life October 12, 1811–July 3, 1900* (Birmingham, 1901).
99 F. A. Blaxill.
100 The financial arrangements of partnership usually started with a round sum divided in fixed proportions. At the end of the year, each partner was credited

with interest on his capital and any surplus divided in fixed proportions to be credited to each partner's account. Dividends and interest were often not paid out but allowed to accumulate, withdrawals being made for living expenses as need arose. An interesting variation is found where a Colchester wine merchant agreed to pay a third of all profits to his 32-year-old clerk, who later became a partner. Agreement between William Smith and John Lay, 3 November 1849 by permission of Richard Wheeler.

101   G. Sturt, *A Farmer's Life with a Memoir of the Farmer's Sister* (Firle, Sussex, 1979).

102   Will of Matthew Argent, Witham, 1796.

103   R. Kenrick, 'Unpublished diary 1839–89', by permission of John Kenrick; A. Kenrick, 'Personal Cash Ledger', by permission of Kenrick and Son Ltd, West Bromwich.

104   Although Quaker meetings officially banned first cousin marriages, seve cases have been found in the local material.

105   R. S. Shaen, 'Unpublished diary 1800–1855', John Johnson Collection, Bodleian Library, Ms 18 and 19. The marriage of Southey and Coleridge to the Fricker sisters may also be recalled.

106   H. Sebastian, 'A brewing family in Essex' (Coggeshall Women's Institute, n.d.), by permission of the author.

107   Isaac Reckitt, DQB.

108   William Bentall, 'Unpublished Diary, 1807', ERO D/F 1/2.

109   H. W. Dickinson, *Matthew Boulton 1728–1809* (Cambridge, 1937). Note: this marriage was before marriage to a deceased wife's sister was made illegal.

110   Shaw letters, no. 4, BUL.

111   *James Allen Ransome, The Story of His Life* (Ipswich, 1880), IRO; Birmingham, Essex and Suffolk Files.

112   M. Anderson, 'The social implications of demographic change, 1750–1950' (1985), unpublished paper by permission of the author.

113   Birmingham, Essex, Suffolk and Witham Files. Given the type of source, this data is unreliable, for example, still-births and infant deaths are often unrecorded. Nevertheless the general trends are clear: completed family size for the second half of the eighteenth century in England is estimated at 5.43. E. A. Wrigley and R. S. Schofield, 'English population history from family reconstitution – summary results, 1600–1799', *Population Studies*, 37 (1983).

114   Phipson Children, *A Tribute to a Father's Memory* (Birmingham, 1864).

115   R. B. Beckett, *John Constable's Correspondence: the Family at East Bergholt 1807–1837* (London, 1962).

116   H. Sebastian.

117   W. Bentall.

118   R. S. Shaen.

119   G. J. Holyoake, *60 Years of an Agitators Life* (1900).

120   Jane Ransome Biddell, 'Unpublished poems, 1808–1833', IRO HA2/D/1.

121   Mrs W. Byng Kenrick (ed.), *Chronicles of a Nonconformist Family. The Kenricks of Wynne Hall, Exeter and Birmingham* (Birmingham, 1932), p. 215.

122   Elizabeth Anne Wheler (née Galton), 'Memorials of my Life', 2 vols., vol. 1. By permission of Mr John Moilliet.

123   R. J. Morris, 'The middle class and the property cycle during the industrial revolution', in T. C. Smout (ed.), *The Search for Wealth and Stability* (1979).

124   H. C. Colman, *Jeremiah James Colman: A Memoir* (1905).

125   K. Pearson, *The Life, Letters and Labours of Francis Galton*, 3 vols. (Cambridge, 1914), vol. I, 1822–53.

126   Witham File; Census whole sample.

127   J. Webb, 'Lines Written by my Father on his First Residence at Kitwell, After his Purchase of It', *Prose and Verse* (1824).

Chapter 5 'A man must act': men and the enterprise

1 H. C. Colman, *Jeremiah James Colman: A Memoir* (1905), p. 28.
2 W. A. Armstrong, 'The use of information about occupation', in E. A. Wrigley (ed.), *19th Century Society: Essays in the use of quantitative methods for the study of social data* (Cambridge, 1972). The difficulties in standardizing occupational titles are confronted in the sophisticated analysis by R. J. Morris. See his unpublished paper, 'The distorting lens: multi-dimensional codes and sources, the poll books and directories for the 1830s' (December 1983).
3 Census of Great Britain, *The Population Returns of 1831* (1832), p. 2.
4 For a sociological discussion of this point see: F. Bechoffer and B. Elliott, 'Petty property: the survival of a moral economy', in F. Bechoffer and B. Elliott (eds.), *The Petite Bourgeoisie: Comparative studies of the uneasy stratum* (1981).
5 Census of 1851: 1 in 8 sample of all Colchester.
6 Census of 1851: all of Witham, Essex.
7 Census of 1851: Havering-atte-Bower, Essex.
8 Census of 1851: Stowlangtoft, Suffolk. An 'open' parish had many landlords including some freeholders with cottages; a 'closed' parish tended to be in the hands of large landlords or great estates.
9 Census of 1851: Edgbaston sample.
10 W. White, *Directory of Ipswich 1844* (Newton Abbot, 1970); W. White, *History, Gazetteer and Directory of the County of Essex* (Sheffield, 1848); *Edgbaston, Directory and Guide 1853* (Birmingham 1853); Birmingham Census Sample.
11 Well illustrated in the ground plan for Marriage's Mill, East Hill, Colchester. Thanks to Dudley White of Ardleigh, Essex for this point.
12 For the comparison see: *Distribution of occupational groups as a percentage of the middle class*: (1851)

	Northampton (%)	Oldham (%)	Shields (%)
Professions	21	12	16
Employers	44	71	60
Tradesmen	35	17	23
	100	100	99

In Northampton and Shields, small shopkeepers and clerks formed a 'mass social tail', while in Oldham there was a sharp break with small farmers and shopkeepers behaving in more 'working-class' ways, e.g. keeping fewer servants. J. Foster, *Class Struggle and the Industrial Revolution: Early Industrial Capitalism in three English towns* (1974), p. 163.

13 Wiener, quoting Perkin, sees the differences between professionals and manufacturers as leading to the former's identification with gentry partly because of their more settled, less fluctuating income. But in this early period and at provincial level, at least, this is unconvincing. M. J. Wiener, *English Culture and the Decline of the Industrial Spirit: 1850–1980* (Cambridge, 1982), p. 15.
14 Isaac Taylor, *Self Cultivation Recommended* (1817), pp. 17, 42.
15 Warrington Academy is the best known. It was run as a family enterprise by the Aiken family. Anna Laetitia Aiken (1743–1825) one of the daughters with her schoolmaster husband set up a boys' school in Suffolk where some of the well known men of the Essex and Suffolk upper middle class were educated.

As Mrs Barbauld, her writings for children were influential; she was personally known to Ann and Jane Taylor. B. Rogers, *Georgian Chronicle: Mrs Barbauld and her Family* (1958). Several such schools have been identified in the local areas.

16 R. E. Schofield, *The Lunar Society of Birmingham: A Social History of Provincial Science and Industry in 18th century England* (Oxford, 1963).

17 N. Hans, *New Trends in Education in the Eighteenth Century* (1951). The Quaker Ransome iron manufacturing family of Ipswich decided to leave the third generation, Robert, at a Quaker boarding school because there he was neither too studious nor too slack – a good mixture for business. David Ransome personal communication.

18 An unusual example of a woman who ran a successful school of navigation is K. R. Alyer, *Mrs Janet Taylor: 'authoress and instructress in navigation and nautical astronomy' 1804–1870* (1982), Fawcett Papers, no. 6.

19 M. D. and R. Hill, *Public Education: Plans for the Government and Liberal Instructions of Boys in Large Numbers; as practiced at Hazelwood School* (2nd edn, 1825).

20 D. Newsome, *Godliness and Good Learning* (1961).

21 Charity Commissioners Reports: 1824, H.C.xiv; 1835, H.C.xxi; 1837–8, H.C.xxv; 1815–37, H.C. vol. xxxv.

22 See, for example, the career of George Airy who became the Astronomer Royal. Son of a farmer who turned exciseman on moving to Colchester in 1810, he was sent to a private academy where geography, arithmetic, bookkeeping, slide rule, mensuration and algebra were taught. While there, he was able to closely observe a steam engine in the brewery owned by a fellow student's father and he also experimented with optics before moving on to the reformed grammar school for more classical studies. Through his mother's brother, Arthur Biddell, a wealthy farmer near Ipswich, he met the elderly slavery reformer, Thomas Clarkson, who sponsored his application to Cambridge. W. Airy, *Autobiography of Sir George Biddell Airy* (Cambridge, 1896).

23 Birmingham Statistical Society, 'Report on the state of education in Birmingham', *Journal of the Statistical Society of London*, 3 (1840).

24 W. Lean, 'Scholars at his school', compiled by J. H. Lloyd, BRL 662590.

25 King Edward VI School Birmingham, Governors Order Book 1798–1818; 1818–32; 1832–41; 1842–50. All schools mss. permission of Mr Walkington, Secretary to the Governors of King Edward VI School, Birmingham.

26 King Edward VI School, Governor's Order Book 1798–1810; 1818–32; 1832–41.

27 BC (30 October 1823).

28 ABG (7 June 1830); King Edward VI School. Governor's Order Book 1832–41.

29 BC (11 March 1824).

30 BC (23 October 1823).

31 King Edward VI School, Birmingham 'Secretary's Register 1838–1857'.

32 K. Pearson, *The Life, Letters and Labours of Francis Galton*, 3 vols. (Cambridge, 1914), vol. I, 1822–53, p. 20.

33 T. W. Hill, *Remains of the Late Thomas Wright Hill* (1859); M. D. and R. Hill, *Public Education*; R. and G. B. Hill, *The Life of Sir Rowland Hill and the History of Penny Postage*, 2 vols. (1880); R. and F. Davenport-Hill, *The Recorder of Birmingham: A Memoir of Matthew Davenport Hill* (1878); F. Hill, *An Autobiography of Fifty Years in Time of Reform. Edited with Additions by His Daughter Constance Hill* (1893).

34 See particularly F. Hill, ibid.

35 C. G. Hey, 'Rowland Hill and Hazelwood School, Birmingham', BRL 660912, p. 14.

36 R. Hill, p. 89; W. H. Ryland (ed.), *Reminiscences of Thomas Henry Ryland* (Birmingham, 1904).

37 Birmingham and Edgbaston Proprietary School, *Deed of Settlement 1838* (Birmingham, 1840); Birmingham and Edgbaston Proprietary School, *Report and Resolutions* (Birmingham, 1838); Birmingham and Edgbaston Proprietary School, *Report of the Proceedings at the Distribution of the Medals and Certificates of Honour at the Close of the Annual Examination, 1841* (Birmingham, 1841).

38 S. Lines, *A Few Incidents in the Life of Samuel Lines* (Birmingham, 1858), p. 13.

39 A. F. J. Brown, 'Voluntary public libraries', in W. R. Powell (ed.), *A History of the County of Essex* (bibliography) (1959).

40 Birmingham Brotherly Society, *Minutes* (Birmingham, 1835); Young Men's Christian Association, *The Chief End of Life: a New Year's Address to Young Men* (Birmingham, 1850).

41 Essex and Suffolk File.

42 William Pattisson, a Congregationalist, and Henry Crabb Robinson, an Anglican, were apprenticed to a Colchester lawyer. They kept up a running debate on political and intellectual affairs in the heady days of the 1790s. Witham File.

43 W. and H. Raynbird, *On the Agriculture of Suffolk* (1849), p. 96.

44 A. F. J. Brown, *Essex at Work* (Chelmsford, 1969), p. 63.

45 L. Caroe, 'Urban change in East Anglia in the 19th century', unpublished Ph.D. thesis, University of Cambridge (1969), p. 72.

46 B. Mason, *Clock and Watchmaking in Colchester* (1969).

47 Essex and Suffolk File. In retailing it was possible to treat each transaction separately rather than being integrated into larger chains of finance and control as in manufacture.

48 Census of 1851: 3 Colchester clusters.

49 Birmingham Wills.

50 W. White, *Ipswich*.

51 L. I. Redstone, *Ipswich Through the Ages* (Ipswich, 1969); A. F. J. Brown, *Colchester 1815–1914* (Chelmsford, 1980).

52 Anon. 'Unpublished diary of a farmer's wife on the Warwick/Leicester border' (18 April 1823), BUL, Heslop Collection, MS10/iii/15, 1823.

53 A. F. J. Brown, 'Jonas Asplin – Prittlewell 1826–28', in *Essex People 1750–1900: From their diaries, memoirs and letters* (Chelmsford, 1972); Robert Bretnall, 'Unpublished diary' (1846).

54 G. Torrey, *Chelmsford Through the Ages* (Ipswich, 1977), p. 58.

55 J. Drake, *The Picture of Birmingham* (Birmingham, 1825), p. 69.

56 J. Gilbert (ed.), *Autobiography and Other Memorials of Mrs Gilbert*, 2 vols. (1874), vol. 1, p. 21.

57 J. J. Green, *The History of a Country Business at Stanstead in the County of Essex 1687–1887* (Ashford, 1887).

58 *Whitelock's Book of Trades*, 1831, quoted in D. Alexander, p. 207.

59 W. Beck, *Family Fragments Respecting the Ancestry, Acquaintance and Marriage of Richard Low Beck and Rachel Lucas* (Gloucester, 1897); E. A. Blaxill, *These Hundred Years 1838–1938: A Brief History of the Progress of Kent, Blaxill and Co. Ltd. of Colchester* (Colchester, 1938).

60 J. J. Green.

61 E. Shewell, *Memoir of the late John Talwin Shewell* (Ipswich, 1870).

62 R. Fletcher, *The Biography of a Victorian Village: Richard Cobbold's Account of Wortham, Suffolk* (1977).

63   Rev. Kenrick, *Memoir of the Rev. John Kentish* (Birmingham, 1854), pp. 9–10.
64   J. Hurnard, *A Memoir: Chiefly Autobiographical with Selections from his Poems* (1883).
65   M. Fawcett, *What I Remember* (1927).
66   M. White, *Directory of Essex*.
67   W. Goodwin, 'Unpublished diaries, 1785–1809', IRO HD365 1–3; L. Barton (ed.), *Selections from the Poems and Letters of Bernard Barton* (Woodbridge, 1849); G. Rickword, *Social Life in Bygone Colchester* (Colchester, 1975).
68   See the clear example of the Greenwood family in *Halstead and District Local History Society Newsletter*, 3 no. 10 (December 1979).
69   Witham File.
70   T. Vigne and A. Howkins, 'The small shopkeeper in industrial and market towns', in G. Crossick (ed.), *The Lower Middle Class in Britain* (1977).
71   H. N. Dixon, 'Reminiscences of an Essex country practitioner a century ago', *Essex Review*, xxv (1916).
72   Miller Christy, 'The history of banks and banking in Essex', *Journal of the Institute of Bankers* (October 1906). Colchester, Ipswich, Halstead and Woodbridge had two banks each; Chelmsford and Bury three. Distribution of banks in Essex shows the importance of coastal trade and the silk industry since farmers were much slower to use banks. L. Caroe, p. 48.
73   L. S. Presnell, *Country Banking in the Industrial Revolution 1760–1830* (Oxford, 1956), p. 12.
74   Essex File. J. Oakes, 'Unpublished diary 1778–1795', WSRO HA 521/1–14.
75   J. Oakes, 1789–90.
76   ibid. (19 November 1800).
77   A. Moilliet, 'Memoranda', by permission of J. L. Moilliet.
78   Up to £5000 according to the diary of a bank manager (Yorkshire). See A. Vernon, *Three Generations: the Fortunes of a Yorkshire Family* (1966).
79   ibid., p. 69.
80   The power of a banker in a small community through his ability to grant credit and his vulnerability to any slur on his reputation is magnificently portrayed in the figure of Bulstrode in George Eliot's *Middlemarch*.
81   Essex and Suffolk File; J. Oakes; J. Hanson, 'Unpublished diary 1777–1839', by permission of Jean Harding, Great Bromley, p. 116.
82   J. Oakes (December 1826).
83   A. Moilliet.
84   A. F. J. Brown, *Colchester 1815–1914* (Chelmsford, 1980).
85   W. Hawkes Smith, *Birmingham and its Vicinity as a Manufacturing and Commercial District* (Birmingham, 1836), p. 2.
86   J. Booker, *Essex and the Industrial Revolution* (Chelmsford, 1974).
87   S. Timmins (ed.), *The Resources, Products and Industrial History of Birmingham and the Midland Hardware District* (1866), preface.
88   W. Hutton, *History of Birmingham (Continued to the Present Time by his Daughter Catherine Hutton)* (1819); General Foods Ltd, *The Food Makers: A History of General Foods Ltd* (Banbury, 1972), p. 5. Bird invented the custard for his wife who was allergic to eggs.
89   W. Hutton, p. 132.
90   C. Behagg, 'Custom, class and change: the trade societies of Birmingham', *Social History*, 4 no. 3 (October 1979).
91   Although even in the eighteenth century large-scale iron furnaces required heavy investment, it has been argued that of the ten iron works near Birmingham in 1812, each had cost over £50,000 to establish. T. Ashton, *Iron and Steel in the Industrial Revolution* (Manchester, 1951), p. 100.

92   E. Roll, *An Early Experiment in Industrial Organisation Being a History of the Firm of Boulton and Watt 1775–1805* (1968).

93   W. Hawkes Smith, p. 16.

94   R. Samuel, 'The workshop of the world: steam power and hand technology in mid-Victorian Britain', *History Workshop Journal*, no. 3 (spring 1977).

95   J. L. Moilliet and B. M. D. Smith, *A Mighty Chemist: James Keir of the Lunar Society* (Birmingham, 1982).

96   Swinney quoted in S. Timmins, p. 211.

97   S. Smiles, *Lives of Boulton and Watt* (1865).

98   General Foods Ltd.

99   Matthew Boulton found himself besieged with requests to take in sons of well-to-do families, S. Pollard, *The Genesis of Modern Management* (1965), p. 149.

100 W. King, *Arthur Albright, Notes of His Life October 12, 1811–July 3, 1900* (Birmingham, 1901); D. C. Coleman, *Courtaulds: An Economic and Social History*, 2 vols. (Oxford, 1969), vol. I.

101 H. W. Dickinson, *James Watt* (Cambridge, 1935); E. Robinson, 'Training captains of industry: the education of Matthew Robinson Boulton, 1770–1842 and the younger James Watt', *Annals of Science*, 10 (1954).

102 J. Bisset, 'Reminiscences of James Bisset', Leamington Public Library, CR 1563/247.

103 W. Hutton; S. Smiles.

104 T. Clark Jnr. 'Leaflets, newspaper cuttings etc. relating to Thomas Clark Junior and Clark's metallic hothouse works Birmingham 1816–1863', BRL 520452. This pattern is also discussed in relation to Chance Bros. in R. H. Trainor, 'Authority and social structure in an industrial area: a study of three Black Country towns 1840–1890', unpublished Ph.D. thesis, University of Oxford (1981).

105 A. Kenrick, 'Unpublished diary 1787–1789', BRL 110/24; R. A. Church, *Kenricks in Hardware, a Family Business 1791–1966* (Newton Abbot, 1969).

106 Birmingham Wills; Birmingham Directories.

107 J. Evans, *The Endless Webb: John Dickinson and Co. Ltd* (1955).

108 D. R. Grace and D. C. Phillips, *Ransomes of Ipswich: A History of the Firm and Guide to its Records* (Reading, 1975), p. 4.

109 P. K. Kemp, *The Bentall Story: Commemorating 150 Years Service to Agriculture 1805–1955* (1955).

110 D. C. Colman.

111 W. C. Aitken, 'Brass and brass manufactures', in S. Timmins, p. 359.

112 S. L. Courtauld, vol. 2, p. 37.

113 S. Smiles.

114 A. Moilliet.

115 Plan of William Bentall's house and iron foundry, Heybridge, Essex, 1815, ERO T/B 229/1.

116 W. H. Ryland (ed.), *Reminiscences of Thomas Henry Ryland* (Birmingham, 1904), p. 50.

117 H. N. Dixon, 'Unpublished diary, 1846', by permission of Dr Denholm, Witham, Essex; F. Boot and A. Davenport, *The Creation of a Village: the Story of Tiptree* (Marks Tey, 1977).

118 J. L. Moilliet and B. M. D. Smith, p. 50.

119 E. Roll, p. 145.

120 J. Glyde, *Suffolk in the 19th Century: Physical, Social, Moral, Religious and Industrial* (c. 1855), p. 331.

121 J. Obelkevich, *Religion and Rural Society: South Lindsey 1825–1875* (Oxford, 1976), p. 96.

122   See, for example, changes in the function of wills. H. Benham, *Some Essex Water Mills* (Colchester, 1976).

123   A. F. J. Brown, 'Joseph Page – Farmer, Fringringhoe', *Essex People 1750–1900 from their diaries, memoirs and letters* (Chelmsford, 1972).

124   Henry Hunt, quoted in A. D. Harvey, *Britain in the Early 19th Century* (1978), p. 237.

125   William Marshall estimated that the farmer ought to at least double the £25 yearly income of a labourer in Suffolk, e.g. £50 per annum which would require upwards of 60 acres. W. Marshall, *The Review and Abstract of the County Reports to the Board of Agriculture*, Eastern Department (1818), vol. III.

126   A. Young, *General View of the Agriculture of the County of Essex* (1807), vol. I, p. 45. About 40 per cent of farms in Essex were between 100 and 250 acres. C. Shrimpton, 'The landed society and the farming community in Essex in the late 18th and early 19th centuries', unpublished Ph.D. thesis, University of Cambridge (1969), p. 310.

127   B. A. Holderness, 'Agriculture and industrialization in the Victorian economy', in G. E. Mingay (ed.), *The Victorian Countryside*, 2 vols. (1980), vol. 1.

128   Quoted in M. C. Wadhams, 'The development of buildings in Witham from 1500 to circa 1800', *Post-Medieval Archeology*, 6 (1972).

129   Census of 1851, all of Witham.

130   J. Oakes; A. F. J. Brown, 'Jonas Asplin', in *Essex People*.

131   Leases customarily ran for multiples of seven years. Arthur Biddell, farming over 1000 acres near Ipswich claimed that during his tenancy running from 1808 to 1860, rent was not even discussed with his landlord, the Earl of Bristol, 'nor lease, nor agreement, paper or parchment'. H. Biddell, 'A short biography of Arthur Biddell' (Ipswich, 1912), IRO qs Playford 9.

132   Seabrook/Bunting family papers, by permission of Mary Mallawaratchi of Colchester.

133   Robert Bretnall, 'Unpublished diary 1846', ERO D/DBs F38.

134   J. Thirsk and J. Imray, 'Suffolk farmers at home and abroad', in J. Thirsk and J. Imray (eds.), *Suffolk Farming in the Nineteenth Century* (Ipswich, 1958), p. 165.

135   John Player, *Sketches of Saffron Walden and its Vicinity* (Saffron Walden, 1845).

136   A. F. J. Brown, 'Joseph Page', in *Essex People*.

137   William Bentall, 'Unpublished diary, 1807', ERO DF 1/30.

138   E. L. Jones, 'Agriculture 1700–1780', in R. Floud and D. McClosky (eds.), *The Economic History of Britain since 1700*, 2 vols. (Cambridge, 1981), vol. 1, p. 78.

139   W. and H. Raynbird, *On the Agriculture of Suffolk* (1949), p. 254.

140   James Allen Ransome, *The Story of His Life* (Official Directory, Ipswich, 1880).

141   W. and H. Raynbird, p. 305.

142   J. Cullum, *The History and Antiquities of Hawstead and Hardwick* (1813), p. 258.

143   J. Harriott, *Struggles Through Life Exemplified*, 2 vols. (1807), vol. 1.

144   WEA, 'The Story of Coggeshall 1700–1900', (typescript, n.d.); John Saville, 'Primitive accumulation in early industrialization in Britain', *Socialist Register* (1969), **vi**, p. 251.

145   J. Glyde, 'The autobiography of a Suffolk farm labourer', published in *The Suffolk Mercury* (1894).

146   Robert Bretnall (4 July 1846).

147 J. Gyford, 'Men of bad character: property crime in Essex in the 1820s', unpublished M.A. thesis, University of Essex (1982).
148 East Essex Agricultural Society, *Rules and Regulations: with prizes and rewards offered by the society* (Colchester, 1840).
149 S. P. Watson, 'Nineteenth century Witham: the role of local government', unpublished B.A. thesis, Department of History, University of Essex (1978).
150 AZ 'On the comparative advantages of keeping married and unmarried servants upon farms', *Farmers' Magazine*, 3 no. 9 (February 1802), p. 6.
151 For a more extended discussion see: L. Davidoff, 'The role of gender in "the first Industrial Nation": agriculture in England 1780–1850', in R. Crompton and M. Mann (eds.), *Gender and Stratification* (Cambridge, 1986).
152 M. Karr and M. Humphrey, *Out on a Limb: An Outline History of a branch of the Stokes Family 1645–1976* (Ongar, Essex, 1976).
153 W. and H. Raynbird, p. 132.
154 Seabrook/Bunting.
155 J. Cullum, p. 252.
156 *Select Committee on Agriculture,* Minutes of evidence (1833), vol. IV, Q. 10624. See also K. Snell, *Annals of the Labouring Poor: Social Change and Agrarian England 1660–1900* (Cambridge, 1985), p. 87.
157 R. Fletcher, *The Biography of a Victorian Village Richard Cobbold's Account of Wortham, Suffolk, 1860* (1977).
158 F. H. Groome, *Two Suffolk Friends* (1895), p. 35.
159 See R. Blomfield, 'The Farmer's Boy', in *Poems* (1845); William Cobbett, quoted in H. Perkin, *The Origins of Modern English Society* (1969), p. 93.
160 W. Green, *Plans of Economy or the Road to Ease and Independence* (1804), p. 10.
161 M. J. Peterson, *The Medical Profession in Mid-Victorian London* (Berkeley, 1978); R. E. Franklin, 'Medical education and the rise of the general practitioner, 1760–1860', unpublished Ph.D. thesis, University of Birmingham (1950); Birmingham Directories.
162 Dr Dixon of Witham refused to make up his own drugs as did Lydgate the progressive doctor in George Eliot's *Middlemarch*.
163 R. E. Franklin; *Birmingham Aris's Gazette* of 1825 carries advertisements for such courses; K. D. Wilkinson (ed.), *The Birmingham Medical School* (Birmingham, 1925).
164 Birmingham File; J. Penfold, *The History of the Essex County Hospital, Colchester 1820–1948* (Colchester, 1984).
165 G. Manning Butts, A Short History of the Birmingham Law Society 1818–1968 (Birmingham, 1968).
166 Mason was related by marriage to the artist John Constable's family in Dedham. Essex and Suffolk File; M. Miles, 'Eminent practitioners: the new visage of county attornies C.1750–1800', in G. Rubin and D. Sugerman (eds.), *Law, Economy and Society: Essays in the History of English Law 1750–1914* (1984).
167 Witham File; Suffolk Mercury, *Public Men of Ipswich and East Suffolk: A Series of Personal Sketches* (Ipswich, 1875).
168 'Records and minutes of the Birmingham Law Society' (1818), by permission of the Birmingham Law Society.
169 ibid., 1828–47.
170 ibid. (19 August 1837).
171 Nathaniel Lea, 'Unpublished memorandum book 1837–1838'. 'Unpublished ledger book, No. 1 1835–1845', by permission of Mr. I. C. Lea.
172 Witham File.
173 J. Penfold, 'Charles Boutflower F.R.C.S: Surgeon in Wellington's army and

Hon. Surgeon to the Essex and Colchester Hospital', *History of Medicine*, 7 nos. 1/2 (spring/summer, 1976), p. 14.

174 J. Oxley-Parker, *The Oxley-Parker Papers: From the letters and diaries of an Essex family of land agents in the 19th century* (Colchester, 1964).

175 Birmingham File; Essex and Suffolk File.

176 W. White, *History, Gazeteer and Directory of the County of Essex* (Sheffield, 1848); Musson's Map of Colchester (1848).

177 W. Withering (ed.), *The Miscellaneous Tracts of William Withering to which is prefixed a memoir* (1822); T. W. Peck and K. D. Wilkinson, *William Withering of Birmingham* (Bristol, 1950).

178 It is significant that the banker was willing to thus invest in a medical career. Quoted in R. E. Franklin, p. 68.

179 H. N. Dixon, 'Reminiscences of an Essex county practitioner a century ago', *Essex Review*, **xxiii** (1914).

180 Adèle Galton, Letters to her brother John Howard Galton, BRL, Galton Coll. 30b. Letter no. 35 (May 1833); K. Pearson.

181 W. J. Reader, *Professional Men: The Rise of the Professional Classes in Nineteenth Century England* (1966), p. 1.

182 Birmingham File.

183 John Bensusan-Butt, personal communication.

184 See 'Setting the scene'.

185 Census of 1851 – Edgbaston; Birmingham File.

186 Witham File; Janet Gyford, personal communication.

187 F. M. L. Thompson, *Chartered Surveyors: the Growth of a Profession* (1968).

188 M. Anderson, 'Preparation and analysis of a machine readable national sample from the enumerators books of the 1851 Census of Great Britain', *Report to the Social Science Research Council* (January 1980), HR. 2066, p. 11.5.

189 Census of Great Britain, *Parliamentary Reports – Occupational Abstract 1841*, part I: England and Wales (1844), p. 193.

190 G. J. Holyoake, *Sixty Years of an Agitator's Life* (1900).

191 J. E. Oxley, *Barking Vestry Minutes and Other Parish Documents* (Colchester, 1955), p. 222.

192 John Perry, 'Unpublished diary', Box T, FHL.

193 Census of Great Britain, *Parliamentary Reports, Occupational Abstract 1841*, p. 193.

194 Birmingham Law Society, 'Records and minutes' (11 November 1838).

195 J. Penfold, *Essex and Colchester Hospital*; B. Drew, *The Fire Office: Being the History of the Essex and Suffolk Equitable Insurance Society, Ltd. 1802–1952* (1952).

196 Witham File.

197 G. Crossick, 'The emergence of the lower middle class in Britain: a discussion', in G. Crossick (ed.), *The Lower Middle Class in Great Britain* (1977).

198 T. A. Finigan, unpublished 'Journal of T. A. Finigan, Birmingham Town Mission, 1837–1838', BRL 312749.

199 ibid.

200 J. Oakes (21 August 1800).

201 Quoted in D. Lockwood, *The Blackcoated Worker: A Study in Class Consciousness* (1956), p. 123.

202 William Banks Austin, 'Unpublished diary, 1851–1852' (21 July), BRL 710101.

203 E. Gaskell, *North and South* (Oxford, 1977), pp. 75, 80.

204 R. J. Morris, 'The economic history of the middle class', unpublished paper delivered to the Conference on the Middle Class, University of Leeds (1983).

Chapter 6 'The hidden investment': women and the enterprise

1   Census of Great Britain, 1851; *Population Tables*, part 2, vol. 1 (1854).
2   Will Smith, archivist Greater London Council, personal communication.
3   M. P. Medlicott, *No Hero, I Confess: a nineteenth century autobiography* (1969).
4   A. Clark, *Working Life of Women in the Seventeenth Century*, 3rd edn (1982). I. Pinchbeck, *Women Workers and the Industrial Revolution 1750–1850*, 2nd edn (1981).
5   G. E. Evans, *The Horse in the Furrow* (1960); 'Account Book of Mrs Mann, Arthur Biddell, Housekeeper 1814–1917', IRO HA2; Jane Ransome Biddell, Unpublished commonplace book, IRO HA2/D/1 and 2.
6   Quoted in E. W. Martin, *The Secret People: English Village Life after 1750* (1954), p. 243.
7   J. Player, *Sketches of Saffron Walden and its Vicinity* (Saffron Walden, 1845), p. 57.
8   For a fuller discussion of this point see: L. Davidoff, 'The role of gender in "the First Industrial Nation": agriculture in England 1780–1850', in R. Crompton and M. Mann (eds.), *Gender and Stratification* (Oxford, 1986).
9   There is some debate about the origins and timing of the phasing out of women's field labour in the Eastern counties. The point here, however, is that the subject at the time was discussed mainly on moral grounds. K. D. Snell, 'Agricultural seasonal unemployment, the standard of living and women's work in the South and East, 1690–1860', *Economic History Review*, 34 no. 3 (1981).
10 J. Glyde, *Suffolk in the 19th Century: Physical, Social, Moral, Religious and Industrial* (c. 1855), p. 367.
11 J. Obelkevich, *Religion and Rural Society: South Lindsey 1825–1875* (Oxford, 1976), p. 50.
12 A. Whitehead, 'Kinship and property; women and men: some generalizations', in R. Hirschon (ed.), *Women and Property; Women as Property* (1983).
13 The marriage settlement which included 'restraint on anticipation' (that is to discourage fortune hunters), shows clearly how both the notion of dependency and expectation that capital would follow daughters out of the kinship line were built into gentry and upper middle-class institutions. T. Murphy, 'Female shadow, male substance: women and property law in 19th century England', unpublished paper, by permission of the author.
14 W. Beck, *Family Fragments Respecting the Ancestry, Acquaintance and Marriage of Richard Low Beck and Rachel Lucas* (Gloucester, 1897), p. 8.
15 J. B. Elshtain, *Public Man, Private Woman: Women in Social and Political Thought* (Princeton, 1981).
16 J. Glyde, *Suffolk*, p. 324.
17 Birmingham Wills.
18 S. D'Cruze, 'The society now surrounding us: Colchester and its middling sort, 1780–1800', unpublished M.A. Thesis, University of Essex (1985), p. 56. In the sample of wills there was a reversal of this trend post-1830 when more widows, once again, were left to their own discretion.
19 A pattern strikingly illustrated in the wills of Isaac and Ann M. Taylor. Ann left voluminous directions for disposal of her books, clothes and trinkets to named children and grandchildren, including leaving her wedding ring, earrings and mother's hair to Jemima which 'I recommend to her particular care', PRO Prob. 11/1773 and 1764. This male/female pattern of legacies is confirmed in S. D'Cruze, and for the US in S. Lebsock, *The Free Women of Petersburg: Status and Culture in a Southern Town 1784–1860* (New York, 1984).

20   H. Dixon, 'Unpublished diary' (26 November 1845), by permission of Dr
     Denholm.
21   J. Oxley-Parker, *The Oxley-Parker Papers: From the Letters and Diaries of
     an Essex family of land agents in the 19th century* (Colchester, 1964).
22   There were legal debates on the status of widows in relation to husbands'
     partnerships. See J. Collyer, *A Practical Treatise on the Law of Partnership*
     (1840), p. 26.
23   Letter to R. Arkwright (5 May 1828), ERO D/DAr. C7/9.
24   J. Harriott, *Struggles Through Life Exemplified*, 2 vols. (1807), vol. 1, p. 329.
25   C. Shrimpton, 'The landed society and the farming community of Essex in
     the late 18th and early 19th centuries', unpublished Ph.D. thesis, University
     of Cambridge (1966), p. 233.
26   C. Chalklin, *The Provincial Towns of Georgian England: A Study of the
     Building Process 1740–1820* (1974), p. 242; J. Field, 'Bourgeois Portsmouth:
     social relations in a Victorian dockyard town 1815–1875', unpublished Ph.D.
     thesis, University of Warwick (1979), p. 132.
27   J. E. Oxley, *Barking Vestry Minutes and other Parish Documents* (Colchester,
     1955).
28   Mrs Henstridge Cobbold, 'Inventory of house and estate, 1849', IRO HA2/
     A2/886.
29   Philip Hills, personal communication.
30   Nathaniel Lea, 'Unpublished memorandum book, 1837–8', by permission of
     Mr I. C. Lea.
31   Therefore the importance of 'love and friendship' as a location for women's
     consciousness but also its limitations. See Caroll Smith Rosenberg, 'The female
     world of love and ritual: relations between women in nineteenth century
     America', *Signs*, 1 no. 1 (autumn 1975).
32   J. Oxley, p. 30.
33   R. Scase and R. Goffee, *The Real World of the Small Business Owner* (1980),
     p. 94. See also J. Finch, *Married to the Job: Wives' incorporation in men's
     work* (1983).
34   M. Karr and M. Humphreys, *Out on a Limb: An Outline History of a branch
     of the Stokes Family, 1645–1976* (Ongar, Essex, 1976), p. 39.
35   Jeremiah Howgego, 'Unpublished diary, 1829–1832', by permission of V.
     Sheldrake.
36   S. L. Courtauld, *The Huguenot Family of Courtauld*, 3 vols. (1957), vol. 2,
     p. 13.
37   E. De Selincourt, *Dorothy Wordsworth: A Biography* (Oxford, 1933), p. 183.
38   T. A. B. Corley, *Quaker Enterprise in Biscuits: Huntley and Palmers of
     Reading: 1822–1972* (1972).
39   ibid.
40   W. Hutton, *The Life of William Hutton, Stationer of Birmingham and the
     History of his Family* (1816).
41   A. E. Fairhead, *The Fairhead Series 1–10* (n.d.), ERO, p. 3.
42   T. Cross, *The Autobiography of a Stage-Coachman*, 2 vols. (1861), vol. 2,
     p. 162.
43   L. Maw, *A Tribute to the Memory of Thomas Maw: by his widow* (1850),
     p. 20.
44   Based on eighty-three cases from both areas.
45   M. Bayly, *The Life and Letters of Mrs Sewell* (1889), p. 104.
46   J. Wentworth Day, 'A Victorian family's inventive genius', *Country Life* (2
     May 1963), p. 962.
47   M. Bayly, p. 36; a pattern confirmed in George Eliot's *Adam Bede* where the
     farmer's wife, Mrs Poyser, has taken Hetty Sorrel, her husband's niece, to

train in dairying and also given a home to her own orphaned niece, Dinah, in return for household help.

48 ABG (4 January 1830).
49 Birmingham File, see Joseph Sturge.
50 Census of 1851: Witham.
51 Census of 1851: whole sample.
52 E. J. Morley, *The Life and Times of Henry Crabb Robinson* (1935); Wordsworth's daughter Catherine was named for Catherine Buck. She was the daughter of a wealthy Bury St Edmund's brewer, see R. G. Wilson, *Greene King: A Business and Family History* (1983).
53 S. L. Courtauld, vol. 2, p. 27.
54 E. J. Robson, *A Memoir of Elizabeth Robson, late of Saffron Walden* (1860), p. 37.
55 J. Bisset, 'Reminiscences of James Bisset', Leamington Public Library, CR 1563/247.
56 Walker's Charity in Fyfield Essex, *Charity Commission Reports*, vol. XVIII (1833).
57 W. Beck, p. 2.
58 E. Gibbins, *Records of the Gibbins Family also a few reminiscences of Emma J. Gibbins and letters and papers relating to the Bevington family* (Birmingham, 1911), appendix I.
59 J. Oxley-Parker, p. 128.
60 J. Perry, 'Unpublished diary 1829–1832', FHL, Box T (August 1838).
61 Mary Alice Parker, 'Unpublished diary 1867', by permission of William Lister.
62 T. Cross, vol. 1, p. 113.
63 B. Mason, *Clock and Watchmaking in Colchester* (1969).
64 Essex and Suffolk File; Birmingham File. An interesting fictional mid century account of a woman taking over the family bank is Mrs Oliphant's *Hester*, first published 1883 (1984).
65 J. A. Watson, *Savills: A Family and a Firm 1652–1977* (1977).
66 Robert Bretnall, 'Unpublished diary 1846', ERO D/DBs F38.
67 R. B. Beckett, *John Constable's Correspondence: the Family at East Bergholt 1807–1837* (1962).
68 M. Smith, *The Autobiography of Mary Smith, Schoolmistress and Nonconformist* (Carlisle, 1892).
69 M. Bayly, p. 166.
70 IJ (24 June 1809).
71 J. Oxley Parker.
72 Mary Hardy, *Diary* (Norfolk Record Society, 1968).
73 J. M. Strickland, *Life of Agnes Strickland* (1887).
74 J. Glyde, 'The autobiography of a Suffolk farm labourer', in *Suffolk Mercury* (1894), p. 74.
75 M. Bayly, p. 33.
76 *The Lady's Magazine*, published from 1770 to 1830 (price 6d), debated women's use of their property as a prominent theme. Information from E. Copeland, Pomona College, California.
77 M. A. Hedge, *Life or Fashion and Feeling: A Novel* (1822), p. 75.
78 ibid., p. 62.
79 G. Crabbe, 'The Parish Register', *Poems* (Cambridge, 1905).
80 S. Pollard, *The Genesis of Modern Management* (1965), p. 146.
81 E. L. Jones, *Agricultural and Economic Growth in England, 1650–1815* (1967).
82 George Eliot, 'Mr Gilfil's love story', in *Scenes from Clerical Life*, 2 vols. (Edinburgh, 1856), vol. 1, p. 158.
83 J. Oxley Parker, p. 107.

84   M. Bayly, p. 31.
85   The only money Catherine Marsh ever earned was readings of handwriting to raise money for charity. L. E. O'Rorke (ed.), *The Life and Friendships of Catherine Marsh* (1917), p. 25.
86   A. T. Gilbert, *Autobiography and other Memorials of Mrs Gilbert*, 2 vols. (1874), vol. I, p. 108.
87   J. Perry (December 1838).
88   M. J. Shaen, *Memorials of Two Sisters: Susanna and Catherine Winkworth* (1908), p. 13.
89   QQ in *Youth's Magazine or Evangelical Miscellany* (1820), p. 370 (pseudonym for Jane Taylor).
90   E. L. Edmunds, *The Life and Memorials of the Late W.R. Baker* (1865), p. 4.
91   M. Smith, p. 169.
92   Mrs C. Hutton Beale, *Reminiscences of a Gentlewoman of the Last Century* (Birmingham, 1891).
93   Elizabeth A. Wheler, 'Memorials of my life', 2 vols., by permission of Mr J. L. Moilliet; E. Darwin, *A Plan for the Conduct of Female Education in Boarding Schools* (1797); M. McNeil, 'A contextual study of Erasmus Darwin', unpublished Ph.D. thesis, University of Cambridge (1979).
94   Phipson Children, *A Tribute to a Father's Memory* (Birmingham, 1864).
95   In this emphasis we would differ from the conclusions drawn by M. J. Peterson, 'No angel in the house: the Victorian myth and the Paget women', *American Historical Review* (June 1984).
96   Rebecca Solly Shaen, 'Unpublished commonplace book', John Johnson Collection, Bodleian Library, Oxford, Ms 18 and 19.
97   F. H. Erith, *Ardleigh in 1796: Its Farms, Families and Local Government* (East Bergholt, Essex, 1978).
98   A. Shteir, '"The Fair Daughters of Albion" and the popularization of British botany', Paper delivered at the British Society for the History of Science (March 1982), p. 8.
99   M. A. Hedge, *Affections Gift to a Beloved God-child* (Colchester, 1819), p. 22.
100 J. Obelkevich, p. 53.
101 IJ (24 June 1809).
102 A. Watkins, *Extracts from the Memoranda and Letters of Ann Watkins* (Ipswich, 1888), p. 3.
103 E. Shore, *Journal of Emily Shore* (1891), pp. 220, 352.
104 E. A. Wheler; Amelia Moilliet, 'Memoranda', both by permission of J. L. Moilliet.
105 Harriet Walker, 'Journal of a tour made in the spring of 1837', IRO HD/236/3/5.
106 Suffolk File; A. Smart and S. B. Attfield, *Constable and His Country* (1976).
107 A. F. J. Brown, 'Voluntary public libraries', in W. R. Powell (ed), *A History of the County of Essex* (bibliography) (1959). However, a water colour of the village reading room at Writtle shows a woman and three children seated at a table. Corder collection, ERO T/B 228.
108 Quoted in J. Glyde, *The Moral, Social and Religious Condition of Ipswich in the Middle of the 19th Century* (1971), p. 173.
109 Hilda Sebastian, 'A brewing family in Essex', typescript prepared for Coggeshall Women's Institute (n.d.), by permission of the author.
110 Census of 1851: whole sample.
111 E. Gaskell, *Cranford* (1980), p. 130.
112 Census of 1851.
113 M. Reeves, *Sheep Bell and Ploughshare: the Story of Two Village Families* (1980).

114 ABG (10 July 1820).
115 W. Lean, 'Scholars at his school', compiled by J. H. Lloyd, BRL 662590; Birmingham Directories File.
116 R. and G. B. Hill, *The Life of Sir Rowland Hill and the History of Penny Postage*, 2 vols. (1880); F. Hill, *An Autobiography of Fifty Years of Reform* (1893); D. Gorham, 'Victorian reform as a family business: the Hill Family', in A. S. Wohl (ed.), *The Victorian Family, Structure and Stress* (1978).
117 J. Manton, *Mary Carpenter and the Children of the Streets* (1976).
118 Birmingham Statistical Society, 'Report on the state of Education in Birmingham', *Journal of the Historical Society of London*, 3 (1840); King Edward VI School, Birmingham, Governors Order Book, 1832–41, 1842–50, by permission of Mr Walkington, Secretary to the Governors.
119 R. Fletcher, *The Biography of a Victorian Village: Richard Cobbold's Account of Wortham, Suffolk* (1977).
120 J. Manton, *Sister Dora: The Life of Dorothy Pattison* (1971), p. 137.
121 M. L. Smith, 'Witham schools' (Witham, n.d.), p. 6.
122 J. Manton, *Mary Carpenter*.
123 R. and G. B. Hill, vol. 1, p. 142.
124 Essex Directories File.
125 A. E. Morgan, *Kith and Kin* (Birmingham, 1896), p. 9.
126 E. T. Phipson, *A Memorial of Mary Anne Phipson* (Birmingham, 1877), Phipson Children.
127 I. Southall, W. Ransom and M. Evans (eds.), *Memorials of the Families of Shorthouse and Robinson and Others Connected with Them* (Birmingham, 1902).
128 Census of 1851: Birmingham.
129 E. T. Phipson.
130 Phoebe Penn's sister had married the Bristol school proprietor Lant Carpenter, father of Mary Carpenter.
131 A. W. Matthews, *Life of Sarah Bache* (1900), p. 20.
132 ibid., pp. 71, 92.
133 E. A. Wheler, vol. I, p. 56.
134 L. Davidoff, 'The separation of home and work? Landladies and lodgers in 19th and early 20th century England', in S. Burman (ed.), *Fit Work for Women* (1979).
135 Witham File.
136 J. E. Tuffs, *Essex Coaching Days* (Letchworth, n.d.).
137 T. Cross, vol. 2, p. 206.
138 B. Mason.
139 J. Booker, *Essex and the Industrial Revolution* (Chelmsford, 1974), p. 32.
140 M. Girouard, *Victorian Pubs* (1975), p. 28 (our italics).
141 P. Mathias, *The Brewing Industry in England 1700–1830* (Cambridge, 1959).
142 G. Sturt, *A Farmer's Life with a Memoir of the Farmer's Sister* (Firle, Sussex, 1979), p. 26.
143 B. Harrison, *Drink and the Victorians: The Temperance Question in England 1815–1872* (1971), p. 46.
144 E. Edwards, *The Old Taverns of Birmingham* (Birmingham, 1879), p. 82.
145 W. White, *Directory of Ipswich* (1844).
146 F. H. Erith.
147 J. A. Chartres, 'Country tradesmen', in G. E. Mingay (ed.), *The Victorian Countryside*, 2 vols., vol. 2, p. 308.
148 Census of 1851: Witham.
149 D. Alexander, *Retailing in England During the Industrial Revolution* (1970).
150 S. D'Cruze, "'. . . To Acquaint the Ladies": women proprietors in the female

clothing trades, Colchester c. 1750–1800', unpublished paper (1985), by permission of the author, pp. 2, 3, see *The Local Historian*, **17** no. 3 (1986).

151 J. Howgego, p. 28.

152 G. Torrey, *Chelmsford Through the Ages* (Ipswich, 1977), p. 59.

153 John Pudney, unpublished diary of an Essex farmer 1757–1823, ERO T/P 116/62.

154 J. Taylor, 'Prejudice', in *Essays in Rhyme on Morals and Manners* (1816), p. 6.

155 G. J. Holyoake, *Sixty Years of an Agitator's Life* (1900), p. 10.

156 W. H. Ryland (ed.), *Reminiscences of Thomas Henry Ryland* (Birmingham, 1904).

157 W. White, *History Gazetteer and Directory of the County of Essex* (Sheffield, 1848).

158 R. Fletcher.

159 For example, Bernard Barton's sister, Maria Hack, published books for children such as *The Discovery and Manufacture of Glass: Lenses and Mirrors*. All her books were published by Harvey and Darton, the children's book publishers who gave Ann and Jane Taylor their start.

160 Marianne Nunn, *Dictionary of National Biography*; C. Porteous, 'Singing the praises of women', The *Guardian* (22 December 1982).

161 J. S. Curwen, *Memorials of John Curwen: with a Chapter on his home life by his daughter* (1882).

162 M. J. Shaen, p. 39 (her italics). Note George Eliot began her literary career by doing translations.

163 J. Oxley, p. 222.

164 'Minute Book of the Committee of the Protestant Dissenting Charity School, 12 vols. (1761–1922), 1836–47, BRL 471911.

165 J. Penfold, 'Early history of the Essex County Hospital', unpublished manuscript by permission of the author (1980), p. 13.

166 J. Lown, 'Gender and class during industrialization: a study of the Halstead silk industry in Essex, 1825–1900', unpublished Ph.D. thesis, University of Essex (1984).

167 Colchester Castle Club records.

168 M. Hardy.

169 Anon., unpublished diary of a farmer's wife on the Warwick/Leicester border (1823), BUL, Heslop Collection, Ms 10/iii/15, 1823.

170 Birmingham File.

171 G. Crabbe, p. 215.

172 D. C. Coleman, *Courtaulds: An Economic and Social History*, 2 vols. (Oxford, 1969), vol. 1, p. 126.

173 This point is forcefully argued in J. Newton, 'Pride and Prejudice: power, fantasy and subversion in Jane Austen', *Feminist Studies*, **4** no. 1 (February 1978).

174 For example Dillwyn Sims, apprenticed to a miller in Ipswich before joining Ransomes, the agricultural engineering firm. DQB.

175 The Hayward family of Colchester, personal communication, Paul Thompson; the Beadel Family of Witham, Witham File; for the Savills of Chigwell see J. A. Watson.

176 At the artisan level note the male usurpation of funeral arrangements through joinery and the making of coffins over women's traditional function of laying out the dead.

177 For Suffolk see G. E. Evans, *The Horse in the Furrow* (1960); Hannah More's barbed portrait of the 'strong minded' Miss Sparkes in *Coelebs in Search of a Wife* highlights her unfeminine interest in the stables. See Chapter 3.

178 J. D. Sykes, 'Agriculture and science', in G. E. Mingay (ed.), *The Victorian Countryside*, 2 vols. (1980), vol. 1.

179 A. Richards and J. Robin, *Some Elmdon Families* (Cambridge, 1975).

180 We are grateful to Deborah Cherry for allowing us to read her unpublished manuscript, 'Women artists'; R. Parker and G. Pollock, *Old Mistresses: Women Art and Ideology* (1981).

181 S. Lines, *A Few Incidents in the Life of Samuel Lines, Senior* (Birmingham, 1858).

182 J. Blatchly, *Isaac Johnson 1754–1835* (Suffolk Record Office, 1979), p. 9.

183 Samuel Williams, DNB. He illustrated an edition of Jeffrey Taylor's, *The Farm*.

184 W. Beck.

185 D. Stroud, *Humphrey Repton 1752–1818* (1962).

186 William Jackson Hooker was the first director of Kew Gardens. He, his son and son-in-law were eventually knighted for their contributions to horticulture. His daughter, wife of the latter, illustrated the journal edited by the Hooker family. N. Scourse, *The Victorians and their Flowers* (1983). See also John Claudius Loudon's enterprise, Chapter 3.

187 D. Allen, 'The women members of the Botanical Society of London; 1836–1856', *The British Journal for the History of Science*, **13** no. 45 (1980), p. 247.

188 D. Allen, *The Naturalist in Britain: A Social History* (Harmondsworth, 1978), p. 167.

189 E. Mann, *An Englishman at Home and Abroad 1792–1828* (1930), p. 201.

190 S. L. Courtauld, vol. 1, p. 44; D. C. Coleman, vol. 2, p. 469.

191 J. Manton, *Mary Carpenter*, p. 39.

192 See N. Stock, *Miss Weeton's Journal of a Governess*, 2 vols. (Newton Abbot, 1969), vol. 1, p. 23.

193 J. Perry (August 1838) (his italics).

194 H. Sebastian, personal communication.

195 R. D. Best, *Brass Chandelier: A Biography of R.H. Best of Birmingham* (1940), p. 25.

196 K. Pearson, *The Life, Letters and Labours of Francis Galton*, 3 vols. (Cambridge, 1914), vol. 1, p. 124.

197 Birmingham File; Essex and Suffolk File.

198 Halstead and District Local History Society Newsletter, **3** no. 10 (December 1979).

199 F. Prochaska, *Women and Philanthropy in 19th Century England* (Oxford, 1980), p. 106.

200 Census of 1851 – Edgbaston; Ratebook for Edgbaston.

201 It should be kept in mind that the wills sample starts in 1780 when there were fewer professional and salaried posts than in 1851, the date of the census. But the point still stands.

202 59 per cent of adult female relatives lived with male household heads and 41 per cent in households with a woman head, compared to the 80 per cent male and 20 per cent female household heads in the whole sample. Sisters living with salaried single males made up a fifth of all adult sisters living with their unmarried brothers. Salaried men tended to be younger and less well off than other occupations. Census sample – whole. For an important discussion of spinsters in nineteenth-century Britain see M. Anderson, 'The social position of spinsters in mid-Victorian Britain', *Journal of Family History*, **9** no. 4 (1984).

203 F. Parkin, 'Social closure as exclusion', in *Marxism and Class Theory: a Bourgeois Critique* (1979), p. 53. On the more general meaning of gender and hereditary practices see, C. Delphy and D. Leonard, 'Class analysis, gender

analysis and the family', in R. Crompton and M. Mann (eds.), *Gender and Stratification* (1986).

204 Mrs S. Stickney Ellis, *The Women of England: Their Social Duties and Domestic Habits* (1839), p. 463.

Introduction to Part Three

1 Census sample. These large numbers of visitors in middle-class households are confirmed in A. Howe, *The Cottonmasters: 1830–1860* (Oxford, 1984).

2 Richard Wall, 'The household: demographic and economic change in England 1650–1970', in R. Wall, J. Robin and P. Laslett, *Family Forms in Historic Europe* (Cambridge, 1983), p. 511.

3 Census sample – all areas.

Chapter 7 'Our family is a little world': family structure and relationship

1 F. Hill, *An Autobiography of Fifty Years in time of Reform*, edited with additions by his daughter Constance Hill (1893).

2 R. B. Beckett, *John Constable's Correspondence: the Family at East Bergholt 1807–1837* (1962).

3 V. K. Pichanick, *Harriet Martineau: the Woman and her Work, 1802–76* (Ann Arbor, 1980), p. 238; Rebecca Solly Shaen, 'Unpublished diary 1800–1855', John Johnson Collection, Bodleian Library Ms 18 and 19, p. 276.

4 It has been calculated that a family of two parents and eight children produces forty-five sets of permutations and 28,500 potential relationships, J. Bossard, *The Large Family System* (Philadelphia, 1956).

5 R. S. Shaen, p. 24.

6 M. Anderson, 'The social implications of demographic change, 1750–1950', unpublished paper, by permission of the author (1984), p. 25.

7 M. S. Hartman, 'Child-abuse and self-abuse: two Victorian cases', in *History of Childhood Quarterly*, 2 no. 2 (1974).

8 Robert Greenwood, Commonplace Book, ERO D/DQ24.

9 William Henry Pattisson, letter to Henry Crabb Robinson, 20 February 1800, DWL.

10 Birmingham, Essex, Suffolk and Witham Files; This compares with roughly two-thirds of the general population up to 1800. See E. A. Wrigley and R. S. Schofield, 'English population history from family reconstitution: summary results 1600–1799', *Population Studies*, 37 (1983), p. 168.

11 Census sample. The higher percentage of men older than their wives in the local files may be due to the preponderance of the upper middle class.

12 Bundle of letters from Adèle Booth née Galton to John Howard Galton, 1805–33, BRL Galton Collection, mss 306; Bundle of letters from Sophia Brewin née Galton to John Howard Galton 1805–33, Galton Collection, BRL mss. 307.

13 Rev. C. B. Tayler, *Edward or Almost an Owenite* (1840), p. 15.

14 J. Priestley, *Autobiography* (new edn, Bath, 1970), p. 87.

15 Of course, inflation has to be kept in mind. T. W. Hill, *Remains of the Late Thomas Wright Hill* (1859), p. 120.

16 A. G. Gardiner, *The Life of George Cadbury* (1923), p. 23.

17 W. H. Ryland, (ed.), *Reminiscences of Thomas Henry Ryland* (Birmingham, 1904), p. 83.

18 E. A. Wheler (née Galton), 'Memorials of my life', 2 vols., by permission of Mr J. L. Moilliet.

19 J. Luckcock, *Annual Address to the teachers of the Old and New Meeting Sunday Schools* (Birmingham, 1819), p. 18.

20 W. King, *Arthur Albright. Notes of his Life March 12, 1811–August 3, 1900* (Birmingham, 1901), p. 24.

21 A. Kenrick, 'Unpublished diary 1787–89', BRL 110/24.

22 W. King, p. 46.

23 Henry Dixon, 'Unpublished diary' (13 May 1843), by permission of Dr Denholm.

24 H. Allen, *A Beloved Mother by her Daughter: the Life of Hannah S. Allen* (1884), p. 18.

25 J. Harriott, *Struggles Through Life Exemplified*, 2 vols. (1807), vol. 1, p. 338.

26 M. Bayly, *The Life and Letters of Mrs Sewell* (1889), p. 51. Charlotte Brontë expressed grave doubts about marriage in these terms just before her own wedding; see M. Shaen, *Memorials of Two Sisters: Susanna and Catherine Winkworth* (1908), pp. 117–18.

27 M. Syms, 'Unpublished letters and reminiscences' by permission of the late Margaret Wilson (14 December 1807).

28 J. Seabrook, 'Commonplace .book' 1832–56, by permission of Mary Mallawaratchi.

29 R. S. Shaen, p. 168.

30 W. H. Ryland.

31 R. S. Shaen, p. 233.

32 ibid., p. 238.

33 Information supplied by Owen H. Wicksteed.

34 E. Mann, *An Englishman at Home and Abroad 1792–1828* (1930), p. 196.

35 C. Marsh, *The Life of the Rev. William Marsh* (1867).

36 E. A. Wheler, vol. 1, p. 171.

37 Bundle of letters from Sophia Brewin, no. 32.

38 Bundle of letters from Samuel Tertius Galton to John Howard Galton 1805–41, BRL Galton Collection, 315, no. 33; ibid., no. 31.

39 J. Bevan Braithwaite, *Memoirs of Anna Braithwaite* (1905), p. 36.

40 R. S. Shaen, p. 290.

41 Mrs S. Stickney Ellis, 'Behaviour to husbands', in *The Wives of England, their Relative Duties, Domestic Influence and Social Obligations* (1843).

42 (See Appendix 1). Note how the form of this poem is identical to Ann Taylor's 'My Mother'. J. Luckcock, *Sequel to Memoirs in Humble Life*, including the period from 1809–25 (Birmingham, 1825), pp. 49–51.

43 J. A. James, *The Family Monitor, or a help to domestic happiness*, in T. S. James (ed.), *The Works of John Angell James*, 17 vols. (Birmingham 1860–4), vol. 12, p. 108.

44 R. S. Shaen, p. 242; A headmaster at Winchester, born 1803, was one of eleven children who between them had ninety-three children and 256 grand-children; C. A. E. Moberley, *Dulce Domum: George Moberly, His Family and Friends* (1911).

45 The importance of this structure – compounded by step-siblings – is described in relation to Freud's family which exhibited many of the same features as the early Victorian English middle class, E. Jones, *The Life and Work of Sigmund Freud* (Harmondsworth, 1964), pp. 36–40.

46 H. Allen.

47 Rev. A. Dallas, *Incidents in the Life and Ministry* (1871).

48 E. Hodder, *The Life of Samuel Morley* (1887), p. 183.

49 S. L. Courtauld, *The Huguenot Family of Courtauld*, 3 vols. (1957), vol. 2, p. 72.

50 W. Hutton, *The Life of William Hutton, Stationer of Birmingham and the History of his Family* (1841), p. 113.

51   E. Conder, *Josiah Conder: A Memoir* (1857), p. 179.
52   W. Beck, *Family Fragments* (Gloucester, 1897), p. 67.
53   S. L. Courtauld, vol. 2, p. 19.
54   C. M. Wakefield, *Thomas Attwood* (1885), p. 92.
55   Mrs W. B. Kenrick (ed.), *Chronicles of a Nonconformist Family: the Kenricks of Wynne Hall, Exeter and Birmingham* (Birmingham, 1911), p. 220.
56   E. Conder, p. 113.
57   E. Gibbins, *Records of the Gibbins Family also a few reminiscences of Emma J. Gibbins and letters and papers relating to the Bevington Family* (Birmingham, 1911), p. 220. Arthur Young adored his youngest daughter, 'Bobbin', who made up to him for an unsatisfactory marriage. She died at age 14, which contributed to his religious conversion in middle age. M. Betham-Edwards, *The Autobiography of Arthur Young* (1898).
58   Alaric Watts, 'The Youngling of the Flock', quoted in Jane Ransome Biddell, Manuscript Book of Poems, IRO HA2/D/1.
59   L. C. Sier, *The Blomfields of Dedham and Colchester* (Colchester, 1924), pp. 27, 43.
60   C. Sturge, *Family Records* (1882), p. 47.
61   H. Allen, p. 8.
62   Bundle of letters from Miss L. A. Patterson to John Howard Galton 1804–20, Galton Collection, BRL mss. 369, no. 79.
63   E. Mann, p. 49; J. Oxley-Parker, *The Oxley-Parker Papers: From the Letters and Diaries of an Essex Family of Land Agents in the 19th Century* (Colchester, 1964).
64   Jeremiah Howgego, 'Unpublished diary, 1829–1832', by permission of V. Sheldrake, 13 July 1833.
65   E. Gibbins, p. 23.
66   E. Conder, p. 180.
67   M. G. Fawcett, *What I Remember* (1924); J. Manton, *Elizabeth Garrett Anderson* (1965).
68   Rev. J. G. Breay, *Memoir of the Rev. John George Breay Minister of Christ Church Birmingham, with correspondence and sermon*, 5th edn (Birmingham, 1844), pp. 352–3.
69   E. A. Wheler, vol. 2, p. 325.
70   M. Marsh, p. 340.
71   See, for example, R. and G. B. Hill, *The Life of Sir Rowland Hill and the History of Penny Postage*, 2 vols. (1880), vol. 1, p. 66.
72   I. Southall, W. Ransome and M. Evans (eds.), *Memorials of the Families of Shorthouse and Robinson and others connected with them* (Birmingham, 1902), p. 48.
73   Rev. J. G. Breay, p. 369.
74   H. N. Dixon (13 January 1842).
75   J. C. Reid, *Thomas Hood* (1963), p. 195.
76   D. M. Armitage, *The Taylors of Ongar: Portrait of an English Family of the 18th and 19th Centuries* (Cambridge, 1939).
77   J. Luckcock, *Sequel to Memoirs in Humble Life*.
78   S. L. Courtauld, vol. 2.
79   H. N. Dixon (14 April 1847).
80   J. Seabrook.
81   M. Slater, *Dickens and Women* (1983).
82   ECS (30 January 1935).
83   Mrs Bayly, p. 122.
84   A. and J. Taylor, *Original Poems for Infant Minds* (1865).
85   H. C. Alexander, *Richard Cadbury* (1906), p. 83.
86   This compares with an average of 39.3 at last birth for the whole population

estimated through parish reconstitution, E. A. Wrigley and R. S. Schofield, p. 174.

87 Brightwen Family, DQB; D. McLaren, 'Marital fertility and lactation 1570–1720', in M. Prior (ed.), *Women in English Society 1570–1720* (1985).

88 Thanks for this interpretation to Oriel Sullivan, Department of Sociology, University of Essex.

89 William Bentall's children by his second wife, Mary Hammond, Bentall Family Bible, by permission of Michael Bentall.

90 A. Gilbert, *Autobiography and Other Memorials of Mrs Gilbert*, 2 vols. (1874), vol. 1, p. 128.

91 E. Gibbins.

92 A. Kenrick.

93 See, for example, Mrs Musgrove in Jane Austen's *Persuasion* (1818), and its centrality in Mrs Gore's novel, *Pin Money* (1843).

94 M. Marsh, pp. 403–4.

95 D. Gorham, *The Victorian Girl and the Feminine Ideal* (1982), p. 67.

96 A. Moilliet, 'Memoranda', by permission of Mr J. L. Moilliet.

97 M. Jesup, *Selections from the Writings of Mary Jesup* (1842), p. 38.

98 L. A. G. Strong, *A Brewer's Progress 1757–1957* (1957).

99 P. H. Chevasse, *Advice to Mothers on the Management of their Offspring* (Birmingham, 1840), p. 97. *Advice* sold 460,000 copies and was quickly followed by *Advice to Wives on the management of themselves during the periods of pregnancy, labour and suckling* (Birmingham, 1843) which sold 390,000. The figures are from G. W. Craig, 'The Old Square: a chapter of bygone local medical history', in *Birmingham Medical Review*, X (1935). p. 102.

100 L. E. O'Rorke (ed.), *The Life and Friendships of Catherine Marsh* (1917), p. 11.

101 M. Marsh, p. 18.

102 H. Allen, p. 111.

103 A. Moilliet.

104 C. Southall, *Records of the Southall Family* (1932), p. 105.

105 R. S. Shaen, p. 266.

106 Quoted in C. Binfield, *So Down to Prayers: Studies in English Non-conformity 1780–1920* (1977), p. 49.

107 Mrs C. Hutton Beale, *Reminiscences of a Gentlewoman of the Last Century* (Birmingham, 1891), p. 116.

108 R. S. Shaen, pp. 242, 302.

109 S. Knight, *Memoir of Sarah Knight, Wife of Thomas Knight of Colchester* (1829), p. 23.

110 E. A. Wheler, vol. 1, p. 5.

111 Mrs. S. Stickney Ellis, *Mothers of England their Influence and Responsibility* (n.d.), p. 3.

112 The 'dear young family' of an Essex shopkeeper's wife, with their constant interruptions left few opportunities for making (religious) memorandums. M. Jesup, p. 43.

113 M. Bayly, p. 122.

114 G. J. Holyoake, *Sixty Years of an Agitator's Life* (1900), p. 15.

115 Jane Ransome Biddell, 'A Reply for Some Versos', 1836, in unpublished Book of Poems, IRO HA2/D/1.

116 M. Marsh, p. 158.

117 J. H. Plumb, 'The new world of children in 18th century England', in N. McKendrick, J. Brewer and J. H. Plumb (eds.), *The Birth of a Consumer Society: the Commercialization of 18th Century England* (1982).

118 C. C. Hankin (ed.), *Life of Mary Ann Schimmelpenninck*, 3rd edn (1859).

119   A. and J. Taylor, 'Rhymes for the Nursery', in *The Poetical Works of Ann and Jane Taylor* (1877).
120   J. Hurnard, *A Memoir: Chiefly Autobiographical* (1883).
121   E. Gibbins, appendix I.
122   C. Sturge.
123   Mrs W. Byng Kenrick, p. 137.
124   E. Mann, p. 27.
125   J. Evans, *The Endless Webb: John Dickinson and Co. Ltd. 1804–1954* (1955).
126   J. Luckcock, *Sequel to Memoirs in Humble Life*, p. 51.
127   A. M. Taylor, *Reciprocal Duties of Parents and Children* (1818), p. 42.
128   A. Smith, 'Pocket diaries 1837–1846', *East Anglian Miscellany* (1928).
129   S. Chitty, *The Woman Who Wrote Black Beauty: A Life of Anna Sewell* (1971).
130   J. J. Green, 'Some extracts from the diary of Susanna Day, a Quakeress of Saffron Walden', *Essex Review*, **xviii** (1909).
131   A. and J. Taylor, *Original Poems for Infant Minds* (1815).
132   William H. Pattisson to Henry Crabb Robinson, letter (20 February 1800), DWL.
133   J. Hurnard, p. 117.
134   J. Perry, unpublished diary (June 1824), FHL Box T.
135   A. Camps, *The Diary and Work of Mrs Amy Camps* (1893), p. 9.
136   J. Webb, 'Lines to My Father on His Birthday', *Prose and Verse* (1824).
137   D. Gorham, p. 41.
138   L. E. O'Rorke, pp. 16, 23.
139   L. Barton, *Selections from the Poems and Letters of Bernard Barton* (Woodbridge, 1849); this substitution is the theme of George Eliot's novella 'Amos Barton', *Scenes from Clerical Life Collected Works*, 24 vols. (1856), vol. 1.
140   A. M. Taylor, p. 128.
141   Anon., *A Brief Sketch of the Life of Anna Backhouse* (1852), p. 24.
142   E. Shore, *Journal of Emily Shore* (1891); A. R. Mills, *Two Victorian Ladies: More Pages From the Journals of Emily and Ellen Hall* (1969).
143   M. Slater.
144   A. Moilliet.
145   Will of Daniel Till of Witham, Essex, ERO.
146   D. Gorham, pp. 44–7.
147   George Eliot, 'Brother and Sister', in *The Spanish Gypsy, Collected Works* (1901), p. 587.
148   M. A. Hedge, *My Own Fireside* (Colchester, 1832), pp. 114–25.
149   I. Taylor (ed.), 'To a Brother on His Birthday', in *Memoirs, Correspondence and Poetical Remains* (1831).
150   C. E. Tonna, *Personal Recollections* (1847). See a classical statement by a Suffolk Evangelical cleric, Rev. C. B. Tayler, 'A Sister's Love', *May You Like It* (1823).
151   R. S. Shaen, p. 311.
152   C. Sturge.
153   O. A. Sherrard, *Two Victorian Girls* (1966), p. 180.
154   See J. Dunn, *Sisters and Brothers* (1984).
155   R. B. Beckett.
156   R. S. Shaen; these conflicts of interest are superbly portrayed in the struggle between Mrs Tulliver, the miller's wife, and her husband's feckless sister in George Eliot's *Mill on the Floss* (1860).
157   E. M. Forster, *Marianne Thorton: A Domestic Biography 1797–1887* (1956), pp. 114–27.
158   J. W. Ley, *The Dickens Circle; a narrative of the novelist's friendships* (1918).
159   R. S. Shaen, pp. 288, 276.

160 For a description see, E. De Selincourt, *Dorothy Wordsworth: A Biography* (Oxford, 1933).
161 H. Martineau, *Autobiography*, 3 vols. (1877), vol. 1, p. 99.
162 N. Anderson, 'The marriage with a deceased wife's sister bill controversy: incest anxiety, and the defence of family purity in Victorian England', *Journal of British Studies*, 21 no. 2 (1982). Harriet Martineau's only novel, *Deerbrook* (1839), centres on a man who is in love with his wife's sister.
163 A. J. Guerard, quoted in M. Slater, p. 89.
164 R. S. Shaen, p. 188.
165 Jane Ransome Biddell, 'Lines Composed in Christ Church Place, Ipswich' (1809), and 'Verses on the Death of a Dear and Only Sister' (1810).
166 C. Sturge, p. 27; M. G. Jones, *Hannah More 1745–1833* (Cambridge, 1952).
167 J. Dunn; for the continued strength and ambivalence of the sister relationship see, T. McNaron, *The Sister Bond: A Feminist View of a Timeless Connection* (New York, 1985).
168 R. B. Beckett, p. 306.
169 M. Bayly.
170 John Webb to Elizabeth Webb Savill, letter (26 June 1799), ERO, D/DUcd C6.
171 Wills, total sample. Childless couples are undoubtedly over represented since when there were children a will might be thought less necessary.
172 M. Karr and M. Humphrey, *Out on a Limb: An Outline History of a Branch of the Stokes Family 1645–1976* (1976).
173 C. Marsh, p. 123.
174 Quakers officially prohibited first cousin marriages but this seems to have been broken several times in the local records.
175 W. Beck, p. 143.
176 Samuel Savill, correspondence with the Sayer-Walkers, ERO D/DUcdC6.
177 John Hanson, 'Unpublished journal, 1822 to 1829', by permission of Jean Harding.
178 Census: whole sample.
179 W. Bentall, 'Unpublished diary of a farmer, 1807', ERO D/F 1/30.
180 Mary Mallawaratchi, unpublished records of the Seabrook and Bunting Family, Colchester, Essex.
181 H. N. Dixon.
182 Hannah Pattison to Henry Crabb Robinson, letter (16 July 1803), DWL.
183 M. A. Hedge, p. 126.
184 R. S. Shaen, p. 259.
185 E. Conder, 'The principle use of birthdays is in the case of absent friends, to have a set time to remember them *specially*', p. 104.
186 A. Wohl, 'Sex and the single room: incest among the Victorian working class', in A. Wohl (ed.), *The Victorian Family: Structure and Stresses* (1978).
187 Rev. C. B. Tayler, 'The Mother', *May You Like It* (1823), p. 180.
188 This seems to have been particularly true for men growing to maturity in mid century. See L. Davidoff, 'Class and gender in Victorian England', in J. L. Newton, M. Ryan, J. Walkowitz (eds.), *Sex and Class in Women's History* (1983); S. Chitty, *The Beast and the Monk: A Life of Charles Kingsley* (1974).
189 R. S. Shaen, p. 318.

Chapter 8 'My own fireside': the creation of the middle-class home

1 E. Shore, *Journal of Emily Shore* (1891), p. 22.
2 L. E. O'Rorke (ed.), *The Life and Friendships of Catherine Marsh* (1917), p. 15.

3   A. Camps, *The Diary and Work of Mrs Amy Camps, with extracts from her writings* (1893), 1 May 1844.

4   Susannah Tabor Savill, unpublished Commonplace Book, Savill Coll., ERO, D/DUcd.

5   A. T. Gilbert, *Autobiography and Other Memorials of Mrs Gilbert*, 2 vols. (1879), vol. I, p. 68; F. M. L. Thompson, *Hampstead, Building a Borough 1650–1964* (1974), p. 241.

6   D. Cannadine, 'The aristocracy and the towns in the nineteenth century: a case study of the Calthorpes and Birmingham, 1807–1910', unpublished D. Phil. thesis, University of Oxford (1975); *Lords and Landlords: The Aristocracy and the Towns 1774–1967* (Leicester, 1980).

7   M. Girouard, *Life in the English Country House: A Social and Architectural History* (New Haven, 1978).

8   A. T. Gilbert, vol. 1, p. 157.

9   Corder Collection, Rolleston Farm, Writtle 1846–64, ERO T/B.228.

10 Count Pecchio, *Semi-Serious Observations of an Italian Exile During His Residence in England* (1833), p. 19.

11 R. S. Shaen, unpublished diary 1800–55, Bodleian Library, Oxford, John Johnson Coll. Ms 18 and 19, 1834, p. 279.

12 W. Green, *Plans of Economy on the Road to Ease and Independence* (1804), p. 20.

13 L. Davidoff, 'The rationalization of housework', in D. Barker and S. Allen (eds.), *Dependency and Exploitation in Work and Marriage* (1976).

14 C. Binfield, *So Down to Prayers: Studies in English Nonconformity 1780–1920* (1971), p. 38.

15 J. Luckcock, *Hints for Practical Economy in the Management of Household Affairs* (Birmingham, 1834), p. 18.

16 J. Burnett, *A History of the Cost of Living* (Harmondsworth, 1969).

17 *Census of Great Britain, 1851: Tables of the Population and Houses*, p. xxxvi.

18 J. Glyde, *Suffolk in the 19th Century: Physical, Social, Moral, Religious and Industrial* (1855), p. 39.

19 J. C. Loudon, *A Treatise on Forming, Improving and Managing Country Residences*, 2 vols. (1806), vol. 1, p. 146.

20 H. Repton, 'View from my own cottage in Essex', *Fragments on the Theory and Practice of Landscape Gardening* (1816).

21 For the social implications see the novel, E. Eden, *The Semi-Detached House* (1859).

22 J. Seabrook, 'Unpublished commonplace book' (*c.* 1830), by permission of Mary Mallawaratchi.

23 J. Stovin, *Journals of a Methodist Farmer 1871–1875* (1982), p. 182.

24 A. D. Harvey, *Britain in the Early 19th Century* (1978).

25 C. W. Chalklin, *The Provincial Towns of Georgian England: A Study of the building process 1740–1820* (1974).

26 Essex and Suffolk File.

27 J. Hill and R. K. Dent, *Memorials of the Old Square* (Birmingham, 1897).

28 J. Drake, *The Picture of Birmingham* (Birmingham, 1825), p. 45.

29 R. Palmer (ed.), *A Touch on the Times: Songs of Social Change 1770–1914* (Harmondsworth, 1974), pp. 78–9.

30 C. Pye, *A Description of Modern Birmingham* (Birmingham, 1818), p. 74.

31 T. R. Slater, 'Family, society and the ornamental villa on the fringes of English country towns', *Journal of Historical Geography*, 4 no. 2 (1978); for Colchester see, George Rickword, *Social Life in Bygone Colchester* (Colchester, 1975); J. Bensusan-Butt, Colchester, personal communication.

32 Census sample: Essex and Suffolk.

33 L. C. Cryer, *A History of Rochford* (1978).

34 Rev. C. B. Tayler, 'A Merchant's Wife', in *May You Like It* (1823), p. 104.
35 C. Fox and J. Melville, unpublished typescript: 'Diary of a Visit to Bingley Hall, Birmingham' (1819), BRL 669392, p. 20.
36 J. Bensusan-Butt, *The House that Boggis Built: A Social History of the Minories* (Colchester, 1972).
37 W. Bentall, plan of iron works and house at Heybridge, 1815, ERO T/B 229/1.
38 R. B. Beckett, *John Constable's Correspondence: The Family at East Bergholt 1807–1837* (1962).
39 B. Walker, 'Some eighteenth century Birmingham houses and the men who lived in them', *Birmingham Archeological Society Transactions*, 53 (1932).
40 In the 1790s, James Oakes remodelled his Bury St Edmund's home when he turned to full-time banking and included a new bank parlour. J. Oakes, 'Unpublished diary' (April 1790), WSRO, HA521/1–14 (see Chapter 6).
41 E. Marshall, *A Biographical Sketch* (1900), p. 20.
42 Charity Commissioners, *Reports on Charities and Education of the Poor in England and Wales*, 1815–37, vol. xxxv.
43 Janet Gyford, personal communication.
44 A. F. J. Brown, *Essex at Work* (Chelmsford, 1969), p. 160.
45 W. Withering, *The Miscellaneous Tracts of William Withering M.D., F.R.S. to which is prefixed a memoir by his son* (1822), p. 74.
46 L. I. Redstone, *Ipswich Through the Ages* (Ipswich, 1969), p. 125.
47 G. Torrey, *Chelmsford Through the Ages* (Ipswich, 1977), p. 71; J. Drake, pp. 69, 34.
48 Clause XIII, 7 and 8 George II, IV, Cap. 29. The distinction is important since conviction for burglary of a dwelling house automatically led to a death sentence, while from a shop, warehouse or counting house the sentence was transportation, imprisonment or whipping. We are indebted to Janet Gyford for drawing our attention to this legislation.
49 B. Harrison, *Drink and the Victorians: the temperance question in England 1815–1872* (1971), p. 46.
50 M. Briggs, *The English Farmhouse* (1953).
51 N. Harvey, *A History of Farm Buildings in England and Wales* (Newton Abbot, 1970), p. 76.
52 E. Mercer, *English Vernacular Houses: A Study of the Traditional Farmhouses and Cottages* (1975), p. 74.
53 R. Baker, 'On the farming of Essex', reprint from *Journal of the Royal Agricultural Society* (1844), p. 31.
54 J. C. Loudon, vol. I, p. 250.
55 Lavenham Rectory, 'Plans for an extension' (1828), WSRO 806/2/14.
56 E. A. Wood, *A History of Thorpe-le-Soken to the year 1890* (Thorpe-le-Soken, 1975).
57 F. H. Erith, *Ardleigh in 1796: Its farms, families and local government* (East Bergholt, 1978).
58 Rev. J. Bramston, *Witham in Older Times*. Two lectures delivered at Witham Literary Institute (Chelmsford, 1855), p. 48.
59 C. Marsh, *The Life of the Rev. William Marsh* (1867).
60 H. H. Horton, *Birmingham: A Poem in Two Parts* (Birmingham, 1851), p. 87.
61 *Edgbaston Directory and Guide* (Birmingham, 1853).
62 G. Yates, *An Historical and Descriptive Sketch of Birmingham* (Birmingham, 1830), p. 247.
63 D. Cannadine, *Lords and Landlords*, p. 214.
64 *Edgbaston Directory*, introduction.

65 T. Ragg, *Scenes and Sketches from Life and Nature: Edgbaston and other poems* (Birmingham, 1847), p. 128.

66 W. Hutton, *History of Birmingham continued to the present by his daughter Catherine Hutton* (1819), p. 141.

67 D. Cannadine, 'The aristocracy and the towns'.

68 J. Bisset, 'Reminiscences of James Bisset', Leamington Public Library, CR 1563/246–251.

69 C. Southall, *Records of the Southall Family* (1932). Mark Rutherford in his novel, *Catherine Furze* (1896), documents the damaging potential of the separation between home and work for an East Midlands ironmonger's family in the 1840s.

70 W. King, *Arthur Albright, born 12th March 1811. Died 3rd July 1900. Notes of his Life* (Birmingham, 1901).

71 J. Burnett, p. 112.

72 ABG (23 August 1830).

73 L. Davidoff, J. L'Esperance and H. Newby, 'Landscape with figures: home and community in English society', in A. Oakley and J. Mitchell (eds.), *The Rights and Wrongs of Women* (Harmondsworth, 1976).

74 R. Gover, 'The gardenesque garden', in Victoria and Albert Museum, *The Garden: A Celebration of 1,000 Years of British Gardening* (1979).

75 e.g. ABG (24 August 1840); quoted in A. F. J. Brown, *Colchester in the 18th Century* (Colchester, 1969), p. 20.

76 T. Clark Jnr., 'Leaflets, newspaper cuttings etc. relating to Thomas Clark junior and Clark's metallic hothouse works Birmingham 1813–63', BRL 520452.

77 J. C. Loudon, *The Greenhouse Companion: Comprising a General Course of Greenhouse and Conservatory Practice* (1829), p. 1.

78 W. H. Ryland (ed.), *Reminiscences of Thomas Henry Ryland* (Birmingham, 1903), p. 43.

79 Samuel Gross, 'Unpublished diary, 1829–1831', IRO 31/8/3.5–5.1.

80 D. Allen, *The Victorian Fern Craze: A History of Pteideomania* (1969).

81 J. Luckcock, 'My House and Garden: Lime Grove, Edgbaston' (1828), BRL 375948 (n.p.).

82 N. Scourse, *The Victorians and their Flowers* (1983).

83 E. A. Wood, p. 113.

84 A. Young, *General View of the Agriculture of the County of Essex* (1807), p. 43.

85 A. T. Gilbert, vol. I, p. 285.

86 J. Luckcock, 'My House and Garden'; The importance of trees as 'a kind of family monument, a bid for personal immortality' is noted by Keith Thomas, *Man and the Natural World: Changing Attitudes in England: 1500–1800* (1983), p. 218; See also Jane Austen's use of trees as a symbol of stable culture associated with land which would have appealed to Luckcock. A. Duckworth, *The Improvement of the Estate: A Study of Jane Austen's Novels* (Baltimore, 1971), p. 54.

87 J. Luckcock, ibid., (n.p.).

88 K. Sanecki, 'Tools of the trade', in Victoria and Albert Museum.

89 J. Harvey, 'Nurseries, nurserymen and seedsmen', in ibid.; J. Harvey, *Early Gardening Catalogues* (1972).

90 L. Barton (ed.), *Selections from the Poems and Letters of Bernard Barton* (Woodbridge, Suffolk, 1849), p. 294.

91 M. Syms, 'Unpublished letters and reminiscences', Letter of 3 October 1809. By permission of the late Margaret Wilson.

92 'Bundle of letters from Isabella Galton, née Strutt to her son Theodore Howard Galton 1825–76' BRL Galton Collection, 434.

93   J. Stovin, p. 115.
94   Rev. J. Creighton, 'A father's advice to his daughter', *The Youth's Magazine or Evangelical Miscellany* (1820), p. 67.
95   M. Cadbury, 'Ms book of Childhood reminiscences. The happy days of our childhood', BRL Cadbury Collection 466/344.
96   A. F. J. Brown, 'Jonas Asplin', in *Essex People 1750–1900* (Chelmsford, 1972), p. 138.
97   Jane Loudon, *Gardening for Ladies* (1840), p. 244.
98   J. Hurnard, 'The setting sun', quoted in R. Hamilton, *James Hurnard: A Victorian Character* (Cambridge, 1946), p. 63.
99   C. Phythian-Adams, 'Rural culture', G. Mingay (ed.), *The Victorian Countryside*, 2 vols. (1981), vol. 2.
100 E. Cadbury, 'Letters from Richard Tapper Cadbury and his wife Elizabeth to the family 1806–55', BRL Cadbury Collection 466/300/1–21 (27 August 1824); M. Cadbury, n.p.
101 A. Pease, *Rachel Gurney of the Grove* (1907), pp. 134–5.
102 Jane Loudon, p. 7.
103 G. Darley, 'Cottage and suburban gardens', in Victoria and Albert Museum, p. 155; L. Davidoff, 'His cabbages and her pinks: men, women and the English garden', unpublished paper (1984).
104 James Oakes (1789).
105 J. C. Loudon, *The Suburban Gardener and Villa Companion* (1838), p. 680.
106 L. Davidoff, 'The rationalization of housework'; J. T. Bunce, *Birmingham Life Sixty Years Ago*, articles for the Birmingham Weekly Post (Birmingham, 1899). See particularly the article dated 15 April 1899.
107 H. More, *Coelebs in Search of a Wife, Comprehending of Domestic Habits and Manners, Religion and Morals*, 2 vols. (1809), vol. II, p. 169.
108 J. Luckcock, *Hints for Practical Economy in the Management of Household Affairs*, p. 5.
109 G. Crabbe, 'The Parish Register', in *Poems* (Cambridge, 1905), p. 169.
110 A. Biddell, in G. Ewart Evans, *The Horse in the Furrow* (1960), p. 93.
111 G. Sturt, *William Smith, Potter and Farmer 1790–1858* (Firle, Sussex, 1978).
112 M. Girouard, *The English Country House: A Social and Architectural History* (New Haven, 1978).
113 A. T. Gilbert, vol. I, p. 23.
114 J. T. Bunce (25 March 1899); for a more commodious but similarly integrated house and enterprise see the merchant house described in an advertisement in ABG (2 February 1804).
115 L. I. Redstone, p. 125.
116 A. T. Gilbert, vol. I, p. 68.
117 M. Cadbury (n.p.).
118 E. Shore, pp. 216–17.
119 In advice on building new farm houses, a parlour was urged as an 'absolute necessity'. T. Stone, *An Essay on Agriculture with a View to Inform Gentlemen of Landed Property Whether Their Estates are Managed to their Greatest Advantage* (Lynn, 1785), p. 243.
120 A. T. Gilbert, vol. 1, p. 52.
121 J. Thirsk and J. Imray, *Suffolk Farming in the Nineteenth Century*, Suffolk Records Society (1958), p. 129.
122 See, for example, the barometers in farmhouses, documented in J. Cullum, *The History and Antiquities of Hawstead and Hardwick* (1813), p. 258.
123 Anon., 'Diary of a farmer's wife on the Warwick/Leicester border' (1823), BUL, Heslop Collection, Ms 10/iii/15; see also Royal Institute of British Architects, *Rooms Concise: Glimpses of the Small Domestic Interior 1500–1850*, RIBA exhibit (1981).

124   Quoted in J. Burnett, *A History of the Cost of Living*, p. 159.
125   J. Priestley, 'Inventory of house and goods destroyed during the riots, 1791', BRL 174683; W. Hutton, 'Inventory of household goods etc. at High Street and Bennetts' Hill, destroyed in the riots 1791', BRL 145428.
126   J. Pudney, 'Unpublished diary of a farmer near Kelvedon, 1757–1823', ERO T/P   116/62.
127   Mahogany imported from the Empire had replaced the darker, heavier indigenous oak of the seventeenth century. Estate of Simcox as described in ABG (15 March 1830); Estate of William Marsh, ABG (27 July 1840); *Sale Catalogue of the Neat Household Furniture of the late Bernard Barton* (26 July 1849).
128   M. I. Fowler, 'One hundred years ago', *Essex Review* (July 1932); Witham File.
129   J. Luckcock, *Hints for Practical Economy*, p. 26.
130   J. Hurnard, *A Memoir. Chiefly Autobiographical* (1883), p. 10.
131   Nathaniel Lea, 'Unpublished ledger book No. 1, 1835–45', by permission of Mr I. C. Lea.
132   'A collection of letters concerning the family of Benjamin and Candida Cadbury 1806–51', BRL 614280. Candia Cadbury to her mother (3 March 1829); the marriage of Emma Cadbury to Thomas Gibbins also provided the occasion for home improvements. E. Gibbins (ed.), *Records of the Gibbins Family and a few reminiscences of Emma J. Gibbins, and letters and papers relating to the Bevington family* (Birmingham 1911), appendix I.
133   T. M. Hope, *The Township of Hatfield Peverel: Its History, Natural History and Inhabitants* (Chelmsford, 1930), pp. 152–5. R. S. Shaen, 1822; personal information Elaine Strutt.
134   J. Burnett, *A Social History of Housing*; J. Taylor, 'The life of a looking glass', *Contributions of QQ* (1845).
135   C. Davidson, *Woman's Work is Never Done: A History of Housework in the British Isles 1650–1950* (1982). A. Ravetz, 'The Victorian coal kitchen and its reforms', *Victorian Studies*, **XI** no. 4 (June 1978).
136   H. Biddell, 'Thomas Clarkson and Playford Hall: reminiscences and recollections', IRO 9q3 Playford.
137   Coal gas was used primarily for public lighting in streets and shops and was not available for domestic use until after mid century.
138   Anon., *Passages in the Life of a Young Housekeeper Edited by Herself* (1862).
139   G. Mingay, *Arthur Young and His Times* (1975).
140   L. R. Cryer, *A History of Rochford* (1978), p. 29; for the struggle over water supplies and drainage in Colchester, see Andrew Phillips, *Ten Men and Colchester* (Chelmsford, 1985), pp. 23–31.
141   L. Wright, *Clean and Decent* (1940).
142   C. P. Fox and J. Melville.
143   R. Rawlinson, *The Public Health Act: Report of Birmingham* (1849), pp. 26, 31.
144   J. Glyde, *The Moral, Social and Religious Condition of Ipswich in the Middle of the 19th Century* (1971), p. 47.
145   G. Rosen, 'Disease, debility and death', in M. Wolf and H. Dyos (eds.), *The Victorian City, Images and Realities*, 2 vols. (1974), vol. 2.
146   D. Sperber, *Rethinking Symbolism* (Cambridge, 1975).
147   R. M. Anthony, 'A diary of 1803', *History Today*, **16** (1966), pp. 477, 482.
148   G. M. Young, *Victorian England: Portrait of an Age* (Oxford, 1966), p. 7.
149   A. M. Taylor, *Practical Hints to Young Females on the Duties of a Wife, a Mother and a Mistress of a Family* (1815), p. 54.
150   'Account book of Mrs Mann, housekeeper to the family of Arthur Biddell' (1814–17), IRO HA2/A5/1.

151 ABG (3 January 1820).
152 Quoted in the first paragraph of the first issue, *Magazine of Domestic Economy* (1835).
153 J. Luckcock, *Hints*, pp. 16–17.
154 Mary Young, 'Account books 1818–1819'; 'Cashbook 1833–1844'; 'Common Place Books 1823–1827', London Museum Library.
155 J. Manton, *Elizabeth Garrett Anderson* (1965).
156 *Select Committee on Agriculture*, IV (1833), Q. 10632.
157 J. Thirsk and J. Imray, 'Suffolk farmers at home and abroad', in *Suffolk Farming in the 19th Century* (1958), p. 129; Ryland, *Reminiscences*, p. 30.
158 Richard Wheeler of Lay and Wheeler, Colchester Wine Merchant, interview.
159 E. A. Wheler, née Galton, 'Memorials of my life', 2 vols., vol. I, p. 68. By permission of Mr J. L. Moilliet.
160 For the meaning attached to the serving of food and its importance in rituals of order, see Mary Douglas, 'Deciphering a meal', *Daedulus*, 101 (1972).
161 J. Austen, *Pride and Prejudice* (Oxford, 1980), p. 58.
162 H. Martineau, *Deerbrook*, 2nd edn (1983).
163 M. Young.
164 J. Player, *Sketches of Saffron Walden and Its Vicinity* (Saffron Walden, 1845), p. 18.
165 A. Vernon, *Three Generations: the Fortunes of a Yorkshire Family* (1966), p. 101.
166 L. Barton, p. xxiv.
167 M. Howitt, *Mary Howitt, An Autobiography* (1889), p. 120.
168 C. Davidson; for a detailed description of goffering a baby's cap see E. M. Forster, *Marianne Thorton: A Domestic Biography 1797–1887* (1956), p. 179.
169 Reckitt Family, DQB.
170 C. Davidson, p. 158.
171 N. Mutton (ed.), 'An engineer at work in the West Midlands. The diary of John Urpeth Raistick for 1820', *Journal of West Midlands Regional Studies*, special publication, no. 1 (Wolverhampton, 1969).
172 Shaw Letters, BUL *passim*.
173 M. E. Fox, *Mary Pease. A Memoir by her daughter* (1911), p. 21.
174 A. Watkins, *Extracts from the Memoranda and Letters of Ann Watkins* (1888), p. 4.
175 R. S. Shaen, 'Diary' (1854), p. 318.
176 E. Higgs, 'Domestic service and household production', in A. John (ed.), *Unequal Opportunities: Women's Employment in England 1800–1918* (1986).
177 Census Sample: all areas.
178 S. Cadbury to E. Cadbury, 'A collection of letters concerning the family of Benjamin and Candia Cadbury, 1806–1851' (26 November 1846).
179 E. Gibbins (ed.), p. 135.
180 A. M. Taylor, *Practical Hints*, p. 38.
181 E. Gibbins (ed.), p. 191.
182 J. Gerard, 'Family and servants in the country-house community in England and Wales 1815–1914', unpublished Ph.D. thesis, University of London (1982).
183 Census: Colchester sample.
184 J. J. Hecht, *The Domestic Servant Class in 18th Century England* (1956).
185 K. D. M. Snell, *Annals of the Labouring Poor: Social Change and Agrarian England 1660–1900* (Cambridge, 1985), p. 326.
186 A. Vernon, *Three Generations: the Fortunes of a Yorkshire Family* (1966); Anon., *Passages in the Diary of a Young Housekeeper*.
187 Mrs Gaskell, letter to her daughters from 'Crix' (December, 1847), thanks to Elaine Strutt.

188 L. Davidoff, in A. Sutcliffe and P. Thane (eds.), *Essays in Social History II* (Oxford, 1986).
189 M. Young.
190 A bundle of letters from Adèle Booth née Galton to John Howard Galton, 1805–33, BRL Galton Collection 306, no. 12, 25; C. Marsh, *The Life of Rev. Wm. Marsh* (1867).
191 E. Gibbins (ed.), appendix I, p. 251; M. Cadbury (n.p.).
192 J. Hardy, 'The diary of Julius Hardy, button-maker of Birmingham 1788–93', transcribed and annotated by A. M. Banks, BRL 669002, p. 36.
193 Anon., 'Diary of a farmer's wife' (5 November 1823).
194 O. R. Sherrard, *Two Victorian Girls* (1966), p. 201.
195 A. Fraser-Tytler, *Commonsense for Housemaids* (5th edn 1869), p. 21.
196 C. Cadbury, A Collection of Letters (7 March 1829).
197 M. Jesup, *Selections from the Writings of Mary Jesup* (1842), p. 47.
198 A. Vernon, p. 101; Mrs Gaskell has one of her old fashioned ch⌐˙   ɔ say that if servants can read, such 'edge tools' will see the French ʌevolution enacted in England. 'My Lady Ludlow', *Round the Sofa* (1859).
199 Mary Young, 'Agreements with servants', commonplace book.
200 F. Hill, *An Autobiography of Fifty Years in Time of Reform*, edited with additions by his daughter Constance Hill (1893), p. 328.
201 Mrs S. Stickney Ellis, *The Women of England* (1st pub. 1839, n.d.), p. 173.
202 J. A. James, *The Family Monitor, or a Help to Domestic Happiness* (1st pub. 1828), in T. S. James (ed.), *The Works of John Angell James*, 17 vols. (Birmingham, 1860–4), vol. 12, p. 125.
203 M. Young.
204 M. Jesup, p. 19.
205 M. Marsh, *Memorials of a Beloved Mother* (Birmingham, 1837), p. 372.
206 L. E. O'Rorke (ed.), *The Life and Friendships of Catherine Marsh* (1917), pp. 68–9.
207 'Minute Book of the Ladies Committee of the Protestant Dissenting Charity School, 1845–91', 5 vols., BRL 471926.
208 'A small ray of genius' Radio 4 (23 December 1983); Rev. H. Thompson, *The Life of Hannah More* (1838), p. 314.
209 E. Gibbins (ed.), appendix I.
210 'Bundle of letters from Miss L. A. Patterson to John Howard Galton 1807–1818', BRL Galton Collection, 369, letters 8, 14.
211 M. Cadbury (n.p.).
212 For a discussion of the effects of servants on middle-class consciousness see, L. Davidoff, 'Class and gender in Victorian society: the diaries of Arthur J. Munby and Hannah Cullwick', in J. L. Newton, M. P. Ryan and J. R. Walkowitz (eds.), *Sex and Class in Women's History* (1983).
213 G. H. Pike, *Charles Haddon Spurgeon: Preacher, Author and Philanthropist* (1886).
214 E. Mann, *An Englishman at Home and Abroad, 1792–1828* (1930); the effects on young working-class men and women of *being* in service should also be kept in mind. There were 2171 servants in the census sample making up one-quarter of the individuals in middle-class households (see p. 463).
215 E. A. Wheler, vol. I, p. 91.
216 R. S. Shaen, p. 305.
217 H. More, vol. 2, p. 178.

Chapter 9 'Lofty pine and clinging vine': living with gender in the middle class

1 The eighteenth century seems to be the culmination of a slow process going back to the sixteenth century, see N. Elias, *The Civilizing Process: The History of Manners* (Oxford, 1978); J. Quinlan, *Victorian Prelude: A History of English Manners, 1700–1830* (1941).

2 Robert Bretnall, 'Unpublished diary 1846', ERO D/DBs F38.

3 O. R. Sherrard, *Two Victorian Girls* (1966), p. 201.

4 H. N. Dixon, 'Reminiscences of an Essex county practitioner a century ago', *Essex Review*, xxiii (1914), p. 6.

5 Rev. J. Fielding, *A Series of Letters Addressed to the Church and Congregation Assembling at the Great Meeting Coggeshall* (Coggeshall, 1815), p. 82.

6 E. Edwards, 'The electroplate trade and Charles Askin', unpublished Mss. BRL 294924, pp. 32–3.

7 A. J. Peacock, *Bread or Blood: A Study of the Agrarian Riots in East Anglia in 1816* (1965), p. 14.

8 H. N. Dixon, 'Unpublished diary' (1 December 1846), by permission of Dr Denholm.

9 Mary Hardy, 2 August 1776, *Diary* (1968).

10 J. Hurnard, *A Memoir: Chiefly Autobiographical* (1883); A. Vernon, *Three Generations: the Fortunes of a Yorkshire Family* (1966), p. 34.

11 J. Harriott, *Struggles Through Life Exemplified*, 2 vols. (1807), vol. 1, p. 287.

12 J. Burnett, *A History of the Cost of Living* (Harmondsworth, 1969).

13 E. Boyce, *The Belgian Traveller – Being a Complete Guide Through Belgium and Holland* (1827), p. 42.

14 G. Sturt, *William Smith, Potter and Farmer 1790–1858* (Firle, Sussex, 1978).

15 V. Martindale, *The Life and Work of Harriet Martineau* (1957), p. 136.

16 J. Hanson, 'Unpublished diary 1777–1839', thanks to Jean Harding, Great Bromley, Essex.

17 E. A. Wheler, née Galton, 'Memorials of my life 1808–1906', 2 vols., vol. 1, p. 91, by permission of Mr J. L. Moilliet.

18 Mrs C. Hutton Beale, *Reminiscences of a Gentlewoman of the Last Century* (Birmingham, 1891), p. 62.

19 T. Binney, *Town Life or a Youth from the Country* (1868).

20 P. Unwin, *The Publishing Unwins* (1972), p. 12.

21 G. Torrey, *Chelmsford Through the Ages* (Ipswich, 1977), p. 61.

22 Records of the Seabrook and Bunting Families, by permission of Mary Mallawaratchi.

23 A Birmingham banker's son was packed off to the continent after indiscretion in love, but this failed to silence local gossips. 'Bundle of letters from Sophia Brewin née Galton to John Howard Galton', 1805–33, BRL, Galton Collection, no. 307; 'Bundle of Letters from Adèle Booth née Galton to John Howard Galton 1805–33', BRL, Galton Collection, no. 306.

24 Rev. M. Seaman, 'The privileges of the righteous and the woes of the wicked', sermon preached at St Peter's, Colchester (17 August 1828). See also A. Clarke, 'Rape or seduction? A controversy over sexual violence in the nineteenth century', in London Feminist History Group, *The Sexual Dynamics of History* (1983).

25 J. Harriott, vol. 1, p. 343.

26 ibid., p. 330.

27 E. Shore, *The Journal of Emily Shore* (1891), p. 178.

28 For example, Elizabeth Bennett's visit to Darcy's Derbyshire home, in *Pride and Prejudice*. The Leasowes was the home of the popular poet William Shen-

stone and was a favourite for 'party excursions' from Birmingham. W. Hutton, *History of Birmingham* (1819), p. 130; Mary Hardy.

29 J. Oxley Parker, *The Oxley Parker Papers: From the Letters and Diaries of an Essex family of land agents* (Colchester, 1964).

30 T. W. Peck and K. D. Wilkinson, *William Withering of Birmingham* (Bristol, 1950), p. 172.

31 For the extensive transport network provided locally see J. E. Tuffs, *Essex Coaching Days* (Letchworth, n.d.).

32 W. Bridges Adams, *English Pleasure Carriages: Their Origin, History, Varieties, Materials, Construction, Defects, Improvements and Capabilities* (1837).

33 A. F. J. Brown, *Witham in the 18th Century* (Witham, 1968).

34 J. Harriott, vol. 1, p. 276.

35 E. Edwards, *Personal Recollections of Birmingham and Birmingham Men* (Birmingham, 1877); E. A. Wheler, vol. 1, p. 25.

36 J. Austen, *Pride and Prejudice* (Oxford, 1980), p. 28.

37 E. Gibbins (ed.), *Records of the Gibbins Family also a few reminiscences of Emma J. Gibbins and letters and papers relating to the Bevington family.* (Birmingham, 1911), appendix 1.

38 Mrs W. B. Kenrick (ed.), *Chronicles of a Nonconformist Family. The Kenricks of Wynne Hall, Exeter and Birmingham* (Birmingham, 1932), p. 137.

39 C. Willett and P. Cunnington, *Handbook of English Costume in the Nineteenth Century* (1959), p. 381.

40 'One letter from Samuel Galton to Hubert Galton 1802', BRL Galton Collection, no. 278; Mrs E. L. Edmunds, *The Life and Memorials of the Late W.R. Baker* (1865), p. 8.

41 R. S. Shaen, 'Unpublished diary 1800–1855', John Johnson Collection Ms 18 and 19, Bodleian Library, Oxford, p. 273.

42 'Bundle of letters from Sophia Brewin née Galton to John Howard Galton 1805–33', BRL Galton Collection, no. 307, letter 24.

43 H. N. Dixon, 'Unpublished diary', by permission of Dr Denholm (11 November 1843).

44 E. Mann, *An Englishman at Home and Abroad 1792–1828* (1930).

45 E. Morley, *The Life and Times of Henry Crabb Robinson* (1935); contrast also William Wordsworth's walking adventures in Europe with Dorothy's role as mother's help to an elder brother: E. De Selincourt, *Dorothy Wordsworth: A Biography* (Oxford, 1933).

46 Ann Taylor Gilbert, *Autobiography and Other Memorials of Mrs Gilbert*, 2 vols. (1874), vol. 1, p. 107.

47 E. Gibbins (ed.), p. 25.

48 R. S. Surtees, 'Analysis of the hunting field', in E. W. Bovill (ed.), *The England of Nimrod and Surtees 1815–54* (Oxford, 1959), p. 91.

49 Quoted in R. J. White, *Life in Regency England* (1963), p. 53.

50 D. Wilson, *A Short History of Suffolk* (1977), p. 129.

51 A. F. J. Brown, *Essex at Work* (Chelmsford, 1969); C. Clark, *Tiptree Races: A Comic punning poem* (Maldon, 1833).

52 S. Golding, 'The importance of fairs in Essex, 1759–1850', *Essex Journal*, 10 no. 3 (1975), p. 53.

53 'Bundle of letters from Violetta Galton née Darwin to John Howard Galton 1807–1818', BRL Galton Collection, no. 317, letter 4.

54 AGB (6 January 1840).

55 R. D. Storch, '"Please to Remember the Fifth of November": conflict, solidarity and public order in Southern England 1815–1900', in R. Storch (ed.), *Popular Culture and Custom in Nineteenth Century England* (1982).

56 J. W. Shorthouse, 'Unpublished diary 1853', BRL 612498.

57 Mrs L. Benton, *Recollection of New Street in the Year 1877* (Birmingham, 1877), p. 4.
58 'Bundle of letters from Sophia Brewin née Galton to John Howard Galton', letter 10.
59 E. Mann, p. 201.
60 Mary Hardy (February 1778).
61 J. Perry, 'Unpublished diary 1818–1842', FHL, Box T (11 July 1824).
62 Robert Bretnall (January 1848).
63 L. Taylor, *Mourning Dress: A Costume and Social History* (1983), p. 25.
64 E. Gaskell, *North and South* (1977), p. 266.
65 Jeremiah Howgego, 'Unpublished diary 1829–1834', by permission of V. Sheldrake.
66 J. Glyde, *The Moral, Social and Religious Conditions of Ipswich in the Middle of the 19th Century* (1971), p. 38.
67 J. C. Loudon quoted in J. S. Curl, *The Victorian Celebration of Death* (Newton Abbot, 1972), pp. 82–3.
68 Birmingham General Cemetery Company, *Articles of Association* (Birmingham, 1857); *Showell's Dictionary of Birmingham* (1st published 1885, 2nd edn Wakefield, 1969); J. Glyde.
69 D. C. Courtauld, *Courtaulds, An Economic and Social History*, 2 vols. (Oxford, 1969); L. Taylor.
70 A. Moilliet, 'Memoranda, 1819–28', by permission of Mr J. L. Moilliet.
71 Robert Bretnall (2 March 1847); Amelia Opie, the Quaker convert from Norwich, was an indefatigable trial-goer, C. L. Brightwell, *Memorials of the Life of Amelia Opie* (1854).
72 This has been called 'the great masculine renunciation'. It has recently been suggested that this was more complex and far from complete, see E. Wilson, *Adorned in Dreams: Fashion and Modernity* (1985), p. 29.
73 T. B. Dudley (ed.), *Memoir of James Bisset* (Leamington Spa, 1904), p. 71.
74 G. Sturt.
75 J. A. James, *The Young Man's Friend and Guide through Life to Immortality* (1851), p. 188.
76 G. E. Mingay (ed.), *Arthur Young and His Times* (1975), p. 216.
77 George Betts, 'Unpublished diary 1772–1827', IRO HD 79/AF2/1.1–39.
78 J. Perry (March 1838).
79 W. Beck, *Family Fragments Respecting the Ancestry, Acquaintance and Marriage of Richard Low Beck and Rachel Lucas* (Gloucester, 1897).
80 W. H. Ryland (ed.), *Reminiscences of Thomas Henry Ryland* (Birmingham, 1904), pp. 52–3.
81 A. Vernon.
82 P. Cunnington and A. Buck, *Children's Costume in England from the Fourteenth to the end of the Nineteenth Centuries* (1965).
83 Borrowed from men's trousers, or 'knickerbockers', C. Willett Cunnington, *English Women's Clothing in the 19th Century* (1937), p. 21.
84 E. A. Wheler, vol. 1, pp. 90–1.
85 C. Willett Cunnington and P. Cunnington, p. 381.
86 IJ (10 May, 1823).
87 A. Camps, *The Diary and Work of Mrs Amy Camps* (1893), 20 June 1819; H. S. Allen, *A Beloved Mother by her Daughter: the Life of Hannah S. Allen* (1884).
88 J. Taylor, *The Contributions of QQ* (1845), p. 383.
89 R. Burls, *A Brief Review of the Plan and Operations of the Essex Congregational Union* (Maldon, 1848).
90 Rev. E. P. Hood, *Thomas Binney: His Mind Life and Opinions* (1874), p. 151.
91 E. Conder, *Josiah Conder: A Memoir* (1857), p. 349.

92   M. A. Hedge, 'The village sabbath', *My Own Fireside* (Colchester, 1832), p. 33.
93   M. A. Hedge, *Affections Gift to a Beloved God-Child* (1819), p. 91.
94   E. J. Morley, p. 205; Ann Plumptree had been a friend of Amelia Opie. While in France she had an affair with Mary Wollstonecraft's lover, Captain Imlay.
95   E. Gibbins (ed.), appendix 1, p. 265.

Chapter 10 'Improving times': men, women and the public sphere

1   J. Bisset, 'Reminiscences of James Bisset', Leamington Public Library, 5 vols., CR 1563/247–251; T. B. Dudley (ed.), *Memoir of James Bisset* (Leamington Spa, 1904). Bisset's story is drawn mainly from these two sources.
2   J. Bisset, ibid., vol. 2, n.p.
3   Bisset officiated at the ill-fated dinner which preceded the Priestley riots. On his membership of the Society for Free Debate see J. Money, *Experience and Identity: Birmingham and the West Midlands 1760–1800* (Manchester, 1977), p. 116.
4   J. Bisset, *A Poetic Survey Round Birmingham* (Birmingham, 1800), p. 14.
5   J. Bisset, ibid., opening address.
6   T. B. Dudley (ed.), *Memoir of James Bisset*, p. 77.
7   ibid., p. 79.
8   J. Bisset, *Quaint Remarks and Comic Strictures on Birmingham's Fine Arts. The Birmingham Society of Fine Arts, A Poetic Effusion* (Leamington, 1829).
9   ABG (10 October 1830).
10   J. Habermas, 'The public sphere: an encyclopedia article', *New German Critique*, 1 no. 3 (1974). Thanks to G. Eley for this reference.
11   J. Brewer, 'Commercialization and politics', in N. McKendrick, J. Brewer and J. H. Plumb (eds.), *The Birth of a Consumer Society. The Commercialization of Eighteenth-Century England* (1983), p. 219.
12   R. J. Morris, 'A year in the public life of the British bourgeoisie', unpublished manuscript (1985).
13   R. J. Morris, 'Voluntary societies and British urban elites, 1780–1850: an analysis', *The Historical Journal*, 26 no. 1 (1983), p. 101.
14   Birmingham Infant School, 'Minute Books 1825–31 and Annual Reports', BRL 300098.
15   K. Clarke, 'Public and private children: infant education in the 1820s and 1830s', in C. Steedman, C. Unwin, and V. Walkerdine (eds.), *Language, Gender and Childhood* (1985).
16   Birmingham Infant School, 6th Annual Report 1831 in 'Minute Book 1831–66 and Annual Reports', BRL 300090.
17   Birmingham Infant School, 'Minute Books 1825–31'.
18   Birmingham Botanical and Horticultural Society, 'Minute Book' 17 July 1829–6 June 1836, BUL 2/1/1/1.
19   J. Luckcock, *Sequel to Memoirs in Humble Life* (Birmingham, 1825), p. 92.
20   Birmingham Botanical and Horticultural Society.
21   This finding in Birmingham, Essex and Suffolk is confirmed by M. B. Simey, *Charitable Effort in Liverpool in the Nineteenth Century* (Liverpool, 1951).
22   Mrs W. Byng Kenrick (ed.), *Chronicles of a Nonconformist Family. The Kenricks of Wynne Hall, Exeter and Birmingham* (Birmingham, 1932), pp. 226–7.
23   Birmingham Botanical and Horticultural Society (4 October 1833).
24   Birmingham Botanical and Horticultural Society, 'Minute Book August 1836–July 1846), BUL 2/1/1/2 (2 January 1837).
25   *Select Committee Report on Public Walks and Places of Exercise* (1833) (448), vol. XV, p. 9.

26 Birmingham Botanical and Horticultural Society (22 October 1845).
27 J. Drake, *The Picture of Birmingham* (Birmingham, 1825), pp. 58–9.
28 See, for example, Society for the Protection of Property of Manufacturers and Others, *Rules and Orders* (Birmingham, 1840).
29 Peter King, 'Prosecution associations in Essex, 1740–1800', unpublished paper, by permission of the author.
30 ECS (10 May 1834).
31 Notice of meeting held at the Blue Posts, Witham (10 May 1798), thanks to J. Gyford for this reference.
32 On the ironmasters see T. S. Ashton, *Iron and Steel in the Industrial Revolution*, 2nd edn (Manchester, 1951), especially the chapter on 'Ironmasters'. On the Birmingham Law Society see 'Records and Minutes of the Birmingham Law Society 1818–57', by permission of the Birmingham Law Society; W. and H. Raynbird, *On the Agriculture of Suffolk* (1849).
33 K. Hudson, *Patriotism with Profit: British Agricultural Societies in the 18th and 19th Centuries* (1972).
34 D. E. Allen, *The Naturalist in Britain: A Social History* (Harmondsworth, 1978).
35 A. Ryland, Notes from an unpublished journal, permission of Mrs R. Waterhouse.
36 John Cadbury, tea and coffee merchant, was the chairman of the Birmingham markets and fairs committee and headed the sub-committee which was responsible for the new Market Hall. T. Insull, *John Cadbury 1801–89* (Birmingham, 1979).
37 J. Thirsk and J. Imray, 'An improved corn and cattle market in Saxmundham', *Suffolk Farming in the Nineteenth Century* (1958).
38 ECS (5 December 1834).
39 J. M. Roberts, *The Mythology of Secret Societies* (1972).
40 D. Knopp and G. P. Jones, *The Genesis of Freemasonry* (Manchester, 1947), p. 141.
41 J. M. Roberts, p. 52.
42 *By-Laws of the Angel Lodge, Colchester*, no. 59 of Ancient Free and Accepted Masons (Colchester, 1835); Bro. J. F. Watson, *A History of British Union Lodge No. 114, Ipswich 1762–1962* (Ipswich, 1962); J. H. Joseph and H. J. Boocock, *Early Records of St Paul's Lodge of Free and Accepted Masons, No. 43 1764–1863* (Birmingham, 1904).
43 J. Gillis, *Youth and History: Tradition and Change in European Age Relations 1770–Present* (1974), p. 78.
44 D. Wright, *Woman and Freemasonry* (1922).
45 J. Bensusan-Butt, 'Freemasonry', private local history collection, Colchester.
46 ibid.; Essex and Suffolk File.
47 J. M. Roberts.
48 A. F. J. Brown, 'Joseph Page, farmer of Fringrinhoe, 1799–1803', *Essex People 1750–1900 from their diaries, memoirs and letters* (Chelmsford, 1972).
49 E. Edwards, *The Old Taverns of Birmingham* (Birmingham, 1879), p. 5.
50 E. Pickard, 'Some account of my own Life', BRL Mss 22/11.
51 E. Edwards, p. 5.
52 M. E. Speight, 'Politics in the Borough of Colchester 1812–1847', unpublished Ph.D. thesis, University of London (1969), p. 167.
53 E. Edwards.
54 B. Harrison, *Drink and the Victorians: The Temperance Question in England 1815–72* (1971); P. Clark, *The English Alehouse: A Social History 1200–1830* (1983); M. Girouard, *Victorian Pubs* (1975).
55 E. Mann, *An Englishman at Home and Abroad 1792–1828* (1930), p. 28.

56   Watercolour of the Writtle Reading Room and Library, Corder Family
     Records, ERO T/B 228.
57   Birmingham Philosophical Institution, *Reports* (Birmingham, 1834, 1835,
     1840).
58   J. Taylor, *Display*, 6th edn (1817), p. 41.
59   J. Penfold, *The History of the Essex County Hospital, Colchester 1820–1948*
     (Colchester, 1984).
60   S. P. Watson, 'Nineteenth century Witham: the role of local government',
     unpublished B.A. thesis, University of Essex (1978).
61   J. Drake, *The Picture of Birmingham* (Birmingham, 1825), p. 78.
62   H. More, *Coelebs in Search of a Wife Comprehending of Domestic Habits
     and Manners, Religion and Morals*, 2 vols., 9th edn (1809), vol. 2, p. 20.
63   R. I. and S. Wilberforce, *Life of William Wilberforce*, 5 vols. (1838), vol. 5,
     p. 264.
64   See, for example, E. Fry, *Memoir of the Life of Elizabeth Fry*, edited by two
     of her daughters, 2 vols. (1847), vol. 1, pp. 299–300. Catherine Cappe made
     very similar arguments, see C. Cappe, *Thoughts on the Desirableness and
     Utility of Ladies visiting the Female Wards of Hospitals and Lunatic Asylums*
     (1816).
65   *Youth's Magazine or Evangelical Miscellany*, new series (1816–27), 1820 QQ
     (Jane Taylor), p. 370.
66   M. A. Hedge, *Affections Gift to a Beloved God-child* (1819), p. 27.
67   A. Summers, 'A home from home: Women's philanthropic work in the
     nineteenth century', in S. Burman (ed.), *Fit Work for Women* (1979).
68   J. A. James, *Female Piety or the Young Woman's Friend and Guide Through
     Life to Immortality*, 5th edn (1856), p. 130.
69   *The Birmingham Monthly Argus and Public Censor*, 2 no. 11 (June 1829).
70   H. N. Dixon, 'Unpublished diary, 1840–1850' (5 June 1842), by permission
     of Dr Denholm.
71   A. Camps, *The Diary and Work of Mrs Amy Camps with Extracts from her
     Writings* (1893).
72   'James Allen Ransome, the Story of His Life', *The Official Directory for
     Suffolk* (1880).
73   Anon., *Passages in the Life of a Young Housekeeper* (1862), p. 19.
74   A. R. Mills, *Two Victorian Ladies* (1969). The politics of husband hunting
     was a favourite target of novelists like Trollope and Thackary.
75   E. A. Wheler, 'Memorials of my life 1808–1906', 2 vols., vol 1, p. 180, by
     permission of Mr J. L. Moilliet.
76   Birmingham File.
77   T. S. James (ed.), *The Collected Works of John Angell James*, 17 vols. (Birm-
     ingham, 1860–4), *The Family Monitor or a Help to Domestic Happiness*, vol.
     12, p. 42.
78   E. Gibbins, *Records of the Gibbins Family Also Reminiscences of Emma J.
     Gibbins and Letters and Papers Relating to the Bevington Family* (Birm-
     ingham, 1911), appendix I, p. 263.
79   A. Moilliet, 'Memoranda', by permission of Mr J. L. Moilliet.
80   e.g. Birmingham Society for the Protection of Young Females and Suppression
     of Juvenile Prostitution (Birmingham, 1840). The importance of *informal*
     organization should not be underestimated. In Colchester, the wife of an
     opulent Congregational Whig corn merchant held regular tea parties which
     were 'reunions of all that was most serious in the town'. G. Rickword, *Social
     Life in Bygone Colchester* (Colchester, 1975), p. 37.
81   Personal communication, Marion Glastonbury.
82   H. C. Colman, *Jeremiah James Colman: A Memoir* (1905), p. 92.

83 P. K. Kemp, *The Bentall Story: Commemorating 150 Years Service to Agriculture 1805–1955* (1955), p. 21.

84 See, for example, the Ransomes in Ipswich, the Sturges and James in Birmingham. Essex, Suffolk and Birmingham File.

85 F. K. Prochaska, *Women and Philanthropy in Nineteenth Century England* (Oxford, 1980), pp. 26–7.

86 ABG (30 July 1821).

87 ABG (22 April 1833).

88 A. Moilliet, 'Memoranda'.

89 Birmingham Ladies Negro's Friend Society, 'Reports 1845–89', BRL 98614.

90 C. Pye, *A Description of Modern Birmingham* (Birmingham, 1818), p. 25.

91 A. F. J. Brown, *Colchester 1815–1914* (Chelmsford, 1980), p. 95.

92 Personal communication from Mrs Joan Hall, archivist to the Birmingham General Hospital.

93 John Penfold, 'Early history of the Essex County Hospital', unpublished paper, by permission of the author. (T. Clark Jnr, the Birmingham greenhouse manufacturer referred to the items sold at bazaars as 'lady manufacture'. 'Leaflets, newspaper cuttings etc. relating to Thomas Clark Junior and Clark's metallic hothouse works, Birmingham, 1813–63', BRL 520452.)

94 IJ (7 June 1823).

95 For a full assessment of women's financial contribution see F. K. Prochaska, especially chs. 1–3.

96 J. Penfold.

97 J. Oakes, Unpublished diary 1778–1827, WSRO HA 521/1–14, (27 April 1800).

98 A. Kenrick, 'Diary 1787–89', BRL 100/24; R. A. Church, *Kenricks in Hardware: A Family Business 1791–1966* (Newton Abbot, 1969).

99 Mrs W. B. Kenrick (ed.).

100 R. Kenrick, 'Unpublished diary 1839–89', by permission of Mr John Kenrick.

101 ibid.

102 West Bromwich Temperance and Education Mission, 'Selected papers', by permission of Kenrick and Son, Ltd, W. Bromwich.

103 R. Kenrick.

104 C. Kenrick, 'Unpublished diary 1854–59', 3 vols., BUL, Austen Chamberlain collection AC1/1/1–3.

105 G. Malmgreen, 'Anne Knight and the radical sub-culture', *Quaker History*, 71 no. 2 (autumn 1982).

106 E. Conder, *Josiah Conder: A Memoir* (1857), p. 318; Alex Tyrrell uses this quotation as the starting point for a discussion of the ways in which 'woman's mission' legitimated increasing public involvement for women in pressure group politics. A. Tyrrell, '"Women's Mission" and pressure group politics in Britain (1825–60)', *Bulletin of the John Rylands University Library of Manchester*, 63 no. 1 (autumn 1980).

107 M. P. Ryan in *Cradle of the Middle Class: The Family in Oneida County New York 1790–1865* (Cambridge, 1981) discusses the importance of women's unpaid contribution and argues that women exerted real social power through the associations. See particularly, 'The era of association between family and society 1825–45'.

108 A. Moilliet, 'Memoranda'.

109 E. Shore, *Journal of Emily Shore* (1891), p. 203.

110 W. H. Ryland (ed.), *Reminiscences of Thomas Henry Ryland* (Birmingham, 1904), p. 40.

111 Quoted in D. Reid, 'Popular theatre in Victorian Birmingham', in L. James, D. Bradby and B. Sharralt (eds.), *Performance and Politics in Popular Drama*

(Cambridge, 1980), p. 75; J. E. Cunningham, *Theatre Royal: The History of the Theatre Royal Birmingham* (Oxford, 1950).

112 The Playgoer, *The Theatre Royal Colchester – A Century's History* (Colchester, 1912).

113 J. A. James, *Youth Warned* (Birmingham, 1824), includes the response from Parker.

114 J. E. Cunningham.

115 J. Austen, *Mansfield Park* (Harmondsworth, 1966).

116 S. Roberts, 'Gentlemen and players: the Romford Philanthropic Theatre, 1831', *Essex Journal*, 2 no. 1 (January 1967). The local press provides evidence of amateur dramatics, e.g. ABG (19 April 1790).

117 D. Reid.

118 J. T. Bunce, *Joseph Gillott 1799–1872* (Birmingham, 1872).

119 W. Weber, *Music and the Middle Class* (1975).

120 E. Edwards, *Some Account of the Origin of the Birmingham Musical Festivals and of James Kempson the Originator* (Birmingham, 1881), p. 5.

121 ibid. In 1777 the clerk, James Kempson, was offered the post of clerk and choirmaster at St Paul's Birmingham, typical of the kinds of possibilities which opened up for men.

122 J. Money, p. 84.

123 ABG (28 June 1790).

124 J. Drake, pp. 56–7; E. A. Wheler, vol. 1, p. 52.

125 ABG (7 August 1820).

126 J. Stimpson, *A Short Description of the Grand Organ in the Town Hall, Birmingham* (Birmingham, 1846); J. T. Bunce, *The Birmingham General Hospital and Triennial Music Festivals* (Birmingham, 1858).

127 J. T. Bunce, ibid., p. 75.

128 E. A. Wheler, Elizabeth Anne found herself sleeping in the attic to facilitate the guests, vol. 2, p. 87.

129 J. T. Bunce, *The Birmingham General Hospital*; ABG advertised family tickets, e.g. (27 April 1840).

130 ABG (27 March 1820).

131 ABG (16 November 1840).

132 ABG (27 February 1840).

133 ECS (30 January 1835).

134 S. Chitty, *The Woman who Wrote Black Beauty: A Life of Anna Sewell* (1971).

135 J. W. Shorthouse, 'Unpublished diary, 1853', BRL 612498.

136 A. Thackray, 'Natural knowledge in cultural context: the Manchester model', *American History Review*, no. 79 (1974), p. 678.

137 Birmingham Philosophical Institute.

138 Quoted in A. Thackray, p. 688.

139 R. J. Morris, 'Middle class culture 1700–1914', in D. Fraser (ed.), *A History of Modern Leeds* (Manchester, 1980), p. 214.

140 George Eliot in *Mill on the Floss* describes Mrs Tulliver and her sisters going over the fine linen in her cupboard that she has collected and has to part with (1860). Sophia Galton's classification of her home and garden has been cited in ch. 6, K. Pearson, *The Life and Letters of Francis Galton*, 3 vols. (Cambridge, 1914), vol. 1, fn, p. 124.

141 T. Fawcett argues that it was unusual for women to be allowed into anatomical lectures. 'Lecturing in literary and philosophical societies', unpublished paper, Sheffield Conference on Provincial Culture (1981).

142 J. Drake, p. 36; W. Smith, *A New and Compendious History of the County of Warwick from the earliest period to the present time* (Birmingham, 1830), p. 352.

143 R. and G. B. Hill, *The Life of Sir Rowland Hill and the History of Penny Postage*, 2 vols. (1880), vol. I, p. 82; T. W. Hill, *Remains of the Late Thomas Wright Hill* (1859). Isaac Taylor in Colchester also gave lecture series on scientific subjects including astronomy for which Jane and Ann helped produce visual aides. A. T. Gilbert, vol. 1.

144 A. Galton, 'Letters to her brother John Howard 1805–33', BRL Galton Coll. 306; S. T. Galton, 'Letters to his brother John Howard 1803–20', BRL Galton Coll. 315.

145 A. F. J. Brown, 'Voluntary public libraries', in W. R. Powell (ed.), *A History of the County of Essex* (bibliography) (1959), p. 316; M. Tylecote, *The Mechanics Institutes of Lancashire and Yorkshire before 1851* (Manchester, 1957).

146 In 1850, it was claimed, while the West Riding had a Literary Institute to every 867, Suffolk had only one to every 22,481 people. J. Glyde, *Suffolk in the 19th Century: Physical, Social, Moral and Industrial* (1855).

147 Birmingham Philosophical Institute, see the report for 1834; *Suffolk Chronicle* (26 April 1846), thanks to Philip Hill for this reference.

148 R. K. Dent, *The Society of Arts and the Royal Birmingham Society of Artists* (Birmingham, 1918), p. 5; J. Hill and W. Midgley, *The History of the Royal Birmingham Society of Artists* (Birmingham, 1928); Birmingham Society of Arts, 'Collection of circulars, leaflets etc. relating to the Birmingham Society of Arts and School of Design 1821–45', BRL 265350.

149 R. K. Dent, p. 3; P. Cunningham, 'The formation of the schools of design 1830–50 with special reference to Manchester, Birmingham and Leeds', unpublished Ph.D. thesis, University of Leeds (1979); T. Fawcett, *The Rise of English Provincial Art* (Oxford, 1974).

150 Birmingham Society of Arts.

151 D. Cherry, 'Women Artists', unpublished mss (1983). We are grateful to Deborah Cherry for permission to read this mss.

152 J. Hill and W. Midgley.

153 ABG (29 March 1790).

154 E. J. Hobsbawm, *The Age of Capital* (1977), p. 286; C. Hall, 'Private persons versus public someones: class, gender and politics in England, 1780–1850', in C. Steedman, C. Unwin and V. Walkerdine (eds.), *Language, Gender and Childhood* (1985).

155 J. Barrell, *English Literature in History 1730–80. An Equal Wide Survey* (1983).

156 See, for example, T. Carlyle on the dignity of work, *Past and Present* (1843). For a discussion of the effects of such ideas see A. Howe, *The Cotton Masters 1830–60* (Oxford, 1984).

157 T. Ashton, *Iron and Steel in the Industrial Revolution*, 2nd edn (Manchester, 1951). G. H. Wright, *Chronicles of the Birmingham Chamber of Commerce 1813–1913 and of the Birmingham Commercial Society 1783–1812* (Birmingham, 1913).

158 C. M. Wakefield, *Life of Thomas Attwood* (1885).

159 H. H. Horton, *Birmingham. A Poem in two parts dedicated to William Scholefield MP* (Birmingham, 1851), p. 78.

160 M. E. Speight.

161 D. Fraser, *Urban Politics in Victorian England* (Leicester, 1976).

162 M. E. Clive, *Caroline Clive. From the diary and family papers of Mrs Archer Clive 1801–73* (1949).

163 J. Howgego, 'Unpublished diary 1832–1834', by permission of V. Sheldrake; further information from Philip Hill.

164 ABG (5 July 1830).

165 F. White and Co. *History and General Directory of the Borough of Birmingham* (Sheffield, 1849), p. 36.

166   A. Phillips, *Ten Men and Colchester: Public Good and Private Profit in a Victorian Town* (Chelmsford, 1985); M. Berman, *Social Change and Scientific Organization: The Royal Institution 1799–1844* (1978), pp. 146–91.
167   ABG (9 August 1830).
168   *Birmingham Journal* (16 February 1839). For an account of the Incorporation dinner see C. Hall. Tyrrell documents the description of one gallery in the Birmingham Town Hall as 'The Ladies Gallery' in the report of a public meeting in 1835, A. Tyrrell, p. 202.
169   A. F. J. Brown, *Colchester*. This was a well established tradition, used by aristocratic ladies among others. See E. Eden, *The Semi-Attached Couple*, 2nd edn (1979), p. 215.
170   The screen is on display at the Holly Trees Museum, Colchester.
171   IJ (6 July 1820).
172   M. Girouard, *The Return to Camelot: Chivalry and the English Gentleman* (New Haven, 1981).
173   IJ (6 July 1820).

Epilogue

1   P. Stallybrass and A. White, 'Bourgeois hysteria and the carnivalesque', in *The Politics and Poetics of Transgression* (1986).
2   J. L. Newton, 'Making – and remaking – history: another look at patriarchy', *Tulsa Studies in Women's Literature*, 3 (spring/fall 1984); J. L. Newton, *The Dispute Between the Sexes: Gender, Sexuality and Class in the 1840s* (forthcoming).
3   D. Hilliard, 'UnEnglish and unmanly: Anglo-Catholicism and homosexuality', *Victorian Studies*, 25 no. 2 (winter 1982).
4   L. Davidoff, 'Class and gender in Victorian England', in J. L. Newton, M. Ryan, J. Walkowitz (eds.), *Sex and Class in Women's History* (1983); S. Chitty, *The Beast and the Monk: A Life of Charles Kingsley* (1974).
5   C. Forder, 'A historical perspective on women and property law', unpublished paper, Women and Property Conference, University of Sussex (May 1983).
6   M. Vicinus, *Independent Women: Work and Community for Single Women 1850–1920* (1985). Michael Anderson, for example, poses the question as to why single women did not enter occupations and become economically independent. He answers that they did not have access to capital, yet we know that many nominally owned property. 'The social position of spinsters in Mid-Victorian Britain', *Journal of Family History* (winter 1984).
7   J. Bowles, *Remarks on Modern Female Manners* (1802), p. 13.
8   Rev. R. Cobbold, *The Character of Woman*, lecture for the benefit of the Governesses Benevolent Institution (13 April 1848).
9   'Lines on marriage', in J. Seabrook, commonplace book, 1830–56, by permission of M. Mallawaratchi.
10   'The Cipher', found in Hutton Beale Collection BRL 116/2; Alexander, Sims and May collection, IRO HD827:4747.
11   B. Taylor, *Eve and the New Jerusalem: Socialism and Feminism in the 19th Century* (1983).
12   The same experience which radicalized the American female delegates, Elizabeth Cady Stanton and Lucretia Mott, B. Taylor, p. 282; M. Ramelson, *The Petticoat Rebellion: A Century of Struggle for Women's Rights* (1972), pp. 72–3; G. Malmgreen, 'Anne Knight and the radical sub-culture', *Quaker History*, 71 no. 2 (autumn 1982).
13   For example in Chelmsford notice had been given that all duly qualified unmarried females were entitled to vote for Members of Parliament, CC (30 July 1831).

14   A. T. Gilbert, *Autobiography and Other Memorials of Mrs Gilbert*, 2 vols. (1974), vol. 2, pp. 185–6.

15   J. Conder (ed.), 'Remonstrance', *The Associate Minstrals* (1813), p. 95.

16   J. Taylor, *Memoirs, Correspondences and Poetical Remains* (1831), pp. 98–9.

17   J. Taylor, *The Contributions of QQ* (1845), p. 341; J. Taylor, *Memoirs*, p. 295; A. T. Gilbert, *Sketches from a Youthful Circle* (1834); for further discussion see L. Davidoff, *Life is Duty, Praise and Prayer: Some Contributions of the New Women's History* (1981).

18   L. E. O'Rorke (ed.), *The Life and Friendships of Catherine Marsh* (1917), pp. 21, 64. For the importance of birth cohorts in placing women's responses see E. Showalter, *A Literature of their Own: British Women Novelists from Brontë to Lessing* (1982).

19   W. J. Gregg, 'Why are women redundant?', *Literary and Social Judgements*, 2nd edn (1869); J. Boucherett, 'How to provide for superfluous women', in J. Butler (ed.), *Women's Work and Women's Culture* (1869), p. 45.

20   M. J. Peterson, 'The Victorian governess: status incongruence in family and society', in M. Vicinus (ed.), *Suffer and be Still: Women in the Victorian Age* (1980). L. Davidoff, 'The English Victorian governess: a study in social isolation', unpublished paper (1971).

21   L. Holcombe, *Wives and Property: Reform of the Married Women's Property Law in Nineteenth-Century England* (Oxford, 1983). R. Strachey, *The Cause: A Short History of the Women's Movement in Great Britain* (1978).

22   J. S. Mill, *On the Subjection of Women*, new edn with H. Taylor, *Enfranchisement of Women* (1983), with introduction by K. Soper.

23   Published anonymously in the *Westminster Review* (July 1851) which Mill later credited to Harriet Taylor.

24   Candia Cadbury to Hannah Cadbury (n.d.), 'A collection of letters concerning the family of Benjamin and Candia Cadbury 1806–1851', BRL 614280.

25   Provincial middle-class women did not have as many opportunities for engaging in the formal status rituals of 'Society' as their aristocratic or upper middle-class metropolitan counterparts. See L. Davidoff, *The Best Circles: 'Society', Etiquette and the Season* (1986).

Select bibliography

This is a bibliography of mainly secondary sources. Much of the primary and local material is referenced in the footnotes. We have regretfully also excluded individual and family biographies, business histories of particular firms, histories of organizations, contemporary journals, Parliamentary Reports and all fiction. Place of publication is London unless otherwise indicated.

General

Books
Alexander, D., *Retailing in England during the Industrial Revolution*, 1970.
Allen, D. E., *The Naturalist in Britain: A Social History*, 1978.
Allen, D. E., *The Victorian Fern Craze: A History of Pteridomania*, 1969.
Altick, R. D., *The English Common Reader*, Chicago, 1963.
Anderson, M., *Approaches to the History of the Western Family 1500–1914*, 1980.
Ardener, S. (ed.), *Women and Space*, 1981.
Ashton, T. S., *An Economic History of England: the 18th Century*, 1955.
Ashton, T. S., *Iron and Steel in the Industrial Revolution*, Manchester 1924, 2nd edn, 1951.
Bamford, T. W., *The Rise of the Public Schools*, 1967.
Barley, M. W., *The House and Home: A Review of 900 years of house planning and furnishing in Britain*, 1971.
Barrell, J., *English Literature in History 1730–80: An Equal Wide Survey*, 1983.
Bayne-Powell, R., *Housekeeping in the 18th Century*, 1956.
Bayne-Powell, R., *English Country Life in the 18th Century*, 1935.
Bebb, E. D., *Nonconformity and Social and Economic Life 1660–1800*, 1935.
Bennett, J., *The History of Dissenters from the Revolution to the Year 1808*, 1833.
Benson, J., *The Penny Capitalists: A Study of 19th Century Working Class Entrepreneurs*, 1983.
Berg, M., *The Age of Manufacturers, 1700–1820*, 1985.
Best, G. F. A., *Temporal Pillars: Queen Anne's Bounty, the Ecclesiastical Commissioners and the Church of England*, Cambridge, 1964.
Binfield, C., *Belmont's Portias: Victorian Nonconformity and Middle Class Education for Girls*, Dr Williams Trust, 1981.
Binfield, C., *So Down to Prayers. Studies in English Nonconformity 1780–1920*, 1977.
Bossard, J., *The Large Family System*, Philadelphia, 1956.
Bovill, E. W., *The England of Nimrod and Surtees 1815–1854*, 1959.

Bradley, I., *The Call to Seriousness: the Evangelical Impact on the Victorians*, 1976.

Bratton, J. S., *The Impact of Victorian Children's Fiction*, 1981.

Briggs, M. S., *The English Farmhouse*, 1953.

Bristow, E. J., *Vice and Vigilance. Purity Movements in Britain since 1700*, Dublin, 1977.

Brown, F. K., *Fathers of the Victorians: The Age of Wilberforce*, Cambridge, 1961.

Brundage, A., *The Making of the New Poor Law: the Politics of Enactment and Implementation 1832–1839*, 1978.

Burman, S. (ed.), *Fit Work for Women*, 1979.

Burnett, J., *A Social History of Housing 1815–1970*, 1980.

Burnett, J., *A History of the Cost of Living*, 1969.

Burnett, J., *Plenty and Want*, 1966.

Butler, M., *Romantics, Rebels and Reactionaries: English Literature and its Background 1760–1830*, Oxford, 1981.

Butler, M., *Jane Austen and the War of Ideas*, Oxford, 1975.

Cannon, J., *Aristocratic Century: the Peerage of 18th Century England*, Cambridge, 1984.

Chadwick, O., *The Victorian Church*, part I, 1966.

Chalkin, C. W., *The Provincial Towns of Georgian England. A Study of the Building Process 1740–1820*, 1974.

Charles, L. and Duffin, L. (eds.), *Women and Work in Pre-Industrial England*, 1985.

Chesterman, M., *Charities, Trusts and Social Welfare*, 1979.

Church, R. A., *Economic and Social Change in a Midland Town. Nottingham 1815–1900*, 1966.

Clark, Alice, *Working Life of Women in the Seventeenth Century*, 3rd edn with new introduction by M. Chaytor and J. Lewis, 1982.

Cockerall, H. A. L. and Green, E., *The British Life Insurance Business 1547–1970: An Introduction and Guide to Historical Records in the U.K.*, 1976.

Colby, V., *Yesterday's Woman: Domestic Realism in the English Novel*, Princeton, 1974.

Cott, N. F., *The Bonds of Womanhood. 'Woman's Sphere' in New England 1780–1835*, Yale, 1977.

Crouzet, F. (ed.), *Capital Formation in the Industrial Revolution*, 1972.

Curl, J. S., *The Victorian Celebration of Death*, Newton Abbot, 1972.

Dale, R. W., *History of English Congregationalism*, 1907.

Davidoff, L., *The Best Circles: 'Society', Etiquette and the Season*, 1986.

Davidoff, L., *Life is Duty, Praise and Prayer: Some Contributions of the New Women's History*, 1981.

Davidson, C., *Woman's Work is Never Done: A History of Housework in the British Isles 1650–1950*, 1982.

Davis, D., *A History of Shopping*, 1966.

Delamont, S. and Duffin, L. (eds.), *The 19th Century Woman: Her Cultural and Physical World*, 1978.

Delphy, C., *Close to Home: a Materialist Analysis of Women's Oppression*, 1984.

Douglas, A., *The Feminization of American Culture*, New York, 1978.

Douglas, M., *Implicit Meanings: Essays in Anthropology*, 1975.

Duckworth, A., *The Improvement of the Estate: A Study of Jane Austen's Novels*, Baltimore, 1971.

Duman, D., *The Judicial Bench in England 1727–1875: the Reshaping of a Professional Elite*, 1982.

Dunn, J., *Sisters and Brothers*, 1984.

Dyos, H. J. and Wolff, M. (eds.), *The Victorian City. Images and Realities*, 2 vols., 1973.

Eagleton, T., *The Function of Criticism*, 1984.

Elias, N., *The Civilising Process: the History of Manners*, Oxford, 1978.

Elshtain, J. B. (ed.), *The Family in Political Thought*, Brighton, 1984.

Elshtain, J. B., *Public Man, Private Woman. Women in Social and Political Thought*, 1981.

Emsley, C., *British Society and the French Wars 1793–1815*, 1979.

Fawcett, T., *The Rise of English Provincial Art*, Oxford, 1974.

Faxon, F. W., *Literary Annuals and Gift Books*, Surrey, 1973.

Finch, J., *Married to the Job: Wives Incorporation in Men's Work*, 1983.

Foster, J., *Class Struggle and the Industrial Revolution. Early Industrial Capitalism in Three English Towns*, 1974.

Fraser, D. (ed.), *A History of Modern Leeds*, 1981.

Fraser, D., *Urban Politics in Victorian England*, Leicester, 1976.

Fraser, D. and Sutcliffe, A. (eds.), *In Pursuit of Urban History*, 1984.

Gash, N., *Aristocracy and People: Britain 1815–1865*, 1979.

Gay, J. D., *The Geography of Religion in England*, 1971.

Gentle, R. and Field, R., *English Domestic Brass 1680–1810 and the History of its Origins*, 1975.

Gilbert, A. D., *Religion and Society in Industrial England: Church, Chapel and Social Change 1740–1914*, 1976.

Gillis, J., *For Better for Worse: British Marriages 1600 to the Present*, Oxford, 1985.

Gillis, J. R., *Youth and History. Tradition and Change in European Age Relations 1770 to the Present*, 1974.

Girouard, M., *The Return to Camelot. Chivalry and the English Gentleman*, New Haven, 1981.

Girouard, M., *Life in the English Country House: A Social and Architectural History*, Harmondsworth, 1980.

Girouard, M., *Victorian Pubs*, 1975.

Goody, J., Thirsk, J. and Thompson, E. P. (eds.), *Family and Inheritance: Rural Society in Western Europe 1200–1800*, Cambridge, 1976.

Gorham, D., *The Victorian Girl and the Feminine Ideal*, 1982.

Gough, R., *The History of Myddle*, 1981.

Gramsci, A., *Selections from the Prison Notebooks* edited and translated by Hoare, Q. and Nowell Smith, G., 1971.

Gray, R. A., *The Labour Aristocracy in Victorian Edinburgh*, Oxford, 1976.

Grubb, I., *Quakerism and Industry Before 1800*, 1930.

Haig, A., *The Victorian Clergy*, 1984.

Hans, N., *New Trends in Education in the 18th Century*, 1951.

Hareven, T. K., *Family and Kin in Urban Communities 1700–1930*, New York, 1977.

Hareven, T. K., *Family Time and Industrial Time: The Relationship*

Between the Family and Work in a New England Industrial Community, Cambridge 1982.

Harrison, B., *Drink and the Victorians*, 1971.

Harrison, J. F. C., *The Second Coming: Popular Millenarianism 1780–1850*, 1979.

Harvey, A. D., *Britain in the Early 19th Century*, 1978.

Harvey, N., *A History of Farm Buildings in England and Wales*, Newton Abbot, 1970.

Heasman, K., *Evangelicals in Action. An Appraisal of their Social Work in the Victorian Era*, 1962.

Hecht, J. J., *The Domestic Servant Class in 18th Century England*, 1956.

Heeney, B., *A Different Kind of Gentleman: Parish clergy as professional men in early and mid Victorian England*, Connecticut, 1976.

Hennell, M., *Sons of the Prophets: Evangelical Leaders of the Victorian Church*, 1979.

Hirschman, A. O., *The Passions and the Interests: Political Arguments for Capitalism before its Triumph*, Princeton, 1977.

Hobsbawm, E. J., *The Age of Capital 1848–75*, 1977.

Hobsbawm, E. J., *The Age of Revolution: Europe 1789–1848*, 1962.

Hobsbawm, E. J. and Ranger, T. (eds.), *The Invention of Tradition*, Cambridge, 1983.

Holcombe, L., *Wives and Property. Reform of the Married Women's Property Law in 19th Century England*, 1983.

Hole, C., *The English Housewife in the 17th Century*, 1953.

Hollowell, P., *Property and Social Relations*, 1982.

Hont, I. and Ignatieff, M. (eds.), *Wealth and Virtue*, Cambridge, 1983.

Hopkins, J., *A Woman to Deliver Her People: Joanna Southcott and English Millenarianism in an era of revolution*, Austin, Texas, 1982.

Howe, A., *The Cotton Masters 1830–60*, 1984.

Hudson, K., *Patriotism with Profit: British Agricultural Societies in the 18th and 19th Centuries*, 1972.

Hunt, B. C., *The Development of the Business Corporation in England 1800–1867*, Cambridge, Mass., 1936.

Ignatieff, M., *A Just Measure of Pain. The Penitentiary in the Industrial Revolution 1750–1850*, 1978.

Isichei, E., *Victorian Quakers*, Oxford, 1970.

Jaggar, A. M., *Feminist Politics and Human Nature*, Brighton, 1984.

Jarrett, D., *England in the Age of Hogarth*, 1976.

Jones, E. L. (ed.), *Agriculture and Economic Growth in England 1650–1815*, 1967.

Jones, G. S., *Languages of Class: Studies in English Working Class History 1832–1982*, Cambridge, 1983.

Joyce, P., *Work, Society and Politics. The Culture of the Factory in Later Victorian England*, Brighton, 1980.

Katz, M. B., *The People of Hamilton, Canada West. Family and Class in a mid 19th Century City*, Cambridge, Mass., 1975.

Kerridge, E., *The Farmers of Old England*, 1973.

Knoop, D. and Jones, G. P., *The Genesis of Freemasonry*, Manchester, 1974.

Kussmaul, A. S., *Servants in Husbandry in Early Modern England*, Cambridge, 1981.

Laqueur, T. W., *Religion and Respectability. Sunday School and Working Class Culture 1780–1850*, New Haven, 1976.

Lawson, M. S., *The Rise of Professionalism: A Sociological Analysis*, Berkeley, 1977.

Lawton, R., *The Census and Social Structure: An interpretative guide to 19th century censuses for England and Wales*, 1978.

Leavis, Q. D., *Fiction and the Reading Public*, 1932.

Lebsock, S., *The Free Women of Petersburg: Status and Culture in a Southern Town 1784–1860*, New York, 1984.

Littleton, A. C. and Yamey, B. S., *Studies in the History of Accounting*, 1956.

McClatchey, D., *Oxfordshire Clergy 1777–1869*, 1960.

McCord, N., *The Anti Corn Law League 1838–46*, 1958.

Macfarlane, A., *Reconstructing Historical Communities*, Cambridge, 1977.

McKendrick, N., Brewer, J. and Plumb, J. H. (eds.), *The Birth of a Consumer Society: The Commercialization of 18th England*, 1982.

McLeod, H., *Religion and the People of Western Europe 1789–1970*, Oxford, 1981.

McNaron, T., *The Sister Bond: A Feminist View of a Timeless Connection*, New York, 1985.

Marshall, G., *In Search of the Spirit of Capitalism: An Essay on Max Weber's Protestant Ethic Thesis*, 1982.

Martin, E. W., *The Secret People: English Village Life After 1750*, 1954.

Mathias, P., *The Transformation of England*, 1979.

Mathias, P., *The Brewing Industry in England 1700–1830*, Cambridge, 1959.

Mercer, E., *English Vernacular Houses: A Study of the Traditional Farmhouses and Cottages*, 1975.

Milne, J. D., *Industrial and Social Position of Women in the Middle and Lower Ranks*, 1857.

Mineka, F. E., *The Dissidence of Dissent. The Monthly Repository 1806–38*, North Carolina, 1944.

Mingay, G. E., *The Victorian Countryside*, 2 vols, 1980.

Mingay, G. E., *Rural Life in Victorian England*, 1977.

Mingay, G. E., *English Landed Society in the Eighteenth Century*, 1976.

Mingay, G. E., *The Gentry: The Rise and Fall of a Ruling Class*, 1976.

Mingay, G. E., *Enclosure and the Small Farmer in the Age of the Industrial Revolution*, 1973.

Mintz, S., *A Prison of Expectations: the Family in Victorian Culture*, New York, 1983.

Mitchell, J. and Oakely, A. (eds.), *The Rights and Wrongs of Women*, 1976.

Moers, E., *Literary Women*, 1978.

Moers, E., *The Dandy. Brummel to Beerbohm*, 1960.

Newsome, D., *The Parting of Friends: A Study of the Wilberforces and Henry Manning*, 1966.

Newsome, D., *Godliness and Good Learning: Four Studies in a Victorian Ideal*, 1961.

Newton, J. L., *Women, Power and Subversion. Social Strategies in British Fiction 1778–1860*, Athens, Georgia, 1981.

Obelkevich, J., *Religion and Rural Society: South Lindsey 1825–75*, Oxford, 1976.

Okin, S. M., *Women in Western Political Thought*, 1980.

Ortner, S. and Whitehead, H., *Sexual Meanings: the Cultural Construction of Gender and Sexuality*, Cambridge, 1981.

Owen, D., *English Philanthropy 1660–1960*, 1965.

Parkin, F., *Marxism and Class Theory: a Bourgeois Critique*, 1979.

Parry, N. and Parry, J., *The Rise of the Medical Profession: A Study of Collective Social Mobility*, 1976.

Perkin, H., *The Origins of Modern English Society 1780–1880*, 1969.

Peterson, M. J., *The Medical Profession in mid-Victorian London*, Berkeley, 1978.

Pinchbeck, I., *Women Workers and the Industrial Revolution 1750–1850*, 1930.

Plumb, J. M., *The First Four Georges*, 16th edn, 1981.

Pollard, S., *The Genesis of Modern Management*, 1965.

Poovey, M., *The Proper Lady and the Woman Writer. Ideology as Style in the Works of Mary Wollstonecraft, Mary Shelley, and Jane Austen*, Chicago, 1984.

Porter, R., *English Society in the 18th Century*, Harmondsworth, 1982.

Powis, J., *Aristocracy*, Oxford, 1984.

Presnell, L. S., *Country Banking in the Industrial Revolution*, Oxford, 1956.

Prior, M. (ed.), *Women in English Society 1500–1800*, 1985.

Prochaska, F. K., *Women and Philanthropy in 19th century England*, Oxford, 1980.

Quinlan, M. J., *Victorian Prelude: A History of English Manners 1700–1830*, 1941.

Rae, G., *The Country Banker, His Clients and Work from an Experience of 40 Years*, 1976.

Raistrick, A., *Quakers in Science and Industry*, 1950.

Raynes, H. E., *A History of British Insurance*, 1948.

Read, D., *The English Provinces 1760–1960*, 1964.

Reader, W. J., *Professional Men. The Rise of the Professional Classes in 19th Century England*, 1966.

Reiss, E., *Rights and Duties of Englishwomen*, Manchester, 1934.

Rendall, J., *The Origins of Modern Feminism: Women in Britain, France and the U.S. 1780–1860*, 1985.

Roberts, D., *Paternalism in Early Victorian England*, 1981.

Roberts, J. M., *The Mythology of the Secret Societies*, 1972.

Rosa, M. W., *The Silver Fork School: Novels of Fashion Preceeding Vanity Fair*, Washington, New York, 1936.

Royal Institute of British Architects, *Rooms Concise: Glimpses of the Small Domestic Interior 1500–1850*, RIBA Exhibit, 1981.

Rubin, G. R. and Sugarman, D. (eds.), *Law Economy and Society 1750–1914: Essays in the History of English Law*, 1984.

Ryan, M. P., *Cradle of the Middle Class. The Family in Oneida County New York 1790–1865*, Cambridge, 1981.

Sachs, A. and Wilson, J., *Sexism and the Law: A Study of Male Beliefs and Judicial Bias*, 1978.

Scase, R. and Goffee, R., *The Real World of the Small Business Owner*, 1980.

Schochet, G. J., *Patriarchism in Political Thought*, Oxford, 1975.

Scourse, N., *The Victorians and their Flowers*, 1983.

Sennett, R., *The Fall of Public Man*, Cambridge, 1974.

Showalter, E., *A Literature of Their Own. British Women Novelists from Brontë to Lessing* 1982

Simon, B. and Bradley, I. (eds.), *The Victorian Public School*, Dublin, 1975.

Simey, M. B., *Charitable Effort in Liverpool in the 19th Century*, Liverpool, 1951.

Simpson, M. A. and Lloyd, T. H. (eds.), *Middle Class Housing in Britain*, Newton Abbot, 1977.

Slater, M., *Dickens and Women*, 1983.

Smith, B., *Ladies of the Leisure Class: The Bourgeoises of Northern France in the 19th Century*, Princeton, 1981.

Smythe, C., *Simeon and Church Order: A Study of the Origins of the Evangelical Revival in Cambridge in the 18th Century*, Cambridge, 1940.

Soloway, R. A., *Prelates and People: Ecclesiastical Social Thought in England 1783–1852*, 1969.

Spiers, M., *Victoria Park Manchester: a 19th Century Suburb in its Social and Administrative Context*, Manchester, 1976.

Spiller, R. E., *The American in England During the First Half Century of Independence*, Philadelphia, 1976.

Stacey, M. and Prior, M., *Women, Power and Politics*, 1981.

Stacey, N., *English Accountancy: A Study in Social and Economic History 1800–1954*, 1954.

Stone, L., *The Family, Sex and Marriage in England 1500–1800*, 1981.

Taylor, B., *Eve and the New Jerusalem. Socialism and Feminism in the 19th Century*, 1983.

Thacker, C., *The History of Gardens*, 1979.

Thomas, K., *Man and the Natural World: Changing Attitudes in England 1500–1800*, 1983.

Thompson, E. P., *The Making of the English Working Class*, 1963.

Thompson, F. M. L., *Chartered Surveyors. The Growth of a Profession*, 1968.

Thompson, F. M. L., *English Landed Society in the 19th Century*, 1963.

Thorne, B. (ed.), *Rethinking the Family: Some Feminist Questions*, 1982.

Tilly, L. and Scott, J., *Women, Work and Family*, 1978.

Tomkins, J. M. S., *The Popular Novel in England 1770–1800*, 1932.

Trudgill, E., *Madonnas and Magdalens. The Origins and Development of Victorian Sexual Attitudes*, 1976.

Trumbach, R., *The Rise of the Egalitarian Family. Aristocratic Kinship and Domestic Relations in 18th century England*, New York, 1978.

Vance, N., *The Sinews of the Spirit. The Ideal of Christian Manliness in Victorian Literature and Religious Thought*, Cambridge, 1985.

Vicinus, M., *Independent Women. Work and Community for Single Women 1850–1920*, 1985.

Victoria and Albert Museum, *The Garden: A Celebration of One Thousand Years of British Gardening*, 1979.

Walkowitz, J. R., *Prostitution and Victorian Society. Women, Class and the State*, Cambridge, 1980.

Warner, M., *Alone of all her sex. The myth and cult of the Virgin Mary*, 1976.

Watt, M. H., *The History of the Parson's Wife*, 1943.

Weber, W., *Music and the Middle Class*, 1975.

Weeks, J., *Sex, Politics and Society. The Regulation of Sexuality Since 1800*, 1981.

White, R. J., *The Age of George III*, 1968.

White, R. J., *Life in Regency England*, 1963.

Wiener, M. J., *English Culture and the Decline of the Industrial Spirit 1850–1980*, Harmondsworth, 1985.

Wilbur, E. M., *A History of Unitarianism in Transylvania, England and America*, Cambridge, Mass., 1952.

Wilson, E., *Adorned in Dreams: Fashion and Modernity*, 1985.

Wilson, R. G., *Gentlemen Merchants. The Merchant Community in Leeds 1700–1830*, Manchester, 1971.

Wohl, A. (ed.), *The Victorian Family, Structure and Stress*, 1978.

Woodward, J. and Richards, D. (eds.), *Health Care and Popular Medicine in 19th Century England*, 1977.

Wright, D., *Woman and Freemasonry*, 1922.

Wright, L., *Clean and Decent*, 1960.

Wrigley, E. A., *Identifying People in the Past*, 1973.

Articles

Alexander, S., 'Women, class and sexual difference in the 1830s and 1840s: some reflections on the writing of a feminist history', *History Workshop Journal*, no. 17, spring 1984.

Allen, D., 'The women members of the Botanical Society of London 1836–1856', *The British Journal for the History of Science*, 13 no. 45, 1980.

Anderson, B. L., 'Money and the structure of credit in the 18th century', *Business History*, XII no. 1, 1970.

Anderson, B. L., 'Provincial aspects of the financial revolution of the 18th century', *Business History*, XI no. 1, January 1969.

Anderson, M., 'Household structure and the industrial revolution: mid-19th century Preston in comparative perspective', in P. Laslett and R. Wall (eds.), *Household and Family in Past Time*, Cambridge, 1972.

Andrew, D., 'The code of honour and its critics: the opposition to duelling in England 1700–1850', *Social History*, 5 no. 3, October 1980.

Armstrong, W. A., 'A note on the household structure of mid-19th century York in comparative perspective', in P. Laslett and R. Wall (eds.), *Household and Family in Past Time*, Cambridge, 1972.

Bechhofer, F. and Elliott, B., 'Petty property: the survival of a moral economy', in F. Bechhofer and B. Elliott, *The Petite Bourgeoisie: Comparative Studies of the Uneasy Stratum*, 1981.

Binfield, C., 'Congregationalisms' Baptist grandmothers and Methodist great aunts: the place of family in a felt religion', *The Journal of the United Reformed Church History Society*, 2 no. 1, 1978.

Blumin, S. M., 'The hypothesis of middle-class formation in 19th century

America. A critique and some proposals', *American Historical Review*, 90 no. 2, 1985.

Bordieu, P., 'Marriage strategies as strategies of social reproduction', in R. Forster and O. Ranum (eds.), *Family and Society*, 1976.

Cannadine, D., 'Civic ritual and the Colchester Oyster Feast', *Past and Present*, no. 94, February 1982.

Cannadine, D., 'Victorian cities: how different?', *Social History*, 2 no. 4, 1977.

Carré, B., 'Early Quaker women in Lancaster and Lancashire', Centre for N.W. Regional Studies Occasional Paper, no. 5, *Early Lancaster Friends*.

Chaytor, M., 'Household and kinship: Ryton in the late 16th and early 17th century', *History Workshop Journal*, no. 10, 1980.

Church, C., 'Victorian masculinity and the Angel in the House', in M. Vicinus (ed.), *A Widening Sphere: Changing Roles of Victorian Women* (1982).

Clark, K., 'Public and private children: infant education in the 1820s and 1830s', in C. Steedman, C. Urwin and V. Walkerdine (eds.), *Language, Gender and Childhood*, 1985.

Colley, L., 'The apothesis of George III: loyalty, royalty and the British nation 1760–1820', *Past and Present*, no. 102, February 1984.

Cott, N. F., 'Passionlessness: an interpretation of Victorian sexual ideology, 1790–1850', *Signs*, 4 no. 2, 1978.

Crozier, D., 'Kinship and occupational succession', *The Sociological Review*, new series, 13, 1965.

Cunningham, H., 'The language of patriotism', *History Workshop Journal*, no. 12, autumn 1981.

Darrow, M. H., 'French noblewomen and the new domesticity', *Feminist Studies*, 5 no 1, spring 1979.

Davidoff, L., 'Mastered for life: servant and wife in Victorian and Edwardian England', in A. Sutcliffe and P. Thane (eds.), *Essays in Social History*, Oxford, 1986.

Davidoff, L., 'The role of gender in the "First Industrial Nation": agriculture in England 1780–1850', in R. Crompton and M. Mann (eds.), *Gender and Stratification*, 1986.

Davidoff, L., 'Class and gender in Victorian society: the diaries of Arthur J. Munby and Hannah Cullwick', in J. L. Newton, M. Ryan and J. Walkowitz (eds.), *Sex and Class in Women's History*, 1983.

Davidoff, L., 'The rationalization of housework', in D. Barker and S. Allen (eds.), *Dependency and Exploitation in Work and Marriage*, 1976.

Davidoff, L. and Hall, C., 'The architecture of public and private life: English middle class society, in a provincial town 1780–1850', in D. Fraser and A. Sutcliffe (eds.), *The Pursuit of Urban History*, 198.

Davidoff, L., L'Esperance, J. and Newby, H., 'Landscape with figures: home and community in English society', in A. Oakley and J. Mitchell (eds.), *The Rights and Wrongs of Women*, Harmondsworth, 1976.

Delphy, C. and Leonard, D., 'Class analysis, gender analysis and the family', in R. Crompton and M. Mann (eds.), *Gender and Stratification*, 1986.

Feinstein, C., 'Capital accumulation and the industrial revolution', in R. Floud and D. McClosky (eds.), *The Economic History of Britain Since 1700*, vol. 1, 1700–1860, Cambridge, 1981.

Fox-Genovese, E., 'Property and patriarchy in classical bourgeois political theory', *Radical History Review*, nos. 2–3, 1977.

George, C. H., 'The making of the English bourgeoisie 1600–1750', *Science and Society*, no. 4, winter 1971.

Gray, R. Q., 'Bourgeois hegemony in Victorian Britain', in J. Bloomfield (ed.), *Class, Hegemony and Party*, 1977.

Grubb, E., 'The Evangelical movement and its impact on the Society of Friends', *Friends Quarterly Examiner*, 1924.

Habermas, J., 'The public sphere: an encyclopaedia article', *New German Critique*, 1 no. 3, 1974.

Hall, C., 'Private persons versus public someones: class, gender and politics in England, 1780–1850', in C. Steedman, C. Urwin and V. Walkerdine (eds.), *Language, Gender and Childhood*, 1985.

Hall, C., 'Gender divisions and class formation in the Birmingham middle class, 1780–1850', in R. Samuel (ed.), *People's History and Socialist Theory*, 1981.

Hall, C., 'The early formation of Victorian domestic ideology', in S. Burman (ed.), *Fit Work for Women*, 1979.

Hall, P. D., 'Family structure and economic organization: Massachusettes merchants 1700–1850', in T. Harayen (ed.), *Family and Kin in Urban Communities 1700–1930*, New York, 1977.

Hall, S., 'The problem of ideology – Marxism without guarantees', in B. Matthews (ed.), *Marx: A Hundred Years On*, 1983.

Hall, S., 'Rethinking the "base and superstructure metaphor"', in J. Blomfield (ed.), *Class, Hegemony and Party*, 1977.

Harris, O., 'Households and their boundaries', *History Workshop Journal*, no. 13, spring 1982.

Harrison, B., 'Philanthropy and the Victorians', *Victorian Studies*, no. 9, 1966.

Hausen, K., 'Family and role-division: the polarisation of sexual stereotypes in the 19th century', in R. Evans and R. Lee (eds.), *The German Family: Essays on the Social History of the Family in 19th and 20th Century Germany*, 1981.

Hueckel, G., 'Agriculture during industrialization', in R. Floud and D. McClosky (eds.), *The Economic History of Britain Since 1700*, vol. 1, 1700–1860, Cambridge, 1981.

Hughes, E., 'The professions in the 18th century', in D. A. Baugh, (ed.), *Aristocratic Government and Society in 18th Century England*, New York, 1975.

Hunt, M., 'Hawkers, bankers and mercuries: women and the Enlightenment, *Women in History*, no. 9, spring 1984.

Inglis, K. S., 'Patterns of religious worship in 1851', *Journal of Ecclesiastical History*, XI no. 1, 1960.

Inkster, I., 'Marginal men: aspects of the social role of the medical community in Sheffield 1790–1850', in J. Woodward and D. Richards (eds.), *Health Care and Popular Medicine in 19th Century England*, 1981.

Jordanova, L. J., 'Natural facts: a historical perspective on science and sexuality,' in C. MacCormack and M. Strathern (eds.), *Nature, Culture and Gender*, Cambridge, 1980.

Kelly, J., 'The doubled vision of feminist theory', in J. L. Newton, M. Ryan and J. Walkowitz (eds.), *Sex and Class in Women's History*, 1983.

McLeod, H., 'White collar values and the role of religion', in G. Crossick (ed.), *The Lower Middle Class in Britain*, 1979.

Malmgreen, G., 'Anne Knight, and the Radical sub culture', *Quaker Education*, 71 no. 2, autumn 1982.

Medick, H., 'The proto-industrial family economy: the structural function of household and family during the transition from peasant society to industrial capitalism', *Social History*, 1 no. 3, 1976.

Medick, H. and Sabean, D., 'Interest and emotion in family and kinship studies: a critique of social history and anthropology', in H. Medick and D. Sabean (eds.), *Interest and Emotion: Essays on the Study of Family and Kinship*, Cambridge, 1984.

Miles, M., 'Eminent practitioners: the new visage of country attornies 1750–1800', in G. Rubin and D. Sugarman (eds.), *Law, Economy and Society: Essays in the History of English Law 1750–1914*, 1984.

Minchinton, W. E., 'The merchants in England in the 18th century', in B. Supple (ed.), *The Entrepreneur*, 1954.

Mitchell, S., 'The forgotten woman of the period: Penny Weekly Family Magazines of the 1840s and 1850s, in M. Vicinus (ed.), *A Widening Sphere: Changing Roles of Victorian Women*, 1982.

Morris, R. J., 'Middle-class culture 1700–1914', in Fraser, D. (ed.) *A History of Modern Leeds* (1981).

Morris, R. J., 'Voluntary societies and British urban elites 1780–1850: an analysis', *The Historical Journal*, 26 no. 1, 1983.

Morris, R. J., 'The middle class and the property cycle during the industrial revolution', in T. C. Smout (ed.), *The Search for Wealth and Stability*, 1979.

Morris, R. J., 'In search of the urban middle class. Record linkage and methodology: Leeds 1832', *Urban History Yearbook*, 1976.

Neale, R. S., 'The bourgeoisie, historically, has played a most revolutionary part', in E. Kamenka and R. S. Neale (eds.), *Feudalism, Capitalism and Beyond*, Whitstable, 1975.

Neale, R. S., 'Class and class consciousness in early 19th century England', in R. S. Neale (ed.), *Class and Ideology in the 19th Century*, 1972.

Obelkevitch, J., 'Proverbs and social history', in P. Burke and R. Porter (eds.), *Essays in the Social History of Language*, Cambridge, 1986.

O'Brien, P. K., 'British incomes and property in the early 19th century', *Economic History Review*, 2nd series, 12 1959–1960.

Pederson, J. S., 'The reform of women's secondary and higher education: institutional change and social values in mid and late Victorian England', *History of Education Quarterly*, 1979.

Peterson, M. J., 'No angel in the house: the Victorian myth and the Paget women', *American Historical Review*, 89 no. 3, 1984.

Pocock, J. G. A., 'Early modern capitalism: the Augustan perception', in E. Kamenka and R. S. Neale (eds.), *Feudalism, Capitalism and Beyond*, Whitstable, 1975.

Pythian-Adams, C., 'Rural culture', in G. Mingay (ed.), *The Victorians Countryside*, vol. II, 1980.

Rapp, R., Ross, E. and Bridenthal, R., 'Examining family history', *Feminist Studies*, 5 no. 1, 1979.

Ravetz, A., 'The Victorian coal kitchen and its reformers', *Victorian Studies*, 11 no. 4, 1968.

Redlich, F., 'Economic development, entrepreneurship and psychologism: a social scientists critique of McClellands "Achieving Society", *Explorations in Entrepreneurial History*, 1, 1963–4.

Rogers, N., 'Money, land and lineage: the big bourgeoisie of Hanovarian London', *Social History*, 4 no. 3, 1979.

Rosaldo, M., 'The use and abuse of anthropology: reflections on feminism and cross-cultural understanding', *Signs*, 5 no. 3, spring 1980.

Rubinstein, W. D., 'The Victorian middle classes: wealth, occupation and geography', *Economic History Review*, 30, 1977.

Rubinstein, W. D., 'Wealth, elites and the class structure of modern Britain', *Past and Present*, no. 76, August 1977.

Ryan, M. P., 'The empire of the mother: American writing about domesticity 1830–60', *Women and History*, nos. 2–3, 1982.

Ryan, M. P., 'Femininity and capitalism in ante bellum America', in Z. Eisenstein (ed.), *Capitalist Patriarchy and the Case for Socialist Feminism*, New York, 1979.

Samuel, R., 'Workshop of the world: steam power and hand technology in mid-Victorian Britain', *History Workshop Journal*, no. 3, 1977.

Saville, J., 'Primitive accumulation and early industrialization in Britain', *The Socialist Register*, vi, 1969.

Saville, J., 'Sleeping partnership and limited liability 1850–1856', *Economic History Review*, 2nd series, 8, 1956.

Schoenwald, R. L., 'Training urban man: a hypothesis about the Sanitary Movement', in M. Wolff and H. Dyos (eds.), *The Victorian City: Images and Realities*, vol. II, 1973.

Seed, J., 'Theologies of power: Unitarianism and the social relations of religious discourse 1800–1850', in R. J. Morris (ed.), *Class, Power and Social Structure in British Nineteenth Century Towns*, Leicester, 1986.

Seed, J., 'Unitarianism, political economy and the antinomies of liberal culture in Manchester 1830–50', *Social History*, 7 no. 1, 1982.

Slater, T. R., 'Family society and the ornamental villa on the fringes of English country towns', *Journal of Historical Geography*, 4 no. 2, 1978.

Smeaton, J. S., 'Origins of the Society of Civil Engineers', in T. P. Hughes (ed.), *The Development of Western Technology since 1500*, New York, 1964.

Smith-Rosenberg, C., 'Sex or symbol in Victorian purity: an ethnohistorical analysis of Jacksonian America', in J. Demos and S. Boocock (eds.), *Turning Points: Historical and Sociological Essays on the Family*, Chicago, 1978.

Smith-Rosenberg, C., 'The female world of love and ritual: relations between women in 19th century America', *Signs*, 1 no. 1, 1975.

Spring, D., 'Aristocracy, social structure and religion in the early Victorian period', *Victorian Studies*, VI no. 3, 1963.

Spring, E., 'Law and the theory of the affective family', *Albion*, 16, 1984.

Thomas, D., 'The social origins of marriage partners of the British peerage in the 18th and 19th centuries', *Population Studies*, 26, part 1, 1972.

Vigne, T. and Howkins, A., 'The small shopkeeper in industrial and market towns', in G. Crossick (ed.), *The Lower Middle Class in Britain*, 1977.

Whitehead, A., 'Kinship and property: women and men: some generalizations', in R. Hirschon (ed.), *Women and Property: Women as Property*, 1983.

Yamey, B. S., 'Scientific bookkeeping and the rise of capitalism', *Economic History Review*, 2nd series, 1 nos. 2 and 3, 1949.

Yeatman, A., 'Women, domestic life and sociology', in C. Pateman and E. Gross (eds.) *Feminist Challenges: Social and Political Theory*, 1986.

Unpublished material

Anderson, M., 'Preparation and analysis of a machine readable national sample from the Enumerators Books of the 1851 census of G.B., SSRC Report HR2066, January 1980.

Arnstein, W. L., 'The Victorian family and the Roman Catholic revival', Paper presented to the Anglo American Conference of Historians, London, 1982.

Auchmuty, R., 'Victorian spinsters', Australian National University, Ph.D., 1975.

Balda, W. D., '"Spheres of Influence": Simeon's Trust and its implications for Evangelical patronage', University of Cambridge, Ph.D., 1981.

Clark, K., 'Infanticide and the medical profession', Paper presented at the University of Warwick Social History seminar, 1980.

Corfield, P. J., 'The social and economic history of Norwich 1650–1850', University of London, Ph.D., 1975.

Fawcett, T., 'Lecturing in literary and philosophical societies', Paper presented to the Sheffield Conference on Provincial Culture, 1981.

Field, J., 'Bourgeois Portsmouth: social relations in a Victorian dockyard town 1815–75', University of Warwick, Ph.D., 1979.

Forder, C., 'A historical perspective on women and property law', Women and Property Conference, University of Sussex, May 1983.

Freer, D., 'Business families in Victorian Leicester: a study in historical sociology', University of Leicester, M.Phil., 1975.

Gatrell, V. A. C., 'The commercial middle class in Manchester 1820–75', University of Cambridge, Ph.D., 1971.

Gerard, J., 'Family and servants in the countryhouse community in England and Wales 1815–1914', University of London, Ph.D., 1982.

Hall, P. D., 'Family structure and class consolidation among the Boston Brahmins', State University of New York at Stonybrook, Ph.D., 1973.

Higgs, E., 'Gender, occupations and work in the 19th century occupational census', Paper presented to the Social History Society Conference, January 1985.

Honeyman, K., 'Origins of enterprise: a study of social mobility in the industrial revolution', University of Nottingham, Ph.D., 1976.

Kaplan, C., 'Language, gender and history', Paper presented to the History Workshop, London seminar, 1982.

Koditschek, T. S., 'Class formation and the Bradford bourgeoisie', University of Princeton, Ph.D., 1981.

McNeil, M., 'A contextual study of Erasmus Darwin', University of Cambridge, Ph.D., 1979.

Meikle, S., 'Issues of masculinity and feminity in three novels by George Eliot', University of Leicester, Ph.D., 1981.

Morris, R. J., 'A year in the public life of the British bourgeoisie', unpublished manuscript, 1985.

Morris, R. J., 'The making of the British middle class', Paper presented to the social history seminar, Birmingham University, 1979.

Morris, R. J., 'Organization and aims of the principal secular voluntary organizations of the Leeds middle class 1830–51', University of Oxford, D.Phil, 1970.

Murphy, T., 'Female shadow, male substance: women and property law in 19th century England', unpublished paper, 1982.

Pope, N. F., 'Charitable activities and attitudes in early Victorian England with special reference to Dickens and the Evangelicals', University of Oxford, D. Phil, 1975.

Reid, C. O., 'Middle class values and working class culture in 19th century Sheffield', University of Sheffield, Ph.D., 1976.

Rosman, D. M., 'Evangelicals and culture in England 1790–1833', University of Keele, Ph.D., 1978.

Russell, A. J., 'A sociological analysis of the clergyman's role with special reference to its development in the early 19th century', University of Oxford, D.Phil, 1970.

Schneid, J., 'The problem of criminal conversation: a study of Victorian sexual attitudes', unpublished paper, 1975.

Scott, J. W., 'Is gender a useful category of historical analysis?', unpublished paper, 1985.

Seed, J., 'The role of unitarianism in the formation of Liberal Culture 1775–1851', University of Hull, Ph.D., 1981.

Shteir, A., '"The Fair Daughters of Albion" and the popularization of British botony', Paper presented at the British Society for the History of Science, 1982.

Tozer, M., 'Manliness: the evolution of a Victorian ideal', University of Leicester, Ph.D., 1978.

Valenze, D., 'Women preachers in 19th century England', Paper presented to the History Workshop Conference on Religion and Society, 1983.

Worsnop, J., 'A re-evaluation of "the problem of surplus women" in 19th century England, in the context of the history of gender', University of Essex, M.A., 1983.

Birmingham

Books

Allen, G. C., *The Industrial History of Birmingham and the Black Country 1860–1927*, 1929.

Cannadine, D., *Lords and Landlords: the Aristocracy and the Towns 1774–1967*, Leicester, 1980.

Court, W. H. B., *The Rise of Midland Industries 1600–1838*, Oxford, 2nd edn, 1953.

Gill, C., *History of Birmingham*, vol. I. *Manor and Borough to 1865*, Oxford, 1952.

Flick, C., *The Birmingham Political Union and the Movement for Reform in Britain 1830–39*, Connecticut, 1978.

Hennock, E. P., *Fit and Proper Persons: Ideal and Reality in 19th Century Urban Government*, 1973.

Hutton, W., *History of Birmingham Continued to the Present Time (1819) by his Daughter Catherine Hutton*, 1819.

Langley, A. S., *Birmingham Baptists Past and Present*, 1939.

Little, B., *Birmingham Buildings. The Architectural Story of a Midland City*, Newton Abbot, 1971.

Money, J., *Experience and Identity. Birmingham and the West Midlands 1760–1800*, Manchester, 1977.

Prosser, R., *Birmingham Inventors and Inventions*, Birmingham, 1881.

Pugh, R. E. (ed.), *The Victoria County History of Warwick*, vol. VII, *The City of Birmingham*, Oxford, 1964.

Schofield, R. E., *The Lunar Society of Birmingham. A Social History of Provincial Science and Industry in 18th Century England*, Oxford, 1963.

Skipp, V., *A History of Greater Birmingham – Down to 1830*, Birmingham, 1980.

Smith, J. S., *The Story of Music in Birmingham*, Birmingham, 1945.

Timmins, S. (ed.), *The Resources, Products and Industrial History of Birmingham and the Midland Hardware District*, 1866.

Trinder, B., *The Industrial Revolution in Shropshire*, 1973.

Articles

Allen, B. M., 'Priestley and the Birmingham Riots', *Transactions of the Unitarian Historical Society*, **5** no. 2, 1932.

Behagg, C., 'Masters and manufacturers: social values and the smaller unit of production in Birmingham, 1800–1850', in G. Crossick and H. G. Haupt (eds.), *Shopkeepers and Master Artisans in Nineteenth Century Europe*, 1984.

Behagg, C., 'Custom, class and change: the trade societies of Birmingham', *Social History*, **4** no. 3, October 1979.

Briggs, A., 'The background of the Parliamentary reform movement in three English cities 1830–1832', *Cambridge Historical Journal*, 1952.

Briggs, A., 'Press and public in early 19th century Birmingham', *Dugdale Society Occasional Papers*, no. 8, 1949.

Briggs, A., 'Thomas Attwood and the economic background of the Birmingham Political Union', *Cambridge Historical Journal*, 1948.

Buckley, F., 'The Birmingham glass trade 1740–1833', *Transactions of the Society of Glass Technology*, **11**, 1927.

Chaloner, W. H., 'Dr Joseph Priestley, John Wilkinson and the French Revolution', *Transactions of the Royal Historical Society*, 5th series, no. 8, 1958.

Craig, G. W., 'The Old Square: a chapter of bygone local medical history', *Birmingham Medical Review*, **X**, 1935.

Fraser, D., 'Birmingham and the corn laws', *Transactions of the Birmingham Archeology Society*, **82**, 1965.

Money, J., 'The schoolmasters of Birmingham and the West Midlands 1750–90', *Historie Sociale – Social History*, **X** no. 1, 1976.

Reid, D., 'Popular theatre in Victorian Birmingham', in L. James, D. Bradby and B. Sharratt (eds.), *Performance and Politics in Popular Drama*, Cambridge, 1980.

Reid, D., 'The decline of Saint Monday 1766–1876', *Past and Present*, no. 71, 1976.

Walker, B., 'Birmingham directories', *Birmingham Archeological Society Transactions and Proceedings*, **58**, 1934.

Unpublished material

Bailey, M. H., 'The contribution of Quakers to some aspects of local government in Birmingham 1828–1902', University of Birmingham, M.A., 1952.

Bushrod, E., 'The history of Unitarianism in Birmingham from the mid 18th century to 1893', University of Birmingham, M.A., 1954.

Cannadine, D., 'The aristocracy and the towns in the 19th century: a case study of the Calthorpes and Birmingham 1807–1910', University of Oxford, D.Phil, 1975.

Cunningham, P., 'Art and social control in early Victorian Birmingham', Paper presented to the Sheffield Conference on Provincial Culture, 1981.

Cunningham, P., 'The formation of the schools of design 1830–50 with special reference to Manchester, Birmingham and Leeds', University of Leeds, Ph.D., 1979.

Franklin, R. E., 'Medical education and the rise of the general practitioner', University of Birmingham, Ph.D., 1950.

Frost, M., 'The development of provided schooling for working class children in Birmingham 1781–1851', University of Birmingham, M.Litt., 1978.

Hooper, A. F., 'Mid Victorian Radicalism: community and class in Birmingham 1850–80', University of London, Ph.D., 1979.

Lane, J., 'Apprenticeship in Warwickshire 1700–1834', University of Birmingham, Ph.D., 1977.

Mole, D. E. H., 'The Church of England and society in Birmingham 1830–66', University of Cambridge, Ph.D., 1961.

Ram, T. W., 'The social evolution of five dissenting communities in Birmingham', University of Birmingham, Ph.D., 1972.

Smith, D., 'A comparative study of class relationships and institutional orders in Birmingham and Sheffield with particular reference to the spheres of education, industry and politics', University of Leicester, Ph.D., 1980.

Trainor, R. H., 'Reports of the death of the middle class in industrial districts are greatly exaggerated: the Black Country 1830–1900', Paper presented to the urban history conference, 1983.

Trainor, R. H., 'Authority and social structure in an industrialized area: a study of three Black Country towns 1840–90', University of Oxford, Ph.D., 1981.

Essex and Suffolk

Books

Bax, C., *Highways and Byways in Essex*, 1939.
Benham, H., *Some Essex Water Mills*, Colchester, 1976.
Blaxill, A. E., *The Non-Conformist Churches of Colchester*, Colchester, 1948.
Booker, J., *Essex and the Industrial Revolution*, Chelmsford, 1974.
Bramston, J., *Witham in Olden Times*, Chelmsford, 1855.
Brown, A. F. J., *Chartism in Essex and Suffolk*, Chelmsford, 1982.
Brown, A. F. J., *Colchester 1815–1914*, Chelmsford, 1980.

Brown, A. F. J., *Essex People 1750–1900: from their diaries, memoirs and letters*, Chelmsford, 1972.

Brown, A. F. J., *Colchester in the 18th Century*, Colchester, 1969.

Brown, A. F. J., *Essex At Work*, Chelmsford, 1969.

Brown, A. F. J., *Witham in the 18th Century*, Witham, 1968.

Burls, R., *A Brief Review of the Plan and Operation of the Essex Congregational Union*, 1848.

Cockerill, C. and Woodward, D., *Colchester as a Military Centre*, Colchester, 1978.

Cromwell, T., *History and Description of the Ancient Town and Borough of Colchester*, Colchester, 1825.

Cryer, L. R., *A History of Rochford*, 1978.

Cullum, J., *The History and Antiquities of Hawstead and Hardwick*, 1813.

Dale, M. A., *The Annals of Coggeshall in the County of Essex*, Coggeshall, 1863.

Dickin, E. P., *A History of Brightlingsea: A Member of the Cinque Ports*, Brightlingsea, 1939.

Eastment, W., *Wanstead Through the Ages*, Letchworth, 1969.

Edwards, A. C., *A History of Essex*, 1978.

Erith, F. H., *Ardleigh in 1796: Its farms, families and local government*, East Bergholt, 1978.

Essex County Telegraph, *The Story of Layer-de-la-Haye*, Colchester, 1934.

Fitch, S. H., *Colchester Quakers*, Ipswich, n.d.

Fletcher, R., *The Biography of a Victorian Village: Richard Cobbold's Account of Wortham, Suffolk*, 1977.

Glyde, J., *The Moral, Social and Religious Condition of Ipswich in the Middle of the 19th Century*, 1971.

Glyde, J., *Suffolk in the 19th Century: Physical, Social, Moral, Religious and Industrial*, c. 1855.

Griggs, Messers, *General View of the Agriculture of the County of Essex*, 1794.

Klaiber, A., *The Story of the Suffolk Baptists*, 1931.

Marshall, W., *The Review and Abstract of the County Reports to the Board of Agriculture: Eastern Department*, 1818.

Mason, B., *Clock and Watchmaking in Colchester*, 1969.

Neale, K., *Essex in History*, 1977.

Page, W. and Round, J. H. (eds.), *The Victoria History of the County of Essex*, 1907.

Peacock, A. J., *Bread and Blood: A Study of the Agrarian Riots in East Anglia in 1816*, 1965.

Phillips, A., *Ten Men and Colchester*, Chelmsford, 1985.

Raynbird, W. and H., *On the Agriculture of Suffolk*, 1849.

Redstone, L. I., *Ipswich Through the Ages*, Ipswich, 1969.

Rickword, G., *Social Life in Bygone Colchester*, Colchester, 1925.

Rowntree, C. B., *Saffron-Walden – Then and Now*, Chelmsford, 1951.

Torrey, G., *Chelmsford Through the Ages*, Ipswich, 1977.

Tuffs, J. E., *Essex Coaching Days*, Letchworth, n.d.

Vaughan, E., *The Essex Village in Days Gone By*, Colchester, 1930.

West, F., *A Sketch of the History of Nonconformity in Braintree and Bocking*, 1891.

Wilkinson, F. W., *A History of Leyton*, Leytonstone, 1897.

Wilson, D., *A Short History of Suffolk*, 1977.

Wood, E. A., *A History of Thorpe-le-Soken to the Year 1890*, Thorpe-le-Soken, 1975.

Wright, T., *The History and Topography of the County of Essex*, 1836.

Young, A., *General View of the Agriculture of the County of Essex*, 1807.

Articles

Baker, R., 'On the farming of Essex', *Journal of the Agricultural Society*, 1844.

Christy, M., 'The history of banks and banking in Essex', *The Journal of the Institute of Bankers*, October 1906.

D'Cruze, S., '"To Acquaint the Ladies": women traders in Colchester c.1750 to c.1800', *The Local Historian*, 17 no. 3, 1986.

Dixon, R. W., 'Reminiscences of the Old Dissent in Witham', *Transactions of the Congregational Society*, V 1911–12.

East, F. J., 'The Quaker brewers of Saffron Walden', *Essex Countryside*, 20, April 1927.

Golding, S., 'The importance of fairs in Essex, 1759–1850', *Essex Journal*, 10 no. 3, 1975.

Laver, H., 'Cheese making in Essex', *Essex Naturalist*, viii, 1893.

Neale, K., 'Chingford enumerated: the village community at the census of 1851', *Essex Journal*, 3 no. 1, January 1968.

Snell, K. D., 'Agricultural seasonal unemployment, the standard of living and women's work in the south and east, 1690–1860', *Economic History Review*, 34 no. 3, 1981.

Wadhams, M. C., 'The development of buildings in Witham from 1500 to c. 1880', *Post-Medieval Archeology*, 6, 1972.

Unpublished material

Caroe, L., 'Urban change in East Anglia in the 19th century', University of Cambridge, Ph.D., 1966.

Davies, S. T., 'History of Witham', unpublished manuscript, 1869.

D'Cruze, S., 'The society now surrounding us: Colchester and its middling sort 1780–1800', University of Essex, M.A., 1985.

Gyford, J., 'Men of bad character: property crime in Essex in the 1820s', University of Essex, M.A., 1982.

King, P,, 'Prosecution associations in Essex 1740–1800', unpublished paper, Cambridge, 1983.

Shrimpton, C., 'The landed society and the farming community of Essex in the late 18th and early 19th centuries', University of Cambridge, Ph.D., 1966.

Speight, M. E., 'Politics in the Borough of Colchester 1812–1847', University of London, Ph.D., 1969.

Turner, J., 'The Colchester poll books – voting behaviour and politics in Colchester 1832–1852', University of Essex (Department of History), B.A., 1979.

Watson, S. P., 'Nineteenth century Witham: the role of local government', University of Essex (Department of History), B.A., 1978.

WEA Coggeshall, 'The story of Coggeshall 1700–1900', typescript, n.d.

Index

The index is divided into two parts. The first part is an **index of people**. Many of the entries are of families and individuals from the areas of research and where this is helpful brief biographical details are included. These are intended to help the reader to understand the relationships between members of families and to show some of the networks and relationships between families.

Entries in italics refer to individuals who are not named in the text but were important sources of information.

Other entries refer to nationally known figures or to contemporary scholars and historians.

The second part is an **index of subjects**.

People index

Adelaide, Queen (wife of William IV) 154
Albright, Arthur (b. 1811: manufacturer: Quaker: Birmingham) 218, 249
Attwood, Thomas (b. 1783: banker: Anglican: Birmingham) 15
Austen, Jane 385, 404, 438

Bache, Sarah (b. 1770: school proprietor: Unitarian: Birmingham) 297–8, 371
Barmby, J. 50
Barton, Bernard (b. 1784: bank clerk and poet: Quaker: Suffolk) 375, 386; friends and library 156,158, 160; income 212; views on: death 146; domesticity 178, 347; gardens 373; parenthood 179; women preaching 139
Barton Lucy (b. 1808: daughter of Bernard Barton, married Edward Fitzgerald, author)
Bentall, William (b. 1779: farmer and iron manufacturer: Goldhanger, Essex) 221, 251, 354, 365–6
Bentham, Jeremy 185, 235
Biddell, Arthur (b. 1783: farmer and land agent: Anglican: Ipswich, Suffolk: husband of Jane Ransome Biddell: agent to Thomas Clarkson) 375
Biddell, Jane Ransome 225, 273, 292; investment 278; reading 160;

views on: Byron 159; domesticity 178, 342–4; sisterhood 351–2; writing 88–9
Binfield, Clyde 77
Binney, Thomas (b. 1798: Independent minister: City of London) 118, 414
Bisset, James (b. 1761: japanner and museum-keeper: Anglican: Birmingham) 416–19; collecting 283; education 249–50; protection society 424; suburbs 369
Blomfield, Bezaliel 119
Blood, Howell Pattisson 265; *see also* Pattisson family
Boulton, Matthew (b. 1728: manufacturer: Anglican: Birmingham) 288; Birmingham Lunar Society 235; partnership 250; public role 445; Soho factory 39, 249, 366; wives 221
Boutflower family (Charles and William Marsh (sons of Charles)) 121, 263
Braithwaite, Anna 138–9
Braybrooke, Lord 49
Breay, Rev. John G. (b. 1796: clergyman: Anglican Evangelical: Birmingham) 87–8,110, 125
Bretnall, Robert (b. 1775: farmer: Anglican: Witham, Essex) 255, 397–8, 400

Bretnall, Sarah (wife of Robert) 410
Brewer, Rev. 132
Bright, John 140
Brightwen, Robert and Mary 335, 337–8
Buck, Catherine (wife of Thomas Clarkson) 282
Bunting, John 354; see also Seabrook family
Burgess, William 118–19
Burke, Edmund 28
Burnett, John 24, 361
Byron, George Gordon, Lord 27, 159–60

Cadbury family (retailers and manufacturers: Quakers: Birmingham) 43, 51,52–9, 227, 324, 335, 373, 374, 382, 390, 394, 404, 454; Richard Tapper (b. 1768: retailer); Elizabeth Head (b. 1768: wife of Richard Tapper); Benjamin Head (b. 1798: son of Richard: retailer); Candia Wadkin (b. 1803: wife of Benjamin); John (b. 1801: son of Richard: retailer and manufacturer); Candia Barrow (b. 1805: wife of John); Richard (b. 1835: son of John); Maria (b. 1838: daughter of John); George (b. 1839: son of John); see also Cadbury family tree 53; Gibbins family for Emma Cadbury Gibbins, daughter of Richard Tapper
Calthorpe family 84, 264, 422
Camps, Amy (b. 1800: sick visitor: Evangelical: Colchester) 88, 100, 122, 141–2, 144, 146, 346, 413–14, 431
Cannadine, David 359
Caroline of Brunswick (wife of George IV) 149–5, 448
Carpenter family: Lant 294, 297; Mary (daughter of Lant) 294
Charlesworth, Rev. John (b. 1782: vicar: Evangelical: Suffolk) 93, 137
Charlesworth, Maria (b. 1819: author: Evangelical) 147
Charlotte, Princess (daughter of George IV) 153
Chaytor, Miranda 31
Chevasse, Pye Henry 307, 340
Clark, Alice 273
Clark, Thomas junior (b. 1794: manufacturer: Unitarian: Birmingham) 157–8, 250, 370
Clarkson, Thomas (b. 1760: anti-slavery reformer: retired near

Ipswich) 112, 138, 381; see also Buck, Catherine
Cobbett, William 22, 260
Cobbold, Rev. Richard (b. 1797: rector: Wortham, Suffolk' 213
Coleby family 221; see also Ransome family; Reckitt family
Colman, Jeremiah 432
Conder, Eliza (wife of Josiah) 436
Conder, Josiah (b. 1789: publisher and editor: Independent: London) 66, 178, 330
Constable family (Anglicans: Dedham, Essex) 65, 160, 223, 284, 350, 352, 366; Golding (corn factor and miller); his children: Ann (b. 1768); Patty (b. 1769); Golding (b. 1774); John (b. 1776: artist); Mary (b. 1781); Abram (b. 1783: corn factor and miller)
Corder, William 402
Corfield, Penelope 24
Cotton, Nathaniel 166
Courtauld family (silk manufacturers: Unitarians: Essex): George (b. 1761: married Ruth Minton) 207, 251, 280, 330; Louisa (daughter of George) 334; Samuel (b. 1793: son of George): church rate issue 98; mill 201; Queen Caroline affair 153–4; start in business 280, 308, 311; training 249, 251; see also sibling, cousin and partnership marriage chart
Cowper, William 18, 26, 103, 162–7, 172; influence 91–2, 149, 157–9; views on: domesticity 112; paternalism 20; rural idyll 28, 181
Crabbe, George 287–8, 307
Crozier, Dorothy 31–2

Darwin, Charles 312
Darwin, Erasmus 235, 263, 290; see also Galton family
Dawson, Rev. George 162
D'Cruze, Shani 276
Dickens, Charles 36, 334, 348, 351
Dixon, Henry (b. 1787: doctor: Independent: Witham, Essex) 48, 90, 102, 252, 262–4 passim, 277, 333, 334, 355, 399, 405, 430
Douglas, Ann 126
Duman, Daniel 206

Edgeworth, Maria 160, 235
Eliot, George 288, 348–9
Ellis, Sarah Stickney 180–5, 188, 315, 340–2 passim

Fielding, Rev. 101, 122
Finigan, T. H. 268
Fitzgerald, Edward
Foster, John 24
Fry, Elizabeth 138, 139, 294, 429–30

Galton family (manufacturers and
bankers: Quakers:
Birmingham) 102–3, 245, 264;
domesticity 226; education 291,
343; garden 373; reading 158,
160; servants 342, 394; Samuel (b.
1753) 206; *Mary Ann
Schimmelpenninck* (b. 1778:
daughter of Samuel); Sophia (b.
1782) 327; Samuel Tertius (b.
1783: son of Samuel: married Violetta
Darwin, daughter of Erasmus
Darwin) 226, 331, 333; *Adèle* (b.
1784: daughter of Samuel); John
Howard (b. 1794: son of
Samuel) 323–4; *Elizabeth Anne
Wheler* (b. 1808: daughter of Samuel
Tertius); *Lucy* (daughter of Samuel
Tertius: married into Moilliet family;
Francis (b. 1822: son of Samuel
Tertius) 227, 312
Gardner family (brewers: Anglican:
Coggeshall, Essex): William (b.
1803) 223–4; Elizabeth (b. 1815: his
wife) 293
Garrett family (iron manufacturers and
maltsters: Evangelical/
Independents: Leiston and
Aldeburgh, Suffolk): Richard (b.
1779) 215, 222; Newson (b. 1812:
son of Richard: father of Elizabeth
Garrett Anderson and Milicent
Garrett Fawcett) 222, 243, 332;
Louisa (wife of Newson) 384
Gaskell, Elizabeth 270, 293, 390, 408
George III 19,152
George IV 19, 21,150–5
Gibbins family (bankers and
manufacturers: Quakers:
Birmingham) 245; Joseph (b. 1756:
banker) 103; Martha Bevington
(wife of Joseph) 77, 338; *Thomas*
(b. 1796: son of Joseph: married
Emma Cadbury); Emma
Cadbury 58, 283, 415; Martha
(daughter of Joseph) 405; Elizabeth
(daughter of Joseph) 217
Gilbert, Alan 76–7
Gilbert, Joseph (minister: Independent:
husband of Ann Taylor) 66; see
also Taylor family tree

Gilbert, Josiah (newphew of
Joseph) 67
Gisborne, Thomas 112, 170
Gorham, Deborah 339
Grubb, Sara 138
Gurney, John Joseph 87, 137–8, 242

Hanson, John 206
Harrison, Brian 300
Harvey, D. W. 49–50
Hedge, Mary Ann (b. 1776: author:
Evangelical: Colchester) 355;
views on: brother/sister
relationship 349;
domesticity 178, 287;
femininity 414, 430; Nature 291;
subscription 212; vicars 122
Hedge, Thomas (brother of Mary
Ann) 299
Hemans, Felicia 161
Hill family (school proprietors:
Unitarians: Birmingham) 160, 235,
237–9, 294, 295, 324, 333, 392, 443;
Thomas Wright (b. 1763: school
proprietor: married Sara Lea) 297,
443; *Matthew Davenport* (b. 1792:
schoolmaster/lawyer: son of
Thomas); Rowland (b. 1795:
schoolmaster then founder of the
penny post: son of Thomas) 27
Hodson, Rev. George 84
Holyoake, George 225, 266, 304
Hood, Thomas 28
Hook, Rev. Walter Farquar 85
Howgego, Jeremiah (b. 1780: baker
and confectioner: Anglican:
Ipswich, Suffolk) 102, 446–7
Hutton, Catherine (b. 1756: writer:
daughter of William) 290, 444
Hutton, William (b. 1723:
manufacturer and historian:
Unitarian: Birmingham) 78, 162,
248

James, Rev. John Angell (b. 1785:
clergyman: Independent:
Birmingham) 75, 85, 103, 123,
126–30; influence on Phipson
sisters 297; influenced by: Ellis,
Sarah Stickney 181; More,
Hannah 158; views on: church
organization 131–3; church rates
issue 99; dress 411; family 109,
113, 328; philanthropy 430, 432;
servants 392; social order 92–4
passim; theatre 437;
women 114–16 *passim*, 143–4

Keir, James (b. 1735: father of Amelia Moilliet) 251, 252, 348; *see also* Amelia Moilliet

Kenrick family (manufacturers: Unitarian: Birmingham) 36, 43, 217, 219, 225, 250, 311, 324, 330, 338, 344, 361, 387, 434–5; *Archibald* (b. 1760); *Rebecca Smith* (b. 1770: wife of Archibald); *Archibald* (b. 1798: son of Archibald); *Rebecca* (b. 1799); *Marianne* (b. 1801: daughter of Archibald and Rebecca: married cousin Samuel Kenrick); *Caroline* (daughter of Archibald (junior))

Kent, John 203

Knight, Anne (b. 1876: anti-slavery and feminist reformer: Quaker: Chelmsford) 452–3

Kussmaul, Ann 67

Lean, William and Hannah 236, 294, 295

Lloyd family (bankers: Quaker: Birmingham) 43, 103, 138–9, 245

Loudon, Jane Webb (b. 1807: daughter of Thomas Webb: wife of John Loudon: writer on gardening for women) 188, 189, 346, 374

Loudon, John (b. 1783: landscape gardener and designer) 180–2, 188–92, 370, 375, 377, 409

Luckcock, James (b. 1761: manufacturer: Unitarian: Birmingham) 13–18, 36, 43, 334; garden 372; 'Hints for Practical Economy in the Management of Household Affairs' 361; views on: domesticity 20, 155; education of girls 384; fashion 375; marriage 324, 328; 'rural idyll' 20

Mackintosh, Richard 102

McLeod, Hugh 79, 108

Malthus, Thomas 15, 185

Marsh family (clergy: Evangelical: Colchester and Birmingham): William (b. 1775) 79–80, 368, 378; banks collapse 121; campaign with Richard Cadbury 56; Camps, Amy 122, 141; Chartism, opposition 93, 94–5; Evangelical network 83; femininity 137; masculinity 110, 111; morality 92; patronage 119; theatre 437; Maria Tilson (b. 1779: wife of William) 327; family life 123–5; 340; patronage 102; views on: conversion 90;

fatherhood 333; motherhood 343; 'rural idyll' 157; Catherine (b. 1818: daughter of William and Maria: writer and philanthropist): family life and philanthropy 124–5, 289, 346–7, 393; reading 90; views on: fatherhood 89, 110; home 358; politics 93, 95, 453

Martineau, Harriet 160, 180–1, 185–8, 321, 351, 385

Martineau, Robert (brother of Harriet: b. 1799: manufacturer: Unitarian: Birmingham) 36, 321; *see also* Kenrick family

Mill, James 154

Mill, John Stuart 454

Moilliet family (bankers: Birmingham) 247, 291; Amelia (daughter of James Keir: wife of John Lewis) 161–2, 339, 340, 348, 409; *John Lewis* (banker)

More, Hannah 167–72; Coelebs in search of a wife 123; Evangelical revival 81–2; influence 158, 184; old age 393; views on: gardens 373; philanthropy 429; society based on land 181; theatre 437; women and domesticity 116, 149, 352, 375, 395

Morgan, Rev. Thomas 296

Morris, Robert 24, 32, 195–6, 226, 443

Oakes family (bankers: Anglican: Bury St Edmunds) 269; James (b. 1741) 245–6, 254, 375; Orbell (b. 1768: son of James: friend of Arthur Young) 247

Obelkevich, James 107,108

Parker, John Oxley 288

Parkes, Joseph 237

Parkin, Frank 315

Pattisson family (attorneys: Independent, later Anglican: Witham, Essex) 244, 366; William Henry (b. 1775) 104, 142–3, 341, 345, 355, 378, 408; Jacob Howell (b. 1803: son of William) 48, 208, 214, 262, 265, 267; *Charlotte Luard* (b. 1817: wife of Jacob); Howell Pattisson Blood 265

Paul, St 108,139, 179, 429

Penn, Phoebe 297–8

Perry, John (b. 1781: draper: Quaker: Ipswich, Suffolk) 216, 267, 289, 346

Perry, Maria Kincey (wife of John: aunt

of Robert Ransome's wife and of Isaac
Reckitt's wife); *see also* Ransome
family
Phipson family (Independents:
Birmingham) 43, 109, 134; Joseph
(b. 1778: manufacturer) 223; Mary
Ann (b. 1811: daughter of Joseph:
school proprietor) 296–7, 298
Pinchbeck, Ivy 273
Player, John 178–9
Priestley, Joseph (b. 1733: clergyman/
chemist: Unitarian: Birmingham):
Birmingham library 156;
home 43; income 120;
influence 15; New Meeting 96,
297; riots 15, 19, 42; views on:
chapel management 135; female
education 145; marriage 324;
social millenium 442
Prince Regent *see* George IV
Prochaska, Frank 135, 313

Ransome family (iron manufacturers:
Quaker: Ipswich, Suffolk) 205,
251; James (b. circa 1789) 222, 431;
Jane (b. 1790: married Arthur
Biddell) *see* Biddell family; Robert
(b. 1795: married Sarah Coleby,
Maria Perry's niece and sister of Ann
who married Isaac Reckitt) 216,
221; James Allen (b. 1806: son of
James) 255–6, 329, 331; Hannah
(b. 1813: daughter of James: married
Stafford Allen) 87, 221
Reckitt family: Isaac (b. 1792: miller
and starch manufacturer: Quaker:
Lincolnshire: married Ann Coleby,
niece of Maria Perry) 221
Repton, Humphrey 310, 361, 370
Robinson, Henry Crabb (b. 1775:
attorney and man of letters:
Independent: Bury St Edmunds/
London: friend of Cowper,
Wordsworth and Catherine Clarkson
née Buck) 282, 355, 378, 414–15
Round family (publishers and bankers:
Anglican: Colchester) 50, 246, 247
Ryan, Mary 30, 117
Ryder, Henry 84
Ryland family (manufacturers:
Unitarians: Birmingham) 36, 43,
104, 212, 252; *William* (b. 1731);
Thomas (b. 1769: son of William);
Thomas Henry (b. 1810: son of
Thomas: married Caroline Clark,
sister of Thomas Clark Junior);
Samuel 104; Louisa (daughter of
Samuel) 104; *Arthur* (b. 1807:

cousin of Thomas Henry: lawyer:
married into Phipson family)

Savill family (wool merchants:
Independent: Bocking, Essex): John
(b. 1780: Independent
minister) 119; *Samuel Webb* (b.
1800: attorney: cousin of John)
Savill, Maria (b. 1817: from family of
builders, architects and surveyors:
Chigwell, Essex) 284
Scott, Walter, Sir 27, 28, 68, 158
Seabrook family (farmers: Anglicans:
Boreham and Tolleshunt D'Arcy,
Essex) 254–5, 258; *see also*
Bunting, John
Sewell, Mary Wright (b. 1797: Quaker:
farmer's daughter: commercial
traveller's wife: writer on
domesticity) 86–7, 89, 146–7, 159,
342
Sewell, Anna (b. 1829: daughter of
Mary Wright Sewell: author of
Black Beauty)
Shaen family (Unitarian: Hatfield
Peverel, Essex) 221, 224, 325–9
passim, 341, 350, 351, 355–6, 380,
383, 395, 404; Samuel (b. 1783: non-
practising attorney and gentleman
farmer); Rebecca Solly (b. 1782:
wife of Samuel); Rebecca Shaen Solly
(b. 1812: daughter of Samuel and
Rebecca: married cousin Henry
Solly); Samuel (b. 1819: son of
Samuel and Rebecca); Benjamin (b.
1819: son of Samuel and Rebecca);
William (b. 1821: son of Samuel and
Rebecca: well-known radical
lawyer: married Emily Winkworth)
see Winkworth, Catherine; Louisa
(b. 1823: daughter of Samuel
(junior)); Louisa (b. 1780: sister of
Samuel (senior)); Hepzibah (sister of
Samuel (senior))
Shewell, John Talwin 91–2, 242
Shore, Emily 291
Simeon, Charles 83, 140
Smith, Adam 20, 26
Southall, Thomas (b. 1794: retailer:
Quaker: Birmingham) 56, 297, 369
Spooner family 84; Isaac, Rev. 120;
William, Archdeacon of
Coventry 84
Spurgeon, Charles 141, 240, 394
Stael, Madame de 161
Stapleton, Dr 65
Stone, Lawrence 21
Strutt family 65

Sturge, Edmund and Joseph
(merchants: Quaker:
Birmingham)   218
Sumner, Archbishop   84

Tayler, Rev. Charles (b. 1797: curate:
Evangelical: Hadleigh,
Suffolk)   95, 138, 154, 160
Taylor family (Independents:
Colchester, Essex)   59–69, 89, 97,
172–7, 234, 334, 337, 345, 359, 377,
383; *Isaac* (b. 1759: engraver and
Independent minister); *Ann Martin*
(b. 1757: author: wife of Isaac); Ann
(b. 1782: daughter of Isaac and Ann
Martin: author) *see* family entries
and   147, 158, 335, 343, 405, 452–3;
Jane (b. 1783: daughter of Isaac and
Ann Martin: author) *see* family
entries, and   105, 147, 161, 289,
303, 343, 349, 405, 453; *Isaac* (b.
1787: son of Isaac and Ann Martin:
author and inventor); *see also* Taylor
family tree   60
Thackeray, William Makepeace   117
Thompson, Edward   30, 97
Thompson, F. M. L.   359
Thomson, James   28, 157
Thornton, Henry   108, 109

Victoria, Queen   154, 447

Watkins, Ann   101
Watt, James (b. 1736: manufacturer and
engineer: Presbyterian)   249–52
passim
Webb, Thomas (Birmingham
businessman: father of Jane Webb
Loudon)   227
Whitehead, Ann   275
Wilberforce, Samuel (Bishop of
Oxford: son of William)   123
Wilberforce, William   81–2, 83, 84,
91, 153, 407, 429
William IV   154, 447
Winkworth, Catherine (b. 1827:
translator and hymn-writer:
Independent: Manchester: friend of
Mrs Gaskell and sister of Emily
(wife of William Shaen))   305
Withering, William (b. 1741: physician:
Anglican: Birmingham)   263, 366
Wollstonecraft, Mary   19, 117, 155,
170–1
Wordsworth family   19, 280, 351, 352;
Dorothy (sister of William); *Mary*
(wife of William); *William* (poet)

Young, Arthur   27, 157, 204, 253,
254, 290, 371, 382, 411

Subject index

accounting 20, 199, 201–5, 383–4; *see also* professions

advertising 241–2, 248

ageing 225–8, 255, 342, 346, 348

agriculture *see* farms and farming

Anglican Evangelicals: beliefs and development 81–9 *passim*; Clapham sect 81–2, 108, 140; clergy 118, 111–13; Cowper, William 163; dress 413–14; gentility 28; morality 110, 437–8; networks 99; parish 83, 99; 'Saints, The' 84, 85, 124; social origins 73–5, 81; Tractarian opposition 85, 99; *see also* Camps, Amy; churches and chapels; Marsh family; More, Hannah; religion; Wilberforce, William

Anglicans 82 (Tables 1 and 2); Birmingham 42–3; church membership 130; clergy 103–4, 120–1; Colchester 49; disestablishment 98; Evangelical challenge 81–3; growth of nonconformity 23, 99; morality 74; networks 99; patronage 102; politics 97–9; social status 24 (Table 1), 104; Tractarians 85, 99, 451; women 107–8, 304; *see also* churches and chapels; religion

annuities 211–12, 277

anti-slavery movement 25, 92, 102–3, 112, 429, 433–4, 436

apprenticeship and training 222–5; banking 246; doctors 261, 290; dressmaking and millinery 302; family's role 62, 65, 249, 281–2; farmers 258; lawyers 290; manufacture 249; professions 262, 264; retailing 52, 242

architecture 232, 246, 358–9, 361–9, 375–80

aristocracy: dress 410; friendship networks 33; housing 359, 377; leadership and values 21, 51, 360; middle-class challenge 103; middle-class view 22; patronage 49, 199, 419, 422; primogeniture 205; servants 389; *see also* gentry

arts 239, 289–90, 309–10, 416, 444–5; *see also* literature; music

assurance 205, 213–14, 264

bankruptcy 77, 102, 201, 203, 208, 241

banks and banking 207–9, 245–7, 366; *see also* Galton family; Moilliet family

Baptists 24 (Table 1), 80, 82 (Tables 2 and 3), 105; *see also* nonconformists

beauty 28, 189, 191–2, 414

bible societies 83, 84, 144, 430, 433

Birmingham Botanical and Horticultural Society 422–4

Birmingham Infant School Society 421–2

Birmingham Lunar Society 235, 263, 290, 312

bloodsports 110, 112, 405–6

book societies *see* literary societies

botanic gardens 370, 422–4

brewing 300, 365, 385

capital: banks 245; capital clubs 250; liquidity 195, 206, 207; personal sources 208; women's contribution 33, 58, 278, 279

Captain Swing riots 50–1

Carrs Lane chapel, Birmingham (Independent): growth 85–6; social life 100; Sunday school 128, 143–4; women 131–3; *see also* James, Rev. John Angell

census 204, 230; 1851: grandparents 354; innkeepers 299; manufacture 248, 251; middle-class households 24, 34, 231; professions 260; religion 76, 80; schools 296; servants 388; widows and single women 313; women 272–3; visitors 321

chapels *see* churches and chapels

Chartists 50, 93–5

childbirth: lying-in societies 434; medical care 307; religious view of 114; *see also* illegitimacy; pregnancy

children 343–8; adolescence 100, 344–5; Cadbury family 52, 56–7; care of: breastfeeding 336–8, 399; children's help 64; servants 339, 391, 394–5; Taylor family 63, 175–6; women's role 281; discipline 331, 340, 343, 347;

family enterprise 52, 251;
gardening 373; gender
differences 65, 344, 398–9; girls'
help with housekeeping 385, 387;
illness and mortality 52, 61,
330–1, 339; inheritance 210–11;
morality 21–2; nurseries and
accommodation 375, 377, 380;
play 26, 64, 281, 343–4, 351;
spiritual training 88, 124, 179, 340;
Taylor family 63, 64; see also
education; family; fatherhood;
motherhood
choral societies 438–9
Christ Church, Birmingham
(Anglican) 79, 84, 104
churches and chapels: building 78–9,
85, 104, 127; organization 131–40;
266; rates 85, 98;
subscriptions 135; tithes 83, 98,
367; see also Carrs Lane chapel;
Christ Church; New Meeting; Old
Meeting; religion; St Martin's
church; St Peter's church; St
Thomas' church; Witham
Congregational church
'civil society' 416, 419
Clapham sect 81–2, 108, 140; see also
More, Hannah; Wilberforce,
William
class: class consciousness:
Freemasons 426;
masculinity 409, 413; middle-class
relationships with working
class 50, 275, 423–4; religious
basis 74–5, 76–7, 81, 83, 105;
retail trade 243–4, 303; servants and
employers 389;
occupation 229–34; social status:
Anglicans 104; bankers 246;
professionals 264–5; retail
trade 243–4; salaried
workers 267–8, 269; theories 13,
30, 107, 450; see also aristocracy;
gentry; social mobility; working class
clergy 118–23; daughters 89, 146,
346–7; education 290;
Freemasons 426; gardens 371;
housing 80, 123, 127, 367, 368;
income 120–1, 127;
inheritance 218; numbers 233
(Table 4); patronage 102, 393;
servants 388, 393; social
status 49, 103–4;
superstition 25–6; teaching 282;
views of: Evangelicals 83–5;
Independents 86;

masculinity 111, 113;
Quakers 87; wives 123–6, 129,
286; work 78–81; see also churches
and chapels; James, Rev John
Angell; Priestley, James; professions;
Marsh, Rev William; religion
clubs 15, 239, 250, 286, 416, 417, 419;
see also voluntary associations
Coelebs in search of a wife (Hannah
More) 123, 158, 167–72, 401
commerce see trade
commercial travellers 26, 248
communications see newspapers and
journals; transport
Congregations see Independents
consumption (tuberculosis) 22, 65,
339
consumption: family and 360–1,
375–6, 384; farmers and 254;
importance of 29–30, 51, 320;
services 196–7
Corn Laws 49, 203
courtship 23, 66, 100, 219–21, 323,
324, 326–7
coverture 200–1, 276, 315
credit: development 20;
manufacturing 249; sources 24
(Table 1), 208, 250; women's
access 278

death: child illness and mortality 52,
61, 330–1, 339; funerals 103, 154,
321, 408–9, 427; illness and
mortality 22, 61, 65, 357; religious
view 77, 87, 90, 146
demography: age of marriage 222,
233, 323, 333, 335–8, 346; family
size 223, 224, 281, 328–9, 335–8,
380; household size 319–20;
middle-class population 23–4;
mortality 52, 61, 322, 339;
occupation and class 229–34;
population figures 23–4, 39, 47,
50, 256; see also census
design 239, 249–50
Dissenters see nonconformists
division of labour by gender 13;
church activities 142–3; men's
work 229–71, 274–5, 308–12; see
also accounting; clergy; doctors;
estate management; farming;
lawyers; teachers; women's
work 25, 29, 274, 288, 308–15;
employment 116, 183–4, 241, 265,
272–5, 293–304; see also
dressmaking; innkeepers; midwives;
milliners; retail trade; teachers;
family enterprise 33, 52, 200–1,

210, 250–1, 279–89;
marginalization 195, 272, 279,
304–8, 310; support to men's
work 13, 264, 267; bankers'
wives 247; Cadbury family 52,
57, 227; clergy wives 123–6, 129,
136–7; farmers' wives 260, 306;
lawyers' wives 283; lodgers 282;
salaried men's wives 267, 268, 269,
283; teachers' wives 283;
workhouse 305; see also children;
domesticity; housekeeping;
housework; literature; motherhood;
philanthropy; single women;
widows
doctors: child health 339–40;
development of profession 307,
340; education 261, 290; housing
366; life assurance 213;
numbers of 233 (Table 4);
patronage 102, 263;
superstition 25–6; see also Dixon,
Henry; health; professions
domestic service see servants
domesticity: Cotton's view 166;
Cowper's view 165–6;
farmers 258; idealization 451,
454; literature 155–92; men's 33,
333; Bisset 418; Cadbury 56–7;
Luckcock 17, 20; Shewell 91;
monarchy 152–3; professional
men's wives 287; Queen Caroline
affair 150–5; rationalization 27;
religious justification 90, 108–9,
112–13, 115–16, 323;
retirement 225–8; women's
role 275, 296, 305, 313; see also
housekeeping; motherhood
dower 209, 276
dress 410–15; clothing clubs 432;
court 21; mourning 408; Quaker
headgear 386; servants 392;
women 395, 404; see also
dressmaking; laundry; needlework
dressmaking 284, 302–4, 313; see also
needlework
drink and drunkenness 400; see also
brewing; inns and innkeepers

education: boys' 24, 65, 234–40, 290,
294, 344–5; fathers' role 331;
gender differences 65, 281–2,
291–2, 340, 344; girls' 59, 183,
186, 188, 289–93; mothers'
role 175–6, 235, 291–2;
nonconformists excluded 99;
philanthropy 420; religion
and 294, 297; self-education 239,

292, 442–4; Taylor family 65;
teachers 120–1, 145, 265, 266, 285,
293–9, 313; women's role 281–2;
see also apprenticeship and training;
schools; Sunday schools
estate management 199, 202, 204; see
also professions
evangelicalism: children 343;
femininity 114–18;
masculinity 108–13;
morality 87; Puritan doctrine 21;
revival 51,78–9, 93–5;
salvation 25, 73, 114; see also
Anglican Evangelicals; Baptists;
churches and chapels;
Congregationals; nonconformists
Evangelicals see Anglican Evangelicals
executors 211, 214, 264; see also
inheritance

fairs 241, 406
family: apprentices 223–5, 249,
281–2; business networks 56,
215–19, 223–4, 255, 352; credit and
capital 250; definitions 28–35,
321–2, 361; dependants 101,
313–15, 354; economic
activity 195, 199, 250–1; see also
family enterprise; education 235,
291–2; extended family 56, 321–2,
341–2; girls' contribution to
housekeeping 65, 125, 282, 347,
385, 387; ideology 21, 74, 83, 99,
108–9; income and
expenditure 23–4, 284–5, 324,
360–1, 378–80, 384;
inheritance 218–19;
intergenerational relationships 329:
aunts and uncles 223, 281, 321,
353; fathers and daughters 332–3;
346–8; fathers and sons 332;
grandparents 354; mothers and
daughters 338, 341, 346; mothers
and sons 340–1, 338; parents and
sons 345–6; networks 119, 289,
419; patriarchy 322, 333; prayers
and worship 89, 108–9, 124, 331,
359, 383; professions 263;
relationships 59: brothers 352;
brothers and sisters 125, 282, 311,
314, 322, 348–53; brothers and
sisters-in-law 351, 352–3; deceased
wife's sister 352; sibling and cousin
marriage 219–21, 348, 352, 353,
354; sisters 351–2; religious
training and role 88, 108–9, 124,
179, 340; size 223, 224, 281, 322,
328–9, 335–8, 380; women 114; see

also children; domesticity; fatherhood; friendship; housing; kinship; marriage; motherhood

family enterprise 31–2, 198–228; Luckcock family 16–17; men's role 228–71; women's role: capital 33, 58, 279; labour 24, 25, 33, 58, 162, 195, 267, 268, 272–315, 451

farms and farming 253–60; accounting and rationalization 202, 204, 256, 383–4; break-up of paternalism 199; capital 245; development 44–7, 196, 273–4; dress 410; family's work 283, 284, 288–9, 306–7; gardens 371; housing 367, 377–8; labourers: allotments 48–9; Captain Swing riots 50–1; separation from farmer's family 256–7, 377–8; social status 22, 274; wages 83, 234, 240, 256; manufacturers 252; numbers 232, 233 (Table 4), partnership and inheritance 218; retail trade 240; retirement 226; social status 49, 233 (Table 4), 286, 399; voluntary associations 286, 425, 427; women excluded 273–4

fatherhood 329–35; discipline 331, 343, 347; recreation 331, 360, 343; relationships with children 345–8; religious view 89, 109; Taylor family 174

femininity: anti-slavery movement 429, 433, 436; beauty 414; brothers' influence 349; class and 30; contradictions 322; development 29, 450–1; dress 413–15; drinking and swearing 400–1; emotional nature 408; gardening 374; gentility 315, 344; home-centred and dependant 25, 90, 315, 319, 323; idealization 19; Luckcock family 17–18; 'Nature' 27; private sphere 68, 137–40, 451; Queen Caroline affair 151–5; religious basis 74, 77, 90, 110, 114–18; romantic ideal 28; sexuality 401; spiritual equality 430; views of 33, 323: Bentham, Jeremy 185; Loudon, John 190–2; Martin, Ann Taylor 173–4; More, Hannah 170–1; *see also* division of labour by gender; domesticity; motherhood

feminism 29, 452–4; development 13; Garrett family 332; Knight, Ann 436, 452–3; Martineau, Harriet 186; More, Hannah 171; Owenism 94; 'woman question' 75

festivals 26, 257, 359, 375, 377, 432

food and meals: consumption and costs 361, 384; cooking and preparation 284, 380–1, 383, 391; labourers and workmen 289, 432; mealtimes 385; table manners 375–6, 399; *see also* drink and drunkenness

franchise: Birmingham Political Union 43; Reform Act 1832 19, 97–8; servants 199; women's suffrage 452

Freemasons 199, 208, 426–7

French Revolution: political effects 18–19, 96; religious effects 51, 74–5, 82, 92, 95

friendship 33, 199; banking 247; business networks 215–19; education 235; marriage 179, 221, 354; Quakers 56, 86–7; religious networks 99–103; salaried posts 266; single women and young men 282; voluntary associations 419; women's role 281, 402–3

funerals 103, 154, 321, 408–9, 427

furnishings 375–80

gardens: ideal of 17, 361; Loudon, Jane Webb 189; Loudon, John 188–92; parks and botanic gardens 370, 422–4; professional development 310

gender difference: appearance 410–15; childhood 65, 344, 385, 387, 398–9; class and 30; development 450–1; education 281, 290–1, 340, 344; families: Bissets 416–19; Cadburys 52; Luckcocks 17–18; family enterprise 223; gardening 310, 373–4; gentility 398–9; homemaking 387; hospitals and prison 429; inheritance 209–13, 218–19; leisure 405–10; literature 149; marriage 179, 183; mobility and travel 403–5; pay 295; professions 264; public life 445–9; religion: church activities 142–3; church membership 86, 107–48;

justification for 74–5, 114, 126;
religious life 90–2; servants 391;
subordination of women 114;
teachers 145, 265, 285, 293–9, 313;
views of 20–1, 29: Bentham,
Jeremy 185; Martineau,
Harriet 185; More,
Hannah 168–72; Quaker 139;
voluntary associations 416, 421,
422, 428–9; see also division of
labour by gender; domesticity;
education; femininity; masculinity;
men; women
gentility 397–401; changes in 73,
113; collecting cards 430;
consumption and 360, 375–6;
Cowper's view 164; education
for 289–90; femininity and 315,
344; funerals 409; middle-class
value 28, 30; motherhood 338;
public houses 300; reading 156;
religion 76, 105; spread of by
servants 25; Taylor, Ann
Martin 172–3; teachers 285;
women's work 184, 274, 388
gentry: Anglican Evangelicalism 73;
dress 410; housing 359, 362, 377;
influence 51; land as basis of
wealth 19–20, 198, 205–6, 253;
landscape gardening 370;
masculinity 110; middle-class
challenge 49, 103, 113, 252;
middle-class imitation 226;
primogeniture 205; professions
replacing role 262; Witham 48
guilds 22, 25, 32, 249
governesses 313, 453

Hazelwood School 235, 237–8, 294,
295, 343
health: child illness and mortality 52,
61, 330–1, 339; hospitals 141, 306,
429, 434; hygiene 90, 382–3, 386,
399; illness and mortality 22, 61,
65, 357; philanthropy 420;
separation of health care and
professional medicine 307; servants
illness 390; vaccination 287, 339;
see also ageing; childbirth; death;
doctors; pregnancy; public health
housekeeping: Cadbury family 52,
57; clergy wives 124; conflict with
religious life 90–1; girls'
contribution 65, 125, 282, 347,
385, 387; rationalization 27, 383–4,
392–3; shopping 385–6; Taylor
family 63, 176; training
for 281–2; see also domesticity;

dressmaking; food and meals;
housework; servants
housework 380–8 passim; see also
housekeeping; servants
housing 357–96; children's
accommodation 375, 377, 380;
clergy homes 80, 123, 127, 367,
368; furnishings 241–2; home as
workplace: banking 245–6;
doctors 366; farmers 253, 257;
inns 300; lawyers 366;
manufacture 365; professions 263;
salaried 267; trade 242, 283; ideal
of 17; Loudon, John 188–92;
'offices' 232, 319; rental
accommodation 357–8, 369;
retirement 226; separation of home
and work 181; farms 367;
manufacture 251; salaried
workers 267; servants
accommodation 389–90; see also
gardens; lodgers; suburbs
hygiene 90, 382–3, 386, 399

ideologies see beauty; domesticity;
family; femininity; masculinity;
rationalism; romanticism; 'rural
idyll'; Utilitarianism
illegitimacy 321, 398, 402
income 23–4, 195; annuities 211–12,
277; clergy 120–1, 127; family
income and expenditure 284–5,
324, 360–1, 378–80, 384;
pensions 212, 251; salaried
posts 265–71; subscriptions 212,
277, 361, 423; teachers 294–5, 313;
wages: labourers 88, 234, 240, 256,
257, 390; women's work 313
Independents (Congregationals) 82
(Tables 2 and 3); beliefs 74, 85–6;
church organization 131–5 passim;
conflict between family and
religion 101; growth 80, 85;
networks 99; services 80, 86, 89;
social status 24 (Table 1), 104;
women's rights 132–3; see also
Carrs Lane Independent chapel;
churches and chapels; James, Rev.
John Angell; nonconformists;
religion; Taylor family
inheritance 24 (Table 1); farms 254;
illegitimate children 321;
manufacturing 250; marriage
networks 218, 221–2; provision
for dependants 205–13, 218;
salaried men 268–9; widows 293,
299: care of property for
children 254, 276, 284

inns and innkeepers 233 (Table 4),
299–301, 367, 427–8
insurance: banking 245, 277;
fire 205, 214, 367
investment 195; for
dependants 211–15; middle-class
status 24 (Table 1);
women's 277–8, 279–80, 423; see
also capital; inheritance; insurance

joint stock companies 32;
manufacture 250; mistrust 200,
201; schools 236, 201; voluntary
associations 422–3; see also
partnerships
journals see newspapers and journals

King Edward's Grammar School,
Birmingham 99, 236–7, 294–5,
366
kinship 31, 32–3, 321; banking 246;
business networks 206, 215–19,
275; education 235;
farming 254–5; professions 263;
Quakers 86–7; religious
networks 99–103; salaried
posts 266; women's role 281; see
also family; family enterprise

labour: family enterprise; family's
work 24 (Table 1), 242; women's
work 33, 58, 195, 267, 268,
272–315; labourers see farms and
farming
land: basis of wealth 19–20, 198,
205–6, 253; ownership 253; see
also estate management
landlords 253, 357–8, 369
language: Esquire 422; names and
naming 31, 222, 401; occupation
and status 230; proverbs and Old
Wives Tales 27; swearing 77,
400–1; womanhood and women's
work 33, 149, 273
laundry 386–7
lawyers 261–2; development of
profession 214; education 290;
housing 366; inheritance
patterns 206; law societies 262,
425; morality 22; numbers 233
(Table 4); social status 265; women
and wives 283, 445; see also
Pattisson family; professions
leisure: bloodsports 110, 112, 405–6;
Cowper's view 164–5;
dancing 436–7; families and
fathers 331; gardening 370–5;
Guy Fawkes 407;

holidays 359–60; housing, effect
on 362, 375; needlework 387;
racing 406; reading and
writing 63–4, 155–7;
retirement 225–8; trials 410;
voluntary associations 436–45;
walking and riding 27–8, 403; see
also fairs; festivals; markets;
weddings
libraries 156, 292, 306, 420
life assurance 205, 213–14, 264
limited liability 200–1
'Lit. and Phils.' see literary societies
literature: activity for women 125,
145–7, 304–5; domestic ideology
and 180–92; garden in 373; ideas
spread by 51, 78; influence on
gender difference 149, 292–3; local
writers 172–9; middle class
and 155–62; views of:
brothers 352; brothers and
sisters 348–9; clergy 122;
daughters 347–8;
women 116–17; see also Barton,
Bernard; Cowper, William; Hedge,
Mary Ann; literary societies; More,
Hannah; Taylor family; Thomson,
James
literary societies 157, 159, 292, 420,
428, 442–4
lodgers 361; apprentices 242, 264,
282; farm labourers 256–7;
supplement to income 299; see also
inns and innkeepers

manufacture 29; Birmingham 36–7,
196, 247–52; development 195–6,
199; farmers in 254;
housing 365–6; men in 311–12;
numbers involved 232–3; voluntary
associations 420–1; waged
labour 234; women in 273,
304–8, 311–12; woollen
industry 44, 253; see also Cadbury
family; family enterprise
'market, the' 20–1, 32, 165, 198–200
markets 241, 286, 407
marriage 322–9; age of 222, 233,
323, 333, 335–8, 346; business
networks 206, 217–19, 222;
changes in 23; clergy 123–6;
cousin marriage 219–21, 353;
idealization 179; Masonic
view 426; Quaker view 86, 219;
Queen Caroline affair 152;
religious networks 100, 119,
219–21; separation 277; sex and
sexuality 26–7; sibling

marriage 219–21, 348, 352, 354; weddings 407–8; women's 'trade' 273; *see also* children; courtship; domesticity; femininity; housekeeping; housework; motherhood

Marxism 29–30

masculinity (manliness): activities associated with 33, 312; appearance 414; aristocratic ideal 110; business competence 205, 214–15; class and occupation 30, 229, 269, 270–1, 272; contradictions 322; development 29, 450–1; dress 410–13; drinking and swearing 400–1; duelling 21; economic success 334–5; education for 235; farmers 260; Freemasons 426; gardening 373–4; military ideal of 19; political independence 199; public life 319; Queen Caroline affair 151; rational thought 27; religion and 73, 74, 86, 107–14, 401; romantic ideal 28; sexuality 401–2; views of: Cowper, William 164, 166; Luckcock, James 15, 17–18; More, Hannah 169; *see also* fatherhood; men

meals *see* food and meals

medicine *see* doctors; health

men: dress 410–13; leisure 405–10; marriage 323–5; mobility and travel 403–5; occupation 30, 231–4, 308–12; patriarchy 322, 333; politics 73, 445–9; religious role 107–23, 131–6, 140; servants and 390–1, 392; voluntary associations 416–49; women's support 13, 52, 57, 91; *see also* domesticity; division of labour by gender; fatherhood; masculinity

Methodists 82 (Tables 2 and 3); Evangelical challenge 81–2; numbers 80, 81; Primitive Methodists 105, 107; social status 24 (Table 1), 73; women's role 137

middle class: definition 18–28; internal divisions 24 (Table 1), 233 (Table 4); moral authority 30; numbers of 31

midwives 307–8

millinery 302–4, 313

monarchy: changing views of 19,

152–3; Cowpers view of 164; Queen Caroline affair 149–55

'moral economy' 15, 20–2, 111–12, 207, 208; patriotism 164; *see also* morality; paternalism; patronage; trusteeship; stewardship

morality: education for 289; fashion 386; garden as metaphor 373; gender difference 450; 'good taste' 191–2; masculinity 199; middle-class 13, 25–6; motherhood 339, 434; Queen Caroline affair 154; religious basis 74, 86, 87–9, 93, 104–5, 110–11; replacing religion 184; theatre 437–8; women's role 117; women's work 90, 274; work and 21–2, 112; *see also* 'moral economy'

motherhood 335–43; clergy wives 129; conflict with religious life 139; education 175–6, 235, 291–2; Evangelical view 114, 116; professionalism 58; Puritan view 114; religious instruction 88, 179, 124, 340; Taylor family 63, 66, 173–5; teaching housekeeping 340; *see also* childbirth; children; domesticity; housekeeping; pregnancy

music 438–42

mutual societies 213, 264

names and naming 31, 121, 222, 273, 401; *see also* language

Napoleonic wars: blockade affects trade 44; economic effects 195; farming affected 253; fear of invasion 68; rationalization 26; social effects 19, 244; taxation and mapping 204; threat to Essex and Suffolk 50

needlework 289, 387; *see also* dressmaking

New Meeting, Birmingham (Unitarian): church organization 134–6; church rate issue 99; clergy income 120; conflict with Anglicans 96; philanthropy 101; Ryland family 104; Sunday school 144–5, 297; *see also* Priestley, Joseph

newspapers and journals 48, 156, 187, 419

nonconformists (Dissenters): Anglican response 95–9; Birmingham 42–3; business and 21–2, 203; church rates

issue 98; clergy 120–1;
Colchester 49; conversion 85,
87, 90; domesticity 21–2;
education 235; Freemasons 426;
growth 23, 85; hymns 89–90;
politics 19, 49, 74–5, 85, 92–5;
social effects 76; women 304; *see
also* Baptists; churches and chapels;
Congregationals; evangelicalism;
Methodists; Puritans; Unitarians

Old Meeting, Birmingham
(Unitarian) 99, 131
Owenites 50, 93–5
Oxford Movement (Tractarians) 85,
99, 451

parks 370, 422–4
partnerships 24 (Table 1), 200–5
passim; coverture 200, 315; family
and kinship 206, 217–22;
farming 254; manufacturing 250;
professions 263; schools 236,
237–8, 294; training for 222–5;
women in 277, 451; *see also* joint
stock companies
paternalism: break-up of 199;
Cowper, William 20, 21, 165; farm
labourers 251, 257; philanthropy as
development of 432–3; religious
basis 73, 86, 113
patriarchy 322, 333
patrilineality 31, 222, 273
patriotism 19, 164
patronage: aristocracy 33, 49, 199;
church 83–5, 102; clergy 119;
friendship and family
networks 355; middle-class
independence from 199, 419;
professions 262–3; salaried
posts 266; schools 235;
servants 393; voluntary
associations 422
pensions 212, 251
philanthropy: clergy wives 124, 130,
393; evangelicalism 25, 43, 78;
kinship and 101; Luckcock,
James 17; middle-class activity 50;
single women 59, 141, 431–2,
435–6; voluntary associations 420,
429–36; women's activity 66, 116,
135, 171–2, 313
philosophical societies *see* literary
societies
physicians *see* doctors
poetry *see* Barton, Bernard; Byron,
George Gordon, Lord; Cowper,
William; Crabbe, George; Hemans,

Felicia; Taylor, Ann Martin;
Thomson, James
politics: alignments 23; Essex and
Suffolk 49–50; middle-class access
to power 73–5 *passim*;
nonconformity 13, 19, 23, 81, 85,
92–7 *passim*, 164; voluntary
associations 445–9; women
and 445–9; *see also* Chartists;
franchise; French Revolution;
Owenites; Radicals; Tories; Whigs
pregnancy: family size 52, 63, 223,
281, 335–8; sexuality 27; *see also*
childbirth; illegitimacy
Priestley riots, 1791 15, 19, 42; *see
also* Priestley, Joseph
primogeniture 205–6
prisons 144, 429, 430
production *see* manufacture; trade
professions 260–5;
development 196–7;
domesticity 287; dress 410;
farming and 254;
inheritance 211, 213, 277; market
system 20; numbers
involved 232, 233 (Table 4);
occupation 30; servants 388;
societies 199, 446; status 233–4,
244; *see also* accounting;
architecture; banks and banking;
clergy; doctors; estate management;
lawyers; surveyors; teachers
property: gentility and 113; middle-
class forms of 20, 24 (Table 1),
195, 205; protection societies 424;
public role of property
ownership 446; voluntary
associations 420–1; women's
property rights 18, 187–8, 210,
275–9, 314, 315, 446, 451;
coverture 200–1, 276, 315;
dower 209; inheritance 209–13,
276; investment 279–80, 423; *see
also* land
'public and private' 13, 32–4, 454;
consumption 29–30;
housing 319–20, 264–9; men's
preparation for public life 445–9;
religion 103–4, 107–8, 136–8, 144;
science 312; women excluded from
public life 176, 416–49 *passim*
public health: cemeteries 409;
sanitation 382–3; water
supplies 382
public houses *see* inns and innkeepers
Puritans: cleanliness 399;
domesticity 114, 323; family 107,

108–9; gender difference 25;
revival 21

Quakers 82 (Tables 2 and 3);
Birmingham public life 43;
business life 203; dress 386;
gender difference 139–40;
leisure 442; middle-class
membership 74, 81;
networks 56, 86–7, 99–103 passim,
216–17, 219; social status 24
(Table 1); women 137–40, 313; see
also Cadbury family; Galton family;
Gibbins family; nonconformists

Radicals 13, 19, 23, 24 (Table 1), 43,
49–50, 96–7, 153
rationalism: 'Lit. and Phils.' 442;
science 26, 205, 291, 312;
Unitarians 26, 96, 442;
Utilitarianism 186, 235, 238, 343
rationalization 13, 26–7, 202–5;
accounting 20, 199, 202, 383–4;
childcare 281, 343; dress 411–12;
education 238; farming 256;
Galton family 312;
housekeeping 27, 383–4, 392–3;
housing 358–9, 375; literary
societies 442–3; Loudon,
John 190; Taylor, Isaac 62–3;
Unitarians 96
reading 63–4, 155–92
Reform Act, 1832 19, 50, 97
religion 76–148; business and 21–2,
111–12, 207, 208; children's
religious training 88, 124, 179, 340;
Christ, views of 86, 87, 173;
domesticity justified 90, 108–9,
112–13, 115–16, 323; education
and 294, 297; femininity
justified 74, 77, 90, 110, 114–18;
gender difference 74–5, 114, 126;
hymns 89–90; masculinity
justified 73, 74, 86, 107–14, 401;
men's place in 107–23, 131–6, 140;
networks 99–103, 119, 219–21;
parish 78, 83, 99, 279; prayer 88,
89, 90–1, 108–9, 124, 331, 359, 383;
sects see named religions;
services 80, 86, 89;
superstition 25–6; tracts 83, 142,
144, 167; women's place in: church
organization 119, 130–40; lay
women 107, 140–8; spiritual
equality 131; see also Anglicans;
Anglican Evangelicals; Baptists;
churches and chapels; clergy;
Congregationals; evangelicalism;

Independents; Methodists;
nonconformists; Puritans; Quakers;
Tractarians; Unitarians
retail shops see trade
retirement 91, 225–8, 233 (Table 4),
255; see also ageing
romanticism: beauty 28, 189, 191–2,
414; Byron, George Gordon,
Lord 159–61; childhood 343;
dress 412; individualism and anti-
urbanism 27–8; Scott, Sir
Walter 159–61; see also 'rural idyll'
'rural idyll': housing 360, 361, 363,
369; romantic view of 27–8; rural
culture and superstition 26, 27;
views of 20, 157–8, 164, 178, 189

St Martin's church, Birmingham
(Anglican Evangelical) 84–5
St Peter's church, Colchester (Anglican
Evangelical) 80, 83; see also Marsh,
Rev. William
St Thomas' church, Birmingham
(Anglican Evangelical) 80, 84–5,
95, 111, 120; see also Marsh, Rev.
William
'Saints, The' 84, 85, 124
salaried posts 198–9, 265–7; numbers
employed 233 (Table 4);
widows 277; wives' role 283;
women excluded 279, 306
schools 283; accommodation 366;
Edgbaston Proprietory
School 238; Hazelwood
School 235, 237–8, 294, 295, 343;
King Edward's Grammar
School 99, 236–7, 294–5, 366;
philanthropy 421–2; see also
education; Sunday schools; teachers
science: development of taste 190;
education 235, 249–50; religious
belief and 26, 291;
technology 205; voluntary
associations 199, 420, 425, 428,
442; women excluded 274, 310,
312, 425
securities 204–5; see also life
assurance
servants 388–96; childcare 339, 391,
394–5; costs of 361; farm servants
see farms and farming – labourers;
female employment of male
servants 391–5 passim;
franchise 199; increase in
numbers 375; male servants 393;
rural culture 26; salaried
staff 267, 269; separate

accommodation 377; social
mobility 25, 280; wet nurses 337
sex and sexuality: attitudes 26–7, 90,
401–3; attitudes to women 170,
322, 430; feminine delicacy 341;
interfamily relationships 356;
brothers and sisters 351, 352;
fathers and daughters 347;
marriage as control 323–4; master
and servant 390–1; Queen
Caroline affair 150–5
sexual difference see gender difference
sexual division of labour see division of
labour by gender
single women: brothers and 350, 351,
352; dependance on
family 313–15; gentility 274;
investment 211–12;
lodgings 358; occupations 293;
philanthropy 59, 431–2, 435–6;
religious life 100, 122, 125;
servants 388; service to
family 67, 329, 342, 347;
'spinster' 273; 'surplus' 114, 325,
453; see also Cadbury, Maria;
Camps, Amy; Hedge, Mary Ann;
Taylor, Jane; widows
smuggling 203
social life: children's 343–4; church
networks 48, 100; family
networks 356; London
society 21; men's business
networks 230, 417; rooms
for 377, 385; social circle 24 (Table
1), 64; visiting 292, 321; see also
leisure
social mobility 21–3, 104, 118, 240,
257–8
societies see voluntary associations
spinsters see single women
sponsorship see patronage
stewardship 33, 73–4, 86, 441–2
subscriptions 135, 212, 277, 361, 423
suburbs: Edgbaston 43, 57, 127,
368–9; Loudon, John 188–92;
separation of home and work 57,
58, 232, 251; social status 24
(Table 1); see also housing; gardens;
urban development
Sunday schools: Carrs Lane
chapel 128, 143–4; clergy
families 124, 147; development of
salaried posts 266;
evangelicalism 78; New
Meeting 144–5; self-
education 239, 292; teacher
training 15; voluntary

associations 420; women 430,
431–2
superstition 25–7, 92, 286–7, 402
surgeons see doctors
surveyors 265; see also professions

taxation: income tax 23, 204;
rates 204; tithes 83, 98, 204, 367;
wartime 253
teachers: clergy 120–1; gender
differences 145, 265, 285, 293–9,
313; growth of profession 266; see
also apprenticeship and training;
education; professions
Test and Corporation Acts 96, 97
theatre 437–9, 442
tithes 83, 98, 204, 367
Tories 23, 24 (Table 1), 43, 49, 153,
446–7
Tractarians (Oxford Movement) 85,
99, 451
tracts 83, 142, 144, 167
trade 240–4; business
organization 200;
merchants 202, 365, 410; numbers
involved 233 (Table 4);
rationalization 26; retail trade:
housing and
accommodation 366–7;
shopping 385–6; social status 105;
trade tokens 208; women 283,
302–4; separate from
manufacture 248; voluntary
associations 420–1; see also family
enterprise
transport: coach travel 47–8, 299,
301, 403–4; improvements 321,
345, 364; links with London 50,
241; market activity improved 44,
240, 253, 255; professional
practices 263; railways 301;
travel for pleasure 383; women
restricted 286
trusts and trusteeship 24, 33;
dower 209, 276; fatherhood 334;
lawyers 208, 214; non profit 200;
religious influences 73–4;
schools 236; voluntary
societies 422; women and
property 209–11, 277, 451
tuberculosis 22, 65, 339

Unitarians 82 (Tables 2 and 3);
Birmingham public life 43;
childcare 343; church
government 134–5; church
rates 98; clergy 118, 121; 'Lit. and
Phils.' 442–3; social status 24

(Table 1), 104; Sunday schools 144–5, 297; women's rights 134–5; see also churches and chapels; Hill family; Kenrick family; Luckcock, James; Martineau, Harriet; New Meeting; nonconformists; Old Meeting; Priestley, Joseph; religion; Shaen family; Utilitarianism

urban development: Birmingham 37–43, 50, 51, 156, 196, 231–2, 247–8, 362–3: Edgbaston 368–9, 383; civic improvements 447; Colchester 47–8; development of retail trade 240–2; see also gardens; housing; public health; suburbs

Utilitarianism: Bentham's view of women 185; Hazelwood School 238, 343; Mill's view of women 454; scientific education 235; Unitarians 145; women's rights 186

voluntary associations 416–49; Birmingham Lunar Society 235, 290, 312; creditworthiness 208; farming societies 255–6; law societies 262, 425; preparation for public life 23, 199; religious societies 83, 84, 100, 140, 144; salaried posts 266, 269; self-improvement 239; social status 24 (Table 1); women excluded 278, 292, 310; see also clubs; literary societies

volunteers 424–5

wages see income
weddings 407–8
weights and measures 204
Whigs 24 (Table 1), 43, 49, 448
widowers 328, 347–8
widows: dependance on family 285, 313; farming 254; Freemasons 426; inheritance 200–1, 209–13, 276–7, 284, 293, 299; investment 211–12,

293; numbers 322; occupation 230, 287–8; public life 126, 137
wills see inheritance
Witham Congregational chapel 133–4
workhouse 305
women: appearance and dress 413–15; Chartism 50; education 289–93; Freemasons 426–7; gentility 360; health care by women 307–8; leisure 405–10; mourning and funerals 408–9; philanthropy 429–36; property 18, 187–8, 210, 275–9, 314, 315, 466: coverture 200–1, 276, 315; dower 209; inheritance 209–13, 276; investment 279–80, 423; public life 19, 104, 447–9; religion: church organization 119, 130–40; lay women 107, 140–8; spiritual equality 131; servants, education and control 117, 391–5 passim; suffrage 452; travel 403–5; voluntary associations 416, 421–45 passim; see also division of labour by gender; domesticity; family; femininity; feminism; gender difference; housekeeping; literature; marriage; motherhood; pregnancy; single women; widows
work: attitudes 22–3, 111–12; occupation 30, 231–4, 308–12; see also accounting; clergy; division of labour by gender; doctors; lawyers; manufacture; professions; salaried posts; teachers; trade
working class: breast feeding 399; exploitation 195; femininity 415; housing 359; manufacturing 251; Methodism 73; middle-class mistrust 275; public gardens 423–4; public houses 300; religion 76, 79; servants and masters 391; social mobility 21–3; superstition 25–6; teachers 295; wage contract 202; see also farms and farming – labourers